George W. Clark

The Gospel of Matthew

a popular commentary upon a critical basis, especially designed for pastors and

Sunday schools - Vol. 1

George W. Clark

The Gospel of Matthew
a popular commentary upon a critical basis, especially designed for pastors and Sunday schools - Vol. 1

ISBN/EAN: 9783337285425

Printed in Europe, USA, Canada, Australia, Japan

Cover: Foto ©Lupo / pixelio.de

More available books at **www.hansebooks.com**

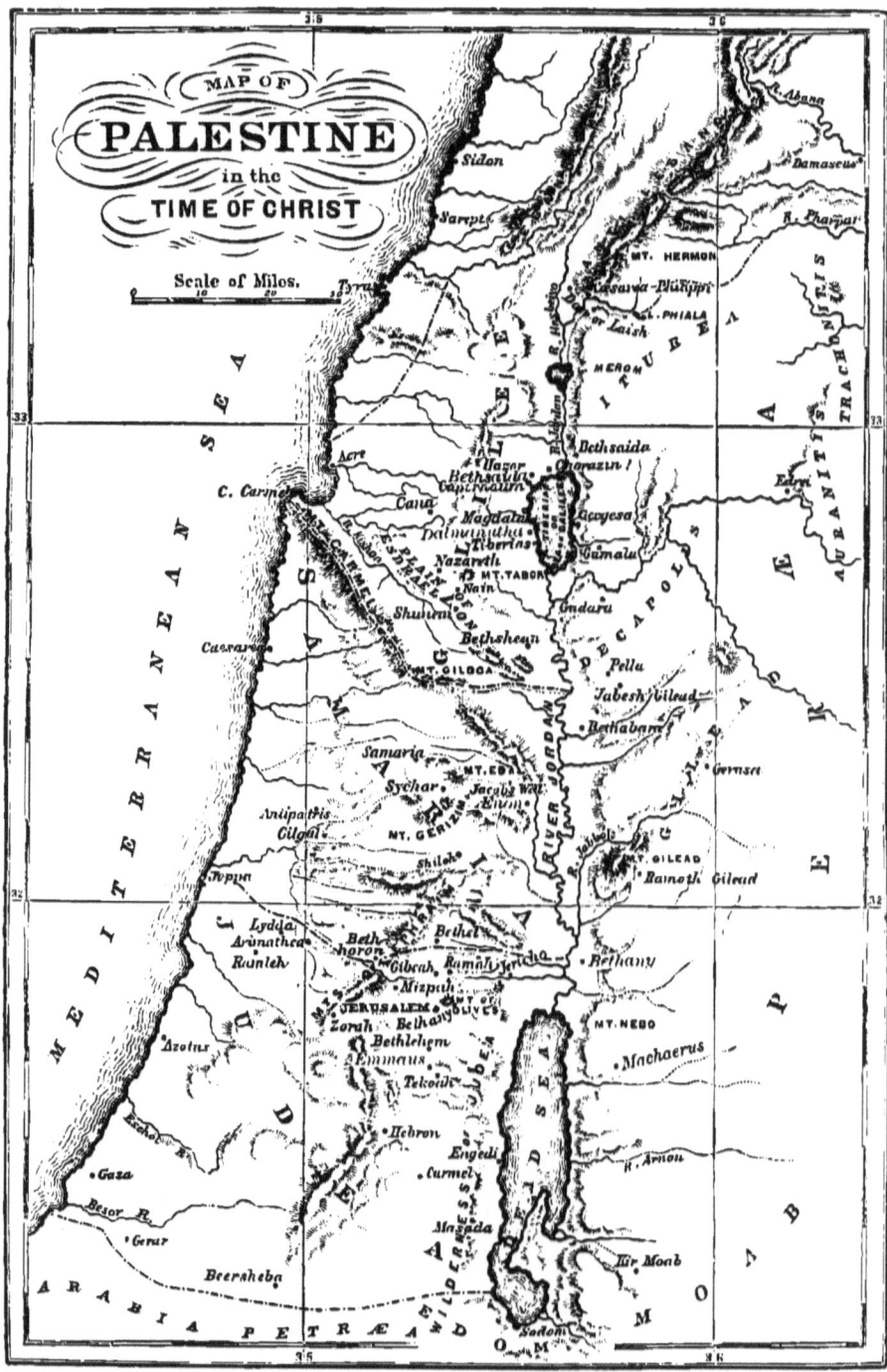

A People's Commentary

THE
GOSPEL OF MATTHEW

A POPULAR COMMENTARY UPON A CRITICAL
BASIS, ESPECIALLY DESIGNED FOR PASTORS
AND SUNDAY SCHOOLS ◇◇◇◇◇◇◇◇◇◇◇◇◇

BY

GEO. W. CLARK, D. D.
Author of "A New Harmony of the Gospels," etc.

A NEW AND REVISED EDITION

PHILADELPHIA
AMERICAN BAPTIST PUBLICATION SOCIETY
1420 Chestnut Street
1896

PREFACE.

———•◆•———

FIFTEEN years ago, the author became deeply impressed with the want of Notes on our Common Version for Sabbath-Schools and Bible-Classes somewhat different from any then existing. Impressions became convictions, and convictions have been earnestly carried out. One result is the volume now given to the public.

The aim has been to write a popular commentary on a critical basis; to explain the meaning of words, idioms, and phrases of the original; to exhibit the drift and object of the discourse or narrative in each particular place, the arguments used, the connection of thought as well as the general scope of the whole Gospel; thus presenting and illustrating the ideas, both doctrinal and practical, of the inspired word.

It has also been the endeavor to avoid prolixity on the one hand and great brevity on the other. The mere detailing, therefore, of various views has not generally been attempted, but what has seemed to be the true one stated. Where, however, it seemed necessary, different views have been presented and discussed. Difficult passages have received attention, and no point on which a commonly intelligent Sunday-school teacher might wish light has been intentionally passed over. The latest results of exegetical and textual criticism, and of recent discovery, have been sought and incorporated in the notes. And, to make all as clear to the eye as possible, several kinds of type are used.

The Chronology and Harmony of the Gospels have been kept in view, and wherever Matthew has come in contact with the other Evangelists, differences have been noted and difficulties explained. Thus, the individuality and independence of Matthew are really the more clearly seen, while a view of the four sides of the sacred narrative is thus obtained. For those wishing a tabular exhibit of these sides and relations, the Synoptical View of the Four Gospels is given (p. xiii.), presenting the arrangement adopted by the author in his Harmony.

Brief Remarks or suggestions are added at the end of each chapter, and the sentiment confirmed by references from other portions of Scripture. Almost every verse is thus remarked upon, the whole forming by itself a brief practical and doctrinal commentary on the Gospel. To some this will doubtless form the most useful portion of the work. Its design is to aid teachers in giving a practical turn and point to their instructions.

The division of chapters into verses, first introduced into the English Bible by the Genevan version (New Testament, A.D. 1557; the whole Bible, 1560), often interferes with the connection of thought, and impedes a quick and intelligent view of many passages. The paragraph form has therefore been adopted; and, to aid the eye and facilitate study, subjects or leading events have been placed at the head of principal paragraphs or divisions.

Many teachers and advanced scholars prefer to explain Scripture by Scripture. Carefully selected references have therefore been placed in the margin. These, in connection with those given in the Notes and Remarks, are believed to constitute this the most complete reference Matthew published. The object is not to do away with close and attentive study, but rather to excite and aid it.

In preparing this work the author has called to his aid all the helps within his reach, the earlier and later critical and popular Commentaries: Harmonies of the Gospels, Books of Travels, Histories of the Church and of Doctrines; Treatises on the Life of Christ, and Grammatical Authorities on the New Testament. His thanks are specially due to Professor T. J. Conant, D.D., of Brooklyn, N. Y., for facilities in consulting rare and valuable works.

In sending forth this volume, the author is sensible that it falls short of that perfect standard which has been his aim. But if others are excited by it to share in these spiritual treasures, his highest anticipations will be realized, and he will rejoice that God is glorified.

BALLSTON SPA, N. Y., May, 1870.

REVISED EDITION.

After twenty-five years, since the publication of this volume, the author has again gone over it, making some necessary changes, corrections, and additions, and bringing it up as near as possible to the present state of textual criticism. An index has been provided for this as for the other volumes of the series.

HIGHTSTOWN, N. J., March, 1896.

INTRODUCTORY REMARKS

GENERAL REMARKS UPON THE FOUR GOSPELS.

The *four Gospels* were written during the last sixty years of the first century of the Christian era. They bear the evident marks of that particular age, its peculiar impress of thought and reasoning, and the special forms of the Greek language then prevalent among Jewish writers. The severest scrutiny has not been able to detect in them any trace of a later age. Indeed, their high character, and their superiority to the Christian literature of the age immediately succeeding, show that they could not have been the product of that age; and at the same time point unmistakably to the training which the Apostles received under the ministry of Jesus and to the gifts and inspiration of the Spirit bestowed upon them and their followers.

It is a well-attested fact that the four Gospels were received by the early churches as *authoritative inspired writings*. Clement of Rome, supposed by many to be the fellow-laborer of Paul, and mentioned in Phil. 4:3, in his Epistle to the Corinthians, written probably about A.D. 68, but not later than A.D. 97, quotes passages to be found in the first three Gospels, but makes no reference to the fourth Gospel, as he wrote either before or about the time that the latter appeared. Ignatius, in a letter written just before his martyrdom between A.D. 107 and 116, quotes several passages from the Gospels of Matthew and John; and Polycarp, in a letter written about the same time, makes several quotations from the Gospel of Matthew, and gives indirect but valid testimony to the Gospel of John. Barnabas, who wrote a little earlier, probably in the last decade of the first century, quotes from Matthew with apparent reference to Luke and John. One of his quotations from Matthew is introduced by, "It is written," the usual formula of citing an authoritive divine revelation, thus treating it as a part of the Holy Scriptures. Justin Martyr, in his Apology and Dialogue, A.D. 139, speaks of the "Memoirs of the Apostles," "composed by his Apostles and followers, which are called Gospels," and says that they were read in connection with the prophets of the Old Testament in the assemblies of Christians on the Lord's day, thus placing the Gospels by the side of the Prophets in authority.

INTRODUCTORY REMARKS.

As early as A.D. 170, two Harmonies of the Gospels had been prepared by two learned men respectively: Theophilus, pastor at Antioch in Syria, and Tatian, who had been a disciple of Justin Martyr. Tatian called his *Diatessaron*, that is, the Gospel according to the four. Irenæus, a disciple of Polycarp, and pastor at Lyons A.D. 177, refers to the general use of the four Gospels as authoritative records. He quotes about 400 passages from them and says, "Such is the certainty in respect to the Gospels that even the heretics bear testimony to them." The Muratorian fragment, written about A.D. 170, describes the Gospels of Luke and John as the third and fourth. The first lines of the fragment which referred to Matthew and Mark have perished, though the imperfect sentence, with which it begins, evidently applies to Mark. Thus the order of the Gospels was the same then as now. Clement of Alexandria, President of the celebrated Catechetical school at Alexandria, about A.D. 190, one of the most learned men of his age, and who had traveled much and had made extensive researches and enjoyed the instruction of many of the best teachers who had either seen the Apostles or those who had received from them instruction, speaks of "the four Gospels which have been handed down to us" in contrast to an apocryphal Gospel used by certain heretics. Tertullian, in his work against Marcion, about A.D. 208, mentions four Gospels, two of them as the work of the Apostles John and Matthew, and two of apostolic men, Luke and Mark and defends their apostolic origin and authority.

So also we have in the writings of heretics and pagans important testimony to the general reception of the Gospels by the early Christians as authoritative inspired writings. Irenæus thus speaks of heretics appealing to them, "Every one of them endeavors to establish his doctrine by making these his point of departure." Valentinus, in the early part of the second century, quotes the Gospels, especially that of John. A disciple of the latter, named Ptolemy, quotes from Matthew and John; and another follower, named Heracleon, wrote a commentary on the Gospel of John. So also Basilides, between A.D. 117 and 138, wrote a work to explain the Gospels; and Marcion, about the middle of the second century, first made use of the four Gospels, and afterward rejected all except Luke, and that mutilated to suit himself; and Tatian as early as A.D. 170 wrote, as already noticed, a harmony of the Gospels. Celsus, a heathen writer, wrote against Christianity about the middle of the second century. He shows a knowledge of the four Gospels, and treats them as written by the disciples of Jesus. So also did Porphyry in the third century, and the Emperor Julian in the fourth. Both heretical and pagan writers would have treated the Gospels as fabrications of a later age if it had been possible. They could not deny that they were written by the Apostles and apostolic men; and their treatment of them is an evidence that they were received by the churches as inspired records.

It may be added that the Syriac Peshito Version, which was confessedly not made later than the close of the second century, and probably near the middle, and the old Latin Version, made as early as the middle of the second century, and probably earlier, each contain the four Gospels. But these suppose their Greek originals before them, and that they had had a previous history, and were regarded as constituting a part of the Holy Scriptures.

THE UNITY OF THE GOSPELS.

The four Gospels present only *one divine record, but from four points of view.* Early Christian writers noticed this design, and were accustomed to explain and illustrate it and the peculiarities of the Gospels by the Cherubim of Ezekiel (ch. 1). Thus to Matthew was assigned the symbol of the man, to Mark that of the lion, to Luke that of the ox, and to John that of the eagle. If we may indeed use these symbols, I would suggest the lion as pointing to the kingly office of Christ as presented by Matthew; the ox to the priesthood of Christ, the *laboring* victim and priest, as presented by Mark; the man to the humanity of Christ, the Redeemer and Mediator, as presented by Luke; and the eagle to the prophetical office of Christ, the deep, spiritual Teacher, as presented by John.

I can not better close this brief reference to the Gospels than by giving Professor Ellicott's condensed summary of the principal points in which the four evangelical narratives are distinguished from each other

"I. In regard to their *external features* and *characteristics*

"The *point of view* of the first Gospel is mainly Israelitic; of the second, Gentile; of the third, universal; of the fourth, Christian.

"The general *aspect*, and, so to speak, *physiognomy* of the first, mainly, is Oriental; of the second, Roman; of the third, Greek; of the fourth, spiritual.

"The *style* of the first is stately and rhythmical; of the second, terse and precise; of the third, calm and copious; of the fourth, artless and colloquial.

"The most striking *characteristic* of the first is symmetry; of the second, compression; of the third, order; of the fourth, system.

"The *thought* and *language* of the first are both Hebraistic; of the third, both Hellenistic; while in the second, the thought is often Occidental, though the language is Hebraistic; and in the fourth, the language is Hellenistic, but the thought Hebraistic.

"II. In respect to their *subject-matter* and *contents:*

"In the first Gospel we have narrative; in the second, memoirs; in the third, history; in the fourth, dramatic portraiture.

"In the first we have often the record of events in their accomplishment; in the second, events in their detail; in the third, events in their connection; in the fourth, events in relation to the teaching springing from them.

"Thus in the first, we more often meet with the notice of impressions; in the second, of facts; in the third, of motives; in the fourth, of words spoken.

"And lastly, the record of the first is mainly collective and often antithetical; of the second, graphic and circumstantial; of the third, didactic and reflective; of the fourth, selective and supplemental.

"III. In respect to their *portraiture of our Lord*, the first Gospel presents Him to us mainly as the Messiah; the second, mainly as the God-man; the third, as the Redeemer; the fourth, as the only-begotten Son of God."—*Professor Ellicott's Lectures on the Life of Christ*, p. 46, note.

THE WRITER OF THE FIRST GOSPEL.

Matthew, the writer of the first Gospel, was also called Levi, the son of Alphæus. Mark 2:14; Luke 5:27. See on Matt. 9:9. His residence was at Capernaum, and his profession a publican, or receiver of customs at that port on the Sea of Galilee under the Roman Government. His great humility is shown in styling himself "Matthew the Publican," ch. 10:3; in his comparative silence in regard to leaving all and following Jesus, and to the great feast he gave at his house, both of which are told us by Luke (5:28, 29). His name appears for the last time in the New Testament among the eleven in Acts 1:13. Tradition assures us that he preached the Gospel for several years in Palestine. The earlier traditions state that he died a natural death; but a later one says that he suffered martyrdom in Ethiopia.

THE LANGUAGE IN WHICH MATTHEW WROTE.

Papias of Hierapolis, in the beginning of the second century, tells us that Matthew "wrote his Words of Jesus in Hebrew (that is, Aramaic), and each according to his ability interpreted it." His statement is confirmed by Irenæus, Eusebius, Origen, Epiphanius, Jerome, and others.

But the Greek copy of Matthew appears to be an original work, not a translation; for—

1st. The quotations of Matthew from the Old Testament conform most generally with the Septuagint Greek Version.

2d. The verbal correspondence between the Gospel of Matthew and those of Mark and Luke, especially in their report of the sayings of Jesus, is difficult to account for on the supposition that the Gospel of Matthew is a translation.

3d. All the Versions, even the Peshito Syriac, the language in which the Gospel is said to have been originally written, conform to the present Greek text.

4th. All the quotations of the early writers are from the Greek copy.

And further it should be noted:

1st. That at the time when Matthew wrote, Greek was fast superseding the Hebrew, even in Palestine, and was understood by the mass of the people;

that Greek was more suitable for a book of permanent and universal value; and that James and the author of the Epistle to the Hebrews wrote to the Jews in Greek.

2d. That Epiphanius, although he asserts that Matthew wrote his Gospel originally in Hebrew, speaks of it as that used by the Nazarenes and Ebionites.

3d. That Jerome thought he had discovered the Hebrew Gospel of Matthew in the one used by the Nazarenes; but afterward he found reason to doubt it.

4th. That although so many of the early writers assert that Matthew originally wrote his Gospel in Hebrew, yet we do not find that any of them ever used it or saw it. Hence if there ever was a Hebrew copy, it must have been lost very early, soon after the destruction of Jerusalem.

The above facts and statements can be harmonized in two ways. *First*, we may suppose Matthew to have written his Gospel both in Hebrew (Aramaic) and Greek. Or, *second*, we may regard the Greek text as the original, and the Hebrew Gospel as drawn from it and more or less disfigured; and the assertion of an original Hebrew text to rest on a misunderstanding of Papias. Tischendorf very satisfactorily explains the latter theory as follows:

"From the Epistle of Paul to the Galatians, we gather that thus early there was a Judaizing party. This party spirit broke out even more fiercely after the destruction of Jerusalem. There were two parties among these Judaizers: the Nazarenes and the Ebionites. Each of these parties used a Gospel according to Matthew, the one party using a Greek text and the other a Hebrew. That they did not scruple to tamper with the text is probable from that very sectarian spirit. The text, as we have certain means of proving, rested upon our received text of Matthew, with, however, occasional departures, to suit their arbitrary views. When, then, it was reported in later times, that these Nazarenes, who were one of the earliest Christian sects, possessed a Hebrew version of Matthew, what was more natural than that some person or other thus falling in with the pretensions of this sect, should say that Matthew was originally written in Hebrew, and that the Greek was only a version of it? How far these two sects differed from each other no one cared to inquire; and with such separatists as the Nazarenes, who withdrew to the shores of the Dead Sea, it would not have been easy to attempt.

"Jerome supports us in this clearing up of Papias' meaning. Jerome, who knew Hebrew, as other Latin and Greek fathers did not, obtained in the fourth century a copy of this Hebrew Gospel of the Nazarenes, and at once asserted that he had found the Hebrew original. But when he looked more closely into the matter, he confined himself to the statement that many supposed that this Hebrew text was the original of Matthew's Gospel. He translated it into Latin and Greek, and made a few observations of his own on it.

"From these observations of Jerome, as well as from other fragments, we must conclude that this notion of Papias—in which several learned men of our day agree—that the Hebrew was the original text of Matthew, can not be substantiated; but, on the contrary, this Hebrew has been drawn from the Greek text, and disfigured, moreover, here and there with certain arbitrary changes. The same is applicable to a Greek text of a Hebrew Gospel in use among the Ebionites. This text, from the fact that it was in Greek, was better known to the church than the Hebrew version of the Nazarenes. But it was always regarded, from the earliest times, as only another text of Matthew's Gospel. This explains what Papias had said about several translations of Matthew."—TISCHENDORF'S *When were our Gospels written?* pp. 114–117.

TIME OF THE WRITING.

The *time* when Matthew wrote his Gospel can not be exactly determined. The early Christian writers are unanimous in their testimony that he wrote first of the Evangelists. It must have been several years after the crucifixion (ch. 27 : 8 ; 28 : 15), and before the destruction of Jerusalem (ch. 24 : 15). Some think it was composed as early as A.D. 37; others as late as A.D. 63. The most probable date is somewhere between A.D. 42 and A.D. 58.

SPECIAL DESIGN.

Matthew *wrote for Jewish converts.* Hence there are fewer interpretations of Jewish customs, laws, and localities than in the other Gospels. He was familiar with the Hebrew Scriptures, and deeply imbued with their spirit. His *chief design* seems to have been to give such an account of the history of Jesus as to show that he was *The Messiah foretold by the prophets*, the *Spiritual King* of the *Israel of God*. Hence he gives his lineage as the Son of David, and the account of the wise men of the East who acknowledged his kingly office and presented to him royal homage and royal gifts. He exhibits the kingly manner and power of Jesus in all that he did. It was by his word (ch. 8 : 8, 16 ; 15 : 23 ; 24 : 35), illustrating the Scriptures, "Where the word of a king is, there is power." In the decisions of the final judgment he is represented as king (ch. 25 : 34); and the Gospel closes with a declaration of sovereign power and with a royal command and promise, ch. 28 : 18–20.

In the accomplishment of this design, Matthew selects those items in the history of Jesus which are best suited to his purpose. Especially does he record those events in which the prophecies of the Old Testament were fulfilled. Thus he begins his Gospel by appealing to a genealogical record of acknowledged authority among the Jews, proving that Jesus, according to prophecy and the universal expectation of the Jews, was the Son of **David**

In his miraculous conception, in the place of his birth, in his exile in Egypt, in the massacre at Bethlehem, and in his residence at Nazareth, Matthew points out marked and distinct fulfillments of prophecy.

So also does he show that John the Baptist came as the harbinger of Christ, and that he was the Elijah that should come, according to prophetic announcements.

Proceeding to the ministry of Jesus, Matthew points to his dwelling at Capernaum, his healing the sick and bearing the sorrows of the comfortless, his retiring from public observation, and his unostentatious character and manner, the hardness of heart exhibited by the Jews, the use of parables by Jesus, and the hypocrisy and traditions of the Scribes and Pharisees, as fulfilling the predictions of the prophets. So also in the last days and sufferings of Christ, Matthew shows Scripture to have been fulfilled in the triumphal entry into Jerusalem, in the desecration of the temple by the buyers and sellers, in the children in the temple singing hosannas to Jesus as the Son of David, in the Jewish people rejecting Jesus, the head-stone of the corner, in his approaching sufferings (ch. 26 : 24, 54), in the scattering of his disciples, in disposing of the thirty pieces of silver for the potter's field, and in the soldiers parting the raiment of Jesus and casting lots upon his vesture.

The resurrection of Jesus he proves by the testimony of reliable witnesses, and gives the Jewish account of the disappearance of the body of Jesus, a simple statement of which was enough to prove its untruthfulness.

Thus does Matthew prove that Jesus was unmistakably the Messiah foretold by Scripture. His argument was complete and incontestable to the Jew who placed unlimited confidence in the sure word of prophecy.

ARRANGEMENT.

Matthew's Gospel bears marks of a *definite arrangement*. He groups and classifies, giving particularly the *sayings* of Jesus, not always in their chronological order, but rather according to their nature and to the purpose he had in view in proving Jesus to be the Messiah. His style and manner is very much what we would naturally expect from one who, as a publican, had been accustomed to arrange, classify, and make systematic reports. The principal divisions are:

1. The nativity and infancy of Jesus, chs. 1, 2.
2. The ministry of John the Baptist; the baptism and temptation of Jesus, ch. 3–4 : 11.
3. The beginning of Christ's ministry in Galilee; sermon on the mount, and a group of miracles, ch. 4 : 12–9 : 38.
4. His Apostles commissioned and sent forth to preach the gospel of his kingdom, ch. 10.
5. The relation of Jesus to different classes, to John and his disciples, to

the Pharisees, to humble inquirers and to his followers. The enmity of the Pharisees taking an organized form, chs. 11, 12.

6. A series of parables on the nature of his kingdom, followed by an account of his miracle-working power, chs. 13, 14.

7. The increased opposition of the Pharisaic party, ch. 15–16 : 12.

8. Revelation to his disciples of his sufferings, ch. 16 : 13–17 : 23.

9 Duty of his followers in relation to civil government, and to one another, especially in regard to offenses, ch. 17 : 24–18 : 35.

10. Last journey from Galilee to Jerusalem, chs. 19, 20.

11. The triumphal entry into Jerusalem. Opposition of the Scribes and Pharisees, who are denounced, chs. 21–23.

12. Discourse on the destruction of Jerusalem, his second coming, and the end of the world, chs. 24, 25.

13. The sufferings and death of Jesus, chs. 26, 27.

14. His resurrection, ch. 28.

NOTE TO THE REVISED EDITION.

The first three Gospels are called the Synoptic Gospels, meaning those *looking together*, since they view Christ from a similar standpoint, relating similar events in similar language. The question regarding their original sources is an interesting one, but largely theoretical. Doubtless an oral gospel preceded the written ones. Memory was cultivated, both by teachers and pupils. It often took the place of the written page. Jewish rabbins had their oral law in their memory, and could also repeat large portions of their sacred writings. So we must believe that the apostles and early teachers held in memory much of our Lord's words and deeds, which they related in similar language. To this must be added the element of inspiration. Jesus had promised the apostles that the Spirit would bring all to their remembrance which he had said to them (John 14 : 26). We should also expect the Spirit's guidance in the design and selection of matter of each Gospel.

In regard to Matthew's Gospel I incline to the belief that he wrote it first in the Aramaic and then in the Greek, the latter not a mere translation of the former; and that Matthew's Gospel was the earliest of the four. This accords with the testimony of early Christian writers, the order in which they are early named, and were placed in the canon. It agrees also with the Divine plan, that the Gospel was to the Jew first (Matt. 10 : 5, 6; Rom. 1 : 16). Josephus did the same with his Jewish War, of which the Greek copy only remains. When the Greek Matthew was circulated among Christians, who were largely Gentiles and Grecian Jews, it naturally superseded the Hebrew.

"Matthew is the opening book—the Genesis—of the new covenant. . . The Gospel according to Matthew conducts us from the position of the Old Testament to that of the New" (*Dr. H. G. Weston*). And Matthew prepares the way for Mark and Luke; and the Synoptics for John.

SYNOPTICAL VIEW OF THE FOUR GOSPELS.

The chronology of the Gospels is in many respects undetermined. The duration of Christ's ministry is much disputed. It continued at least two and one half years; for John in his Gospel mentions three Passovers, John 2 : 13; 6 : 4; 13 : 1. If the feast (or "a feast of the Jews") mentioned in John 5 : 1 be also regarded as a Passover, then his public ministry continued about three years and a half. But if the feast was that of Purim (Esther 9 : 26), as many suppose, occurring a month before the Passover of John 6 : 4, then must we assign the shorter term to his public ministry. Although certainty may not be attained, yet the amount of labor that Jesus performed, and the time required for his three preaching tours throughout Galilee, before the Passover mentioned in John 6 : 4, incline us to regard the feast of John 5 : 1 as also a Passover. In accordance with this view the following table is arranged, and the probable chronological order and harmony given; but where either is quite doubtful, or beset with special difficulty, the references are printed in **heavy type**. The reasons for the arrangement are given by the author in his HARMONY OF THE GOSPELS.

I. EVENTS CONNECTED WITH THE BIRTH AND CHILDHOOD OF JESUS.

A period of about thirteen and a half years, from B.C. 6 to A.D. 8.

SECT.	SUBJECT	MATT.	MARK.	LUKE.	JOHN.
1.	Luke's Preface			1 : 1-4	
2.	John's Introduction				1 : 1-14
3.	The Genealogies	1 : 1-17		3 : 23-38	
4.	Annunciation of John's Birth			1 : 5-25	
5.	Annunciation of the Birth of Jesus			1 : 26-38	
6.	Mary visits Elizabeth			1 : 39-56	
7.	The Birth of John the Baptist			1 : 57-80	
8.	An Angel appears to Joseph	1 : 18-23			
9.	Birth of Jesus	1 : 24, 25		2 : 1-7	
10.	The Visit of the Shepherds			2 : 8-20	
11.	The Circumcision			2 : 21	
12.	Presentation in the Temple			2 : 22-38	
13.	Temporary Return to Nazareth			2 : 39	
14.	Again at Bethlehem; Visit of the Magi.	2 : 1-12			
15.	Flight into Egypt	2 : 13-15			
16.	Herod's Massacre of the Children	2 : 16-18			
17.	Return and Residence at Nazareth	2 : 19-23		2 : 40	
18.	Childhood of Jesus			2 : 41-52	

II. ANNOUNCEMENT AND INTRODUCTION OF CHRIST'S PUBLIC MINISTRY.

About one year, from the spring of A.D. 26 to that of A.D. 27.

19.	The Ministry of John the Baptist	3 : 1-12	1 : 1-8	3 : 1-18	
20.	The Baptism of Jesus	3 : 13-17	1 : 9-11	3 : 21-23	
21.	The Temptation	4 : 1-11	1 : 12, 13	4 : 1-13	
22.	Testimony of John to Jesus				1 : 15-34

SECT. SUBJECT.	MATT.	MARK.	LUKE.	JOHN.
23. Jesus gains Disciples; returns to Galilee...............	....	....	....	1: 35–51
24. The Marriage at Cana.................	....	....	....	2: 1–11
25. Visits Capernaum	....	....	....	2: 12

III. FROM THE FIRST PASSOVER OF CHRIST'S PUBLIC MINISTRY UNTIL THE SECOND.

One year, from April, A.D. 27, to April, A.D. 28.

SECT. SUBJECT.	MATT.	MARK.	LUKE.	JOHN.
26. At the Passover; the Traders expelled.	....	....	....	2: 13–25
27. Visit of Nicodemus..................	....	....	....	3: 1–21
28. Jesus remains in Judea	....	....	....	3: 22–24
29. Further Testimony of John the Baptist.	....	....	....	3: 25–36
30. John Imprisoned	....	....	3: 19, 20	....
31. Jesus departs for Galilee............	4: 12	1: 14	4: 14	4: 1–4
32. Discourses with the Woman of Sychar.	....	....	....	4: 5–42
33. Teaches publicly in Galilee..........	4: 17	1: 14, 15	4: 14, 15	4: 43–46
34. Heals a Nobleman's Son.............	....	....	....	4: 46–54
35. Rejected at Nazareth................	4: 13	....	4: 16–30	....
36. Makes Capernaum his Residence.....	4: 13–16	....	4: 31	....
37. Four called as Constant Attendants...	4: 18–22	1: 16–20	....	....
38. A Demoniac healed in the Synagogue.	....	1: 21–28	4: 31–37	....
39. Heals Peter's Wife's Mother........	8: 14–17	1: 29–34	4: 38–41	....
40. First Preaching Tour throughout Galilee....	4: 23–25	1: 35–39	4: 42–44	....
41. The Miraculous Draught of Fishes....	....	....	5: 1–11	....
42. Sermon on the Mount.................	5: 1–7: 29	....	....	....
43. A Leper healed......................	8: 1–4	1: 40–45	5: 12–16	....
44. Heals a Paralytic....................	9: 2–8	2: 1–12	5: 17–26	....
45. The Call of Matthew.................	9: 9	2: 13, 14	5: 27, 28	....

IV. FROM THE SECOND PASSOVER UNTIL THE THIRD.

From April, A.D. 28, to April, A.D. 29.

SECT. SUBJECT.	MATT.	MARK.	LUKE.	JOHN.
46. At the Passover; Heals the Impotent Man........	....	....	....	5: 1–47
47. Plucking the Ears of Grain...........	12: 1–8	2: 23–28	6: 1–5	....
48. Healing the Withered Hand..........	12: 9–14	3: 1–6	6: 6–11	....
49. Withdraws to the Sea of Galilee......	12: 15–21	3: 7–12	....	....
50. The Twelve Apostles chosen..........	....	3: 13–19	6: 12–16	....
51. The Sermon in the Plain	....	....	6: 17–49	....
52. Healing of the Centurion's Servant...	8: 5–13	....	7: 1–10	....
53. Raises a Widow's Son at Nain........	....	....	7: 11–17	....
54. John's Message to Jesus.............	11: 2–19	....	7: 18–35	....
55. Upbraiding the Cities of Galilee......	11: 20–30	....	....	....
56. Anointed by a Penitent Woman......	....	....	7: 36–50	....
57. Second Circuit of Galilee	....	....	8: 1–3	....
58. A Blind and Dumb Demoniac healed..	12: 22–37	3: 19–30	....	....
59. A Sign demanded of Jesus............	12: 38–45	....	....	....
60. Christ's Mother and Brethren........	12: 46–50	3: 31–35	8: 19–21	....
61. Parable of the Sower................	13: 1–23	4: 1–25	8: 4–18	....
62. Other Parables spoken to the Multitude	13: 24–35	4: 26–34	....	....
63. Wheat and Tares explained; and other Parables to the Disciples......	13: 36–53	....	....	....
64. The Tempest stilled	8: 18, 23–27	4: 35–41	8: 22–25	....
65. The Two Demoniacs of Gadara.......	8: 28–9: 1	5: 1–21	8: 26–40	....
66. Matthew's Feast.....................	9: 10–13	2: 15–17	5: 29–32	....
67. Discourse on Fasting................	9: 14–17	2: 18–22	5: 33–39	....
68. Jairus's Daughter; the Bloody Issue.	9: 18–26	5: 22–43	8: 41–56	....
69. Healing of the Blind and Dumb......	9: 27–34	....	....	....
70. Second Rejection at Nazareth........	13: 54–58	6: 1–6	....	....
71. Third Circuit of Galilee..............	9: 35–38	....	....	....
72. The Twelve endowed and sent forth .	10: 1–42	6: 7–11	9: 1–5	....
73. They go forth; Third Tour continued.	11: 1	6: 12, 13	9: 6	....
74. Herod's Opinion of Jesus; John's Beheadal................	14: 1–12	6: 14–29	9: 7–9	....

SYNOPTICAL VIEW OF THE GOSPELS.

SECT.	SUBJECT.	MATT.	MARK.	LUKE.	JOHN.
75.	Return of the Twelve............	....	6 : 30, 31	9 : 10	....
76.	Feeding the Five Thousand........	14 : 13-21	6 : 32-44	9 : 10-17	6 : 1-14
77.	Jesus walks on the Sea...........	14 : 22-36	6 : 45-56	....	6 : 15-21
78.	Discourse at Capernaum...........	....	....	....	6 : 22-71

V. FROM THE THIRD PASSOVER UNTIL THE ENSUING FEAST OF TABERNACLES.

Six months, from April to October, A.D. 29.

SECT.	SUBJECT.	MATT.	MARK.	LUKE.	JOHN.
79.	Jesus continues in Galilee........	....	....	....	7 : 1
80.	Traditions of the Elders...........	15 : 1-20	7 : 1-23	....	....
81.	The Canaanitish Woman...........	15 : 21-28	7 : 24-30	....	....
82.	Deaf and Dumb Man, etc., healed..	15 : 29-31	7 : 31-37	....	....
83.	Feeds the Four Thousand.........	15 : 32-39	8 : 1-9	....	....
84.	A Sign again demanded...........	15 : 39-16 : 4	8 : 10-12	....	....
85.	The Leaven of the Pharisees......	16 : 4-12	8 : 13-21	....	....
86.	Blind Man healed.................	....	8 : 22-26	....	....
87.	Visit to the region of Cæsarea Philippi.	16 : 13-20	8 : 27-30	9 : 18-21	....
88.	Jesus foretells his Death..........	16 : 21-28	8 : 31-9 : 1	9 : 22-27	....
89.	The Transfiguration...............	17 : 1-13	9 : 2-13	9 : 28-36	....
90.	Healing the Dumb Demoniac......	17 : 14-21	9 : 14-29	9 : 37-43	....
91.	Jesus again foretells his Death....	17 : 22, 23	9 : 30-32	9 : 43-45	....
92.	The Sacred Tribute................	17 : 24-27	9 : 33	....	....
93.	Contention among the Disciples...	18 : 1-14	9 : 33-50	9 : 46-50	....
94.	Dealing with an Offended Brother, etc.	18 : 15-20	....	....	....
95.	On Forgiveness...................	18 : 21-35	....	....	....
96.	Still continues in Galilee..........	....	....	....	7 : 2-9
97.	Goes to the Feast of Tabernacles..	....	....	9 : 51-56	7 : 10
98.	Concerning following Jesus.......	8 : 19-22	....	9 : 57-62	....

VI. FROM THE FEAST OF TABERNACLES TILL CHRIST'S ARRIVAL AT BETHANY, SIX DAYS BEFORE THE FOURTH PASSOVER.

Six months, less six days.

SECT.	SUBJECT.	MATT.	MARK.	LUKE.	JOHN.
99.	Jesus at the Feast; teaches publicly..	....	....	....	7 : 11-8 : 1
100.	The Woman taken in Adultery.....	....	....	....	8 : 2-11
101.	Further Public Teaching...........	....	....	....	8 : 12-59
102.	Seventy instructed and sent forth..	....	....	10 : 1-16	....
103.	Return of the Seventy.............	....	....	10 : 17-24	....
104.	Reply to a Lawyer; Good Samaritan...	....	....	10 : 25-37	....
105.	Jesus at the House of Martha and Mary.	....	....	10 : 38-42	....
106.	How to pray......................	....	....	11 : 1-13	....
107.	Heals a Dumb Demoniac..........	....	....	11 : 14-36	....
108.	Jesus Dines with a Pharisee......	....	....	12 : 37-54	....
109.	On Hypocrisy, Worldliness, etc....	....	....	12 : 1-59	....
110.	Slaughter of Certain Galileans.....	....	....	13 : 1-9	....
111.	A Blind Man healed on the Sabbath..	....	....	....	9 : 1-41
112.	The Good Shepherd...............	....	....	....	10 : 1-21
113.	Jesus at the Feast of Dedication...	....	....	....	10 : 22-39
114.	Retires beyond Jordan.............	....	....	....	10 : 40-42
115.	Heals an Infirm Woman on the Sabbath	....	....	13 : 10-21	....
116.	Journeying and Teaching; warned against Herod..................	....	....	13 : 22-35	....
117.	Jesus hears of Lazarus' Sickness...	....	....	....	11 : 1-6
118.	Dines with a Chief Pharisee.......	....	....	14 : 1-24	....
119.	Requirements of Discipleship.....	....	....	14 : 25-35	....
120.	Lost Sheep, Lost Silver, Prodigal Son..	....	....	15 : 1-32	....
121.	Parable of the Unjust Judge.......	....	....	16 : 1-13	....
122.	The Rich Man and Lazarus........	....	....	16 : 14-31	....
123.	Teaches Forbearance, Faith, etc...	....	....	17 : 1-10	....
124.	Goes to Bethany and Raises Lazarus...	....	....	....	11 : 7-46
125.	Retires to Ephraim................	....	....	....	11 : 47-54
126.	Passes through Samaria and Galilee..	....	....	17 : 11-19	....
127.	On the Coming of the Kingdom of God.	....	....	17 : 20-37	....
128.	The Importunate Widow, etc......	....	....	18 : 1-14	....
129.	Finally leaves Galilee; on Divorce...	19 : 1-12	10 : 1-12	....	....
130.	Blesses Little Children............	19 : 13-15	10 : 13-16	18 : 15-17	....
131.	The Rich Young Ruler.............	19 : 16-30	10 : 17-31	18 : 18-30	....

SECT.	SUBJECT.	MATT.	MARK.	LUKE.	JOHN.
132.	Laborers in the Vineyard	20:1-16			
133.	Third Time foretells his Death	20:17-19	10:32-34	18:31-34	
134.	The Ambitious Request of James and John	20:20-28	10:35-45		
135.	Healing Two Blind Men near Jericho	20:29-34	10:46-52	18:35-43	
136.	Zaccheus; the Ten Pounds			19:1-28	
137.	Jesus sought at Jerusalem				11:55-57
138.	Arrives at Bethany Six Days before the Passover			19:28	12:1, 9-11

VII. THE LAST PASSOVER WEEK.

Seven days, April 2nd to April 8th, A.D. 30.

139.	*First Day of the Week.* Public Entry into Jerusalem	21:1-11	11:1-11	19:29-44	12:12-19
140.	Certain Greeks desire to see Jesus	21:17	11:11		12:20-36
141.	*Second Day of the Week.* The Barren Fig-tree	21:18, 19	11:12-14		
142.	The Temple Cleansed	21:12-16	11:15-19	19:45-46; 37, 38	
143.	*Third Day of the Week.* Withered Fig-tree	21:20-22	11:20-26		
144.	In the Temple; the Two Sons	21:23-32	11:27-33	20:1-8	
145.	The Wicked Husbandmen	21:33-46	12:1-12	20:9-19	
146.	Marriage of the King's Son	22:1-14			
147.	Tribute to Cæsar	22:15-22	12:13-17	20:20-26	
148.	Concerning the Resurrection	22:23-33	12:18-27	20:27-40	
149.	The Great Commandment	22:34-40	12:28-34		
150.	Christ the Son of David	22:41-46	12:35-37	20:41-44	
151.	Last Discourse to the Jews	23:1-39	12:38-40	20:45-47	
152.	The Widow's Mite		12:41-44	21:1-4	
153.	Reflections on the Unbelief of the Jews				12:37-50
154.	Discourse on the Mount of Olives	24:1-51	13:1-37	21:5-36	
155.	The Ten Virgins; the Talents	25:1-30			
156.	Graphic Scene of the Judgment	25:31-46			
157.	*Fourth Day of the Week.* The Rulers conspire	26:1-5	14:1, 2	22:1, 2	
158.	The Supper and Anointing at Bethany	26:6-16	14:3-11	22:3-6	12:2-8
159.	*Fifth Day of the Week.* Preparation for the Passover	26:17-19	14:12-16	22:7-13	
160.	*Sixth Day of the Week.* The Passover; Contention of the Twelve	26:20	14:17	22:14-18, 24 30	
161.	Washing the Disciples' Feet				13:1-20
162.	The Traitor pointed out; Judas withdraws	26:21-25	14:18-21	22:21-23	13:21-30
163.	Jesus foretells the Fall of Peter			22:31-38	13:31-38
164.	Institutes the Lord's Supper (1 Cor. 11:23-26)	26:26-29	14:22-25	22:19, 20	
165.	Valedictory Discourse				14:1-31
166.	" " Continued				15:1-27
167.	" " Concluded				16:1-33
168.	Christ's Intercessory Prayer				17:1-26
169.	Again foretells the Fall of Peter	26:30-35	14:26-31	22:39	18:1
170.	The Agony in Gethsemane	26:36-46	14:32-42	22:40-46	18:1
171.	Betrayal and Apprehension	26:47-56	14:43-52	22:47-53	18:2-11
172.	Jesus before Annas				18:12-14, 19-23
173.	Peter thrice denies Christ	26:58,69-75	14:54,66-72	22:54-62	18:15-18, 25-27
174.	Jesus before Caiaphas	26:57,59-68	14:53,55-65	22:54,63-65	18:24
175.	The final Formal Examination	27:1	15:1	22:66-71	
176.	Jesus led to Pilate	27:2	15:1	23:1	18:28
177.	Remorse and Suicide of Judas (Acts 1:18, 19)	27:3-10			
178.	Jesus before Pilate	27:11-14	15:2-5	23:2-5	18:28-38
179.	Jesus before Herod			23:6-12	
180.	Again before Pilate; Barabbas	27:15-26	15:6-15	23:13-25	18:39, 40

SYNOPTICAL VIEW OF THE GOSPELS.

SECT.	SUBJECT.	MATT.	MARK.	LUKE.	JOHN.
181.	Scourged and delivered to be crucified.	27 : 26-30	15 : 16-19	23 : 25	19 : 1-16
182.	Led away to be crucified	27 : 31-34	15 : 20-23	23 : 26-33	19 : 16, 17
183.	The Crucifixion	27 : 35-44	15 : 24-32	23 : 33-43	19 : 18-27
184.	Phenomena attending his Death	27 : 45-56	15 : 33-41	23 : 44-49	19 : 28-30
185.	The Burial	27 : 57-61	15 : 42-47	23 : 50-56	19 : 31-42
186.	*The Seventh Day of the Week.* Sepulchre sealed and guarded	27 : 62-66	....	....	....

VIII. FROM CHRIST'S RESURRECTION TILL HIS ASCENSION.

Forty days, April to May, A.D. 30.

SECT.	SUBJECT.	MATT.	MARK.	LUKE.	JOHN.
187.	*The First Day of the Week.* The Resurrection	28 : 2-4	....	....	....
188.	Women visit the Sepulchre	28 : 1	16 : 1-4	24 : 1, 2	20 : 1, 2
189.	Vision of Angels	28 : 5-8	16 : 5-8	24 : 3-8	....
190.	Peter and John at the Sepulchre	....	....	24 : 12	20 : 3-10
191.	Jesus appears to Mary Magdalene	....	16 : 9	....	20 : 11-17
192.	Meets the Other Women	28 : 9, 10	....	....	....
193.	Report of the Women	....	16 : 10, 11	24 : 9-11	20 : 18
194.	Report of the Watch	28 : 11-15	....	....	....
195.	Appears to Two Disciples and to Peter (1 Cor. 15 : 5)	....	16 : 12, 13	24 : 13-35	....
196.	*Evening at the Close of the First Day of the Week.* Appears to Ten Apostles (1 Cor. 15 : 5)	....	16 : 14	24 : 36-49	20 : 19-25
197.	*Evening at the Close of the First Day of the Next Week.* Appears to Eleven Apostles	....	....	....	20 . 26-29
198.	Appears to Seven Apostles	....	....	....	21 : 1-23
199.	Appears to above Five Hundred (1 Cor. 15 : 6)	28 : 16	....	....	....
200.	He is seen of James; then of all the Apostles, 1 Cor. 15 : 7; Acts 1 : 3-8	28 : 16-20	16 : 15-18	....	....
201.	The Ascension (Acts 1 : 9-12)	....	16 : 19, 20	24 : 50-53	....
202.	John's Conclusion of his Gospel	....	....	....	20 : 30, 31; 21 : 24, 25

THE FOUR GOSPELS; THEIR DIVINE RELATION.

The careful and devout student of the Gospels will observe a relation between them; and that it was no accident that they are what they are and where they are. The following from Dr. H. G. Weston's "Gospel According to Matthew" (p. 8) is well worth pondering:

"What then are the Gospels? They are histories of redemption as accomplished in the life, death, burial, and resurrection of our Lord Jesus Christ. They are neither memoirs nor chronicles, but histories, presenting the redemptive work of Christ in its successive aspects and stages. Each Gospel prepares the way for its successor, each telling afresh the story of the life, death, and resurrection from its own point of view, each presenting its own phase of the history of redemption, its own stage of the redemption in process, each beginning at a higher level than the preceding. The Gospels are vitally related to one another, and the four constitute an organic whole."

A FEW RECENT WORKS REFERRED TO IN THESE NOTES,

AND ACCESSIBLE TO GENERAL READERS.

ALEXANDER, DR. J. ADDISON. Commentary on Matthew. Charles Scribner & Co., 654 Broadway, New-York.

ALFORD, DR. HENRY. The Four Gospels, with a Critical and Exegetical Commentary. Harper & Brothers, New-York.

BENGEL, DR. J. A. Gnomon of New Testament. A New Translation by Professors C. T. Lewis and M. R. Vincent. Perkinpine & Higgins, Philadelphia.

COLEMAN, DR. L. Ancient Christianity Exemplified. Lippincott & Co., Philadelphia.

CONANT, DR. T. J. The Gospel by Matthew, Revised with Critical and Philological Notes. Also, The Meaning and Use of *Baptizein*, Philologically and Historically Investigated. American Bible Union, 32 Great Jones Street, New-York.

ELLICOTT, DR. C. J. Historical Lectures on the Life of Christ. Gould & Lincoln, Boston.

HACKETT, DR. H. B. Illustrations of Scripture. Gould & Lincoln, Boston.

HERZOG, DR. Real Encyclopädie. A translation of this work from the German may be expected from Professor Howard Osgood, D.D.

KITTO, DR. J. Cyclopædia of Biblical Literature. Third Edition. Edited by Dr. W. L. Alexander. J. B. Lippincott & Co., Philadelphia.

LANGE, DR. J. P. Commentary on the Gospel according to Matthew. Translated from the German, with Additions, by Dr. P. Schaff. Charles Scribner, New-York.

LYNCH, LIEUT. WILLIAM F. United States Expedition to the Jordan and the Dead Sea. Philadelphia, Baltimore, and London.

MEYER, DR. H. A. W. Critical and Exegetical Commentary. A Translation from the German, to be published by T & T. Clark, Edinburgh.

NAST, DR. WILLIAM. Commentary on Matthew. Poe & Hitchcock, Cincinnati.

OLSHAUSEN, DR. H. Biblical Commentary on the New Testament. First American edition; revised by Dr. A. C Kendrick. Sheldon & Co., New-York.

ROBINSON, DR. E. Biblical Researches in Palestine, etc. Crocker & Brewster, Boston.

SMITH, DR. W. Dictionary of the Bible. American Edition; revised and edited by Professor H. B. Hackett, D.D. Hurd & Houghton, New-York.

STIER Dr. R. Words of the Lord Jesus. Revised American Edition. N. Tibbals & Son, New-York.

THOLUCK, DR. A. Sermon on the Mount. T. & T. Clark, Edinburgh.

THOMSON, DR. W. M. The Land and The Book. Harper & Brothers, New-York.

TISCHENDORF, Dr. C. When were Our Gospels Written? American Tract Society, New-York.

TRENCH, PROFESSOR R. C. Notes on Parables; on Miracles. D. Appleton & Co., New-York.

WHEDON, DR. D. D. Commentary on the Gospels. Carlton & Porter, New-York.

WORDSWORTH, DR. CHARLES. The New Testament, with Notes. Scribner & Co., New-York.

THE GOSPEL ACCORDING TO MATTHEW.

CHAPTER I.

The royal genealogy of Jesus.

1 THE book of the ^ageneration of Jesus Christ, ^bthe son of David, ^cthe son of Abraham.

^a Lk. 3. 23. etc.; Ge. 5. 1.
^b ch. 22. 42-45; Is.

The Gospel. The name Gospel is compounded of two Anglo-Saxon words, *god*, *good*, and *spell*, history, story, news, that is, *good news*, or *tidings*, which is a translation of the Greek term applied as a title to the four inspired histories of the life and teaching of Christ. It is thus found in the greatest number of ancient manuscripts, and was doubtless very early applied to the four narratives of our Lord. This narrative, as written and delivered by Matthew, is very appropriately inscribed, *The Gospel according to Matthew.* The simplicity of the title is in harmony with God's word and works everywhere, and with the style of the book. The word *saint*, so often applied to Matthew, and placed before his name in the inscription of his Gospel, is an addition of a late date, and the product of a vitiated taste which delights in useless epithets, and can not bear the simplicity of truth. It is worthy of note that while the New Testament teaches that all believers are saints (Acts 9: 13, 32, 41; 26: 10; Rom. 1: 7; 8: 27), yet nowhere is the term applied to any of them individually as a distinguishing epithet.

CHAPTER I.

Matthew begins his Gospel by tracing the descent of Jesus *from* Abraham, the father of the faithful, and *through* David, from whom the Messiah was to descend. Then he briefly records the circumstances of his miraculous birth, announced by an angel, and in fulfillment of an ancient prophecy. Thus by his genealogy and birth is he shown to be the Messiah foretold and foreshadowed by the prophecies and types of the Old Testament. In his genealogy we have proof of his humanity; in his miraculous birth, of his divinity. Not only the first chapter, but the whole Gospel, forms a series of historical arguments for the Messiahship of Jesus.

I. THE INSCRIPTION OF THE CHAPTER.

1. The book. The word translated *book* originally signified the inner bark of the *papyrus*, one of the most ancient kinds of writing material. It was thence applied to any writing, and particularly to a roll or scroll of linen, papyrus or parchment, the ancient form of a volume, written inside and unrolled for reading.

A PARCHMENT.

The meaning of the word here is very nearly expressed by *document* or *record*. **Generation.** The same word in the original as that translated *birth* in ver. 18. Some regard the expression, *The book of the generation* as equivalent to *genealogy, genealogical table*, and thus an inscription of the sixteen following verses. Others, with far less reason, take it to mean *book of nativity* in the sense of history, and applied as a title to the whole Gospel. It is better, however, to take it in its more obvious and natural sense, *The record of the birth* To what, then, is it a title? Plainly to the first chapter alone. For the expression in ver. 18, "Now the birth of Jesus was on this wise," indicates the continuing of the account of the Savior's birth, while the transition in ch. 2 : 1, "Now when Jesus was born," denotes the completion of the record.

Jesus Christ. Jesus was the personal name of our Lord, being the Greek form of Joshua, or rather of Jeshua, as the name was written after the Babylonish captivity, and means *Savior*, or more strictly, *Jehovah his help* or *salvation*. Joshua is referred to under the name of Jesus twice in the New Testament, Acts 7 : 45; Heb. 4 : 8. It is the name commonly applied to our Lord in the Gospels. We shall therefore generally use this name to designate him in these notes. The writers of the Epistles usually call him "the Lord," "the Lord Jesus," or "the Lord Jesus Christ," thus indicating him as their risen Lord, their anointed and spiritual king, and their divinely appointed Ruler and Savior. See on ver. 21. **Christ,** that is, *anointed*, his official name corresponding to the Hebrew *Messiah*. In the Old Testament, the latter had been used of prophets (Ps. 105 : 15); of high-priests (Lev. 4 : 3, 5); and of kings (1 Sam. 24 : 6, 10); because all these persons were consecrated to their office by *anointing* with oil. From such passages as Ps. 2 : 2, Dan. 9 : 24, 25, it became common among the Jews to apply it to the expected deliverer. See John 1 : 41, and 4 : 25. It was preëminently appropriate to our Lord, as the *consecrated* or *anointed* one, having received the spiritual anointing, the Holy Spirit without measure, and combining in himself the three offices of prophet, priest, and king. The Jews speak of the Messiah; Christians speak of him as the Christ. Our Savior is not once called *Messiah* by any writer in the New Testament, while *Christ* is very frequently applied to him. It is generally used as an official title in the Gospels, pointing to the one that was to come (ch. 11 : 3), foretold by the prophets. The Greek word *Christ*, passing from a title, is commonly used as a proper name in the Epistles and in all but a few instances in the Acts. In the Gospels it appears thus only at the beginning or the ending (ver. 16; ch. 27 : 17; Mark 1 : 1; John 1 : 17), and once in the mouth of our Lord himself, John 17 : 3. One object of the following genealogical table, and the account of our Savior's birth, was to show that he was the Christ.

The son of David, the son of Abraham. *Son* in both instances refers to Jesus Christ, and, according to a Hebrew manner of speaking, is equivalent to *descendant*. Son was variously used among the Jews, meaning a male child, a grandson, an adopted son, one taking the place of a son, a disciple; and in a wider sense, a descendant. Jesus is called the son or descendant of both David and Abraham, because the promise had been made to both, Ps. 89 : 35, 36; 132 : 11; Gen. 12 : 3; 22 : 18; 26 : 4. *Son of David* had become a special title of the Messiah (see on ch. 12 : 23; 21 : 9); and *son of Abraham* pointed to that seed in whom all nations should be blessed. Matthew, in tracing the genealogy of Jesus through the royal line of David to Abraham, clearly indicates the character of his Gospel. He wrote specially for Jewish Christians, while Luke, in ascending to Adam, wrote for the race. Mark begins with styling Jesus as the Son of God; Matthew represents him as the Son of Man and the Messiah. His may be called in a special sense, the *Messianic Gospel*.

2–17. THE GENEALOGICAL TABLE, in which the ancestry of Jesus is traced from Abraham through the royal line of David. Luke 3 : 23–38.

It was customary with the Jews to keep such registers in their own families, and it was a peculiar glory of the Jewish people that, while the history of other nations was involved in obscurity and fable, theirs could be traced in an unbroken line to the beginning of the race, 1 Chron. chaps. 1–4; Gen. 5 : 1 and 6 : 9. Josephus speaks thus of his own genealogy: "I give the descent of our family, exactly as I find it written in the public records." The royal family of David would of course have its public record, probably at Bethlehem, the place of David's birth, and of Joseph's, and Mary's, enrollment, Luke 2 : 4, 5. Matthew very likely was led by the Holy Spirit to give us a copy of such a family, or public, document. Thus the Jewish readers of his Gospel could verify his statement, by going and examining the record for themselves.

The genealogy as here given, however, presents various difficulties: First, in regard to several omissions; Second, in comparing it with that given by Luke; Third, in its arrangement into three divisions of fourteen generations each.

First, the names of Ahaziah, Joash, and Amaziah are omitted, which, according to 1 Chron. 3: 11, 12, should come in between Joram and Ozias (ver. 8); also the name Jehoiakim should be inserted between Josias and Jechonias (ver. 11), 2 Kings 24: 6. There must have been a sufficient reason for these omissions. The Jews, who were the best and most capable judges, did not object to them. Matthew, in copying his genealogy from the family or public records, was responsible only for the accuracy of the copy. This was legal evidence that Jesus was the descendant of David, and the legal heir to his throne. The names between Joram and Ozias may have been stricken out because they were the near descendants of the wicked Jezebel, and unworthy links in the royal chain. We know that Joash was, at his death, deemed unworthy of burial in the sepulchres of the kings, 2 Chron. 24: 25. For like reasons other omission may have been made. These, however, did not impair the genealogy as a whole, since such omissions were common among the Jews, as now among the Arabians; and the words *beget, son,* and *daughter,* were well understood to have frequently the wider reference to descendants. "Furthermore, as in geography the distances of places are, without any violence to truth, described sometimes by longer and sometimes by shorter stages, so with the steps of generations in a genealogy—among the Hebrews as well as among others."—*Bengel.*

Second, Luke, in his genealogical table of our Lord (ch. 3: 23–38), has given an entirely different list from that of Matthew between David and Christ. According to Matthew, the father of Joseph, Mary's husband, was Jacob, a descendant of David through the royal line of Solomon, and the kings of Judah; but according to Luke, Joseph's father was Heli, whose descent is traced through Nathan to David. Various explanations have been given. (1) A very ancient one is the supposition that by the Jewish levirate law (Deut. 25: 6)—that when a man died without children, his brother should marry his widow—the two lines had converged into one. Thus Julius Africanus, according to Eusebius (E. H. 1. 7), suggested that Heli and Jacob were step-brothers, and that the former dying childless, the latter married his widow, and was the real father of Joseph. Ambrosius, however, supposed that Heli was the real, and Jacob the nominal, father. This explains the difference; yet it has been objected that, in either case, only the *legal* father of Joseph (Deut. 25: 6) would have been mentioned, and also that the levirate law did not apply to step-brothers by the same mother. (2) Another explanation, which is worthy of notice more for its ingenuity than for any thing else, is proposed by Arthur C. Hervey, in Smith's Dict. of the Bible ("Genealogy of Jesus Christ"), which supposes both genealogies to be those of Joseph. Matthew's is Joseph's genealogy as *legal* successor to David's throne, exhibiting the successive heirs to his kingdom. Luke's is Joseph's *private* genealogy, showing his *real* birth. Lord Hervey supposes that on the failure of Solomon's line in Jechonias, Salathiel, of the house of Nathan, became heir to David's throne, and that he and his descendants were transferred to the royal genealogical table, according to Jewish law laid down in Num. 27: 8–11. The other divergences of the two genealogies are explained on the same principle. Matthew, he supposes, had two sons, Jacob and Heli. But Jacob, the father of Mary the mother of Jesus, dying without male issue, the succession to David's throne devolved on Joseph, the son of Heli. For more on this see Smith's as above, and Alexander's Kitto, "Genealogy of Jesus Christ." (3) A better explanation is that which supposes that Matthew gives the paternal genealogy, and Luke the maternal. This is the view most commonly adopted, and one supported by much ancient authority. Jesus was but the *reputed* son of Joseph, and hence so far but the *reputed* descendant of David. It was necessary to the strict fulfillment of prophecy that Mary should be of the house of David. And such was the fact, Luke 1: 27, 32. While it was important that the right of Jesus to the throne of David should be shown through the royal line, it was equally important that his connection "as concerning the flesh," should be traced through the line of Mary. Genealogical

MATTHEW I.

2 ^d Abraham begat Isaac: and ^e Isaac begat Jacob: 9. 7; 11. 1; Jer 23. 5.
3 and ^f Jacob begat Judas and ^g his brethren: and   ^e Ge. 12. 3; 22. 18;
 ^h Judas begat Phares and Zara of ⁱ Thamar; and   Gal. 3. 16.
  ^k Phares begat Esrom: and Esrom begat Aram: ^d Ge. 21. 2, 3.
                                                  ^e Ge. 25. 26.

---

tables are indeed unusual in the case of women, but this difficulty is more than overcome when we consider the greatness of Jesus. The genealogy of Luke is not so much that of Mary as of her most illustrious and ever blessed Son. Moreover, if she was an heiress, as many suppose, then such a table must of necessity exist. In that case she must marry in her own tribe (Num. 36: 6-9); and her husband must himself enter her family, and have as it were two fathers. This is especially applicable to Joseph, the husband of Mary. Matthew, speaking of his *real* father, says, "Jacob *begat* Joseph;" while Luke, regarding him as having entered the family of Mary, styles him, "the son of Heli." This supposition also explains Mary's journey to Bethlehem, where, as an heiress, she with her husband would be registered. The two names, Salathiel and Zorobabel, are the same in both (Matt. 1 : 12; Luke 3 : 27); but their position in the two tables points to different persons bearing the same names, but living at different times.

Third, Matthew divides his table into three divisions of fourteen generations each. The object of this was doubtless to assist the memory, as well as to present the *growth* of the genealogical line through the patriarchs to David, its *power* through the royal line to the captivity, its *decline* from the captivity to Joseph, the carpenter. This is thus but a summary of the names here given without reference to any that may, for good reasons, have been omitted in the table. **All the generations** (ver. 17) more probably refers to the first clause of the verse, and may strictly mean all the links between Abraham and David; but if it be extended to the whole verse, it may, without any violence, mean all that are here given. Some difficulty has been found in making fourteen in each division; and different arrangements of the names have been made. The best arrangement makes the first division begin with Abraham and end with David; the second, to begin with David and end with Josiah; the third, to begin with Jechonias, ending with Jesus. While David is evidently included in the first and second divisions, no name is mentioned at the *removal* to Babylon which can well be repeated. Josiah was too early to be included in the third division; and the reference to the begetting of Jechonias about the time of the removal would indicate him as the starting-point of that division.

2. Judas and his brethren. Judas is the Greek form of Judah. But why are the brethren of Judah named, and not those of Abraham, Isaac, and Jacob? Doubtless because the former were the children of the promise, but the latter were not. As all the sons of Jacob inherited the blessing of their father, it was fitting to recognize the brethren of Judah and thus the whole of Israel, though it had been foretold that from Judah Shiloh should come, Gen. 49 : 10.

3. Thamar. The four women mentioned by Matthew in his genealogy, Thamar, Rahab, Ruth, and Bathsheba, were objectionable according to Jewish law, but chosen of God to be among the ancestors of Christ. Ruth, though a Gentile, chose to be numbered with the people of God, and was an example of piety. The faith of Rahab is recorded in the Epistle to the Hebrews (11 : 34). The others doubtless repented of their grievous sins, and were accepted of God, through faith in the coming Redeemer. Christ, however, derives his glory from himself, and not from his ancestors. It is not they who honor him, but rather he that honors them. His condescension, too, is the more wonderful, the lower he descended in the scale of honor in taking on himself our nature. Thus would he humble both Jewish and human pride, and illustrate his sovereignty in choosing the despised and base of the world, "that no flesh should glory in his presence," 1 Cor. 1 : 29. And did not God intimate, by adopting Thamar and Rahab, Canaanitish women, and Ruth the Moabitess, into the line of the ancestors of Christ, that through him the Gentiles should be saved, and so united to his people as to be "one flock and one shepherd"?

MATTHEW I.

4 and Aram begat Aminadab: and Aminadab begat
5 Naasson: and Naasson begat Salmon: and Salmon begat Booz of ᶦRachab: and Booz begat Obed of
6 ᵐRuth: and Obed begat Jesse: and ⁿJesse begat David the king.
 And ᵒDavid the king begat Solomon ᵖof her
7 *that had been the wife* of Urias: and ᑫSolomon begat Roboam: and ʳRoboam begat Abia: and Abia
8 begat Asa: and Asa begat Josaphat: and Josaphat
9 begat Joram: and Joram begat Ozias: and Ozias begat Joatham: and Joatham begat ˢAchaz: and
10 Achaz begat Ezekias: and ᵗEzekias begat Manasses: and Manasses begat Amon: and Amon
11 begat Josias: and ᵘJosias begat Jechonias and his brethren, about the time they were ˣcarried away to Babylon.
12 And after they were brought to Babylon, ʸJechonias begat Salathiel: and Salathiel begat ᶻZoroba-
13 bel: and Zorobabel begat Abiud: and Abiud begat
14 Eliakim: and Eliakim begat Azor: and Azor begat Sadoc: and Sadoc begat Achim: and Achim begat
15 Eliud: and Eliud begat Eleazar: and Eleazar be-
16 gat Matthan: and Matthan begat Jacob: and Jacob begat ᵃJoseph the husband of Mary, ᵇof whom was born Jesus, ᶜwho is called Christ.

ᶠ Ge. 29. 35; 49. 8-12.
ᵍ Ge. 35. 22-26.
ʰ Ge. 38. 27, etc.; 46. 12.
ᶦ Ge. 38. 6.
ᵏ Ru. 4. 18, etc., 1 Chr. 2. 5, 9, etc.
ˡ Jos 6. 22-25.
ᵐ Ru. ch. 2. to ch.4
ⁿ 1 Sam. 16. 1, 11-13; 17. 12.
ᵒ 2 Sam. 12. 24, 25.
ᵖ 2 Sam. 11. 26, 27
ᑫ 1 Chr. 3. 10, etc.
ʳ 1 Ki. 11. 43.
ˢ 2 Ki. 15. 38.
ᵗ 2 Ki. 16. 20; 20. 21; 1 Chr. 3. 13.
ᵘ 1 Chr. 3. 15, 16.
ˣ 2 Ki. 24, 14-16; 25. 11.

ʸ 1 Chr. 3. 17, 19.
ᶻ Ezra 3. 2; 5. 2; Ne. 12. 1.

ᵃ Lk. 1. 27.
ᵇ Mk. 6. 3; Lk. 1. 35; 2. 7. 11.
ᶜ ch. 27. 17.

5-6. Rachab—David. Some suppose certain omissions between Rahab and David, such as were common in Hebrew genealogies. But Matthew agrees exactly with the line given in Ruth 4: 18-22. It is possible that some unimportant names were omitted in both, as the verb *beget* does not necessarily denote, in all cases, immediate succession, but may express the relation of ancestor and descendant. But it is better to account for the 366 years between Rahab and David by supposing the parents very old at the birth of their children. Rahab was young when she hid the spies (Joshua 6: 23); Boaz was far advanced in life when he married Ruth (Ruth 3: 10); and Jesse was very old when he became the father of David, 1 Sam. 17: 12-14.

David the king. Called the king to show the beginning of the royal line, as a type of Messianic royalty, and because his throne is given to Christ, Luke 1: 32.

11. About the time—carried away_to Babylon. Nebuchadnezzar first took Jerusalem B.C. 606, three years after the death of Josiah, 2 Kings 24: 1; Dan. 1: 1. Seventy years from this date Cyrus made his decree for re-building the temple and the restoration of the Jews, Ezra 1: 1-4. The storm was gathering in Josiah's reign, which resulted in the removal to Babylon, though it was delayed on account of his piety and his zeal in reforming the people and suppressing idolatry, 2 Kings 22: 19, 20; 23: 26, 27. *Babylon*, capital of the empire of Babylonia, was a celebrated city situated on both sides of the Euphrates. Its walls are described as 60 miles in circumference, entered by 100 brazen gates, 25 on each side.

12. Jechonias. Jeremiah (22: 29, 30) had prophesied of Coniah or Jehoiachin, or as here, Jechonias, "Write this man childless," and that no man of his seed should prosper, sitting on the throne of David. How then could come of him Jesus, the Messiah? It may be answered :

First, that the prophet spoke of him not as an individual, for he had children; but as a king, for none of his children became king. He was the furthest in descent from David, who reigned in Judah. So it seems to be explained in Jer. 22: 30. But if this does not fully satisfy the mind, it may be said, *secondly*, that

17 So all the generations from Abraham to David *are* fourteen generations: and from David until the carrying away into Babylon *are* fourteen generations: and from the carrying away into Babylon unto Christ *are* fourteen generations.

The Divine origin and the birth of Jesus.

18 NOW the ᵈ birth of Jesus Christ was on this wise: When as his mother Mary was espoused to Joseph, before they came together, she was found
19 with child ᵉ of the Holy Ghost. Then Joseph her husband, being ᶠ a just *man*, and not willing ᵍ to

ᵈ Lk. 1. 27, etc.

ᵉ Lk. 1. 35; Gal. 4. 4, 5.
ᶠ Lk. 2. 25.
ᵍ Deu. 24. 1.

Jesus was not of the seed of Joseph, but of Mary, whose descent is traced through Nathan, to David. He had only a legal claim to the throne of David through Joseph, his reputed father.

18–25. ACCOUNT OF THE BIRTH OF JESUS. Found only in Matthew. Compare Luke 2: 4–21.

This account probably corresponds with the time of Mary's return from visiting Elisabeth. It should be noted that, in ver. 16, Matthew did not say, *Joseph begat Jesus*, but that he was "the husband of Mary, of whom was born Jesus," thus intimating that Joseph was not his father. Matthew, therefore, next proceeds to give such an account of his real birth as will explain his language, and show his divine origin.

18. **On this wise.** After this manner. **Espoused.** Betrothed. Jewish parents were wont to arrange in regard to the marriage of their children, sometimes according to the previous choice of the son, and with some regard to the consent of the daughter, Gen. 24: 4, 39, 58; Jud. 14: 2, 3. A dowry was given by the suitor to the parent and brethren of the bride. The interval between betrothal and the celebration of marriage was generally ten or twelve months, Deut. 20: 7; Jud. 14: 8. During this time the betrothed remained at her father's house.

Joseph resided at Nazareth, as also did Mary (Luke 1: 26; 2: 4), and followed the occupation of a carpenter, to which Jesus was also trained, Mark 6: 3. See on ch. 13: 55. But little is said of him in the Gospels, the last reference being that of his return from the Passover when Jesus was twelve years of age. What was his age when he married, and when he died, are alike unknown. That he died before the crucifixion is quite certain from what is related in John 19: 27, and from the absence of his name in those passages in the Gospels where allusion is made to Mary and the brethren of Jesus.

Little is said of **Mary** by the Evangelists after their account of the birth of Jesus. No intimation is given of her sinlessness from birth, which is now a doctrine of the Romish Church. The Scriptures teach positively that all the race have fallen in Adam, with the exception of Christ, and that they can be saved only through him, Acts 4: 12; Rom. 3: 10, 23; Gal. 3: 22; 1 John 1: 8. The entire silence of the New Testament after the first chapter of the Acts in regard to her, and the language of Jesus recorded in ch. 12: 46–50, Luke 2: 49, 50, and John 2: 4, are alike against this doctrine and that of making her an object of worship. See on ch. 2: 11, and Luke 1: 47, where Mary confesses her own need of a Savior. She appears at the cross (John 19: 25, 26), but is not mentioned in connection with the resurrection. Her name appears for the last time in the N. T. in Acts 1: 14. How long she lived after this, and where she died, are unknown. Tradition is very conflicting on these points. One is, that she went to Ephesus with the Apostle John, and died there in the year 63.

Of the Holy Ghost. *Ghost* in older English signifies spirit, but in the English of the present day is applied almost exclusively to the apparition of a departed human spirit. Hence *Holy Spirit* is the better designation of the third person of the Godhead. Jesus was not begotten by ordinary generation; but his

make her a public example, was minded to put her away privily. But while he thought on these things, behold, ᵇ the angel of the Lord appeared unto him in a dream, saying, Joseph, thou son of David, fear not to take unto thee Mary thy wife:

ᵇ ch. 2. 19; Lk. 1. 11, 26; 2. 9.

body was created by the direct power of God, Luke 1 : 35; Heb. 10 : 5. The Evangelist carefully guards the purity and innocence of Mary, in that he says that this occurred "before they came together."

19. The Jews regarded betrothed persons as husband and wife, and unfaithfulness was treated as adultery. Hence Joseph is styled **her husband.** See "thy wife," in ver. 20.

A just man. Upright, righteous. The word *just* has been falsely explained as meaning kind, tender-hearted, but no such use of the word can be found in the New Testament. His *being just* is the reason for putting her away. So Dr. Conant, and others.

A public example; by punishment, being stoned to death, Deut. 22 : 23, 24. But according to the highest critical authorities, it should read, *expose her openly*. Though Joseph's sense of right led him to decide upon a divorce, yet he was unwilling to expose her openly to shame and punishment. Mary had doubtless told him all the circumstances, but he was unable to share her faith. Suspicious yet uncertain, and well knowing the virtuous character of Mary in the past, it would have been unjust in him to have proceeded to the extreme measures of the law (Deut. 22 : 23, 24), or to have exposed her to shame by a public divorce. **Privily.** *Privately*. The law of Moses gave the husband the power of divorce. He could give a bill of divorcement publicly, assigning the reason, or he could give a private kind of divorce in which no reason would be assigned, and the dowry would not be forfeited. Joseph, unwilling to do the former, "was minded," rather *desirous*, to do the latter, in which case the child might be regarded as his son. His mind was yet in doubt, and he still undecided as to what to do.

20. **But while he thought,** etc. The inward struggle continues. Thus God subjected both Mary and Joseph to trial, and Christ to humiliation. Mary, supported by strong faith and the words of the angel Gabriel, could well endure for a time suspicion. Joseph could not act hastily against one he so tenderly loved, and in a case so closely affecting his own happiness, character, and reputation. He kept revolving these things in his mind. God at length came to his relief. God causes his chosen people in every age to pass through trial, but at the proper time he comes to their rescue.

The angel of the Lord. The angel of the Lord, or the angel Jehovah, is the usual title of the second person of the Godhead, in the Old Testament; but here *an angel* (for so it is in the original) probably refers to the angel Gabriel, who appeared to Mary, Luke 1 : 26. *Angel* means *messenger*, Luke 9 : 52. It is applied to prophets (Isa. 42 : 19), to priests (Mal. 2 : 7), and even to inanimate objects, Ps. 104 : 4. But generally in the Bible the word is applied to a race of intelligent beings of a higher order than man, who surround the Deity, and are messengers or agents in administering the affairs of the world, and are sent forth to minister to those who shall be heirs of salvation, Dan. 10 : 20, 21; Acts 7 : 30; Heb. 1 : 14. The existence of angels accords with reason as well as with revelation. As we behold in creation a descending order of beings below man, so it is natural to suppose that there is an ascending order above man toward the infinite God.

In a dream. God has employed various ways in revealing his will, by dreams, visions, assuming a human appearance, angels, direct announcement, etc. Revelation by dreams was common under the old dispensation, and appears to have been the lowest mode of divine communication. How the true was distinguished from the false we know not. God, however, who gave the dream, enabled the dreamer to recognize it as from Him. Mary received the highest order of revelation, an open announcement by the angel Gabriel; Joseph, the lowest order by an unnamed angel in a dream. To her the communication was of a future event; to him of a present fact. Christ having come and finished his sacrificial

^l for that which is conceived in her is of the Holy
21 Ghost. ^k And she shall bring forth a son, and thou
shalt call his name JESUS: for ^l he shall save his
22 people from their sins. Now all this was done that
it might be fulfilled which was spoken of the Lord
23 by the prophet, saying, ^m "Behold, a virgin shall
be with child, and shall bring forth a son, and they

^l ver. 18.
^k Lk. 1. 31.
^l Dan. 9. 24-26; John 1. 29; Ac. 3. 26; 4. 12; 5. 31; Tit. 2. 14; 1 John 3. 5.
^m Is. 7. 14.

---

work, the Holy Spirit having been sent, and the Scriptures completed, revelation by dreams, visions, etc., is no longer needed.

Son of David. Descendant of David. See on ver. 1. This title would remind Joseph of his royal descent, and prepare his mind for the announcement of the Messiah. **Mary thy wife.** He is also reminded of the relation subsisting between him and Mary his betrothed, and he is exhorted to consummate the marriage. The reason why he should not fear to take her to him is given in what follows. **Conceived.** Begotten by the miraculous power of the Holy Spirit. It was fitting that the creative power of God should be exercised in the second Adam, as well as in the first, Luke 1: 35.

21. Bring forth a son. "It is a slight but significant difference between this and the similar assurance made to Zecharias (Luke 1 : 13), that the pronoun *to thee* is omitted here, because our Lord was to be brought forth not to Joseph, but to God."—J. ADDISON ALEXANDER. **Shalt call.** Expressing what he should do by divine appointment. **Jesus.** See on ver. 1. His name was prophetic of the divine *salvation* of which he would be the author, Heb. 5 : 9.

He shall save his people. *He* is emphatic. He alone shall save; salvation shall only be through him. Here do we see the general meaning of his name, and why he was so called. By *his people* Joseph doubtless understood the Jews, but in its wider and spiritual application, it included the whole Israel of God, of all ages and from all nations. We have thus the true and spiritual character of Christ presented before his birth.

From their sins. Here is brought to view the spiritual nature and design of Christ's office and work. It is not said from any temporal calamity, or any earthly power, but from their sins. It is a salvation from sin itself; yet salvation from sin includes salvation from the effects of sin—guilt, punishment, and misery. Notice also that salvation and holiness are inseparable. Christ does not save his people *in* their sins, but *from* their sins. There is no salvation except from sin; and we have no evidence that we are his people, unless we are saved from the power and dominion of sin. Thus this verse brings to view the great work of the Redeemer: Jesus the only Savior; his people, the saved; from what they are saved, their sins; and all that he did, and does, and shall do, for their salvation, by his life, death, resurrection, the Holy Spirit in renewal and sanctification, his intercession, his grace and power in their behalf, their future bodily resurrection and glorification, and their presence and participation with him in heaven.

22. Now all this was done. The language not of the angel but of the Evangelist. Literally, *and all this has come to pass*, the perfect being used in the Greek. It is characteristic of Matthew to point out the fulfillment of prophecy, ch. 2 : 6, 15, 18, 23; 3 : 3; 4 : 14; 8 : 17; 12 : 17, etc.

That it might be fulfilled. *In order that it might be*, etc., is the uniform meaning of this phrase in the New Testament, referring to the direct fulfillment of some prediction, type, or typical prophecy. We catch here a glimpse of a twofold reason for the fulfillment of prophecy: First, that the power, truth, and faithfulness of God should not be compromised; Second, that his purposes as revealed should be carried out. Hence it is said, "Now all this was done that," etc. Types and prophecies are not the cause of events, but simply the revelation of God's will concerning them.

Of the Lord by the prophet. Rather, "*by* the Lord," as the author of the prediction, and "*through* the prophet," as the medium of its communication.

B.C. 5. MATTHEW I. 25

24 shall call his name Emmanuel," which being interpreted is, ⁿGod with us. Then Joseph being raised from sleep did as the angel of the Lord had bidden
25 him, and took unto him his wife: and knew her not till she had brought forth ᵒher firstborn son: and he called his name JESUS.

ⁿ Is. 8, 9, 10.
John 1:14.
9.
1 Tim. 3.

ᵒ Ex. 13:2; Num. 8.17; Lk. 2. 7, 21

23. Behold a virgin shall be, etc. More exactly, *the virgin*, the particular one in whom the prophecy was fulfilled. This prediction is recorded in Isa. 7 : 14, and announced to Ahaz, king of Judah, about 742 B.C. The land of Judah was invaded by the two kings of Israel and Syria. Isaiah is directed by the Lord to go to Ahaz, who was greatly alarmed, and announce to him his deliverance, and the overthrow of both Syria and Israel. As a pledge or token that these things should come to pass, the prophet was directed by the Lord to mention a sign, namely, a virgin should have a son and should call his name Immanuel, and before he should arrive to years of discretion, the kings of Israel and Syria should be cut off. The prediction seems to have an immediate reference to an event which was shortly to take place. Yet Matthew unmistakably points to its fulfillment in the child Jesus. This difficulty is best explained, we think, by regarding this prediction as a typical prophecy, having a double reference, first to some birth soon to take place in the ordinary course of nature; and secondly, to the miraculous incarnation of our Lord. The prophecy included both, as type and antitype, strengthened rather than weakened by the former, as both the prediction and type concentrated in Christ. The principle here involved, we believe, is the explanation of those passages which the old expositors interpreted in a double sense, and which many modern commentators explain as a mere accommodation. Olshausen has well remarked: "But the difficulty can be removed by our acknowledging in the Old Testament prophecies a twofold reference to a present lower subject, and to a future higher one. With this supposition we can everywhere adhere to the immediate, simple, grammatical sense of the words, and still recognize the quotations of the New Testament as prophecies in the full sense. And it belongs in the peculiar arrangement and adjustment of Scripture, that the life and the substance of the Old Testament were intended as a mirror of the New Testament life, and that in the person of Christ particularly, as the representative of the New Testament, all the rays of Old Testament ideas and institutions are concentrated as a focus."

Some suppose the immediate fulfillment of the prophecy to be related in Isa. 8 : 1-4. But the child was not called Immanuel. Others suppose the birth of a child of Ahaz to be intended. Certainty can not be attained in regard to this. But while it is uncertain what child is meant in Isaiah's day, Matthew clearly declared Jesus to be the child to whom both the prophecy and type pointed. In Mary and Jesus was a literal fulfillment, Luke 1 : 34, 35.

Immanuel. A Hebrew word, meaning *God with us*, and quite synonymous with Jesus, the meaning of which includes both Jehovah and salvation. See on ver. 1. As applied to the child of Isaiah's day, it was simply expressive of God's presence with the Jews to deliver them. But the full meaning of the name was only realized in Christ, the incarnate God, the God-man. Many names among the Jews had been compounded of Jehovah or God and some other word. Thus Isaiah means, "the salvation of Jehovah;" Elijah, "Salvation of God;" Eli, "my God;" Eliab, "God is Father;" Eleazar, "help of God." In none of these instances, however, does the name indicate divinity connected with the persons so called, no more than Immanuel did in the child so named in Isaiah's day. Yet in so common a practice may we not see the longing of the ancient people of God for the promised seed, the "man with Jehovah"? Gen. 4 : 1. The use of Jehovah or God in the name of the Jews, therefore, so far from militating against a higher sense, was but preparatory and prophetic, a preparation of suitable language to express an incomprehensible fact, types, prophetic longings, and prophecies of that One, who was truly and emphatically IMMANUEL, GOD

3

Visit of the Magi.

II NOW when ᵖ Jesus was born in Bethlehem of Judæa in the days of Herod the king, behold, there   ᵖ Lk. 2. 4–7.

MANIFESTED IN THE FLESH. John 1 : 14

24, 25. Joseph was obedient to the heavenly vision, and immediately married Mary with the usual Jewish ceremonies. Her virginity continued, however, till the birth of Jesus. The language here, as well as subsequent history, implies that she continued to live after the birth of her first-born, as the wife of Joseph, ch. 2 : 13, 20.

Her first-born son. The oldest manuscripts and the best critical authorities read, *a son*, omitting the words, *her first-born*. That Jesus was her first-born is, however, distinctly taught throughout the whole account of his birth, and distinctly stated by Luke (ch. 2 : 7). This passage, in connection with the one referred to in Luke, shows that there was nothing repugnant in the idea that Mary might have had other children, and indeed affords a presumption that she had. The language, *And knew her not till*, is rather *against* than *for* her perpetual virginity. See ch. 13 : 55; Luke 2 : 7. **His name Jesus.** Joseph conferred it upon him in accordance with the divine command, on the eighth day, at the time of his circumcision, Luke 2 : 21.

REMARKS.

1. A preparation had been going on in the world's history for the coming of Christ. Toward him all events were converging through the families of Abraham and David, ver. 1; Gal. 4 : 4. So let our hearts converge through every human affection toward Jesus, John 6 : 68.

2. How fleeting is human life! One generation passeth away and another cometh, vers. 2–16; Ps. 90 : 12. Though our names may not be handed down to posterity, let us see to it that they are written in heaven, Luke 10 : 20; Phil. 4 : 3.

3. Pious ancestors do not confer holiness on their children. Some of the links between David and Christ were wicked men. Yet even they were made to do their part toward bringing the Messiah into the world, ver. 8–12; ch. 3 : 9; Ezek. 18 : 20.

4. The miraculous birth of Jesus is typical of the second birth in man. In his birth was the united operation of the Holy Spirit and the word; so the believer is born of the Spirit, and begotten by the word of truth, ver. 18; John 3 : 5; James 1 : 18.

5. As through woman came the fall, so by means of woman came salvation from the consequences of the fall, ver. 21; Gal. 4 : 4; 1 Tim. 2 : 14.

6. Christ is the only Savior from sin, ver. 21; John 12 : 32; 14 : 6; Acts 4 : 12.

7. In Joseph we have an example of patience and kindness. Like him we should be careful lest our sense of justice lead us, in our ignorance, to do that which is most unjust. God will make known the path of duty to those who commit their affairs to him, vers. 19, 20; Ps. 112 : 4; Prov. 3 : 5, 6; Isa. 26 : 7.

8. In fulfilling the promises in the coming of Christ, God has given us a pledge that all his promises shall be fulfilled. For Christ is the embodiment of all promises—all being "yea and amen in Christ Jesus," vers. 22, 23; 2 Cor. 1 : 20.

9. Christ is the Immanuel, *the God with us*, to his people, ver. 22; ch. 28 : 20; John 1 : 14; Rom. 9 : 5; 2 Cor. 5 : 19; Col. 2 : 9; Rev. 21 : 3.

10. Many of God's gems are found amid poverty and obscurity. God honored Mary, an obscure virgin, betrothed to a carpenter, as the mother of the heir of all things, vers. 24, 25; Heb. 11 : 6; James 2 : 18.

CHAPTER II.

Having given the genealogy of Jesus, and an account of his miraculous birth, Matthew proceeds to relate how the representatives of the Gentile world came and paid homage to Jesus, who had been born at Bethlehem; how Jesus was carried into Egypt, thus escaping the murderous designs of Herod; and how he returned thence and resided at Nazareth—all in fulfillment of prophecy, showing that he was the Messiah foretold in the Old Testament Scriptures.

1-12. Visit of the Wise Men from the East, who do homage to Jesus and offer him gifts. Recorded only by Matthew. Joseph and Mary, with Jesus, had probably been to Nazareth (Luke 2: 39), and returned to Bethlehem to reside there. See on vers. 11, 22.

1. Now when Jesus was born. Jesus having been born. For a detailed account of his birth see Luke 2: 1-20. Much has been written in regard to the time of the Savior's birth. The exact day and year can not be ascertained with certainty. Dionysius the Small, a Scythian by birth and an abbot at Rome, in the year A.D. 526, published an Easter cycle, in which he fixed the birth of Christ to the 754th year of Rome. This is the era from which it has been common to reckon. But it has long been admitted that Dionysius made an error of at least four years. According to Josephus and Dion Cassius, Herod the Great died in the 750th year of Rome, probably a few days before the passover of that year. If Christ was born that year, the event would thus be four years before the common era. But Jesus must have been born several months before the death of Herod. The coming and the visit of the wise men, the stratagem of Herod, the murder of the infants, and the flight into Egypt, were all embraced in this period, all which would seem to indicate that the common era is too late by at least five years. Jesus must have been born at least in the autumn before Herod's death. Some learned men fix it one or two years earlier. See on ver. 16.

But greater doubt hangs over the day of Christ's birth. It is a historical fact that early Christians did not commemorate the birth of Christ. Clement of Alexandria, A.D. 215, mentions some who designated the 20th of May as the day of our Savior's birth. Others regarded the 19th or 20th of April as the birthday. Oriental Christians in the third and fourth centuries kept the 6th of January as the day of the Savior's baptism and birth. The twenty-fifth of December was solemnized in the fourth century in the West, as the birth-festival, and this day came soon to be looked upon as the day of birth. The latter day is not supported by the circumstances of the case. The census or registering, which was taking place at our Savior's birth (Luke 2: 1-4), and which made it necessary for every man and woman to repair to the homestead of the family, thus occasioning long and innumerable journeys, would hardly be carried on in mid-winter. Neither is it probable that the shepherds would then be "abiding in the field, keeping watch over the flock by night." According to Talmudical writers, the flocks were brought in from the fields about the beginning of November, and driven out again about March. Greswell in his Dissertations upon the harmony of the Gospels, endeavors to show that our Savior's birth, baptism, and death were each at the time of the passover. This theory commends itself to the pious heart, but it is after all only a conjecture. It is enough for us to know that the inspired writers did not record the day of our Savior's birth, and it is well to leave it where the Holy Spirit has left it.

Bethlehem of Judah. In distinction from another Bethlehem in Galilee, in the tribe of Zebulun, mentioned in Josh. 19: 15. Bethlehem, which signifies "house of bread"—fitting name for the place where "the bread of life" was born—so called perhaps on account of its fertility, was a small town about six miles south of Jerusalem. Its earlier name, Ephratah, which means "land" or "region," probably included its environs. Its earliest notice by the sacred historian is Gen. 35: 16-20, when Jacob was bereaved of his beloved Rachel. It was the scene of the touching story of Ruth and the ancestral seat of the house of David. It was called the city of David (Luke 2: 4), because it was the place of his nativity. It was situated on an eminence. The hills around it were clothed with vines, fig-trees, and almonds, and the valleys bore rich crops of grain. It was fortified by Rehoboam (2 Chron. 11: 6), but remained an unimportant place (Mic. 5: 1), not even mentioned by Joshua and Nehemiah among the cities of Judah. Modern travelers speak of the fertility of the surrounding region. At present Bethlehem is a small but populous town, containing about 4000 inhabitants, mostly belonging to the Greek Church.

Herod the king. Judea was a province of the Roman empire, and this person was Herod the Great, the son of Antipater, an Idumæan or Edomite, who was born at Ascalon, Judea, 71 B.C. Various accounts are given of his ancestry, some holding that

2 came wise men ⁿ from the East to Jerusalem, saying, ʳ Where is he that is born King of the Jews? for

ᵗ Ge. 25. 6; 1 Kl. 4. 30.
ʳ ch. 21. 5; Ps. 2. 6

he was of the stock of the principal Jews, who came out of Babylon into Judea, and others that he was a half Jew, and of a proselyte family. See on ver. 22. He was declared king of Judea by a decree of the Roman senate, about 41 B.C., and for thirty-seven years reigned under the supremacy of Rome. On account of his distinguished exploits in war, his marked ability in governing and defending the country, and his works of public improvements, he is called Herod the Great. He strove to ingratiate himself into the favor of the Jews by acts of munificence and generosity, and thus he began to build the temple at Jerusalem; while at the same time he courted the favor of Rome by concessions to heathenism, and building an amphitheatre without the walls of Jerusalem, in which the Roman combats with wild beasts and gladiators were exhibited. He, notwithstanding, failed to gain the affection of his subjects, who were prejudiced against him as a foreigner, and hated him for his concessions to heathen customs and for his numerous cruelties. Josephus represents him as "a man of great barbarity and a slave to his passions." The murder of the infants at Bethlehem was but one of his many acts of like nature. His reign, however, was very successful. For thirty years Judea was undisturbed by war. The world, too, was at peace, under Augustus, the Roman Emperor. It was a fitting time for the coming of the Prince of Peace. The last forty days of his life were spent at Jericho and the baths of Callirrhoe. The visit of the wise men must have therefore been before this; for they found him at Jerusalem.

Wise men from the east. *Magians.* This term was originally applied to a priestly caste of the ancient Persians, who cultivated astrology, medicine, and the like. An order of them existed at Babylon, of which Daniel was made president, Dan. 2 : 48. The name was afterward applied to eastern philosophers in general, who followed them in cultivating the sciences. They were widely known as *wise men*, and were supposed to possess secret knowledge both in science and religion. The term which was first used in a good sense, was also used afterward in a bad sense. The wise men here mentioned belonged to the former and earlier class; Simon Magus to the latter and corrupt class, Acts 8 : 19. The particular part of *the east* from which these wise men came is unknown. The east may mean Arabia, Persia, Parthia, or Babylonia. It more naturally points to the countries beyond the Euphrates, of which Persia formed a part, where the Magian philosophy had its chief seat. It has been calculated that they could not have been less than four months in coming from their distant home to Jerusalem. The narrative implies that they came from a distance, and that they were Gentiles. The Jews called Christ king of Israel; the Gentiles, king of the Jews, ch. 27: 29, 42; John 1 : 49; 12 : 13; 18 : 33.

To Jerusalem. It was natural for the wise men to come to Jerusalem, the capital of Judea, on their mission. Their arrival must have been after the circumcision of Jesus, and his presentation in the temple, Luke 2 : 23–38. The case of Ezra (Ezra 7 : 9) shows that the journey from beyond the Euphrates could be accomplished in four months. *Jerusalem* signifies dwelling or foundation of peace. It was once called Salem, and was the abode of Melchizedek, Gen 14 : 18. It was afterward called Jebus, Jud. 19 : 10. When David reduced it, the hill Zion was also called the city of David, 2 Sam. 5 : 6, 9. After it came into the possession of the Israelites, the sacred writers apply Jerusalem to the whole city as its common name. It was destroyed by the Chaldeans, but rebuilt by the Jews on their return from exile. Herod expended large sums in its embellishment. It was built on four hills: Zion on the south, which was the highest, and contained the citadel and palace; Moriah on the east, on which stood the temple; and Acra and Bezetha, north of Zion and covered with the largest portion of the city. Jerusalem is near the middle of Palestine, about thirty-five miles from the Mediterranean, and about twenty-five miles from the Jordan and the Dead Sea. Its elevation is 2610 feet above the former sea, and 3927 feet above the latter.

2. He that is born King of the Jews. So the Gentiles styled the Mes-

we have seen *his star in the east, and are come to   Is. 9. 6, 7.

siah. See on preceding verse. The language here implies that he was recently born. Doubtless there was at this time a general expectation throughout the east of a new and universal empire to arise in Judea. Suetonius, a Roman historian, speaks of it in his life of Vespasian (chap. 4), and Tacitus alludes to the same. Josephus and Philo, Jewish historians, also mention a similar expectation. This expectation must be traced to the belief universally held by the Jews of the coming Messiah. They were then spread throughout the known world; the greater part of the ten tribes remained in the east, and many proselytes had been made from among the sincere inquirers of all countries. These were looking for a Messiah who should be a temporal prince, deliver them from bondage, and rule over the world. The wise men were assured that the king of the Jews was born; their only inquiry was, *Where?*

Have seen his star. More exactly, *We saw his star.* It was *his* star. What kind of a star it was, and how the wise men could distinguish it as *his,* we are not told. A beautiful and ingenious theory based on astronomical calculations, first made by Kepler, is held by some of the most learned modern commentators. It is found that a conjunction of the planets Jupiter and Saturn took place in the year of Rome 747, first on the 20th of May, and again October 27th, and November 12th—or, according to more recent calculations, December 5th. The conjunctions occurred in the constellation Pisces, just in that part of the heavens in which, according to astrological science, signs betoken the greatest and most notable events. During the six months the planets kept near together. Alford, on this passage, supposes that the wise men saw the first of these conjunctions; then took their journey, arriving at Jerusalem in a little over five months; and going to Bethlehem, in the evening, the November conjunction being before them in that direction, and arriving there at eight o'clock, at which time it would be in the meridian. This would fix our Savior's birth at about six years before our common era. Others, having ascertained that the Chinese astronomical tables record the appearance of a new star, two years later, conclude that our Lord was born four years earlier than the usual era. Supposing that the wise men observed *both* of these, might harmonize with the fact that Herod caused all the children of Bethlehem, of two years old and under, to be put to death. The appearance of these rare phenomena about the time of the Savior's birth is remarkable, and especially in that part of the heavens, *Pisces, The Fishes,* which was supposed to be connected with the Jews. And it is argued in favor of this theory, that God adapts himself in his providence to the imperfect knowledge and conceptions of men; that accordingly he directed the devout minds of these wise men, through their knowledge of astronomical science, to the Messiah; and that there is no reason for supposing a miracle, so long as the appearance of the star can be explained by science and history.

While this explanation may satisfy some minds, to our own it seems to partake too much of speculation. It does not seem fully to accord with the fact that they knew it to be the Messiah's star, and with the statement that the star led them forward, "till it came and stood over the place where the child was," ver. 9. Moreover, the definite term *star,* in the original, though applying to any star, planet, comet, or meteor, would hardly be used to designate the conjunction of the greater planets. It seems more probable that they were Gentile philosophers who had been led to the knowledge of the true God; and that God had favored them with some revelations of himself, as he did Melchizedek, Abimelech, and others. This accords well with the divine communication given them, mentioned in ver. 12. Whatever the star was, there was probably some divine influence exercised on their minds, and its going before them leads rather to the conclusion that it was a meteor, low in the atmosphere, prepared and explained in some way to them by God, which led them first to Jerusalem, and then to the very house where Jesus was at Bethlehem. This accords best with the whole narrative. See on ver. 9.

In the east. In the eastern coun-

3 worship him. When Herod the king had heard *these things*, he was troubled, and all Jerusalem
4 with him. And when he had gathered all 'the chief priests and ᵘscribes of the people together, ˣhe demanded of them where Christ should be

* Num. 24. 17.

ᵗ 2 Ch. 36. 14.
ᵘ 2 Chr. 34. 13.

ˣ Mal. 2. 7.

---

try. The star was thus west of them when they saw it at their own homes in the east.
To worship him. To do him homage. The word translated *worship* literally means *to kiss the hand to any one*, as an expression of reverence and homage. According to Herodotus (i. 134) the ancient oriental and Persian mode of salutation was, between persons of equal rank, to kiss each other on the lips; when the difference of rank was slight, they kissed each other on the cheek; when one was much inferior, he fell upon his knees, touched his forehead to the ground, or prostrated himself, kissing at the same time his hand toward the superior. The word was especially applied to express this oriental form of salutation to a superior, by prostration of the face to the ground. It thus denoted the reverence paid to teachers and the homage paid to kings. When the object of this homage was God, it denoted worship, adoration. (See 1 Kings 19 : 18; Hos. 13 : 2; John 14: 24; 1 Cor. 14 : 25, and Dr. Conant on this passage and on Job 31 : 27.) We know not how great was the knowledge of these wise men concerning the newborn King of the Jews. There is nothing in the word, translated worship, that demands any thing more than that they would pay the homage usually accorded to kings. Herod doubtless so understood them, and this was what he professed a desire to do, ver. 8. They also had come to do homage, not to God, but to a great king that had been born in the land. When our common version was made, the word worship was applicable to men as well as to God ; and when referring to men, it meant to respect, to honor, to treat with civil reverence. Thus in Luke 14 : 10 to "have worship" means to "have honor."
3. **Herod—troubled.** When Herod heard of the coming of these sages of the east, of the star and their inquiry, he was troubled. He was about seventy years old, and therefore the more easily troubled in regard to himself and son. He was also a usurper, and had come to power through bloodshed and crime; he was hated by his subjects; the Pharisees had predicted a revolution and the destruction of his family. He was, therefore, the more alarmed when he heard that the expected King of the Jews was born.
All Jerusalem. The friends of Herod shared his fear. His enemies dreaded his cruelties. There was great excitement. The people were afraid of offending him and feared fresh wars and tumults. The whole population of Jerusalem therefore unite with Herod in the alarm. And they stay with Herod and go not up to Bethlehem.
4. **Chief priests and scribes of the people.** Probably the Sanhedrim, the highest civil and ecclesiastical court of the Jews. It consisted of seventy-one or two members, including the chief priests, the elders, and scribes of the people. The mention of elders is similarly omitted in ch. 20 : 18. It appears to have been quite common to designate the Sanhedrim by two of its component orders, ch. 26 : 3; 27 : 1. The *chief priests* included the heads of the twenty-four classes into which David divided the priests (1 Chron. 24 : 7–18), the high-priest who was president, if he were a suitable person, and probably his deputy and his surviving predecessors. The elders were men of rank and influence chosen from among the people. The *scribes* were learned men, whose business it was to preserve, copy, and expound the Scriptures and the traditions. They were also called lawyers (ch. 22 : 35; Mark 12 : 28), and doctors of the law, Luke 5 : 17, 21. They were not a religious sect, though most of them belonged to the Pharisees. The son of R. Nehemiah was probably present at this council, who doubtless remembered the prophecy said to have been uttered by his father—that the coming of the Messiah could not be delayed more than fifteen years.
Demanded of them. *Inquired of them:* for so the original means. They were the ones who would be supposed to know about the king of the Jews,

5 born. And they said unto him, In ʸBethlehem of Judea: for thus it is written by the prophet,
6 ᶻ'And thou, Bethlehem, *in* the land of Juda, art not the least among the princes of Juda: for out of thee shall come a Governor, ᵃthat shall rule my people Israel.'
7 Then Herod, when he had privily called the wise men, inquired of them diligently
8 what time the star appeared. And he sent them to Bethlehem, and said, Go and search diligently for the young child; and when ye have found *him*, bring me word again, ᵇthat I may come and worship him also.
9 When they had heard the king, they departed; and, lo, ᶜthe star, which they saw

ʸ Ge. 35. 19; Ru. 1. 19; 1 Sam. 16. 4.
ᶻ Mic. 5. 2; John 7. 42.
ᵃ Rev. 2. 27; 19. 15.

ᵇ 2. Sam. 15. 7-12; Pro. 26. 24, 25.
ᶜ Ps. 23. 12; 2 Pet. 1. 19.

and the prophecies concerning him and his birth. Herod, therefore, consults them. He makes the question of the wise men his own: **where Christ should be born.** In the original, *The Christ*, not the proper name, but the official title of the promised Deliverer.

5. By the prophet. Micah 5 : 2. The Sanhedrim answers by quoting a prophecy, which unmistakably referred to the Messiah. By referring to Micah, there will be found a verbal difference between the original prophecy and that here given. The evangelist, however, does not quote the language of the prophet, but merely gives the answer of the Sanhedrim to Herod. The idea of the passage is freely given. And as the inquiry had reference only to the *place* of the Messiah's birth, the answer settles that point alone: he should be born at Bethlehem.

6. Land of Judah. In Micah it is Bethlehem, Ephratah. Bethlehem came to be applied to the town; and Ephratah, its ancient name, which means region, district, was applied to the adjacent district. It was preëminently the district or land of Judah, as the place out of which should come forth the expected Governor of Israel.

Not the least among the princes of Judah. Not by any means the least. The princes were the *chiefs* of families. Micah uses *thousands of Israel*, denoting the civil divisions into which the people were divided. The term *thousands* was sometimes applied to the district where they resided, and thence to the town where the chief resided. The term *chief* was sometimes used in like manner, first for their families, and then for their cities. So here the term *princes* means the towns where they resided. The meaning of both Micah and Matthew is, that, though Bethlehem be one of the smallest cities of Judah, yet it shall not be the smallest in honor, for out of it shall come the Messiah. The birth of Jesus has made Bethlehem ever memorable. **Rule.** The idea is of ruling, as a shepherd does his flock; feed, protect, and control. Jesus is the shepherd, the governor of his people. As such he leads, watches over, provides, and directs them.

7. Privily. Privately, secretly. **Inquired diligently.** Herod was not satisfied with knowing the *place* and the *time* of the birth of the child. He wished also more accurate information in regard to his parents, and the very house where he was, so that he might the more easily destroy him. Possibly he desired the wise men to return, so that he might destroy them also. He completely deceived them by his hypocrisy. The character of such men as Herod, their cruelty, pride, and deceit, is well described in Ps. 10 : 4-10; 55 : 21. **Worship him.** A hypocritical pretext. Do him *homage* as in ver. 2.

9. **Lo, the star went before them.** *Lo, behold*, introduces something new and unexpected, and suggests the sudden reäppearance of the *star;* from which it seems evident that it was not a planet, or a conjunction of planets, but a luminous meteor in the atmosphere prepared by God expressly for guiding them not only to Bethlehem but to the very house where the child lay. **In the east.** That is, the star which they saw while in the eastern country. It is quite probable that they had lost sight of the star before they arrived at Jerusa-

in the east, went before them, till it came and stood 10 over where the young child was. When they saw the star, they rejoiced with exceeding great joy. 11 And when they were come into the house, they saw the young child with Mary his mother, and fell down and worshiped him: and when they had opened their treasures, ᵈ they presented unto him

ᵈ Ps. 45. 8; 72. 10, 15; Is. 60. 6.

lem. That it appeared to them in their own country, and then disappeared, is favored by the words, *the star which they saw in the east*, and by ver. 2, literally, *we saw in the east*, and also by their great joy in again beholding it, ver. 10. They therefore came to the chief city of the Jews to inquire where their great King was born. Having ascertained the place of his birth, they at once proceed according to a common eastern custom, by night, and lo, the star which they had seen in their own country goes before them, and conducts them to the very spot where Jesus lay. God performed a miracle, but he called in the exercise of their faith and their accompanying works. They showed their faith not merely by starting on their journey, but by continuing it to Jerusalem, by their diligent inquiry, and their hastening to Bethlehem. God then rewarded their faith, having sufficiently tried it, by guiding it directly to the object of their search. And so will he ever reward the faithful.

10. **Rejoiced.** The cause of their joy was not merely because they saw the star going before them, but because it *came and stood over where the young child was*. To see the star standing still thus, indicating the end of their long and tiresome journey, and the house where lay the infant King of the Jews, whom they should so quickly see and pay their homage to, was enough to inspire them *with exceeding great joy*.

11. **The house.** The place indicated by the star, where they then lived. Hither they may have removed from the stable where Jesus was born, soon after the visit of the shepherds, Luke 2:16. Some suppose that they returned to Nazareth immediately after the presentation in the temple (Luke 2:22, 39), and thence came back to reside at Beth'lehem. See further on Luke 2:39. It would seem that they resided some time at Bethlehem after the nativity.

Fell down and worshiped. According to the usual manner of showing respect to a superior (Esth. 8:3), they fell down and did homage to the King of the Jews. It is quite probable that they did him more than mere political homage. This was probably their object when they started on their journey, possibly when they inquired of Herod; but as they came and saw the child, it is not unreasonable to suppose that God, who had guided them, gave them also some insight into the spiritual and divine nature of Jesus, as he did to Simeon and Anna (Luke 2:25-38), and that with this inward knowledge they paid him religious homage—adoration. Notice here that Mary holds a subordinate position in this verse and in verses 13, 14, 20, 21. This is directly opposed to the traditions and superstition of the Romish Church in regard to her.

Opened their treasures. The bags and boxes containing their gold, etc. In eastern countries those that called on kings and other distinguished persons, brought gifts, Gen. 43:11; 1 Sam. 9:7-9. The Queen of Sheba came to Jerusalem with presents for Solomon, of spices, gold, and precious stones, 1 Kings 10:2. The custom still continues in the east. **Frankincense.** A product of Arabia and India. It was a valuable white resin or gum of bitter taste, obtained from a tree by making incisions in the bark, highly fragrant, and used in sacrifices and in the services of the temple, Lev. 2:16; 16:13. **Myrrh.** A precious gum, obtained in the same manner as frankincense, from a tree eight or nine feet high, growing in Africa and Arabia. Its name denotes bitterness, but its smell is not disagreeable. It was employed in perfumes, in improving the taste of wine, in embalming the dead, and as an ingredient of the holy ointment. Ex. 30:23; Esth. 2:12; John 19:39; Mark 15:23. These valuable gifts probably afforded to Joseph and Mary the means of support on their jour-

B.C. 4.   MATTHEW II.   33

12 gifts; gold, and frankincense, and myrrh. And being warned of God *in a dream that they should not return to Herod, they departed into their own country another way.   *ch. 1. 20.

Flight into Egypt; Herod's cruelty; The return to Galilee.

13 And when they were departed, behold, the angel of the Lord appeareth to Joseph in a dream, saying, Arise, and take the young child and his mother, and flee into Egypt, and be thou there until I bring thee word: for Herod will seek the young child to
14 destroy him. When he arose, he took the young child and his mother by night and departed into
15 Egypt: and was there until the death of Herod: that it might be fulfilled which was spoken of the Lord by the prophet, saying, ᶠ 'Out of Egypt have I called my son.'   ᶠ Hos. 11. 1.

ney to Egypt. In their presentation by the wise men, we see some of the representatives of the Gentile world doing homage to Christ. "We may also combine a symbolical interpretation of the three-fold gift. Thus, the myrrh, as precious ointment, may indicate the prophet and balm of Israel; the incense, the office of the high-priest; the gold, the splendor of royalty."—LANGE.

12. **Warned of God.** *Having received a divine response; being admonished by God.* In the original, the expression seems to imply a previous inquiry. The same word is used in ver. 22. The wise men were doubtless in the habit of constantly seeking divine direction. They may also have become suspicious of Herod's intentions. But they looked to God, and he took care of them and of his Anointed. And so will he do to all who commit their ways to him, Ps. 37: 5; Prov. 3: 6. Being divinely admonished **in a dream** (see on 1: 20), they *withdrew* or *retired* by another way to their own country.

13-15. THE FLIGHT INTO EGYPT. Only in Matthew.

13. **The angel.** See on ch. 1: 20. **Arise, take the young child.** The command was immediate; he arose and departed the same night into Egypt, as is indicated by the words in ver. 14, **When he arose,** etc., which more literally translated is, *And he arose and took the young child.* Egypt was at that time a Roman province, independent of Herod, much inhabited by Jews, about sixty miles south-west from Bethlehem. The Greek language was spoken there. The Jews had there a temple and many synagogues. The Greek translation of the Old Testament, called the Septuagint, was made there. It formed a near, convenient, and indeed the only possible refuge for Jesus and his parents. God had wonderfully prepared this land where the children of Israel had suffered oppression, to be the refuge of the new-born Messiah.

14. **When he arose.** *And having arisen,* or *and he arose* without delay. The fact that he started by night shows the promptness and haste of his withdrawal.

15. **Until the death of Herod.** Herod's death is generally thought to have occurred very soon after the flight into Egypt. In regard to the time of his death, see on ver. 19.

That it might be fulfilled. A divine purpose fulfilled, as expressed by the Lord through the prophet. See on ch. 1: 22, 23. The prophecy here cited is found in Hos. 11: 1. It was originally written of Israel in Egypt, and is best explained by regarding it a typical prophecy. Though literally referring to Israel, it is typically fulfilled in the child Jesus. The children of Israel are regarded as one man, as God's son. They are so called in Exod. 4: 22; they are there also styled his first-born.

34 MATTHEW II. B.C. 4.

16 Then Herod, when he saw that he was mocked of the wise men, was exceeding wroth, and sent forth, and slew all the children that were in Bethlehem, and in all the coasts thereof, from two years old and under, according to the time which he had
17 diligently inquired of the wise men. Then was fulfilled that which was spoken by ^g Jeremy the

^g Jer 31, 15; Prov. 28. 15-17.

Israel is thus a type of Christ, who is in the highest sense the Son of God. Both were strangers in Egypt, and both were called forth by the command of God. Jesus, too, the true first-born, fulfilled the case of the people he represented, "In all their afflictions he was afflicted," Isa. 63 : 9. His people, the body, is one with him, their head. Christ is the sum and substance of Old Testament types and prophecies.

16-18. THE MASSACRE OF THE CHILDREN OF BETHLEHEM. Only in Matthew.

16. **Mocked.** Treated disrespectfully, trifled with. "Outwitted, made a fool of."—LANGE. This expresses the feeling of Herod; the wise men had no such design. **Exceeding wroth.** He was *very angry* both because he felt that he had been trifled with, and also because he had failed to ascertain more about Jesus, in order that he might certainly kill him.

Slew all the children. *All the boys;* for so the original means. Herod's object was to destroy the lately born King of the Jews; and hence he did not need to kill any but the male children. **In all the coasts thereof.** All the borders thereof. The word coast now means the margin of land next to the sea, as *sea-coast.* Here it means the vicinity, borders, adjacent district. This is ordinarily its meaning in Scripture. **From two years old and under.** The exact length of time here indicated is doubtful. Some suppose that all the male children under two years of age were slain. Others, according to Jewish reckoning, suppose two years to mean *entering the second year.* A child that had entered the second year would be called two years old. The latter supposition is probable. Matthew would doubtless speak of time according to Jewish reckoning. The Evangelists thus speak of our Savior's death. The parts of the three days that he was under the power of death are called three days. Herod thought he knew the age of Jesus from the time the star appeared. He therefore slew all that were about his age, according to the time he had exactly learned from the wise men, probably going a little beyond, so as to make his death the more certain. This was among the last acts of Herod's cruelty, probably but a few weeks, or possibly days, before his death.

The number of children slain could not have been large. Bethlehem was a very small town, and the families bordering upon it were probably few. There were not probably in all more than three hundred inhabitants. Dr. Hackett supposes that the number of children slain did not exceed twelve or fifteen. Yet Voltaire, seizing upon an unreliable tradition, puts them down at fourteen thousand! So many and atrocious were Herod's cruelties that it is not strange that Josephus makes no mention of this. Herod had marked his whole reign with blood, had murdered a brother-in-law, one of his wives, and three sons, the last son five days before his own death. At about the time of the massacre at Bethlehem, above forty zealots were burned alive at Jerusalem, at the command of Herod, because they had destroyed his golden eagle erected over the gate of the temple. This execution took place on the night of the 12th of March. Again, Herod probably gave this order secretly, and it might not have been known to Josephus. The calling the wise men, *privily,* etc., in ver. 7, favors this view. And finally, if Josephus did know it, he would not, as a Jewish historian, wish to give direct testimony to the truth of Christianity. No argument can therefore be drawn from the silence of Josephus. The most careful historians relate only a few of the events that have occurred. The slaying of the children of Bethlehem, though it showed Herod's great wickedness, was among his many cruelties

18 prophet, saying, 'In Rama was there a voice heard, lamentation, and weeping, and great mourning, Rachel weeping *for* her children, and would not be comforted, because they are not.'
19 But when Herod was dead, behold, an angel of the Lord appeareth in a dream to Joseph in Egypt,
20 saying, Arise, and take the young child and his mother, and go into the land of Israel: for [h] they
21 are dead which sought the young child's life. And he arose, and took the young child and his mother,

[h] Ps. 76. 10; Ex. 4. 19.

only as a drop in the ocean, and would never have been recorded except for its connection with the life of Jesus.

17. Then was fulfilled. Notice it is not said as in ch. 1 : 22, or in verse 15 of this chapter, "that it might be fulfilled." Those had reference to the *designs* of God in respect to the Messiah; this, to the consequences of Herod's cruelty. The former were the positive designs of God; the latter the permission of wickedness on the part of man.

18. Jeremy. Jeremiah. The quotation from Jer. 31 : 15. **Rama,** signifying *eminence,* is the name of several towns situated on hills. The *Rama* here referred to, was a city of Benjamin, about six miles north of Jerusalem, and on the road to Samaria. It must not be confounded with Ramah, in Mount Ephraim, the place of Samuel's birth, residence, and burial. Drs. Robinson and Hackett both find it in the modern village El-Ram, on a conical hill a little east of the road above mentioned. There are ruins of broken columns, large hewn stones, and an ancient reservoir. The village is almost deserted.

Fulfilled, etc. The Evangelist evidently points to the fulfillment of a prediction. It must be explained similarly to those already noticed in ch. 1 : 22 and 2 : 15, as a typical prophecy. Its primary reference (Jer. 31 : 15) is to the captivity of the Jews to Babylon after the conquest of Jerusalem by Nebuzaradan. Rachel, the mother of Benjamin, is represented as bewailing her children. Her voice is vividly represented, in poetic imagery, as coming, as it were, from her sepulchre near Bethlehem, and is carried northward beyond Jerusalem, and is heard at Rama, where the captives were collected, ready to be sent to Babylon, Jer. 40 : 1. It must be remembered that the tribes of Judah and Benjamin were closely united, after the revolt of the ten tribes. But the prophecy extended not merely to Jewish captives of Jeremiah's day, but to the destruction of the innocents in Messiah's time. The atrocious deed of Herod fills Bethlehem and its vicinity with lamentation. The fact that Herod was aiming at the life of the King of the Jews, the spiritual and temporal hope of the world, only increases the intensity of the crime. The awfulness of the deed, the horror and pungent grief produced by it, are strikingly represented by the figure of Rachel bewailing her cruel bereavement in her grave, which was "in the way to Bethlehem," Gen. 35 : 19. Such bewailing among eastern women was most violent, Jer. 9 : 17, 18. Omit the words, **lamentation, and.**

19–23. THE RETURN FROM EGYPT AND THE RESIDENCE AT NAZARETH. Found only in Matthew.

19. Herod was dead. Died at Jericho in the seventieth year of his age and the thirty-seventh year of his reign, of a most painful and loathsome disease. An eclipse of the moon which occurred about the same time fixes his death in the spring of the 750th year of Rome, B.C. 4. According to Josephus, about the time of the passover, who gives an account of his terrible death. (Joseph. *Antiq.* xvii. 8, 5, and *Jewish War,* i. 33, 5, 6, 7).

20. Land of Israel. The land given to Abraham and his seed forever. Israel was applied to the twelve tribes until the time of Rehoboam. From that time to the captivity, the ten tribes that revolted and followed Jeroboam were called *Israel,* in distinction from the two tribes, Judah and Benjamin, which were called Judah. But after the Babylonish captivity the general name was again applied to all who traced their descent to Jacob. Land of Israel therefore applied to the whole of Palestine.

22 and came into the land of Israel. But when he heard that Archelaus did reign in Judea in the room of his father Herod, he was afraid to go thither: notwithstanding, being warned of God in a

i ch. 3. 13; Lk. 2. 39.
k John 1. 45; Ac. 2. 22.

They are dead. Some suppose here a verbal reference to Exod. 4 : 19. The language was doubtless familiar to Joseph, and would remind him that He who protected Moses was watching over the young child Jesus. The phrase, *They are dead*, refers especially to Herod. But others who were with him in spirit had also died. Antipater, the son of Herod, and heir-apparent to the throne, who had procured the death of his two elder brothers to clear his way to the succession, would probably be very active in seeking the destruction of Jesus, and in advising the murder of the children of Bethlehem. But his father, five days before his own death, had him put to death.

21. Arose—and came into the land of Israel. The time of Joseph's sojourn in Egypt must have been short, probably only a few months, or possibly a few weeks, since Herod died soon after the slaughter of the infants, and Joseph's return was soon after the death of Herod.

22. He heard that Archelaus did reign. After the death of Herod, Archelaus received half of his kingdom, including Judea, Idumæa, and Samaria, with the title of *Ethnarch*, which means governor of a nation or province. The remaining half was divided between Herod Antipas and Herod Philip, each receiving the title of *Tetrarch*, that is, governor of a fourth part of a province; the former having the regions of Galilee and Peræa, and the latter Batanæa, Trachonitis, and Auranitis. The title of ethnarch, though superior to tetrarch, was inferior to that of king. After a reign of nine years, Archelaus was banished by the Roman Emperor Augustus, on account of his oppression and cruelty. At the commencement of his reign, he massacred three thousand Jews at once in the temple. He died in Gaul, whither he was banished A.D. 6. After him Judea had no more a native king. Shiloh had come, and the sceptre departed, Gen. 49 : 10. It was placed under Roman governors, who resided at Cesarea. The successive governors during the life of Jesus were, Coponius, Ambivius, Annius Rufus, Valerius Gratus, and Pontius Pilate. The following table shows at a glance the

HEROD THE GREAT. Died B.C. 4.
Married

Mariamne, 2d wife.	Mariamne, 5th wife.	Malthace, 6th wife.	Cleopatra, 7th wife.
Aristobulus. Died B.C. 6.	Herod Philip. First Husband of Herodias, Matt. 14 : 3.	ARCHELAUS. Matt. 2 : 22. Deposed A.D. 6.	HEROD ANTIPAS. Luke 3 : 1. Matt. 14 : 3-6. Deposed A.D. 40.	HEROD PHILIP. Luke 3 : 1. Died A.D. 34.
HEROD AGRIPPA I. Died A.D. 44. = Herodias. Acts 12 : 23-35. Matt. 14 : 6.			
HEROD AGRIPPA II. Acts 25 : 13, 26. The last of the Herods. Died A.D. 95.	Berníce. Acts 25 : 13, 23; 26 : 30.	Drusilla. Acts 24 : 24.	

several individuals of Herod's family mentioned in the New Testament, and their relation to Herod the Great.

He was afraid to go thither. Knowing that Archelaus was like his father, a suspicious and cruel tyrant. He "seemed to be so afraid lest he should not be deemed Herod's own son that he took especial care to make his acts prove it." So said the Jewish deputies

dream, he turned aside ¹ into the parts of Galilee: 23 and he came and dwelt in a city called ᵏ Nazareth: that it might be fulfilled which was spoken by the Prophets, He shall be called ¹ a Nazarene.

ch. 26. 71; Judg. 13. 5; Ps. 22. 6; Is. 53. 3; Ac. 6. 14; 24. 5.

to Augustus. Joseph. Antiq. xvii. 11, 2. Joseph may have heard of his recent cruelties. **Warned of God.** See on ver. 12. While Joseph was troubled and seeking divine guidance, he is honored the fourth time with a revelation of God's will. In a dream God directs him to turn aside to Galilee. That he at first intended to go to Judea is a circumstantial argument that he had, before his flight into Egypt, made Bethlehem his residence. **Parts of Galilee.** Galilee consisted of Upper and Lower Galilee.—DR. CONANT: "*The parts of Galilee* may refer to the divisions of country embraced within its bounds." Palestine was at this time divided into three parts: Galilee on the north, Samaria in the middle, and Judea on the south. Joseph could live in safety in Galilee under Herod Antipas, who was comparatively a mild prince, and who, not being on good terms with Archelaus, would be slow to deliver up to him the young child Jesus. This, however, is on the supposition that Jesus and his parents were known to Archelaus; but this probably was not the case. Jesus doubtless lived in obscurity and quiet, unknown to royalty and unsuspected by the Herods.

23. **Nazareth.** Means *a branch*, a fit name of the place where the Branch (Isa. 11:1; Zech. 3:8; 6:12) should live and grow up. This was a small city in Lower Galilee, about seventy miles north of Jerusalem, and nearly half-way from the Jordan to the Mediterranean. It was situated on a side of a hill (Luke 4:29), a small place, not even named in the Old Testament, nor by Josephus, and was in no good repute, John 1:46. It is first noticed as the residence of Mary (Luke 1:26), and from this time became the usual residence of Jesus till he entered his public ministry. Of the modern city, Dr. Hackett who visited it in 1852, says, "Nazareth is situated just north of the great plain of Esdraelon, among the lovely hills at the extremity of the Lebanon mountains. It is hidden from view till you look down upon it from the adjacent heights. It lies along the western edge of a ravine, which, narrow for the most part, flows in a waving line through the mountains, enlarging itself somewhat in front of the town, and falling into the great plain on the south-east. The present Nazareth belongs to the better class of eastern villages. It has a population of nearly three thousand, a few of them Mohammedans, but most of them Christians of the Latin and Greek order."—*Hackett's Scrip. Illustrations*, p. 310.

He shall be called a Nazarene. This prediction has afforded the learned much difficulty, as the word Nazarene is not found in any passage of the Old Testament. (1.) Some suppose the quotation is from some lost book or prophecy. (2.) Others, that the word Nazarene is equivalent to Nazarite, and that Samson was typical of Christ, Jud. 13:5. But the Savior's life and character were inconsistent with the supposition that he was a Nazarite, Matt. 11:19. (3.) Others suppose a verbal reference to the Hebrew word *Netser*, applied to the Messiah in Isa. 11:1 (compare Isa. 60:21), which signifies a *sprout*, *branch*, from which Nazareth is probably derived. They suppose that Nazareth received its name on account of the brushwood or shrubs abounding in the surrounding districts. They regard the prophecy literally fulfilled in Christ being called a Nazarene, that is, a branch. (4.) But the more probable mode of solving the difficulty is the supposition that Matthew refers not to any single prediction, but to the general language of the prophets in regard to the Messiah under the title of the Branch, and especially to his lowly and despised condition, which the term Nazarene had come to represent, Jer. 23:5; 33:15; Isa. 53: 2; Zech. 6:11. This accords with the *plural*, **prophets.** David (Ps. 22:6; 69:7-12) and Isaiah (Isa. 49:7; 53: 2, 3) had foretold that the Messiah should be reproached and despised. Now, the people of Nazareth were held, at the time of our Savior, in contempt (John 7:52), and that too, by even the people of small neighboring towns, as is evident from the question of Nathanael of Cana, John 1 : 46. Hence Nazarene was a term implying reproach. As applied to Christ, it was expressive of his humble and despised condition. The evangelist thus saw the several allusions of the prophets to the lowliness of the Messiah concentrated in that expressive word, Nazarene. Instead of repeating such predictions as, *He is despised and rejected of men*, he expresses the substance by saying, *He shall be called a Nazarene*. His humiliation and sufferings, as the Nazarene, most completely fulfill all that the prophets had thus spoken.

REMARKS.

1. Christians are not called upon to celebrate the birthday of Christ. Had God intended its observance, he would not have left it in doubt, ver. 1; Gal. 4 : 10, 11.

2. True science is in harmony with religion, and subservient to Christ and his kingdom. The sages of the east used their knowledge in connection with the star, the word of God, and the direction of the scribes in finding Jesus, ver. 2; Rom. 1 : 20.

3. Christ was the star that was to come out of Jacob (Num. 24 : 17); and symbolized by the star which the wise men saw, ver. 2; Rev. 22 : 16.

4. What honor did God confer on the only-begotten Son, in ordering a star to appear as a signal of his birth, in calling the wise men of the east to do him homage, and in the several revelations concerning him to Joseph and the wise men, vers. 2, 12, 13, etc.

5. Christ is most truly the King of the Jews—the King of his spiritual Israel, ver. 2; compare John 18 : 36, 37; Ps. 72 : 11.

6. The young child Jesus troubles Herod and all Jerusalem with him. So is the weakest child of God a troubler to Satan and to the kingdom of darkness.

Princes and people may well tremble if they find themselves hostile to Christ, ver. 2; James 4 : 7; Ps. 2 : 9-12; Rev. 18 : 9, 10, 19; 19 : 11-16.

7. Some point others to Christ without going to him themselves. Thus did Herod and the Jews. Let us beware of their sin and condemnation, vers. 5, 6, 8; 1 Cor. 3 : 19, 20.

8. God will guide those who seek the Savior and use the appointed means. The wise men found Jesus by following the star, by prayer for direction, and by inquiring of God's professed people and consulting his word, ver. 9; Prov. 3 : 6.

9. In Herod, the Sanhedrim, and the wise men we have a striking representation of some of the ways in which men treat Christ and the Gospel. Some with the greatest hostility; others, who have enjoyed the greatest advantages, with indifference; while a third class, with perhaps fewer privileges, look to Christ as their Prophet, Priest, and King, and consecrate their all to him, vers. 1-11; 1 Cor. 1 : 26-28.

10. Mary is not an object of worship. The "young child" was the object of their search and adoration, ver. 11; Rev. 22 : 9.

11. As in the former chapter we saw the connection of Christ with Abraham and the Jews, so in this we behold the relation of the Gentile world to Christ. The wise men were the representatives of the pious Gentiles of all time doing homage to Christ. Christ was "the light to the Gentiles," as well as "the glory of Israel," ver. 11.

12. They who seek and faithfully follow divine direction will most likely escape the snares of the most crafty, ver. 12; Prov. 11 : 5.

13. Christ is the substance of Old Testament prophecies. Their fulfillment in Christ proves his Messiahship, and the inspiration of the Scriptures, vers. 6, 15, 23; Luke 24 : 27.

14. As Jesus was preserved in Egypt, so shall the church be in the world. He who watched over the infant Jesus and gave four revelations to Joseph, will watch over his people. They are in Christ, one with him here and hereafter, vers. 14, 15, 20; ch. 16 : 18; John 17: 20-23; Rom. 12 : 5.

15. Trials are made to carry out the divine purposes. The various sufferings of Joseph and Mary in Bethlehem, Egypt, and Nazareth were steps in fulfilling prophecy and the purposes of God, vers. 13, 23.

16. It is God's part to direct; man's to obey. Joseph is warned, and the same night starts for Egypt. "Duties are ours; events are God's," vers. 13, 14, 20, 21.

17. In Herod's conduct we see the opposition of the kingdom of darkness against Christ, Ps. 2 : 1, 2. Herod re-

A.D. 26. MATTHEW III. 59

Ministry of John the Baptist.

III. ᵐ IN those days came John the Baptist, preach-

ᵐ Lk. 3. 2–5.
ⁿ ch. 5. 3, 10; 11. 11, 12; 13. 11, 24; 18. 1–4, 23; 23,

built the temple with great splendor, yet sought to kill the Prince of life. So many give largely to build houses of worship, but in their hearts are opposed to Christ's spiritual kingdom, vers. 16–18.

18. Let us be thankful that we live under a free government, and enjoy religious liberty, vers. 16–18.

19. God knows how at the right moment to deliver the godly and thwart the designs of his enemies, vers. 12, 13, 19; 2 Pet. 2 : 9.

20. How great the host of God's foes who have perished utterly. He maketh the wrath of man to praise him, ver. 20; Ps. 76 : 10; compare Exod. 4 : 19; Prov. 21 : 30.

21. Nazareth reminds us of the lowly condition of Christ and of Christianity in the world. Christians inherit a participation in the reproaches of Christ here, as well as in his glory hereafter, ver. 23; 2 Tim. 2 : 12; 1 Pet. 2 : 19–24.

CHAPTER III.

Having given an account of the birth and infancy of Jesus, and the events of his life which led to his residence at Nazareth, all in striking fulfillment of prophecy, the evangelist proceeds at once to relate the ministry of John and the baptism of Jesus. John's coming, in fulfillment of prophecy, his recognition and baptism of Jesus, the descent of the Spirit, and the declaration of the Father, still further point to him as the Messiah. Thus, through the baptism of John was the ministry of Jesus introduced.

1–12. JOHN'S PREACHING AND BAPTISM. Mark 1 : 1–8; Luke 3 : 1–18.

1. **In those days.** While Jesus was still residing in obscurity at Nazareth, referring to ch. 2 : 23. An interval of about twenty-seven years had elapsed between the coming of Jesus to Nazareth and the public appearance of John. The Evangelists have passed over this period with almost total silence, as if to make the obscurity and the public ministry of Jesus the more striking. We have only a brief notice of his visit to Jerusalem with his parents at twelve years of age, (Luke 2 : 41–51); a passing remark that Jesus "increased in wisdom and knowledge, and in favor with God and man" (Luke 2 : 52), and allusions to the fact that Joseph was a carpenter, and that Jesus wrought at the same occupation, ch. 13 : 55 and Mark 6 : 3.

Came John. The name *John* in Hebrew means *one whom Jehovah has graciously given*. For an account of his birth, see Luke ch. 1. As John was six months older than Jesus, it is not improbable that he entered on his public ministry as much earlier. This would make him about thirty years of age, Luke 3 : 23. And this supposition is the more probable in the light of the Mosaic law, which required priests to be of the age of thirty before commencing the duties of their office. Luke fixes the time of his public appearance in the fifteenth year of Tiberius Cæsar, which was the 779th year of Rome, or A.D. 25. See on Luke 3 : 1. From the autumn of this year to that of 780 was a sabbatical year, the year of our Lord's baptism, as well as of a good portion of the ministry of John. At what season of the year John's ministry began is unknown. Quite likely in the spring or summer.

The Baptist. The baptizer. This title was evidently familiar to the Jews. Matthew speaks of John the Baptist, without any explanation, as a person well known. So also did Herod, Mark 6 : 14. Josephus also says (Antiq. xviii. 5, 2) that he was "called," or rather "surnamed the Baptist." John was indeed *the Baptizer*, the institutor of a *new* ordinance, which had special reference to Christ. John's baptism was not founded on the ceremonial purifications of the old dispensation; neither was it an offshoot of proselyte baptism; for the latter appears not to have originated till after the destruction of the temple. Neither Josephus nor Philo, nor the Apocrypha, nor the Jewish Targums or rabbinical books, say any thing of proselyte baptism, though they all speak of proselytes. The earliest mention of it is in the Babylonish Talmud, a Jewish commentary of about the sixth century of the Christian era. In Herzog's *Real Encyclopädie*, (Art. "Proselyten") vol. xii. pp. 245–6, we find the following decided declaration of its late origin:

ing in the wilderness of Judea, and saying, Repent
2 ye: for ᵃ the kingdom of heaven is at hand. For

13; 25, 1, 14;
Dan. 2. 44; Lk.
9. 2: 10. 9-11.

"The institution of a strictly proselyte baptism, as an independent initiatory act, will not, according to these investigations, date higher perhaps than toward the close of the first century of the Christian era; nay, there are strong grounds for assigning it a somewhat later date. The oldest evidence for it is in the Babylonian Gemara (completed about five hundred years after Christ), Jebam, 46, 1. 'If a proselyte has submitted to circumcision but has not been baptized, "he is," says Rabbi Eliezer, "a proselyte; for so we find it to have been with our ancestral fathers, who were circumcised but not baptized." But if one is baptized and not circumcised, Joshua says, "he is a proselyte; for so we find it to have been with our ancestral mothers, who were baptized but not circumcised." But the wise men [that is, the greater number] declare both to be an indispensable condition.'"

The New Testament also makes no reference to proselyte baptism, but indirectly teaches its non-existence. In reply to our Lord's inquiry, "The baptism of John, whence was it?' from heaven or of men?" (ch. 21 : 25), no such embarrassment would probably have been felt like that which existed among the chief priests and elders, if they could have pointed to proselyte baptism. The inquiry made to John, "Why baptizest thou?" (John 1 : 25) plainly implies that baptism was a new rite; and this is confirmed in John 1 : 33, where the Baptist expressly declares that he received his commission to baptize from God himself. See Dr. Chase in *Christian Review*, Oct. 1863, pp. 510, 529.

John the Baptist was the forerunner of Christ, the preparer of his way, "as the light of the sun, which, though not yet risen, still fills the heavens with a light which presages his glorious appearing." Hence Mark styles the ministry of John *the beginning of the Gospel of Jesus Christ*, Mark 1 : 1-5. This ministry consisted in preaching and baptizing. John's preaching was the beginning of Christian preaching (compare ch. 3 : 2; Mark 1 : 7, 15), and his baptism the beginning of Christian baptism. The baptism of Christ, and after that, the disciples of Jesus baptizing by his authority, connect the baptism of John with the final commission of our Lord.

Preaching. Proclaiming, announcing publicly. We are not to suppose John making set discourses to well-regulated audiences, but traveling the country and heralding his brief messages, first to individuals, families, and small companies, wherever found; and afterward to crowds who flocked to hear him. **Wilderness of Judea.** The word *wilderness* or *desert*, in the New Testament, denotes merely an uninclosed, untilled, and thinly inhabited district. It was applied to mountain regions, to districts fitted only for pasture, and to tracts of country remote from towns and sparsely settled. The wilderness of Judea was in the eastern portion of Judah, in the neighborhood of the Jordan and the Dead Sea. It was rocky and mountainous, but abounding in pastures for flocks. Several towns and small places situated in this district are mentioned in Josh. 15 : 61, 62, and Jud. 1 : 16.

2. Repent. This word means *to change one's mind*. It expresses an inward change of views and feelings, and implies a sorrow for sin (ch. 11 : 21; 2 Cor. 7 : 10); a turning to God (Acts 3 : 19; 26 : 20); and a change of conduct or outward reformation as the fruits, ch. 3 : 8; Acts 26 : 20. Another word translated *repent* occurs in the New Testament a few times. Unlike the former and more common word, it does not denote a change of mind that is deep, durable, and productive of consequences, but rather a feeling of regret, of sorrow, or remorse for something done. See ch. 27 : 3; 2 Cor. 7 : 8; Matt. 21 : 29, 32.

Kingdom of heaven. This phrase is used in the New Testament only by Matthew, and is equivalent to "Kingdom of God," of the other Evangelists. The same thing is expressed by "kingdom of Christ," or simply "kingdom." Eph. 5 : 5; Heb. 12 : 28. The prophets had represented the Messiah as a Divine King (Ps. 2 : 6; Isa. 11 : 1; Jer. 23 : 5; Zech. 14 : 9; Mic. 4 : 1-4; 5 : 2), and especially Daniel (Dan. 2 : 44; 7 : 13, 14), who had spoken of "a kingdom which the God of heaven would set up." Hence, *kingdom of heaven*, or *of God*, be-

3 °this is he that was spoken of by the prophet Esaias, saying, ᵖ'The voice of one crying in the wilderness, ᵠ Prepare ye the way of the Lord, make his 4 paths straight.' And the same John ʳ had his raiment of camel's hair, and a leathern girdle about

° Mal. 3. 1.
ᵖ Is. 40. 3.
ᵠ Lk. 1. 76.
ʳ Mk. 1. 5, 6.

came common among the Jews to denote the kingdom or reign of the Messiah. Their own theocracy was also typical of it. They indeed perverted the meaning of prophecy, and expected an earthly and temporal kingdom, the restoration of the throne of David at Jerusalem, and the actual subjugation of all nations. John the Baptist, Jesus, and the apostles, however, rescued the phrase from error, and gave it its full and true meaning. This *kingdom, reign,* or *administration* of the Messiah is spiritual in its nature (John 18 : 36; Rom. 14 : 17); and is exercised over, and has its seat in, the hearts of believers, Luke 17 : 21. It exists on earth (ch. 13 : 18, 19, 41, 47); extends to another state of existence (ch. 13 : 43; 26 : 29; Phil. 2 : 10, 11); and will be fully consummated in a state of glory, 1 Cor. 15 : 24; Matt. 8 : 11; 2 Pet. 1 : 11. It thus embraces the whole mediatorial reign or government of Christ on earth and in heaven, and includes in its subjects all the redeemed, or as Paul expresses it (Eph. 3 : 15), "the whole family in heaven and earth." *Kingdom of heaven* and *church* are not identical, though inseparately and closely connected. The churches of Christ are the external manifestations of this kingdom in the world.

The Jews understood John to announce that the kingdom or the reign of the Messiah was approaching. His views of that kingdom were doubtless imperfect, but he was quite free from the errors of his countrymen. His preaching repentance showed that he apprehended its spiritual nature, and saw that an inward change with its external fruits was necessary in order to become a true member of it. Hence the reason he urged for repenting; "for the kingdom of heaven **is at hand.**" Literally *has drawn near,* that is, *now near, at hand,* in the birth of Jesus, etc. For the force of the verb translated at hand compare ch. 26 : 45; Luke 21 : 20.

3. By the prophet Esaias. Through the prophet Isaiah. The quotation is made by Matthew and is found in Isa. 40 : 3. John applies the prediction to himself in John 1 : 23. The figure here used is founded on an eastern custom of sending persons to prepare the way for the march of a monarch through a wild and uncultivated region. This consisted of leveling hills, filling valleys, putting roads in order, and getting every thing in readiness. "When Ibrahim Pasha proposed to visit certain places on Lebanon, the emeers and sheiks sent forth a general proclamation, somewhat in the style of Isaiah's exhortation, to all the inhabitants, to assemble along the proposed route and prepare the way before him. The same was done in 1845, on a grand scale, when the present Sultan visited Brusa. The stones were gathered out, crooked places straightened, and rough ones made level and smooth."—DR. THOMSON, *The Land and the Book,* vol. i. p. 106. Such was the character of John's ministry. He went before to announce the coming of the Messiah, and to "make ready a people prepared for the Lord," Luke 1 : 16, 17. He rebuked the proud, exposed hypocrites, called men to repentance, and directed them to a coming Savior.

His preaching was indeed **the voice of one crying,** of short duration, but exciting attention, and the place of his preaching **the wilderness.** The prediction was thus remarkably fulfilled in John. Many regard it as a typical prophecy fulfilled, first in the return of the Jews from the Babylonish captivity, and then more remotely, and at the same time more strikingly, in John the Baptist. Such a view is possibly, but not absolutely necessary. We have here an authoritative exposition of its meaning and application.

Of the Lord. In the Hebrew, *of Jehovah,* a decisive evidence of the supreme divinity of Christ.

4. **Raiment of camel's hair,** etc. John's garb and manner of life, as well as character and preaching, were like those of Elijah. 2 Kings 1 : 8; Mal. 4 : 5, 6; Matt. 11 : 14; Luke 1 : 17. It was common for prophets to wear a coarse outer garment, Zech. 13 : 4. John's raiment was of coarse cloth woven from

his loins; and his meat was locusts and wild honey.
5 Then went out to him Jerusalem, and all Judea,
6 and all the region round about Jordan, and were

the long, shaggy hair of the camel, which was shed every year. "The coat or mantle of camel's hair is seen still on the shoulders of the Arab who escorts the traveler through the desert, or of the shepherd who tends his flock on the hills of Judea, or in the valley of the Jordan. It is made of the thin, coarse hair of the camel, and not of the fine hair, which is manufactured into a species of rich cloth."—*Hackett's Illustration of Scrip.* p. 104. *Girdles* were a regular part of the dress, used in binding the garments, which were loose and flowing around, the loins (Luke 12 : 35), and were of linen, silk, or even silver, and sometimes gold. A *leathern* girdle was a very ordinary one, and here serves to indicate the *austerity* of John.

His meat. His *food;* so the old English word meat means. **Locusts** were voracious winged insects, closely resembling the grasshopper; and were *clean* for the Jew, and might be used

for food, Lev. 11 : 22. They were roasted and sometimes boiled, or salted and preserved, and eaten by the poorer classes of the people, as at the present day. "It is well known that the poorer class of the people eat them cooked or raw, in all the eastern countries where they are found."—*Hackett, as above.*

Wild Honey. This was probably found in the trees and rocks of the wilderness. Some suppose it to be a *honey dew,* or sweet gum which flows from certain trees of the east. But it is doubtful whether the honey-producing tree ever grew in Palestine, though it is said to be found in Arabia. The honey of the wild bee was abundant, and often found in hollow trees and clefts in the rock, Lev. 20 : 24; Deut. 32 : 13; Ps. 81 : 16; 1 Sam. 14 : 26. It is still found in large quantities where

John sojourned, and came preaching. Thus the raiment and food of John were those of the poorer class; and indicated his humble condition, his austere and self-denying manner, and, being in harmony with his stern warnings and requisitions, rendered his preaching the more effective.

5. **Jerusalem.** The people of Jerusalem. **All Judea.** The people from the rest of Judea besides Jerusalem. Great multitudes. We sometimes use the expression, It is known to *all,* when we mean it is generally known. **Region round about Jordan.** On both sides of the river, and adjacent to it. Jerusalem as the metropolis is mentioned first, though the region about Jordan was doubtless the scene of his first success. The singular appearance of John, his prophetic address and manner of life, his stern and earnest preaching, and the general expectation of the immediate coming of the Messiah, all concurred to call great multitudes after him.

6. **Were baptized.** The word *baptize* is the Greek *baptizo,* transferred into our language and the termination altered. The literal meaning of the original Greek is to *dip, plunge, immerse.* "All lexicographers and critics of any note," says Prof. Stuart, "are agreed in this." "This word," says Dr. Conant (Revised Version of Matthew and Notes), "expressed a particular act, namely, *immersion* in a fluid or yielding substance. The word had no other meaning; it expressed this act alone, either literally or in a metaphorical sense, through the whole period of Greek literature." So also the learned Lutheran scholar, Dr. Meyer, in his Critical Commentary on the New Testament, says of *Baptizontai* in Mark 7 : 4, that it "is not to be understood of *washing the hands,* but of immersion, which the word in classic Greek and in the New Testament everywhere means; therefore here, according to the context, *to take a bath.* So also Luke 11 : 38." Again, in his Commentary on the Acts (p. 336) he says, "Immersion was a thoroughly essential part of the baptismal symbolism."

Its figurative meaning is based on this

ground meaning, and always expresses an idea of immersion. In this sense it may be translated plunge, immerse, overwhelm, or whelm. Thus Josephus speaks of a certain one being "plunged (baptized) by drunkenness into stupor and sleep." * Chrysostom, an eminent Greek writer of the Christian Church, in the fourth century, exclaims in one place, "How are we immersed (baptized) in wickedness."† And Plutarch, who was born in the year fifty after Christ, says of a certain one that he was "overwhelmed (baptized) with debts, amounting to fifty millions."‡ (See Mark 10 : 39; Luke 12 : 50.)

In the Septuagint, a Greek version of the Old Testament (made about two hundred and eighty-five years before Christ), we find the Hebrew word *tabal*, (טָבַל) which Gesenius in his Lexicon says means *to dip, to dip in, to immerse*, translated by the Greek word *baptizo* in 2 Kings 5 : 14, "Then he went down and dipped himself seven times in the Jordan." The Hebrew word is also found in Job 9 : 31, "Thou shalt plunge me in the ditch," or more correctly, "into the pit;" Gen. 37 : 31, "Dipped the coat in the blood;" Lev. 9 : 9, "He dipped his finger in the blood;" Deut. 33 : 34, "Let him dip his foot in oil;" Ezek. 23 : 15, "In dyed (dipped) attire upon their heads;" that is, dyed according to the common custom among the ancients of dipping any thing into a dye in order to color it. It is also found in Exod. 12 : 22; Lev. 4 : 6; 14 : 6, 51; Num. 19 : 18; Josh. 3 : 15; Ruth 2 : 14; 1 Sam. 14 : 27; 2 Kings 8 : 15, and is in each case translated in our Common Version by the word *dip*.

Dr. Conant, in his exhaustive treatise on the meaning and use of *baptizein*, has for ever set at rest both the literal and figurative meaning of this word. After quoting examples where it is used, from Greek writers in almost every department of literature and science, belonging to various religions and to many different countries, through a long succession of ages, he says, "From the preceding examples it appears that the ground-idea of this word *is to put into or under water* (or other penetrable substance), so as *to immerse* or *submerge;* that this act is always expressed in the literal application of the word, and is the basis of its metaphorical uses. . . . In all, the word has retained its ground meaning without change. From the earliest age of Greek literature down to its close (a period of about two thousand years), not an example has been found in which the word had any other meaning. There is no instance in which it signifies to make a partial application of water by *affusion* or *sprinkling*, or *to cleanse, to purify*, apart from the literal act of immersion, as the *means* of cleansing or purifying." And again he says, "In the age of Christ and his Apostles, as in all periods of the language, it was in common use to express the most familiar acts and occurrences of every-day life; as, for example, *immersing an ax in water* to harden it; *wool in a dye* to color it; *an animal in water* to drown it; a ship *submerged* in the waves; rocks *immersed* in the tide; and (metaphorically) *immersed in cares, in sorrow, in ignorance, in poverty, in debt, in stupor and sleep*," etc.

In addition to this the incidental and figurative allusions to baptism in the New Testament, the places of its administration, and the accompanying circumstances, accord with and confirm the meaning of the word. Thus, John first baptized in the river Jordan, a place offering facilities for the immersion of the multitudes who resorted to him. Afterward we find him baptizing in Ænon, "because there was much water there," John 3 : 23. In the account of the Eunuch's baptism we have the movements of the candidate and the administrator, immediately preceding and following the action of baptizing, "they went down into the water," "they came up out of the water," Acts 8 : 38, 39. *Baptizo* in the original text of the New Testament is only followed by the prepositions *in* and *into*, when connected with the word denoting the element. *In* (Greek, *en*) denotes the locality or element *in* or within which the act is performed, as "and were all baptized of him in the river Jordan," Mark 1 : 5. See note on ver. 11. *Into* (Greek, *eis*) denotes the act of passing into the element in which the rite is performed, Mark 1 : 9, which see. All these point unmistakably to immersion.

The Apostle Paul represents baptism as a *burial*, "We are buried with him by baptism" (Rom. 6 : 4; Col. 2 : 12); and to the Corinthians he says (1 Cor. 10 : 1, 2) that the Israelites "were all baptized unto Moses in the cloud and in the

---

* Antiquities of the Jews. x. 9, 4.
† Discourse v. on Titus. 33.
‡ Life of Galba. xxi.

baptized of him in Jordan, confessing their sins. 7 But when he saw many of the Pharisees and Sad-

sea." Both of these distinctly mark and require immersion as the act in baptism.

The Greeks, who certainly understand their own language, hold that *baptizo* means *immerse*, and have practiced immersion from the first introduction of the Gospel among them till the present time. De Stourdza, a native Greek scholar, and one of the most learned of the present age, says, "The verb *baptizo* has, in fact, but one application. It signifies literally and always to *plunge*. Baptism and immersion are therefore identical." And again, "The distinctive character of the institution of baptism is immersion, which can not be omitted without destroying the emblematical meaning of the sacred rite, and without contradicting, at the same time, the etymological meaning of the word which serves to designate it."

Prof. A. N. Arnold, formerly a missionary to Greece, in a letter to me writes, "The modern word expresses immersion neither more clearly nor less clearly than the ancient. Whether used as a sacred or a common word, it means, as it always did, immersion. The Greeks are not accustomed to say that baptism is administered by sprinkling, in the Roman Catholic and most Protestant churches, but that they have *substituted sprinkling in the place of baptism*. As a common word *baptizo* has always the meaning to immerse. I remember, for example, reading many years ago in a Greek newspaper, an account of the mode of preparing gun-cotton. The cotton was to be dipped (baptized) in a certain liquid. The figurative use of the word is always founded on this meaning. To baptize one's pen in gall, is a common form of expressing a severe criticism or a sarcastic style. The Greek Church *really* practices immersion and insists upon it. I was well acquainted with a learned English deacon, who wished to join the Greek Church, but was not willing to be immersed—rebaptized, as he regarded it, and could not be received on any other terms. He afterward joined the Roman Catholic Church. Two things, however, ought to be stated. The first is that, while strenuously insisting on immersion as the only baptism, they are not quite so particular as we are to make the immersion absolutely complete. The child is dipped naked into the font up to the chin or mouth, and then the priest with his hands sends a wavelet over the projecting head. This they acknowledge to be an abuse; but it pleases the mother, and saves a little risk of the child swallowing water. The other thing to be noted is that, in the Russian branch of the Greek Church, Roman Catholics may be received without baptism, the chrism (corresponding to confirmation in the English Church) only being administered. But this indulgence is not extended to Protestants, and is limited to the national church of Russia, into which this innovation was substituted for the ancient strict requisition, through the influence of Nikon, in spite of much opposition, a little after the middle of the seventeenth century. See Stanley's History of the Eastern Church, p. 460." For a discussion of the word and subject, see Dr. Conant's BAPTIZEIN, Carson on Baptism, and kindred works.

In Jordan. In the river Jordan. This is the chief river of Palestine running from north to south. It is formed by the junction of three rivers before it enters the "waters of Merom," now lake of Huleh. Issuing from this lake the Jordan flows nine miles to the sea of Galilee, through which its course may be traced over twelve miles to its lower end. Thence it pursues its crooked course to the Dead Sea. Lieutenant Lynch, of the United States Navy, who traversed the river in 1848, found that although the distance from the Sea of Galilee to the Dead Sea is but sixty miles in a straight line, it is two hundred miles by the course of the river. It rushes over not fewer than twenty-seven rapids, and many others less precipitous. Its current is usually swift and strong. Its width varies at different points from seventy-five to two hundred feet, and its depth from three to twelve feet.

Confessing their sins. Freely, fully, publicly. John required repentance in those baptized of him (ver. 8); and hence Mark says that he preached "the baptism of repentance," Mark 1:4.

A.D. 26.   MATTHEW III.   45

ducees come to his baptism, he said unto them, *O generation of vipers, who hath warned you to flee
8 from the wrath to come? Bring forth therefore fruits meet for repentance: and think not to say
9 within yourselves, We have Abraham to *our* father: for I say unto you, that God is able of these stones

* Lk. 3. 7-9; Rom. 5. 9; Thess. 1. 10.

Consequently confession of sin was required. In the act of baptism they professed to be penitent, to enter on a new life, and to be preparing for the Messiah. Compare Rom. 6 : 4.

7. Pharisees and Sadducees. The two principal parties among the Jews at that time, religious and also political, originating about one hundred and fifty years before Christ. The *Pharisees* were noted for their rigid observance of the letter of the law and of their traditions. Among their leading characteristics were formality, ostentation, self-righteousness, and hypocrisy. The *Sadducees* rightly rejected all traditions, but unhappily denied many of the important truths of revelation, ch. 22 : 23 ; Acts 23 : 8. They were mostly men of rank, wealth, and education; but the Pharisees were more numerous, and had greater influence with the people. It is evident, from John's address to them, that they came to receive, not to oppose, his baptism; but they came to him from unworthy motives, probably because others did, wishing to be in the popular current. They were unworthy subjects—they came not "confessing their sins." After receiving his faithful reproofs, most of them went away impenitent, and without baptism at his hands. See ch. 21 : 25; Luke 7 : 30.

Generation of vipers. Brood of vipers, denoting persons both deceitful and malignant; hypocritical and holding pernicious doctrines and principles; hence injurious to others and especially exposed to coming wrath. See on ch. 12 : 34. The viper is a very poisonous serpent. See Acts 28 : 3-6. **Who hath warned you,** etc. An expression of surprise and distrust. How is it that sinners so hardened and hypocritical as you should be induced to flee? What has moved you to this, when you think yourselves the "children of Abraham," and the models and teachers of the people? You who teach others, who hath warned you and shown you that *you* must flee? **To flee.**

By repentance and baptism. **Wrath to come.** Impending wrath, the punishment which was to be visited upon those who rejected the kingdom of heaven and neglected preparation. The Jews expected troublous times in connection with the appearance of the Messiah. The prophets foretold it. See Mal. 3 : 1; 4 : 5; Isa. 60 : 12; 63 : 1. As a prophet John referred to the wrath coming on the Jewish nation at the destruction of Jerusalem, and upon all the wicked at the general judgment. 1 Thess. 1 : 10; Matt. 24 : 21, 38, 39.

8. Bring forth therefore fruits. Bring forth works, let your course of life be such as to show your sincerity; and **meet for repentance,** suited and becoming such a change. Forsake as well as confess your sins, Luke 3 : 11-14. Show by your lives the reality of a thorough change of views and purposes. Bring forth humility, meekness, patience, love, faith, mercy, and every good work, consistent with and expressive of repentance. See on ver. 2, and ch. 7 : 16-20.

9. And think not, etc. Imagine not that you may say, etc. Put away all confidence in hereditary privileges, and that you shall be saved simply because you are the descendants of Abraham. The Jews, and especially the Pharisees, thought that, as children of Abraham, they were partakers of the promise made to him, and consequently possessed the favor of God. John 8: 33, 39. **Abraham to our father.** Rather, *for* our father. **God is able of these stones.** God, who created Adam out of the dust of the earth, can now form from these stones men who shall be spiritually and truly the children of Abraham. See Gal. 3: 6, 7. John doubtless pointed to the stones on the banks of the Jordan. These were the most unlikely material; so God could take the most unpromising persons, Gentiles and the most notoriously wicked, and make them suitable subjects of the Messiah. John condemns

10 to raise up children unto Abraham. And now also the ax is laid unto the root of the trees: therefore every tree which bringeth not forth good fruit is
11 hewn down, and cast into the fire. ¹I indeed baptize you with water unto repentance, ᵘ but he that cometh after me is mightier than I, whose shoes I am not worthy to bear; ᵛ he shall baptize you with

ᵗ Mk. 1. 8; Lk. 3. 16; John 1. 15, 26; Ac. 11. 16; 19. 4.
ᵘ Lk. 1. 17.
ᵛ Ma'. 3. 2; John 1. 33; Ac. 1. 5; 2, 2–4; 1 Cor. 12. 13.

the erroneous views of hereditary piety, then prevalent; and teaches that, under the new dispensation, not descent but repentance was necessary to the privileges of sonship.

10. **And now also the ax is laid.** Already lies at the root of the tree, ready for use. Aimed not at the branches, but at the root. The object

ORIENTAL AX.

is not to prune, but to cut down. From this time every one is to be dealt with according to his individual character. Inward repentance and the corresponding outward righteousness, are now required. Men are not to be judged by their birth or their professions, but by their hearts and lives. If deficient and wanting in these, they are to be cut down from the very roots, like barren trees for firewood. **Is hewn down.** Without delay. The execution is to be immediate. **Cast into the fire.** The punishment. Into unquenchable fire, ver. 12; Heb. 6 : 8.

11. **Baptize you with water.** According to the original, *in water*. In the sixth verse the same preposition is translated "*in* Jordan." The Greek preposition *en*, with *baptizo*, in connection with the immersing substance, never means *with* but always *in.* See Conant's BAPTIZEIN, sect. iii. 2. Meyer on this passage says, "*En (in)* is, in accordance with the meaning of *baptizo* (immerse), not to be understood instrumentally, but, on the contrary, as *in*, in the element wherein the immersion takes place." There is as much propriety in translating, *immerse with Jordan*, as *immerse with water.* **Unto repentance.** Into a profession of repentance. John made repentance a condition to baptism; his baptism implied a profession of repentance in those receiving it. It was a symbol of this change of heart and life: a public symbolical declaration to the world that they were in a state of true repentance, and henceforth would live a new life.

He that cometh after me; the Messiah. A contrast between himself and Christ who was immediately to follow. **Whose shoes I am not worthy to bear.** Whose sandals, etc. Sandals

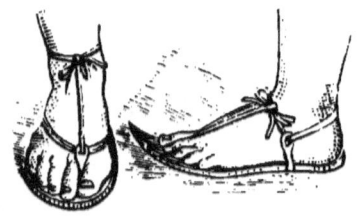

SANDALS.

were coverings of the bottom of the feet, bound to the feet with straps. At first they were of wood, afterward of leather or skins of animals dressed. As stockings were not worn, the feet became soiled; and hence on entering a house, the sandals were taken off, and laid away by the lowest servant, so that the feet might be washed. The newly acquired slave was also to show his submission by such menial service. Hence the loosing, tying, or carrying the sandal became proverbial to express the humblest service. The general meaning is, He that cometh after me is so much greater in authority and power, and so distinguished, that I am unworthy to do him the humblest service.

Shall baptize you with the Holy Ghost and with fire. Literally, *in the Holy Spirit and fire*, there being no preposition in the original before *fire;* and the preposition *en (in)* being used after baptize as at the beginning of this verse. This was literally fulfilled on the day of Pentecost, Acts 2 : 2-4; 1 : 5. The words, *and of fire*, as well as the external appearance of *tongues as of fire*, express symbolically the fiery, the vehement, ardent, and active power of the Holy Spirit, and as manifested in those receiving this baptism, the fiery zeal and fervor, connected with the gift of tongues and other gifts, then conferred upon them. Such an overwhelming and all-pervading descent of the Holy Spirit, with outer manifestations of fire, could aptly be styled a baptism in the Holy Spirit and fire. Cyril of Jerusalem, who lived in the fourth century of the Christian era, referring to the promise of our Lord, "Ye shall be baptized in the Holy Spirit not many days hence," very justly says, "For as he, who sinks down in the waters and is baptized, and is surrounded on all sides by the waters, so also they were completely baptized by the Spirit."—*Instruction* VIII., *on the Holy Spirit*, ii. 14.

Many commentators refer these words to the baptism of the righteous in the Holy Spirit, and of the wicked in fire. Thus Lange explains as follows, "He will either entirely immerse you in the Holy Spirit as penitents, or, if impenitent, he will overwhelm you with the fire of the judgment (and at last with hell-fire.)" So also Neander, who says, "As John's followers were entirely immersed in the water, so the Messiah would immerse the souls of believers in the Holy Spirit. . . . And this Spirit-baptism was to be accompanied by a baptism of fire. Those who refused to be penetrated by the Spirit of divine life should be destroyed by the fire of divine judgments." The passages generally quoted for this symbolical use of the word fire are Mal. 4 : 1 ; Matt. 25 : 41 ; Jude 7 ; Rev. 20 : 14, 15 ; 21 : 8. It is thought that this interpretation agrees better with verse 12, where there is a distinct reference to both the righteous and the wicked. But as Alford remarks, it is only "apparently (to the superficial reader) borne out by verse 12." The language plainly refers to one class, for "the Holy Spirit" and "fire" are closely united in the pronoun *you* and by the conjunction *and*, "He shall baptize *you* in the Holy Spirit *and* fire." It is unnatural and harsh to suppose a reference to two classes of persons.

If it be objected that these Pharisees were not baptized in the Spirit, and hence as *you* refers to them, a different baptism must be meant, it may be answered, that John had just said, "I baptize *you*," and yet the Pharisees generally rejected John and his baptism. The use of the word is general and indefinite. He shall baptize those that be shall baptize in the Holy Spirit and fire. Besides, the prophecy was evidently fulfilled on the day of Pentecost. The language of Jesus, "Ye shall be baptized in the Holy Spirit not many days hence" (Acts 1 : 5), plainly referred to the Pentecostal season. If it be objected that no fire then appeared, but only "tongues as of fire," it may be answered that the presence of material fire was not necessary to the fulfillment of the prophecy, fire being used in the Scriptures so frequently in a symbolical sense.

It appears also that this baptism refers, not to the common influence of the Spirit, but to his miraculous influences and gifts; for Jesus had before the Pentecostal season breathed upon the disciples, saying, "Receive ye the Holy Spirit," John 20 : 22. And it was when the Holy Spirit fell on Cornelius and his company, and they spake with tongues, that Peter remembered the Pentecostal season, and the Savior's promise of the baptism of the Spirit, Acts 11 : 16. See also Acts 10 : 44-46. And Paul in 1 Cor. 12: 13; speaking of spiritual gifts, says, "For by one Spirit we were" (not "are," as in the common version) "all baptized into one body." From such passages it would seem that the baptism in the Holy Spirit and fire, in its broadest application, must be referred to the miraculous influences of the Holy Spirit, communicated on the day of Pentecost and on other seasons.

On these occasions and in these wonderful gifts Christ showed that he was the dispenser of the Spirit, and that his kingdom would be carried on through the power of the Spirit, John 16 : 7-14. Thus he gave a pledge that the Comforter should be given to believers in all ages.

John, also, by contrasting his baptism in water with that in the Holy Spirit and fire, showed the superiority of Christ's office, work, and power over his own. As spirit and fire are more powerful, penetrating, and subtle than water, so Christ's work would be higher, more spiritual and profoundly searching

12 the Holy Ghost, and *with* fire: ᶻ whose fan *is* in his hand, and he will thoroughly purge his floor, ʸ and gather his wheat into the garner; but he will burn up the chaff with ᶻ unquenchable fire.

ˣ Is. 30. 24; Mal. 3. 3.
ʸ ch. 13. 30, 43; Is. 65, 15, 16: Mal. 4. 1.
ᶻ Mk. 9. 43-48.

The baptism of Jesus.

13 THEN cometh Jesus ᵃ from Galilee to Jordan unto John, to be baptized of him.

ᵃ ch. 2. 22; Lk. 2. 39.

---

than his; consuming the dross and producing a higher spiritual life, with all the attendant fruits and blessings.
12. **Whose fan.** A winnowing shovel, with which the mingled wheat

WINNOWING SHOVEL OR FAN.

and chaff was thrown up against the wind; thus the chaff was blown away, while the grain fell in a heap. Christ is thus represented as bearing the winnowing shovel in token of the separating and purifying power of his doctrines. **Thoroughly purge his floor.** Thoroughly cleanse the contents (grain, etc.,) of his threshing-floor, by separating the wheat and the chaff. Believers are to be separated, even by severe measures, from both unbelievers and also their remaining sins. The threshing-floor was a circular piece of ground in the open field, leveled, and beaten down or paved. An elevated ground was generally selected, for the purpose of having the benefit of the wind. That of Ornan the Jebusite was on Mount Moriah, 1 Chron. 21 : 15, 28, 30. The grain was trodden by oxen or horses, Deut. 25 : 4; or beaten by a threshing-machine, drawn over it by horses or oxen, Isa. 41 : 15; Amos 1 : 3. **The wheat.** The righteous, true believers. **The garner.** Granary, storehouse. **The chaff.**

The wicked, unbelievers. **Unquenchable fire.** Fire that will not be put out, fire that utterly consumes. See Isa. 66 : 24; Mark 9 : 43-48. Thus Christ will gather the righteous into his heavenly kingdom, and consign the wicked to everlasting punishment. Matt. 25 : 34, 41, 46.

13-17. THE BAPTISM OF JESUS. Mark 1 : 9-11; Luke 3 : 21, 22. Jesus, who had taken upon himself the form of a servant, and was made in the likeness of men commences his public ministry, by placing himself on a level with man, and receiving the baptism of repentance, and thereby the public testimony of his Father's approval.

13. **Then cometh Jesus.** It is supposed that John had been preaching and baptizing about six months. The exact time of Christ's baptism is unknown. Ancient tradition very generally places it in the winter. **From Galilee.** Nazareth of Galilee, Mark 1 : 9. **To Jordan.** Nazareth was seventy miles north of Jerusalem, and not less from the place of our Savior's baptism. The exact spot on the banks of the Jordan where John was preaching is not stated; probably the same as that referred to in verses 5 and 6, where the multitudes came to him for baptism, namely, "in the wilderness of Judea," ver. 1. But the wilderness of Judea did not probably extend to the east of the Jordan, and only a little north of the Dead Sea. The place of his preaching, therefore, answers well to the west bank of the Jordan opposite Jericho, where the Israelites under Joshua crossed the river, and where it was twice miraculously opened by Elijah and Elisha. Bethabara, or rather Bethany, (John 1 : 28) was probably at this point on the east side of the river. Possibly the wilderness of Judea was regarded as extending a little east of the Jordan, John 1 : 28. Or better,

14 But John forbade him, saying, I have need to be
15 baptized of thee, and comest thou to me? And
Jesus answering said unto him, Suffer *it to be so
now;* [b] for thus it becometh us to fulfill all right-
16 eousness. Then he suffered him. [c] And Jesus,

[b] Ps. 40. 7, 8; John 4. 34.
[c] Mk. 1. 10.

John may have made Bethany his headquarters at this time, and baptized both on the eastern and western side of the river, and preaching from either bank. Says Lieutenant Lynch, "Tradition, sustained by the geographical features of the country, make this the scene of the baptism of the Redeemer. And as the ford probably derived its name from the passage of the Israelites with the Ark of the Covenant, the inference is not unreasonable that this spot has been doubly hallowed." And speaking of the pilgrims, who came while he was on the ground, to commemorate the Savior's baptism, he says, "Each one plunged himself, or was dipped by another, three times below the surface, in honor of the Trinity." See *Lynch's Expedition*, pp. 255, 263.

14. But John forbade him. Sought to hinder him. Having doubtless known of the wonderful circumstances connected with the birth of Jesus, as well as something concerning his blameless life, and at the same time by a divine impulse recognizing in Jesus the Messiah, he shrunk from performing the service from a deep feeling of inferiority and unworthiness. See John 1 : 31; 3 : 28, 30. As the less should be baptized by the greater, and as John had probably not been baptized, he would rather receive the ordinance from the hands of Jesus.

15. Thus it becometh us to fulfill all righteousness. In this reply we see the design of Jesus in receiving baptism from John. "Had he omitted this act of obedience, he would have left incomplete that perfect righteousness which, in our nature, he has wrought out. If aught that it became him to fulfill, had been left unfulfilled, something essential would have been wanting."—DR. CONANT. Christ had taken upon him our nature, not only that he might be "made sin for us," but also that he might work out a perfect righteousness, comprehending every holy principle and affection of the heart and entire conformity of life to the divine law. In this reply, Jesus indicates baptism as an act of holy obedience incumbent on every pious individual, and, as such, it became him to receive it and John to administer it. In the neglect of it, there would have been disobedience on the part of both to a divine requirement.

There was also a deep significance in the baptism of Jesus, pointing to the vicarious nature of his great work. It was only as he was connected with a sinful race, he himself being without sin, that he could appropriately submit to baptism. It prefigured not merely his death, burial, and resurrection, Luke 12 : 50; but also his death to sin, that is, to the sins of the people that were laid on him, and his life to righteousness, that is, the new life of all his spiritual people. It prefigured sin, as it were, receiving its death and burial with him, and holiness its resurrection and life. Col. 2 : 12, 13; Eph. 2 : 5; Rom. 6 : 3, 4. 8; Ps. 40 : 12. He that has not truly died with him and risen with him, can have no part, lot, nor life with him.

Christ, being thus closely connected and identified with his people, was their exemplar. And as baptism was to be an ordinance of perpetual obligation in the new dispensation, we see in the baptism of Jesus an example to his followers. What Jesus here sanctions by his example, what he afterward did through his disciples (John 4 : 2), he at last confirms with the complete formula in his last commission, ch. 28 : 19. Thus the baptism of John, though commencing in the dawn of the new dispensation, was substantially the ordinance as carried out by Christ himself. See on ver. 1. John's baptizing in view of the coming Messiah was the first step in the development of the ordinance; Christ's disciples baptizing in the name of Jesus as the Messiah, the second; and the last commission to baptize in the name of the Father, and of the Son, and of the Holy Spirit, the final step which made the ordinance complete

when he was baptized, went up straightway out of the water: and, lo, the heavens were opened unto him, and he saw ᵈ the Spirit of God descending 17 like a dove, and lighting upon him : ᵉ and, lo, a voice from heaven, saying, ᶠ This is my beloved Son, in whom I am well pleased.

ᵈIs. 11. 2: Lk. 3. 22.
ᵉJohn 19. 28–30.
ch. 12. 18 ; 17. 5 ; Ps. 2. 7; Is. 42. 1; Mk. 1. 11; Lk. 9. 35; 2 Pet. 1. 17.

---

as an institution of the churches of Christ. **Then he suffered him.** As soon as John was convinced of duty, he did it.

16. **Went up straightway out of the water.** From the water where he was immersed to the bank of Jordan. The preposition used here in the original means *from ; out of* is the meaning of the preposition found in Acts 8 : 39, and so translated there. The peculiar force of straightway should not be overlooked. He went up immediately; and as soon as he had gone up from the water, behold the heavens were opened. He went up praying (Luke 3 : 21); and on reaching the bank of the river, the miraculous descent of the Spirit occurred.

The heavens were opened. There appeared a parting in the heavens, probably like the parting of clouds by a flash of lightning. See Acts 7 : 56. **Unto him.** To Jesus. **He saw.** Jesus saw. John also witnessed it, John 1 : 32. **Like a dove.** As a dove. The words "as a dove" may refer either to the *shape* or the manner, in which the Spirit descended. Probably the former; for Luke says (3 : 22) that the Spirit assumed a "bodily form like (as) a dove." This was a fit emblem of the pure, gentle, and peaceful character of Jesus and his work. Ch. 10 : 16; 11 : 29; Isa. 61 : 1–3. John adds (1 : 32), "and it abode on him." Thus Jesus received the heavenly anointing, and from this time his ministry actively and officially begins. Ps. 45 : 7; Isa. 11 : 2; 42 : 1; 61 : 1. The descent of the Spirit was also the appointed token for fully making known the Messiah to John, John 1 : 33.

17. **A voice from heaven.** From the Father; specially designed for John as the harbinger of Jesus, in order that he might introduce him as the Messiah to the people. John 1 : 32–34. **My beloved Son.** Not only *my Son*, but emphatically the *Beloved*. The term Son was applied to the Messiah (Ps. 2 : 7, 12), indicating the close and endearing relation he sustained to the Father, and the dignity both of his nature and his office. See also Isa. 42 : 1. **I am well pleased.** Am ever well pleased with him in all respects, as a son and as a Mediator. This testimony to our Lord's sonship and to the pleasure of the Father in him, was repeated at the transfiguration, ch. 17 : 5. See also John 12 : 28–30 ; 2 Pet. 1 : 17.

Thus at the baptism of our Lord we have the manifestation of the three persons of the one God. The Son baptized in Jordan; the Holy Spirit descending upon him in the form of a dove; and the Father proclaiming him as his beloved Son. While Jesus was thus manifested and honored, a threefold honor was bestowed upon the ordinance he had just received. Surely we should not only honor Jesus, but also the ordinance which he, with the Father and Holy Spirit, honored with implicit obedience.

REMARKS.

1. The most eminent servants of God often grow up in the most humble circumstances and labor in the most retired places, ver. 1 : Amos 7 : 14–16.

2. This world is a spiritual wilderness, the kingdom of "the wicked one." ver. 1 ; ch. 13 : 39 ; Eph. 2 : 2 ; 6 : 12 ; 1 John 5 : 19.

3. Christ is a king. His kingly office is no less prominently presented in Scripture than his prophetic and priestly, ver. 2 ; Ps .2 : 6 ; 45 : 6 ; 110 : 1, 2.

4. Christ's kingdom is spiritual and has its seat in the heart ; hence the necessity of entering it with repentance, a deep, thorough change of mind, a confessing and a forsaking of sin, vers. 2, 6 ; Mark 1 : 15 ; Luke 24 : 47.

5. True repentance springs from a sense of the mercy of God as manifested in Christ. John preached repentance ; *for the kingdom of heaven is at hand*, ver. 2 ; Rom. 2 : 4 ; Acts 5 : 31.

6. In John we see the type of the

A.D. 26. MATTHEW IV. 51

The temptation of Jesus.

IV. THEN was *g* Jesus led up of the Spirit into the wil- *g* Lk. 4. 1. 2 ; Acts 8. 39.

law, as our schoolmaster to lead us to Christ. By the severity of his manners and doctrines he "prepared the way of the Lord;" so the terrors of the law prepare the soul, through the convicting Spirit, for the reception of Jesus, vers. 3, 4; Gal. 3 : 24; 2 Cor. 5 : 11.

7. As John's preaching and manner of life corresponded, so should the profession and practice of every Christian. All should put into daily practice the doctrines they preach or profess, ver. 4; ch. 12 : 33.

8. Public confession of sin is the duty of the sinner, since he has been an open transgressor; and is an evidence of repentance, ver. 6; Rom. 10 : 10.

9. Ministers of Jesus and all religious teachers should be like John, neither flatterers, nor self-seekers, nor servants of men, ver. 7; Gal. 1 : 10.

10. Self-righteous formalists are, spiritually, a generation of vipers, cunning, deceitful, malicious, and pernicious, and, as such, especially exposed to divine wrath, ver. 7; ch. 23 : 23. 24, 33.

11. True repentance is attended with reformation of life. It is vain to profess repentance without the attending fruits, or to be baptized without both a change of heart and life, ver. 8; Acts 26 : 20; ch. 7 : 16, 20.

12. We do not enter Christ's kingdom by birth. We must not trust in the piety of our ancestors, any more than in Pharisaical or Sadducean philosophy, ver 8; Luke 13 : 3, 5.

13. There is more hope for the heathen and the most abandoned, than for many of the highly favored and self-righteous, ver. 8; ch. 21 : 31, 32.

14. The wicked are already condemned; the ax is laid at the root of the tree, and except they repent and bring forth fruit to God, they perish, ver. 10; John 3 : 18, 19.

15. John knew nothing of infant baptism. He required repentance well attested, as a pre-requisite to the ordinance, vers. 8–10; Luke 3 : 10–14.

16. Christ is the dispenser of the Spirit and of spiritual gifts, ver. 11; John 16 : 7. And by the Spirit and through the truth, he becomes in this world the great Winnower, separating the race into the righteous and the wicked, ch. 10 : 34–36.

17. Christ is our Judge, and will with equal fidelity spare and reward his people, and punish the wicked, who are but chaff, ver. 12; John 5 : 22; Matt. 25 : 31–46.

18. The most eminent saints feel their unworthiness of the honor put upon them in the service of God, ver. 14; 1 Cor. 15 : 9.

19. Let Christ be our example in baptism, who came such a distance to receive it, and who said, "Thus it becometh *us*," including, in a subordinate sense, all his followers. If it became him to "fulfill all righteousness," it surely becomes us to walk in his ordinances and to obey all his commandments, ver. 15; John 14 : 15; 1 John 5 : 3; Acts 2 : 38.

20. John showed his humility in baptizing Jesus as well as in hesitating and shrinking from it at first. Humility and obedience to God go hand in hand. Disobedience and pride are twin brothers, vers. 14, 15; 1 Sam. 15 : 22.

21. Let us pray for, and strive to possess, the dove-like spirit of Christ, *gentleness, harmlessness, love*, and purity, ver. 16; ch. 10 : 16; Gal. 5 : 22.

22. Christ was truly the Wonderful. What wonders attended him! The star appeared and angels sang at his birth; at his baptism the Spirit descends and the Father speaks, attesting his Messiahship, and approving the ordinance, vers. 16, 17.

23. Heaven is opened to us by the Son, vers. 16, 17; John 1 : 51; 14 : 6.

24. The Triune God is concerned in our salvation. While we bestow on the Persons of the Godhead equal honors, let us accept of Christ as our Mediator, and love him who is accepted and loved by the Father, vers. 16, 17; John 5 : 23; 1 Tim. 2 : 5.

CHAPTER IV.

Matthew now proceeds to record the conflict of Jesus with Satan and his triumph over him; the beginning of his public ministry in Galilee, including

2 derness to be tempted of the devil. And when he had fasted forty days and forty nights, he was af- ᵇ Job. 1. 9–12; 1 Thes. 3. 5; Rev. 2. 10.

the call of four fishermen to be his public attendants; and a summary account of his first missionary tour in that region. His triumph over Satan, his labors in Galilee in fulfillment of prophecy, and his wonderful miracles there, are additional proofs of his Messiahship and Divinity.

1–11. THE TEMPTATION OF JESUS. Mark 1 : 12, 13; Luke 4 : 1–13. He is led by the Spirit into the wilderness; fasts forty days, is tempted by the Devil; angels minister to him.

1. **Then was Jesus.** Immediately after his baptism. **Led up of the Spirit.** From the valley of Jordan by the Spirit. Mark says, "The Spirit driveth him." He was urged on by the Spirit which had just descended upon him. **The Wilderness.** Possibly the Arabian desert of Sinai; but more probably the wilderness of Judea, or of Jericho, the eastern part of Judah, adjacent to the Dead Sea, and extending toward Jericho. It is still one of the most dreary and desolate regions of the whole country. The wildness of certain parts of it is strikingly indicated by Mark, "He was with the wild beasts." The mountain Quarantania, in this wilderness, which tradition has marked as the site of the temptation, is described by Robinson, as "an almost perpendicular wall of rock twelve or fifteen hundred feet above the plain." See on ch. 3 : 1. **To be tempted.** The design of the Spirit in leading him into the wilderness. It was meet that the Second Adam should endure the same trial under which the first Adam fell; so that his power to overcome the Devil and to restore man to his lost state might be manifested. It was also needful that our great High-Priest should be tempted in all points as we are, so that he might thereby be fully prepared to sympathize with, intercede for, and help us, Heb. 2 : 17, 18 ; 4 : 15, 16. **Of the Devil.** By the Devil. The word *devil* (Greek, *diabolos*) means a *traducer*, a false accuser, and answers to Satan of the Old Testament, which means an adversary, Job 1 : 6; Zech. 3 : 1. It is applied to the chief of the fallen spirits, and is descriptive of his character and work, and was the name by which he was familiarly known. He is the prince of the power of the air (Eph. 2 : 2), under whom are the *demons*, who are active in introducing every evil among mankind. He is known also by the name of Beelzebub, the prince of devils or demons, ch. 12 : 24; the old serpent, Rev. 12 : 9. The Scriptures frequently speak of him as a personal agent, ascribing attributes and acts to him, John 8 : 44; 14 : 30; 2 Cor. 11 : 3, 14, 15 ; Eph. 6 : 11, 12; 1 Pet. 5 : 8, 9; 1 John 3 : 8; Rev. 2 : 10; 3 : 9; 20 : 10. Whether he appeared in visible form is not stated, though fairly implied. His *coming to him* (ver. 3), his saying, If thou wilt *fall down and worship me* (ver. 9), his *leaving him* (ver. 11), all render it probable that the Devil appeared in a bodily form, and possibly as an angel of light.

But how was Jesus tempted? In his human nature. Thus it became him, as a man, the Second Adam, to be tempted and to overcome. As a man there was a possibility of falling; as God-man there was no possibility. The human soul of Jesus was free from all tendency to evil; he could, therefore, be tempted only from without. Yet he "was in all points tempted like as we are, yet without sin," Heb. 4 : 15. But since he could not be tempted through evil desires, he was tempted through the senses; and that Satan might bring his temptations the more thoroughly to bear, Jesus *hungered*, he felt the strong cravings of appetite, necessarily resulting from long fasting. He was worn and weak for want of food, thus presenting a rare opportunity for Satan to bring upon him his strongest and most artful temptations.

2. **Fasted forty days and nights.** Some have supposed that he abstained only from bread and ordinary food, but Luke affirms that *he ate nothing*, Luke 4 : 2. His fasting, like that of Moses (Deut. 9, 18), and Elijah (1 Kings 19 : 8), was a total abstinence from all food. In these cases they were doubtless supernaturally supported. A high state of spiritual enjoyment will render a person, for a time, independent of the common necessities of life. Jesus, aside from his union with the second person

3 terward an hungered. And when ⁿthe tempter came to him, he said, ⁱ "If thou be the Son of God,
4 command that these stones be made bread. But he answered and said, ʲ It is written, ᵏ 'Man shall not live by bread alone, ˡ but by every word that proceedeth out of the mouth of God.'

ⁱ ch. 3. 17.
ʲ Is. 8. 20; Ro. 15. 4; Eph. 6 17.
ᵏ Deu. 8. 3.
ˡ Ps. 119. 11; Jer. 15. 16; John 5. 39; 6. 27, 31-35. 63; 20. 31; 2 Tim. 3. 16.

---

of the Trinity, was *full of the Holy Spirit* (Luke 4 : 1), and in this high and perfect state was thus supernaturally sustained. After forty days, according to the design of the Spirit, he hungered, in order that the Devil might have an opportunity of bringing against him his greatest power as a tempter.

3. When the tempter came to him. This does not necessarily indicate the first assault of the Devil, the correct translation being, *And the tempter came*, etc. Both Mark and Luke intimate that Jesus was tempted during the forty days, Mark 1 : 13; Luke 4 : 2. In those recorded we have the kinds of temptation to which he was exposed; and being the last, they were the most signal, forming the climax of all that preceded. In them we have the three principal forms of temptation, the lust of the flesh, the lust of the eyes, and the pride of life, 1 John 2 : 16. They run parallel with the temptation of our first parents in the garden : "When the woman saw that the tree was good for food, that it was pleasant to the eyes, and a tree to be desired to make one wise, she took of the fruit thereof and did eat," Gen. 3 : 6. In the first, our Savior is tempted to unbelief and selfishness; in the second, to presumption and vanity; in the third, to ambition and idolatry.

If thou be the son of God. This temptation had doubtless some reference to the declaration at his baptism, "This is my beloved Son." We need not suppose that the Devil fully understood his divinity or his Messiahship. He had doubtless known something of his history and heard the voice of the Father at his baptism. But as *Son of God* could be applied to angels, and to the spiritual children of God, the tempter might easily have been in doubt. He had, however, witnessed enough to know that Jesus was a remarkable personage, possibly divine. The language in the original is worthy of close study. *Son* is emphatic, but has not the article before it, as in the title *The Son of God*, so often applied to the Messiah. The tempter thus lays emphasis not on his Messiahship, but on *his Sonship*. The expression is equivalent to, *If thou be God's Son*, hence, possessed of extraordinary and supernatural powers, etc. **If thou.** He would have him doubt the reality of his Sonship, and also distrust his Father. As if he had said, "Use the means at your disposal to supply your wants, instead of depending on God, whom you call your Father, but who appears to have forgotten you; *command that these stones be made bread*; and thus you will satisfy your hunger, and at the same time your evidence of your Sonship." Thus the tempter would lead him both to distrust God, and exercise a selfish principle.

4. It is written. As Jesus is tempted as a man, so does he meet the tempter as a man. He meets every temptation exactly as any one else might meet it, by the simple and appropriate use of God's word. To have performed a miracle would have been contrary to his uniform principle of action. With him miracles were for the honor of his Father, for the good of others, and for confirming his mission and doctrine : he never performed one to defend or relieve himself, ch. 20 : 28; 26 : 53, 54. As a prophet he had been led by the Spirit to fasting, and it became him to wait, and not to relieve himself by a miracle, unless divinely directed.

Man shall not live, etc. In the passage here cited (Deut. 8 : 3), Moses tells the people that God, by giving them manna, had taught them that life could be sustained not only by bread but by any thing he might appoint for that purpose. And Jesus, in quoting it, shows his reliance on his heavenly Father's care, and his determination to seek no means to sustain life but such as God should appoint.

Every word that proceedeth out of the mouth of God. Whatever God may appoint, or by what-

MATTHEW IV.

A.D. 26.

5 Then the devil taketh him up ᵐ into the holy city,   ᵐ Ne. 11, 1, 18; Is.
6 and setteth him on a pinnacle of the temple, and   48. 2; Rev. 11. 2.
saith unto him, If thou be the Son of God, cast
thyself down: for it is written, ⁿ 'He shall give his   ⁿ Ps. 34. 7, 20; 91.
angel charge concerning thee: and in *their* hands   11, 12.
they shall bear thee up, lest at any time thou dash

ever means he pleases, John 4: 32, 34. In the expression, *mouth of God*, we have an example of a figurative mode of speaking, common in Scripture, by which terms proper to the bodily frame and to the soul of man are applied to God, Gen. 6: 6; Ex. 33: 23; Ezek. 5: 13. It should be noticed that Jesus makes no reference to his divine sonship. Throughout these temptations, he acts on the full assurance that he is the Son of God, and yet speaks with all the humility and with all the holy and unselfish principle becoming him, as Son of Man. He was not called upon to prove his divine nature to Satan; much less to perform a miracle at his suggestion. Thus in the first temptation, Satan tempted Jesus through the bodily appetite. And thus he approaches mankind everywhere. By this means drunkards, gluttons, and debauchees have become his prey.

5. Then. Luke places this temptation last, but this word *then* seems to fix the order. Luke seems here less careful about the order of *time*, and connects the temptations by simply the conjunction *and*. Our Lord's answer, ver. 10, "Get thee hence," etc., evidently points to the conclusion of the temptations. This is one of many instances of unimportant diversity, and yet substantial agreement, between the Evangelists, which go to confirm the truthfulness of their narrative, Luke 4: 3, 5, 9.

The devil taketh him. A marvelous power was granted the tempter till Jesus uttered the words, *Get thee hence*. Nothing can be determined from these words as to whether the devil did, or did not, transport him through the air. Luke's language (Luke 4: 9), *he brought him*, favors the latter supposition. But both Evangelists leave no doubt that the Devil exerted certain power over Jesus in going to Jerusalem. He went there, and to the pinnacle of the temple, not of his own accord merely, though not against his will, but through the power permitted the devil.

As the Spirit of the Lord caught away Philip (Acts 8: 39), so the devil may have borne away Jesus. **The holy city.** Jerusalem, so called as the place where the temple was situated, and the public worship of God was performed. See Isa. 48: 2; Dan. 9: 24. Modern Jerusalem is called by the Arabs El Kuds, "the holy." **A pinnacle of the temple** was some very high point of the temple buildings, probably either Solomon's porch on the east side, which overlooked the valley of Jehoshaphat or Kidron, or the elevation of the middle portion of the southern portico, looking down at a fearful height of about six hundred feet into the valley of Hinnom. The latter, which Josephus describes as a dizzy height, is the most probable. For further on the temple, see on ch. 21: 12. The word translated *temple* both here and in Luke means not the temple proper, but the whole sacred inclosure, the temple buildings.

6. Cast thyself down. Having failed in leading Jesus to distrust the providence of his Father, the tempter would induce him to presume upon it. Failing to produce selfishness, by addressing the appetite, he would now lead him to vain display and vanity. Having also been repulsed by the word of God, he attempts to use the same weapon in overcoming Jesus: "If thou be the son of God, cast thyself down from this dizzy height: it can not hurt thee; for thou art under thy Father's care, and it is in accordance with his will: for it is written, etc. It will be also a miracle worthy of thee, and a striking proof of thy sonship; and becoming known, will attract the people after thee." **He shall give his angels charge.** This passage (Ps. 91: 11, 12) expresses the care of divine providence over the righteous. And the inference was, that if such a promise had been granted to all righteous persons, it would certainly apply more forcibly to the Son of God. But the devil both

7 thy foot against a stone.' Jesus said unto him, It is written again, ° 'Thou shalt not tempt the Lord thy God.'   ° Deu. 6. 16.

8   Again, the devil taketh him up into into an exceeding high mountain, and showeth him all the kingdoms of the world and the glory of them;   ᵖ John 14. 30; 2 Cor. 4. 4; Eph. 2. 2.

9 and saith unto him, ᵖ All these things will I give thee, if thou wilt fall down and worship me.   ᵠ Jam. 4. 7; 1 Pet. 5. 9.

misquotes it and misapplies it. He omits an important part, "Keep thee in all thy ways," that is, the ways along which God's providence leads the believer. To apply such a promise to acts of rashness, vanity, and ostentation, would be to "tempt the Lord thy God."

·7. **It is written again.** Jesus still as a man combats the Devil by the right use of Scripture. It is worthy of notice that he does not correct the Devil's false quotation and misapplication of Scripture; but simply shows the Devil's false position by quoting another passage. What you advise can not be right; for it is contrary to another portion of God's words, and his truth can not be contradictory.

Thou shalt not tempt the Lord thy God, Deut. 6 : 16. The word *tempt* here means *to put on trial*, put to *the proof, to test*. Thus in Gen. 22 : 1, God is said to have tempted Abraham, in other words, he put his faith and obedience on trial, he tested them. So the Israelites tempted God at Massah, by asking water to drink, and asking in such a spirit that they would judge, from the reception given to their request, "whether the Lord was among them or not," Ex. 17 : 2–7. In the application of this passage, our Savior intimates that he should not put God on trial, by exercising a presumptuous confidence or by needlessly testing his veracity. In every trial connected with the path of duty he could trust God; but he would not put himself needlessly into dangerous circumstances, and thus trifle with his promises.

8. **Again.** Failing in his second assault, the Devil now changes his tactics. He no longer commences with, *If thou be the Son of God;* but as Satan, the great *adversary* of Christ's kingdom, he would lure Jesus with ambition to renounce God and worship him. He would make him a false Christ, such a' Messiah as the worldly Jews expected, a temporal prince with universal dominion.

An exceeding high mountain. What mountain, can not be determined. Some suggest Nebo, from one of whose summits, namely, Pisgah, Moses had a view of the promised land, Deut. 34 : 1–4. Others suggest the Mount of Olives, or one of the high summits north of Jericho. Tradition says Mount Quarantania, on the northern boundary of the plain of Jericho.

All the kingdoms of the world. Not merely Palestine (the term *world* has often a restricted meaning. Acts 11 : 28; Rom. 1 : 8), but also the heathen world, over which Satan exercised spiritual dominion. From the lofty elevation the kingdoms or tetrarchies of Palestine, and adjacent regions, could be seen, and the more distant empires of the world might be suggested by the tempter. The force of the words, **Showeth him all,** etc., rather demand that these kingdoms should have come up before his vision. That there was something supernatural in this, agrees with Luke, who says that the Devil showed all the kingdoms of the world in *a moment of time.*

And the glory of them. The rich countries, large cities, splendid palaces, etc.

9. **All these will I give thee.** Satan now appears in his character as "the prince of this world," (John 12 : 31; 14 : 30; 16 : 11; 2 Cor. 4 : 4). He showed himself also the father of lies, (John 8 : 44); for he had nothing but usurped power; the kingdoms of the world were not his by right, but Christ's (Ps. 2 : 8), and therefore he could not give them.

Fall down and worship me. See on Matt. 2 : 2. Satan wished him to fall down and do him homage, which would be an acknowledgment of his authority and his right to give him the kingdoms of the world. It would also

10 Then saith Jesus unto him, ⁹ Get thee hence, ʳ Satan: for it is written, ˢ 'Thou shalt worship the Lord thy God, and him only shalt thou serve.'

11 Then the devil leaveth him; and, behold, ᵗ angels came and ministered unto him.

⁹ 1 Chr. 21. 1; Job 1. 6.
ʳ Deu. 6. 13, 14; Jos. 24. 14; 1 Sam. 7. 3.
ˢ Lk. 22. 43; Heb. 1. 6, 14.

Our Lord's ministry in Galilee; the call of Peter, Andrew, James, and John. First general preaching tour.

12 ᵘ NOW when Jesus had heard that ˣ John was

ᵘ Mk. 1. 14; Lk. 4. 14; John 4. 1-3.
ˣ Lk. 3. 20; 4. 16-31; John 4. 43.

---

imply a renouncing of God and transferring his allegiance to Satan. The Devil really puts himself in the place of God, and would have Jesus "ask of him," Ps. 2:8. The meaning is well expressed by *worship me*. Our Lord was thus tempted not only to secular power and ambition, but also to devil-worship, idolatry.

10. Get thee hence, Satan. Jesus openly rebukes and repels him, not that he did not know him before, but because the tempter had openly manifested himself and made such a bold disclosure of his object. The thought of grasping at temporal power, of worshiping Satan, and being a temporal and false Messiah, is instantly repelled. God is the only object of worship, and no religious homage and service should be paid to any other. **Thou shalt worship the Lord thy God.** Again Jesus answers as a man, "For it is written," citing Deut. 6:13. Thus does the Savior each time honor the written word, resting upon it with unwavering faith, from which there could be no appeal; and thus does he show us how to resist the Devil. The richness and the power of the divine truth are remarkably shown, from the fact that the Savior found within the compass of a few verses enough to repel all the assaults of the Devil.

11. Then the devil leaveth him. Luke adds (4:13) "for a season." How often the devil assaulted him secretly, or through others, we know not; but he certainly renewed his attacks near the termination of our Savior's ministry on earth. See Luke 22:53; John 14:30. **The angels came and ministered.** "The Savior here appears standing between the two worlds of light and darkness. As the hostile powers fled, heavenly powers surrounded him, and joined in celebrating the victory." — OLSHAUSEN. Ministering spirits had left him to meet the Devil alone. Yet they were anxious spectators, and no sooner is Satan vanquished, than they hasten to rejoice with Jesus and minister to his wants. Some suppose that they supplied him with food, as the angels did Elijah, Kings 19:5, 6. But as the angels appeared and strengthened Jesus in Gethsemane, (Luke 22:43), so here we must not limit their ministration to the supply of material food, but refer it principally, if not altogether, to imparting consolation of soul and supernatural and heavenly support. Heb. 1:14.

12-19. JESUS BEGINS HIS MINISTRY IN GALILEE, Mark 1:14 15; Luke 4:14-30. Between the last paragraph and this a considerable interval occurs. On the return of Jesus from the temptation, John gave renewed testimony to his Messiahship, and the day following pointed him out to two of his disciples, Andrew and probably John. Andrew brings Peter to Jesus, John 1:29-42. Jesus calls Philip and returns to Galilee; Philip finds Nathanael, and brings him to Jesus, John 1:43-51. Three days after was the marriage in Cana; then Jesus visits Capernaum, remaining a few days, after which he goes up to Jerusalem to the passover, and drove the traders out of the temple, John 2:1-25. Nicodemus visits him at night; Jesus leaves Jerusalem, but tarries in Judea, makes disciples, and receives further testimony from John, who was baptizing in Ænon, John 3:1-36.

12. John was cast into prison. *Literally*, John was delivered up, that is, for confinement. He was imprisoned by Herod Antipas, son of Herod the Great, in the castle of Machærus, a fortress on the eastern shore of the Dead Sea. This took place probably in the autumn of 780 from the founding of Rome,

13 cast into prison, he departed into Galilee. And leaving Nazareth, he came and dwelt in Capernaum, which is upon the sea coast, in the borders of Zab-

about eight to twelve months after the baptism of Jesus. See on ch. 14 : 3-5; and John 4 : 35. John's ministry had continued about eighteen months. **He departed into Galilee.** Jesus retired to Galilee, probably *first*, because, having preached the Gospel a few months in Judea, he was becoming sufficiently known, and he did not wish at present to increase the jealousy of the Pharisees by further success. He was aware that his growing popularity was exciting their envy and ill-will, which he wished at present to avoid, John 4 : 1. And *second*, because he would take advantage of the impressions made by the ministry of John on the people there, which would be rather increased than diminished by the treatment he was receiving at the hand of Herod. He could also labor the more quietly in Galilee, than in Judea where the scribes, Pharisees, and priests held general sway. All parts of the country, too, must enjoy his labors.

On this journey, probably, he passes through Samaria, and converses with a woman of Sychar at Jacob's well, and many Samaritans believe on him, John 4 : 4-42. Arriving in Galilee, he again visits Cana, where he heals the son of a nobleman lying ill at Capernaum, (John 4 : 46-54). Exercises his ministry in the synagogues of Galilee, and goes to Nazareth. From John 4 : 35 we learn that it was four months before the harvest, the first-fruits of which were presented on the second day of the paschal week. The journey, therefore, was probably performed in the latter part of November, or early in December.

13. And leaving Nazareth. Luke gives an account of our Savior's visit to Nazareth, and the persecution he received of his townsmen, Luke 4 : 16-30. Hence he left Nazareth and **came and dwelt in Capernaum,** made it the principal place of his residence, Luke 4 : 31. Capernaum was the name of a fountain (Josephus, *Jew. War*, iii. 10, 8), and a town situated on the northwest shore of the sea of Galilee, on the borders of the tribes of Zebulun and Naphtali. It was a thriving commercial place on the road from Damascus to the Mediterranean. This seems to have been the principal residence of Christ during the three years of his ministry. "It is called his own city," ch. 9 : 1. Its name was appropriate for his dwelling-place, meaning *Village of Nahum*, or *consolation*. It was also the residence of Andrew, Peter, James, and John, who were natives of Bethsaida (John 1 : 44), and probably of Matthew. Its present complete desolation forcibly illustrates our Lord's denunciation in ch. 11 : 23. Its name and site are lost.

The most probable suppositions concerning the site of Capernaum are as follows : (1) Dr. Robinson supposes it to have been at *Khan Minyeh*, on the northern borders of the fine plain of Gennesaret, about five miles from the Jordan, where there is a copious fountain, and ruins of some extent still remain. In favor of this site, it may be said, It is on high ground (ch. 11 : 23), near the shore, in the land of Gennesaret, and well located for a customhouse, on the highway between Jerusalem and Damascus. Lieutenant Kitchener and Selah Merrill (1877) favor this site. See on Mark 1 : 21. (2) But Dr. Thomson and others place the site near the head of the lake at *Tell Hum*, about three miles north of *Khan Minyeh*, and about the same distance from the point where the Jordan enters the lake. It is argued that *Hum* is the closing syllable of Capernaum, and that its first part *Caphar*, which signifies a village, has given place to *Tell*, meaning a site or ancient ruin. But no fountain is found nearer than two miles. Tradition of Jews and Arabs, however, fixes Capernaum here. Recent excavations have brought to light extensive ruins, among which is a synagogue in a fine state of preservation, and belonging to an age earlier than that of Christ. It is probably one in which Jesus taught, and possibly performed miracles, but whether at Capernaum is still uncertain.

Upon the sea-coast. By the sea of Galilee. **Zabulon and Nephthalim.** The Greek form of the Hebrew Zebulun and Naphtali, two

ulon and Nephthalim: ⁵ that it might be fulfilled which was spoken by Esaias the prophet, saying,
15 ᶻ ' The land of Zabulon, and the land of Nephthalim, by the way of the sea, beyond Jordan, Galilee of
16 the Gentiles; ᵃ the people which sat in darkness saw great light; and to them which sat in the region and shadow of death light is sprung up.'

ʸ Lk. 22. 37; 24. 44.
ᶻ Is. 9. 1, 2.
ᵃ Is. 42. 7; Lk. 2. 32.

---

tribes of the Israelites, which, in the division of the land by Joshua, obtained their lots in the neighborhood of the sea of Galilee, Josh. 19 : 10, 17, 32, 34.

14. That it might be fulfilled, etc. See note ch. 1 : 22. The prediction is found in Isa. 9 : 1, 2. It is freely quoted from the Hebrew in a somewhat abbreviated form, and was a prophecy having direct reference to the Messiah. Matthew points to its fulfillment in the residence of Jesus at Capernaum, and his ministry there and in the surrounding regions. The idea of the prediction was, that the most despised regions of Palestine would enjoy the greatest splendor of that light which was to lighten the nations and be the glory of Israel, Luke 2 : 32.

15. The land of Zabulon and the land of Nephthalim. The northern portion of Palestine is here designated, by the tribes which inhabited it, Zabulon, being the most southern and eastern. It is then designated by its position, **by the way of the sea,** the country near, adjacent to the Sea of Galilee; Naphtali alone, of the two, touched the Sea of Galilee. **Beyond Jordan.** Extending northward beyond the sources of the Jordan. **Galilee of the Gentiles,** or of the nations, Isa. 9 : 1. The Jews distinguished other people from themselves by calling them *the nations,* or *Gentiles.* Galilee was a Hebrew name, meaning a *ring* or *circle,* and was probably first given to a small "circuit" among the mountains of Naphtali (Josh. 20 : 7), where were situated the twenty towns given by Solomon to Hiram, King of Tyre; 1 Kings 9 : 11. The name may contain an allusion to one or more of the circular plains of those mountains. It came afterward to be applied to the whole northern province of the land of Israel, between Phœnicia and Samaria, the Jordan and the Mediterranean. It was divided into two parts, upper or northern, lower or southern. The northern portion is here specially designated "Galilee of the Gentiles," because it bordered on territories inhabited by Gentiles, and especially because it was itself inhabited by a mixed population. According to the testimony of Strabo and others it was inhabited by Egyptians, Arabians, and Phœnicians. It was near to Tyre and Sidon. **Beyond Jordan** may mean beside Jordan, in the vicinity of Jordan; but to refer it to the eastern side of the river is out of the question, as the name "Galilee of the Gentiles" is but the designation of Zabulon and Naphtali. It is, however, better to refer the phrase *beyond Jordan,* with Lange, to the region beyond the source of the Jordan, as the territory of Naphtali extended thither.

16. The people which sat in darkness. An expression representing the ignorance and spiritual degradation of the people, 1 Thes. 5 : 5. "The verb *to sit* aptly denotes a sluggish solitude."—BENGEL. **Saw great light.** Enjoyed the instruction of the Saviour, who was "the light of the world." **The region and shadow of death.** The shadowy region of death. This phrase expressed in a stronger manner the same ideas as *darkness* in the former part of the verse. *Shadow of death* is equivalent to *death shade,* such a dismal darkness as that which reigns in the region of the dead; the deepest night (compare Job 10 : 21, 22). Such were the spiritual destitution and the spiritual ignorance of the people. **Light is sprung up.** Christ has commenced there his ministry. There is here a gradation or climax. The spiritual ignorance and destitution of the people is expressed first by *darkness,* then by **region of the shadow of death;** so the instruction and ministry of Jesus is expressed first by *the light* the people *saw;* then *the light* is represented as already *sprung up,* shedding upon the people its rays of knowledge, peace, and joy. It could be said of the people

17 ᵇFrom that time Jesus began to preach, and to say, Repent: for the kingdom of heaven is at hand.
18 ᶜAnd Jesus, walking by the sea of Galilee, saw two brethren, Simon ᵈcalled Peter, and Andrew his brother, casting a net into the sea: for ᵉthey were

ᵇ Mk. 1. 14, 15: Lk. 4. 14, 15; John 4. 43, 45.
ᶜ Mk. 1. 16-20; Lk. 5. 1-11.
ᵈ John 1. 42.
ᵉ 1 Cor. 1. 27-29.

---

of Northern Galilee that they lived in spiritual darkness; because, *first*, they were far distant from Jerusalem and the temple, the centre of Jewish religious worship; *second*, they contracted much that was impure from their heathen neighbors; and *third*, of their mixed population. Isaiah (ch. 8 : 22; 9 : 1) had foretold that the tribes of Zabulon and Naphtali should be reduced to a very degraded state. That northern district was peculiarly exposed both to the debasing influence of Gentile superstition, and to the attacks of foreign enemies, who commonly entered Palestine from the north, 2 Kings 15 : 29. Yet here in this region Christ especially manifested himself by his doctrines and his miracles. Their degraded condition made their need of salvation the greater, while their freedom from the narrow prejudices and the rigid practices of the inhabitants of Southern Palestine fitted them to attend more freely to the Gospel.

17. From that time. From the time he heard John was cast into prison, ver. 12. Jesus had indeed visited Galilee, stopping a while at Cana and Capernaum (John 2 : 1-12), before John was cast into prison; but now the ministry of his forerunner having ceased, he took up and carried forward the teachings of John, proclaiming, **Repent; for the kingdom of heaven is at hand.** He began by preaching repentance. See on ch. 3 : 2. In this preaching of our Savior, we see a step after John in the unfolding and developing of the kingdom of God. The kingdom of heaven was really at hand, actually present and represented in the person and preaching of our Lord, Mark 1 : 15.

18-22. FOUR DISCIPLES ARE CALLED BY THE SEA OF GALILEE, to be his constant attendants: Peter and Andrew, James and John, Mark 1 : 14-20.

18. Sea of Galilee. Called also the Sea of Tiberias, from a city built by Herod Antipas, on the south-west shore, and named in honor of the Emperor Tiberius (John 6 : 1; 21 : 1); the Lake of Gennesaret (Luke 5 : 1); and, in the Old Testament, the Sea of Chinnereth, from a city and small district on the western shore, Num. 34 : 11. It is twelve and one half miles long, six broad, and 165 feet deep. It is surrounded on all sides by hills, more broken on the western side, from 500 to nearly 2000 feet high. Its waters are pure and sweet, and abound in fish. The Jordan, with a marked current, passes through the middle of the lake. According to Lieutenant Lynch, it is 653 feet below the Mediterranean. It lay in a region the most populous in Palestine. Many populous towns once stood on its shores—such as Tiberias, Bethsaida, Capernaum, Chorazin, etc.; but these with their commerce are gone. Tiberias and Magdala are the only inhabited spots. It is subject, as in the days of our Savior, to sudden squalls and whirlwinds, owing, probably, to the high surrounding hills. An old little boat is said to be the sole representative of the fleets that once covered its waters. It was usual for the Jews to call every expanse of water *a sea*, Luke, whose geographical terms are always more distinctive, calls it generally *a lake*. By this sea Jesus *walked*, not listlessly, but for the purpose of preaching the kingdom of God, and calling certain ones to be his ministers. **Simon called Peter.** Simon is contracted from Simeon, and means *hearkening*; Peter signifies *a rock*, or *stone*, and had been previously given by our Lord to Simon, John 1 : 42. This name was given him in allusion to his hardy character, noted for decision and boldness, and to the most conspicuous position he should hold among the Apostles, in subordination to Christ, as one of the great foundations of the Church. **Andrew.** It is uncertain whether he was the elder brother of Peter. **Casting a net into the sea.** A *casting*-net, distinguished from the large hauling-net mentioned in ch. 13 : 47. They were just commencing their day's or night's labor, and hence their instantly following Christ was the more significant. It was common to fish in the night, John 21 : 1-4.

19 fishers. And he saith unto them, Follow me, and
20 ᶠI will make you fishers of men. ᵍAnd they straightway left *their* nets, and followed him.
21 ʰAnd going on from thence, he saw other two brethren, James *the son* of Zebedee, and John his brother, in a ship with Zebedee their father, mend-
22 ing their nets; and he called them. And ⁱthey immediately left the ship and their father, and followed him.
23 And ᵏJesus went about all Galilee, ˡteaching in

ᶠ Lk. 5. 10, 11; Ac. 2. 38–41.
ᵍ Mk. 10. 28; Gal. 1. 16.
ʰ Mk. 1. 19, 20; Lk. 5. 10
ⁱ ch. 10. 37; Deu. 33. 8, 9.
ᵏ Ac. 10. 38.
ˡ ch. 9. 35; Mk. 1. 39; Lk. 4. 15, 44.

19. **Follow me.** Literally, *Come hither! behind me*, or *Come after me*, as my disciples, my attendants, and the proclaimers of my gospel. They had previously recognized Jesus as the Messiah (John 1 : 41, 42), but had continued to follow their occupation as fishermen. This helps to explain why they were now so ready to arise and follow Jesus. They had before been called to follow him as his disciples; but now they were expressly called as his servants, messengers, or ministers, and they become his constant attendants; although afterward they sometimes went out to fish, when they were near their homes, Luke 5 : 1-11. Thus they were called, *first*, as disciples in general (John 1 : 35–42); *second*, as constant attendants, ministers, evangelists; *third*, among the twelve Apostles, Luke 6 : 14–16; compare Matt. 10 : 2-4. Luke's account (ch. 5 : 1-11) probably refers to an event later than this, though not long after. See on Luke 5 : 1. **Fishers of men.** Preachers of the gospel; winners of souls to Christ. Their former secular calling served as an emblem of their higher spiritual calling.

20. They immediately leave their nets, forsake their calling, and follow Jesus; thus showing obedience, sincerity, and faith.

21. **James the son of Zebedee.** The mention of James first, and also as the son of Zebedee, and then of John as the brother of James, leads to the conclusion that James was the elder brother. John had probably before believed in Jesus as the Messiah; he was doubtless the one who went with Andrew to the dwelling of our Lord, John 1 : 39. He did not then give up his occupation, but doubtless was much with Jesus, and witnessed the events recorded in the second, third, and fourth chapters of his gospel. **Mending their nets.** They were preparing their nets for their day's or night's labor.

22. Like Andrew and Peter, they immediately obeyed the call of Jesus. How beautiful to see brothers going hand in hand in the service of the Lord. But they not only left their nets, but also their father Zebedee. They were young men. John lived seventy years after this, and died at Ephesus, about A.D. 100. James was put to death by Herod, about A.D. 44, and was the first martyr among the Apostles, Acts 12 : 1, 2. It is just to infer from the narrative that Zebedee gave his consent to their leaving.

23–25. JESUS MAKES HIS FIRST CIRCUIT OF GALILEE, with his disciples, preaching the gospel of the kingdom, and working miracles. While the scene of John's gospel was principally in Judea and at Jerusalem, that of the first three gospels was principally in Galilee. In this brief and vivid description we have a specimen of the many similar preaching excursions of our Savior throughout Galilee during his ministry there. The Evangelist sketches the character of his ministry preparatory to giving his sermon on the mount. Compare Mark 1 : 35–39; Luke 4 : 42-44.

23. **Jesus went about all Galilee.** Having called certain disciples to be his constant attendants, he goes forth on a preaching tour. Galilee included all the northern part of Palestine, lying west of Jordan and north of Samaria. Originally the name was applied to a small tract bordering on the northern limits, Josh. 20 : 7; 21 : 32; 1 Kings 9 : 11. In the time of Christ it was divided into Upper and Lower, occupying the region above-named, the former a mountainous country, the latter

their synagogues, and preaching ⁿ the Gospel of the ᵐ Is. 61. 1-3; Mk. 1. 14; Eph. 2. 17.

partly level. It was thickly inhabited (Josephus, *Jewish War*, iii. 3, 2), and contained four hundred and four towns and villages. The inhabitants were brave and industrious, although other Jews looked down upon them as seditious, unpolished, both in their manners and language, and impure from contact with the heathen, Luke 13 : 1; 23 : 6; John 1 : 47; 7 : 52; Mark 14 : 70; see note on ver. 15.

Teaching in their synagogues. Here we get a glimpse of the style of our Lord's ministry. He *taught;* entered the synagogues, and, like a Jewish teacher or rabbi, expounded the Scriptures and instructed the people. Synagogue means *assembly, congregation,* and is applied both to a religious gathering having certain judicial powers (Luke 8 : 41; 12 : 11; 21 : 12; Acts 9 : 2), and to the place where the Jews met for their public worship on ordinary occasions, ch. 6 : 2, 5; Luke 7 : 5. Synagogues appear to have been first introduced during the Babylonish captivity, when the people, deprived of their usual rites of worship, assembled on the Sabbath to hear the law read and expounded. See Neh. 8 : 1-8. Jewish tradition gives them an earlier origin, and Deut. 31 : 11, and Ps. 74 : 8, are cited as evidences of it; the former passage does not necessarily imply it; the latter was evidently written after the destruction of the temple by the Chaldeans, and may mean either that the enemies had put an end to all the holy assemblies, by burning the temple; or it may refer to the burning of other places in a certain sense *sacred,* as Ramah, Bethel, Gilgal, etc., distinguished as seats of the prophets, and where religious assemblies were sometimes held, 2 Chron. 17 : 9; 2 Kings 4 : 23; 1 Sam. 10 : 5-11. In the days of Jesus there was a synagogue in almost every town in Palestine, and wherever Jews resided; and in the larger towns, several. It is said that there were not less then four hundred and sixty or even four hundred and eighty synagogues in Jerusalem. When the Jews were not able or not permitted to have a synagogue in a town, they had their place of prayer outside the town, usually near a stream or the sea-shore, for the convenience of ablution, Acts 16 : 13.

In the synagogues prayers were offered, the law and the prophets were read and expounded. After the reading of the Scriptures, the heads of the synagogues desired such learned and grave persons as might be present to address the people. Our Savior and the Apostles constantly availed themselves of this privilege. The times of meeting at the synagogues were the Sabbath and feast days; and afterward on the second and fifth days of the week. Each synagogue had a community, with its president or ruler (Luke 8 : 49; 13 : 14; Acts 18 : 8, 17) and elders (Luke 7 : 3-5), who might chastise (ch. 10 : 17; Acts 22 : 19; 26 : 11) or expel (John 9 : 34) an offender. See also Mark 5 : 22, and Acts 13 : 15, where the ruler and elders appear to be spoken of indiscriminately as *rulers.* It ought to be added that it is not a matter of certainty how far or how perfect was the organization of the synagogue in the time of Christ. Its organization was probably somewhat changed and developed after the destruction of Jerusalem by the Romans.

Synagogues were generally built on eminences, and in imitation of the temple, with a centre building supported by pillars, with courts and porches. In the centre building or chapel were a pulpit, lamps, and a chest for keeping the sacred books. It was filled up with seats, fronting the pulpit, which stood on a platform toward the western end. Behind the pulpit were the high seats of honor, the "chief seats," where the Scribes and Pharisees loved to sit facing the people, ch. 23 : 6.

The officiating person stood while reading the Scriptures; but when he and others expounded them, they did it sitting, Luke 4 : 20.

Preaching. Announcing publicly, publishing orally, see ch. 3 : 2. **Gospel.** Good news, glad tidings. Thus, it is translated in Luke 8 : 1, "showing the glad tidings of the kingdom of God;" also in Luke 1 : 19; 2 : 10; Acts 13 : 32; Rom. 10 : 15; 1 Thes. 3 : 6. Our English word *Gospel,* when traced back to its original meaning, resembles the Greek word thus translated. It is derived from the Saxon words *god,* good, and *spell,* history, story

kingdom, " and healing all manner of sickness and " Mk. 1. 34.
24 all manner of disease among the people. And
his fame went throughout all Syria. And they
brought unto him all sick people that were taken
with divers diseases and torments, and those which
were possessed with devils, and those which were

tidings, and was thus equivalent to *good news*. Our Savior not only taught, expounded Scripture, and instructed the people in the synagogue, but he announced publicly, wherever he went, the glad tidings that the kingdom of heaven, the reign or administration of the Messiah, was at hand. For an illustration of his teachings and preaching the glad tidings, see Luke 4 : 16–30. On *kingdom of heaven*, see ch. 3 : 2. **Healing all manner of sickness.** Jesus accompanied His preaching with miracles, which were evidences of his Messiahship, and of the truthfulness of his word. **Disease.** Every infirmity among the people.

24. His fame went throughout all Syria. Mark (ch. 1 : 28) says, "all the region round about Galilee." In the New Testament, Syria is the Roman province of which Northern Palestine was the south-western part, extending north and north-east of Palestine, and lying between the Mediterranean on the west, and the Euphrates on the east. His fame, the report of his ministry, especially of his wonderful works, spread throughout this region, especially all along the frequented route between Damascus and the Mediterranean sea, by the way of the Sea of Galilee.

All sick people. All that were sick in the region through which he passed, in the vicinities where he was preaching. The ailments of these sick people are immediately specified, "divers diseases and torments," "possessed with devils," "lunatic," and "palsy." **Torments.** Diseases attended with excruciating pain. **Possessed with Devils.** Possessed with *demons*. An inferior order of evil spirits subject to Satan, their prince, ch. 9 : 34; 25 : 41; Rev. 12 : 9. The original Scriptures recognize but one devil, but many demons. The sacred writers in thus speaking did not merely use the common and popular language of the Jews, without intending to sanction the opinion on which it was founded, but they state, as matters of fact, that persons were actually possessed with one or more demons. Jesus spake to demons as to persons, and they answered as such (Mark 1 : 25; 5 : 8, 9 : 25); demons showed a supernatural knowledge of Jesus (ch. 8 : 29; Luke 4 : 34); they requested to enter, and were permitted to enter, a herd of swine (ch. 8 : 31, 32); our Lord distinguished between the casting out of demons and healing diseases, ch. 8 : 16; Mark 1 : 32–34; Luke 7 : 21. A person might be dumb as a result of demoniacal possession, but not every dumb person was possessed with a demon, ch. 9 : 32, 33; Mark 7 : 32. So nowhere is possession with a demon made identical with any one disease. Yet various mental and bodily disorders are attributed to the agency of the devil and demons, Acts 10 : 38; Luke 9 : 39, 42. The physical frames of individuals are represented as forcibly possessed by a consciousness and will foreign to themselves, Luke 9 : 39; 11 : 14; Mark 7 : 25, 30. The Scriptures therefore teach that Satan and his angels, or demons, have been permitted to take possession of the bodies of some men, and inflict various sufferings upon them.

To the frequent objection, How comes it that similar possessions do not occur at the present day? it may be answered, How is it known that they do not occur even now? We can not prove the negative. It can not be said that in many cases of insanity and the like the malady may not be traced to the direct agency of demons. It is, however, remarkable that we have no cases of demoniacal possession recorded in the Old Testament, and none in the Epistles of the New Testament; and that Josephus speaks of no real possessions, except in the generation in which Christ exercised his ministry. Admitting, therefore, that such possessions are not common, yet was there not a reason for such great external manifestations of Satan's power in our Savior's day? The crisis of the moral history of our

A.D. 28.   MATTHEW IV.   63

lunatic, and those that had the palsy; and he
25 healed them. °And there followed him great multitudes of people from Galilee, and *from* Decapolis, and *from* Jerusalem, and *from* Judea, and *from* beyond Jordan.

° Mk. 3. 7.

---

world was at hand. The devil was permitted to exercise unusual power in temptation on the souls and bodies of men, in order that Christ might show forth his power. "In the fullness of time the kingdom of Satan was openly displayed, that it might be openly conquered. Then, and not till then, there was, if I may so speak, a clear revelation of evil, because men were able to support it in the strength of the Son of God. The Tempter was seen in the fullness of his worldly dominion at the moment he was met and vanquished. . . . . In this way the miracles on the spirit world complete the public signs of Christ's ministry." — WESTCOTT, *Characteristics,* pp. 80, 81.

As God was manifested in the flesh, so may not demons have been permitted to manifest themselves among men and in men? Possibly it was permitted to show what the condition of men would have been without a Savior (Heb. 2 : 14); possibly to show the condition of the finally wicked, tormented by evil spirits who are stronger than they.

Lunatic. Literally *Moonstruck,* probably epileptic. Epilepsy was supposed to become more aggravating with the increase of the moon. The term is now applied in English to an insane person. The Greek word thus translated is found only twice in the New Testament (here and in ch. 17 : 15), and is of doubtful meaning. As epilepsy is sometimes attended with insanity, that form of the disease may possibly be here intended. **Palsy.** A disorder which deprives the limbs of sensation or motion, or both, and makes them useless to the patient; paralysis. It is applied to the paralysis of the whole body; to a paralysis of one side of the body; to a paralysis of all parts below the neck; to the contraction of the muscles in the whole or part of the body, as the *withered hand* (ch. 12 : 10); and to the cramp, which in eastern countries is a fearful malady—the limbs, when seized with it, remain immovable, and the person thus afflicted resembles one undergoing torture. Some suppose the latter to have been the disease of the centurion's servant (ch. 8 : 6). **Healed them.** By miraculous power. The healing of these diseases must be referred to the extraordinary agency of divine power.

25. **Decapolis.** (Greek, *deka,* meaning *ten,* and *polis, city.*) A country in Palestine, which contained ten principal cities, on both sides of the Jordan, principally the eastern, east, and south-east of the sea of Galilee. It was inhabited by many foreigners. In the enumeration of these cities the learned are not agreed. They are generally reckoned as follows: Damascus, Philadelphia, Raphana, Scythopolis, Gadara, Hippos, Dion, Pella, Galasa (Gerasa), Canatha. Only one of these, Scythopolis, was in Galilee; the rest were east of the Jordan, mainly in that part of Palestine occupied by the half tribe of Manasseh. **Beyond Jordan.** The region east of Jordan and south of Decapolis, which was called Perea, from the Greek word *peran,* which means *beyond.*

SUGGESTIONS OR REMARKS.

1. If Christ our Head was tempted, we must not expect to escape temptation, vers. 1-11; ch. 10 : 24.
2. Seasons of great spiritual enjoyment are frequently followed by great temptations, ver. 1; ch. 16 : 17, 22, 23.
3. Solitude is frequently the place and the occasion of temptation. It has its advantages and also its dangers, ver. 1.
4. The proper preparation for trial is to be filled with the Spirit, ver. 1; Luke 4 : 1.
5. Although we should not needlessly expose ourselves to temptations and trials, yet when led into them by the Spirit, we should patiently submit, and trust in his wisdom to direct and his power to sustain, ver. 1; 1 Cor. 10 : 13.
6. What a contrast between the first Adam, who was overcome in the garden, and the second, who overcame in the wilderness, vers. 2-11.

7. The Christian, and especially the young convert, may expect to be tempted to doubt his own adoption and distrust God, ver. 3.

8. Let us trust God for temporal things in extraordinary emergencies, as well as on ordinary occasions; and when tempted with privation, let us look to the full supply, provided in the Gospel, for our spiritual wants. Faith in God will insure victory over the wants of the world, vers. 3, 4; John 6 : 27, 32.

9. The word of God, the sword of the Spirit, is our weapon in temptation, vers. 4, 7, 10; 1 John 2 : 14.

10. When we have overcome the devil in one respect, we should beware lest we be overcome in another; lest our faith be turned into presumption, vers. 5, 6.

11. To pervert Scripture is to follow in the footsteps of the devil. Wicked men love to appeal to Scripture to support and cover up their own crimes. Errorists misquote the word of God, wrest it from its connection, and pervert its meaning, ver. 6; 2 Pet. 3 : 16.

12. We have no right to test God merely for the sake of testing him; nor are we to trifle with his promises and to expect miraculous deliverances, when throwing ourselves into uncommanded dangers, ver. 7.

13. All secularizing of religion is an attempt to take the kingdoms of the world through carnal weapons, a yielding of Christ's cause to the power of the devil. To depend on worldly pomp, vain display, fashion, wealth, fine churches, and the like, is a forsaking and a renouncing of the spiritual nature, power, and weapons of Christ's kingdom, vers. 8-10; Rom. 14 : 17.

14. We should wait God's time and way for receiving that which he intends to bestow. Although all things were Christ's, yet he would not receive them at the hand of Satan. That which seems the easiest and shortest way is not always the best, vers. 9, 10.

15. We should never compromise religion, or withhold from God his due, for the sake of obtaining riches or honor, vers. 9, 10; Prov. 23 : 23.

16. We must resist the devil, and he will flee from us, ver. 10; 1 Pet. 5 : 8, 9; James 4 : 7, 10.

17. Christ's victory over Satan is a pledge of the victory of those that believe in him. He shows that he is able to succor those that are tempted, ver. 11; 1 Cor. 10 : 13; Heb. 2 : 17; 4 : 15.

18. Angels are interested in our salvation, and are anxious spectators of our temptations and sorrows, ver. 11; Heb. 1 : 14.

19. We may, like Jesus, prudently retire from those who wickedly oppose us, and seek more quiet fields of labor, when we are so guided by the Spirit and providence, or when we can do so without sacrificing duty and principle, ver. 12.

20. This world is, by the fall, sunk into the deepest moral night. Christ is the Sun of Righteousness. How highly privileged are any people who enjoy this light, vers. 13, 16.

21. Christ extends his kingdom not by carnal but by spiritual weapons. "It pleased God by the foolishness of preaching to save them that believe," ver. 17; 1 Cor. 1 : 21.

22. Ministers of the Gospel are to be called of God. Jesus called the fishermen of Galilee, whose untutored minds, freed from many of the prejudices of the more cultivated, were the better prepared to receive the instructions of our Lord. After being with Jesus during his ministry, they were not ignorant, but in the highest sense educated, ver. 18-21.

23. Christ calls us to self-renunciation, to spiritual communion with him, to a new life of holy activity, to gospel blessings here and to a blessed home hereafter, vers. 19, 21.

24. We are to follow Christ in faith and labor, in sufferings and cross-bearings, and in all religious privileges and blessings, vers. 19, 22; Luke 9 : 57-62.

25. We should not stop to calculate the worldly loss we may sustain in obeying Jesus, but in all simplicity of heart follow him. Prompt obedience is especially pleasing to God, ver. 22.

26. Like Jesus, let us strive to do good to all; and let us not allow one work to prevent us from doing another; he taught in the synagogues, preached the Gospel in other places, healed all kinds of diseases, and cast out devils, vers. 23, 24.

27. Ministers should especially instruct the people. Jesus taught, etc., ver. 23; 1 Tim. 3 : 2; 2 Tim. 2 : 2, 24.

28. Disease in the body is emblematical of the disease of the soul. As there are many forms of bodily disease, so sin manifests itself prominently in many ways, vers. 23, 24.

29. The demoniacal possessions which were permitted in our Savior's day strikingly present the power of the devil over the unrenewed heart, ver. 24.

30. By his miracles Jesus showed his infinite compassion, the spiritual nature of his kingdom, and his power over sin and the devil, ver. 24.

31. Many may attend the preaching of the Gospel and yet but few of them be benefited. Very few of these multitudes became the true disciples of Jesus, ver. 25.

CHAPTER V

THE SERMON ON THE MOUNT.

THE DISCOURSE recorded in this chapter and the two following ones is so similar to that in the sixth chapter of Luke that many have thought them to be identical. Such was the view generally held by the Greek Church. But Augustine, and after him most of the writers of the Latin Church, held that they were distinct. According to Augustine (*De Consensu Evangelistarum*, ii. 19), Jesus first delivered the longer discourse which Matthew gives, upon the mountain; and after descending to the plain, communicated, in an abridged form, the same truths to the multitude there. Modern interpreters are much divided, though a majority of them regard these discourses as only two different accounts of the same sermon. After careful and patient examination, we have been led to the conclusion that these discourses are distinct, delivered on different occasions; and that the one given by Matthew may be styled *The Sermon on the Mount*, and that by Luke, *The Sermon on the Plain*. The reasons for this view may be briefly stated as follows: 1. The one in Matthew was delivered by Christ *sitting on a mountain* (ch. 5 : 1), that in Luke, *standing in a plain* (Luke 6 : 17). 2. On comparing parallel passages, there is such a difference that it seems evident that the two evangelists were not giving the same discourse. In Matthew there are 107 verses, and in Luke only 30; yet the latter not only connects with his four beatitudes as many *woes* (Luke 6 : 20, 26); but is fuller in several places, Luke 6 : 39, 40, 45. 3. Both discourses, when examined separately, seem complete and connected throughout. From Matt. 8 : 28, *When Jesus had finished these sayings*, it seems evident that the whole discourse just given was delivered at once; so also the one in Luke is natural and closely connected throughout, giving no evidence that it is either the gathered fragments of a longer discourse, or a collection of sayings uttered at different times. 4. Matthew places the sermon *before his call* (ch. 9 : 9), and hence *before* the appointment of the apostles; whereas Luke expressly says that the discourse he gives was delivered after the twelve were chosen. Luke, indeed, is indefinite in regard to the time of this selection, for he uses the phrase, *in these days* (Luke 6 : 12); but this only makes both events indefinite, while *the order*, namely, the selection of the apostles, and then the delivery of the sermon, still remains. The objection, that Jesus would not have delivered two discourses so similar, and repeated the same truths, seems to my mind not only untenable, but frivolous. We can conceive no reason why he might not have spoken these discourses to two different audiences, especially if we suppose that some little time intervened. That he often repeated his sayings is evident from the comparison of many passages. See for instance Matt. 5 : 22 and Luke 12 : 58; Matt. 6 : 9-13 and Luke 11 : 2-4; Matt. 6 : 24 and Luke 16 : 13; Matt. 7 : 13, 14 and Luke 13 : 24; Matt. 16 : 21 and 17 : 22, 23 and 20 : 17-19. It should not be thought strange that our Lord should have repeated the highest and most central truths, when we consider their importance. The same thing has been done by the wisest teachers and by inspired prophets. Compare Jer. 10 : 12-16 with 51 : 15-19. So also Dr. J. A. ALEXANDER and others.

The facts in the case appear to be as follows: The Sermon on the Mount was delivered at the close of our Lord's first general circuit of Galilee, and was followed by the healing of a leper, Matt. 8 : 2-4. Its position in Mark is thus between the 39th and 40th verses of the first chapter; and in Luke just before the 12th verse of the fifth chapter. The Sermon on the Plain was immediately after the selection of the twelve Apostles, and is followed by healing a centurion's servant, Luke 7 : 1-10; Matt. 8 : 5-13. Its position in Mark is immediately after the 19th verse of the third chapter, and in Matthew somewhere between the 17th verse of the

The Sermon on the Mount.

V. AND seeing the multitudes, ᵖ he went up into a mountain: and when he was set, his disciples came 2 unto him: and he opened his mouth, and taught them, saying,

ᵖ Mk. 3. 13; ch. 14. 23.

---

ninth chapter and the 1st verse of the tenth chapter. The first verse of the latter chapter implies that the Apostles had already been selected, and the verses following give their names and their mission.

The character and analysis of the Sermon on the Mount will appear in the notes that follow.

In it we have a specimen of our Lord's teaching, at this time, and preaching the good news of the kingdom of God. Its subject may be briefly stated to be, *The Nature, Subjects, and Principles of the Kingdom of God*. It does not indeed contain a full development of those principles, for the time had not come for this. It was admirably fitted to show men their sins and their need of repentance, and to prepare them to receive the great doctrine of the atonement when more fully presented. When viewed in the light of the Cross, this discourse receives a new lustre.

PRELIMINARY CIRCUMSTANCES.

1. **The multitudes.** The people spoken of in ch. 4 : 25. **He went up into a mountain.** In the original, *the mountain;* doubtless some elevation in the vicinity of Capernaum which may have been familiarly called The Mountain. According to Latin tradition, which, however, can be traced no further back than the 13th century, the Mount of Beatitudes was what is now called the Horns of Hattin (two summits with a depression between them, and hence the name Horns), situated between Mount Tabor and Tiberias, and about seven miles south-west of Capernaum. But there is no positive evidence that this was the place where this discourse was delivered. It is implied by his ascending the mountain that he was just before with the multitude below, at its foot. **He was set.** Sitting was the usual posture in teaching among the Jews, Luke 4 : 20.

His disciples. The word *disciple* means *a learner, a scholar,* one taught by a teacher, ch. 10 : 24. It was applied to the twelve Apostles (ch. 10 : 1), to *true* disciples (John 13 : 35), and after Christ's death, to his professed followers, believers, Christians, Acts 6 : 1, 2; 11 : 26. There was a separation at this time between Christ's disciples and the people (John 4 : 1, 2), yet the term here does not imply that they were all his true followers, John 6 : 66.

2. **He opened his mouth.** An oriental expression indicating the act of beginning a solemn, weighty, and full discourse, Job 3 : 1; Dan. 10 : 16; Eph. 6 : 19. **Taught them.** We have here a model of his teaching. He instructed his disciples in the hearing of the multitude, ch. 7 : 28.

3–12. JESUS SHOWS WHO ARE THE TRULY HAPPY, indicating at the same time in what true happiness consists. These are the subjects of his kingdom. This was a striking and apt beginning of his discourse. All wish to be happy. The first word, "happy," struck a cord that would vibrate in every heart.

3. **Blessed.** This word (Greek *makarios*) means *happy,* and is so translated in John 13 : 17; Acts 20 : 2; Rom. 14 : 22; 1 Peter 3 : 14; 4 : 14. Another word (Greek *eulogetos*) is properly translated *blessed,* which in the New Testament is applied only to God, Mark 14 : 61; Rom. 1 : 25; 2 Cor. 1 : 3. The latter is derived from a verb which means to *speak well of,* to *commend,* and hence to *praise,* to *bless;* and, as applied to God, means worthy of all praise, *adorable, blessed,* with ascriptions of praise and thanksgivings. The passive perfect participle of this verb (*eulogemenos*) also properly means blessed, and, as applied to men, means those blessed or favored of God, ch. 25 : 34. The former is allied to a verb which means to *pronounce happy,* and answers to the Hebrew *ashrey (happy),* derived from a verb, *to go well, to prosper, to be happy.* Our Savior means, that those persons whom he pronounces *happy* are not only in the way to future blessedness, but that they are in the present enjoyment of happiness—happy in their re-

3 ¶ Blessed *are* the poor in spirit: for theirs is the kingdom of heaven.
4 Blessed *are* they that mourn: for they shall be comforted.
5 ʳ Blessed *are* the meek: for ˢ they shall inherit the earth.

q Lk. 6. 20, 21.
r Ps. 25. 9; 37. 11; Eph. 4. 2.
s Ps. 37. 22; Ro. 4. 13.
t ch. 6. 33; Ps. 42. 1, 2.

---

lations and destiny. In the following beatitudes Jesus pronounces those happy whom the world holds to be most unhappy. He runs directly counter to the carnal views of the Jews of his day. **The poor in spirit.** They who feel a deep sense of spiritual poverty, who are lowly in heart, and are conscious of their spiritual ignorance and unworthiness, and of their entire dependence on God. See Isa. 57: 15. Such are happy in contrast to the proud and ambitious, those who aspire after worldly pleasures, riches, and honor. **Theirs is the kingdom of heaven.** Theirs as a *gift*, through divine grace. They are subjects and citizens of the Messiah's kingdom, which is commenced on earth, and is to be consummated in the world to come. They are entitled to the great blessings of Messiah's reign both for time and eternity. See on ch. 3: 2.

4. They that mourn. This can not refer to all kinds of mourning; for the sorrow "of the world worketh death," 2 Cor. 7: 10. It especially refers to those who mourn under a penitent sense of their sins, under a feeling of their spiritual poverty, and exercise a godly sorrow that "worketh repentance unto salvation." But it need not be limited to merely those who mourn over their own sins, but may extend to those who, in addition to this, mourn on account of the sins of others, and who, in sorrowful circumstances and afflictions, mingle their grief with humble hope in God. In contrast to the gay and jovial, those are happy, **for they shall be comforted.** Their sins shall be forgiven; they shall be supported in trial and cheered with the everlasting favor of God. Christ, "the consolation of Israel" (Luke 2: 25), will be their Savior, the Holy Spirit their Comforter (John 14: 16, 17, 26), and the Father their Father and eternal Friend, Rom. 8: 15; 2 Cor. 1: 3. Their joy shall be complete, pertaining both to the present and future state, 2 Cor. 1: 4; 4: 17; Rev. 21: 4.

5. The meek. The gentle and forgiving. Such as are "long suffering," who "forbear in love," and, regulating their passions, are "angry and sin not," Eph. 4: 2, 26. They are those who are made so by grace, and, having felt their spiritual poverty and mourned over sin, have exercised repentance and obtained forgiveness. They are thus prepared to be kind, gentle, and forgiving in their conduct toward others. As to be "poor in spirit" is an element in humility before God, so "meekness" is an element of humility before men; and of true godly "mourning" before the heart itself, and before both God and men. Moses was an example of meekness, Num. 12: 3. Christ declares, "I am meek and lowly in heart," ch. 11: 29. The Jews expected that the Messiah would usher in his kingdom as a great conqueror, with military courage and martial exploits; but he here strikes a blow against their expectations, and declares that the meek **shall inherit the earth.** This had been foretold in Ps. 37: 11; 25: 13. The word in the original may also be translated *the land.* The land of Canaan was promised to Abraham, Isaac, and Jacob, and their posterity. Its peaceful possession was one chief promise of the law (Ex. 20: 12), and became afterward to include the other blessings of the Jewish covenant, when the people had come into the possession of the promised land. See the 37th Psalm, verses 3, 9, 11, 18, 29, 34. As Israel, under the old dispensation, had the promise of the land of Canaan, with its connected blessings, so Jesus holds forth a promised inheritance of his followers. The one is the symbol of the other. "All are yours," 1 Cor. 3: 22. "There remaineth therefore a rest to the people of God," Heb. 4: 9. Christians are to enjoy on earth the millennial glory, Rev. 20: 4–6. The creation itself shall be delivered from bondage of corruption into the glorious liberty of the children of God,

6 Blessed *are* they ʷwhich do hunger and thirst after righteousness: ˣfor they shall be filled.
7 Blessed *are* the merciful: ʸfor they shall obtain mercy.
8 ʸBlessed *are* the pure in heart: for ᶻthey shall see God.

ʷ Ps. 63. 1, 5; Is. 41. 17, 18; John 4. 14; 6. 48-58.
ˣ ch. 6. 14; 18. 33-35; 2 Sam. 22. 26; Eph. 4. 32; Jam. 2. 13.
ʸ Ps. 15. 2; 18. 26;

Rom. 8 : 21. A new earth wherein dwelleth righteousness is to come into existence, 2 Pet. 3 : 13. And the heavenly Jerusalem is to descend, and the tabernacle of God is to be erected among men, Rev. 21 : 2-4. But even now Christians are the only ones who truly enjoy the earth and its blessings. All things work together for their good, Rom. 8 : 28. Godliness is profitable for all things, having promise of the life that now is, and of that which is to come, 1 Tim. 4 : 8.

6. **Hunger and thirst.** Expresses strong, earnest, and even painful desire. As the hungry and thirsty long after food and drink, so do these here described, ardently long after righteousness, Ps. 42:1; John 6:35. **Righteousness.** Holiness; conformity of heart and life to the Divine will. As those who feel their spiritual poverty mourn over sin, and are gentle and forgiving, since they have been forgiven, so also do they earnestly desire perfect conformity to the will of God. This hungering and thirsting is indeed an evidence of their spiritual life. In contrast to those who entertain carnal hopes concerning the Messiah's kingdom, and long for worldly possessions, power, and glory, and are ready to use unjust means to obtain them, these hungering and thirsty souls after righteousness are happy; for **they shall be filled.** They shall be *satisfied*, so as to desire nothing more, as the hungry man is satisfied with food, Ps. 17 : 15. They shall find complete satisfaction in Christ, having his righteousness accounted to them, and being sanctified and conformed to his image, Prov. 21 : 21; Isa. 41 : 17; 60 : 21; 2 Pet. 3 : 13. The fulfillment of this promise begins here and extends to the fully developed holiness of heart and conduct in the future world.

7. **The merciful.** Those who exercise a compassionate love toward the suffering, who make the sorrows of others their own, and who delight in relieving human distress. "The *meek* bear the injustice of the world; the merciful bravely address themselves to the wants of the world."—LANGE. Compare ch. 25 : 34-40; Luke 10 : 30-37. Such are happy; not those who delight in scenes of desolation and sorrow, nor the victorious, who rejoice to execute vengeance on their enemies, and who can withhold sympathy from human sorrow. For **they shall obtain mercy.** A merciful disposition obtains favor from men; thus the common version in Prov. 18 : 24. But that active, compassionate love which is the result of grace in the heart obtains favor from God. "With the merciful thou wilt show thyself merciful," Ps. 18 : 25. See also 2 Tim. 1 : 18; Heb. 6 : 10. As they constantly need mercy so long as they are in this imperfect state, so shall they constantly receive it from the hand of God.

8. **The pure in heart.** Not absolute purity, nor ceremonial, but that inward purity which is produced by the Spirit through faith, Acts 15 : 9. To be pure is to be unmixed, undefiled (Tit. 1 : 15), and when the term is applied to the heart, it means that freedom from defilement, that piety, that internal righteousness which is connected with being born of God (1 Jchn 3 : 9), and with a life of sanctification, ending in complete perfection in the future life, 1 Cor. 13 : 12. In contrast to those hypocrites who affect outward purity, while their hearts are full of corruption and defilement, they who possess this inward and progressive purity are happy; **for they shall see God.** It was the custom of eastern kings to conceal themselves from the view of their subjects (Est. 4 : 11); royal ministers were preëminently called "those that see the king's face"(2 Kings 25 : 19; Est. 1 : 14); and hence "to see the king's face" was regarded as a peculiar favor and honor, 1 Kings 10 : 8. Transferring this image to that higher relation existing between men and our Heavenly King (1 Tim. 6 : 15), the phrase to *see God* expresses the greatest honor and the highest happiness

A.D. 28. MATTHEW V. 69

9 Blessed *are* ª the peacemakers: ᵇ for they shall be called the children of God.
10 ᶜ Blessed *are* they which are persecuted for righteousness' sake: ᵈ for theirs is the kingdom of heaven.
11 ᵉ Blessed are ye, when *men* shall revile you, and per-

73. 1 ; Pro. 22. 11 ; Ac. 15. 9 ; 2 Cor. 7. 1 ; Heb. 10. 22 ; 1 Pet. 1. 22.
ᵇ Job 19. 26. 27 ; Heb. 12. 14.
ᶜ Ps. 122. 6 8 ; Ac. 7. 26 ; Ro. 14. 17–

---

that can be conferred on man. They shall see God in their spiritual enjoyments here, and in blessedness and glory hereafter. The spiritual vision begins with regeneration in the heart (Eph. 1 : 18); it strengthens with the progress of spiritual life (2 Cor. 3 : 18); and it will be perfected in heaven when the soul shall be freed from every impurity. When we shall be like him, *then* we shall see him as he is (1 John 3 : 2), and know him even as we are known. All shall see him as a Judge, but these shall see him as their Friend, Rev. 1 : 7; 22 : 3, 4.

9. **The peacemakers.** Not merely the *peaceful*, nor the *maintainer* of peace, but the *makers of peace.* The word translated *peacemakers* is found nowhere else in the New Testament, but (which is nearly the same) the verb of the same origin occurs in Col. 1 : 20, where it signifies *actively to reconcile,* to make *peace.* In that passage (Col. 1 : 20) we get a view of the highest and most perfect model of a *peacemaker,* Jesus Christ. He makes peace between God and men, and between man and man. Every one of his followers partakes of his spirit and becomes in a certain degree a peacemaker, James 3 : 18. Jesus refers not to mere natural ability, nor to the exertions of unregenerate men, but to the members of his spiritual kingdom, and especially to his messengers of peace (2 Cor. 5 : 20); for he adds, "they shall be called the sons of God." They are peacemakers because they are instrumental both in leading souls to be reconciled to God, and also in effecting reconciliation, peace, and harmony among men. Christ is the Prince of Peace, and his Gospel, universally diffused, received, and obeyed, would produce peace. This beatitude, however, implies that the endeavors of any are noble who strive to maintain peace among men and nations, or to restore harmony wherever it has been interrupted, Gen. 13 : 7, 8; Ex. 2 : 13. In contrast to those who love strife and seek contention, who would propagate religion by conquest and the sword, the peacemakers are happy; for **they shall be called the children of God.** They shall be recognized not merely as *children,* but *sons, children of age :* for such is the meaning here. The God of peace (Rom. 16 : 20; 2 Cor. 13 : 11) is the Father of the sons of peace. They are children by resemblance, by being born of the Spirit, by being partakers of the divine nature, by being representatives and messengers of Christ, and by adoption, 1 John 3 : 1; John 1 : 12; 2 Pet. 1 : 4. When they become entirely conformed to the image of Christ, who, in the highest sense, is *the* Son of God, then shall they answer perfectly to their *name* by which they are called, *sons of God.* In this world, and especially in the next, will they be so considered, recognized, and called.

10. **Persecuted for righteousness' sake.** Having shown who are the truly happy by seven distinguishing characteristics, which are the products of grace in the heart, Jesus proceeds to point them out by the treatment they will receive from a wicked world. They are persecuted, harassed, hard pressed upon, and pursued by repeated acts of enmity, privately and publicly, legally and illegally, for righteousness' sake. By righteousness is meant that conformity of heart and conduct to the divine will which is the product of the Holy Spirit in connection with the human will, that righteousness of Christ which is accounted through faith, and by implication their open profession of godliness. See 2 Tim. 3 : 12. In contrast to those who enjoy worldly pomp and pleasures, victories and military triumphs; these are happy: **for theirs is the kingdom of heaven.** The blessings of Messiah's kingdom in this life, and especially in that to come, are theirs, 2 Tim. 2 : 12; Rev. 20 : 4. See on ver. 3.

11. **Revile and persecute,** etc. Insult with words, and persecute in fact, and falsely say every thing that is evil against you. Slander you. The first

secute *you*, and shall say all manner of evil against
12 you falsely, for my sake : rejoice, and be exceeding
glad : for great *is* your reward in heaven : for so
persecuted they the prophets which were before
you.

13   YE are the salt of the earth : *but if the salt
have lost his savor, wherewith shall it be salted? it
is thenceforth good for nothing, but to be cast out.

19; Ep. 4. 1-3:
b Col. 3. 13-15.
b Phil. 2. 15.
c 2 Tim. 2. 12; 3.
11. 12; 1 Pet. 4.
12-16.
d 2 Thes. 1. 4-7.
e Lk. 6. 22, 23.
f Mk. 9. 49, 50.

Christians were charged with vicious habits and heinous crimes. Nero charged Christians with the burning of Rome. **You ; for my sake.** Jesus now applies his discourse directly to his disciples. They were to possess the characteristics he had pointed out, and be the ones who are truly happy. He, on the other hand, was the personification of righteousness (ver. 10), as it was exhibited in his life and death, and as it is connected with his disciples through faith and by an open profession, Rom. 10 : 10.

12. **Great is your reward.** Not of debt, but of grace. Christians have reason to *rejoice* and *exult* amid persecution, in view of a reward so great and glorious, 2 Cor. 4 : 17. **So persecuted they the prophets.** No new thing was to happen to his disciples. For so was Elijah persecuted, 1 Kings 19 : 1, 2; and Elisha, 2 Kings 2 : 23; and Jeremiah, Jer. 38 : 4-13; and Zechariah, 2 Chron. 24 : 20, 21; and Daniel, Dan. 6 : 11-17. How great was their reward (Heb. 11 : 26), who were hastening to join that great cloud of witnesses, Heb. 12 : 1.

13-16. THE IMPORTANT RELATION OF CHRIST'S DISCIPLES to the world. Their dignity and their high vocation. They are fitted for this by the characteristics just pointed out.

13. **Ye are the salt of the earth.** *Ye*, not the Apostles, for they were not yet selected, but his *disciples*. Jesus rather views his disciples as a whole, in the world; yet what was true of them as a whole, was also true of them individually. Salt was most highly esteemed by the ancients, denoting proverbially one of the most indispensable necessaries of life. " Nothing is more useful than sun and salt," was a current proverb in our Savior's day (Plin. *His. Nat.* xxxi. 9). What salt and sunlight are to the material world in preventing putrefaction and dispelling darkness, Christ's disciples are to our spiritually corrupt and dark world. Elisha healed the unwholesome water by means of salt, 2 Kings 2 : 20. Salt is a preservative; so are the righteous. Ten righteous persons would have saved Sodom, Gen. 18 : 32, 33. A very small remnant saved the people of Judah and the inhabitants of Jerusalem from destruction, Isa. 1 : 9. See on Mark 9 : 49, 50. *Earth*, and *world*, in this and the following verse, are used of mankind generally. **If the salt have lost its savor.** If it has become insipid, tasteless. Maundrell in his travels found salt in the Valley of Salt, south of the Dead Sea, which, while retaining its appearance, had lost its taste. Thomson (*The Land and the Book*, vol. ii. p. 43) says that he saw large quantities of spoiled salt thrown into the street to be trodden underfoot. **Wherewith shall it be salted.** It can be salted from no other source. The remark is hypothetical. If the salt, etc. Salt that has become tasteless can not be restored; it is useless, fit only to be cast away and trodden under foot. So, if Christ's disciples apostatize, if they lose the preserving and sanctifying power of the Gospel in themselves, how shall they recover it? What can save and sanctify, if the truth of God can not? They are useless, and fit only to be cast away as vile and worthless. Jesus does not say that any true disciples will apostatize; but if they should, then their case is hopeless. Compare Heb. 6 : 4; 2 Pet. 2 : 15. Such warnings are part of the means used by the Spirit to keep the elect from entirely falling away. **It is henceforth good for nothing,** etc. Dr. Thomson (vol. ii. p. 44) speaks of salt becoming insipid and useless: " Not a little of it is so impure that it can not be used at all, and such salt soon effloresces and turns to dust; not to fruitful soil, however. It is not only good for nothing itself, but it actually destroys all fertility wherever it is thrown; and this is the reason why it is cast into the street. There is no place about the

A.D. 28. MATTHEW V. 71

14 and to be trodden under foot of men. ᵍ Ye are the light of the world. A city that is set on an hill
15 can not be hid. Neither do men ʰ light a candle, and put it under a bushel, but on a candlestick; and it giveth light to all that are in the house.
16 ⁱ Let your light so shine before men, ᵏ that they may see your good works, and ˡ glorify your Father which is in heaven.
17 ᵐ Think not that I am come to destroy the Law,

ᵍ Pro. 4. 18; John 5. 35; Phil. 2. 15.
ʰ Mk. 4. 21.
ⁱ 1 Pet. 2. 9.
ᵏ Eph. 2. 10; Tit. 3. 8; 1 Pet. 2. 12.
ˡ John 15. 8; 1 Cor. 14. 25; 2 Thes. 1. 11, 12.
ᵐ Ro. 3. 31; 10. 4; Gal. 3. 21.

---

house, yard, or garden where it can be tolerated." The only place is in the street, to be trodden under foot of men.
14. Ye are the light of the world. Christ is himself the light of the world (John 1 : 9, 8 : 12; 9 : 5), and so are his disciples so far as they reflect his light, Phil. 2 : 15. Rather Christ's light is in them; it is in them and shines through them; they do not, like the moon, cast a reflected light, 2 Cor. 3 : 18; 4 : 6. They are his representatives among men, and communicate his truth both by precept and example. Thus they shine by the light of knowledge and holiness derived from him, Eph. 5 : 8. **As a city that is set on a hill can not be hid,** so were they to attract notice. Their relation to the world and their calling were morally high, and correspondingly responsible. It is supposed that our Savior pointed to some city, situated on some neighboring hill. *City* in the English Scriptures denotes *hamlet, village,* as well as a large town. Villages were usually situated on hills, and hence from a mountain several might be seen at once. Some suppose that Jesus pointed to the city of Safet, situated on the highest point of Galilee; but it probably did not then exist.
15. Neither do men light a candle. A lamp. **Under a bushel.** *The* bushel, indicating a familiar household utensil, as the common grain measure, holding about a peck. **But on a candlestick.** On the lamp standard, the support on which the lamp was placed in order that it might give light to all in the house. As the lamp is intended to illuminate, so are Christians intended to diffuse the knowledge of spiritual truth. They should not, therefore, conceal their light and frustrate the divine intention.
16. Let your light so shine. Thus let your light shine like a lamp on its support. Christians are to diffuse divine truth openly and boldly, conspicuous like a city on a hill, like a lamp raised on its support above the ground. **That they may see your good works.** Notice, he does not say *you*, nor your light (these will indeed be seen), but your *good works*. The good works are the fruits, evidence, outward manifestation of the inner life, John 1 : 4. **Glorify your Father.** That others, seeing that God is your Father, may be led to praise him for such a religion, and to imitate your holy example. The usefulness of Christians is designed not only for men's salvation, but thereby for God's glory.
17–20. THE RELATION OF CHRIST TO THE LAW. Christ the fulfiller of the Law. The relation between the new dispensation and the old; Christ and Moses.
17. Jesus had pointed out the happy, in contrast to the carnal views of the Jews; and had spoken of his disciples as the spiritual preservers and lights of the world. He had alluded to persecution for righteousness' sake and for his sake. He was speaking as a lawgiver, with authority.
So imperfect was the knowledge of his disciples, that they might easily misunderstand him, and suppose that he came to subvert the law, and that his teachings were in opposition to the Old Testament Scriptures. He therefore says, **Think not that I am come to destroy the Law or the Prophets.** By the Law or Prophets are meant the writings of the Old Testament, including the five books of Moses, called the Law, and the writings of the prophets, or rest of the Old Testament, Luke 16 : 29; 24 : 27,

LAMP AND ITS STANDARD.

or the Prophets: I am not come to destroy, ⁿ but to
18 fulfill. For verily I say unto you, ᵒ Till heaven and
earth pass, one jot or one tittle shall in no wise pass
19 from the law till all be fulfilled. ᵖ Whosoever
therefore shall break one of ᑫ these least command-
mandments, and shall teach men so, he shall be

ⁿ ch. 3. 15; Heb.
10. 3-12.
ᵒ Lk. 16. 17.
ᵖ Deu. 27. 26; Jam. 2. 10.
ᑫ Lk. 11. 42.

---

44. The carnal Jews also might think that the life and teachings of Jesus, being so opposite to their views of the law and of prophecy, were destructive not only of the law, but also of the prophets, their entire sacred writings. **Destroy.** To put an end to, render null and void. This word has in it the idea of *pulling down.* It is thus figuratively used of the *dissolution* of the body in 2 Cor. 5 : 1; and of a *complete renouncing and forsaking* of a system of belief and practice in Gal. 2 : 18. Christ declares that he came not to pull down, disintegrate, and thus to effect a complete dissolution of the law. He came not to renounce it, treat it as worthless, and consign it to destruction. **But to fulfill.** To bring to pass and accomplish all that the law requires. Jesus fulfilled the law: *First,* by accomplishing, as antitype, the types, shadows, and ceremonies of the Old Testament. All these shadowed him forth as the Lamb of God, the sacrifice offered once for all, with all the attendant blessings, Heb. 10 : 1, 10; Col. 2 : 14. *Second,* by rendering the law and also the injunctions of the prophets a perfect obedience. *Third,* by suffering the penalty of the law and taking away its curse. *Fourth,* by accomplishing in himself and in his kingdom all the predictions of prophecy. *Fifth,* by substituting his spiritual kingdom for the Jewish theocracy, the former being typified by the latter. *Sixth,* by unfolding the *spirit* of the Old Testament teachings, and incorporating all that was imperishable and essential to moral truth in the doctrines and precepts of the new dispensation. *Seventh,* by accomplishing in his people all these spiritual requirements, through the Holy Spirit within them, and through his righteousness accounted to them, Rom. 8 : 3, 4; 3 : 31; 10 : 4. Thus the fulfillment, commenced by Jesus on earth, still goes on, and will be fully accomplished at the time spoken of by Paul in 1 Cor. 15 : 28, when God shall be all in all. Thus Christ fulfills the law in its ceremonial or sacrificial, its moral, its civil, and its prophetical aspects.

18. **Verily.** *Amen, truly,* certainly. Jesus only employed this word at the beginning of his discourses to give them force. As emphatically the Lawgiver of his people, he could speak with an authority above all other teachers. **Verily, I say unto you.** No one else could thus speak. He is also the *Amen,* the faithful and true witness, Rev. 3 : 14. **Till heaven and earth shall pass.** Gen. 1 : 1; 2 : 1. The visible creation will pass away (2 Pet. 3 : 11-13), but God's word endureth forever, 1 Pet. 1 : 25. **One jot or one tittle.** The *jot* or *iota* refers to the smallest Hebrew letter *yŏdh.* *Tittle* refers to the little points, turns, or strokes by which one letter differs from another. The omission of a single letter, or a change in similar-looking letters, would sometimes greatly alter the sense. The expression "jot or tittle" means the *smallest portion.* The minutest portion of revealed truth is precious, and it shall not **pass from the law till all be fulfilled,** till its whole design shall be accomplished, and all things that it requires or foretells shall be effected. See Luke 16 : 17.

19. **Whosoever therefore.** This verse is closely connected with and founded upon the preceding. **These least commandments.** Referring to the minutest portions, the jot and tittle of the law. The Pharisees divided the commands into the great and small, the weighty and the light. Jesus, however, allows not their distinctions; but, adopting his own, refers to the *spirit* rather than to the letter of the law. For the law may be kept in spirit when it is transgressed in the letter. See, for example, Mark 2 : 27, 28; John 5 : 17.

The Gospel is not in conflict with the law. In Christ, the Gospel, and Christians, the law obtains its highest fulfillment. The minutest portion of the law is thus realized in the Gospel. **Shall break—and shall teach men so.** Whosoever shall violate or set aside one

A.D. 28. MATTHEW V. 73

called the least in the kingdom of heaven: but whosoever shall do and teach *them*, the same shall
20 be called great in the kingdom of heaven. For I say unto you, That except your righteousness shall exceed ʳ *the righteousness* of the scribes and Pharisees, ye shall in no case enter into the kingdom of heaven.
21 YE have heard that it was said by them of old

ʳ Ro. 9. 30–32; 10. 2, 3.

of the least of the commands of God in spirit, and teach men so, either by example or precept. This refers principally to religious teachers. "These words are decisive against such persons, whether ancient or modern, as would set aside the Old Testament as without significance, or inconsistent with the New." —ALFORD. **Shall be called the least in the kingdom of heaven.** Shall be recognized by God and others as the least under the administration of the Messiah. There are degrees of attainment in the divine life, grades in the kingdom of heaven, 1 Pet. 2 : 2; Eph. 14 : 13. Jesus does not say that such a one will be rejected; for if he is founded on Christ, though there be wood, hay, and stubble in his building, yet he will be saved as through fire, 1 Cor. 3 : 15. But, on the contrary, they who shall recognize the whole of Scripture as the word of God, and shall attend to its spirit both in their teaching and practice, shall be recognized, as they really are, as **great in the kingdom of heaven.** Such would recognize the close relation between the law and the Gospel, the one preparatory to the other, and the latter absorbing the spirit of the former within itself. The Gospel sheds great light upon our relations to God and man, and gives us deeper views of moral truth, and hence increases personal responsibility. It thus includes the spirit of the law within itself. This may be seen by what follows, when Jesus proceeds to pour the fuller light of the spirit of the Gospel upon the law, thus lifting and expanding its requirements into their full meaning in the life and practice of the Christian to whom, through faith, Christ becomes the end of the law for righteousness, and who by the indwelling Spirit is led into all truth and purity.

20. **For I say unto you.** *For* connects this verse with the last. *For* . . . . except your righteousness shall exceed that of the scribes and Pharisees, who, in attending to the letter of the law, neglect the spirit, and who also make the word of God of no effect through their traditions (ch. 15 : 3–9), ye shall not enter into the kingdom of heaven.

Your righteousness exceed. Your righteousness is to be of a higher order. It is to include both the perfect righteousness which can only be found in Christ, who is the Lord our righteousness, and that which, in submitting to Christ, is manifested in purity of heart and life. **Scribes.** Persons devoted to copying, reading, and expounding the law. Most of them were Pharisees, though some belonged to other sects. **Pharisees.** See on ch. 3 : 7. The scribes and Pharisees were in such high repute that it was a common saying, that if two men only were admitted into heaven, one would be a scribe and the other a Pharisee. Their righteousness, however, was merely external, while inwardly they were full of hypocrisy and iniquity (ch. 23 : 23, 25, 27, 28); it was connected with harshness and oppression (ch. 23 : 4); and with a love of applause, and an unholy ambition, ch. 23 : 5–7.

Shall in no case enter into the kingdom of heaven. Shall not be saved here or hereafter. They shall not become subjects of the Messiah's kingdom, which commences on earth and is perfected in the world of glory; and shall, therefore, share in its blessings neither in this world nor in the world to come. The announcement of a righteousness exceeding that of the scribes and Pharisees, and in contrast with it, leads the Savior to go into some details, expounding the spirit of the law. The sentiment of this verse is thus illustrated by what follows.

21–48. THE LAW SPIRITUALLY EXPOUNDED in contrast to the Pharisaical exposition according to the letter; illustrated by *six examples.*

21. **Ye have heard.** In the public reading and exposition of the law by the scribes. **That it was said by them of old time.** Correctly translated, "to

time, *Thou shalt not kill; and whosoever shall
22 kill shall be in danger of the judgment. But I say
unto you, That ᵗ whosoever is angry with his brother
without a cause shall be in danger of the judgment:
and whosoever shall say to his brother, Raca! ᵘ shall
be in danger of the council: but whosoever shall
say, Thou fool! shall be in danger of hell fire.

* Ex. 20. 13.

ᵗ Eph. 4. 26; 1 John 3. 15.

ᵘ 2 Sam. 6. 20

those of old," or "to the ancients." Jesus is referring to the stress put upon the mere letter of the law by the scribes. They taught that this was the full meaning of the law, as given to the ancient people of God, and as confirmed by tradition. Christ is not speaking in opposition to Moses, or to the Old Testament, but to the false exposition of the Pharisees. Going beyond the mere letter, he shows the spirituality and the depth of the law, which in its application reaches the mind and the heart. Compare Paul's experience, Rom. 7 : 7-12.
THOU SHALT NOT KILL. Ex. 20 : 13. Jesus begins with the *second table* of the law concerning duties to our neighbor; and with the *Law of Murder*, a most obvious precept.
The relation of man to man is more easily apprehended than that of man to God. And if men fail to come up to the requirements of the law in regard to their neighbor, much more would they be likely to fail to meet those higher requirements in regard to God. Indeed, failure in the former would be proof of failure in the latter, 1 John 4 : 20. **And whosoever shall kill,** etc. This was added by the traditions of the scribes, limiting the law to actual murder—the outward act—and making it merely an external legal enactment. **Danger of the judgment.** An inferior court among the Jews; constituted in every city, in conformity with Deut. 16 : 18, consisting, according to Josephus, of seven persons, and having the power of slaying with the sword. Joseph. *Ant.* iv. 8, 14. See next verse.
22. **But I say unto you.** In opposition to Pharisaical teachings, Jesus speaks with authority as an interpreter of the law. He who gave the law was the best fitted to expound it. He shows that the law of murder not only forbade the outward act, but the inward feelings that led to it, extending to causeless anger. The hater of his brother is a moral murderer, 1 John 3 : 15. He proceeds to point out *three degrees* of anger, and three degrees of punishment. **Angry with his brother.** The words **without a cause** are omitted in some of the oldest texts. A want of love is the thing condemned. A holy indignation is consistent with love to **his brother,** *his fellow-man*, on proper occasions, Mark 3 : 5; Eph. 4 : 26. **Of the judgment.** Exposed and justly subject to that spiritual court, even the judgment-seat of Christ. As Jesus is speaking of the spiritual application of the law, so does he here refer to spiritual punishment. "There were among the Jews three well-known degrees of guilt, coming respectively under the cognizance of the local and supreme courts; and after these is set the *Gehenna of fire,* the end of the malefactor, whose corpse, thrown out into the valley of Hinnom, was devoured by the worm or the flame. Similarly, in the spiritual kingdom of Christ, shall the sins even of thought and word be brought into judgment and punished, each according to its degree of guilt, but even the least of them before no less a tribunal than the judgment-seat of Christ."—ALFORD. **Raca.** A Hebrew word expressing contempt, *worthless, vain fellow,* and marks the second grade of anger. The sin condemned is not in the mere utterance of the word, but in the hostility which prompts the utterance. **In danger of the council.** The Sanhedrim, the supreme central court of the Jews, which inflicted death with the disgrace of stoning. See on ch. 2 : 4. This in Christ's kingdom indicates an exposure to a punishment greater than the former. **Thou fool.** This expresses the third grade of angry feeling, and means, *Thou impious, godless one.* Compare Ps. 14 : 1. An expression of angry reproach, and one of the most contemptuous that a Hebrew could employ. The sin, however, was not in the mere word, but in the high degree of anger which led to the expression of so odious an epithet.

23 Therefore ˣ if thou bring thy gift to the altar, and there rememberest that thy brother hath aught against thee ; ʸ leave there thy gift before the altar, and go thy way ; ᶻ first be reconciled to thy brother, and then come and offer thy gift.
25 ᵃ Agree with thine adversary quickly, ᵇ whiles

ˣ Deu. 16. 16, 17.
ʸ Job 42. 8 ; 1 Pet. 3. 7.
ᶻ 1 Tim. 2. 8.
ᵃ Pro. 25. 8 ; Lk. 12. 58. 59.
ᵇ see Job 22. 21 ; Is. 55. 6, 7 ; Heb. 3. 7, 13.

Hell fire. The Gehenna of fire. Gehenna, which is here correctly translated hell, is a Greek word derived from two Hebrew words, and means *Valley of Hinnom*, which was south of Jerusalem. In its lowest part, toward the south-east, the idolatrous Jews sacrificed their children to Moloch, a name of a heathen god worshiped by the Ammonites, into the red-hot arms of whose statue these children were cast alive and burned, 2 Kings 16 : 3 ; Ps. 106 : 38. The name *Tophet* (Jer. 7 : 31) was also given to it, as some suppose, from *toph*, a drum ; drums being beaten to drown the cries of the children offered in sacrifice. On account of the cruel and idolatrous sacrifices that had been offered here, Josiah polluted it (2 Kings 23 : 10) ; and after that it became the place for casting out and burning all the filth and pollution of the city, and the dead bodies of the worst of criminals. Hence the place was called the Gehenna of fire. But this expression, which had primary reference to the burning, especially of the dead bodies of criminals, in the valley of Hinnom—the greatest ignominy that could be inflicted upon them—became to be used by the Jews to represent the place of the punishment of the wicked, Isa. 30 : 33 ; 66 : 24. This is its only use throughout the New Testament, where it is found twelve times, namely, Matt. 5 : 22, 29, 30 ; 10 : 28 ; 18 : 9 ; 23 : 15, 23 ; Mark 9 : 43, 45, 47 ; Luke 12 : 5 ; James 3 : 6. Our Lord thus speaks of it (Mark 9 : 43, 44) as emphatically the future place of torment, where (quoting from Isa. 66 : 24) "their worm dieth not, and the fire is not quenched."

As Jesus presents three grades of anger, so he presents three *degrees*, not *kinds*, of punishment. In the figures used death was inflicted (1) by the sword, (2) by stoning, and (3) with the additional disgrace of burning the body in the fire. So these figures illustrate eternal death in different intensity, with different degrees of horror and disgrace, corresponding to the degrees of guilt.

23. Therefore. Such being the sin and penalty of unholy anger, reconciliations ought to be immediately effected. Whoever has excited his brother's anger should immediately seek to remove it. The sun should not go down on his wrath, Eph. 4 : 26. **If thou bring thy gift to the altar.** Offerings to God were generally presented at the temple, and burned wholly or in part upon the altar. The altar was in the court of the priests, in front of the Holy Place. Jesus speaks of Jewish worship as it then existed. Sacrifices were then a part of worship, Jesus having not yet offered up himself once for all. The same principle applies to Christian worship. He who approaches God through Jesus Christ must strive to be at peace with his brother ; and he who retains enmity against his fellow-man can not be an acceptable worshiper. **That thy brother hath aught against thee.** Is offended, or thinks he has been injured by you. It is not enough to say, *I have nothing against him, or it is only in his imagination.* Real or unreal, you should seek to remove it from your brother, whether he be a Christian brother or a brother man.

24. Leave there thy gift before the altar. "*Before* the altar the offerings are left standing, that is, in the outer court of the Israelites, into which narrow space the people brought their offering, and then withdrew to the outer court of the women."—THOLUCK. It was the part of the priest to receive it *before* the altar, and to offer it *on* the altar. **Go.** Implies haste. **First be reconciled.** Remove first the cause of offense ; make friendly overtures ; do all in your power, and all you ought to do, to effect a reconciliation ; especially be reconciled *thyself*. Compare Mark 11 : 25.

25. Agree with thy adversary quickly. Come to a friendly agreement with thy adversary, thy opponent, one who is going to law with thee, whom thou owest. The word translat-

thou art in the way with him; lest at any time the adversary deliver thee to the judge, and the judge deliver thee to the officer, and thou be cast into 26 prison. Verily, I say unto thee, ᶜ Thou shalt by no means come out thence, till thou hast paid the uttermost farthing.

27 Ye have heard that it was said by them of old 28 time, ᵈ Thou shalt not commit adultery. But I say unto you, That whosoever ᵉ looketh on a woman to lust after her hath committed adultery with her

ᶜ Lk. 16. 26; 2 Thes. 1. 9.

ᵈ Ex. 20. 14; Deu. 5. 18; Prov. 6. 32.
ᵉ Ex. 20. 17; Pro. 6. 25; 2 Pet. 2. 14; 1 John 2. 16.

ed *adversary* means the *adverse party in a suit*, one going to law with another. It here means a *creditor;* one who has just claims on the other. Jesus further enforces the duty of becoming reconciled with our brother man by a legal illustration from the practice of the time, which permitted a settlement of a dispute after the summons had been served, and before the trial. He supposes the adversary to have just legal claims, and in view of the consequences of non-compliance he urges an immediate settlement. **While thou art in the way with him.** According to Hebrew law, no accusation could be listened to by a judge except in the presence of the accused party. According to Roman custom, the accusing party could compel the accused to go with him before the prætor, unless he agreed by the way to settle the matter. The language of our Savior can be explained by either custom. He urges settlement quickly, in the way, before coming before the judge, lest **the judge deliver thee to the officer** of the court, and **thou,** failing to pay the debt and the additional expenses of the trial, **be cast into prison.** Compare Luke 12:58. So a person who indulges unkind feelings toward his fellow-man is summoned and on his way to his Judge; if he does not repent and exercise a spirit of love and reconciliation, he shall be condemned, and cast into eternal condemnation. The *adversary* represents the *offended brother*, and, back of him, *the law of God*, which denounces all wrong feeling and wrong doing to our fellow-man. The *way* represents the *way to the judgment* which all men are traveling. *God* is the *judge*, and the *officer*, probably, the *angels* (ch. 13:39, 49; 1 Thess. 4:16), and the *prison, perdition.*

26. **Uttermost farthing.** The Greek word signifies one of the smallest Roman coins, rather less than two fifths of one cent. Our Lord uses strong language, meaning that the guilty one should suffer the full measure of his punishment; that, as in the future world he should have nothing to pay, so his punishment should have no end. See ch. 18:30, 34, 35.

27. Our Lord passes to the commandments which respect the marriage relation. Commencing with the *Law of Adultery* (Ex. 20:14), he first gives its deeper meaning, and adds certain admonitions, (vers. 29, 30), and then proceeds to the *Law of Divorce.* These two laws should be considered together, since our Savior's exposition of the latter is but a further exposition of the former. It is but the application of the law of adultery to all cases of divorce, making every dissolution of the marriage relation, except where it has been practically broken by fornication, a violation of the seventh commandment.

28. **Whosoever looketh upon a woman.** *Looketh* is emphatic, *gazeth.* See Luke 7:44; Acts 1:9; 3:4. Our Lord speaks especially to *men.* Polygamy and divorce had been permitted to men on account of the hardness of their hearts (ch. 19:8); his language strikes directly at the opinions and customs of his time. Adultery, according to the Old Testament usage, here includes fornication. **To lust after her.** This clause is the *key* to the whole sentence, determining the character of the look, and means, *In order to lust after her.* It refers not to unintentional thoughts and desires, such as may be suggested by the tempter or may involuntarily arise in the heart, and are checked by the watchful and pious soul; but to those that are intentional and

A. D. 28.   MATTHEW V.   77

29 already ᶠ in his heart. ᵍ And if thy right eye offend thee [*or*, cause thee to offend], pluck it out, and cast *it* from thee: for it is profitable for thee that one of thy members should perish, and not *that* thy whole body should be cast into hell. And if thy right hand offend thee, cut it off, and cast *it* from thee: for it is profitable for thee that one of thy members should perish, and not *that* thy whole body should be cast into hell.

31 It hath been said, ʰ Whosoever shall put away his wife, let him give her a writing of divorcement.

ᶠ Ro. 7. 7, 8, 14.
ᵍ Mk. 9, 43–47.

ʰ ch. 19. 3, 9; Deu. 24. 1–4.

---

conscious. It is gazing in order to feed impure desires. **Already in his heart.** He has already committed the act inwardly, in thought and purpose, and in the sight of God who looketh upon the heart. He has by this act broken the seventh commandment. It should be borne in mind that, as our Lord noticed degrees of hatred, in expounding the law of murder, so there are degrees in this sin. The faintest intentional movement of inordinate lust breaks the law; much more, stronger movements, and especially those connected with the outward transgression.

29, 30. In view of the truth just announced in the preceding verse, Jesus teaches the duty of crushing the first beginnings of impure desire, and of sacrificing, if it be necessary, what we count most dear. **The right eye** and **the right hand,** the most valuable of our members, were proverbial expressions for any thing peculiarly dear and valuable. They represent here the occasions to sin, such as our strongest propensities and habits, sensual appetites, pride, vanity, worldly beauty or friendship, covetousness, worldly honors or possessions, or whatever is offensive to God. Most of our Lord's hearers were poor people, who lived by their daily labor, and hence the loss of a right hand would be a greater calamity than that of a right eye. Thus he passes from the weaker to the stronger figure; also from the sight to the act. Better that the dearest and most useful object of life should be sacrificed, than to be led into sin and be lost. **Offend thee.** The correct translation is, *causes thee to offend*. If thy right eye, or thy right hand, is an occasion of falling into sin. **Pluck it out. Cut it off.** Mortify and subdue the passions, evil desires, or inclinations which animate the eye or the hand, let the conflict cost what it may, Col. 3 : 5. Whatever becomes in lets to temptation or instruments to sin, must be sacrificed, or we perish. We must crucify the flesh with its affections and lusts, Gal. 5 : 24. We must do like the surgeon, who cuts off a diseased member in order to save the whole body. **Thy whole body** represents *thy whole being,* just as the hand or eye represents a passion or a part of thy being; the whole man, thyself. **It is profitable for thee.** It is for thy highest interest. Self-denial is enforced here on the ground of the truest self-interest. **Hell.** The place of future punishment. See verse 22.

31, 32. **Whosoever shall put away his wife,** etc. Jesus applies the principle developed from the seventh commandment to the law of divorce. According to the Mosaic law, the wife could not divorce the husband, but only the husband the wife. Moses had permitted divorce (Deut. 24 : 1, 2) in such a way as to restrain a bad practice, which had gone far to annul the original law of marriage, and which still prevails among the Arabs, who by a word may dissolve the marriage tie. He allowed the wife to be divorced only on account of "some uncleanness," and only by a legal document, "a bill of divorcement." Thus Moses did not command to divorce, but rather placed a restriction on the prevailing custom. In the days of our Savior, two opposite interpretations of this law prevailed among the Jews. Rabbi Shammai and his disciples taught that, according to Moses, adultery was the only allowable ground of divorcement; while Hillel and his disciples taught that a wife might be put away for any thing that

32 But I say unto you, That [i] whosover shall put away his wife, saving for the cause of fornication, causeth her to commit adultery: and whosoever shall marry her that is divorced committeth adultery.

33 Again, ye have heard that [k] it hath been said by them of old time, [l] Thou shalt not forswear thyself, 34 but [m] shalt perform unto the Lord thine oaths. But

[i] Mal. 2. 14-16; Lk. 16. 18; Ro. 7. 3; 1 Cor. 7. 10, 11.
[k] ch. 23. 16, 18, 22.
[l] Ex. 20. 7; Num. 30. 2.
[m] Deu. 23. 23; Ecc. 5. 4, 5.

---

amounted to uncleanness in the eyes of the husband, and indeed for any thing displeasing to him in appearance, manner, or dress. Josephus thus loosely states the law (*Jewish Antiq.* iv. 8, 23), "He that desires to be divorced from his wife from any cause whatsoever, and many such causes happen among men, let him in writing give assurance that he will never use her as his wife any more; for by these means she may be at liberty to marry another husband, although, before this bill of divorce was given, she is not permitted so to do." The language of the Savior, **But I say unto you,** implies that the scribes and their party expounded the law with great laxity, favoring the common practice, that whoever wished to put away his wife had merely to give a bill of divorce.

On the contrary, our Savior teaches that the marriage relation should not be dissolved by man. "What therefore God hath joined together, let not man put asunder," ch. 19: 6; Mark 10: 9-11; Luke 16: 18. Adultery, however, is an actual breaking of the marriage tie, and therefore Jesus adds, **save for the cause of fornication.** According to the strict application of the Mosaic law, the guilty party was to be put to death. Thus the breaking of the bond, which had been actually accomplished, was to be publicly accomplished by death. A bill of divorcement would in such a case be only a statement of a fact as actually existing. In accordance with the same principle, Paul teaches, in 1 Cor. 7: 15, that if the marriage tie is actually broken by one party, it may be so regarded and accepted by the other party.

Jesus goes on and states the consequences attending unlawful divorcements. Whoever puts away his wife, save for the cause of fornication, **causeth her to commit adultery.** Dr. Conant has brought out the true meaning of this clause, making it "equivalent to *makes her an adulteress*, in the same sense in which it is said (1 John 5: 10) *he that believeth not God hath made him a liar;* not that God thereby becomes a liar, or that she becomes an adulteress, but simply is treated as such. By repudiating her, for which the only just cause was adultery, he makes her appear as one guilty of that crime." And so whoever marries her thus put away **committeth adultery;** he becomes a partaker with her of an apparent crime, and also sanctions an unlawful sundering of the marriage relation. Compare 1 Cor. 7: 11, where Paul advises the wife that has departed from her husband either to remain unmarried, or to be reconciled to her husband.

33. Our Lord proceeds to expound the *Law of Oaths.* This law is found in Lev. 19: 12, and Deut. 23: 23. **By them of old time.** Rather, *to them of old.* See ver. 21. **Thou shalt not forswear thyself.** Thou shalt not swear falsely. The abuse of oaths was exceedingly common among the Jews of that day. They held that only those were binding in which the name of God, the gold or the sacrifices of the temple were invoked; and that all other oaths might be violated without committing perjury. Laying special stress upon those made in the name of God, they could say, Thou **shalt perform unto the Lord thine oaths,** implying that all others which were made in the name of *creatures,* as heaven, earth, Jerusalem, the temple, etc., were of little or no obligation. See ch. 23: 16. Jesus shows that these distinctions were vain and futile; that the creature is connected with God, and derives all that is lofty and noble from him; and that thus an appeal to the creature is in a certain sense an appeal to the Creator. Heaven is God's throne, the earth his footstool (Isa. 66: 1), Jerusalem his peculiar abode, the central point of the theocracy (Ps. 48: 3), and the head is so much the property and work of God that man can not change the color of a single hair.

35 I say unto you, ⁿ Swear not at all; neither by heaven; for it is ᵒ God's throne: nor by the earth; for it is his footstool: neither by Jerusalem; for it
36 is ᵖ the city of the great King. Neither shalt thou swear by thy head, ᵠ because thou canst not make
37 one hair white or black. ʳ But let your communication be Yea, yea; Nay, nay: for whatsoever is more than these cometh of evil.
38 Ye have heard that it hath been said, ˢ An eye
39 for an eye, and a tooth for a tooth. But I say unto

ⁿ Jam. 5. 12.
ᵒ Ps. 11. 4; Is. 66. 1; Ac. 7. 49.
ᵖ 2 Chr. 6. 6; Ps 48. 2; 76. 2; Jer. 8. 9.
ᵠ Lk. 12. 25.
ʳ Col. 4. 6.

ˢ Ex. 21. 23-25.

34–36. Swear not at all. Swearing is prohibited in the same way as killing. To kill is both lawful and not lawful, and so of swearing. God has sworn by himself (Isa. 45 : 23; Heb. 6 : 13), Jesus without doubt took a judicial oath (ch. 26 : 63, 64), and Paul appeals to God as a witness (1 Thess. 2 : 5; 2 Cor. 11 : 31; Gal. 1 : 20; 2 Cor. 1 : 23), and an angel swears by him who lives forever and ever, Rev. 10 : 6. The lax teachings of the Jewish *rabbis* had resulted in filling common discourse with profane words and thoughtless oaths. The modern orientals "are fearfully profane. Every body curses and swears when in a passion. They swear by the *head*, by their *life*, by *heaven*, and by the *temple*, or what is in its place, the *church*. The forms of cursing and swearing, however, are almost infinite, and fall on the pained ear all day long."—Dr. Thomson in *The Land and the Book*, vol. i. page 284. These modes of swearing were common among the Jews in our Lord's day, and against them he specially makes his attack. That this is the case seems evident from verse 37, "Let your *communication* (that is, your *word, talk, speech, discourse*) be Yea, yea; Nay, nay." Thus our Lord forbids all profanity in common discourse, and teaches that individuals in their intercourse one with another should not confirm their words with an oath. This is especially binding on Christians; their *yea* and *nay* should be as reliable as an oath, and are really so, if they are in a proper spiritual state. A Christian's word should be enough, especially for his fellow-Christians.

Neither by heaven. To swear by that is to swear by God's throne, and Him that sitteth thereon, ch. 23 : 22. So to swear by the earth is to swear by Him whose footstool it is; or by Jerusalem, by Him whose city it is; or by the head, by Him who holds its changes and destiny in his hands. Thus every oath is an appeal to God. Otherwise it is unmeaning; but even then it would be an idle word, and trifling with sacred things.

37. Let your communication be Yea, yea; Nay, nay. Let your word, speech, discourse be truthful and simple, without oaths or profane expletives. The Arabs have a proverb, "Let thy speech be yea or nay, so that you may be truthful to all men." Repetition, among the Hebrews, was used for emphasis, and implied truth and certainty, Gen. 41 : 32; Dan. 5 : 25; John 3 : 3, 5, 11. *Yea, yea*, is a solemn and deliberate affirmative; *Nay, nay*, as solemn a negative. See James 5 : 12. **Whatsoever is more than these cometh of evil.** The need of oaths of any kind is the result of evil, because they indicate either the want of confidence or the want of truthfulness, or both. Were men what they ought to be, there would certainly be in no case any need of them. The first recorded oath was that made by Satan in support of the lie by which he tempted Eve, Gen. 3 : 5. The multiplication of judicial oaths has been found to indicate not only a general distrust among men, but to be productive of falsehood and profanity. The use of them in conversation is proof of a low morality and a fearful depravity of heart. Instead of strengthening the truthfulness of what is said, profanity only weakens it. It shows a want of reverence and love for the Most High, and may well shake our confidence in any who use it. No profane person has any right to regard himself a Christian; and no one can utter an oath in common conversation without transgressing this command of our Lord, "The Lord will not hold him guiltless that taketh his name in vain," Ex. 20 : 7.

38. Jesus passes to the *Law of Retaliation*. **An eye for an eye,** etc., Deut.

you, ¹ That ye resist not evil: ᵘ but whosoever shall smite thee on thy right cheek, ˣ turn to him the 40 other also. And ʸ if any man will sue thee at the law, and take away *thy* coat, let him have *thy* cloak

¹ Le. 19. 18; Is. 50. 6; Pro. 20. 22; 24. 29; John 18. 22, 23.
ᵘ Lk. 6. 29, 30; Lam. 3. 30.

19 : 21; Lev. 24 : 20; Ex. 21 : 24. Moses gave this rule to guide the decision of judges, and as such it is founded in justice. Among a depraved race governments must maintain public order, and protect the lives and property of their citizens, by inflicting punishments corresponding to the injury which one person inflicts upon another. They are ordained by God; and the magistrate bears not the sword in vain, but is a minister of God, an avenger for wrath to him that doeth evil, Rom. 13 : 1–5. Instead of confining this law to magistrates, the Jews extended it to private conduct, and made it a rule for taking private revenge. That Moses did not intend it as a rule for private intercourse is evident from the command, " Thou shalt not avenge, nor bear any grudge against the children of thy people," Lev. 19 : 18. Compare Prov. 24 : 29. Against the Jewish perversion of this law our Lord principally directs his remarks.

39. Resist not evil. Do not retaliate. When any do you evil, return not like for like. This precept is frequently enjoined by the apostles, Rom. 12 : 17, 19–21; 1 Thess. 5 : 15; 1 Cor. 6 : 7; 1 Pet. 3 : 9. These passages are the best exposition of our Lord's injunction. We are not to cherish an unkind or revengeful spirit under injuries, but rather a spirit of forgiveness, of generosity, and of patient endurance. We are to overcome evil with good, and make no resistance except where the honor of God, the good of the injurer, and the good of community require it. The magistrate should faithfully punish wrong; the parent should protect, if possible, his family against violence; and every man has a right of self-defense when life is threatened. Compare Acts 16 : 35–40; 22 : 23 –29; 25 : 9–11; 23 : 2–4. Yet we should not always defend our own lives, especially in religious persecution. God's honor may require that we willingly submit, like Jesus, to a martyr's death, 2 Tim. 4 : 6. Jesus, however, illustrates the principle by four examples, presenting first the strongest manifestation of insolence, and descending to the weakest, and showing the treatment which each should receive. **Evil** is variously referred to the *devil*, an *evil person, wrong*, or *evil*. It can not well refer to the devil in the examples given, nor hardly to an evil person, especially in the last example. Besides, the original Greek presents the usual form of the *abstract*, meaning *evil* in general. The connection, however, shows that it refers to *evil, wickedness*, as it is manifested through individuals, and as it outwardly assails us, in doing us wrong, and in inflicting upon us injuries. "The fundamental idea of the passage is, that Christian love must make us willing to bear twice as much as the world, in its injustice, could demand."—LANGE.

Whosoever shall smite thee on the right cheek. *The first example.* An act of great contempt, personal outrage, and insolence. It was regarded as an affront of the worst sort, and was severely punished by Jewish and Roman laws. **Turn to him the other also,** was a proverbial phrase, expressing submission to insults and injuries, Lam. 3 : 30. This must not be taken too literally, but must be obeyed in the spirit more than in the letter. Thus, Christ himself did not conform literally to this precept (John 18 : 22, 23), though he obeyed it in spirit by yielding up himself to his persecutors and crucifiers, Isa. 50 : 6. Under private and personal outrages we are not to contend and fight; but we should endure them patiently from Christian principle. This does not prevent us from insisting firmly and kindly that justice should be done us, or from rebuking and remonstrating against injustice whenever practiced against us.

40. Sue thee at the law and take away thy coat. *The second example.* From personal violence Jesus descends to the demanding of property by a legal suit. The *coat* or "tunic" was the *undergarment*, made of linen or cotton, and which folded close to the body. The **cloak** or mantle was the outer, the larger, and more valuable garment. It was worn loose around the body, and made of various materials, according to the circumstances of the wearer. It was common-

41 also. And whosoever ˣ shall compel thee to go a   ˣ 1 Pet. 2. 20–21.
42 mile, go with him twain. Give to him that asketh   ʸ 1 Cor. 6. 7.

ly of different sizes, nearly square, six to nine feet long, and about as many broad, and was wrapped around the body, or fastened about the shoulders, and could be thrown off when engaged in labor. It was also used as a blanket or covering, to wrap one's self in at night, hence it was not allowed by the law to be taken by the creditor and retained as a pledge over night, Ex. 22 : 26, 27. This last fact shows the force of the command to yield even the *cloak*. If any one would go to law with thee and take away thy under-garment, rather than contend with him, let him have the out-

CLOAK AND COAT.

er garment also. As in matters of personal violence and wrong we are not to show a retaliating and revengeful spirit, so must we not in legal matters. We are to show a forgiving and generous spirit, in striving to settle disputes in regard to property, preferring to suffer loss ourselves than to engage in a law-suit.

41. **Whosoever shall compel thee.** *The third example.* The word translated *shall compel* is of Persian origin, and is found three times in the New Testament, here, ch. 27 : 32, and Mark 15 : 21, and means *impress, to press into service*. According to the postal arrangement of Cyrus, horses were provided, at certain distances along the principal roads of the empire, so that couriers could proceed without interruption both night and day. If the government arrangements failed at any point, the couriers had authority to press into their service men, horses, or any thing that came in their way which might serve to hasten their journey. A like authority was exercised over the Jews by the Roman governors. The word, originating in this custom, passed from the Persian into the Greek, and into rabbinical language, meaning *compulsory service* in forwarding royal messengers, and also *to press into service* for any purpose. See Dr. Conant on this passage. "The Jews particularly objected to the duty of furnishing posts to the Roman government; and Demetrius, wishing to conciliate the Jews, promised, among other things, that the beasts of the Jews should not be pressed into his service (Josephus, *Antiq.* xiii. 2, 3). Hence our Savior represents this as a burden."—DR. BURTON. Our Lord enjoins that, rather than resist the public authority, or any individual who had the authority to require your attendance and service for a certain distance, you should willingly go twice the distance. The service may be hard, even unjust, and the motives for pressing thee into the service wrong; yet go peaceably. It will be more for your own comfort, as well as for your credit, to submit than to contend. A Roman **mile** was a thousand paces of five feet each.

42. **Give to him that asketh thee.** *Fourth example.* Evil as we meet it in beggars and borrowers. We must bear in mind that Jesus is opposing a retaliating and revengeful spirit, ver. 38. We must not withhold charity from any, out of revenge. He also gives a general rule. Christians should be benevolent, giving willingly according to what they have (2 Cor. 8 : 12), doing good to all, especially to the household of faith (Gal. 6 : 10); yet their benevolence should be wisely distributed, exercised seldom or never toward those who can but will not work (2 Thess. 3 : 10), and always consistently with their duty to their families, 1 Tim. 5 : 8. As the Lord gives not always to those who ask the *very thing* that they ask, but *that which is better* for them (2 Cor. 12 : 8, 9), so the spirit of love and true benevolence should prompt us to give not always that which may be asked, but that which is *best* for the re-

thee, and ᵃ from him that would borrow of thee turn not thou away.

43 Ye have heard that it hath been said, ᵇ Thou shalt love thy neighbor, ᶜ and hate thine enemy.

44 But I say unto you, ᵈ Love your enemies, bless them that curse you, do good to them that hate you, and pray ᵉ for them which despitefully use you

45 and persecute you; that ye may be the children of your Father which is in heaven: for ᶠ he maketh

ᵃ ch. 27. 32; Mk. 15. 21.
ᵇ Ps. 37. 21, 26; 112. 5-9; Prov. 11. 24, 25; Ecc. 11. 1, 2; 2 Cor. 9. 6-15; 1 Tim. 6. 17-19; 1 John 3. 16-18.
ᵇ Le. 19. 18.
ᶜ Deu. 23. 6; Ps. 41. 10.

ceiver. "To give every thing to every one—the sword to the madman, the alms to the impostor, the criminal request to the temptress—would be to act as the enemy of others and ourselves."—ALFORD. Jesus doubtless had also in view the hard-hearted, oppressive, and covetous practices of the scribes and Pharisees (ch. 23 : 14); and he emphatically enjoins the spirit of the law in Deut. 15 : 1-11, which they were violating like their fathers frequently before them, Neh. 5 : 1-5; Ezek. 22 : 7. **Borrow.** Without *usury*, which was forbidden by the law, Lev. 25 : 36, 37; Deut. 23 : 20.

43. Jesus now proceeds to the *Law of Love to our Neighbor*. Having just presented the negative side of duty, he now presents the positive. From the duty of endurance, he proceeds to that of active and outreaching love. **Thou shalt love thy neighbor** was a command of God, Lev. 19 : 18; but thou shalt **hate thine enemy** was never commanded, but was added by Jewish teachers, who thought that hatred to enemies was implied by the command to "love thy neighbor." They also limited *neighbor* to the Jews, and called all Gentiles *enemies*. The word *neighbor* signified literally one living near; and was used in a limited sense, to mean a friend, associate, one belonging to the same country or professing the same religion. In its broader signification it meant a fellow-man. Compare Luke 10 : 29-37. The Pharisees so restricted the term as to exclude not only Gentiles and Samaritans, but also the publican and those who shared not their peculiar views. In the original command it doubtless had primary reference to Israelites; but that it was not to be limited to them, is evident from our Savior's application of it to all mankind. He opposes not the law, but the carnal Jewish interpretation of the law; he rather gives its deep spiritual meaning and its universal appli-

cation. And this was in harmony with the Old Testament requirement, that enjoined love to strangers (Lev. 19 : 34), and kindness to enemies, Prov. 25 : 21. It should, however, be observed, that, while Jesus repeats the law as commonly enjoined by Jewish teachers of his day, he does not thereby sanction the Jewish application of *neighbor* to the *Jew* and of *enemy* to the *Gentile*, but applies these terms to friend and foe in private intercourse.

44. **But I say unto you.** In opposition to this narrow and selfish exposition of love to one's neighbor, and to this wicked appendage of hatred to an enemy, Jesus expounds the law of love. Taking for granted that a friend, and any human being who exercises no hatred toward you, should receive your love, he begins by saying **love your enemies.** This is the ground principle, the disposition from which flows what follows. According to the highest critical authorities, this command should read, *Love your enemies, and pray for them that persecute you*, the omitted clauses being found in Luke 6 : 27, 28. Compare ver. 11, 12 of this chapter. This is not inconsistent with the Old Testament, Ex. 23 : 4, 5; 1 Sam. 24 : 5; Prov. 24 : 17; 25 : 21 (Rom. 12 : 20). Cursing is to be met with blessing, a steady and settled hatred with well-doing, and abusive language and persecution—that is, hostile speech coupled with hostile action—with prayer.

45. **That ye may be children of your Father.** That you may prove yourselves sons of your heavenly Father by showing a likeness to him, and that you are partakers of his benevolent spirit. Jesus enforces the true principle of love from the example of God, who causes the sun to rise and the rain to descend upon all, the wicked as well as the righteous. The sons of God must necessarily be like him in character and life, in spi-

his sun to rise on the evil and on the good, and
46 sendeth rain on the just and on the unjust. ᵍFor
if ye love them which love you, what reward have
47 ye? Do not even the publicans the same? And if
ye salute your brethren only, what do ye more *than*
48 *others?* do not even the publicans so? ʰBe ye
therefore perfect, even ⁱas your Father which is in
heaven is perfect.

ᵈ Ps. 7. 4; 35. 11-14; Pro. 25. 21, 22; Ro. 12. 14. 20.
ᵉ Lk. 23. 34; Ac. 7. 60; 1 Cor. 4. 12, 13; 1 Pet. 3. 9.
ᶠ Job 25. 3; Ps. 145. 9; Ac. 14. 17.
ᵍ Lk. 6. 32.

rit and acts, Eph. 5 : 1, 2. It follows that the love required is not the love of complacency, that which approves of the moral character of all, but the love of benevolence, which desires the true welfare of all. We are to imitate God so far as a son may imitate a father. We are not to usurp a father's authority, and hence we are not to sit in judgment over others, nor execute vengeance on others; but, like true sons, we are to imitate our Father in goodness and love.

46. Jesus enforces this principle of love from the example of wicked men. The sons of God should surely exhibit a higher love than the children of the evil one. If they love only those loving them, what reward have they? What claim have they to extraordinary praise or moral approbation? **Do not even the publicans the same?** The *publicans*, or the collectors of revenue and taxes under the Roman government, consisted of two classes. The first were Roman knights, who levied the revenues of a large district; the second were subordinate collectors, each of whom was required to pay a certain sum to his superior, with the privilege of raising as much more as he pleased for his own benefit. This led to extortion and oppression. The latter class were the publicans of the New Testament. They were also under the additional reproach of being the instruments of a Gentile or heathen power and a foreign despotism. Hence the very name of *publican* was expressive of a depraved and reckless character. Jews engaged in this calling were excluded by their occupation from respectable society, and were naturally thrown into that of wicked and disreputable men. This explains the force of the phrase so frequently used in the Gospels, "publicans and sinners," ch. 9 : 11. To exercise no higher love than men of the most degraded character surely was unworthy of Christ's disciples, and could not be followed by the reward which shall be given to the righteous.

47. **Salute your brethren.** Jesus changes the figure from *love* to *saluting*, *greeting*, which is one of the expressions of love. Salutation among the Jews was more significant than among us, denoting marked friendship and affection, and expressing a desire for the divine blessing to rest upon the person saluted, as, Blessed be thou of Jehovah; may Jehovah be with thee. **Brethren.** Not merely brothers in the strict sense, but also relatives, friends, and fellow-countrymen. The Jews did not salute Gentiles, just as even now, in the east, Mohammedans do not salute Christians. If you only do this, **what do ye more** and better than the worst of men? What do ye that excels, and that should entitle you to special regard? **Do not even the publicans,** or rather, **the heathen so?** The oldest manuscripts have *heathen* or *Gentiles* instead of *publicans*. This only varies the expression, but not the sense. Jesus shows, on the one hand, that the law of love, as falsely expounded by the Pharisees, was nothing more than that of the openly wicked; and, on the other hand, that the true exposition of this law required a higher and holier principle than that which flowed out of selfishness, or mere natural affection.

48. Our Lord now returns to the divine example set forth in verse 45, and exhorts his hearers to imitate their Father in heaven, who is perfect in love. He does not simply repeat what he had said before, but he gives a general and comprehensive rule for his followers. **Be ye therefore perfect.** Take God as your pattern, your model. God gives us a perfect standard and rule of life, Lev. 11 : 44; 1 Pet. 1 : 16. To be *perf et* denotes a moral completeness. Thus, Paul uses the word to denote a full, complete spiritual growth, contrasted with infancy and childhood; and thus it is

properly translated *men* in 1 Cor. 14 : 20, and *fill up* in Heb. 5 : 14. Compare Eph. 4 : 13-15; 1 Cor. 2 : 6. The Greek word, like our word *perfect*, is sometimes used in a relative, and sometimes in an absolute sense. God is absolutely perfect, always full-grown and matured in all his perfections; but man, at the best, is only relatively perfect. Though he may have arrived at spiritual manhood, there is still an opportunity for growth (Eph. 4 : 15); though he enters heaven, he has an eternity before him in which to expand all his moral and spiritual powers, and to increase in knowledge, in wisdom, and in likeness to God. Thus the word perfect, when applied to men, while it denotes a certain completeness and maturity, may be applied to the various degrees of that maturity. This explains how Paul could speak of himself as perfect, when just before he had disclaimed being already perfected, Phil. 3 : 12-15. The distinction between the relative and absolute sense of the word perfect must be borne in mind in the passage before us, "Be ye therefore perfect, even as your Father is perfect." Let it be your aim to attain to the measure of the stature of Christ's fullness, to the full maturity of Christian manhood. Imitate the perfections of God, which are to be imitated by his children; especially his love, which was exercised even toward his enemies, by the gift of his Son, John 3 : 16. And especially by faith be in Christ, perfect and complete in him, who is made unto us righteousness, sanctification, and redemption, Col. 1 : 28; 1 Cor. 1 : 30.

The exact form of the Greek verb translated *be ye* is future. Scholars are very generally agreed that it is a future used imperatively, or at least it includes an imperative sense, and that therefore it is properly translated *be ye*. This is sustained by the passive meaning of the Hebrew future in the ten commandments, and throughout the law of Moses. If, however, it includes a future sense as well as an imperative, it then denotes what Christ's disciples are to be in his kingdom and service. In their aims and efforts, in their connection with Christ by faith, in their growth and maturity, and in their final glorified state, they are to be and they shall be perfect and complete in their being, even as their heavenly Father is perfect and complete in his being.

This is the design, will, and promise of God in regard to his children.

Thus in several instances Jesus expounds the law, showing its deep spiritual meaning. It is only by resting in the perfect work of Jesus, who hath for us brought in everlasting righteousness, that we can rejoice in the spirituality of the law, and become followers of God as dear children. Thenceforth, the law is life, and his commandments are not grievous, 1 John 5 : 3, 4.

REMARKS.

1. It is fitting at times to preach in the fields or on mountain tops, as well as in houses of worship. Ministers should not be sticklers in regard to times and places of preaching, ver. 1.
2. "When Jesus opens his mouth, let us open our hearts."—HEUBNER. Ver. 2; Rev. 3 : 20.
3. True happiness is very different from what the world thinks it to be. Its seat is in the heart, not in any external condition, vers. 3-12.
4. True religion makes men happy; and none can be truly happy without it, vers. 3-12; Eccl. 11 : 9; 12 : 13.
5. The beatitudes present humiliation on the one hand, and exaltation on the other; with present happiness ("Happy the poor," etc.) and future joy and glory ("they shall," etc.), vers. 3-12.
6. All true happiness begins with spiritual poverty, a consciousness of a moral deficiency in ourselves, a self-renunciation that yields the heart up to Christ and the claims of the Gospel, ver. 3; Ps. 51 : 17; Isa. 57 : 15; Luke 4 : 18.
7. The traits brought to view in the first seven beatitudes are blended in Christian character, and are essential to the image of Christ, vers. 3-9; Phil. 2 : 1-8.
8. True happiness is increased rather than diminished by the opposition and persecutions of men. If Christians have internal evidences of God's favor, the hatred of the world is an additional evidence. They are the companions of prophets, and shall be participators in their reward, vers. 10-12.
9. By manifesting the characteristics of the truly happy, Christians become the salt of the earth, and the light of the world, vers. 13-16; Eph. 5 : 8-11.
10. It is the design of God that Christians should exert a saving and preserving influence on their fellow-men; and if they fail of this, they have reason to

fear that the grace of God is not in them. This is specially true of them collectively. That church, or that body of Christians, that fail of this end, is like tasteless salt, and is unworthy of the Christian name, ver. 13; Rev. 3 : 16.

11. It is God's design, also, that Christians should be seen; they are the light of the world, a city set on a hill. The world are looking at them; they can not be hid; and if they do not send forth the light of truth, they belie Christian character, disgrace the Christian name, and do greater injury than if they had never professed godliness, vers. 14, 15; 1 Tim. 6 : 11, 12.

12. Christians should not merely be lights (Phil. 2 : 15), but by being united in Christ and in the truth, should be collectively one great light, reflecting the pure and clear light of their Lord, ver. 14; Eph. 4 : 14–16; 5 : 27.

13. Christian example comes with convincing power to the hearts of men, and is adapted to lead them to honor God, ver. 16; 1 Cor. 14 : 25.

14. The great end in all good works should be the glory of God, ver. 16.

15. Christ is the Lawgiver of his people, vers. 17, 20, 22, 28, etc.

16. Christ's mission was in harmony with the old dispensation. The Gospel is a counterpart of the law. He did not lessen, but by the diffusion of greater light, increased moral obligation. While he was himself the substance of all that was transitory in the law, all that was imperishable and essential to godliness, he incorporated and expounded in the Gospel, and he gives all moral requirements a practical efficacy over the hearts and lives of men by leading them to love and obey them, ver. 17; Eph. 2 : 15; Col. 2 : 14; Rom. 3 : 31; Heb. 10 : 16.

17. We must avoid a false Christian liberty, an Antinomian licentiousness, on the one hand, and a Pharisaical self-righteousness, on the other, vers. 18–20.

18. We ought to guard against the least sins as well as the greatest, ver. 19.

19. Our righteousness must not consist in mere outward observances, nor merely in holding scriptural views and doctrines, but in spiritual worship and faith in Christ who is the end of the law for righteousness, ver. 20; John 4 : 20.

20. Our Lord's deep and spiritual exposition of the law clearly shows that by the deeds of the law no flesh shall be justified, vers. 21–48; Rom. 3 : 20.

21. The law demands conformity of word and thought as well as of deed. Thus, it forbids unholy wrath, and the unchastity of the eye and heart. Anger is a great sin and is allied to murder; obscene words and actions are adultery, vers. 21–30; Prov. 23 : 7.

22. We should seek first to do justice to our fellow-men, if we would be accepted of God, vers. 25–26.

23. Present duty should be performed at once, or the opportunity may be forever lost, ver. 25.

24. We ought to resist the first approaches of sin, and avoid even the appearance of evil, vers. 27–32.

25. Whatever causes us to sin should be renounced and forsaken; and though the sacrifice be great, it will result in our present and eternal gain, vers. 29, 30; ch. 16 : 26, 27; 1 Cor. 9 : 27.

26. All swearing in common conversation is a great sin, and shows great depravity of heart. Official and judicial swearing is often perverted and carried to excess, and is only allowable as a necessity for preventing a greater evil, and when imposed by adequate authority, vers. 33–37.

27. We must not imitate the world in returning evil for evil, but our Heavenly Father in loving our enemies and doing them the highest good. A revengeful spirit is unchristian, vers. 38–48.

28. Forgiving injuries instead of avenging them is a mark of true greatness and goodness, vers. 38–42.

29. The best way of overcoming evil is with good, vers. 38–42; Rom. 12 : 20, 21.

30. It is the glory of Christianity that it makes mankind a common brotherhood, and that it is the only religion that demands love to our enemies. These are evidences of its divine origin, and of its universal adaptation to men, vers. 43, 44.

31. God speaks through nature to men. He teaches lessons of love through the sunshine and the rain, vers. 44, 45; Ps. 104 : 9–24.

32. The highest perfection should be our constant aim, ver. 48; Phil. 3 : 13, 14; 1 John 2 : 1.

CHAPTER VI.

Vers. 1–18. Our Lord proceeds to EXPOUND PRACTICAL PIETY AND TO ENFORCE THE RIGHT WAY OF PERFORMING RELIGIOUS DUTIES. These should be

VI. TAKE heed that ye do not your alms [*or*, righteousness ᵏ] before men, ˡ to be seen of them: ᵐ otherwise ye have no reward of your Father which 2 is in heaven. Therefore ⁿ when thou doest *thine* alms, do not sound a trumpet before thee, as the hypocrites do in the synagogues and in the streets,

ʰ Ge. 17. 1; Le. 11. 44; Lk. 6. 36; 2 Cor. 7. 1; 13. 9, 11; Phil. 3. 12-15; Col. 1. 28; 4. 12; Jam. 1. 4; 1 Pet. 1. 15, 16.
ⁱ Eph. 5. 1.

---

done not to be seen of men, but from a true regard to God. Thus he passes from doctrine to practice, and from action to motive, and shows in this respect the hypocrisy and the formality of the scribes and Pharisees.

1. **Take heed that ye do not your alms.** Your righteousness. The best Greek manuscripts have instead of *alms*, *righteousness;* the latter is considered the true text by the best critics. This verse is thus a general introduction to what follows, a general precept as to righteousness, right doing, or conformity to the will of God, with special reference here to religious duties, good deeds. Take heed, be careful not to do your religious duties, your good deeds, in the sight of men. For this phraseology in other places, see Ps. 106 : 3; Isa. 58 : 2; 1 John 2 : 29; 3 : 7; 3 : 10. The word righteousness is also a connecting link with ver. 20 of the preceding chapter. Jesus had already shown how the righteousness of his disciples should exceed that of the scribes and Pharisees in regard to doctrine and a spiritual observance of the law, and now he is about to show how it is to exceed in regard to practical piety and right motives. He notices three manifestations of this practical righteousness: alms-giving, prayer, and fasting; and warns them against ostentation in their performance. They were to let their light shine (ch. 5 : 16), but not to make a vain display of their good deeds, not to do them **before men, to be seen of them,** as a show to be gazed at. All our duties are to be performed to God, not to men, 1 Cor. 10 : 31. This is the very opposite of all formal and false religions. Mrs. Judson, giving some account of the first Burman convert, says, "A few days ago I was reading with him Christ's Sermon on the Mount. He was deeply impressed and unusually solemn. 'These words,' said he, 'take hold on my very heart; they make me tremble. Here God commands us to do every thing that is good in secret, not to be seen of men. How unlike our religion is this! When Burmans make offerings at the pagodas, they make a great noise with drums and musical instruments, that others may see how good they are. But this religion makes the mind fear God; it makes it of its own accord fear sin.'"

No reward of your Father. You may receive the applause of men, but you can not receive the approbation and favor of God. God will not bless those who rob him of that which is his due.

2-4. First example. In regard to giving alms.

2. **When thou doest thine alms.** Thine acts of mercy toward the poor, in relieving want; acts of charity. The change from *ye* in the preceding verse to *thou* in this is worthy of notice, indicating that each one should engage in this work individually and personally. Our Lord presupposes that his disciples would give alms, and therefore he simply gives direction as to the manner of doing it. The Jew gave one tenth of his income; the Christian, with his greater blessings and privileges, should not fall behind him.

Do not sound a trumpet. A figurative expression, meaning *to make a great display, to attract attention.* Some suppose that the Pharisees gathered the poor together by sounding a trumpet, but there is no evidence of such a practice. Others seek an explanation in the modern custom of beggars in the east, who blow a trumpet before him from whom they ask alms; but there is no evidence of such a custom existing among the Jews of our Savior's day. And others think there is an allusion to the trumpet-shaped money-boxes, and to the ringing of the coin as it fell into them; but this is both far-fetched and unnatural. The language of our Lord here is evidently figurative, representing a boastful and ostentatious display. **Hypocrites.** They who, like stage actors, assume characters that do not belong to them—dissemblers, false

that they may have glory of men. Verily I say
3 unto you, They have their reward. But when thou
doest alms, let not thy left hand know what thy
4 right hand doeth: that thine alms may be in secret:
and thy Father ⁰which seeth in secret himself
ᵖ shall reward thee openly.
5 And when thou prayest, thou shalt not be ᵈ as the
hypocrites *are:* for they love to pray standing in
the synagogues and in the corners of the streets,

ᵏ Ps. 112. 9; Dan. 4. 27; 2 Cor. 9. 9, 10.
ˡ ch. 23. 5, 28; John 12. 43.
ᵐ ch. 10. 41, 42.
ⁿ Ro. 12. 8.

ᵒ Jer. 17. 10.
ᵖ 1 Sam. 2. 30; Lk. 8. 17; 14. 14.
ᵠ Job 27. 8–10; Is. 1. 10–15.

---

pretenders. The scribes and Pharisees were of this class, ch. 5 : 20 ; 23 : 13–15. **In the synagogue.** Where alms were deposited at their religious gatherings. See ch. 4 : 23. **In the streets**, where gifts might be bestowed upon beggars. Thus, they sought the public religious assemblies and the crowded thoroughfares (Acts 9 : 11) for the display of their charities, in order that they **might have glory**, be flattered in public, applauded **of men. They have their reward.** More correctly, *they have in full their reward.* They seek the applause of men, and they already have it; their reward is in full, complete; and they will get no more, Luke 16: 25.

3. Let not thy left hand know. This seems to be a proverbial expression implying privacy, and especially such an absence of ostentation that even one member of the body should not know what another did. Be modest, quiet, and noiseless in doing alms, and make no effort to have them known abroad. "For if it be possible to be thyself unaware, let it be your desire to escape the notice, if you can, of even the hands that give."—CHRYSOSTOM. The spirit of this injunction can be carried out even in those cases where it may be necessary to give alms in public, to excite others. The contrast here between the Pharisaic and the Christian mode of giving alms is brought out not only by this proverbial expression, but also by the pronoun at the beginning of the verse, which is emphatic in the original, **But when** THOU **doest alms.**

4. That thine alms. Implying more than a mere result, a purpose, an aim at privacy, an avoidance of notoriety. **In secret.** Literally, *in the secret place*, where you will not be seen of others. **Thy Father.** Despagne observes that to say in the singular "MY *Father*"

belongs only to the Only Begotten; but "THY *Father*" is said to the faithful also; *Father*, or OUR *Father*, by the faithful. See ver. 9; John 20 : 17. **Seeth in secret.** As well as in public; in the darkness as well as in the light, Ps. 139 : 12. **Shall reward thee.** *Himself* and *openly* (also in vers. 6 and 18) are omitted by most of the latest critics, on the testimony of the oldest manuscripts and other ancient authorities. The reward is thus not limited to any time or way. God will reward as he sees best, both in this world and in the next. A good man will generally be known as such, without any effort of his own to make it known. The reward, too, will be received in his own soul at the time of performing the duty; and especially at the final judgment, ch. 25 : 34–40; Luke 14 : 14; 1 Tim. 5 : 25. Not even a cup of cold water given in the right spirit will lose its reward.

5–13. Second example. In regard to prayer.

5. They who pray to be **seen of men** are evidently **hypocrites;** for prayer is from its very nature addressed not to men, but to God. Jesus assumes that his disciples would pray. **When thou prayest;** rather, *When ye pray*. Prayer is the Christian's vital breath. **Standing.** The usual posture of the Jews in prayer (1 Sam. 1 : 26; 1 Kings 8 : 22; Luke 18 : 11), as also of the Mohammedans of the present day. Our Lord does not condemn the posture, but the ostentation, and the love of it, which showed a depraved heart. The publican prayed standing (Luke 18 : 13), and this posture was frequent among early Christians as well as kneeling, Mark 11 : 25; Acts 9 : 40; 20 : 36; 21 : 5. The **synagogues** were proper places of devotion, but were used by the hypocrites for displaying their for-

that they may be seen of men. Verily, I say unto
6 you, They have tl ir reward. But thou, when thou
prayest, ᵣ enter into thy closet, and when thou hast
shut thy door, pray to thy Father which is in
secret; and thy Father which seeth in secret shall
reward thee openly.
7 But when ye pray, ˢ use not vain repetitions, as
the heathen *do:* ᵗ for they think that they shall be

ʳ ch. 14. 23; Ge.
32. 24; 2 Ki. 4.
33; Ac. 10. 9.

ˢ Ecc. 5. 2.
ᵗ 1 Ki. 18. 26, 29;
Ac. 19. 34.

mal worship. The **corner of the streets,** the widest and most frequented thoroughfares, were finely adapted for a vain display, but most unsuited for devotion. The Jews observed stated hours of prayer. The Scriptures mention three: the *third hour,* answering to our nine o'clock, when the morning sacrifice was offered; the *sixth hour,* at which Peter prayed on the house-top, Acts 10 : 9; and the *ninth hour,* at which time Peter and John went up to the temple, Acts 3 : 1. Compare Ps. 55 : 17, and Dan. 6 : 10. The hypocrites probably took care to be in the synagogues or on the corners of the streets at the hours of prayer, so as to perform their devotions in the most public manner. Thus they appeared to men to pray; but it was only prayer in name, not in reality. **Their reward** is received in full in the praise of men. See ver. 2.

6. **When thou prayest.** As an individual; a change here to the singular from the plural *ye,* of the last verse. **Enter into thy closet.** The Greek word translated closet means literally a *store-room,* and hence a place of privacy. The Jews had their place of retirement, an upper room, where they could pray with the utmost secrecy. This was called the *upper chamber* (ὑπερῷον), Acts 1 : 13; 9 : 37; 20 : 8. A word of more general application is here used, which may include not only the upper chamber of the Jew, but also any retired room or place. Every Christian should have his closet. The desire and love for prayer will prepare the way for selecting a closet, even under the most disadvantageous circumstances. Jesus arose a great while before day, and went into a solitary place and prayed. **Shut thy door.** This is expressive of the strictest privacy, in opposition to the ostentation of the Pharisees. The discourse is not aimed against social or public prayer, but against display in prayer. While our Lord is doubtless treating especially of private prayer, which should not be performed in public places, yet the manner and spirit which he enjoins should be carried into all kinds of prayer. "The *heart* is the closet into which we should *retire* and shut the door, even in public prayer."—QUESNEL. Ps. 4 : 5. **Thy Father, who** both **is, and seeth in secret, shall reward thee.** Both here and hereafter. See ver. 4; Acts 10 : 4; Luke 12 : 2. Thus our Savior teaches that prayer should be performed to God, not to men.

7. **When ye pray.** Mark the change to the plural. The best explanation of this, as well as of the plural form throughout the Lord's Prayer, is that Jesus now proceeds to speak of prayer in general, whether private, family, social, or public. He warns against heathenish abuses. **Vain repetitions.** The word in the original occurs only here in the New Testament, and has been thought by many to be derived from Battus, a Cyrenian king and stammerer, or from a poet of that name, whose poems were full of repetitions. More likely it was formed from the imitation of the natural sound in stammering and babbling. It means using many words and empty repetitions. Two remarkable examples of this heathen practice are found in Scripture; that of the priests of Baal in Elijah's day, who "called on the name of Baal from morning even until noon, saying, O Baal, hear us" (1 Kings 18: 26); and that of the worshipers of Diana at Ephesus in Paul's day, who for the space of two hours cried out with one voice, "Great is Diana of the Ephesians," Acts 19 : 34. The repeating of the same petition many times is still common in the East, both among Mohammedans and nominal Christians. They did this because they thought they would be **heard for**

MATTHEW VI.

8 heard for their much speaking. Be not ye therefore like unto them: for ᵘ your Father knoweth what things ye have need of, before ye ask him.
9 After this manner therefore pray ye: ˣ Our Father
10 which art in heaven, Hallowed be thy name. Thy

ᵘ Ps. 69. 17-19.

ˣ Lk. 11. 2-4.

their much speaking. Deep and intense feelings may lead to repetition, or to spending whole nights in prayer, Matt. 26 : 44; Luke 6 : 12; 2 Cor. 12 : 8. In such cases there are no *vain* repetitions, no *dependence* on much speaking or the length of the prayer; but the earnest wrestling of the soul which prevails, saying, "I will not let thee go, except thou bless me," Gen. 32 : 26. The Jews needed the caution of our Savior, Mark 12 : 40. The Jewish rabbins had a maxim that "every one that multiplies prayer is heard, and that the prayer which is long shall not return empty." Christ's disciples also, in every age, need the caution. One of the most common errors of a corrupt Christianity has been that which our Lord here condemns.

8. Further reasons for avoiding vain repetitions in prayer. The practice rests on ignorance and superstition. It is heathenish. It becomes not the Christian to be **like** the ignorant and superstitious worshiper of false gods. God also **knoweth what things ye have need of before ye ask him.** Prayer is not to instruct nor to inform God; it is to worship him. If God needs not to be informed of our wants, much less does he need a vain repetition of them.

9. In contrast to ostentatious and unmeaning prayers, our Lord gives one which is a model for simplicity, conciseness, and fullness of meaning. This has long been styled by way of eminence, THE LORD'S PRAYER. **After this manner, therefore, pray ye.** Thus pray ye; after this model; not as a form to be adhered to strictly, but as one which may be used, and which will serve as a specimen of acceptable prayer. That our Lord did not give this as a form of prayer to be strictly and of necessity used by his followers appears: 1st, He nowhere intimates any such purpose; 2d, The one in Luke is an equally authoritative form, yet with important variations from the one here given (see Luke 11 : 2-4); 3d, We do not find an instance where Jesus used this prayer or any other as a form; 4th, John 16 : 23, 24 is against the supposition; 5th, In none of the recorded prayers of the apostles do we find a single repetition of this prayer; 6th, We find no trace of its use among the primitive churches. Tholuck remarks, "It does not occur in the Acts, nor in any writer before the third century."

There is no good ground for saying, with some, that our Lord took most of this prayer from Jewish forms. Doubtless it embodied petitions, in essence, of saints in previous ages; yet Jesus needed not to select from these, but could draw from the richness of himself, in whom were all the treasures of wisdom and knowledge.

The Lord's Prayer is commonly arranged into three parts, the *introduction*, the *petitions*, and the *conclusion*. The petitions, consisting of six in number, may be divided into two classes of three each, the first class relating to God, his name, his kingdom, his will; the second to ourselves, our daily want and dependence on the Divine bounty, our sins and need of pardon, our dangers and need of protection. The use of the *plural* teaches us to pray for others as well as for ourselves. It is a striking feature of this model prayer that it begins with God's glory, and then passes to the wants and necessities of the suppliant himself. The latter should ever be subordinate to the former.

Our Father. As Creator (Mal. 2 : 10; Isa. 64 : 8); as Preserver (Ps. 145 : 16); by adoption, Rom. 8 : 15; Eph. 1 : 5. He is the Father of the whole race (Acts 17 : 26), and especially of all his spiritual children, Isa. 63 : 16. This relation between God and his people, though recognized in the Old Testament, is more fully revealed in the New, Rom. 8 : 17. Whoever truly utters this prayer acknowledges these great truths. **Who art in heaven.** Literally, *in the heavens*, a *Hebraistic* usage of this word, frequent in the New Testament, meaning simply *heaven*. In contrast to

kingdom come. Thy will be done, in earth as *it is*
11 in heaven. Give us this day our daily bread. And forgive us our debts, as we forgive our debtors.

frail earthly parents, God is our Father in heaven, which is the throne of his glory (Isa. 66 : 1) and the portion of his children, 1 Pet. 1 : 3–5. Though God is everywhere, he is more immediately present in heaven, Acts 7 : 55, 56. Where this is, we know not. Astronomers suppose a centre of the vast system of worlds, and that centre may be the capital of the universe, "the third heaven," where God dwells. **Hallowed be thy name.** Sanctified, revered, held sacred thy name; in the thoughts of our hearts (1 Pet. 3 : 15), by the words of our lips, and by the works of our hands; everywhere and by all, 1 Cor. 10 : 31. By name is meant not merely the appellation by which God is known, *Jehovah*, but also his *Being* which his name represents, as revealed in his word. Let thy whole Being, thy revealed perfections, be held in holy reverence.

10. Closely connected with the last petition are the two that follow. In the answer of them, the name of God is hallowed. **Thy kingdom come.** The *reign* of God, the *administration* or *kingdom* of the Messiah. See ch. 3 : 2. This petition embraces the full accomplishment of the kingdom of God, which has its seat in the heart, and also all the events which are necessary to this glorious result. The kingdom of grace here and of glory hereafter, in all the successive steps till God will be all in all, 1 Cor. 15 : 28. The meaning of this petition varies, therefore, according to the state and progress of Christ's kingdom.

Thy will be done. *Will* here means that which is willed; purposes, commands. Let thy purposes be accomplished, and thy commands be obeyed. Then will God's name be everywhere hallowed, and the Messiah's kingdom will fully come in the hearts and lives of men.

In earth as it is in heaven. Literally, *As in heaven, so also on the earth.* As submissively, as cheerfully, as fully, and as universally. As it is done by angels, so may it be done by men. Thus are we taught to pray, and consequently to expect and to labor, for the extension of Christ's kingdom over the whole world. In harmony with this is the last commission, ch. 28 : 19, 20; and hence the missionary enterprises for preaching the Gospel to the heathen, and to the spiritually destitute everywhere. Every Christian in some sense should be a missionary.

11. **Our daily bread.** The food, sustenance required for **this day.** The meaning is not materially different if we translate, with some, "Give us this day our *needful* bread." But the translations of some others, "Give us to-day the *bread of to-morrow*," or "*our future bread*," are founded on very doubtful philological grounds, inconsistent with our Savior's exhortation in ver. 34, and unsuited to the petition itself. It should be noted that *this day* can not here mean *day by day*. The Lord gave daily manna to the Israelites, Ex. 16 : 4, 21. Compare Agur's prayer, "Feed me with food convenient (sufficient) for me," Prov. 30 : 8, 9. *Bread* here refers primarily to nourishment for the body; yet as we are made up of body and soul we should not restrict it to material food, but extend it also to the bread of eternal life (John 6 : 34), to heavenly and spiritual nourishment. Compare Dr. Conant's able note on this verse, *Ma'thew, etc.*, p. 30.

12. **Debts.** According to an Aramæan conception (the Aramæan was the vernacular language of Jews in our Savior's day), *sin* is here represented as a *debt.* The supreme love and service of our hearts belong rightfully to God. So far as we come short of this are we debtors to God, and guilty of a breach of moral obligation. Divine justice has claims upon us, and we are exposed to the penalty, which we must bear unless satisfaction is made to God, either by discharging the obligation and repairing the wrong done, or by an atonement which is acceptable to him as an infinitely just and holy Being. As the latter is the only way in which our sins can be forgiven, and as Christ has provided this way by the sacrifice of himself and his perfect righteousness, therefore only the believer in Jesus can truly offer the prayer, *Forgive us our debts.* As

13 And lead us not into temptation, but deliver us from evil. ʸ For thine is the kingdom, and the power, and the glory, forever. ˣ Amen. ᵃ For if

ʸ 1 Chr. 29. 11, 12.
ᶻ Ps. 41. 13; Deut. 27. 16.

we forgive our debtors. In like manner as we forgive those who fail to meet their moral obligations to us. It is the duty of every one to love his neighbor as himself. In so far as he fails of this he is a debtor, a delinquent. Thus are we taught to ask that God would bestow forgiveness upon us in like manner as we exercise the spirit of forgiveness toward others. If we are unforgiving, what is the petition but asking God to withhold forgiveness from us; but if we find a readiness within ourselves to forgive the faults and shortcomings of others, then may we feel the assurance that God for Christ's sake will also forgive us.

13. The sixth petition. **Temptation** means originally *trial*, and is particularly applied to moral trial, or to the test of a person's character or faith (1 Pet. 4 : 12), and in a stronger sense to the trial of one's virtue, a direct solicitation to sin, Luke 4 : 13; 1 Tim. 6 : 9. In the latter sense, God is said to tempt no man (James 1 : 13), yet he may be said to *do* that which he *permits* (compare 2 Sam. 24 : 1 and 1 Chron. 21 : 1); but in the former senses he does tempt or prove men, and especially his children, Gen. 22 : 1; Ex. 15 : 25; Deut. 13 : 3. *Temptation* here means those trials which may lead to the commission of sin; and hence the prayer, **Lead us not;** permit not Satan (Job 1 : 12; 2 : 6) nor others to do it, but so arrange circumstances as not to involve us in such peril. As all affairs of life are under God's control, so he may be said to *bring into temptation;* that is, so to order events that we may be liable and in great danger of sinning, without compelling us to do so. But whatever the temptations God in his Providence may bring upon us, he will give a way of escape, 1 Cor. 10 : 13. This prayer, like all others, is to be offered in submission to the will of God, Matt. 26 : 39.

But deliver us from evil. This with the preceding words form two sides of one petition, one in contrast to the other, and both making it complete. The general idea may be thus expressed, "Lead us not into temptation which exposes us to sin, but deliver us from evil altogether." *Evil* is the abstract noun, and should not be limited to "the evil one," as it includes whatever is morally evil, in every form. The petition looks forward to a complete deliverance from sin and all its consequences. Compare Rom. 8 : 23.

But the Revised and the Improved versions, render, *the evil one*, putting *the evil*, as the alternative reading, in the margin. The word thus translated is not the usual appellation of Satan in the New Testament, the only undoubted example in the Gospels being in Matt. 13 : 19; nor is it applied to him in the Septuagint version of the Old Testament. The Greek Fathers, however, unanimously prefer "the evil one." Their historical and exegetical trustworthiness may be questioned. But let us turn to the whole petition. The first clause, "Bring us not into temptation," naturally suggests not Satan merely, but all exposures to sin. What follows, "but deliver us from evil," is not a separate petition, but is antithetical, and further unfolds the petition itself, referring to evil in general, including the evil one. I prefer therefore to retain "evil" in the text, and place "evil one" in the margin. See Appendix at end of volume. The doxology, **For thine,** etc., is omitted by the best critical authorities. Probably inserted from the ecclesiastical liturgies about the fourth century. Some trace it to 1 Chron. 29 : 11, while others find the germ, as they suppose, in 2 Tim. 4 : 18.

14, 15. A reason for the restriction in ver. 12. The forgiveness of injuries is necessary to the acceptance of our prayers. If we desire forgiveness from God, against whom we are so great sinners, it becomes us to exercise it toward our fellow-men, whose offenses against us are comparatively trifling. If they seek mercy in vain from us, how shall we obtain it from God? ch. 18 : 23–35. The spirit of forgiveness is essential to acceptable prayer, and is an evidence of forgiven sin. It is no arbitrary condition, but so inseparable from right feeling that God conducts himself toward us ac-

ye forgive men their trespasses, your heavenly
15 Father will also forgive you: but ᵇ if ye forgive not men their trespasses, neither will your Father forgive your trespasses.
16 Moreover ᶜ when ye fast, be not, as the hypocrites, of a sad countenance: for they disfigure their faces, that they may appear unto men to fast. Verily, I
17 say unto you, They have their reward. But thou, when thou fastest, ᵈ anoint thine head, and wash thy
18 face; that thou appear not unto men to fast, ᵉ but unto thy Father which is in secret: and thy Father, which seeth in secret, shall reward thee openly.

ᵃ ch. 7. 2; Mk. 11. 25, 26; Eph. 4. 32.
ᵇ ch. 18. 35.
ᶜ Is. 58. 3–5.
ᵈ Ru. 3. 3; Dan. 10. 2, 3.
ᵉ Zec. 7. 3–6; Col. 3. 23.

---

cording to the spirit we cherish, Ps. 18: 25, 26. Judgment without mercy is for him who shows no mercy.

Trespasses. The figure is here changed from that of *debt* (ver. 12) to that of a *lapse, fall,* or *false step*. Sin may be considered either as debt due to God, or as a fall from the straight line of moral rectitude.

16–18. Third example. In regard to fasting.

16. Jesus opposes the formal fasting of the hypocrites, and exhorts his disciples to seek the reality instead of mere appearance. He takes it for granted that his disciples would fast, **when ye fast.** He refers especially to private fasting; notice, in this connection, the change from plural to singular in the next verse, "But *thou* when *thou* fastest." The Pharisees fasted twice in the week (Luke 18: 12), presenting in public a sad, worn, negligent countenance and dress, in order that they might be regarded as persons of superior holiness. See on ch. 9: 14.

Sad countenance. A sour, sullen, morose appearance. To assume expressions of sorrow for the purpose of show is hypocrisy; but a solemn expression of countenance is becoming solemn and serious feelings. What he means by "sad countenance" is further explained by what follows: **for they disfigure their faces,** by putting ashes on their faces, neglecting the ordinary washing and anointing, and the dressing of the hair and beard. Compare Dan. 10: 3; Jon. 3: 5, 6. All this they did for ostentation, that they might **appear unto men to fast.** There is a *contrast* in the original between *disfigure* and *appear*, the two verbs being derived from the same root, "They make their faces *unseemable* that they may be *seen* by men to fast." For this they receive the applause of men, and thus gain their object, and obtain in full **their reward.** See ver. 2.

17. **Anoint thy head and wash thy face.** This can not mean any such anointing and preparation, or any such cheerfulness and gayety as was customary before going to a feast, for that would be deception; but rather that they should dress and appear as usual. Anointing the head was common among the Jews, and neglecting to do it was an indication of sorrow, 2 Sam. 12: 20. In the warm climate of the east it was thought to give softness and brilliancy to the skin, and to be conducive to health. Thus they were not to **appear unto men to fast.** It was to be performed unto God. To do thus quietly and unobtrusively is no deception, but a recognition of the spiritual nature of God, and of the fact that true worship has its seat in the heart. The same principle should be applied to public fasting. There should be no ostentation; it should be done as much to God as if no eye but his saw it. Then will it be accepted and rewarded.

19–34. JESUS WARNS HIS DISCIPLES AGAINST WORLDLINESS, AND EXHORTS THEM TO AN ENTIRE CONSECRATION TO GOD. The connection is natural. Religious display and worldly-mindedness, setting the mind on the world and its treasures, commonly go together. Such was the case with the Pharisees. It was also natural to pass from the idea that our good works should be done only to God, and not to man, to the more

19 ᶠLay not up for yourselves treasures upon earth, where ᵍmoth and rust doth corrupt, and where
20 ʰthieves break through and steal; ⁱbut lay up for yourselves treasures in heaven, where neither moth nor rust doth corrupt, and where thieves do not
21 break through nor steal: ᵏfor where your treasure
22 is, there will your heart be also. ˡThe light of the body is the eye: if therefore thine eye be single,
23 thy whole body shall be full of light. But if thine

ᶠ Pro. 23. 4; Is. 55. 2; John 6. 27; 1 Tim. 6. 17-19.
ᵍ Job 13. 28; Jam. 5. 1-3.
ʰ Hos. 7. 1; Joel 2. 9.
ⁱ Lk. 12. 33, 34; 18. 22; 1 Pet. 1. 4.
ᵏ ch. 12. 34, 35; Col. 3. 1-3.
ˡ Lk. 11. 34, 36.

general idea that all our aims should be heavenly and our consecration to God entire. He enforces this duty: 1st, by an analogy derived from human sight, vers. 22, 23; 2d, by another analogy from a servant and his master, ver. 24; 3d, God, who has given life, will give what is necessary to support it, ver. 25; 4th, and if he feeds the birds and clothes the flowers, much more will he care for his children, vers. 26-30; 5th, undue anxiety is heathenish, and dishonoring to God, ver. 32; 6th, God will take care of those in the future who exercise toward him singleness of affection and a humble faith, vers. 33, 34.

19. Lay not up treasures upon earth. Let not this be your aim and purpose in life. Make not your supreme good of the things that are earthly, dependent on this life and ending with it. Treasures mean not merely precious metals, but *stores* of all kinds. **Moth.** An insect that breeds in neglected clothes, eating their substance and destroying their texture, Isa. 50 : 9; 51 : 8. In the east, where fashions seldom changed, clothes were laid up in large quantities, and formed a considerable portion of a person's wealth, Gen. 45 : 22; 2 Kings 5 : 5, 22. Hence their treasures were in danger of moths. **Rust.** The word in the original has the idea of eating, and means corrosion, the wear and tear which eats into and consumes all earthly treasures. **Doth corrupt.** Consume. **Break through.** More literally, *dig through*, an allusion to thieves digging through the mud, clay, or sun-dried brick walls of which eastern houses were commonly built. Compare Job 24 : 16. The perishable nature of earthly possessions, and our feeble hold upon them, are thus strikingly exhibited, and hence the folly of making them our dependence and chief good.

20. Treasures in heaven. Let your highest aims and your chief good be in heaven. Be "rich toward God" (Luke 12 : 21); live by faith in the enjoyment of the divine favor, and in a living hope of an eternal inheritance (1 Pet. 1 : 4); rich in good works, and laying up for yourselves a good foundation against the time to come, 1 Tim. 6 : 18, 19. The contrast is between the perishable treasures *on earth*, and the imperishable ones *in heaven*. Seek the latter; for, though the enjoyment of them begins on earth, they are beyond this world and this life, and are not subject to change or decay.

21. Where your treasure is. The treasure and the heart must go together. Here is another reason showing that our chief good should be in God. What we value we love. Our hearts will be fixed supremely on our highest good. If our treasure, then, is in this world, our affections are fixed upon it; we have nothing in the future world to engage our love. At death we must leave the decaying treasures of earth, and our hearts be comfortless. But not so if our treasure is in heaven. It is not only imperishable, but the soul enjoys foretastes here, and enters upon its full enjoyment hereafter. The heart and its treasure will be brought together in heaven.

22. Jesus enforces this singleness of affection toward God by a popular illustration of the eye. **The light** (rather *the lamp*) **of the body is the eye.** The light is not the eye itself; but, receiving the light, the eye lightens and guides the body. So the moral sense of the soul receives light from above, for the enlightenment and guidance of the soul, Eph. 1 : 18. **Single.** An eye that does not *see double;* that has a single, distinct, *clear* vision. Then, as a consequence of this singleness of vision, the eye fully performing its office, **thy whole body shall be full of light,**

eye be ᵐ evil, thy whole body shall be full of darkness. If therefore the light that is in thee be darkness, how great is that darkness!

24 ⁿ No man can serve two masters: for either he will hate the one, and love the other; or else he will hold to the one, and despise the other. ᵒ Ye can not serve God and mammon.

25 Therefore I say unto you, ᵖ Take no thought for your life, what ye shall eat, or what ye shall drink; nor yet for your body, what ye shall put on. ᵠ Is

ᵐ Pro. 28. 22; Mk. 7. 22.
ⁿ Lk. 16. 13; Ro. 6. 16-23.
ᵒ Jos. 24. 15; 1 Sam. 7. 3; 1 Ki. 18. 21; Gal. 1. 10; 1 John 2. 15, 16.
ᵖ Ps. 55. 22; Heb. 13. 5, 6.
ᵠ Ro. 8. 32.

23. **Thine eye be evil.** A bad eye; one that is not clear, distinct, single in its vision, but double, confused, and dim. **Full of darkness.** This gives a wrong idea of the original. The true translation is, *Thy whole body shall be dark;* not totally dark, but obscured and dimmed by want of singleness and clearness of the eye. **If therefore the light,** etc. The application of the illustration. If that within thee, which ought to enlighten, is dark and obscured by a bad and confused vision, if the inner eye thus gives not only dim and indistinct but false impressions, how great and terrible the darkness! "The real peril lies in the eye seeing falsely or double, because in that case the light of the sun will only serve to blind, which is worse than utter darkness. The same holds true of the inner eye, when it converts the light of revelation into a blinding and a misleading light."—LANGE. If the eye of thy soul be double and confused in its vision, so that you prefer earthly treasures to the heavenly, or so that you attempt to have your treasure on the earth and also in heaven, which is, indeed, impossible (James 4 : 4), how **great is the darkness;** for you see nothing clearly, and you are deceived by what you do see, Prov. 4 : 19. Let your heart and your treasure, therefore, be together, not on earth, but in heaven.

24. A singleness of affection toward God, and an entire consecration to him, is further enforced by an illustration drawn from domestic life. **No man can serve two masters.** Be wholly devoted to them. His affections and interests would be divided. The reference is to the continued obedience of a bond-servant, and to that true service which presupposes love and attachment. The masters also are supposed to have opposite interests. Hence either he would hate the one and love the other, or he would cleave to the one and despise the other. He would have really but one master; one only would receive his hearty service, while that of the other would be merely outward, with disdain or hatred. In application our Lord says directly and pointedly, **Ye can not serve God and Mammon.** Mammon is a Chaldee word, meaning originally *one's trust,* and hence *riches* as a ground of hope. Compare Mark 10 : 24. It does not appear to have been the name of a Syrian god, as some have supposed. Riches is here personified and treated as a master in opposition to God. No two masters can both receive single-hearted service, especially when they are so opposed as God and the world. How vain the attempt to seek your chief good both on earth and in heaven. Give up such folly, and seek it only in God. Make him thy master, and mammon thy servant.

25. **Therefore,** for this cause, for this reason, that you should be wholly devoted to God and his service, **I,** your teacher with authority, **say unto you** as my disciples, **take no thought,** *be not anxious,* be not concerned about **your life,** etc. Make not your physical and temporal wants the special and great objects of thought and care. The precept has special reference to a concern for the *future,* as is evident from ver. 34, "Take no thought therefore for the morrow." The practice of it should be coupled with prayer (ver. 11; Phil. 4 : 6), and with a faith in God that "all these things shall be added," ver. 33. Godliness, instead of involving the loss of food and raiment, has the promise of the life that now is as well as that which is to come, 1 Tim. 4 : 8. Diligence, industry, foresight, and the use of those

not the life more than meat, and the body than
26 raiment? ʳBehold the fowls of the air: for they
sow not, neither do they reap, nor gather into
barns; yet your heavenly Father feedeth them.
27 ˢAre ye not much better than they? ᵗWhich of
you by taking thought can add one cubit unto his
28 stature? And why take ye thought for raiment?
Consider the lilies of the field, how they grow;

ʳ Job 38. 41; Ps. 104. 11, 12; 147 9.
ˢ ch. 10. 31.
ᵗ ch. 5. 36.

means which God in his providence puts in our hands, are not condemned; but those questions and that concern which implies distrust and unbelief in our Heavenly Father. **Is not the life more than meat** (*food*)? The argument is from the greater to the less. He who gives us life will sustain it; He who made the body will clothe it and provide for it. The argument is the more pointed by being put into the form of a question : Is not life of greater importance than meat? Is not the body of more value than raiment?

26. Jesus proceeds and draws an argument from God's care for the inferior creation, first, in regard to food (vers. 26, 27), and second, in regard to raiment, vers. 28-30. Arguing from the less to the greater, he shows that he who cares for the birds and the flowers will most assuredly provide for his intelligent creatures, and especially his spiritual children. **Behold.** Look at with attention; consider. In the spring, birds are exceedingly numerous in Galilee; partridges, quails, larks, doves, and pigeons. **The fowls of the air.** The birds of heaven. **Barns.** Store-houses of any kind. Though the birds neither sow nor reap, yet they build their nests and seek their food. The exhortation of our Savior is not against labor and industry, but against an undue solicitude in regard to our future support. Notice, he says not *their*, but **your Heavenly Father**, which served to remind them of the relation God stood to them. The translation **yet** is incorrect; it should be **and**. **Better.** More valuable.

27. By a pointed question our Lord shows the weakness of men, and hence the importance of trusting God for food, after, like the birds of the air, doing their part. **Stature.** This word in the original means, primarily, *age*, and, secondarily, *stature*, and may be translated by either. If by the latter, then **the meaning is,** You are not able to add any thing to your height, or to promote your growth; God has charge of this, and regulates the size of your body without any purpose or direct agency of your own. Why then take thought and be concerned about your food, and thus distrust your Heavenly Father? It seems better, however, to translate **age**. It agrees better with the context : Jesus is speaking of life, and of food as necessary to sustain it. It is also an objection to the interpretation, *stature* of the body, that a cubit to one's height is a very great addition, whereas Luke (ch. 12 : 26), in a parallel passage, describes the addition as "that which is least." *Age*, as noticed above, is the primary meaning of the word, which is so translated in John 9 : 21, 23; and Heb. 11 : 11. To the objection that *cubit*, a standard of measure from the elbow to the tips of the fingers, usually reckoned a foot and a half, more or less, was a measure of *space* and not of *time*, it may be replied that terms of length are sometimes applied to time; as in Ps. 39 : 5, "Thou hast made my days as a handbreadth." We also speak of "an inch of time." The allusion here is doubtless to life as a journey or pilgrimage, of which a cubit would be a very insignificant addition. The meaning then is : Who, by taking thought, can make the smallest addition to his appointed pilgrimage on earth? Since, then, you can not do that which is the least, be not unduly solicitous about the rest, but trust your Heavenly Father, and devote yourselves wholly to him.

28. Jesus now passes from food to raiment. He might have drawn his illustration here also from the animal creation, but he descends to the vegetable, and by so doing presents his subject in a more striking light. **Consider.** Observe attentively. **Lilies.** Several varieties of this flower are found in Palestine, usually red, orange, and yellow. They grow wild in the fields,

MATTHEW VI. A.D. 28

29 they toil not, neither do they spin: and yet I say unto you, that "even Solomon in all his glory was
30 not arrayed like one of these. Wherefore if God so clothe the grass of the field, which to-day is, and to-morrow is cast into the oven, *shall he* not much
31 more *clothe* you, ˣ O ye of little faith? Therefore

" 1 Ki 10. 5–7, 23.

ˣ ch. 8. 26.

---

and are noted for their beauty and fragrance (Sol. Songs, 2 : 1, 16 ; 5 : 13 ; 6 : 2, 3). The *kind* of lily here intended has given rise to much speculation. Nothing is known about it; and it is quite unimportant. The *toiling* and *spinning* has reference to sowing, and the gathering of the flax, and the preparing it for clothing. This the lilies can not do; but God does that for them which they are unable to do themselves.

29. **Solomon in all his glory.** The external splendor of his reign (2 Chron. 9 : 15–28), and especially his royal state and dress, as he sat upon the throne of ivory, 1 Kings 10 : 18. **Like one of these.** Even any one of these is clothed in greater beauty and splendor than was Solomon, who was regarded by the Jews as the highest type of human glory. Thus the work of God in nature exceeds the art of man. God clothes the flowers better than it is possible for man to clothe himself. What confidence should this inspire in us toward our Heavenly Father.

30. **Grass.** Herbage generally. The wild flowers grow profusely in the fields of Palestine, and are cut down with the grass. **To-day—to-morrow.** Expresses their brief existence. Under a strong east wind the grass in Palestine withers in two days, and often a south wind causes the herbage to fade in a day. **Is cast into the oven.** Dried grass and the stalks of flowers were used for fuel. The Jews had a kind of earthen or iron oven, shaped like a large pitcher, open at the top, in which they made a fire. When it was well heated, they made a paste of mingled flour and water, and applied it to the outside, where it was quickly baked, and taken off in thin pieces. Ovens were also made by digging a cavity in the ground, and lining it with cement. A fire was built on the floor of this oven, and when the sides were sufficiently heated, thin cakes were stuck upon them and soon baked. "The scarcity of wood in Palestine is very great, especially in the southern part; so that the people are obliged to resort to the use of almost every thing that is capable of being burnt, in order to procure the means of warming their

AN OVEN.

houses in winter, and of preparing their daily food. They not only cut down, for this purpose, the shrubs and larger kinds of grass, but gather the withered grass itself, and the wild flowers, of which the fields display so rich a profusion."—Dr. HACKETT, *Illustration of Scripture*, p. 139.

Shall he not much more clothe you? The argument is from that of less to that of greater value. If your Heavenly Father so beautifies the vegetable kingdom, whose life is so brief, how much more will he provide sufficient covering for you, his servants and his children, since your life on earth is so much longer, and your nature and interests are so much higher and more glorious? **Ye of little faith.** Ye so prone to distrust God, and be careful for your daily food. Having little confidence in God.

31. The application of the argument from the two illustrations just given of God's care, over the birds of the air, and the lilies of the field. Be not, therefore, unduly solicitous about your food and raiment.

32. To be thus anxious is heathenish

ʸ take no thought, saying, ᶻ What shall we eat? or, What shall we drink? or, Wherewithal shall we
32 be clothed? ᵃ for after all these things do the Gentiles seek. For your heavenly Father ᵇ knoweth
33 that ye have need of all these things. But ᶜ seek ye first ᵈ the kingdom of God, and ᵉ his righteousness; ᶠ and all these things shall be added unto
34 you. ᵍ Take therefore no thought ʰ for the morrow: for the morrow shall take thought for the things of itself. Sufficient unto the day is the evil thereof.

ʸ Phil. 4. 6; 1 Pet. 5. 7.
ᶻ ch. 4. 4; Ps. 78. 18-24.
ᵃ Eph. 4. 17.
ᵇ Ps. 37. 18, 19.
ᶜ Ps. 37. 25; Mk. 10. 30.
ᵈ ch. 3. 2.
ᵉ Is. 45. 24; Ro. 3. 21, 22.
ᶠ Ps. 34. 9, 10; Ro. 8. 31, 32; 1 Cor. 3. 22.
ᵍ Ex. 16. 18-20.
ʰ Deut. 33. 25.

and dishonoring to God. **Gentiles.** All besides the Jews; the heathen nations. An essential feature of heathenism is living for the present. Ignorant of God's perfections, and of his paternal care, and of the privileges of his children, they naturally seek after earthly things. Here the Pharisaic Jew and the formal and worldly Christian unite with the heathen in their views and practices. But let it not be so with you, for ye are not ignorant of your Heavenly Father's goodness, infinite knowledge, and almighty power, who **knoweth that you have need of all these things.**

33. Having shown what we should not do, be unduly concerned about even the necessary things of life, he shows what we should do, **seek first the kingdom of God and his righteousness,** make it our one great object of pursuit; make all things subordinate to this; and thus, whether we eat or drink, or whatever we do, do all to the glory of God. This will be indeed laying up treasures in heaven, ver. 20. Seek the spiritual blessings of the Gospel, and that *righteousness,* that conformity to the Divine Will, which God requires, Micah 6: 5, 8. By thus seeking their highest good in God, and striving to do his will and promote his cause, they would receive those very things for which they were so prone to be anxious. **All these things shall be added to you.** All such things as you may need will God bestow. Wealth is not promised, but those things necessary for food and raiment. He who seeks first the kingdom of God, can cast all his care on God, and leave his worldly things, as well as all things, to the will of God. Compare 1 Kings 3: 9-13, where Solomon asks only for wisdom, and riches are added; and 1 Tim. 4: 8; 6: 8; Mark 10: 30.

34. Jesus, after the reasons just given for avoiding undue solicitude about the cares of this life, now repeats the exhortation with an additional reason. **For the morrow.** For the future. Anxiety for food and clothing has reference generally to the future. **The morrow shall take thought,** etc. The morrow will have sufficient cares of its own; do not, then, double the cares of to-day by adding those of the morrow. **Sufficient unto the day.** For the day, each as it comes. **The evil thereof.** Each day has enough care and perplexity; this is true of to-day, and it will be equally true of to-morrow. When it comes, then will be the time to attend to its duties and its sufferings.

REMARKS.

1. The character of religious action is determined by the feelings and motives. The works of the Christian are distinguished from those of the hypocrite in this, that the former are done with a desire to please and glorify God; but the latter for ostentation, and to gain the applause of men, ver. 1; Prov. 23: 7.

2. True Christian charity springs out of love to God and love to men. The former will lead us to exercise it as a service to him; the latter, as a pleasant work and duty we owe the needy; and both, to do it quietly and without display. The spirit of true charity is opposed to all display and self-glorying, vers. 2-4.

3. What need of examination in reference to all our good deeds, since our Father seeth in secret? ver. 4.

4. If our works are done to God and not to men, we shall receive the reward not of men but of God, vers. 4, 6, 18.

VII. JUDGE ¹ not, that ye be not judged.   ¹ Ro. 2. 1; 14. 3,

5. Secret prayer is the duty of every individual; *thou*, when *thou* prayest, enter into *thy* closet, ver. 6.

6. Since prayer is the offering up of our desires to God, it is a perversion to use it for a display, to be seen and heard of men, vers. 5, 6.

7. Since prayer is not intended to inform God, but to enable us to perform our duty as suppliants, our petitions should be simple, short, yet full of meaning. Earnest prayer is always direct and brief; and even when the soul presses its petition like Jacob, it loses not this characteristic in a vain repetition, vers. 7, 8.

8. True prayer is unselfish, extending to all of God's children and the race. It becomes us to say, *our* Father, ver. 9.

9. If we desire above all things the glory of God, the advancement of his cause, and the accomplishment of his will among men, deliverance from sin and temptation, if we feel our daily dependence on God for both temporal and spiritual supplies, and exercise a spirit of forgiveness, then our prayers are acceptable to God through Christ, and will be answered, vers. 9-15.

10. An unforgiving disposition is displeasing to God, and if continued in, will result in everlasting banishment from his presence, ver. 15.

11. A sad and morose countenance is no part of religion, but is often the cloak of hypocrisy, ver. 16; Isa. 58 : 5

12. Fasting, which is a mortification of self through the appetite, and a service we owe to God, is from its nature opposed to ostentation, and is therefore perverted as soon as it is done to be seen of men, ver. 16-18; Zech. 7 : 5, 6.

13. Earthly treasures, which are material and decaying, are unworthy and insufficient to constitute the chief good of our spiritual and immortal nature. Since this can be found only in God and heaven, the avaricious man is guilty of the greatest folly, and insults both God and his own soul, vers. 19, 20.

14. Whatever a man regards supremely is his treasure, his god, ver. 21.

15. If we would have the single eye, our spiritual sight must be enlightened by the Holy Spirit, and fixed on Christ by faith, ver. 22.

16. It is impossible to have two objects of supreme good at once, ver. 24.

17. If a man makes riches or any earthly object his treasure, then it takes the place of Jehovah, and becomes his god, and he becomes an idolater, ver. 24.

18. Formality in religion is not only hypocritical and ostentatious (1-18), avaricious and idolatrous (19-24), but unduly solicitous, distrustful, and unbelieving, ver. 25.

19. It is our duty and privilege as children of a heavenly Parent to depend on God for our daily supplies, ver. 30.

20. God's care over the animal and vegetable portions of creation should dispel all distrust from his children, vers. 26-30.

21. Spiritual ignorance, unbelief, and worldly anxiety go together, ver. 32.

22. The only way to have both earthly and heavenly treasures is to seek first the kingdom of God and his righteousness, ver. 33; Matt 19 : 29.

23. Every day has its cares of earth, and its help from heaven, ver. 34; Deut. 33 : 25.

CHAPTER VII.

1-12. JESUS WARNS HIS DISCIPLES AGAINST A CENSORIOUS SPIRIT, and treats of their conduct toward their fellowmen. The self-righteous spirit of the Pharisee blinded him to his own faults, and led him to judge others severely, Luke 18 : 9. He who does this must expect like treatment from others, and punishment from God, vers. 1, 2. In finding fault with others, when he himself is guilty of greater sins, is inconsistent, and a condemnation of himself, 3-5. Yet it becomes us to discriminate, and not treat the contemptuous opposer as we would the sincere inquirer and the believer, 6. In order to have grace to exercise this charity, to conduct ourselves wisely, and to be faithful to the truth, we should ask what we need of God, whose willingness to give, and whose paternal kindness illustrates and enforces our duty in carrying out the law of love to our fellow-men, 7-12.

1. **Judge not.** Judge not rashly, censoriously, unjustly, the conduct of others. This does not prohibit judicial and official judgments (1 Cor. 5 : 12), nor the mere formation of opinion (16, 20), which is more or less unavoidable, but those voluntary and rash judgments

2 ᵏ For with what judgment ye judge, ye shall be judged: ˡ and with what measure ye mete, it shall be
3 measured to you again. ᵐ And why beholdest thou the mote that is in thy brother's eye, ⁿ but considerest
4 not the beam that is in thine own eye? Or how wilt thou say to thy brother, Let me pull out the mote out of thine eye; ᵒ and, behold, a beam *is* in
5 thine own eye? Thou hypocrite, first cast out the beam out of thine own eye; and then shalt thou see clearly to cast out the mote out of thy brother's eye.

ᵏ 4. 10-13; 1 Cor. 4. 3-5; Jam. 4. 11, 12.
ˡ Ps. 18. 25, 26.
¹ Jer. 51. 24; Obad. 15; Lk. 6. 38.
ᵐ Lk. 6. 41, 42.
ⁿ 2 Chr. 28. 9, 10; John 8. 7-9.
ᵒ Ro. 2. 21.

which are the product of a censorious spirit. **"That ye be not judged."** By God. By avoiding censoriousness you will so far avoid condemnation. But by exercising an unkind spirit toward your neighbor, you will only increase the severity of the judgment of God, Luke 6: 37; John 8: 7; Rom. 14: 10-13. It is also true that they that judge others rashly are themselves judged in like manner by others.

2. The reason more fully stated. **With what judgment ye judge,** etc. You shall be treated as you treat others. The high and strict standard which you apply to your fellow-men shall be applied to yourselves. According to your conduct toward them, shall you receive at the hand of God the same **measure,** either directly or through the instrumentality of men. See Jud. 1: 6, 7; 2 Sam. 22: 26, 27; James 2: 13; Rev. 13: 10. We should be engaged in searching our own hearts rather than in censuring others.

3. The censorious are here addressed pointedly and personally, **Why beholdest thou?** It is common for persons of this spirit to censure those whose defects are by no means equal to their own. This is illustrated by the figure of the eye.

The mote, a *dry particle* of wood, a minute splinter, represents a small fault; **the beam,** a *joist,* a *rafter,* denotes a *large* one. Sin blinds men in regard to their own faults, and warps their judgment, and makes them censorious in regard to others. **Considerest.** Observe attentively, scrutinize. Instead of looking at, staring at the slight obstruction in thy brother's eye, thou oughtest to scrutinize diligently the large one in thine own. The illustration here is an ideal one, and the beam a hyperbolical expression, presenting in a strong light the difference between the faults of the two individuals. Somewhat similar phrases have been found in the writings of the rabbins, and in the classics. Compare Num. 33: 55; Josh. 23: 13. See also Rom. 2: 17, 19, 21.

4. **How wilt thou say.** The illustration is still further applied. With what consistency canst thou say, **Let me pull out,** literally, *cast out,* the mote from thine eye? **Behold.** An expression of surprise, introducing something strange and unexpected. Is it possible that one who has such an obstruction in his own eye should undertake to cast out a small speck from his brother's eye? "Our own sinfulness destroys the spiritual vision which alone can rightly judge sin in others." — THOLUCK.

5. **Hypocrite.** One who assumes to be what he is not. See ch. 6: 2. The censorious formalist shows himself a hypocrite, in that he indulges greater sins in himself than those which he dwells upon and condemns in others. Jesus rebukes him for his folly, and points out the right course to pursue. **First cast out the beam.** Sit first in judgment upon thyself. Direct thy attention first to the correction of thine own faults. Then shalt thou **see clearly,** the obstructions having been removed from thine eye, **to cast out the mote** from thy brother's. You will be able to judge rightly and assist him in the correction of his fault.

6. Jesus, however, would not have his disciples carry their kindness so far and withhold their judgments to such an extent as to become morally lax, and to fail to discriminate between the good and the bad, treating all alike, and thus exposing themselves and the truth unnecessarily to the scorn of the censorious, ma-

MATTHEW VII.   A.D. 28.

6   ᵖ Give not that which is holy unto the dogs,   ᵖ Pro. 9. 7, 8; 23.
    ᵍ neither cast ye your pearls before swine, ʳ lest they   9; Ac. 13. 45, 46.
    trample them under their feet, and turn again and   ᵍ Pro. 11. 22.
    rend you.   ʳ ch. 22. 5, 6.
7   ˢ Ask, and it shall be given you; seek, and ye   ˢ Lk. 11. 9-13; 23.
    shall find; knock, and it shall be opened unto you: 42, 43.
8   for every one that asketh receiveth; and he that

licious, and sensual. **Dogs—swine.** The *dog*, among the Jews, was despised and regarded as unclean (Isa. 66 : 3), and hence the name was used as a term of reproach and contempt (2 Kings 8 : 13), and, on account of their insolent and ravenous manner (1 Kings 14 : 11; Jer. 15 : 3), their name was applied to men of fierce and violent character, Job. 30 : 1; Ps. 22 : 16; Phil. 3 : 2. *Swine* were also regarded as unclean, and their flesh was forbidden as food to the Hebrews, Lev. 11 : 7. On account of their filthy habits, they represented those who were peculiarly low and degraded, 2 Pet. 2 : 22. Thus the dogs and the swine here represent the ferocious and sensual enemies of Christ and his cause.

Holy—pearls. That which is *holy* may refer first to the "holy flesh" of the sacrifices, of which no unclean person was to eat; and then to any thing made sacred by being appropriated to God's service, Lev. 22 : 6. The *pearl* is a silvery, or bluish-white, hard, smooth, shining piece of substance, usually roundish, found in a shell-fish of the oyster kind. They have, in all ages, been held as peculiarly valuable. Both in ancient and modern times strings of the largest pearls have been among the choicest ornaments of eastern monarchs. The pearl here represents what is the most valuable; it is a beautiful image of divine truth, which Christ has intrusted to his disciples. To give that which is holy to dogs, and pearls to swine, is to give the privileges and the truths of the Gospel to its malicious and sensual foes. The justness of this command would at once commend itself to the Jew from the impropriety of giving that which is holy to dogs, and pearls to swine; but Jesus adds an additional reason, **Lest they trample,** etc. Pearls bear a resemblance to peas and acorns, the food of swine. The swine, finding them not food, and being unable to appreciate their value, trample them with their feet, and, in fury and hunger, **turn and rend,** tear, wound, the giver. Some interpreters suppose that while the swine trample the pearls with their feet, the dogs turn and rend the donor; others suppose both to be meant, the distinction having been lost sight of in the last clause. It is more natural to refer it to the swine as above, and it is also in harmony with their voracious nature. The idea here is, Give not your instructions to the malicious and sensual foes of the Gospel, who would treat your messages with blasphemous contempt, lest they make it an occasion for merely exhibiting their ferocious hatred to the truth, and of injury to yourselves, Prov. 9 : 8; 23 : 9; Luke 10 : 10, 11; Acts 13 : 46.

7. To exercise a becoming kindness and charity toward our fellow-men, and at the same time to discriminate properly, so as not to expose ourselves and the truth needlessly to the scorn and contempt of the blasphemous and malicious opposers of the truth, needs grace and wisdom from above. Hence Jesus encourages them to pray. Such an exhortation was also appropriate, after forbidding all undue and unbelieving solicitude in regard to future food and raiment, ch. 6 : 25-34. **Ask, seek, knock.** This threefold repetition presents prayer under different aspects, and forms a climax. To *ask*, is making known our desires to God; to *seek*, is earnestly to implore; and to *knock*, is to persevere in our requests. These commands and promises must, of course, be restricted and explained by the conditions which are elsewhere put upon prayer. It should be made in the name of Christ (John 14 : 13, 14), in faith (Mark 11 : 24), and in accordance with the will of God (1 John 5 : 14).

8. The truth of the preceding verse is here repeated in still stronger terms, not as a promise to be fulfilled in the future, but as a present reality. **Every one that asketh receiveth.** Mark the change from the future tense in the

A.D. 28. MATTHEW VII. 101

seeketh findeth; and to him that knocketh it shall
9 be opened. Or what man is there of you, whom
10 if his son ask bread, will he give him a stone? Or
11 if he ask a fish, will he give him a serpent? If ye
then, being evil, know how to give good gifts unto
your children, how much more shall your Father
which is in heaven give good things to them that
ask him!
12 Therefore all things ᵗ whatsoever ye would that
men should do to you, do ye even so to them: for
ᵘ this is the Law and the Prophets.

ᵗ Lk. 6. 31; Gal. 5. 14.
ᵘ ch. 22. 39, 40; Eze. 18. 7, 8; Zec. 8. 16, 17; 1 Tim. 1. 5.

last verse to the present in this. Not only do they who ask receive in the future, but they actually receive it now. It is a fact in their present and constant experience. **Shall be opened.** The Vatican manuscript and other authorities make this also present, *is opened*. If, however, the future be retained, it then forms a promise that prayer, especially persevering prayer, will be answered. All who ask aright receive either what they ask, or else something better in its place, 2 Cor. 12: 7-9.

9, 10. That prayer will be answered is not only evident from actual experience, but also from the paternal character of God. This is shown by an analogy from the workings of parental affection in fallen man. The argument is from the less to the greater. If human love in the sinful earthly parent will lead him to do good rather than evil to his children, and grant their requests, much more will the pure and divine love of your Heavenly Father lead him to answer the prayers of his children, and bestow upon them good things. The argument is rendered the more forcible by being made interrogatory. **Or what man is there of you.** The meaning is, There is no man among you, however wicked he may be, who, if his son ask bread, would give him a stone, etc. **Bread.** Doubtless the round cake, or loaf, such as is now used in the east, and which bore some resemblance to a round, flat **stone.** Some kinds of **serpents** also resemble some kinds of **fish.** To a hungry child a stone would be useless, and a serpent poisonous. There is thus a gradation in the questions. The most hardened and depraved parent would not deceive his crying, hungry child with a stone, much less with a serpent, which would take his life. It is implied that, instead of practicing a cruel deception, he would endeavor to satisfy the cravings of his child.

11. **If ye then being evil.** Fallen, sinful, and hence selfish. **Know how.** Understand from actual experience how ye give good gifts to your children, **how much more,** indeed, infinitely more, will **your Father,** who is supremely good and merciful, give **good things,** all those things you need, and especially the Holy Spirit, which is the sum of all spiritual blessings (Luke 11 : 13), to those that ask him. If they received the Holy Spirit, then they would have that wisdom and love which would prevent them from exercising a censorious spirit, and also save them from exposing themselves and the truth needlessly to the scorn of depraved and blasphemous opposers, vers. 1-6.

12. Jesus uses the paternal kindness of our heavenly Father to enforce the love which we should ever exercise toward our fellow-men. Inasmuch as ye are infinitely more loved and well treated by your heavenly Parent than any child is by his earthly parent, therefore extend the exercise of your love not only to your children, but to all. Make him an example in your treatment of others, ch. 5 : 48. **Therefore,** introduces the inference from God's treatment of his children, and the conclusion of the first eleven verses of this chapter. **Whatsoever ye would,** etc. Make the case of others your own, and whatsoever ye ought to wish, as honest and righteous men, that they should do to you, do even so to them. **For this is the law and the prophets.** This is, indeed, a practical application of the law, to love our neighbor as ourselves. This is what is required in the Old Testament. Nothing short of this meets the requirement

13 ˣ ENTER ye in at the strait gate: for wide *is* the gate, and broad *is* the way, ʸ that leadeth to destruction, and ᶻ many there be which go in thereat:
14 because [*or*, how] ᵃ strait *is* the gate, and narrow *is* the way, which leadeth unto life, ᵇ and few there be that find it.
15 ᶜ Beware of false prophets, ᵈ which come to you

ˣ Pro. 9. 6; Eze. 18. 27-32; Lk. 13. 24, 25.
ʸ Phil. 3. 18, 19; 2 Thes. 1. 8, 9.
ᶻ Ex. 23. 2.
ᵃ ch. 16. 24, 25; John 15. 18-20; Ac. 14. 22.
ᵇ Lk. 12. 32.

of the law. Different writers have quoted similar sentiments from heathen and rabbinical authors; but while the latter have rather given the negative part of this command, Christ has given the positive. This may be seen by the following comparison of Christ's precept with three of the best examples found in ancient authors:

CONFUCIUS.
What you do not like, when done to yourself, do not do to others.

ISOCRATES.
Do not do to others that which would make you angry if done by others to you.

HILLEL.
Do not unto another what thou wouldst not have another do unto thee. This is the whole law: the rest is mere commentary.

CHRIST.
Therefore all things whatsoever ye would that men should do to you, do ye even so to them: for this is the law and the prophets.

This radical difference will at once be seen: Christ's precept alone commands us to do any thing. Not only are we to avoid doing to others what we in their situation would dislike, but we are to do to them whatever we would reasonably and righteously wish them to do to us. This truth, which was included in the law and prophets, and which was more or less clearly apprehended and expressed by moralists and inspired writers, received its greatest completeness, and its most perfect application, from our Savior; and, as containing the sum and substance of our duty to our fellow-men, may justly be styled the Golden Rule.

13-23. JESUS EXHORTS HIS DISCIPLES TO BE EARNEST IN THE WAY OF SALVATION, and warns them against false teachers, and against making a false profession. Such admonitions are appropriate in concluding such a discourse.

13. **Enter ye in at** (literally *through*) **the strait gate.** Some suppose the gate to be at the end of the way, the gate of heaven. It is more natural, however, to regard it as at the beginning of the journey. This is the order of the figure in both this and the following verse, *first* the *gate* and *then* the *way*. Gate is the entrance of a city or a large inclosure, just as a *door* is of a house or room. **Strait,** that is, *narrow*, the opposite of **wide. Destruction.** Loss, perdition, applicable to both temporal and eternal ruin. I am *destroyed* was a frequent Attic phrase, meaning, "I am undone, ruined." Compare Hos. 13: 9; *lost* in Luke 15: 24, 32. Those who pursue the broad way suffer both temporal and eternal loss. Jesus presents two objects before them, *destruction* and *life*. To the latter the gate is strait or narrow, hence difficult to enter, and the way narrow or contracted, and therefore hard to continue therein; to the former, the gate is wide and the way broad, hence easy to enter the one and walk the other. The figure represents, on the one hand, how difficult it is to begin and to continue heartily to serve God; and on the other, how easy to live a life of sin, requiring only to follow our own depraved inclinations. The difficulty of being saved, as well as the fact that multitudes are pressing on to destruction, are given as a reason of entering in through the strait gate, Luke 13: 24; Prov. 4: 27.

14. Further reason for pressing into the strait gate: not only the straitness of the gate and the narrowness of the way, but the small number that find it. Some of the oldest Greek manuscripts make this an exclamation, "How strait the gate!" The latest and best critical authorities, however, regard it as giving an additional reason, **because,** etc. **Narrow the way.** The word translated *narrow* means pressed together, compressed, contracted, and thus made narrow, and suggests the difficulties of

A.D. 28. MATTHEW VII. 103

in sheep's clothing, but inwardly they are ᵉ ravening
16 wolves. ᶠ Ye shall know them by their fruits. ᵍ Do
   men gather grapes of thorns, or figs of thistles?
17 Even so ʰ every good tree bringeth forth good fruit;
18 but a corrupt tree bringeth forth evil fruit. A good

ᵉ ch. 24. 4, 5, 11, 24; Deu. 13. 3;
ᶠ Jer. 23. 16; Ro. 16. 17, 18; 2 Pet. 2. 1-3.
ʰ Mic. 3. 5; Gal. 2. 4; 2 Tim. 3. 5-9.

the way. **Few that find it.** Notice he does not say, *few go in*, as in the preceding verse; but few *find* it. In speaking of the gates of cities, Dr. Thomson says of some of them, "I have seen these strait gates and narrow ways, 'with here and there a traveler.' They are in retired corners, and must be sought for, and are opened only to those who knock; and when the sun goes down, and the night comes on, they are shut and locked. It is then too late."

Life. Eternal life, in opposition to destruction, John 17 : 3. The difficulties attending a life of piety do not arise from the nature of holiness, but from the depravity of the human heart. To go to hell needs no searching for the way, for all are in it by nature; no exertion to continue therein, for man's natural desires are toward evil continually. But to enter the way that leads to heaven needs searching to find the gate; for none by nature know where it is, and the understandings of all are darkened. And, having discovered the way, it requires exertion on their part to choose it, and to walk therein. The way of holiness is in opposition to human wisdom, and to the natural desires of the heart, and is, therefore, a way of self-denial and effort, ch. 16 : 24, 25; Luke 14 : 33; Phil. 3 : 7-9.

15. The difficulties connected with beginning and living a life of piety show the need of guidance and of religious instruction. But the Pharisees were false teachers, and there would be also false Christian teachers who would deceive, if possible, even the elect, ch. 24: 24. Hence the need of the caution, **beware of false prophets.** A *prophet* means not only one who foretells future events, but also one who speaks in the name of God—a religious teacher. A false prophet is one who falsely professes either to foretell or to teach in the name of the Lord, Jer. 23 : 16, 17, 21. It is a characteristic of such teachers, and as a matter of fact they now **come to you in sheep's clothing,** not in literal sheepskins, like the supposed rough costume of the old prophets, but with the outward appearance of humility, innocence, and piety. **Inwardly ravening wolves.** Inwardly they are selfish, greedy of gain, and eager to seize and devour, John 10 : 12; Acts 20 : 29. A wolf in sheep's clothing very strikingly represents a wicked person making a great profession of religion, yet unable so to dissemble as not to be discovered by the attentive observer. Such, indeed, was the character of the Pharisees (ch. 23 : 25); and the same is true to a greater or less extent of all the religious guides who lead away from the strait gate.

16. How to detect false teachers. **Ye shall know them.** Discover, detect them. **By their fruits.** By their actions, conduct, and practices, and by the effect of their doctrines on others. In their conduct, and in the moral tendency of their teaching, you will discover the selfish and rapacious spirit of the wolf. The wickedness of their hearts will show itself. And this is just what you would expect; for their character is just as little adapted to bring forth humility, love, and all the fruits of the Spirit, as thorns are grapes, or thistles, figs. Hence the question, which is equivalent to a strong negative, "Men do not gather grapes," etc. **Grapes** and **figs** were the choicest and most highly valued fruits of Palestine, Num. 13 : 23, 24. **Thorns** and **thistles** were fruitless and worthless plants. The former represents the whole class of thorny plants; the latter, a particular kind. At the present day the traveler is struck with the number and variety of thorny shrubs and prickly plants in Palestine. The people gather them and use them for fuel.

17. **Even so.** What is true of thorns and thistles is true of every kind of tree. **Good tree.** A tree of good quality, and good for bearing. **Corrupt tree.** Literally, *rotten;* which is hardly the meaning here, since rotten or decayed trees do not usually bear fruit. It rather means, *bad* in quality, in opposition to *good*. Thus, the same Greek word is applied to fish in ch. 13 : 48, and translated *bad*. Jesus here states

tree ʲcan not bring forth evil fruit, neither *can* a
19 corrupt tree bring forth good fruit. ᵏEvery tree
that bringeth not forth good fruit is hewn down,
20 and cast into the fire. Wherefore by their fruits
ye shall know them.
21 ˡNot every one that saith unto me, Lord, Lord,
ᵐshall enter into the kingdom of heaven, ⁿbut he
that doeth the will of my Father which is in
22 heaven. Many will say to me ᵒin that day, Lord,
Lord, have we ᵖnot prophesied in thy name? and
in thy name have cast out devils? and in thy name

ᵉ Eze. 22. 25; Ac.
20. 29.
ᶠ ch. 12. 33. 35.
ᵍ Lk. 6. 43. 44;
Jam. 3. 12.
ʰ Jer. 11. 19; Gal.
5. 22-24; Jam. 3.
17, 18.
ⁱ Gal. 5. 17; 1 John
3. 9. 10.
ᵏ Lk. 3. 9.
ˡ ch. 25. 11. 12;
Hos. 8. 2-4; Lk.
6. 46; 13. 25; Tit.
1. 16; Jam. 1. 22
-27.

a general fact, that good trees do produce good fruit; and bad, worthless trees, evil fruit.

18. The case stated still stronger. Not only is it a general fact, but it must be so. It is impossible for a good tree, from its very nature, to bring forth evil fruit, or for a bad, noxious tree to bring forth good fruit. The heart of man is depraved, and if he is unrenewed, his depravity must affect his whole conduct. This is especially true of false religious teachers. Their depravity will affect their whole faith and practice, and will show itself in their actions, their instructions, in a selfish and wicked spirit, and in false doctrine, 1 John 4 : 1-3.

19. Jesus pursues the figure still further, by which the destiny of these false teachers is suggested. As a matter of common observation, trees that do not produce good fruit are hewn down and converted into fuel. See on ch. 3 : 10. So all these false guides shall be cut off and doomed to unquenchable fire.

20. Jesus returns from the slight digression of the last verse, and applies the comparison to false prophets. **Wherefore,** etc. So then you shall know, recognize, detect them from their fruits, from their actions and conduct, and from the effect of their doctrines on others. Such was doubtless the meaning of *fruits*, as used at the time by our Lord. With the Holy Scriptures, however, completed, those who can read and judge can now not only try the conduct and spirit, but also the doctrines of professed teachers, without even waiting to see what may be the moral effect of their instructions, 1 John 4: 1-3.

21. Jesus passes from false prophets generally to false professors. **Not every one,** not all who make an open profession shall be saved. **Lord,** which is an acknowledgment of him as Master, Sovereign, is repeated not merely for emphasis, but to indicate a common and habitual practice : Not all who are accustomed to call me their Lord. Jesus was doubtless thus called even now by his disciples. **Kingdom of heaven.** As consummated in glory. See ch. 3 : 2. **But he that doeth the will,** etc. He that from the heart doeth what God requires, who heartily obeys the revealed will of God.

22. **Many.** The number of false professors will not be few. **Say to me,** who shall be the judge, 2 Cor. 5 : 10. **That day.** The day of judgment, ch. 11 : 24; Luke 10 : 12-14; 1 Tim. 4 : 8. The prophets frequently used this phrase to express, sometimes the introduction of the Messiah's kingdom, and sometimes its consummation. The repetition of **Lord,** expresses earnestness and importunity. **Prophesied.** Preached, taught in the name of the Lord. The word may here include, though not necessarily, foretelling future events. Saul was among the prophets (1 Sam. 10 : 5-13); Balaam predicted the future glory of Israel (Num. 24 : 4); and Caiaphas the death of Jesus (John 11 : 51). So some of Christ's professed followers have uttered predictions, and yet have been destitute of true piety. **Devils.** Demons. The Scriptures in the original recognize but one devil; all the other fallen spirits, of which he is the head or chief, are called *demons.* They are also spoken of together as the devil and his angels, ch. 25 : 41. **Wonderful works.** The word thus translated implies supernatural power, and is applied in usage to miraculous perform-

A.D. 28. MATTHEW VII. 105

23 done many wonderful works? And ᵠthen I will profess unto them, I never knew you: ʳdepart from me, ye that work iniquity.
24 Therefore ˢwhosoever heareth these sayings of mine, and doeth them, I will liken him unto a wise
25 man, which built his house upon a rock: and the rain descended, and the floods came, and the winds blew, and beat upon that house; and it fell not: for
26 it was founded upon a rock. And every one that heareth these sayings of mine, and doeth them not, shall be likened unto a foolish man, which built his
27 house upon the sand: and the rain descended, and

ᵐ ch. 18. 3.
ⁿ Lk. 11. 28; 1 John 3. 22-24.
ᵒ Mal. 3. 17. 18; 2 Thes. 1. 10. Num. 24. 4; John 11. 51; 1 Cor. 13. 1, 2; Heb. 6. 4-6.
ᵠ Lk. 13. 25, 27; John 10. 14; 2 Tim. 2. 19.
ʳ ch. 25. 41; Ps. 6. 8; 2 Thes. 1. 9.
ˢ Lk. 6. 47-49; Ezek. 13. 13-16.

---

ances. It is better to translate *miracles*. Casting out demons is specified as prominent among the miracles wrought by them. Judas doubtless had some miraculous gifts, and demons were subject to him as well as to the rest of the apostles. And some, doubtless, who have been instrumental in the conversion of souls will be rejected at the day of judgment, 1 Cor. 9: 27; 1 Cor. 13: 1-3.

23. **Profess.** Publicly declare. They had professed to be his; he, in opposition, would profess that he never **knew** them as his true followers. He had never acknowledged them as such. **Depart.** Ye belong not to me; begone then, and take your true place as my enemies. **Iniquity.** Ye who work unrighteousness, who in character and action are opposed to conformity to the law and will of God.

24-27. IN CONCLUSION, JESUS DRAWS A STRIKING CONTRAST between those who obey and those who disobey his instructions. Not only are false teachers and false professors in danger of eternal condemnation at the judgment, but also another larger class, those who are hearers but not doers of the word.

24. **These sayings.** The discourse he was uttering. **Therefore** draws a conclusion from all that he had said. The doing of his words, the acting upon them, implies faith. Works is the evidence of faith; and faith cometh by hearing. **I will liken.** *Shall be likened.* **Wise** means discreet, prudent. **A rock.** Literally, *the rock;* or, who built his house on rock, denoting the class of substance on which the house was built. Some commentators refer this rock to Christ (1 Cor. 3: 11); others to the words of salvation he taught. But he who builds on Christ's words, really builds on Christ.

25. The stability of a good man's hopes further illustrated. True religion will stand every peril, here represented by rain, floods, and wind, whether in life, at death, or at the judgment. **Rain** indicates a shower or storm. **Floods.** The streams, freshet. The imagery here was most vivid before an audience accustomed to the suddenness and fierceness of an eastern tempest. The quantity of water that fell in Palestine between seed time and harvest was very great. At times it descended in torrents. The brooks were suddenly filled, and small streams were swollen into the likeness of rivers, sweeping away houses and cattle that lay in their way. The value of such a foundation is at once seen in that the house, exposed to such a terrible ordeal, **fell not.** The reason given is, **it was founded,** more correctly, *it had been founded* on a rock.

26. He that merely hears these sayings, which Jesus had just been uttering, without acting upon them and obeying them, is like a **foolish** man, one wanting common prudence and foresight, who built his house upon **sand.** Sand denotes the material of his foundation, and represents the works, doctrines, and opinions of men, and all other delusive grounds on which unregenerate men build their hopes for eternity. It is worthy of notice that both *heard*, which was commendable; both built their house, had their religion, and hoped for future safety and happiness; but their foundations were different. The house on the sand could not stand the fierce beating of rain, torrents, and winds, and **it fell.** To represent more forcibly the total ruin of this foolish

the floods came, and the winds blew, and beat upon that house; and it fell: and great was the fall of it. 28 And it came to pass, when Jesus had ended these sayings, ¹the people were astonished at his doctrine: 29 for he taught them as *one* having authority, and not as the scribes.

¹ Mk. 1. 22; Jer. 23. 29; John 7. 4-6.

---

man's house, Jesus adds, **and great was the fall of it.** "The fishermen of Bengal," says Mr. Ward in his *View of the Hindoos*, "build their huts in the dry season on the bed of sand from which the river has retired. When the rains set in, which they do often very suddenly, accompanied with violent north-west winds, the water pours down in torrents from the mountains. In one night multitudes of these huts are frequently swept away, and the place where they stood is the next morning undiscoverable." And thus the man with mere religious knowledge, without the corresponding practice, shall be visited with swift destruction, Prov. 12 : 7; Isa. 28 : 16, 17. Expecting, it may be, to go to heaven, he shall be cast down to hell.

28, 29. The impression made by the discourse upon the people. These verses prove conclusively that the Sermon on the Mount is not a mere collection of our Savior's sayings, as some have supposed, but a single discourse delivered to the multitudes (ch. 4 : 25, and 5 : 1) at the close of his first general circuit of Galilee. **Had ended.** Had finished his discourse. **The people.** In the original, *the multitudes*, ch. 5 : 1. **Astonished at his doctrine.** At his teaching, both its matter and his manner. The reason of this astonishment is given: he taught them as **having authority.** The authority was in himself. He spoke as an authoritative teacher; not as a mere expounder of the law, but as the Lawgiver himself, and as the one who should be their final Judge. The truths he uttered were fitted to make a deep impression; but he uttered them as his own truth ("I say unto you"), and this especially filled them with wonder. **And not as the scribes.** *Their scribes;* the successors of Ezra (Ezra 7 : 6), a class of educated men, whose duty was to preserve, copy, and expound the Scriptures and the traditions. They exerted a commanding influence; but they spoke only with an authority as expounders of the law, arising from their knowledge of the sacred text, and from the sayings and traditions of the Fathers. In showing the spirituality of the law, and the extent of its requirements, Jesus opened the eyes of the people to their shortcomings, and aroused their consciences; but the scribes, dealing in vain and trifling questions, and making void the law through their glosses and traditions (ch. 15 : 1-16), blinded the people and failed to move them to right feeling and action.

REMARKS.

1. A censorious spirit is opposed to Christ, invites a like spirit from others, and is self-condemnatory, vers. 1, 2; 1 Pet. 2 : 23; 1 Cor. 13 : 4-7; Matt. 18 : 33, 34; Rom. 2 : 1.

2. If we put ourselves in the place of our Judge, and thus pronounce rash and harsh judgments on others, we shall bring judgments upon ourselves, vers. 1, 2; Jud. 1 : 6, 7; Rom. 14 : 10; 12 : 19.

3. Sin and selfishness blind men to their own faults, and make them censorious and sharp-sighted in regard to the faults of others, vers. 3, 4; 1 Tim. 5 : 13; 2 Tim. 3 : 6-8.

4. To get right ourselves before God is our first duty; then will we be prepared to set others right. A beam in thine eye unfits thee to take out the mote from thy brother's eye, ver. 5; Rom. 2 : 19-23; Gal. 6 : 1.

5. A knowledge of ourselves is the best preventive of evil speaking, and all censoriousness, ver. 5.

6. We must not form hasty judgments, yet we must so distinguish the characters of men as to adapt our instructions to them. Scoffers must sometimes be let alone, lest our messages drive them to madness and blasphemy, and they prove unnecessarily injurious to themselves and to us, ver. 6.

7. We should ask wisdom from God

to enable us to exercise a right spirit toward our fellow-men, and to do our duty to them, feeling confident that we shall receive what we ask in faith, for Christ's sake, and according to his will, vers. 7-11; James 1 : 5.

8. Parental tenderness, as exhibited among our fallen race, should inspire our confidence in the willingness of our most merciful heavenly Father to answer all those who rightly ask him. Though all should forget their little ones, God will not forget his own, ver. 9; Isa. 49 : 15.

9. Since God is the Father of all, all should act toward one another as brethren. His love and mercy toward us should lead us to exercise a spirit of love and kindness toward others, ver. 12; 1 John 3 : 16.

10. Each one can find in himself the rule of conduct toward his neighbor, ver. 12; Acts 24 : 16; 1 Tim. 1 : 5; Gal. 5 : 24.

11. The difficulties attending the beginning and the continuing a life of piety should not discourage any, but rather excite them to greater earnestness. It is the violent who seize upon the kingdom of heaven, vers. 13, 14; Matt. 11 : 12.

12. Beware lest ye be deceived by appearances, and ye be led to think that there is safety, even for the shortest time, in following the multitude to do evil, ver. 14; Prov. 16 : 25.

13. Though we are not to be censorious or rash in judging, it is our duty to prove all things, and hold fast to that which is good, and decide by the fruits between true and false teachers, as well as between true and false doctrine, ver. 15-20; Jer. 23 : 16; 2 Cor. 11 : 13; 1 Thess. 5 : 21; 2 Tim. 3 : 5.

14. Profession without the corresponding practice is worthless, vers. 21-23; ch. 25 : 11, 12.

15. Christ will be our final Judge, ver. 22; Acts 17 : 31.

16. Doing the will of God is a sure test of our discipleship, ver. 21; John 6 : 40; 1 Thess. 4 : 3.

17. Christ is our Lawgiver, vers. 24, 29; Acts 3 : 21, 22.

18. Those who build on Christ by a living faith and a hearty obedience (the two are inseparable) shall stand against every trial, vers. 24, 25; 1 Pet. 2 : 6.

19. All hopes founded on human merit shall perish; many who now weep, pray, and fast shall be lost because they made these and not Christ their dependence, vers. 26, 27; Isa. 28 : 17; Prov. 11 : 7.

20. Hearing and not doing will only increase our condemnation, ver. 27; John 15 : 22.

21. Take heed lest ye hear these doctrines of our Lord, and wonder, despise, and perish. Rather receive them in faith with true love and admiration, and practice them in life, vers. 28, 29; Acts 13 : 40, 41.

CHAPTER VIII.

By the Sermon on the Mount, Matthew had strikingly presented Jesus as a teacher; his words were in keeping with and confirmatory of his Messiahship. He now proceeds in this and the following chapter to illustrate his miraculous power, by giving a selection of his miracles. These our Lord performed in proof of his divine mission, ch. 11: 4, 5; John 9 : 3-5; 10 : 25, 37; 2 : 22. The Jews generally expected that the Messiah would work miracles, John 7 : 31; Matt. 12 : 38; Luke 11 : 16, 17; so also did John the Baptist, ch. 11 : 3. The miracles of Christ were designated by several words, according to the lights in which they were viewed. When they were specially regarded as evidences of his divine mission, they were called (*semeia*), *signs* (ch. 12 : 39; John 2 : 11); when as the manifestation of supernatural power, they were called (*dunameis*), *mighty works*, corresponding more strictly to the word *miracles* in common English usage (ch. 11 : 20; Mark 9 : 39); when as extraordinary and portending phenomena, exciting astonishment or terror, they were called (*terata*), *wonders* (John 4 : 48; Acts 2 : 22); and when viewed in a still more general and comprehensive light, as something completed and to be reflected on, the natural acts and product of His being, they were called (*erga*), *works* (John 7 : 3, 21). In the Common Version, the first of these is translated variously by the words *signs, miracles,* and *wonders;* the second by *mighty works, mighty deeds, wonderful works,* and *miracles;* the third by *wonders;* and the fourth by *works* and *deeds.*

To get a full and correct conception of the miracles of Christ, they should be viewed in all these aspects. They were not simply the manifestations of a supernatural power, but also the pro-

The healing of a leper, of the Centurion's servant, of Peter's wife's mother, and of many others.

VIII. WHEN he was come down from the mountain, great multitudes followed him.

2 ª And, behold, there came a leper and worshiped

ª Mk. 1. 40-44; Lk. 5. 12-14; Lev.chs. 13. 14; 2 Ki. 5. 11-14.

duct of a power inherent in our Lord, the natural fruits, the outworkings of his own divine nature; they were not merely adapted to deeply impress the mind and excite astonishment or terror, but they were also the signs, the evidences of himself, and of the truth of which he was the embodiment. They were, in fine, the supernatural phenomena produced by his own power in proof of his divine mission. It is not necessary to suppose them either a violation or a suspension of the laws of nature. If they were above nature, they were not against nature. "All phenomena which are not explicable from the known or unknown laws of earthly development are not, for that reason, necessarily violations and suspensions of the laws of nature; rather they are themselves comprehended under a higher general law, for what is divine is truly according to law. That which is not divine is against nature; the real miracle is natural, but in a higher sense."—OLSHAUSEN. Some would have us suppose that the disciples *mistook* natural events for miracles; and others, that the Evangelists relate *myths* or legends, and not histories. But such suppositions are more incredible than miracles themselves.

Such were the miracles of Christ. When, however, we speak of miracles, not of Christ only, but of all the messengers of God, as recorded in the Scriptures, we must generalize our definition. They were supernatural acts and occurrences, wrought by supernatural power either inherent or conferred, in proof of the divine authority of the messengers of God.

1. **Great multitudes.** This verse is closely connected with the foregoing chapter, and is an additional proof that the Sermon on the Mount was a single discourse, delivered at one time and place. Having descended the mountain, many groups, crowds, *great multitudes*, a vast, promiscuous assemblage, follow him.

2-4. HEALING OF A LEPER. Mark 1: 40-45; Luke 5: 12-16.

2. **Behold there came.** This plainly implies that the leper met Jesus on his descent from the mountain. It should be noticed that neither Matthew, Mark, nor Luke fixes the place of this miracle with certainty. **A leper.** A person afflicted with *leprosy*, a most fearful and foul skin disease, peculiar to Egypt, Palestine, Syria, and some other portions of the east. In its worst form it was the most terrible of all diseases, and absolutely incurable. It is described, with certain enactments respecting it, in Lev., chapters 13 and 14. It probably began internally, after which it showed itself in swellings, scabs, bright spots, or slight reddish eruptions, grouped in circles, covered with a shiny scale or scab. The disease was not contagious, though often it became hereditary for generations. Its progress was not generally rapid. A leper from his birth sometimes lived as many as fifty years; while those afterward infected, sometimes as many as twenty. It was inflicted sometimes as a special judgment for sin, and hence was called a *plague* or *stroke*, Num. 12: 10; 2 Kings 5: 27; 2 Chron. 26: 20.

Whether this disease is identical with modern leprosy has been much disputed. The latest testimonies favor the belief that, under certain forms, it continues to prevail. Dr. Thomson (*The Land and the Book*, vol. ii. p. 519) thus describes the most aggravated form, as witnessed at present in Palestine : " The scab comes on by degrees, in different parts of the body; the hair falls from the head and eyebrows; the nails loosen, decay, and drop off; joint after joint of the fingers and toes shrink up and slowly fall away. The gums are absorbed, and the teeth disappear. The nose, the eyes, the tongue, and the palate are slowly consumed; and finally the wretched victim shrinks into the earth and disappears, while medicine has no power to stay the ravages of

him, saying, Lord, if thou wilt, thou canst make
3 me clean. And Jesus put forth his hand, and
touched him, saying, I will; be thou clean. And
4 immediately his leprosy was cleansed. And Jesus
saith unto him, See thou tell no man; but go thy

this fell disease, or even mitigate sensibly its tortures."

This disease is a striking emblem of sin and its effects. The leper was regarded as unclean; he was to rend his garments, let his hair hang down dishevelled, wear garments of mourning as for the dead, and live in exclusion outside the camp or city. So strictly was this last regulation enforced, that neither Miriam, the sister of Moses, nor King Uzziah was exempted from it, Num. 12:15; 2 Chron. 26:21. He was to warn off every one whom he happened to meet by crying, Unclean, unclean! Every one and every thing he touched was defiled. Leprosy was indeed regarded as a living death (Joseph. *Antiq.* iii. 11, 3). Thus, not only was he while diseased to be excluded from society, as if in effect dead, and to wear garments of mourning, as for the dead; but if healed, he was to be cleansed by the same means as for uncleanness through touching or handling the dead, Num. 19:13-20; Lev. 14:4-7. And thus sin affects the soul, pervading the whole being, rendering it unclean, separating it from God, producing spiritual death, unfitting it forever for heaven and the company of the holy, and insuring its eternal banishment, as polluted and abominable. It was indeed wisely ordered that such a type of the sinner should be cleansed immediately after the wonderful discourse of our Lord. That this was an aggravated case of the disease is evident from the language of Luke, "a man full of leprosy;" it covered his whole body from head to foot.

Worshiped him. This expression applies either to adoration to God or to reverence to man. See ch. 2:2. We have no reason for supposing that this leper apprehended the divine nature of Jesus, or that he did more than bow down before him, thereby expressing special respect and reverence. His particular acts of homage are described by Mark (1:40) and Luke (5:12) as kneeling and falling on his face.

Lord. This term was applied as a title of address to God and to man, signifying, according to circumstances, *Sir*, or *Master*, or *Most Revered One*, or *Jehovah*. As the leper bows before this great Teacher and Worker of miracles, the idea of *Master* most appropriately fits his language. **If thou wilt thou canst.** If thou art willing, thou art able. The leper had strong faith in the miraculous power of Jesus, but had a doubt about his willingness to exercise it on such an object, on one so unclean. Contrary to Jewish usage, he had come near to Jesus; but his case was urgent. Would Jesus be willing? Possibly he would yield to his importunity; at best, the leper determined to rest his case on the will of Jesus alone: *If Thou wilt.* **Make me clean.** Cleanse me; heal my leprosy, and thus remove my uncleanness.

3. Jesus immediately showed his willingness to exert, even in this case, his miraculous power, and, contrary to law, he stretched forth his hand and **touched him.** But Christ was himself the Lawgiver and the fulfiller of the law. As it was in harmony with the law of the Sabbath to do good and save life, so was it with the law of leprosy to remove the disease and the defilement. But Jesus himself was purity. He purified, but contracted no uncleanness. Before his power, as symbolized by stretching forth his hand and touching him, the leprosy fled, and the leper was cleansed. How beautiful and striking his language, corresponding to that of the leper, **I will; be thou clean,** or **cleansed.** And instantly his leprosy was cleansed; he was freed from the disease and from its uncleanness; or, as Mark says, "The leprosy departed from him, and he was cleansed."

4. **Tell no man.** Our Lord frequently gave such prohibitions as this, ch. 9:30; 12:16; Mark 5:43; 7:36, etc. His reasons for them were various, according to circumstances. As a general principle, they accorded with his

way, show thyself to the priest, and offer the gift that Moses commanded, for a testimony unto them.
5 ˣ And when Jesus was entered into Capernaum, there came unto him a centurion, beseeching him,
6 and saying, Lord, my servant lieth at home sick of

ˣ Lk. 7. 1–10; Acts 10. 7; Col. 3. 11; Philem. 16.

gentle and modest bearing, and with the peacefulness and spirituality of his kingdom (ch. ˣ 12 : 16–20), which came not with observation, Luke 17 : 20. In some cases he would repress rather than encourage the excitement of the people, who sometimes beset him in such crowds as greatly to trouble him (Mark 3 : 9, 20), and would even make him a temporal king, John 6 : 15. In other cases he doubtless had the good of the persons healed specially in view. In this instance the prohibition was temporary, binding upon him till he should go and show himself to the priest; "See thou tell no one; but go and show," etc. In other words, Go at once to the priest; tell no one, lest thou be delayed from the performance of this duty ; or lest the report reaching him that thou art the man that was healed, he be prejudiced against thee, and from malice he refuse to acknowledge thy cure. That the man disobeyed, greatly to the inconvenience of Jesus, appears from Mark 1 : 45, which suggests still another reason for enjoining silence.

Go show thyself, etc. Go to Jerusalem, where the officiating priests were, present the appointed offerings of purification, according to the law, Lev. 14: 1–32. This would free both Jesus and the one healed from the imputation of any disregard of the Mosaic law. There were two stages of purification, the second beginning on the seventh day after his showing himself to the priest. They consisted of purifying ceremonies and offerings, uniting confessions of sin and pollution with grateful acknowledgment of God's mercy. As the leprosy was a striking type of sin, so the ceremonies of cleansing were typical of the forgiveness of sin and justification through the blood of Christ, and of the anointing of the Holy Spirit for sanctification, Heb. 10: 21, 22; 1 John 2 : 20. **A testimony to them.** To the people that he was cured, and that he might be safely admitted again into society. The leper had been pronounced unclean by the priest, and the priest alone could pronounce him clean, and readmit him into the congregation.

5–13. HEALING OF THE CENTURION'S SERVANT. Luke 7: 1–10. Luke places this immediately after the Sermon on the Plain. There is no inconsistency between the two Evangelists, since Matthew here makes a selection of our Savior's earlier miracles, without strict regard to chronological order, and his language does not closely connect this with the preceding miracle. The prominence of the individual whose servant was healed, the commonness of palsy and the difficulty of its cure, the healing of the individual without touching or even seeing him, may have been some of the reasons for the selection and position of this miracle. **When Jesus was entered.** As he entered. The expression is indefinite. Capernaum had become his principal residence (see ch. 4 : 13) and the centre of his operations. To it he frequently returned from his preaching tours. On one of these occasions, as he entered Capernaum, there came to him a **centurion,** who was a Roman officer commanding a hundred men. He was probably in the service of Herod Antipas, and stationed at Capernaum, as an important provincial town and a place of considerable traffic on the Sea of Galilee, to preserve order there and in the adjacent country. He was a Gentile (ver. 10), but seems to have been strongly attached to the people and worship of Jehovah; and to have regarded Jesus as without doubt a "teacher come from God," and probably as the Messiah, the Redeemer of Israel.

6. **Lord.** This title here expresses great reverence, and an acknowledgment of the high rank and dignity of Jesus as a great teacher, or the Messiah. It is not necessary to suppose that the centurion conceived of him as "God manifested in the flesh." See on ver. 2. **My servant.** Literally, *my boy,* a familiar way of styling a domestic servant. From Luke we learn that he was specially beloved by his master. **Palsy.** In Greek, *a paralytic,* a word which was

7 the palsy, grievously tormented. And Jesus saith
8 unto him, I will come and heal him. The centurion answered and said, Lord, ʸ I am not worthy that thou shouldest come under my roof: but ᶻ speak the word only, and my servant shall be healed.
9 For I am a man under authority, having soldiers under me: and I say to this *man*, Go, and he goeth; and to another, Come, and he cometh; and to my
10 servant, Do this, and he doeth *it*. When Jesus heard *it*, he marveled, and said to them that followed, Verily, I say unto you, I have not found so
11 great faith, no, not in Israel. And I say unto you, That ᵃ many shall come from the east and west, and shall sit down with Abraham, and Isaac, and Jacob,

ʸ Lk. 15. 19, 21.
ᶻ vers. 16, 26; ch. 9. 6, 7; Ge. 1. 1-3; Lk. 4. 35, 36; John 4. 50; 11. 43.

ᵃ Lk. 13. 29; Mal. 1. 11; Gen. 12. 3; Rom. 15. 9-12.

---

applied to one suffering from any morbid relaxation of the nerves, loss of sensation or voluntary motion, including paralysis and apoplexy. See on 4 : 24. The present case was a severe one. He was suffering extreme pain, **grievously tormented;** and Luke adds, "about to die." "Paralysis, with the contraction of the joints, is accompanied with strong pain, and when united, as it much oftener is in the hot climates of the East and of Africa than among us, with tetanus, both causes extreme suffering and would rapidly bring on dissolution."—TRENCH.

7, 8. Jesus at once declared his readiness to come and heal the centurion's servant; but the centurion felt unworthy to have the Savior honor his dwelling with his presence. He not only felt that he was a Gentile, a heathen, but doubtless also his own spiritual lowliness, his deep sinfulness; and hence unworthiness to receive under his roof the great Redeemer of Israel. He would, therefore, have Jesus **speak the word,** or literally, *say in a word*, and his servant would be healed. In the use of a single word he believed Jesus could cure his servant.

9. The reason for thus believing he now states. He knew both what it was to be under authority and what to exercise authority. His power was, indeed, limited; but even his word was promptly and faithfully obeyed. If the word of a subordinate officer like himself received such obedience, how much more the word of one whose rank was so exalted, and who was manifestly a sovereign over all diseases. **Servant.** A different word from the one translated servant in verse 6, and may mean either a soldier attending him as an officer, or a domestic. It properly means a bondman, or slave, though it is also used to express the service of choice and devotion. See 1 Cor. 7 : 21; Gal. 3 : 28; Col. 3 : 11; John 15 : 15; Rom. 6 : 16; 1 Cor. 7 : 23.

10. **Marveled.** Wondered at, and beheld his faith with admiration. As a man, Jesus exercised the various faculties of the human soul. This instance of faith excited the surprise or wonder of his human nature; to his divine nature all was known, nothing was new or strange. **No, not in Israel.** Not even in Israel, the chosen people of God. Israel was applied to the ten tribes after they separated from Judah; but after the captivity it was applied to the whole nation as settled in Palestine. This was the first instance of faith in Christ's power to heal at a distance. And this great faith was found not in some favored Israelite, but in one far less privileged and favored—a Gentile! Faith was a frequent and special object of our Savior's praise, ch. 15 : 28; Luke 7 : 50.

11. **I say unto you.** "Not only do I solemnly declare this Gentile to be more enlightened as to my authority and power than any Jew whom I have met with; but I also solemnly declare that this superiority of faith will one day be exhibited by multitudes."—J. A. ALEXANDER. **From the east and west.** From the Gentiles, not only those near, but also those most distant; from all parts of the earth, Isa. 45 : 6; 49 : 6. **Sit down.** Rather, *recline at table*, according to the custom of the time of reclining upon beds or couches at their feasts or banquets. The blessings of

12 in the kingdom of heaven. But ᵇ the children of the kingdom ᶜ shall be cast out into outer darkness: there shall be weeping and gnashing of teeth. 13 And Jesus said unto the centurion, Go thy way; ᵈ and as thou hast believed, *so* be it done unto thee. And his servant was healed in the selfsame hour.

ᵇ ch. 21. 43; Ro. 2 25–29.
ᶜ ch. 22. 13; Lk. 13. 28; 2 Pet. 2. 17; Jude 13.
ᵈ ch. 9. 29.

---

the Messiah's reign had been represented in prophecy by a feast, Isa. 25 : 6. To recline at table with Abraham, Isaac, and Jacob, the fathers of the nation, was to the Jewish mind a representation of the highest honor and the greatest happiness. "According to Jewish notions, splendid banquets with the patriarchs formed part of the happiness enjoyed in Messiah's kingdom."—MEYER. Many Gentiles shall become spiritual descendants of the fathers in faith (Heb. 11 : 8–10), participators of the **kingdom of heaven**, both below (Col. 1 : 13) and above, Rev. 19 : 9. Compare Luke 14 : 15–24.

12. **The children of the kingdom.** The Jews, the natural heirs of the patriarchs, to whom were committed the oracles of God, whose were the adoption, the covenants, and the promises, but who were disinherited on account of unbelief, Rom. 3 : 2 ; 4 : 11, 12, 16 ; 9 : 4, 31, 32 ; 11 : 7–10, 20. **Outer darkness.** The figure of a feast is still continued. Feasts were always held toward evening, and frequently protracted to a late hour, Luke 12 : 38. When Judas went out from the supper of the Lord it was night, John 13 : 30. The banqueting house is lighted up; within is joy and festivity, but without is darkness. The streets are narrow and filthy, and unillumined by any light whatever. To be cast out into the outer darkness in the chilly night, such as they have in the East; to rove around the filthy streets, exposed to robbers and ferocious dogs, were the opposite of enjoying the feast within, a vivid representation of the spiritual blindness and the miserable condition of those who had been so highly privileged with the law and the prophets, and with the first announcement of the glad tidings of salvation, and yet who were rejected on account of unbelief. Their disappointment and misery are further represented by their **weeping and gnashing,** grinding, grating, **of teeth.** More correctly, *the weeping and the gnashing of teeth,* referring to the well-known misery in hell. They will be like children torn from the feast, and at night cast from the house of their father into the darkness without, where they will be heard giving vent to their disappointment, rage, and grief. Thus is represented not only their spiritual wretchedness and blindness here (Rom. 11 : 8–10), but their terrible doom hereafter, ch. 22 : 13 ; 25 : 30.

13. Having made this application of the centurion's faith to the rejection of Israel and the calling of the Gentiles, he proceeds to heal the servant. **As thou hast believed.** Rather, *As thou didst believe,* in making this request. Jesus does not make faith a ground of merit, but rather a rule by which he gauges his gifts of mercy and grace. The healing corresponded with and was in proportion to his faith, "As thou didst believe, be it done to you." Alexander most strangely remarks that this, and later instances of healing persons on the faith of others who represented and interceded for them, afford "a beautiful analogy in favor of baptizing children on the faith of their parental sponsors"! Much better could he have said that they afford a beautiful analogy of the salvation of certain individuals on the faith of others! But faith by proxy, either in baptism or salvation, is equally unscriptural. We wait to see a single example of either adduced from the word of God. Anything that is not taught in Scripture, and indeed is contrary to Scripture, can not have any scriptural analogy. It is also worthy of notice that the centurion did not represent or stand in the place of his servant; he did not exercise faith for him, but rather for himself, that his servant, whom he tenderly loved, might be restored to him, that he might continue to enjoy his faithful service. **Self-same hour.** The Greek word hour originally meant a definite space of time, fixed by natural laws. Hence it was applied to the seasons of the year, and the divisions of the day, especially to the twelve parts of the day from sunrise to sunset. Here it seems to mean

14 *And when Jesus was come into Peter's house, he saw ʰhis wife's mother laid, and sick of a fever.
15 And he touched her hand, and the fever left her: and she arose and ministered unto them.
16 ᵍWhen the even was come, they brought unto him many that were possessed with devils: and he cast out the spirits with *his* word, and healed all

* Mk. 1. 29–34; Lk. 4. 38–41.
ᶠ 1 Cor. 9. 5.
ᵍ Mk. 1. 32, 34; Ac. 10. 38.

an indefinite short duration, the *time* or *moment* that Jesus uttered the word, *at that instant*, Luke 7 : 6, 10.

From the fuller account of this miracle in Luke 7 : 1; 10, it appears that the centurion first sent the elders of the Jews to Jesus, and then his friends to him, bearing the message which in Matthew seems to have been delivered by the centurion personally. But it was common then as now to speak of a person doing what was done by others under his direction. Thus Jesus is said to baptize, when he only baptized by his disciples, John 4 : 1; see also 19 : 1. Possibly the centurion followed his friends, his earnestness having overcome his modesty.

14–17. HEALING OF PETER'S WIFE'S MOTHER AND MANY OTHERS. Mark 1: 29–34; Luke 4 : 38–41.

14. This miracle, like the preceding, is selected without strict regard to chronological order, and presents an example of a more private and domestic character, and of another common and dangerous disease. **When Jesus was come into the house of Peter.** According to Mark 1 : 29 this took place in the house of Simon and Andrew, immediately after healing a demoniac in the synagogue at Capernaum on the Sabbath. Although Andrew and Peter were natives of Bethsaida, which means a fishery, a house or place for fishing (John 1 : 44), and was applied to two or more villages on the lake, it seems that they had taken up their residence at Capernaum. **Wife's mother.** Mother-in-law. Peter was married. Many years after this, as late as A.D. 57, Paul refers to Peter's wife as living and accompanying her husband on his missionary tours, 1 Cor. 9 : 5. The Romish doctrine of clerical celibacy is unauthorized by Scripture, Heb. 13 : 4. **Laid, sick of a fever.** Lying, prostrate, sick of a fever. In Palestine, fevers were among the most common and the severest inflictions under which the people suffered. The disease in the present instance was a malignant one; for Luke says that she was "taken with a great" or "violent fever." In the vicinity of Capernaum, fevers of a malignant type are still prevalent, especially in the summer and autumn. On entering the house, they tell Jesus of her illness (Mark 1 : 30), and entreat him to exercise his power in her behalf, Luke 4 : 38.

15. As in the case of the leper, at the touch of Jesus the fever left her; and as an evidence of the perfect cure, she arose and **ministered to him.** The most ancient and best authorities read *him* instead of *them*. The fever did not leave her, as is common by natural means, weak and exhausted. As one fully restored, she at once attended to her household duties ; **ministered,** waited on the table, and served Jesus with food.

16. **Even.** Old English for *evening*. According to Mark and Luke it was at the setting of the sun. Various reasons may be given for the people bringing their sick to Jesus in the evening. It was the cool of the day, and therefore the best time for bringing the sick. It was the Sabbath day, and they may have preferred to wait till its close, at the setting of the sun, before bearing their sick to Jesus. During the day it became generally known that he was in the city, and the news of the healing of the demoniac in the synogogue (Mark 1 : 23, 28) spread among the people. Hence, "all the city was gathered together at the door" (Mark 1 : 33); and they brought to him many that were **possessed with devils**, with *demons*, ch. 4 : 24. The demons recognized Jesus as the Christ, crying out, "Thou art the Christ, the Son of God," Luke 4 : 41. **With his word.** With a word. A single word from Jesus was all-sufficient. And he healed **all** that were brought to him, **sick** with various dis-

17 that were sick: that it might be fulfilled which was spoken by Esaias the prophet, saying, ʰ ʻHimself took our infirmities, and bare *our* sicknesses.' ʰ Is. 53. 4; Heb. 9. 28; 1 Pet. 2. 24.

Jesus crosses the lake; stills a storm; heals the Gadarene demoniacs; and returns to Capernaum.

18 ⁱ NOW when Jesus saw great multitudes about him, he gave commandment to depart unto the ⁱ Mk. 4. 35–41; Lk. 8. 22–25.
19 other side. ᵏ And a certain scribe came and said unto him, Master, I will follow thee whithersoever ᵏ Lk. 9, 57, 58.

eases. Here, as well as in ch. 4 : 23, 24, we get a glimpse of the vast number of miracles he performed.

17. Matthew pauses here a moment to show that this was a direct fulfillment of prophecy. This peculiarity of Matthew above the other Evangelists is a strong evidence that he wrote his Gospel especially for the Jews. The prophecy here quoted is found in Isa. 53 : 4. The Evangelist gives a translation of his own, which is in strict accordance with the meaning of the original Hebrew. **Himself took our infirmities, and bare our sicknesses.** He took them upon himself, and bore them himself, lifting up, carrying, and removing them. He was "touched with the feeling of our infirmities." In his compassion for the sick, and in his sympathies for them, he *suffered with* them in his human nature. Thus, he wept at the grave of Lazarus (John 11: 35), and sighed over the deaf man, Mark 7 : 34. What exhaustion of body must his *sympathy*, which was so much purer and more intense than that of other men in their depraved state, have produced in connection with the preaching and labors of the day. It must also be remembered that bodily sickness is a part of the sorrow which sin has occasioned. His miracles were typical of the great work which he was to accomplish for the soul, by taking our place, "being wounded for our transgressions" and "bruised for our iniquities." They shadowed forth also the perfect redemption of our bodies from all the effects of sin, when they should rise incorruptible and immortal. The whole life of Jesus, too, on earth was one of humiliation and suffering, culminating in death upon the cross.

It was only in view of the great fact that he was the Christ, and that he was to make an atonement for sin by taking the sinner's place, that he performed miracles, and went about preaching the Gospel and doing good. By viewing sickness as the effect of sin, and miracles as a part of his work as the Christ, typifying the removal of all the effects of sin, and, in connection with his great sympathy as the Redeemer, producing in him bodily suffering, we see here a beautiful fulfillment of this prophecy. It began to be fulfilled by the removal of the lesser evils of sin. Compare 1 Pet. 2 : 24.

18–27. JESUS EMBARKS UPON THE LAKE AND STILLS THE TEMPEST. Just previous to embarking, some incidents are related, illustrating the nature of Christ's kingdom, and the requirements of discipleship, Mark 4 : 35–41; Luke 8 : 22–25 and 9 : 57–62.

18. **Now when Jesus saw,** etc. And Jesus seeing great, etc. This expression is indefinite as to time, and does not necessarily connect the incidents and miracle here related with the foregoing. It was common for Jesus to be attended with multitudes, and thus there were many times when this could have occurred. The incidents here related come in very aptly after showing the fulfillment of Isaiah's prophecy in Jesus. Alexander thinks he finds here the reason for Matthew's selection of the following miracle, and the attending circumstances, though they probably occurred at a later period. According to Mark 4 : 35, this crossing the lake occurred on the evening after teaching in parables by the sea-side. **Unto the other side.** To the eastern side of the lake.

19. **A certain scribe.** *And one, a scribe, came.* See on ch. 5 : 20. It was a rare occurrence for a scribe to

20 thou goest. And Jesus saith unto him, The foxes have holes, and the birds of the air *have* nests; but ¹ the Son of man ᵐ hath not where to lay *his* head.
21 ⁿ And another of his disciples said unto him, Lord,
22 ᵒ suffer me first to go and bury my father. But

¹ ch. 16. 13; Ps. 80. 17; Dan. 7. 13.
ᵐ 2 Cor. 8. 9.
ⁿ Lk. 9. 59, 60.
ᵒ ch. 19. 29; 1 Ki. 19. 20, 21.

come to Jesus, and offer to become his constant attendant. **Master.** Teacher. **I will follow,** etc. I will become thy constant attendant, sharing with you toils, dangers, difficulties, and successes, everywhere and at all times. This scribe was probably a professed disciple, which is implied in ver. 21 by the words "another disciple," and regarded Jesus as the Messiah; but, like the disciples in general, had wrong views of the nature of Christ's kingdom. He expected a temporal kingdom, and would naturally expect, as one of the constant attendants of Jesus, and a preacher of the glad tidings, to share in its honors and triumphs.

20. The reply of Jesus corrects the scribe's false expectation of comfort and worldly advantage in his service, by showing his own unsettled and homeless condition. Jesus does not forbid him; but rather shows him that, so far from expecting worldly emoluments, he must expect to be a sharer in his poverty and sufferings. Jesus would have him count the cost. It does not appear upon hearing this that he did follow Jesus as a constant attendant. He who is not willing to give up all worldly prospects for Jesus, is not fit to be a minister of the Gospel. See Luke 9 : 60. **The foxes have holes,** dens, lurking-places; and **the birds of the air,** of heaven, **have nests,** shelters, dwelling-places. Even wild and inferior animals have their places of safety and abode; but I am a pilgrim, without property and without a home. **The Son of man.** A favorite name with Jesus, by which he loved to style himself, and yet, with the exception of the expression of the martyr Stephen, who beheld his glorified humanity at the right hand of God (Acts 7 : 56), the name is never applied to him but by himself. It is worthy of notice that in the first three Gospels, where the external life of Jesus is narrated, and his human nature brought out prominently, he more frequently calls himself "the Son of Man;" but in the fourth Gospel, where his inner life and divine being are specially brought to view, he styles himself more frequently "the Son of God," or simply "the Son." Daniel in foretelling Christ's coming with the clouds of heaven, does not say that he saw the Son of Man, but "one like the Son of Man" (Dan. 7 : 13), which implies that, notwithstanding his exaltation and glory, he would come in the form and likeness of a man. See also Rev. 1 : 13 and 14 : 14. This title Jesus applies preëminently to himself as the Messiah, as "God manifested in the flesh," indicating, notwithstanding his divinity, his *true humanity*, and his oneness with the human race. The Jews rightly understood it to mean the Messiah (John 12 : 34), though they did not enter into the fullness of its meaning. He was the Son of Man in the highest sense (Ps. 8 : 3-5; Heb. 2 : 6-9), possessed of all the attributes and characteristics of our common humanity, a perfect and model man, the representative of the race, the second Adam from heaven, 1 Cor. 15 : 45, 47. **Hath not where to lay.** Destitute of a home and its comforts. In following me, therefore, you must expect poverty and hardships. Compare Luke 9 : 52-56.

21. **Another — disciple.** This implies that the scribe was a professed disciple. They were both disciples, at least, in the wider sense of the term, in that they acknowledged his authority as a teacher, and doubtless regarded him as the Messiah, calling him *teacher*, **Lord.** See on ver. 6. **Suffer me.** Permit me. From Luke we learn (Luke 9 : 57-60) that while the scribe made a voluntary offer to become a constant attendant of Jesus, this one received a command, "Follow me." Tradition makes the latter to have been Philip. But he was called long before, John 1 : 43. It could be he only on the supposition that he was becoming slack in the service of Jesus, and that he received the command anew, as in the case of Peter (John 21 : 19), "Follow me." **First to go and bury.** He put a condition on his

Jesus said unto him, Follow me; and let ᵖ the dead bury their dead.
23 And when he was entered into a ship, his dis-
24 ciples followed him. ᑫ And, behold, there arose a

ᵖ Eph. 2. 1; Rev. 3. 1.
ᑫ Mk. 4. 37; Lk. 8. 23.

obeying the command of Jesus; and placed his duty to his father before his duty to Christ. The language implies that his father was dead; not, as some have supposed, that he should go and *wait* till his aged father was dead and buried. The command was immediate, and he indicates his readiness to give immediate obedience so soon as he could perform the funeral rites in burying his father.

22. Jesus did not grant his request. To have done it in this case would have been to acknowledge that the man's duty to his parent was more important than his duty to Christ. Jesus teaches that no duty arising from human relationship should interfere with a duty arising from a positive command of his, requiring immediate obedience. He therefore answers, Follow me, and let the **dead bury their dead.** A few interpreters take *dead*, in both cases, in its literal, physical sense, Let the dead bury one another; which is equivalent to their being left unburied. This would make the words of our Savior mean, Better that your father be left unburied than that you should not give my command the immediate obedience required. It accords, however, better with the compassionate spirit of Jesus to suppose that our Savior meant, not that his father should be left unburied, but that there were others to bury him. The usual interpretation is, therefore, preferable, which regards the word *dead* as used in two senses, the first *spiritual*, as in Rev. 3: 1, the second *literal*. Let the dead in trespasses and sins bury their kindred and friends who are dead in body. As if Jesus had said, Your father has other children, or friends, and they are spiritually dead, and can be of no service in my kingdom; let them attend, then, to his burial; you have an immediate duty to perform higher than any human obligation: "Go thou and preach the kingdom of God," Luke 9: 60. Jesus was ever ready to recognize the claims of filial duty. He himself was subject to his parents in childhood, and on the cross provided a home for his mother. But he could not sanction the conduct of any disciple who would put any duty arising from human relationship before a duty owed to him as the Christ, the Lawgiver of his people. That disciple put forth a wrong principle, and in acting upon it would have done great injury to his own spirituality. In addition to these two, Luke speaks of a third, Luke 9: 61, 62.

23. Matthew now proceeds to relate the miracle of stilling the tempest, to which what just precedes was only incidental and preparatory. Embarking in a **ship**, which was a general name for every grade of merchant or transport vessel, here, probably, a fishing vessel or boat, and propelled both by sails and oars, his **disciples**, those who were his usual attendants, such as Andrew and Peter, James and John, probably the one who had asked permission to go and bury his father, and others, **followed** him into the vessel, to accompany him across the lake. Mark adds that there were other ships with him.

24. **There arose a great tempest.** The word translated *tempest* is translated *earthquake* in ch. 24: 7. It properly means a *shaking, violent agitation*, whether in the water, air, or earth; and here refers to one of those sudden violent squalls or whirlwinds, to which this lake is subject. According to Mark and Luke, it was a great storm of wind. Rev. E. P. Hammond, who visited this lake in 1866, thus describes one of those sudden storms to which it is subject: "It was not long before a fearful storm burst upon us. We were then nearly two miles from the shore, in that part of the sea which is about eight miles wide; but as the fierce waves tossed our boat about like a plaything, it seemed as if the lake suddenly expanded in all directions. I have at different times in my life been in great danger upon the water. I was once upset in a boat on Lake Superior, and had to swim for my life. But never but once, and that when we struck an iceberg in the Atlantic, was I so much alarmed. I really felt we were in danger of going to the bottom. The miserable Arabs seemed to know nothing about managing the boat; and we could not

A.D. 28. MATTHEW VIII. 117

great tempest in the sea, insomuch that the ship was covered with the waves: *t* but he was asleep.
25 And his disciples came to *him*, and awoke him, say-
26 ing, Lord, *save us: we perish! And he saith unto them, *t* Why are ye fearful, O ye of little faith? Then *u* he arose, and rebuked the winds and the
27 sea; and there was a great calm. But the men marveled, saying, *x* What manner of man is this, that even *y* the winds and the sea obey him!
28 *z* And when he was come to the other side, into the country of the Gergesenes, there met him two

t Ps. 44. 22, 23.
s Ps. 46. 1; Ac. 4. 12; 16. 30, 31; Heb. 7. 25.
t ch. 14. 30, 31; Is. 41. 10.
u Job 38. 11; Ps. 65. 7.
x Mk. 4. 41; Lk. 8. 25.
y ch. 14. 25, 32; John 6, 21.
z Mk. 5. 1-21; Lk. 8. 26-40.

---

make them understand a word of our language; and they were as much alarmed as we. One of the ladies was sea-sick. The boat was leaking all the time, and occasionally a large wave paid us an unceremonious visit." The waters were violently agitated, so that the ship **was covered** with the waves that beat in, and was being filled, Mark 4: 37. It is not uncommon for waves to sweep over the deck of a vessel in a storm. **Insomuch that.** So that. **He** is emphatic. While all others were awake and filled with terror, he was asleep, according to Mark, in the hinder part of the ship. He needed sleep on account of the labors of the day; but his sleep and this tempest were simultaneous, so that his disciples might feel their extremity, and be the more deeply impressed with his power over the elements. Like Jonah, he slept in the midst of the storm; but how differently! —the prophet fleeing from duty, Jesus waiting calmly for the exact moment of duty; the prophet the cause, Jesus the allayer of the storm.

25. **Save us; we perish.** How great the tempest thus to terrify his disciples, who were accustomed to fishing and sailing upon the waters of the lake! The words are the cries of intense anxiety, the exclamations of terror, Lord, save us from impending ruin; we are now perishing, we are lost! The destruction which seemed already upon them was the reason for their awakening him, and their cry for help.

26. Jesus first rebukes their troubled hearts. **Why are ye fearful?** or *cowardly?* showing their **want of faith.** They were in great danger, and had not Jesus been on board, there would have been great cause of alarm; but since he was with them, they showed by their alarm that they were of *little faith*, having small confidence in the knowledge and power of Jesus. He then arose and **rebuked the winds and the sea;** commanded the wind not to blow, and the waves of the sea to be still. Some infer from the language that Satan and his demons had caused the storm, and that they are the objects of his rebuke. Jesus speaks, indeed, as to a personal, rational agent, Mark 4: 39. It may be explained, however, by supposing a strong personification. By thus speaking to the wind and sea, he showed that the elements were subject to his bidding. Compare Ps. 106: 9, and 89: 8, 9. And there was a **great calm,** a great stillness; great in contrast to the violent agitation of both air and water which had just subsided. Jesus with his disciples in the ship is a beautiful emblem of the Church tossed and shaken by the tempests of the world, yet always safe; for Jesus is with her to the end. Compare, in contrast, Ezekiel ch. 27, where Tyre is presented under the figure of a vast ship, built, manned, and freighted by the combined skill, strength, beauty, and riches of all nations; but it is broken by the storm and destroyed.

27. **The men marveled.** The men who were in the ship besides Jesus and his disciples; the crew or sailors. They marveled; but alas! it is to be feared they did not recognize the Messiahship of Jesus. So men continue to wonder at the mighty works of God—wonder, despise, and perish.

28-34. HEALING OF TWO DEMONIACS. Mark 5: 1-20; Luke 8: 26-40. The three Evangelists agree in placing this miracle immediately after the stilling of the tempest.

28. **Country of the Gergesenes.** *Gergesenes,* for which reading there is considerable authority, might be explained as identical with the Girgashites, whom

possessed with devils, coming out of the tombs, exceeding fierce, so that no man might pass by that

---

the Israelites under Joshua destroyed, Josh. 3 : 10. Matthew might have called the region, as once inhabited by that tribe, by its ancient name. So also *Gerasene* may be a corruption of the same name. Yet, according to the highest critical authorities, this should be "*country of the Gadarenes;*" and in Mark 5 : 1 and Luke 8 : 26 it should read, "country of the Gerasenes." *Gadara*, now Umkeis, was a city of Perea, a chief city of Decapolis, of considerable importance in the time of Christ. It was on the river Hieromax, about seven miles south-east of the Sea of Galilee; the hill on which it was located has some ruins on the top, and a large number of excavated tombs on its sides. Its territory could well extend to the lake. *Gerasa*, now *Jerash*, on the eastern boundary of Perea, was a town of Decapolis, about forty miles south-east of the scenes of the miracle. Josephus describes it as rich and populous. Ruins now mark its site. Some suppose that a large tract of country adjacent to this city bore its name. Jerome states that in his day the name of Gerasa was given to ancient Gilead. Origen, however, says that a city called Gergesa anciently stood on the eastern shore of the Sea of Galilee. Dr. Thomson thinks he has discovered the ruins of this city, now called *Kersa* or *Gersa*, on the eastern shore of the lake, about midway between the entrance and the outlet of the Jordan. He describes it as " within a few rods of the shore, and an immense mountain rises directly above it, in which are ancient tombs. . . . The lake is so near the base of the mountain, that the swine rushing madly down it could not stop, but would be hurried on into the water and drowned." This is the more probable site, not only of the Gergesa of Origen, but also of the Gerasa of Mark and Luke. The country of Gergesa or Gerasa, probably joined upon that of Gadara; and as the limits of the territory belonging to each city were not very accurately determined, Matthew could call it the country of the Gadarenes, and Mark and Luke the country of the Gerasenes.

Two possessed with devils. With demons. On demoniacal possessions, see ch. 4 : 24. Mark and Luke mention only one possessed with demons. There is no contradiction; for while Matthew speaks of two, the others do not say there were not two, or that there was only one. They only speak of one, without referring to the other, who was probably less remarkable and less prominent. To illustrate take the following example : "In the year 1824, Lafayette visited the United States, and was everywhere welcomed with honors and pageants. Historians will describe these as a noble incident of his life. Other writers will relate the same visit as made, and the same honors as enjoyed, by *two* persons, namely, Lafayette and his son. Will there be any contradiction between these two classes of writers?" Will not both record the truth?"— ROBINSON'S *Harmony of the Gospels*, note on § 57.

The tombs. Having left the dwellings of men, they made their abode in the tombs. The sepulchres of the Hebrews " were generally cut out of the solid rock ; sometimes below the level of the ground, but oftener above the ground, and on the side of mountains. The natural caves, with which the country abounds, were also used for this purpose. "Their size, since they are as large often as a commodious room, and their situation near the traveled paths, cause them to be resorted to as places of shelter for the night. During the winter season, the wandering Arabs sometimes take up their permanent abodes in them."—Dr. HACKETT, *Illus. of Scrip.* pp. 105, 108. Compare Judges 6 : 2. They were **exceeding fierce,** exceedingly ferocious, so that no one **might pass by that way;** no one was able, strong enough, to pass by that way. They had made that road or way impassable for travelers. These are the most terrible cases of demoniacal possessions recorded in the Gospels. No others are represented as possessing such muscular strength, such abandonment of all society, and such savage and uncontrollable ferocity.

29. **Behold** introduces the wonderful fact that these demoniacs, who had made the way impassable, acknowledge the superiority of Jesus. The demons believe and tremble, James 2 : 19, and

29 way. And, behold, they cried out, saying, What have we to do with thee, Jesus, ᵃ thou Son of God? art thou come hither to torment us ᵇ before the time?
30 And there was a good way off from them an herd of
31 many ᶜ swine feeding. So the devils ᵈ besought him saying, If thou cast us out, suffer us to go
32 away into the herd of swine. And he said unto them, ᵉ Go. And when they were come out, they went into the herd of swine: and, behold, the whole herd of swine ran violently down a steep place into the sea, and perished in the waters.

ᵃ ch. 4. 3; Lk. 3. 11; Lk. 4. 41; Ac. 16. 17; Jam. 2. 19.
ᵇ 2 Pet. 2. 4; Jude 6.
ᶜ Le. 7. 11.
ᵈ Job. 1. 10-12; 2. 3-6; Lk. 10. 17.
ᵉ 1 Pet. 3. 22.

show greater knowledge of the character of Jesus than the men of his time. **What have we to do with thee?** Thus the demons speak through the men, so thorough was their control over both body and soul. This phrase is common to the Hebrew and the later Greek (2 Sam. 16 : 10; 19 : 23; 1 Kings 17 : 18 ; John 2 : 4), and means, What is there in common between us? Why interfere with us? Ezra 4 : 3. **Son of God.** As a participator in the divine essence, and therefore possessed of divine power. See on verse 20 above. They had discovered this power, for he had already commanded them to come out, Mark 5 : 8. **Art thou come hither to torment us before the time?** Before *the time* of their doom, the day of judgment. Jesus speaks of "everlasting fire prepared for the devil and his angels" (ch. 25 : 41), Peter, that God had "delivered them over to chains of darkness, reserved for judgment" (2 Pet. 2 : 4); and Jude, that they are "reserved in everlasting chains under darkness unto the judgment of the great day," Jude 6. The demons admit their coming doom, and ask if he, the Son of God, had come to execute it, or rather, to inflict the torture, the torment, the pains of hell, before the time appointed.

30. **A herd of many swine.** About two thousand, Mark 5 : 13. Since swine were unclean to the Jews (Lev. 11 : 7, 8), and they were prohibited from keeping them, (Lightfoot, 315), and since Gadara, according to Josephus, was a Greek city, and many Gentiles inhabited that region, it is probable that the keepers of these swine were Gentiles.

31. **So.** And. Since the demons can not remain in the men, they desire that they may not be sent out of the country (Mark 5 : 10); but that he would **suffer them to go ;** or according to the best critical authorities, *send* them away into the herd of swine. They prefer to possess the bodies of brutes rather than to be sent away from their permitted residence on earth to their residence of darkness below. How they could possess inferior animals is not difficult to imagine, since they so thoroughly possessed the lower and sensual nature of men. They could exert no moral and intellectual influence, as in man; but they could operate through the organs of their bodies, and through their animal and sensual natures.

32. **Go.** Why Jesus granted the request of the demons, we are not informed. The requests of Satan are sometimes granted, Job 1 : 12 ; 2 : 6. By giving them this permission, it was clearly shown that demons do exist, that those possessed with demons were not simply insane, or suffering from mere bodily disease. It showed their power and malice in this particular instance, and hence the greatness of the miracle. According to Mark, their name was *Legion*, which had come to signify an indefinitely large number. The two thousand swine is suggestive of their smallest supposed number; for we must suppose at least as many demons as swine. The swine manifest the power and malignity with which they are possessed by rushing down the steep into the lake, where they perish by drowning. The power of Jesus is thus manifested over the powers of darkness, and their final and utter overthrow is foreshadowed.

This miracle and that of the withered fig-tree which Jesus cursed (ch. 21 : 18–20) are the only ones which resulted in any destruction of property. On this point Dr. Alford remarks : "We may well think that, if God has appointed so

33 ʳ And they that kept them fled, and went their ways into the city, and told every thing, and what was be-
34 fallen to the possessed of the devils. And, behold, the whole city came out to meet Jesus. And when they saw him, ᵍ they besought *him* that he would depart out of their coasts.

ʳ Mk. 5. 14-18; Lk. 8. 37-39.

ᵍ 1 Ki. 18. 17; Job 21. 14; Ac. 16. 39.

many animals daily to be slaughtered for the sustenance of men's bodies, he may also be pleased to destroy animal life, when he sees fit, for the liberation or instruction of souls. Besides, if the confessedly far greater evil of the possession of *men* by evil spirits, and all the misery thereupon attendant, was permitted in God's inscrutable purposes, surely much more this lesser one. Whether there may have been special reasons in this case, such as a contempt of the Mosaic law by the keepers of the swine, we have no means of judging; but it is at least possible." In addition, it may be said, the permission was our Lord's, the destruction of the swine the work of the demons. Our Lord was no more responsible for what the demons did than he is for what wicked men do whom he permits to live and to hold high places in our world. Besides, Christ had a right to send them where he pleased.

33. Astonished and affrighted, the herdsmen fled and went away into the city, and **told every thing,** all that had occurred. They told not only what had happened to the swine, but what had **befallen to the possessed of the devils;** how that the demons had been cast out, and the two men restored to their right minds.

34. **The whole city.** The mass of the people came out to meet Jesus as he was approaching the city. How worldly interests excite men! They see Jesus, and also one who had possibly been a fellow-citizen, yet for a time a raving maniac, living like a wild man and wearing no clothing, but now calmly sitting at the feet of Jesus, clothed, and in his right mind, Luke 8 : 27, 35. But they valued worldly gain above the blessings attending the miracles of Jesus. To their minds the loss of the herd of swine more than counterbalanced the cure of the demoniacs. And besides, they may have feared that similar results would attend other miracles. Other owners of swine may have thought their traffic in danger. Compare Acts 19 : 24-31. They, therefore, besought Jesus to **depart out of their coasts,** their borders. See ch. 2 : 16. Jesus acceded to their request, and let them alone. We do not read of his ever visiting them again.

REMARKS.

1. Christ is the Wonderful—wonderful in his words; wonderful in his deeds; and wonderful in his saving power, ver. 1; Isa. 9 : 6.
2. In leprosy we have a striking type of sin, a most loathsome disease, one deeply seated, gradually showing itself on the surface, progressive, fearfully destructive, incurable by human means (2 Kings 5 : 7), and cutting off the person diseased from the society of the clean, ver. 2.
3. In the leper that came to Jesus we have a type of the sinner seeking Jesus, and saved by him. He *felt* that he was diseased; he *despaired* of human help; he exercised *confidence* in the power of Jesus; and *submitted* to *the will* of Jesus, and was healed, vers. 2, 3.
4. The soldier is encouraged to look to Jesus. Three centurions are specially referred to in the Gospels and the Acts, ch. 27 : 43; Acts 10 : 1. Soldiers came to John the Baptist, Luke 3 : 14; ver. 5.
5. The centurion presents a beautiful example of faith. A belief on testimony; an unwavering confidence in the power of Jesus, and that his power was not limited to time and place; showing itself in earnest entreaty, and connected with divine compassion, vers. 6-9.
6. We also have in the centurion a striking exhibition of humility. What thoughts does he have of himself, notwithstanding his prosperous circumstances and his honorable station, and what high veneration for Jesus! Humility rests on faith, and is inseparable from it, ver. 8.
7. The centurion's faith was condemnatory of the unbelief of the Jews. It was a foreshadowing of that faith by which the Gentiles should surpass Israel, vers. 10, 11; Rom. 9 : 31, 32.

IX. AND he entered into a ship, and passed over, [h] [h] ch. 4. 13.
and came into his own city.

---

8. External advantages, and pious parents and friends, give no title to the privileges and blessings of God's people, either here or hereafter, vers. 11, 12.

9. Faith in Jesus receives an immediate answer, though the evidence of it may not be seen at the moment. By inquiry the centurion found that the answer of Jesus to his prayer of faith was immediate, ver. 13; Acts 9 : 11.

10. They who are restored to spiritual health should use their strength in ministering to Christ and his people, ver. 15.

11. The whole life of Jesus was a continued scene of humiliation and sufferings, culminating in his death upon the cross. There was a close connection between his active and passive obedience, ver. 17; Phil. 2 : 6-8.

12. In sickness and death we can rest on Jesus as our Consoler, Sustainer, and Deliverer, vers. 14-17; Acts 7 : 55-60.

13. How great the condescension and poverty of Jesus! He had no place where he might lay his head, ver. 20.

14. All who would follow Jesus should count the cost. They must be willing, if necessary, like him, to be homeless, ver. 20; Luke 14 : 27-33.

15. Honest poverty is no disgrace. It is no dishonor to be like Christ in our earthly condition, ver. 20.

16. Not every profound scholar, though a Christian, should be a preacher of the Gospel, vers. 19, 20.

17. Duties to Christ should occupy the first place. Our ease, comforts, interests, or even human friendships and obligations, should not interfere with our obedience to the commands of Christ, vers. 21, 22; ch. 10 : 37-39.

18. In the stilling of the tempest we have a four-fold illustration—of Christ with his people of every age; Christ with his church, against which the gates of hell shall not prevail; Christ with the believer through the voyage of life; and Christ with the repenting sinner, allaying his fears with his word of forgiveness, vers. 23-27.

19. Faith will tranquilize the soul amid the greatest trials and dangers, and, so far as is for our good, will result in tranquillizing or bettering our external circumstances, vers. 26, 27; Isa. 26 : 3.

20. Christ is Lord of the elements. He will deliver them from the curse of sin, and subject them to the good of his children, ver. 26; Rom. 8 : 18-23.

21. The powers of hell are subject to the word of Jesus. They can not go beyond his permission, vers. 28-32; Luke 10 : 18, 19.

22. In the demoniacs of Gadara we see a type of those who are under the spiritual power of Satan. "Thus do they break asunder the bonds of reason and gratitude, and sometimes of authority, and even of shame; and thus driven on by the frenzy of their lusts and passions, they are so outrageous as to injure others, and to wound themselves."—DODDRIDGE. Ver. 28; Jude 12, 13, 16.

23. We also see the power of Christ. Salvation is possible to the most desperate, vers. 29-32; Heb. 7 : 25.

24. Christ may permit our property to be taken from us, either in mercy or in judgment, ver. 32.

25. In the drowning of the swine, we see the destructive nature of the devil's power. The wicked shall perish, ver. 32.

26. The modern rationalist and skeptic, like the Gadarenes, find fault with Jesus for healing the maniacs and destroying the swine, ver. 33.

27. Christ often answers the prayer of the wicked, "Depart from us, for we desire not the knowledge of thy ways," and leaves them to perish, ver. 34.

CHAPTER IX.

1. This verse presents the sequel to the healing of the demoniacs of Gadara. Jesus, taking those at their word who besought him to depart from their borders, **entered into a ship,** rather *the ship* in which he came hither, and passed over the lake and came to **his own city,** Capernaum, ch. 4 : 13.

2-8. HEALING OF A PARALYTIC AT CAPERNAUM. Mark 2 : 1-12; Luke 5 : 17-26. In this and the preceding chapter we have a good illustration of Matthew's manner of grouping events. See HARMONY OF THE GOSPELS, by the AUTHOR.

2. **And behold.** These words introduce the remarkable miracle and circumstances that follow, which are, however, more fully related by Mark and Luke. They do not necessarily connect the miracle in point of time

Jesus heals a paralytic at Capernaum.

2 ¹ And, behold, they brought to him a man sick of the palsy, lying on a bed: and Jesus seeing their faith said unto the sick of the palsy, Son, be of 3 good cheer; thy sins be forgiven thee. And, behold, certain of the scribes said within themselves, 4 This *man* blasphemeth. And Jesus ʲ knowing their thoughts said, Wherefore think ye evil in your

¹ Mk. 2, 3-12; Lk. 5. 18-26; ch. 12. 25; Ps. 139. 2; Ac. 3. 6.

ʲ Ps. 139. 2; ch. 12. 25; Mk. 12. 15; Lk. 9. 47.

with the healing of the demoniacs. Luke is indefinite; "it came to pass on a certain day," Luke 5:18. So is also Mark. Matthew, doubtless, selected this miracle as closely associated with his own call, which occurred immediately after, ver. 9. **They brought to him.** There were four men, as we learn from Mark 2:3 and Luke 5:18. Jesus was teaching in a certain house, Mark 2:1. **A man sick of the palsy.** The translation of one Greek word, which may be rendered *a paralytic*, one who had lost the power of muscular motion. See on 4:24; 8:6. **Lying on a bed.** Probably a pallet, or perhaps a rug or mere blanket. It was light. Jesus afterward commanded him to take it up and walk, ver. 6. **Seeing their faith.** Perceiving their faith by what they did. From the other Evangelists we learn that, being unable to come near to Jesus on account of the multitude, they went upon the housetop, and let the palsied man down through the tiling on his couch into the midst before Jesus. It is implied by what follows that the palsied man also exercised faith; perhaps he directed the men what to do. **Son.** *Child.* A title of condescension and kindness, and in this case expressive of an endearing spiritual relation just formed between Jesus and the sick man. **Be of good cheer.** Take heart, take courage. **Thy sins be forgiven.** It seems that this disease had awakened in him a sense of sin; possibly it had come upon him on account of some special sinful indulgence. Jesus, perceiving his burdened soul, his penitence in the sight of God, and his faith in him as the Messiah, addressed first his spiritual nature and attended to the deeper and more dangerous disease of sin. His words, "Thy sins are forgiven," gave peace to the sick man's soul, and were designed to teach those who heard that he came not to remove the *lesser evils* only, but also *sin*, which is the root of all. They were also a pledge to the palsied man, whose body and spirit doubtless reacted on each other, that his disease would in due time be healed. In our Savior's miracles there was doubtless a close connection between bodily healing and spiritual healing. Thus, the cleansed Samaritan "glorified God" (Luke 17:16); the impotent man, after he was made whole, was commanded to "sin no more" (John 5:14); the one born blind *believed* so soon as Jesus made known to him that he was the Son of God (John 9:35-38); and the blind man near Jericho, having received his sight, "followed" Jesus, "glorifying God," Luke 18:43. In James 5:14, 15 we also find a close relation recognized between the raising of the sick and the forgiving of his sins. We must not suppose, however, that Jesus adopted the Jewish notion that every suffering was caused by some specific sin. Such a notion he elsewhere condemns, John 9:3; Luke 13:2-5.

3. **Certain of the scribes.** See ch. 2:4. From Luke we learn that there were present Pharisees and doctors or teachers of the law from every village of Galilee, and Judea and Jerusalem. Certain of these expounders of the law and spiritual guides of the people **said within themselves,** "reasoning," as Mark has it, "in their hearts," **This man blasphemeth.** The word translated blaspheme primarily signified to speak evil, slander; and in its scriptural application to God, to speak irreverently, impiously to or of Him, also to arrogate to one's self what is the prerogative of God. The latter is the meaning here. The Scribes thought that Jesus blasphemed by usurping (in his words and acts) the prerogative of God to forgive sins, Luke 5:21.

4. **Jesus knowing their thoughts.** Omniscience was an evidence of the Messiahship of Jesus. He knew what was in man, John 2:25. "When Bar Covan declared himself Messiah, the

5 hearts? For whether is easier, to say, *Thy* sins be
6 forgiven thee; or to say, Arise, and walk? But that ye may know that the Son of man hath power on earth to forgive sins (then saith he to the sick of the palsy), Arise, take up thy bed, and go unto
7 thine house. And he arose, and departed to his
8 house. But when the multitudes saw *it*, they marveled, and glorified God, which had given such power unto men.

The call of Matthew, and the feast at his house; discourse concerning fasting.

9 ᵏ AND as Jesus passed forth from thence, he saw

ᵏ Mk. 2. 14; Lk. 5. 27, 28.

---

rabbins quoted Isa. 11 : 3, and examined him to see if he could reveal the secrets of their hearts. He failed, and they slew him."—WHEDON. **Wherefore think ye evil,** etc. Why ponder such evil things concerning me? Why revolve in your hearts such evil thoughts in attributing blasphemy to me, because I claim the power of forgiving sin? Do not my wonderful miracles sustain my claim?
5. **For whether is easier.** For which is easier. To perform miracles is as really the work of God as to forgive sins. But it should be noticed that Jesus does not ask which is the easier *to do;* but "which is easier *to say*, Thy sins are forgiven; or *to say*, Arise, and walk." To these fault-finding scribes, it would appear easier to pronounce a man's sins forgiven than to pronounce a palsied man whole and sound. In the latter case, if the diseased man was not healed, his claim would not be sustained, and he would be shown to be an impostor; but in the former case, the evidences whether his sins were forgiven or not would be spiritual and unseen, and hence his claim could not be so easily disproved. See TRENCH *on the Miracles*, p. 169.
6, 7. Jesus, however, proposes to give an external proof of his power as the Messiah to forgive sins, by performing a miracle on the palsied man. Here do we see the wisdom of Jesus in first pronouncing the man's sins forgiven, and then giving a proof of his power and putting an end to all caviling by the miracle that immediately follows. **Son of Man.** The Messiah. See on ch. 8 : 20. **Power on earth.** The *authority* and consequent *power*, not only in heaven, but also on earth, the place where sins are committed and forgiven;

see ch. 28 : 18. At his command the palsied man **arose and departed to his house.** Jesus thus sustained his claim, and gave a new evidence that he was God manifested in the flesh. He did not account it robbery to be equal with God, Phil. 2 : 6.
8. Matthew now describes the effect of this miracle on the people who witnessed it. **They marveled.** The most ancient Greek manuscripts have here a word which means *were afraid* or *feared*. They were filled with religious awe at such an exhibition of divine power. It does not describe the effect on the Scribes. They were cavilers, and were determined to be pleased with nothing. But the common people, of whom the multitudes were mostly composed, feared and **glorified God,** made him glorious by grateful and adoring praise. The reason of their fear and their praise was, that God **had given such power unto men.** The power not only of healing diseases, but also of forgiving sin. They appear to have had no conception of the divine nature of Jesus. **Unto men.** To mankind. They were convinced by the miracle that Jesus possessed such power. But they regarded him as a man, and hence they would naturally conclude that the same power might be possessed, under the proper circumstances, by other men. They therefore recognized this power as a gift of God to mankind; and did not then perceive its true ground, the divinity of Jesus, God manifested in the flesh, 1 Tim. 3 : 16.
9–17. THE CALLING OF MATTHEW, AND THE FEAST AT HIS HOUSE. The conversations concerning our Lord's treatment of publicans and sinners, and concerning fasting, Mark 2 : 13–22; Luke 5 : 27–39.
9. **And as Jesus passed forth from**

a man, named Matthew, sitting at the receipt of custom: and he saith unto him, ¹ Follow me. And he arose, and followed him.

10 ᵐ And it came to pass, as Jesus sat at meat in the house, behold, many publicans and sinners came and
11 sat down with him and his disciples. And when

ch. 4. 18–22; Jno. 1. 43–45; 8. 12.
ᵐ Mk. 2. 15–17; Lk. 5. 29–32; ch. 11. 19.

---

thence. The first three Evangelists agree in placing the call of Matthew immediately after the miracle just narrated. Jesus went forth to the sea-side (Mark 2 : 13), and passing along, he saw **Matthew,** whom Mark and Luke call *Levi.* In none of the four lists of the apostles, however, is the name of Levi found; but in one of them (ch. 10 : 3) we have the name of *Matthew the publican.* The three narratives clearly relate the same circumstances, and point to Matthew as identical with Levi. All difficulties are obviated by supposing that he had a double name, like Peter, Paul, or Mark; and that he speaks of himself as he was familiarly known as an apostle, and as he ever regarded himself and his life after his conversion, *a gift of Jehovah,* for so the name Matthew means; and that Mark and Luke designated him by the name by which he was commonly known before his conversion. **Sitting at the receipt of custom.** At the place of receiving custom, which may have been a regular custom-house or a temporary office. The revenues which Rome derived from the conquered countries consisted chiefly of tolls, tithes, harbor duties, tax for the use of public pasture lands, and duties for the use of mines and salt-works. See on ch. 5 : 46. *Sitting,* Dr. Thomson remarks, is the usual posture of the people of this country at all kinds of work. Our Savior's call, **Follow me,** does not necessarily imply that this was Matthew's first acquaintance with Jesus. Like Andrew and Peter (ch. 4 : 18, 19, and John 1 : 40–42), he had doubtless before this heard Jesus and witnessed his miracles, and recognized him as the Messiah. Like them, he seems to be called not as a mere disciple, nor yet as one of the apostles, but as one of his constant attendants, a preacher of the Gospel, an evangelist. Like them, Luke tells us, *he left all* and followed him,

Luke 5 : 28. Matthew modestly says, "he arose and followed him."

10. Matthew proceeds to relate two conversations that occurred during a feast at his house. It is not necessary to

RECLINING AT TABLE.

suppose that this took place immediately after his call. A little time may have intervened. **As Jesus sat at meat.** Reclined at table, according to the custom of the time, on a couch, resting on the left arm. **In the house.** Of Matthew, Luke 5 : 29. Luke records that this feast was provided by Matthew himself; probably with the purpose of both honoring Jesus, and of bringing his former associates under his teaching and influence. We have here another instance of the modesty (see ver. 9) of Matthew. He makes such a slight reference to this "great feast" which he had provided that, if it were not for the accounts of Mark and Luke, we would be left in doubt whether it were a feast or a common meal, and whether it was at the house of Matthew or at the house where Jesus dwelt at the time. **Many publicans and sinners.** Tax-gatherers and vicious persons. The publicans were peculiarly odious among the Jews, and their employment was attended with so much corruption and fraud that they were ranked among the

the Pharisees saw *it*, they said unto his disciples, Why eateth your Master with publicans and sin-
12 ners? But when Jesus heard *that*, he said unto them, They that be whole need not a physician, but
13 they that are sick. But ⁿ go ye and learn what *that* meaneth, ᵒ 'I will have mercy, and not sacrifice:' for I am not come to call the righteous, but sinners to repentance.

ⁿ ch. 12. 3, 5, 7; Lk. 10. 28.
ᵒ 1 Sam. 15. 22; Pro. 21. 3; Hos. 6. 6; Mic. 6. 6–8.

---

basest and the most depraved. See on ch. 5 : 29.

11. The Pharisees could not but acknowledge the unblemished character of Jesus; they could not charge him with sin. But they thought he associated with unsuitable persons; they condemned his familiar intercourse with those whom they excommunicated from their synagogues. But instead of coming out frankly, they oppose him underhandedly, captiously asking his disciples, "Why eateth your **master,** your *teacher*, with publicans and sinners?" This at least seemed to them as inconsistent with his high pretensions as a religious teacher.

12. Jesus hearing it, answers it himself. The correct text reads, *And hearing it he said*, omitting **Jesus** and **unto them** (Mark 2 : 13). **They that are whole need not a physician, but they that are sick.** These publicans and sinners were diseased with sin; they therefore needed his attentions as the great Physician of the soul. The fact that they were vile and notorious sinners only made his attentions the more necessary. And if any were really righteous, as the Pharisees imagined they were, then they did not need his healing and saving power. The Pharisees thus misunderstood the great object of his mission, that he came into the world to save sinners.

13. Jesus further vindicates himself, and condemns the principle on which the Pharisees acted, by quoting Hos. 6 : 6. **Go** and **learn.** You have not yet learned what you ought to have known, and what is so plainly taught in Scripture. A severe reproach for their ignorance. **I will have mercy,** etc. I desire mercy and not sacrifice. *Mercy* is the exercise of kindness and compassion toward the needy and the suffering. In opposition to *mercy is sacrifice*, which here represents all ceremonial observances. The meaning is: I desire mercy more than the most careful attention merely to external rites. Sacrifices were indeed appointed by God; to offer was a part of obedience; but they were not so important as a merciful disposition. Their most exact observance was only acceptable to God when they were expressive of a penitent, forgiving, and merciful heart. And if at any time the two came in conflict, the external observance must give way to the internal. The Scribes and Pharisees were therefore in the wrong. Their religion lay in the careful observance merely of external ceremonies. They carried this so far that they even neglected to exercise mercy, and do good to the bodies and souls of publicans and sinners, for fear of contracting outward defilement. It was in the true spirit of this Scripture that Jesus associated with this forsaken and despised class of men, in order that he might do them good and save their souls; for he came not **to call the righteous, but sinners.** The idea of the passage is better presented by translating, *I come not to call righteous men, but sinners.* He does not say that there are any absolutely righteous men, but rather implies the contrary. He came not to call men as unfallen and holy beings, but as sinners. **Repentance** is not found in the oldest manuscripts, and is therefore omitted by the highest and latest authorities. It is, however, found in Luke's account (Luke 5 : 32), and is explanatory of our Savior's language as more briefly given by Matthew and Mark. To call righteous men to repentance would be absurd, but sinners would be reasonable and becoming. He was, therefore, but carrying out the object of his mission, as well as exemplifying the true spirit of piety, in associating with and preaching to publicans and sinners.

14. Another conversation occurs. While Jesus and his disciples were enjoying a day of feasting, the Pharisees

14 Then came to him the disciples of John, saying, ᵖ Why do we and the Pharisees fast oft, but thy
15 disciples fast not? And Jesus said unto them, Can ᑫ the children of the bridechamber mourn, as long as the bridegroom is with them? but the days will come, ʳ when the bridegroom shall be taken from
16 them, and ˢ then shall they fast. ᵗ No man put-

ᵖ Mk. 2. 18–22 ; Lk. 5. 33–39 ; 18. 12.
ᑫ Ps. 45. 14. 15; John 3. 29 ; Judg. 14. 10. 11.
ʳ Lk. 24. 13–21; John 16. 6. 20-22.
ˢ Ac. 13. 2, 3; 14. 23.

---

and the disciples of John were fasting, Mark 2 : 18. This coincidence made the difference between Jesus and his disciples and the Pharisees and the disciples of John the more conspicuous. Hence the question which follows. Had the **disciples of John** possessed the spirit of the great forerunner, and obeyed his precepts, they would all have become followers of Christ, John 1 : 29–36 ; 3 : 27–34. But even while John was yet baptizing, they showed a spirit of rivalry (John 3 : 26), and after his imprisonment departed still further from the spirit of his instructions. They maintained a separate party (see also Acts 19 : 4, 5), and probably practiced a sort of austere and rigid morality, and in some points resembled the better part of the Pharisees. Both they and the Pharisees came to Jesus and questioned him in regard to fasting, Mark 2 : 18. This gives the clue for harmonizing Matthew and Luke, the former stating that the disciples of John, the latter, that the Pharisees—who had just before been conversing with Jesus—put the question. Both parties were among the questioners.

Fast oft. The only stated fast enjoined by Moses was that of the great day of atonement. Lev. 16 : 29. Other fasts were added after the destruction of the first temple, Zech. 7 : 5 ; 8 : 19 ; that of the fourth month, commemorating the capture of Jerusalem by the Chaldeans, Jer. 52 : 6, 7 ; that of the fifth month, commemorating the destruction of the temple, Jer. 52 : 12, 13 ; that of the seventh month, commemorating the murder of Gedaliah, 2 Kings 25 : 25 ; Jer. 41 : 1, 2 ; that of the tenth month, commemorating the beginning of the siege of Jerusalem by Nebuchadrezzar, Jer. 52 : 4 ; that of Esther, on the 13th of the twelfth month, commemorating the deliverance of the Jews on that eventful day, Esther 9 : 31 ; 4 : 16, 17. The Pharisees also observed two weekly fasts (Luke 18 : 12), on the second and fifth day, Monday and Thursday. The disciples of John doubtless observed the stated fasts of the Jews, and imitated their teacher in respect to his rigid habits and fastings ; for John came neither eating nor drinking, ch. 11 : 18. His imprisonment would also be an additional incentive to fasting. **But thy disciples fast not.** Notice again the want of frankness. They now complain to him of his disciples, as in ver. 11 they complained to his disciples of him. By their question they showed that they had difficulty in harmonizing his professions as a great teacher sent from God, and the neglect of fasting, upon which they laid so much stress.

15. Jesus replies to the inquiry by presenting three illustrations, showing how unbecoming it would be for his disciples to fast at that time. **Children of the bride-chamber.** *Sons*, etc. These were the male attendants of the bridegroom, who upon the day of marriage went with him to the house of the bride (Jud. 14 : 11), in order to bring her home. The marriage feast lasted seven days. Could it be expected that the sons of the bride-chamber, the attendants on the bridegroom, would mourn on a nuptial occasion? Nothing would be more unsuitable. Christ had been represented as the bridegroom by John (John 3 : 29), and also long before by the prophets, Ps. 45 ; Isa. 54 : 5 ; 62 : 5. And now Jesus announces himself as the glorious Bridegroom, and here represents his disciples as his friends. How unsuitable for them to fast while he was with them! It became them to rejoice at his presence. But the time is coming when he shall be taken from them ; and **then shall they fast.** Fasting on proper occasions will then be becoming. He does not teach that they should have stated days for fasting ; for the principle he lays down is, that fasting is becoming only when there is a reason, an occasion for it. He merely announces the general fact, that they shall fast, implying that there would be trials and dangers attend-

teth a piece of new cloth unto an old garment, for that which is put in to fill it up taketh from the 17 garment, and the rent is made worse. Neither do men put new wine into ᵘ old bottles: else the bottles break, and the wine runneth out, ˣ and the bottles perish: but they put new wine into new bottles, and both are preserved.

ᵗ John 16. 12; 1 Cor. 3. 1. 2.
ᵘ Job 32. 19.
ˣ Jos. 9. 4.

Raising of Jairus' daughter; healing of a woman with an issue of blood, of two blind men, and of a dumb demoniac.

ʸ Mk. 5. 22–43; Lk. 8. 41–56.

18 ʸ WHILE he spake these things unto them, be-

ing them, making such a service suitable.

16. The second illustration, drawn from the familiar art of patching, in which he gives an instance of what no one of his hearers would think of doing. **New cloth.** Unfulled cloth; cloth not yet dressed, or fulled, and liable to shrink upon being wet; and hence, if put on an old garment would take from it by shrinking, and a worse rent would be made. There is an unfitness in thus patching an old garment with unfulled cloth. It would be an act of unheard-of folly. But equally unfit, equally an act of folly, would it be to unite fasting, which is a sign of sorrow, with the joyous work of my disciples, while I, their Lord, am with them. You must not expect in my kingdom a mere patching up of the old dispensation, but a complete renovation, and one harmonious and congruous in all its parts.

17. The third illustration, drawn from the common experience and practice of putting up wine in our Savior's day. **Bottles.** Bags or vessels for holding, preserving, and transporting liquids were then made not of glass, but of the skins of animals. Dr. Hackett, in his *Illustrations of Scripture* (p. 48), says, "The use of skin bottles prevails still very extensively in all parts of western Asia... At Cairo I saw them at almost every turn in the streets, and on the backs of the water carriers between that city and Bulak, its port on the Nile. After that, I met them constantly, wherever I traveled, both in Egypt and Syria. They are made of skins of animals, especially of the goat, and in various forms. They are more commonly made so as to retain the figure of the animal from which the skin is taken. . . . That bottles of this shape have been used in the eastern countries from the earliest antiquity, that they were common in the days of the patriarchs and the Pharaohs, I had an interesting proof in one of the tombs near the Ghizeh pyramids. Among the figures on the walls, I saw a goat-shaped bottle, as exactly like those now seen in Cairo as if it had been painted from one of them by a modern artist. It was not a 'bottle' in our sense of the word, but 'water-skin,' according to the Hebrew, which Abraham took and placed on the shoulder of Hagar, when he sent her forth into the desert, Gen. 21 : 14." Wine bottles, or rather wine-skins, are mentioned in Josh. 9 : 4, 13, which were "*old*, and *rent*."

Old bottles, or *skins*, being dry, cracked, and rotten, are unsuited for holding **new wine,** which would ferment, expand, and **break,** *burst* them. But the new bottles, or skins, being stronger and less rigid, and capable of expansion, are properly used for that purpose. As it was unbecoming to put new wine in old bottles, so was it unbecoming for his disciples to fast while their Lord and Teacher was with them. Jesus intimates in this illustration, as well as in the last, that the new dispensation was not to be mixed up with the old. The doctrines and the spirit of Christ's kingdom were not to be joined with the forms of the Mosaic law, much less to those of Pharisaical and traditional corruption. The Gospel, like the new wine, must have its new forms and means for its preservation and propagation.

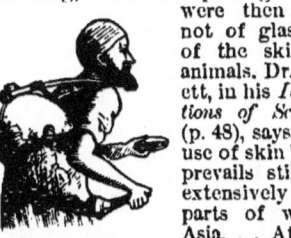

SKIN BOTTLES.

hold, there came a certain ruler, and worshiped him, saying, My daughter is even now dead: but come and ᵃ lay thy hand upon her, and she shall
19 live. And Jesus arose, and followed him, and *so did* his disciples.
20 ᵃ And, behold, a woman, which was diseased with an issue of blood twelve years, came behind *him,*
21 and ᵇ touched the ᶜ hem of his garment: for she said within herself, If I may but touch his garment,
22 I shall be whole. But Jesus turned him about, and

ᶻ Ac. 4. 30.

ᵃ Mk. 5. 25; Lk 8. 43.
ᵇ ch. 14. 36; Mk. 3. 10.
ᶜ Num. 15. 38, 39.

18–26. RAISING OF JAIRUS' DAUGHTER, AND THE HEALING OF A WOMAN WITH AN ISSUE OF BLOOD. The accounts of these two miracles are interwoven, the latter having been performed while Jesus was on his way to work the former, Mark 5 : 22–43; Luke 8 : 41–56.

18. **While he spake these things** in the house of Matthew, there came to him a **certain ruler,** as Mark and Luke inform us, of the synagogue, and named Jairus. The ruler of the synagogue presided over the assembly, convening it, preserving order, and invited readers and speakers. See Acts 13 : 15. **Worshiped him.** Bowed down to him; did him reverence. How much religious homage there was in this we have no means of knowing. See on ch. 8 : 2. Mark (ch. 5 : 22) and Luke (ch. 8 : 41) describe him as falling at the feet of Jesus. **My daughter is even now dead.** *Has just now died.* "My little daughter lieth at the point of death," Mark 5 : 23. "He had one only daughter, about twelve years of age, and she lay a dying," Luke 8 : 42. As she was in this state when her father left her, he may on reaching Jesus have given vent to his fears by the strong statement, she "has just now died;" and then have explained himself, by saying that she was at the point of death, or dying. He seems to have thought that personal contact, the *laying his hand on her*, was necessary. His faith, though strong, was not of so high a type as that of the centurion at Capernaum, ch. 8 : 8–10.

19. Upon receiving the application of Jairus, Jesus **arose** from the table in the house of Matthew, where he had been conversing with the Pharisees and the disciples of John, and started on his errand of mercy, accompanied by his **disciples,** those who were his constant attendants, together with those who held him to be a teacher sent from God. Much people also followed him and thronged him, Mark 5 : 24. **Followed him.** Was following him. This marks the time and place of the miracle upon the woman which is now narrated.

20. **A woman** having a disease which, according to the law, rendered her unclean. The details of her peculiar malady are unnecessary. Its continuance is especially noted, **twelve years.** She had probably been possessed of wealth and had moved in good society; but the expenses of many physicians and their remedies had reduced her to poverty; she had suffered much, and her disease instead of becoming better had grown worse, Mark 5 : 26. How pitiable her condition! Excluded from society, and suffering from what was regarded an incurable disease! But she had heard of Jesus, and she had faith in his power to heal her. She approached him from **behind,** both from a sense of her unworthiness and her uncleanness, and also to escape observation, and **touched the hem of his outer garment.** It was not the *hem*, but the *fringe*, as the Greek should be here translated, which she touched. The Jews were commanded to wear blue fringes on the borders of their garments, to remind them that they were the true people of God, Num. 15 : 38, 39.

21. Her faith is vividly presented by revealing what were the thoughts of her heart. While she was pressing through the crowd, she said within herself, **If I may but touch,** if I only touch, **his garment,** no matter what part of it, **I shall be made whole** from my disease. Like Jairus, she thought there must be some contact with Jesus. He thought there was virtue in the laying on of his hand; she, in but touching his garment; but yet both traced the

when he saw her, he said, Daughter, be of good comfort; ᵈ thy faith hath made thee whole. And the woman was made whole from that hour.

23 ᵉ And when Jesus came into the ruler's house, and saw ᶠ the minstrels and the people making a noise,
24 he said unto them, ᵍ Give place: for the maid is not dead, but sleepeth. And they laughed him to

ᵈ Mk. 10. 52; Lk. 7. 50; 8. 48; 17. 19.
ᵉ Mk. 5. 38; Lk 8. 51.
ᶠ See 2 Chr. 35. 25; Jer. 9. 17.
ᵍ Ac. 9. 40; 20. 10.

---

power back to Jesus himself. There may be true faith, and even strong faith, amid much superstition.

22. The other Evangelists relate that Jesus asked who touched him, when the woman came forward and made confession of what she had done and the cure effected in herself. **Daughter.** A term of tender kindness. **Be of good comfort.** Be of good cheer, the same as in ver. 2. **Thy faith,** etc. Her faith, as a condition, as a means, resulted in a cure; Christ was the cause. His power was exerted according to her faith. Jesus was not confined to any one mode of healing. In this instance a simple touch of his garment was followed by a cure, which was adapted to impress the people with his wonderful power. In like manner God wrought special miracles by the hand of Paul, Acts 19: 11, 12.

23. Matthew now returns to the miracle upon the ruler's daughter. In his brevity he passes over a number of incidental circumstances related by Mark and Luke; among others, the one that, after hearing that the daughter was dead, he suffered no one to follow him but Peter, James, and John, Mark 5: 37. These were the three honored disciples, the witnesses of the Savior's transfiguration (ch. 17: 1), and of his agony in Gethsemane, Mark 14: 33. Coming to the house of the ruler, he found **the minstrels,** the pipers or flute-players, who were generally hired, especially by the wealthy, on such occasions, and **the people,** probably the relatives and friends of the family, **making a noise** by their various expressions of grief. The custom of mourning for the dead and at funerals is alluded to in such passages as Eccle. 12: 5; Jer. 9: 17; 16: 6, 7; Ezek. 24: 17. Similar customs still prevail in the east. Dr. Hackett, in his *Illustrations of Scripture* (page 122), remarks: "It is customary, when a member of a family is about to die, for the friends to assemble around him, and watch the ebbing away of life, so as to remark the precise moment when he breathes his last; upon which they set up instantly a united outcry, attended with weeping, and often with beating upon the breast, and tearing out the hair of the head. . . How exactly, at the moment of the Savior's arrival, did the house of Jairus correspond with the condition of one, at the present time, in which death has just taken place! It resounded with the same boisterous expressions of grief for which the natives of the east are still noted. The lamentation must have commenced also at the instant of the child's decease; for when Jesus arrived he found the mourners already present, and singing the death-dirge. . . . . . Matthew speaks of 'minstrels' as taking part in the tumult. The use of instruments of music at such times is not universal, but depends on the circumstances of the family. It involves some expense, which can not always be afforded. Mr. Lane mentions that it is chiefly at the funerals of the rich among the Egyptians that musicians are employed to contribute their part to the mournful celebration. The 'minstrels,' therefore, appear very properly in this particular history. Jairus, the father of the damsel to whom Christ restored life, since he was a ruler of the synagogue, must have been a person of some rank among his countrymen. In such a family the most decent style of performing the last sad offices would be observed."

24. Jesus says to the mourners, **Give place,** retire, withdraw, implying that their services were not needed; **for the maid,** the little girl, **is not dead, but sleepeth.** He does not mean to say that her death is only apparent; for he uses the same language respecting Lazarus, which he explains to mean death, John 11: 11, 14. In relation to his power death was but a sleep; he had only to speak the word, and the dead would come to life like one awaking from sleep. Her death, too, was not permanent, but transient, like a sleep from which she

25 scorn. But when the people were put forth, he went in, and took her by the hand, and the maid
26 arose. ʰ And the fame hereof went abroad into all that land. ʰ ver. 31; ch. 4. 24.
27 And when Jesus departed thence, two blind men followed him, crying, and saying, ⁱ *Thou Son of*
28 *David, have mercy on us.* And when he was come into the house, the blind men came to him. And Jesus saith unto them, ᵏ Believe ye that I am able to do this? They said unto him, Yea, Lord. ⁱ ch. 12. 23; 15. 22; Mk. 10. 47, 48; Ro. 1. 3; Rev 22. 16. ᵏ John 11. 40.
29 Then touched he their eyes, saying, ˡ According to ˡ ch. 8. 3, 13.

should be speedily awakened. The company of mourners were so certain that the child was dead, and understanding neither the language nor the power of Jesus, **laughed him to scorn.** They laughed at him in derision or scorn.

25. The crowd of noisy mourners, the deriders of Jesus, are put forth. Only Peter, James, and John, with the father and mother of the child, remain with Jesus in the house, Mark 5 : 40. Entering the room where the child was, he takes her by the hand and says, in their Hebrew or Aramæan language, *Talitha cumi*, which is interpreted, Damsel, I say unto you arise, Mark 5 : 41. She arose and walked, and Jesus commanded that something should be given her to eat, Mark 5 : 42, 43.

26. **The fame thereof.** *This report*, a more exact translation. This is the first instance of Christ raising the dead of which we have an account. It would naturally excite the wonder of the people more than any other of his miracles. It was indeed the mightiest exhibition thus far given of the power of Jesus. No wonder, then, that this report went through all that region of country.

27–31. HEALING OF TWO BLIND MEN. Related only by Matthew.

27. It would seem to the passing reader that this and the following miracle occurred immediately after the raising of the daughter of Jairus. A more careful examination shows that the connection is not necessarily so close. The words **Jesus departed thence** may mean from that city, or that part of the country. It is also in harmony with the last verse to suppose that a little time intervened.

Two blind men. It is not strange that persons suffering from blindness should be together, or that two of them should go together to Jesus; especially when it is remembered, that blindness was common, then as now, in the east. It was probably caused by the fine particles of flying dust and sand entering the eyes and inflaming them, and also by sleeping in the open air, and exposing the eyes to the noxious night dews. The objection to Matthew, and the insinuation that he saw things double, because he speaks of miracles performed on persons in pairs (ch. 8 : 28; 20 : 30), are frivolous and wicked. **Son of David.** Descendant and successor of David on the throne of Israel. The angel of the Lord had previously applied the title to Joseph, ch. 1 : 20. It seems to have been a popular designation of the Messiah (ch. 22 : 42), and by the use of it the blind men acknowledged the Messiahship of Jesus. Our Lord did not employ this title in speaking of himself, doubtless because it would favor the idea of an earthly reign and kingdom, and might lead the people to desire, as on one occasion (John 6 : 15), to make him king. The titles, "the Son of Man," "the Son of God," were of deeper significance, and less liable to be perverted. See on 8 : 20, 29. **Have mercy.** Have pity, show compassion.

28. **The house.** Whether this was the house of Peter, or the one Jesus inhabited, or some other house at Capernaum, or some house elsewhere, is not stated, and is unimportant. It appears that the blind men followed Jesus in the way, and persevered in following him, even into the house, whither he was going. He probably delayed the healing, in order to draw forth an exhibition of their faith; for upon their coming to him in the house he asks, **Believe ye that I am able to do this?** Have you faith in my power or ability to work this miracle?

29. The blind men having affirmed their faith, Jesus touched their eyes, granting a cure corresponding to the

A.D. 28, 29.   MATTHEW IX.   131

30 your faith be it unto you. And ^m their eyes were opened. And Jesus straitly charged them, saying,
31 ⁿ See *that* no man know *it.* ^o But they, when they were departed, spread abroad his fame in all that country.
32 ^p As they went out, behold, they brought to him
33 a dumb man possessed with a devil. And when the devil was cast out,^q the dumb spake: and the multitudes marveled, saying, It was never so seen in
34 Israel. But the Pharisees said, ^r He casteth out devils through the prince of the devils.

Our Lord's third general circuit of Galilee. His compassion for the people.

35 ^s AND Jesus went about all the cities and villages, ^t teaching in their synagogues, and preaching

^m Ps. 146. 8; Is. 42. 2, 7.
ⁿ ch. 8. 4; 12. 16; 17. 9.
^o Mk. 7. 36.
^p see ch. 12. 22; Lk. 11. 14.
^q Is. 35. 6.
^r ch. 12. 24; Mk. 3. 22; Lk. 11. 15.
^s Mk. 6. 6.
^t ch. 4. 23.

---

measure of their faith: **According to your faith.** Faith was no ground of merit, but a condition on their part to a cure. In this instance, the fact that Jesus attempted a cure showed that he knew that they had faith; and the result showed the strength of their faith.

30. Their eyes were opened. Were healed. The sight of the eye was no longer closed, but opened to the perception of external objects, 2 Kings 6 : 17; Isa. 35 : 5. So the mouth is said to be opened, Luke 1 : 64; and also the ears, Mark 7 : 35. **Straitly charged.** Sternly charged them. The word thus translated expresses strong and earnest emotion, amounting even to sternness. The reasons for charging to let no one **know it** were probably such as these: 1. That the people might not become so excited as to attempt to make him king, and to rebel against their temporal rulers; 2. that the wrath of the Pharisees might not be too greatly aroused against himself, as his hour had not yet come; 3. that his time and strength might not be too much overtaxed by the multitudes who would naturally gather after him, on hearing the report of the men who had been blind; 4. that he might exhibit his own gentle and modest bearing, and the nature of his kingdom, which came not with observation. See on 8 : 4.

31. The result was, the blind men go out and **spread abroad his fame** through all that region. It was indeed the outburst of gratitude and love; but it was nevertheless disobedience. Though an error of affection, it was wrong. "To obey is better than sacrifice, and to hearken than the fat of rams," 1 Sam. 15 : 22.

32-34. Healing of the Dumb Demoniac. This miracle is narrated only by Matthew. A similar one is related in ch. 12 : 22, and one by Mark (ch. 7 : 32), but both manifestly at different times and with varying circumstances.

32. As they, the blind men, **went out.** The miracle was wrought immediately after the preceding. **A dumb man,** etc. A man dumb, possessed with a demon. *Possessed,* etc., is explanatory of his dumbness. He became dumb in consequence of the possession. Hence the case was peculiar, the disease complicated.

33. The dumb spake. In consequence of the demon being expelled. Prophecy was thus fulfilled (Isa. 35 : 5, 6), and additional evidence was given that Jesus was the Christ. **It was never so seen.** The multitudes wondered at seeing both the demon cast out and the dumb speaking, and they affirm that such a thing had never before been witnessed among the people of **Israel**, or in their history as a nation.

34. The Pharisees could not deny the greatness of the miracles; but wishing to prevent the people from receiving Jesus as the Messiah, and as an expression of their own prejudice and hatred, ascribe them to the power of Satan. **Through the prince of devils.** By or through the agency, power, or authority of Satan, who is the prince or chief of the demons. See on 12 : 22-30.

35-38. The compassion of Jesus for the multitude. It is quite generally

the Gospel of the kingdom, and healing every sickness and every disease among the people. ⁿ But when he saw the multitudes, he was moved with compassion on them, because they fainted, and were scattered abroad, as sheep having no shepherd. Then saith he unto his disciples, ˣ The harvest truly is plenteous, ʸ but the laborers *are* few; ᶻ pray ye therefore ᵃ the Lord of the harvest, ᵇ that he will send forth laborers into his harvest.

36
37
38

ⁿ Mk. 6. 34.
ˣ Lk. 10. 2; John 4. 35.
ʸ Phil. 2. 19-21; Col. 4. 11.
ᶻ 2 Thes. 3. 1.
ᵃ John 20. 21; Eph. 4. 11.
ᵇ Lk. 10. 1, 2; 1 Cor. 12. 28.

thought that this paragraph opens with an account of Christ's third missionary tour through Galilee, the first being described in ch. 4 : 23, and the second by Luke, 8 : 1-3.

35. Regarding this as our Lord's third circuit through Galilee, it is but incidentally referred to in Mark 6 : 6. The description is very similar to that in ch. 4 : 23. He visits towns of every size, **cities and villages**, preaching the good news and working many miracles. Omit, **among the people.**

36. **Multitudes** attend his ministry as on his former journey, and on other occasions, both to hear him and to witness his miracles. Seeing such crowds of people attending him, **he was moved with compassion;** with pity on account of their low spiritual condition, which he forcibly illustrates with the figure of sheep without a shepherd. **Fainted and were scattered abroad.** Rather, *they were harassed and scattered.* They were *vexed, harassed* with the burdensome traditions and grievous exactions of the scribes and Pharisees; and thus *scattered* by their negligence to their spiritual wants, and by their extortions and oppressive injustice. Having become wearied and distrustful of their religious guides, they were like sheep having no shepherd, wandering and ready to follow any one who would promise to guide them and afford them relief. Compare Zech. 11 : 15-17; Luke 11 : 46.

37. **Then,** on that occasion, when he was specially moved with compassion toward the multitude, who had no competent religious teachers. Possibly when the crowds had become the greatest, toward the end of this missionary journey. Addressing his disciples, he now represents the spiritual condition of these multitudes by the figure of a harvest perishing for want of reapers. **The harvest truly is plenteous.** It indeed is great, but the laborers are few.

They are too few to gather it. What will it avail, then, if there are not enough to reap it? There are vast multitudes who need the Gospel, but how few the preachers! Jesus afterward addressed the same language to the seventy, Luke 12 : 2. As the first verse of the next chapter implies that the twelve apostles had already been chosen, may we not suppose these words were addressed to them soon after, or at the time, of their selection? If such be the case, then the word **disciples** in this verse refers to the twelve.

38. But how shall this great want be supplied? How shall this vast harvest be garnered? By prayer for laborers to the **Lord of the harvest.** Christ is the Lord of the harvest, ch. 10 : 1; 13 : 37. He is God manifested in the flesh. Thus, while he spoke of God, and was so understood by his disciples, he also spoke of himself. They afterward, when they were enlightened, so understood it. John 20 : 21; Eph. 4 : 11-15. **The Harvest** primarily referred to the multitude before him; but in its wider sense it included the whole world. **Send forth.** Expresses an earnest and urgent sending forth of laborers. Pray that the Lord of the harvest will, by the power of his Spirit, *impel and urge forth* laborers, so overcoming their natural unwillingness to engage in such a work, and so laying upon them the duty and the necessity, that they shall go forth feeling and saying, "Woe is me if I preach not the Gospel," 1 Cor. 9 : 16.

REMARKS.

1. In the case of the palsied man, we have a striking illustration of perseverance in going to Jesus, ver. 2.
2. A sense of sin connected with faith in Christ is attended with his compassion and forgiveness, ver. 2; Ps. 103 : 3; Isa. 35 : 3, 4; 40 : 2.

3. The cavillings of the wicked against Christ are groundless, vers. 3–7; John 10 : 37, 38.
4. Christ has power to forgive sins, vers. 5–7; Heb. 9 : 26; Acts 3 : 26; 5 : 31.
5. Christ is divine, vers. 5–7; 1 Tim. 3 : 16. Heb. 1 : 3; 4 : 13; Rev. 2 : 23.
6. One of the uses of the miracles of Jesus was to manifest and prove his full power as the Messiah, vers. 6, 7; John 20 : 30, 31.
7. The condescension and grace of Jesus is limited to no class of men. Matthew, though a publican, and engaged in an infamous business, is called to be a disciple, a constant attendant, and afterward an apostle, ver. 9; ch. 15 : 21, 22, 28; Luke 4 : 25–27; Acts 13 : 46; 18 : 6.
8. Young converts will recommend Jesus to their former associates, and strive to bring them under his influence, ver. 10; John 1 : 41; 4 : 28, 29.
9. It is proper to mingle with the wicked in order to do them good, vers. 10–12; 1 Cor. 9 : 19–22.
10. The Pharisees saw that Jesus and his disciples were not as the publicans and sinners; so let there ever be a marked distinction between Christians and the world, vers. 10, 11; Acts 4 : 13.
11. Christ is the physician of heartfelt sinners, not of self-righteous hypocrites. Where there is a sense of sin there is hope, ver. 12; Luke 18 : 9–14; 24 : 47.
12. Mercy is the greatest and best sacrifice. Without the spirit of Christ, a kind and compassionate disposition, all external religious performances are but an empty name, ver. 13; Mic. 6 : 6–8; 1 Cor. 13 : 1.
13. Fasting must be observed on suitable and proper occasions, vers. 15–17; ch. 17 : 21; 1 Cor. 7 : 5.
14. So there is a suitable time and manner for the performance of every duty, vers. 14–17; 1 Cor. 14 : 40.
15. Christian doctrines and precepts are not only true and right in themselves; but in their nature fitted to man, and adapted to his various circumstances and wants, vers. 14–17; 1 Cor. 3 : 2; Heb. 5 : 14.
16. Christianity is a spiritual religion; its ordinances and practices are exponents of, and in harmony with, its spirituality. Patch not its spirituality and liberty with a carnal and slavish legalism; nor the new wedding garment with our own righteousness, ver. 16; John 4 : 24; 2 Tim. 3 : 5.

17. In affliction we should repair to Jesus, who will be spiritually present, to sympathize, aid, and bless, vers. 18, 19; Heb. 4 : 15, 16.
18. The young may die. Let them seek Jesus at once. Let parents be stimulated to faithfulness, ver. 18; Eccle. 12 : 1; Eph. 6 : 4.
19. When all other physicians fail, Jesus is the great Physician who has never failed to effect a cure, vers. 20–22; 2 Chron. 16 : 12, 13; Jer. 8 : 11, 22.
20. Many a trembling, sin-sick soul has alone, and unknown to others, exercised faith in Jesus and been made whole, vers. 20, 21; Nah. 1 : 7.
21. The touch of this woman was no ordinary touch, for many were touching and pressing upon him. So by prayer and faith we may touch Jesus. Our importunity can not irritate him, nor the greatness of our sins debar his blessing, vers. 20–22, 13; Luke 18 : 1–8.
22. Jesus has determined that those who enjoy his saving grace shall acknowledge him before others, ver. 22; Rom. 10 : 9, 10; Ps. 116 : 13, 14.
23. The dead in Christ are but asleep, ver. 24; Acts 7 : 60; 1 Cor. 15 : 6, 18; 1 Thess. 4 : 13–15.
24. In raising the dead, Jesus showed his power to raise dead souls to life, and at last to raise the bodies of his followers, ver. 25; John 5 : 21.
25. The ridicule and scorn of unbelievers need not impede the faithful servant of God in his work, ver. 24; Isa. 51 : 7.
26. The fame of Jesus can not be suppressed. The Gospel must and will spread, vers. 26, 31; Rom. 10 : 18.
27. Christ is the enlightener of blind souls. It is in recognizing him as the Christ that we may receive our sight, vers. 27–30; John 9 : 39.
28. Jesus often tries the reality and strength of faith, for the good of the suppliant, and for the good of others, ver. 28; 1 Pet. 1 : 7.
29. Faith and confession go together. We should confess Christ according to his direction. Young Christians sometimes err in a zeal not according to knowledge, vers. 30, 31; John 15 : 14.
30. The dumb demoniac represents those whose bodily infirmities have their seat in the soul, ver. 32.
31. Christ often saves those who are regarded beyond the reach of hope, ver. 33.
32. Honest men will acknowledge a

Mission of the twelve Apostles.

X. AND [d] when he had called unto *him* his twelve disciples, he gave them power *against* unclean spirits, to cast them out, and to heal all manner of sickness and all manner of disease.

[d] Mk. 6. 7; Lk. 9. 1; Ac. 3. 12, 16.

---

power in the Gospel. The miracles of Jesus were convincing except to those who were unwilling to be convinced, ver. 33; 1 Cor. 14 : 24, 25.

33. Hypocrites, the worldly wise, and the determined opposers, will, when they can not deny the power of Christ, ascribe it to the basest means and the vilest motives, ver. 34; Isa. 32 : 6.

34. Jesus continues in his work; nothing impedes him; an example to all his followers, ver. 35; Heb. 12 : 1, 2.

35. Christ, as our High-Priest, still exercises compassion over the race, who without him are like sheep without a shepherd, ver. 36; Heb. 2 : 17; Isa. 53 : 6.

36. An increase of preachers of the Gospel and earnest laborers in the great harvest-field must be sought by earnest prayer. We are taught to expect that they will be sent forth in proportion to the faith and urgency of our prayers, 37, 38.

CHAPTER X.

In this chapter we have THE MISSION OF THE TWELVE APOSTLES AND OUR SAVIOR'S CHARGE TO THEM, Mark 6 : 7-13; Luke 9 : 1-6. They had previously been selected as apostles. We must distinguish between their becoming disciples (John 1 : 35-45), their call to be constant attendants, preachers, or evangelists (ch. 4 : 17-22), and their call, appointment, or selection as apostles, Mark 3 : 14; Luke 6 : 13. They are now empowered to work miracles, and sent forth on their immediate mission, with appropriate instructions.

1. EMPOWERING THE TWELVE TO WORK MIRACLES, Luke 9 : 1.

1. **And when he had called,** etc. Connected with what precedes. Having compassion on the multitude because they were in want of religious teachers (ch. 9 : 36-38), he calls to him his twelve disciples and gives them **power against,** rather *authority*, with the consequent power *over* **unclean spirits,** etc. See on ch. 9 : 6. Their number corresponded with the twelve tribes of Israel. Compare ch. 19 : 28. The number twelve is significant, and frequent in Scripture. Twelve sons of Israel; twelve stones of the Urim and Thummim on the breastplate of the high-priest (Ex. 28 : 17-21); twelve loaves of show-bread (Lev. 24 : 5-8); the altar and the twelve pillars which Moses erected by Mount Sinai (Ex. 24 : 4); the altar of twelve stones, by Elijah (1 Kings 18 : 31); the twelve spies who went to search the promised land (Num. 13 : 1; Deut. 1 : 23); the twelve stones taken from the bed of the Jordan (Josh. 4 : 3), etc. So, also, the woman with a crown of twelve stars (Rev. 12 : 1), and the new Jerusalem with twelve foundation-stones, Rev. 21 : 14. "The careful student of Scripture must be struck with the frequency of the use of certain numbers, especially 3, 4, 7, 10, and 12, in significant connection with sacred ideas and things from Genesis to Revelation. It is impossible to resolve all this into accident or unmeaning play. . . . Number is expressive of order, symmetry, proportion and relativity. 1 is the symbol of unity or oneness; 2, of antithesis or polarity; 3, of synthesis, of the uncreated *Divinity*, the *Holy Trinity* (compare Num. 6 : 24-26; Isa. 6 : 3; Matt. 28 : 19; 2 Cor. 13 : 14); 4, of *humanity*, or the created *world* as the revelation of God (think of the four corners of the earth, the four seasons, the four points of the compass, the four elements, the four gospels). From this may be explained the symbolical significance of 7, or 3+4, and of 12, or 3×4. Seven, being the union of 3 and 4, is the signature of the relation of God to the world, or the covenant (the Hebrew word for *seven* signifies also an *oath*, Gen. 21 : 27; 26 : 33, and the verb, *to swear*, 'since seven,' as Gesenius explains, 'was a sacred number, and oaths were confirmed either by seven victims offered in sacrifice, Gen. 21 : 28, or by seven witnesses or pledges'). . . . Twelve, being the product of 3 and 4, symbolizes, from the twelve patriarchs and twelve tribes down to the twelve foundations and twelve gates of

A.D. 29. MATTHEW X. 135

2 Now the names of the twelve apostles are these; The first, *e* Simon, who is called Peter, and Andrew *e* Mk. 3. 16–19; Lk. 6. 12–16.

the heavenly Jerusalem, the indwelling of God in the human family, or the interpenetration of the world by the Divinity. Ten is the number of harmony and completeness, as in the ten commandments." —DR. SCHAFF, in *Lange's Com.* Jesus gave them power, delegated power or authority. It was not over spirits in general, but limited to *unclean* spirits, fallen angels. The extent of this power is specified, **to cast them out,** or more exactly, *so as* to cast them out. They were also empowered to heal every sickness and every infirmity. They were thus to exercise miraculous power similar to that of Jesus. They received all the power and instructions they needed for their immediate work, and no more. Afterward they were more fully instructed, enlightened, and endowed with power from on high.

2–4. THE NAMES OF THE TWELVE APOSTLES.

2. **Apostles.** This word primarily signifies *persons sent forth.* Using this term, Jesus gave it to the twelve whom he selected from among his disciples, Luke 6 : 13. In the Gospels they are more commonly called *the twelve* (Luke 18 : 31), or *the twelve disciples* (ch. 20 : 17), or simply *disciples*, ch. 14 : 15 and Luke 9 : 12. "They were, during the whole period which the Gospels embrace, *disciples*, and are therefore so called. But after the advent of the Paraclete, in the Acts and Epistles they are never called disciples, but apostles."—BENGEL. A necessary condition to their apostleship was that they had seen the Lord, and were witnesses of him and his resurrection, Acts 1 : 8, 21; 1 Cor. 9 : 1; Acts 22 : 14, 15. They could, therefore, have no successors. Four catalogues of the apostles are given in the New Testament, each divided into three classes, and the classes being the same in each, and the leading name of each class the same. Thus, Peter heads the first class, Philip the second, James the third, and Judas Iscariot stands the last, except in the Acts, where his name is omitted because of his apostasy and death. The following table shows the four arrangements, with their connectives:

	MATTHEW 10 : 2.	MARK 3 : 16.	LUKE 6 : 14.	ACTS 1 : 13.
1	Simon Peter,	Simon Peter,	Simon Peter,	Peter,
2	And Andrew,	And James, son of Zebedee,	And Andrew,	And James,
3	James, son of Zebedee,	And John,	And James,	And John,
4	And John.	And Andrew.	And John.	And Andrew.
5	Philip,	And Philip,	And Philip,	Philip,
6	And Bartholomew,	And Bartholomew,	And Bartholomew,	And Thomas,
7	Thomas,	And Matthew,	And Matthew,	Bartholomew,
8	And Matthew.	And Thomas.	And Thomas.	And Matthew.
9	James, son of Alpheus,	And James, son of Alpheus,	James, son of Alpheus,	James, son of Alpheus,
10	And Lebbeus Thaddeus,	And Thaddeus,	And Simon Zelotes,	And Simon Zelotes,
11	Simon the Canaanite,	And Simon the Canaanite,	And Judas, brother of James,	And Judas, brother of James.
12	And Judas Iscariot.	And Judas Iscariot.	And Judas Iscariot.	

Thus, Matthew enumerates the apostles two by two, probably with reference to their being sent out in *pairs*, Mark 6 : 7; Mark and Luke, one by one; and Luke in the Acts, mixedly.

The first Simon who is called

his brother; James *the son* of Zebedee, and John his
3 brother; Philip, and Bartholomew; Thomas, and

Peter. More correctly, *First Simon,* etc., there being no article in the original; first in order of enumeration, it implies no superiority of rank. The place assigned Peter, however, at the head of each of the four lists of the apostles is significant. He was among the first who recognized Jesus as the Messiah (John 1 : 40–42); and with Andrew, his brother, the first called to be a constant attendant of Jesus. He appears frequently as spokesman of the apostles, as in ch. 16 : 16, in the name of the twelve, he says, " Thou art the Christ, the Son of the living God." He was also the chief speaker on the day of Pentecost, and also the first to carry the Gospel to the Gentiles, Acts ch. 10. He was indeed prominent and foremost among the apostles, but not *over* them or *above* them. That he had no superiority of rank is evident from 1 Pet. 5 : 1, where he describes himself as " a fellow-elder;" and from the fact that Paul speaks of him as one of the "pillars" together with James and John (Gal. 2 : 9); that he was intrusted with the Gospel to the circumcision, as Paul was to the uncircumcision; and that Paul rebuked him as an equal, Gal. 2 : 7, 8, 11. That the apostles were all equal in rank appears from declarations of our Lord, ch. 18 : 18; 19 : 27, 28; 20 : 25, 26 28 : 23 : 8; John 20 : 21; Acts 1 : 8.

Simon Peter was a native of Bethsaida, in Galilee, and was the son of Jonas, and by occupation a fisherman. After his marriage he lived at Capernaum. When first introduced to Jesus he re-received the Aramæan surname, *Cephas,* which is equivalent to the Greek *Petros,* meaning a stone. See ch. 4 : 18. *Simon,* Hebrew *Simeon,* means *hearing, answer.* The most we know of Peter is derived from the Gospels and the Acts of the Apostles. The latter book traces him to the Council at Jerusalem. After that he was with Paul at Antioch (Gal. 2 : 11), labored at Corinth (1 Cor. 1 : 12; 3 : 22), and at Babylon, where he wrote his first epistle, 1 Peter 5 : 13. According to a tradition which may be considered in the main reliable, he visited Rome and suffered martyrdom under the reign of Nero.

Andrew is a name of Greek origin, but was in use among the Jews. It is derived from a word which means *man,* and may have been applied to Peter's brother on account of his manly spirit. He was a disciple of John the Baptist, as was doubtless John, Peter, and others, who were afterward called to be apostles. Very little is related of him by the Evangelists. He appears in connection with feeding the five thousand (John 6 : 8), afterward as the introducer of certain Greeks to our Lord (John 12 : 22), and also with Peter, James, and John, asking for an explanation of what Jesus had said concerning the destruction of the temple, Mark 13 : 3. Of his subsequent history and labors nothing is certainly known. Tradition assigns Scythia, Greece, and Thrace as the scenes of his ministry. He is said to have been crucified at Patræ in Achaia.

James the son of Zebedee. The name is the same as that of the patriarch Jacob, meaning *supplanter.* Custom has applied in our language the name James to three persons in the New Testament, and Jacob to the patriarch. This James is called the greater, or the elder; and it is worthy of notice that he is never mentioned in the New Testament apart from John his brother. They were styled by our Lord, Boanerges, or *Sons of Thunder,* probably on account of their energetic and zealous disposition, Mark 3 : 17. They with Peter alone were present at the Transfiguration (ch. 17 : 1); at the restoration to life of Jairus' daughter (Mark 5 : 42); and in the garden of Gethsemane during the Savior's agony, Mark 14 : 33. With Andrew, they listened in private to our Lord's discourse on the fall of Jerusalem, Mark 13 : 3. James also was the first martyr among the apostles, being slain with the sword by Herod Agrippa I., Acts 12 : 2. Clement of Alexandria says that the officer who conducted him to the tribunal was so influenced by his bold declaration of faith as to embrace the Gospel and to avow himself a Christian; whereupon he also was beheaded at the same time.

John, whose name means, *graciously given by Jehovah,* was, next to Peter, the most noted of the apostles, and characterized with a wonderful mingling of

Matthew the publican; James *the son* of Alphæus, and Lebbæus, whose surname was Thaddæus; 4 Simon the Canaanite, and Judas Iscariot, who also betrayed him.

---

gentleness and firmness. He belonged to a family of influence, as is evident from his acquaintance with the high-priest (John 18 : 15), and was in easy circumstances, since he became responsible for the maintenance of his Lord's mother, John 19 : 26, 27. After the ascension of our Lord, he resided at Jerusalem. About A.D. 65 he removed to Ephesus, and for many years labored in Asia Minor. He survived all the apostles, and died at Ephesus A.D. 100; being then, according to Epiphanius ninety-four years old, but according to Jerome, a hundred.

3. **Philip** was also a native of Bethsaida, a disciple of John the Baptist, and called by our Lord the day after the naming of Peter (John 1 : 43, 44). He is mentioned in connection with feeding the five thousand; as introducing with Andrew certain Greeks to Jesus; and as asking after the last supper, "Lord, show us the Father, and it sufficeth us," John 6 : 5–7; 12 : 21; 14 : 8–10. Tradition says that he preached the Gospel in Phrygia, and suffered martyrdom at Hierapolis in Syria. Philip is a name of Greek origin, meaning lover of horses. He doubtless had also a Hebrew name.

Bartholomew. The Hebrew form is Bar-Tholmai, or son of Tholmai, the latter meaning *rich in furrows*, or *cultivated fields*, the whole name implying, as some suppose, son of a rich field, rich fruit. It is the patronymic, as is generally supposed, of Nathanael of Cana of Galilee. In the first three Gospels, Philip and Bartholomew are constantly named together, while Nathanael is nowhere mentioned; while in the fourth Gospel Philip and Nathanael are similarly combined, but nothing is said of Bartholomew, John 1 : 45; 21 : 2. According to tradition, he labored in India, and was crucified either in Armenia or Cilicia.

Thomas was also called *Didymus*, both meaning *a twin*, the former Aramæan, the latter Greek, John 11 : 16. He was probably from Galilee. He was impulsive (John 11 : 16), of an inquiring mind (John 14 : 5, 6), and slow to be convinced. John 20 : 24–29. Tradition affirms that he preached the Gospel in India, and the Syrian Church there claim him as their founder, and call themselves by his name.

Matthew the publican (ch. 9 : 9) is the same with Levi, son of Alpheus, Mark 2 : 14. For further account of him see introductory remarks to this Gospel.

James, son of Alpheus, is also called James the less, or the younger, Mark 15 : 40. His father is probably not the same with the father of Matthew, but is generally thought to be identical with Cleophas, Luke 24 : 18; John 19 : 25. Alpheus and Cleophas are but different ways of expressing the same Hebrew name. The mother of James was Mary, supposed to be a sister of our Lord's mother, John 19 : 25; Luke 24 : 10. He had a brother Joses, ch. 27 : 56.

Lebbeus, whose surname was Thaddeus, is also called Judas, Luke 6 : 16. He was the "Judas not Iscariot" (John 14 : 22); brother of James the less, and author of the epistle bearing the name of Jude. It has been common to regard Lebbeus and Thaddeus as allied names, being derived from Hebrew or Aramæan words, the former denoting *heart*, the latter *breast*, and hence denoting *the hearty, the courageous*. But the words "Lebbeus, whose surname was" are omitted in the best text.

4. **Simon the Canaanite.** Or *the Cananite* (Greek *kananaios*), an inhabitant of Cana. But more probably the name corresponds with the Greek *kananites*, a zealot, according to its Hebrew etymology. He is called Simon Zelotes by Luke in his Gospel and in the Acts, probably on account of his former zeal for the law, and possibly as expressive of his character. The name also distinguished him among the apostles from Simon Peter. It has been thought that he took it from his having belonged to a political sect known among the Jews as zealots; this was probably not the case, as the party bearing that name do not appear in Jewish history till after the time of Christ. See further on Luke 6 : 15. He is not mentioned in the New Testament out of the four catalogues.

Judas Iscariot, that is, *Judas, man*

5 ᶠThese twelve Jesus sent forth, and commanded them, saying, ᵍGo not into the way of the Gentiles, and into *any* city of ʰthe Samaritans enter ye not: 6 ⁱbut go rather to the ᵏlost sheep of the house of

ᶠ Mk. 6. 7-11; Lk. 9. 1-5.
ᵍ Ac. 1. 8.
ʰ 2 Ki. 17. 24; John 4. 9-20.

---

of Karioth, probably a native of Karioth, a small town in the tribe of Judah, Josh. 15 : 25. He was probably the only one of the apostles who was not a Galilean. His father's name was Simon, John 6 : 71. He carried the bag, and was accustomed to appropriate part of the common stock to his own use, John 12 : 6. The climax of his sins was the betrayal of his Lord, which was speedily followed by hanging himself. His despised and infamous character doubtless accounts for the position of his name as last on each of the catalogues of the Evangelists. It was a part of infinite wisdom that Christ should have chosen his betrayer among the twelve. God works even through wicked men, as in the case of Balaam. The churches of Christ must not expect absolute purity on earth; some of the chaff will remain among the wheat. The defection of those who have been regarded great in the church will not cause its ruin.

5–42. THE IMMEDIATE MISSION OF THE APOSTLES TO THE LOST SHEEP of the house of Israel, and our LORD'S CHARGE TO THEM. Only in Matthew.

5–6. THEIR IMMEDIATE MISSION TO THE JEWS.

5. These twelve Jesus sent forth. Two by two, Mark 6 : 7. **Commanded them.** Charged them, as their great leader, their Lord. **Go not into the way of the Gentiles.** Into the way to Gentiles; direct not your course to them. **Into any city.** More exactly, *into a city* **of Samaritans enter *ye* not.** The charge in regard to the Samaritans differs from that in regard to the Gentiles. They were not to direct their course toward the latter; but they might find it necessary, in carrying out their mission, to pass through the territory of the former, yet they were not to enter into a city of theirs, especially in the capacity of religious teachers and Christ's apostles.

The Samaritans inhabited the country between Judea and Galilee, and were the descendants of heathen colonists from Babylonia, Cuthah, Ava, Hamath, and Sepharvaim, whom Shalmanezer, king of Assyria, sent into the country, after he had taken Samaria and carried away the better portion of the ten tribes, and of the remnant of Israelites left behind, whom they intermarried. A mixed people as well as a mixed religion was the result, 2 Kings 17 : 24–41. On the return of the Jews from the Babylonish captivity, the Samaritans requested permission to assist them in rebuilding the temple. This they were denied, after which they opposed the Jews and greatly retarded their work, Ezra 4 : 1–5; Neh. 2 : 10, 19; 4 : 1–3. Later still, Manasseh, son of the high-priest, married the daughter of Sanballat, the governor of Samaria, and Nehemiah would not allow him to perform the functions of the priest's office, but drove him from the city, Neh. 13 : 28. Accordingly, the Samaritans, under Sanballat, reared a temple on Mount Gerizim, and Manasseh acted there as high-priest. This served to deepen the hatred between the Jews and the Samaritans, and render it perpetual, John 4 : 9; 8 : 48. The temple on Mount Gerizim was destroyed by Hyrcanus about 129 B.C.; but the Samaritans still regarded the place sacred, and as the proper place of national worship, John 4 : 20, 21. They rejected all the sacred books of the Jews except the Pentateuch. A few families of the Samaritans now remain at Nablous, the ancient Shechem. They have a very ancient manuscript of the Pentateuch, are strict observers of the law, keeping the Sabbath and the ancient festivals, and are expecting the Messiah.

6. Lost Sheep. Scattered and wandering without a shepherd, ch. 9 : 36. **House of Israel.** Family of Israel, the descendants of Jacob, the Jews, the whole nation consisting of the tribes of Judah and Levi and those of other tribes incorporated with them. Their mission on which they were now sent was not permanent, but temporary. It was preliminary, limited, and preparatory. It was meet that the Gospel should be preached first to God's ancient chosen people. The restriction was at length taken off, and their mission extended to Samaria, and to the Gentiles, ch. 28 : 19; Acts 1 : 8. The

A.D. 29.   MATTHEW X.   139

7 Israel. ¹ And as ye go, preach, saying, ᵐ The king-
8 dom of heaven is at hand. ⁿ Heal the sick, cleanse
the lepers, raise the dead, cast out devils. ᵒ Freely ye
9 have received, freely give. ᵖ Provide neither gold
10 nor silver, nor brass in your purses, nor scrip for
your journey, neither two coats, neither shoes, nor
yet staves: ᑫ for the workman is worthy of his
meat.

ⁱ ch. 15-24; Ac. 3. 26; 13. 46.
ᵏ ch. 9. 36; Is. 53. 6; Jer. 50. 6; Eze. 34. 5, 6, 16; 1 Pet. 2. 25.
ˡ Lk. 9. 2.
ᵐ ch. 3. 2; 4. 17; Lk. 10. 9.
ⁿ Mk. 6. 13.
ᵒ Ac. 3. 6; 20. 33-35.

working of miracles in connection with preaching the good news of the kingdom (ver. 1) was their present qualification; the endowments of the Holy Spirit in addition to these, the qualification for their permanent work, their mission to all nations, Luke 24 : 49; Acts 1 : 21. See on vers. 1 and 2. Compare Col. 1 : 25-29.

7, 8. THE PURPOSE OR OBJECT OF THIS MISSION to announce the Messiah, and to accompany it with miracles as credentials of their commission and evidences of the truth they proclaimed.

7. **And as ye go.** And going, **preach,** announce, proclaim. This is the purpose of your going, the object of your mission. They were to take up and bear the proclamation as announced by John the Baptist, and afterward by Jesus himself, namely, the kingdom, reign, administration of the Messiah at hand. See on ch. 3 : 2; 4 : 17.

8. Their preaching was to be confirmed by miracles similar to those wrought by Christ himself, ch. 4 : 23; 8 : 16. Doing good to the bodies of men would prepare the way for doing good to their souls. **Lepers.** See ch. 8 : 2. **Cast out devils,** demons. See ch. 4 : 24. Some ancient manuscripts omit the words **Raise the dead,** others of high authority give them before *cleanse the lepers.* We have no account of their raising the dead during the Savior's life, the first recorded instance, by any of the apostles, being that of Dorcas by Peter, Acts 9 : 36. Though the power may have been delegated to them, they may not have been called upon to exercise it till after the ascension of our Lord. **Freely give.** Make not either your preaching or your power of working miracles a means of gain. As you have received your commission and power freely, gratuitously, so exercise it gratuitously for the good of others. Compare Acts 8 : 18-23.

9, 10. THE PROVISION FOR THEIR JOURNEY. They are to rely on God for their daily supply. The instructions contained in vers. 9-15 were repeated with slight variations to the seventy, Luke 10 : 4-12.

9. **Provide.** Procure no equipment. Provide no additional money than that you may now have with you. Jesus names three current metals which formed the money of the day, gold, silver, brass, or copper. The compound of copper and zinc which forms our brass does not appear to have been known to the ancients; but bronze, compounded of tin and copper, was extensively used. Though the word translated brass was sometimes used to designate bronze, yet in the New Testament copper is generally intended, and is doubtless the metal meant here. They were not to procure even the smallest amount. **Purses.** *Girdles* or belts which kept their long, flowing dress together. The folds of the girdle served as a pocket or purse to carry money.

10. **Nor scrip,** or bag, generally made of leather, for carrying provisions,

SCRIP OR BAG.

1 Sam. 17 : 40. **Nor two coats,** tunics, under-garments, worn next to the skin, mostly with sleeves, and reaching generally to the knees. They were not to incumber themselves with a change of raiment. **Shoes,** sandals. See ch. 3 : 11. They were to have no extra sandals. **Staves.** This should be in the singular, *staff.* If they had a staff, they could take it; but they were not to procure

11 And into whatsoever city or town ye shall enter, inquire who in it is worthy; and there abide till
12 ye go thence. And when ye come into an house,
13 salute it: ʳ and if the house be worthy, let your peace come upon it: ˢ but if it be not worthy, let
14 your peace return to you. And whosoever shall not receive you, nor hear your words, when ye depart out of that house or city, shake off the dust
15 of your feet. Verily I say unto you, It shall be

ᵖ Mk. 6. 8-11; Lk. 22-35.
ᵍ Lk. 10. 7.
ʳ Lk. 10. 5.
ˢ Ps. 35. 13.

---

one for the journey. Make no preparation, but go just as you are; for this reason, **the workman,** the laborer, **is worthy of his meat,** his sustenance, all that is necessary to sustain life, his living. "At this day the farmer sets out on excursions quite as extensive, without a para (about a fourth of a cent) in his purse; and the modern Moslem prophet of Tarshiha thus sends forth his apostles over this identical region. Neither do they encumber themselves with two coats. They are accustomed to sleep in the garments they have on during the day, and in this climate such plain people experience no inconvenience from it."—*The Land and the Book,* vol. 1, p. 533. It is implied that their wants would be supplied, that they should trust God, whose messengers they were, and that the support they should receive from those to whom they bore their message was not an act of charity, but of gratitude, justly their due. The care of Providence over them during this mission was doubtless an encouragement during their whole subsequent life. See Luke 22 : 35.

11-15. DIRECTIONS AS TO THEIR CONDUCT TOWARD THE PEOPLE.

11. **Town,** village. **Inquire,** search out, **who in it is worthy,** a man of piety and hospitality, and who will be likely to receive you and your message. There they were to **abide,** or remain, till they departed **thence,** out of the city, town, or village. This would be for their comfort, and convenient for those who resorted to them. It would also show that they were grateful for the hospitality, and not fastidious in regard to their living.

12. More particular direction for introducing themselves into the family. A **house** should be *the house,* that is, of the one who should be supposed to be worthy, ver. 11. **Salute it.** Use the customary forms of politeness among the Jews, namely, "Peace be to this house," Luke 10 : 5; 1 Sam. 25 : 6. The salutation was both a prayer and a blessing, and shows the spirit with which they should enter their temporary home.

13. **If the house be worthy.** If they prove themselves to be so by welcoming you and your message, then they shall enjoy the **peace,** the blessings you have invoked upon them; but if they reject you, or slight your message, thus proving themselves unworthy, then let your blessing **return to you.** It shall not rest on that family; but you shall enjoy the rich reward of having done your duty.

14. Direction as to how they should act toward those who should reject them. **Whosoever.** A person or persons; a family or a city. Whoever should reject them, and not receive their message, then, going out of that house or city, they should **shake off the dust** of their feet. The Pharisees were accustomed to shake off the dust of the heathen, when they returned from a foreign country to their own land, by which act they renounced all fellowship with Gentiles, and proclaimed that the very dust of those foreign countries was polluting to their own. So Jesus enjoins upon his disciples the same act, signifying that the very dust of the places where the rejecters of the Gospel lived was unclean to them, much more those rejecters themselves. They should free themselves from their dust, much more from all fellowship and intercourse with them. They must treat them as heathen, renouncing not only all intercourse, but all participation of criminality and condemnation in rejecting the Gospel. See Mark 6 : 11. Thus, Paul shook off the dust of his feet against his persecutors at Antioch in Pisidia (Acts 13 : 51), and shook out his garments against the Jews at Corinth, Acts 18 : 6; Neh. 5 : 13.

more tolerable for the land of Sodom and Gomorrah in the day of judgment, than for that city.
16 ᵗ Behold, I send you forth as sheep in the midst of wolves: ᵘ be ye therefore wise as serpents, and
17 ˣ harmless as doves. But ʸ beware of men: for ᶻ they will deliver you up to the councils, and ᵃ they
18 will scourge you in their synagogues; and ᵇ ye shall

ᵗ Lk. 10. 3.
ᵘ Ge. 3. 1; Lk. 21. 15; Ac. 23. 6.
ˣ 1 Cor. 14. 20; Phil. 2. 15; 1 Thes. 5. 22.
ʸ Mic. 7. 5.
ᶻ ch. 24. 9; Mk. 13. 9; Lk. 21. 12
ᵃ Ac. 5. 40.

15. More tolerable for Sodom and Gomorrah. These cities were types of aggravated sins (Gen. 13 : 13; 18 : 20; Jude 7), and of terrible retribution, Deut. 29 : 23; Isa. 13 : 19; Jer. 49 : 18; Amos 4 : 11; 2 Pet. 2 : 6. Yet their doom would be less dreadful at the day of judgment than that of those who should reject the Gospel message. The greater the light, the greater the guilt and the greater the punishment. The doomed cities of the plain had enjoyed but the dim light that gleamed from the preaching of Lot; the Jews had their law, their prophets, John the Baptist, and, to climax all, the preaching of Christ and his apostles. In rejecting these their crime was greater than that of the worst of heathen.

16-23. JESUS FOREWARNS THEM OF PERSECUTION, and instructs them in regard to their conduct. This forms the second part of our Lord's charge to the apostles. In its predictions it extends beyond the immediate mission before them to the trials of their whole ministry. Yet the germs of these trials they began doubtless to experience at once.

16. **Behold, I send you forth.** *I* in the original is emphatic. *Send you forth* is the verb from which *apostle* is derived. The meaning, therefore, is, "Behold, I am he who *apostles* you, constitutes you my apostles, sending you forth in the midst of great dangers." Apostles were literally persons sent forth. See on ver. 2.

As sheep in the midst of wolves. Sheep and wolves are natural enemies; the one is innocent and defenseless, the other malicious and cruel. The apostles were indeed *sheep* of "the good Shepherd" (John 10 : 11), precious and valuable to him who sent them forth. The figure gives an impressive image of them as Christ's precious ones, meek and innocent, unarmed and defenseless, in the midst of cruel foes. Therefore he exhorts them to use the prudence or discretion of serpents, and the simplicity or guilelessness of doves. It is not the malignant cunning of the serpent (Gen. 3 : 1 ; 49 : 17) that is referred to, but the prudence, wisdom, for which he is noted in avoiding dangers, **wise as serpents. Harmless.** The word thus translated means *unmixed, simple, pure* from all taint of evil, guileless. The dove is the emblem of innocence and purity, and at the baptism of Jesus the visible, bodily emblem of the Holy Spirit, Luke 3 : 23. The particular trait here enjoined is simplicity or guilelessness of character and motive. With the prudence of the serpent combine the simplicity of the dove. Thus will you be cautious and sharp-sighted, pure in motive, and guileless in action.

17. **Beware of men.** The thought of the preceding figures expanded. The *wolves* are *men.* By taking heed, and being cautious in regard to them, they would exercise the wisdom of serpents. **Deliver you up,** by civil process, **to the councils;** not to *the council,* or sanhedrim, which was the supreme national court of the Jews, but to *councils* (without the article), the lower courts. Some suppose them to be the *courts of seven* established in every city, in conformity to Deut. 16 : 18, and explained by Josephus (*Antiq.* iv. 8, 14). Others, that they were the tribunals connected with the synagogues, commonly known as "the council of three," who could punish by scourging. Both may be intended; this, however, is unimportant, since the idea simply is, that they should be arraigned before courts of justice. Scourging was in accordance with the Mosaic law, and limited to forty stripes (Deut. 25 : 2, 3); the criminal was made to lie upon the ground, and was scourged with a whip of three lashes, not more than thirteen blows being given, which was equal to thirty-nine stripes. This was the forty save one which Paul received, 2 Cor. 11 : 24. Compare Acts 22 : 24. It is said that scourging was actually inflicted in the synagogues at public worship.

18. **And ye shall be brought,** etc.

be brought before governors and kings for my sake, ᶜfor a testimony against them and the Gen-
19 tiles. ᵈBut when they deliver you up, take no thought how or what ye shall speak: for ᵉit shall be given you in that same hour what ye shall
20 speak. ᶠFor it is not ye that speak, but the Spirit
21 of your Father which speaketh in you. ᵍAnd the brother shall deliver up the brother to death, and the father the child: and the children shall rise up against *their* parents, and cause them to be put to
22 death. And ʰye shall be hated of all *men* for my name's sake: ⁱbut he that endureth to the end shall

ᵇ Ac. 12. 1; 24. 10; 25. 7, 23; 2 Tim. 4. 16.
ᶜ 2 Tim. 1. 8; Rev. 6. 9.
ᵈ Dan. 3. 16-18; Mk. 13. 11-13.
ᵉ Ex. 4. 12; Ac. 4. 8-13; 2 Tim. 4. 17.
ᶠ 2 Sam. 23. 2 Ac 6. 10.
ᵍ vers. 35. 36; Lk. 21. 16.
ʰ ch. 24. 9; John 17. 14; 1 John 3. 13.

To bring out the gradation of thought and the emphasis, read rather, "And before governors also, and kings, shall ye be brought." In addition to being arraigned before courts, ye shall be brought before governors also, such as the Roman governors of provinces—for example, Pilate (ch. 27: 2), Felix (Acts 23: 24), Festus (Acts 25: 1)—and before kings, such as were dependent on the emperor of Rome, or perhaps the emperor himself, Acts 12: 1; 25: 23; 25: 12. Civil rulers generally are meant. **For a testimony against them.** This should be translated *to them*, not *against them*. This testimony was of Christ, **for my sake,** and of his truth. It was to *them*, that is, the Jews, and to the **Gentiles.** Some prefer to regard *them* as referring to the governors and kings, and *Gentiles* to the nations, the meaning of the word *Gentiles*, over which they ruled. A great object and result was thus obtained through persecution. When they were delivered up to these persecuting Jewish magistrates, and when they were brought before Gentile governors and kings, then could they give their testimony for Christ. Compare Phil. 1: 12-14. It was *to* them for salvation if they believed, as in the case of Sergius Paulus (Acts 13: 7, 12), or for condemnation if they rejected it, Acts 24: 25. In giving this testimony by their word, conduct, and sufferings they would have an opportunity of exercising the simplicity and guilelessness of doves. The inspiration of the Spirit, which he goes on to promise, would also enable them to act thus.

19, 20. Jesus directs them to depend entirely on the Holy Spirit in these trying emergencies. **Take no thought.** Be not unduly solicitous, be not anxious, ch. 6: 25. **How,** the manner; **what,** the matter of your defense. Words would be given them at the exact time needed, **that same hour.** See Acts 4: 8-12. And even more than this, they should be specially inspired, and completely under the control of the Spirit as instruments, so that it should not be they that speak, but the Spirit of their Father speaking in them. We have here the inspiration of the apostles on certain occasions stated in the strongest possible terms. The promise of our Savior gave them, however, no encouragement to preach generally without any forethought or previous preparation. It can not be used to support any such practice.

21. Persecution would become so severe, that even the tenderest relationship would not form a barrier. Brother would deliver up to the magistrate brother; the father, the child, and even children would rise up against parents. The result of such judicial proceedings would be death. Early church history shows the fulfillment of these predictions.

22. The violent hatred displayed in disregarding the nearest earthly ties, and causing brothers, children, and parents to be put to death for his name's sake, will be general. Christians will be **hated of all;** that is, by all but themselves. "The friendship of the world is enmity with God," James 4: 4. Christianity is exclusive, and therefore Christians were hated by both Jews and Gentiles. It proclaimed salvation through Jesus alone. The Jewish theocracy was superseded by a spiritual kingdom, and all that was indestructible and essential to man's duty in the law was incorporated in the Gospel. The Jew would, of

23 be saved. But ᵏ when they persecute you in this city, flee ye into another: for verily I say unto you, Ye shall not have gone over the cities of Israel, ˡ till the Son of man be come.

ˡ ch. 24. 13; Ro. 2. 7; Heb. 6. 11; Jam. 1. 12; Jude 20, 21; Rev. 2. 10
ᵏ ch. 12. 15; Ac. 8. 1; 9. 25; 14. 6.

---

course, hate a system destructive of his own, and one which shut him out of salvation, except through a hearty reception of faith in its doctrines. Pagans tolerated each other; their systems of religion were local and limited in their claims, confined to tribes, nations, and countries. They could even worship each other's gods. But they could not tolerate Christianity, which proclaimed itself a universal religion; and exclusive, in that it was the only true religion; and exterminating, in that it condemned all idolatry, and waged war with all other religions as embraced in the kingdom of darkness. Pagans, therefore, hated Christians, and regarded them in the language of Tacitus, the Roman historian, as exercising "enmity to the human race." The doctrines and claims of the Gospel, which are so repugnant to the human heart, aroused the hatred not only of the Jews and pagans, but of all other opposers not included in these two classes.

But Jesus adds a comforting promise, and encourages them with the prospect of final triumph. **He that endureth,** perseveres faithful **to the end of** the trials through which he is called to pass, **shall be saved,** fully and finally delivered from them. "The end" to every believer is the end of life, 1 Cor. 1: 8; Heb. 3: 6, 14; 6: 11; Rev. 2: 26. He shall be saved from sin and all its consequences, temporal and eternal, physical and spiritual. "'Enduring to the end' is the proper evidence of the reality and solidity of the Christian profession, 'drawing back unto perdition' exposes the want of foundation."—P. SCHAFF. See on ch. 24: 13.

23. Jesus directs them to avoid dangers by escape. See examples in Acts 8: 1; 9: 24, 25; 13: 51; 14: 6; 20: 1. By exercising a wise discretion in this respect, they would show the wisdom of the serpent. **Flee ye into another.** *Flee into the other,* the next city in order, which they had not visited. Persecution would thus result in spreading the Gospel, Acts 8: 4; 14: 7. They had no time to lose in needlessly braving persecution. Their mission required due haste. **The Son of Man.** The title which Jesus loved especially to apply to himself as the Messiah. See on ch. 8: 20. They should not end their mission in visiting the cities of Israel until the Son of Man **be come.**

Various interpretations have been given to the expression *till the Son of Man be come.* Some, referring this passage to the particular mission on which the apostles were now sent forth, suppose that Jesus would follow them as he did the seventy (Luke 10 : 1), and that he therefore means, until the Son of Man overtake you. The great objection to this view is, that Jesus had just been foretelling persecutions, which were never endured till after our Savior's personal ministry. The persecution and the coming of the Son of Man must therefore refer to some period later.

Others refer the fulfillment of the passage to the resurrection of Christ, when the Son of Man came with power (ch. 28 : 18) to establish his kingdom on earth, Judaism having been ended at the crucifixion, its rites and its whole service rendered null and void, after which also the cities of Israel were no longer the circumscribed field of apostolic labors. Others still regard the passage as pointing to the outpouring of the Spirit when the Son of Man came in power by the Holy Spirit, fully establishing his kingdom among men. The objection to the first view, however, holds good against these. We have no account of the apostles suffering persecution till after the descent of the Spirit, and the large ingathering of believers into the church at Jerusalem.

It is, however, very generally referred to the destruction of Jerusalem, according to which the meaning of the passage is, that the apostles will not be able to complete their mission in visiting all the cities of Israel before the Son of Man shall come by his providence, and put an end to the Jewish state, and the externalities of the Jewish dispensation, by the destruction of Jerusalem. It is argued that this view, both in point of time and in regard to persecution, meets the requirements of

24 ^m The disciple is not above *his* master, nor the
25 servant above his lord. It is enough for the disciple that he be as his master, and the servant ⁿ as his lord. If ^o they have called the master of the house ^p Beelzebub, how much more *shall they call*

^l ch. 16. 28; 24. 27, 30; 25. 13; 26. 64.
^m John 13. 16; 15. 20.
ⁿ Heb. 12. 2–4.
^o ch. 12. 24, 26, 27; John 8. 48, 52.

---

the prophecy, that in the twenty-fourth chapter of this Gospel we find the first apostolic period used as a type of the whole age of Christianity, and the vengeance on Jerusalem a type of the final coming of our Lord. Yet it is objected to this, that the destruction of Jerusalem is nowhere called *the coming* of Christ.

Hence others have referred this saying of our Lord to his second coming. And yet we meet an objection here, that this extends the time too far distant, since the language of Christ implies that his coming would occur while the apostles were still living, and that before it they would scarcely visit all the cities of Israel.

The greatest objection to any of these views I conceive to be, that they are not comprehensive enough. They lose sight of a great principle in prophecy, namely, that it often points not only to the final event itself, but also to types of that event, thus including at times a series of events, all ranging under one description, and fulfilled by one prophecy. Thus, the reign of Solomon is a type of the glory and the durability of the reign of Christ, the Son of David, Ps. 72. The return of Israel from their captivity at Babylon is linked in prophecy with the future triumph and glory of spiritual Israel. See also an illustration of this principle in ch. 1 : 23.

According to this principle, the prediction of this passage may extend, as that in ch. 16 : 27, 28 may, and that 24 : 30, 31, certainly does extend to the second and final coming of Christ. The destruction of Jerusalem is made typical of the judgment following his second coming; and although the former event is not in so many words called the coming of Christ, yet his providential coming is implied. So also, as the ascension of Jesus is made to illustrate in some respects the manner of his second coming (Acts 1 : 11), I can see no objection to supposing that his rising from the dead, with the connecting wondrous circumstances, such as the earthquake and the descent of the angel (ch. 28 : 2–4), were also in some respects typical of that coming. See also ch. 28 : 18. Neither would I seriously object to regarding the pentecostal outpouring of the Spirit as typical of the power and glory of Christ's kingdom, as connected with his second coming. The disciples in this their first mission doubtless received like treatment with their Lord. They doubtless were rejected by many, treated with cold indifference, and even insulted; which were the germs and the types of their future persecutions. It is by no means probable that they went over the **cities** of Israel, the *towns* and *villages*, before the resurrection. Neither is it probable that they themselves had visited them all before the destruction of Jerusalem, A.D. 70, as their attention had long before that event been directed to Jews living out of Palestine and to the Gentiles. In connection with the destruction of Jerusalem were the ruin and the extinction of many cities, towns, and villages of Palestine, some of which doubtless had never been visited by the apostles. Thus, at the second coming of Christ there will be found a literal fulfillment of the prediction. Jesus would have them exercise all proper haste; for however diligent and faithful they might be, there would be some cities which would never receive a visit from them. Compare ch. 16 : 27, 28, and 24 : 30, 31.

24–39. THE THIRD PART of the discourse in which JESUS GIVES APPROPRIATE INSTRUCTIONS AND ENCOURAGEMENTS in view of persecution.

24, 25. Persecution is to be expected. In suffering they are only sharers with Christ. They should not, therefore, murmur, but rather be satisfied and comforted. These thoughts are enforced by a three-fold illustration, bringing out a three-fold relation between Christ and his followers, *disciple* and *teacher* (ch. 23 : 8), *servant* and *lord* (Luke 12 : 35–37, 45–48), *master of the house* and *household* (Eph. 3 : 15; Matt. 21 : 33–37; 26 : 26–29). The disciple must not expect

26 them of his household! ᵠ Fear them not therefore: ʳ for there is nothing covered, that shall not be re-
27 vealed; and hid, that shall not be known. ˢ What I tell you in darkness, *that* speak ye in light: and what ye hear in the ear, ᵗ *that* preach ye upon the housetops.
28 ᵘ And fear not them which kill the body, but are not able to kill the soul: but rather fear him which

ᵖ Mk. 3. 22.
ᵠ Pro. 29. 25; Is. 51. 7, 8; 1 Pet. 3. 14.
ʳ Mk. 4. 22; Lk. 8. 17; 12. 2, 3.
ˢ ch. 13. 34; Lk. 8. 10.
ᵗ Pro. 1. 20, 21; 8. 1-5.
ᵘ Lk. 12. 4-10.

---

better treatment than his teacher, nor the servant than his lord. And if they apply the most opprobrious epithets to the master of the house, how much more will they do it to the household, the family. They will have less respect for them than for him. **Beelzebub.** According to the original it is *Beelzebul*, a name by which Satan, the prince of the devils, is called by the Jews, ch. 12: 24. It is variously explained. Thus, by some it is supposed that the name Baalzebub, *lord of flies*, the fly-god of Ekron (2 Kings 1: 2), was changed to Baalzebul or Beelzebul, *lord of dung*, dung-god, expressive of contempt, and applied to Satan as the prince of all idolatry and all impurity. But although Lightfoot (*Hor. Heb.* Matt. 12: 24; Luke 11: 15) has shown that *zebul* occurs in the Talmudic writers, in the sense of *dung, filth*, and is by them applied in this sense to idols, yet in the Hebrew Scriptures it never occurs in that sense, but means a *habitation, a house*. Hence, others suppose Beelzebul to mean, *lord of the habitation, master of the house*, and thus applied to Satan as the lord of idolatry, or demons and the kingdom of darkness; and that Jesus in this passage had just represented himself in contrast as the true "master of the house," and lord of the kingdom of light. The latter is the more probable explanation. Satan is the great usurper. The epithet, in the mouth of a Jew, was one of the most contemptuous he could use.

26-33. Reasons for encouragement and for not fearing their persecutors.

26. Since, therefore, ye are to be partakers of my sufferings, and also of my triumphs, **fear them not,** although ye be hated, reviled; and persecuted, **for there is nothing covered,** etc. A proverbial saying, implying that truth, though covered up and hid for a time, shall be brought to light, diffused, and vindicated. It was Christ's design that his gospel should be displayed, not concealed. It shall be known and acknowledged. Nothing which had been taught in secret was to be withheld, but all announced publicly. The secret designs, too, of their enemies would also be made known, exposed to the light of truth, and condemned at the judgment, Eph. 4: 13; 1 Cor. 4: 5.

27. The principal thought of the preceding verse expanded and enforced. **What I tell you in darkness,** etc. Speak *publicly* that which I have told you *privately, clearly* what ye have heard in *parables, openly* in the light of day what ye have heard *secretly*, in the darkness of night. **What ye hear,** whispered, as it were, **in the ear, that preach,** proclaim like a public herald **upon the housetops.** The roofs were flat, upon which the people in the evening were accustomed to sit. It is still a custom in the east to make public proclamation from the housetops. In the evening, after the people have returned home from their labors, the public herald ascends the highest roof, and the most convenient for the purpose, and makes his proclamation.

28. Another reason why they should be bold, and fearless of their persecutors: The latter can only do them external injury, while God's power extends over their spiritual nature, and hence is the true object of reverential fear. **Fear not them.** *Be not afraid*, in opposition to the holy and reverential *fear* which should be exercised toward God. **Soul,** the inner spiritual nature, in opposition to **body.** Notice also that men may **kill** the body, but not the soul, which is immortal. That still lives, though the body be dead. The soul and body are together not said to be *killed*, but *destroyed*, that is, ruined, made to perish **in hell,** in *Gehenna*, the place of future torment, which punishment is distinctly stated to be everlasting in ch. 25: 46. "I am

29 is able to destroy both soul and body in hell. Are not two sparrows sold for a farthing? and one of them shall not fall on the ground without your 30 Father. ᵛBut the very hairs of your head are all 31 numbered. Fear ye not therefore, ye are of more 32 value than many sparrows. ʷWhosoever therefore shall confess me before men, him will I confess also 33 before my Father which is in heaven. But whosoever shall deny me before men, him will I also deny before my Father which is in heaven.

ᵛ 1 Sam. 14. 45; Lk. 21. 18; Acts 27. 34.
ʷ Rom. 10. 9, 10; Rev. 3. 5; 2 Tim. 2. 12.

destroyed" was a common Attic phrase, meaning, "I am undone, ruined," or, according to Passow, "I am in the last degree miserable or unfortunate." Compare Job 19 : 10 ; Hos. 13 : 9. On Gehenna, see ch. 5 : 22.

Some very able commentators have very strangely supposed that Satan is presented in the last part of this verse as the destroyer of souls and the object of fear. But an exhortation to fear the devil would be out of place in this connection. The disciples are exhorted to fear *him who is able to* destroy both soul and body in hell, which can refer only to God, whom James declares (James 4 : 12) to be " the one Lawgiver and Judge, who is able to save and destroy." No such ability is ascribed to Satan or to any created being. Satan is nowhere represented as administering the punishments of hell; but is himself condemned to suffer punishment with the wicked there. Compare 2 Pet. 2 : 4.

29-31. Still another reason for not fearing their persecutors: His disciples are under the protection and providential care of their heavenly Father. As, therefore, they should exercise a godly, reverential fear toward the Almighty, so also they should exercise a childlike trust in him as their heavenly Father.

29. **Are not two sparrows?** The word translated *sparrows* means little birds generally, including sparrows especially, which were very abundant, small, and cheap. **Farthing.** The word thus translated designates a Roman copper coin, worth a cent and a half. So minutely does your heavenly Father watch over all events, that even one of these **shall not fall to the ground,** shall not die, without your Father's permission. They are still abundant in Palestine, sometimes brought to market and sold as food. " The sparrows," says Dr. Hackett (*Scripture Illus-*

trations, p. 94), "which flutter and twitter about dilapidated buildings at Jerusalem, and crevices of the city walls, are very numerous. In some of the more lonely streets they are so noisy as almost to overpower every other sound."

30, 31. **But the very hairs of your head,** etc. *Your* is in the Greek emphatic, and in marked contrast to what had just been said of the sparrows: But *you*, even the hairs of your head, etc. A proverbial expression, showing in the most forcible language the special providential care of God over his children. Their very hairs, and the smallest things that pertain to them, are precious; and they are watched over and cared for. How much **more value than many sparrows** are they who have an intelligent and immortal nature, and have been redeemed by such a costly price as the precious blood of Christ! 1 Pet. 1 : 18, 19. The argument is from the less to the greater, very similar to that in ch. 6 : 26. Compare 1 Sam. 14 : 45 ; Luke 21 : 18 ; Acts 27 : 34.

32, 33. Yet another reason for encouragement and boldness amid persecution : Fidelity will be approved and rewarded ; the unfaithful and the deniers of his name shall be rejected and punished. **Whosoever.** The application is made general : *Every one.* **Confess me before men.** Shall acknowledge me as the Messiah, his Lord and Teacher. **Him will I confess,** as my disciple, **before my Father,** as their Intercessor, as their Judge, and in the glories of the heavenly kingdom. But those who **deny** him, refuse to own him as their Lord and Teacher, the Messiah, he will also **deny,** reject, and disown as his at the judgment, before his Father and the holy angels. The confession must be true and genuine, indicative of the state of the heart as united in a spiritual, living union with Christ. So also

34 ˣ Think not that I am come to send peace on
35 earth: I came not to send peace, but a sword. For
I am come to set a man at variance ʸ against his
father, and the daughter against her mother, and
the daughter-in-law against her mother-in-law.
36 And ᶻ a man's foes *shall be* they of his own house-
37 hold. ᵃ He that loveth father or mother more than
me is not worthy of me: and he that loveth son or
38 daughter more than me is not worthy of me. ᵇ And
he that taketh not his cross, and followeth after me,

ˣ Lk. 12. 49. 51-53.

ʸ ver. 21; ch. 24. 10.

ᶻ Ps. 41. 9; 55. 13, John 13. 18; Gal. 4. 29.

ᵃ Lk. 14. 26.

ᵇ ch. 16. 24-26; Mk. 8. 34.

---

the denial must be indicative of a heart that really refuses to receive Christ and acknowledge him as Lord. Hence "the Lord will not confess the confessing Judas, nor deny the denying Peter." "We may observe that both in the Sermon on the Mount (ch. 7: 21-23) and here, *after mention of the Father*, the Lord describes *himself* as the Judge and Arbiter of eternal life and death."—ALFORD.

34-36. Jesus further teaches that strife and persecution are to be expected as a necessary consequence of his coming, and the proclamation of the Gospel.

34. **Think not,** do not entertain the mistaken idea that I am come to establish a temporal kingdom, diffusing prosperity, tranquillity, and peace upon the earth. **I came not to send peace but a sword.** There can be no peace between truth and error, light and darkness. The mission of Christ was aggressive, and so also is the Gospel aggressive. It has for its object the overthrow of the kingdom of darkness, and the rescuing of men from the power of sin and Satan. The truth, the word of God, is indeed a sword, a spiritual weapon, sharper than any two-edged sword (Heb. 4: 12), and wherever proclaimed will separate and cause divisions, conquering and making friends or arousing the hostility of obstinate foes, a savor of life unto life to the one and a savor of death unto death to the other, 2 Cor. 2: 16. The ultimate object of the Gospel is *peace*, peace with God, and then peace among men. But in a world of sin, like ours, this can only be attained through conflict. Strifes and divisions are, therefore, necessary results, arising from the cruel and rebellious nature of evil.

35, 36. The idea of the preceding verse expanded. The separating power of the *sword* would be seen in the cutting asunder the tenderest relations, and setting at variance members of families.

"The terms to **set at variance with** indicate a direct influence from the Lord; hence, the son, the daughter, and the daughter-in-law are here the representatives of Christ. It has not inaptly been suggested, that these special terms have been selected because the younger members and the female portion of households were commonly first to embrace the Gospel."—LANGE. **Daughter-in-law.** *Bride,* young wife. The words of our Savior here strikingly correspond with Micah 7: 6, and are regarded by some commentators as a quotation.

37-39. Jesus still further fortifies the minds of his disciples in view of stripes and persecutions, which should cut asunder the dearest relations of life, by teaching them that their love to him must be supreme, and that they must sacrifice any human attachment if it comes in conflict with duty and love to him.

37. **He that loveth,** etc. A man must have a love and devotion to Christ, as his Lord and Savior, combining both his human and divine natures, such as he could not lawfully exercise toward any human being, even father or mother, son or daughter. It is above, and higher than mere earthly attachments. The latter must yield to the former, if they come in conflict. Obedience to parents is a Christian duty, yet even they must be disobeyed if that be necessary to obedience to Christ. Even separation from father and mother, son and daughter, and the sacrifice of home and all the tenderest ties of kindred, must be submitted to, if necessary to allegiance to Jesus. **Not worthy of me.** Not fit to be my disciple.

38. **He that taketh not,** etc. The prominent idea in cross-bearing is the reproach endured. Taking his cross and following are inseparable. The suffering

39 is not worthy of me. *He that findeth his life shall lose it; and he that loseth his life for my sake shall find it.
40 *He that receiveth you receiveth me, and he that
41 receiveth me receiveth him that sent me. *He that receiveth a prophet in the name of a prophet shall receive a prophet's reward; and he that receiveth a righteous man in the name of a righteous man shall

* Lk. 17. 33; John 12. 25; Phil. 1. 20, 21.
* ch. 25. 40; Lk. 10. 16; John 13. 20; 2 Cor. 5. 20.
* John 12. 44–49; 2 John 9.
* 1 Ki. 17. 10, 16; 18. 4; 2 Ki. 4. 8; 2 Tim. 1. 16–18.

---

of such trials and persecutions, and the cutting asunder the tenderest ties, were indeed a spiritual crucifixion. The language of Jesus here is prophetic of his own sufferings. It was doubtless very expressive to his disciples when he uttered it, and was well fitted to prepare their minds for his sufferings and death. Yet that great event served to give an intensity of meaning to this and similar passages, and to throw new light on the self-denials and self-sacrifices, the inner and outer struggles pertaining to the Christian life, John 12: 16; Rom. 6: 6; Gal. 2: 20; 5: 24. The language is an allusion to that severest and most disgraceful Roman punishment, in which the malefactor was often compelled to bear his own cross to the place of execution, thus vividly portraying the duty of Christ's disciples to follow him through all trials that his cause and truth should demand. Every one has **his** own **cross**, which he must **take** willingly, and **follow after** Christ, not after the world or any object of his selfish inclination. This is indeed a test of discipleship; for if he does it not, he is **not worthy,** not fit to be his disciple. A wise man once seeking to explain the cross, took two slips of wood, a long and a short one, and said, "The long piece is the will of God; the short piece is your will. Lay your will in a line with the will of God, and you have no cross; lay it athwart, and you make a cross directly."

39. Jesus now compresses in a single sentence the trials and rewards of true discipleship, and the consequences of putting any object, even life itself, above him. The word translated **life** is the same as that which is rendered *soul* in verse 28, it having the twofold use, expressing both the natural *life* and the *soul*. The contrast here is between the natural life which pertains to the body and to this world, and the inner spiritual life which pertains to the soul, and which commences here by faith, and will be consummated in the world to come. **Findeth** in contrast to **loseth** has in it the sense of *saveth*. **He that findeth his life,** making the life of his body his great object, and saving it by rejecting me, shall **lose** his higher spiritual life, by falling short of it, and by being condemned to eternal death. But he that **loseth his life,** making Christ and his cause paramount to the life of the body and all that pertains to it in this world, ready even to die if needs be, and perchance laying it down for his sake, **shall find it,** shall attain to a higher, spiritual, eternal life, and thus save his soul. Thus Jesus encourages them to faithfulness to him, even though it should result in martyrdom.

40–42. In conclusion, Jesus states that they are HIS REPRESENTATIVES, and that they who heartily receive them shall be sharers in their reward.

40. **He that receiveth you,** etc. You are my representatives, even as I am my Father's representative. He, therefore, that receiveth you, not merely to his house and board, but also to his heart, welcoming you as my apostles, and consequently your message, receives both me and my Father. What honor and what blessedness! ch. 25: 34–40.

41. **A prophet.** One divinely commissioned to foretell future events, make known the will of God, or teach religious truth. **A righteous man.** A pious, godly person. He that receiveth such **in the name,** that is, as a prophet, having reference to his professed office and character, and as a righteous man, because he is a righteous man, with reference to his professed character, shall be sharers in their reward. It must be not a mere external reception, but a hearty reception of them, and consequently of their message, 1 Kings 17: 14–16. They may not always be what they profess, yet if they are received in the name of prophets or righteous men, the corresponding reward will follow. They who honor the

A.D. 29.   MATTHEW X.   149

42 receive a righteous man's reward. ʰ And whosoever shall give to drink unto one of these little ones ⁱ a cup of cold *water* only in the name of a disciple, verily I say unto you, ᵏ he shall in no wise lose his reward.

ᵍ ch. 16. 27; 25. 34–40.
ʰ ch. 18. 3–6, 10; Mk. 9. 44.
ⁱ 2 Cor. 8. 12.
ᵏ Phil. 4. 15–19; Heb. 6. 10.

---

office, though a Judas fills it, and receive him, supposing him to be a prophet, and because he is a prophet, shall be rewarded equally as if it had been a Peter, a James, a John, or Christ himself.

42. Even the smallest act of kindness will receive its appropriate reward. **Little ones.** Disciples, even the humblest. Perhaps the lambs, the young converts, or the less advanced disciples, ch. 11 : 11; Zech. 13 : 7. Compare ch. 18 : 10. There seems to be a certain gradation observed—the apostles, a prophet, a righteous man, little ones. **A cup of cold water only.** The cheapest refreshment and the smallest service that can be rendered to a disciple, **in the name,** because he is **a disciple,** shall be recompensed. Christ will note every such act, and will also see that the *doer* does not lose *his* reward.

REMARKS.

1. Christ calls those to preach the Gospel who are adapted to the work, and qualifies them with gifts and graces. This, however, does not preclude the necessity of mental discipline, etc., ver. 1; 1 Tim. 4 : 13.
2. As Christ sent forth the apostles to do good both to the bodies and souls of men, so now preachers of the Gospel should show an interest both in the temporal and spiritual welfare of their hearers, ver. 1; Acts 3 : 6, 7.
3. Christ chose his apostles, and he still chooses his ministers, principally from men in plain and humble circumstances, both for his own glory and the good of mankind, they being generally better adapted to reach the masses of men, vers. 2–4; 1 Cor. 1 : 20–24, 27–29.
4. A person may exercise the office of minister, he even blessed in the work, and receive the approbation of his brethren, and yet be unconverted, ver. 4. Compare 1 Cor. 9 : 27.
5. As the apostles were first sent forth to the lost sheep of the house of Israel, so Christ still, by his providence and Spirit, appoints to ministers their fields of labor; and wherever that may be, they should seek after those who are, and are to be, God's chosen people, vers. 5, 6; Acts 13 : 2–4; 18 : 10; 16 : 6, 9.
6. Ministers are the heralds of the Gospel, preaching not themselves, but Christ, and the message he gives them, ver. 7; 2 Cor. 4 : 1, 2, 5.
7. Ministers are not to set a price upon the Gospel, but freely do good to all, ver. 9; Acts 8 : 18–20.
8. Present duty should not be delayed in order to be better able to perform it. The accumulation of property is no prerequisite to preaching the Gospel, vers. 9, 10; Gal. 1 : 16.
9. Ministers of the Gospel should go forth to their work, depending on God for a supply of their temporal wants; trusting that he for whom they labor will provide, from time to time, all that may be necessary, vers. 9, 10; 1 Cor. 9 : 8–11; 3 John 7.
10. It is the duty of Christians and churches to make a practical acknowledgment of the truth that the laborer is worthy of his hire, by giving their pastors a liberal support, ver. 10; 1 Cor. 9 : 13, 14; 2 Cor. 11 : 7, 8; 3 John 8.
11. Ministers are to seek the godly for associates and companions, so that they may not identify the Lord's cause with the unworthy; yet their message extends to the chief of sinners, ver. 11; Acts 16 : 15. Compare 1 Cor. 5 : 11.
12. Ministers are also to be courteous, exercising good-will to all, and praying for the peace of those among whom they labor, vers. 12, 13; Col. 3 : 15. See also Ruth 2 : 4; Jer. 29 : 7.
13. They must also bring the Gospel into the family, to children and domestics as well as parents, to all indeed that are able to understand its claims. The piety of parents, however, does not include that of their children, nor their right to baptism, the Lord's Supper, and church membership, ver. 13; ch. 3 : 7–10; Prov. 9 : 12; Ezek. 18 : 20.
14. They who do not receive the ministers of the Gospel as Christ's ministers, withholding from them the welcome of their hearts and the support that is their due, and especially those

XI. AND it came to pass, when Jesus had made an end of commanding his twelve disciples, he departed thence to teach and to preach in their cities.

who reject their message, are guilty of greater sin, and exposed to a more fearful punishment, than are the inhabitants of Sodom, vers. 14, 15; also vers. 10, 40.

15. In a wicked world like ours it is necessary that ministers be wise as well as good; discreet as well as bold; gentle as well as courageous, ver. 16. Compare Rom. 16 : 19; 1 Cor. 14 : 20; Phil. 2 : 15.

16. No amount of gentleness of character, purity of motive, or discretion of action will at all times save the faithful minister from open opposition or bitter persecution, vers. 17-19; Acts 5 : 40; 2 Tim. 3 : 12.

17. The apostles were inspired to speak in their own defense; how much more would they be to write for Christians of every age, vers. 19, 20; Acts 4 : 8; Eph. 3 : 3; 1 John 4 : 6.

18. Persecution, when it does come, must be faithfully endured for Christ's sake, and in view of the final reward, ver. 22; ch. 24 : 13; 2 Tim. 4 : 6-8.

19. Persecution is to be avoided, if it can be consistently with duty. Christ's cause elsewhere may demand our flight, ver. 23; Acts 17 : 13, 14.

20. We should expect and be willing to receive treatment from the world similar to that which Christ bore, vers. 24, 25.

21. We should leave ourselves, if in the path of duty, in the hands of Christ, who knows all our trials, and will fully vindicate our cause, ver. 26.

22. The Gospel is intended to be preached openly; its truth is not to be kept in darkness, ver. 27; ch. 28 : 19.

23. God is to be feared rather than men, ver. 28; Acts 4 : 19; 5 : 29.

24. Both body and soul of the finally lost will suffer in hell, ver. 28.

25. God exercises a particular providence over all his creatures, especially his children, vers. 29-31; Luke 12 : 6, 7.

26. Christ's treatment of men in the coming world will correspond to their treatment of him in this world, vers. 32, 33; 2 Tim. 2 : 12.

27. Though many households are saved through the individual faith of their members (Acts 10 : 33, 44 ; 16 : 15, 34, 40), yet the Gospel is a divider of many, vers. 34-36.

28. The faithful preaching of the Gospel results in bringing men to Christ, or in arousing a more decided opposition to Christ, ver. 35.

29. Love to Christ must be supreme; kindred, friends, and life itself must be subordinate. Failure here will result in losing the soul, vers. 37-39.

30. Self-sacrifices are necessary to true discipleship, ver. 38.

31. A close union subsists between Christ and his people, vers. 40-42; John 17 : 23.

CHAPTER XI.

1. This verse properly belongs to the preceding chapter. When Jesus had finished charging or instructing his disciples he **departed thence.** Commonly supposed to be from Capernaum; but not probable, as it appears from 9 : 35 that Jesus delivered this charge to the twelve while he was performing his third missionary tour through Galilee. **Their cities.** The cities and towns of Galilee. Mark (6 : 30) and Luke (9 : 10) mention the return of the twelve from their mission.

2-6. THE MESSAGE OF JOHN THE BAPTIST AND THE REPLY OF JESUS, Luke 7 : 18-23. Having given an account of the apostles being sent forth on their first mission, and the charge of Jesus to them, Matthew now goes back a little in the history (Luke 7 : 18), and relates an incident in the life of John the Baptist. The inquiry of John and the answer of Jesus, together with his discourse on the occasion to the multitude, bring to view the evidences of his Messiahship (vers. 4-6); the position of John in the divine arrangement and his relation to Jesus (7-15); the treatment that he and John received of the men of their day (16-19); the woes that would come upon them for rejecting so much light, and such evidences of his Messiahship (20-24); the divine sovereignty in revealing spiritual truth to babes (25-27); and the affectionate invitation to all who were groaning under spiritual bondage to come to him for rest, 28-30.

Message from John the Baptist to Jesus; his answer; and his discourse to the multitude.

2 ¹ NOW when John had heard in the prison the
3 works of Christ, he sent two of his disciples, and
said unto him, ᵐ Art thou he that should come, or

¹ Lk. 7. 18–35; ch. 14. 3; Lk. 3. 19, 20.
ᵐ Gen. 3. 15; 49. 10; Num. 24. 17; Deu. 18. 15–18; Dan. 9. 24, 26; Is. 29. 18; 35. 4–6; 42. 7.

---

2. In the prison, ch. 4 : 12. According to Josephus (*Ant.* b. 18, c. 5, s. 2), John was imprisoned in the castle of Machærus, a fortress in the southern extremity of Perea, east of the Dead Sea, and, next to Jerusalem, the strongest fortress of the Jews, being surrounded on all sides by deep valleys. **Works of Christ.** Rather, *works of the Christ*. Matthew uses his official name. He holds up Jesus as the Messiah; so, doubtless, many were calling him, and by this appellation John may have heard of him. It was through his own disciples (Luke 7 : 18) that John heard of the works which were characteristic of the Messiah, particularly the recent miracle of restoring to life the widow's son at Nain, Luke 7 : 11–17. **Sent two of his disciples.** According to the highest critical authorities, it should read *by his disciples;* that there were *two* of them we learn from Luke 7 : 19. John's disciples still adhered to him, though he was in prison and had fully accomplished his mission, ch. 9 : 14. A separate organization was kept up long after his execution, Acts 19 : 3. Indeed, a sect bearing the name of "John's Disciples" exists to the present day in the east, which is opposed alike to Judaism and to Christianity.

3. He that should come. He that comes. An appellation of the Messiah, which appears to have become quite common (ch. 3 : 11 ; John 11 : 27); and probably had its origin in ancient prophecy, Ps. 40 : 7; 118 : 26; Mal. 3 : 1; Matt. 21 : 9; Heb. 10 : 37. The meaning of the question is, "Art thou he that comes, the Messiah who has been so long expected, or look we still for another?" or, in the stronger sense of the Greek word, "Look we for one of another kind, a different sort of a Messiah?" Possibly, as the later Jews afterward adopted the view of two Messiahs, a conquering Messiah and a suffering Messiah, so John, in this hour of his trial, may have entertained a vague idea that possibly there might be another, who should the more completely fulfill the predictions of the prophets.

Various reasons have been given for this inquiry of John. Some think that he asked it for the sake of his disciples, whose minds he wished to satisfy in regard to the Messiahship of Jesus. But to this it is objected that the answer was sent to John himself. Others suppose that doubt existed for some reason or other in John's own mind. And still others think that his inquiry denoted impatient zeal, and implied an intimation to Jesus to assert his Messiahship still more plainly, and that our Savior's reply was a rebuke similar to that given to Mary, John 2 : 4.

But whatever view we adopt, we must beware of supposing that John had no higher ideas of the kingdom of God than those which were common at that time among the Jews. That he had conceptions of its spiritual nature, is evident from his preaching. See ch. 3 : 7–12; John 1 : 29–31, 34; 3 : 27–36. It seems also evident that the reason of the inquiry must be found principally in John himself; for the answer was sent to *him*, and the import of it was comforting, strengthening, and corrective. While it administered a gentle rebuke, it was adapted to confirm his faith. Having been confined in prison several months, cut off suddenly from active labor, and hearing many reports of Jesus, some vague and some distorted by the prejudices of his disciples, it was not strange that he should have been dejected, like many eminent saints before him, brooding over his own troubles and the slow progress of the kingdom of God. In this his hour of darkness, he felt that he needed more light and more strength. Not that he doubted his own office as forerunner, nor that he had any good reason to doubt the divine commission of Jesus, nor any of the declarations he had made concerning him; but he felt the inward need of a new confirmation of his own faith, by a fresh declaration from Jesus himself. And this was just

4 do we look for another? Jesus answered and said unto them, Go and show John again those things 5 which ye do hear and see: the blind receive their sight, and the lame walk; the lepers are cleansed, and the deaf hear; the dead are raised up, and the 6 poor have the Gospel preached to them. And blessed is *he* whosoever shall not ⁿ be offended in me.
7 ᵒ And as they departed, Jesus began to say unto

ⁿ ch. 13. 55–57; 15. 12–14; Is. 8. 14, 15; Rom. 9. 32, 33; 1 Cor. 2. 14; 1 Pet. 2. 8.
ᵒ Lk. 7. 24.

---

what he received. This view also makes the analogy between John and his prototype, Elijah, complete. The one was cast into prison by Herod, the other driven into the wilderness by Ahab, and both during their trial were dejected and desponding, 1 Kings 19 : 1–4, 14. Doubtless also the disciples of John needed similar, and possibly greater encouragement, and a severer rebuke than did their master. That the answer of Jesus resulted in their good also, appears from the fact that, when John was beheaded, they "took up the body and buried it, and came and told Jesus," ch. 14 : 12.

4. Instead of a direct reply, Jesus commands them to **go and show to John,** *report, make known* to him, the miracles and the preaching of Jesus, which were the evidences of his Messiahship and an exact fulfillment of prophecy, Isa. 29 : 18 ; 35 : 5, 6 ; 61 : 1–3. What an example of modesty and humility does Jesus present in his reply! He says not, Report the miracles that I am working, but **what ye hear and see.** **See** refers specially to the miracles which were wrought in the presence of John's disciples, Luke 7 : 21. **Hear** may refer to accounts of other miracles from eye-witnesses; but its special reference is to the preaching of the good tidings to the poor.

5. Jesus specifies the more signal things they heard and saw, which were the signs of his ministry. **The dead are raised.** They may have witnessed the raising of the dead, or they may have received accounts from reliable witnesses of the raising of the daughter of Jairus (ch. 9 : 18–26), and of the widow's son at Nain, Luke 7 : 11–15. The miracles were significant, and symbolical of the healing of the soul. They were attended with spiritual blessings, and indeed were the external signs of inward cures to those who exercised faith in Jesus as the Redeemer. **The poor.** The lowly, the humble, of low estate, including the idea of being afflicted and distressed. Reference is evidently made to Isa. 61 : 1, and to that class of persons who combined external poverty with humility and a sense of spiritual want. See Luke 4 : 18. **The Gospel.** The good tidings of eternal salvation. Pharisees and philosophers and false religionists had overlooked the poor and the lowly. Stier observes that with *the dead are raised* is united *the poor are evangelized,* or *have the Gospel preached to them,* as being a thing hitherto unheard of and strange.

6. **Blessed.** *Happy* in his condition, his relations and destiny. See ch. 5 : 2. Shall not be offended in me. Rather, *at me,* as an occasion of offense, of dissatisfaction and dislike. The meaning is, Happy is he to whom I shall not prove a stumbling-block, who shall not *take offense* at my character, conduct, or words, so as to desert and reject me. See ch. 5 : 29. Mark how carefully put are the words. They are not personal to John himself, nor do they imply that he had really taken offense at Jesus. So far as he remained steadfast, they were full of comfort; but so far as he desponded or wavered in his faith, they were full of warning of what might result from such a condition of mind and course of conduct.

7–30. Jesus makes this an occasion of uttering a discourse to the multitude.

7–15. THE CHARACTER OF JOHN, HIS POSITION IN THE DIVINE ARRANGEMENT, AND HIS RELATION TO JESUS, Luke 7 : 24–30.

7. **As they departed.** As the disciples of John were departing, so as not to appear to flatter him through them, Jesus began to speak of him in the highest terms of commendation. This shows that John had not gone far in wavering; and we may justly infer that the answer of Jesus dispelled all darkness and despondency that may have

A.D. 29.   MATTHEW XI.   153

the multitudes concerning John, *r* What went ye
out into the wilderness to see? *q* A reed shaken
8 with the wind? But what went ye out for to see?
r A man clothed in soft raiment? behold, they that
9 wear soft *clothing* are in kings' houses. But what
went ye out for to see? A prophet? yea, I say

r ch. 3. 1–3, 5.
q Eph. 4. 11.

r ch. 3. 4.

possessed his mind. Bengel remarks, "The world praises to the face, censures behind the back; divine truth the opposite." Jesus doubtless intended to prevent the people putting a wrong construction on John's inquiry, and from supposing that he in any sense retracted his testimony in regard to Jesus. He also had an opportunity of affirming the character and high position of John, and showing the wicked treatment that both his forerunner and himself had received, of pronouncing woes upon unbelievers, and extending gracious invitations to those who were in a condition to receive him. Instead of beginning with positive assertions, he wisely commences with certain interrogations, which lead to the most positive affirmations. Referring to the time when they went forth into the wilderness to the preaching and baptism of John, he asks, **But what went ye out into the wilderness to see?** The word translated *see* is very expressive, meaning *to behold, to gaze at,* as a public show or spectacle. **A reed shaken with the wind?** Surely not a reed shaken by the wind? Some suppose that Jesus refers to reeds as a common product of the wilderness of Judea, and which grew in abundance on the banks of the Jordan: surely it was not to see the rustling reeds of the desert? Others regard the language as descriptive of John: surely ye did not go out to see a man, fickle, wavering and unstable? The latter suits the context the best; for Jesus began to speak concerning John, and he proceeds to the most positive assertions. It also accords with the figurative style of the east. The meaning is, Ye did not go out to see a man who was wavering and easily influenced, like the reeds of the wilderness shaken by the wind; for you found John to be a firm and decided character. Think not, therefore, that he is any way different now; or that he has changed his views in regard to the great truths and doctrines he then expressed.

8. **But** if ye did not go out to see such a character, **what,** then, **went ye out to see? Soft raiment?** Luxurious clothing, a mark of effeminacy and the very opposite to John's dress, ch. 3: 4? It is evident that this was not their object; for they would not have gone into the wilderness to find one in costly and luxurious clothing, but rather to king's palaces. The meaning is, Ye did not go out to see a man in luxurious dress, and of effeminate habits and character, like those who dwell in the palaces of kings, and especially at the court of Herod; for you found John bold, stern, and inflexible, austere and self-denying, and not one disposed to flatter from motives of expediency, selfishness, or cowardice. Think not, then, that he has been influenced by any such motives in sending his recent inquiry to me; or that the inquiry itself indicates any such trait in his character. Jesus appeals to John's well-known character, and to the esteem in which he was held by the multitude when he was in the height of his ministerial success. These were a sufficient answer to the supposition that he was either fickle, selfish, or cowardly.

9. **But** if ye went not out to see a luxurious and effeminate person, *why,* then, went ye out to see? Anticipating their reply, he asks, **a prophet?** for all held John as a prophet, ch. 21: 26. This he affirms **Yea,** and adds, **more than a prophet.** A *prophet* was not only one who foretold future events, but also one who was divinely commissioned as a religious teacher, or who instructed men as to the will of God. John was more than an ordinary prophet. The reason for this assertion is given in the following verse.

10. **For** is implied, but is omitted in

154   MATTHEW XI.   A.D. 29.

10 unto you, *and more than a prophet. For this is *he* of whom it is written,^t Behold, I send my messenger before thy face, which shall prepare thy way before
11 thee. Verily I say unto you, Among them that are born of women there hath not arisen a greater than John the Baptist: notwithstanding he that is least in "the kingdom of heaven is greater than he.
12 *And from the days of John the Baptist until now the kingdom of heaven ᵞ suffereth violence, and the
13 violent take it by force. ᶻ For all the Prophets and

* ch. 14. 5; 17. 12, 13; 21. 26; Lk. 1. 15-17, 76.
t Mk. 1. 2.

* Zech. 12. 8; Gal. 4. 1-7.
⸱ Lk. 16. 16.
ʸ Lk. 13. 24; John 6. 27.
ᶻ Lk. 24. 27, 44; Ac. 3. 22-24.

---

the best text. He quotes Mal. 3 : 1. The quotation is according to the sense of the prophecy, not in its exact language. John was the messenger of God who was to prepare the way before the Lord, even the messenger or Angel of the Covenant. He was, in other words, *the forerunner of the Messiah*, and thus superior to all of his predecessors. He was himself the subject of prophecy (one of the two messengers or angels spoken of by Malachi), the nearest of all the prophets to the Messiah, and indeed the preparer of his way. The prophets had spoken of Christ from afar; they had *pointed men toward* Christ; but John *announced* his immediate coming (ch. 3 : 2, 3, 11 ; Luke 1 : 76) and *introduced* Christ, John 1 : 35, 36. Christ was the Bridegroom; John the friend of the Bridegroom, his groomsman, John 3 : 29. Thus, he enjoyed a distinction never before conferred on any prophet (this verse) or even on any man (next verse). **Prepare thy way.** Fully make ready for thy advent. **Before thy face.** Immediately before thee.

11. **Born of women.** From the human race, among mankind. **Greater than John.** None enjoyed the distinction that he enjoyed, his relative position to the Messiah as explained in the preceding verse. It does not necessarily mean that he excelled all others in piety and purity of character. **He that is least,** etc. Literally, *He that is less,* that is, than all the rest in the kingdom of heaven. This in English is equivalent to *He that is least.* **Greater than he.** Than John the Baptist. They who are in the kingdom of heaven constitute the Bride of Christ. Inasmuch as the Bride enjoys a greater distinction than the friend of the Bridegroom, so the weakest and the least distinguished in Christ's kingdom enjoys a distinction above John, the harbinger and groomsman of Christ. Some suppose the passage to mean, He that is less than John, his inferior in all other respects, yet, by virtue of his being in the kingdom of heaven, is greater, more important and distinguished than he. The former interpretation is to be preferred, as the most natural.

12. Jesus continues his glowing discourse concerning John, describing the wonderful effects of his ministry. **From the days of John.** From his public appearance as a preacher. **The kingdom of heaven.** The reign, administration, rule, or kingdom of the Messiah. See ch. 3 : 2. **Suffereth violence.** Is assaulted as by storm by those who would prematurely hurry its development, as may have been the case with John, and as was the case of those who would make Jesus king, or have him assert a temporal power (compare John 6 : 15, and 7 : 3-5); and by those also who were rushing forth by multitudes, seeking the blessings and the privileges of that kingdom, Matt. 3 : 5; 4 : 23-25; 8 : 1 ; 9 : 36. **Take it by force.** The violent, they who are truly eager and earnest, seize upon it, some indeed improperly, and hence unsuccessfully, but many pressing in enjoy its privileges, Luke 16 : 16. Thus, from the days of John the kingdom of heaven began to be present, and men began to press into it.

13. **For.** A reason given for what had been said. No wonder that such results had followed; for until John the kingdom of heaven had been only predicted; but he had proclaimed it as actually present, and indeed he was the Elijah that was to come. The **prophets** and **the Law** comprised the whole body of testimony under the old dispen-

14 the Law prophesied until John. And if ye will receive *it*, this is ^a Elias, which was for to come.
15 ^b He that hath ears to hear, let him hear.
16 ^c But whereunto shall I liken this generation? It is like unto children sitting in the markets, and
17 calling unto their fellows, and saying, We have piped unto you, and ye have not danced; we have
18 mourned unto you, and ye have not lamented. For ^d John came neither eating nor drinking, and they

^a Mal. 4. 5, 6; Mk. 9. 11-13; Lk. 1. 17.
^b Lk. 8. 8.
^c Lk. 7. 31-35.

^d ch. 3. 4.

sation (ch. 5 : 12), and is sometimes expressed by law, prophets, and psalms, Luke 24 : 44. The order of the Greek is, "For all the prophets and the law until John prophesied." They *predicted*, he *proclaimed* the advent of the Messiah and his kingdom; opened the gates as it were, by his preaching.

14. This is Elias. Rather *he*, that is, John, *is the Elijah*. *Elias* is the Greek mode of writing the Hebrew *Elijah*. Jesus affirms that the prediction of Malachi (Mal. 4 : 5) was fulfilled in John, who came "in the spirit and power of Elijah," Luke 1 : 17. This was different from the general belief and expectation of the Jews, who were looking for the appearance of Elijah himself. Jesus, therefore, knowing that the prophecy was differently understood by his hearers, said, **If ye will receive it,** If ye are willing to receive it. The account of Elijah is found in 1 Kings chs. 17-21; 2 Kings chs. 1, 2. This accords with John's denial that he was actually Elijah, John 1 : 21. He was not Elijah himself, but the Elijah who should come, whose coming had been predicted, and who was typified by the prophet Elijah. See ch. 17 : 10-13; Mark 9 : 11-13.

15. He that hath ears, etc. A proverbial expression, calling to candid and solemn attention. Whoever can hear, let him hear and understand this concerning John and the coming of the kingdom of heaven.

16-19. How the ministry of John and of Jesus had been respectively received; or the childish treatment they had received of that generation, Luke 7 : 31-35.

16. But whereunto, etc. Implying that they had not ears to attend to and understand what he had just taught in regard to John, and himself. **This generation.** The people of this time, especially the leaders, the scribes and Pharisees, Luke 7 : 30. They are like to children who, sitting in the markets, imitate in their plays the scenes of actual life, now of marriage and now of funerals, and yet are unable in any way to please one another. The ancient **markets** were places of public resort, where people congregated for business or for conversation, and the children for amusement. **Unto their fellows.** Rather, *To the others;* that is, other children. This agrees with Luke (7 : 32) where the children are represented as "calling to one another."

17. When they had **piped,** played on the flute a lively and joyful tune, the others had not **danced** to the music. It was customary among the Jews, Greeks, and Romans, to play the flute at marriage dances. And then changing their play, they had **mourned,** *sung dirges* as at a funeral, and yet even then the others, being determined to be satisfied and pleased with nothing, had **not lamented,** had not *beat the breast* as an expression of grief on such occasions. Compare Luke 18 : 13; 23 : 48. These two sets of children represented the childish, freakish, and ill-humored conduct of the scribes and Pharisees toward John and Jesus. Neither of them really represent Christ and his forerunner; for, as Dr. Schaff remarks, they "could with no degree of propriety and good taste be represented as playmates and comrades of their wayward contemporaries."

18. Jesus now applies the illustration just given. **Neither eating nor drinking.** John was abstemious and austere in his habits, not living on ordinary food, but on locusts and wild honey (ch. 3 : 4); yet the people, especially the scribes and lawyers, ascribed it to demoniacal instead of divine influence, saying, **He hath a demon.** See on ch. 4 : 24.

19. The Son of Man. The Mes-

19 say, He hath a devil. *The Son of man came eating and drinking, and they say, Behold a man gluttonous and a winebibber, ᶠa friend of publicans and sinners. ᵍBut wisdom is justified of her children.
20 ʰTHEN began he to upbraid the cities wherein most of his mighty works were done, because they
21 repented not: Woe unto thee, Chorazin! woe unto thee, Bethsaida! ⁱfor if the mighty works which

*Lk. 5. 29, 30; 7. 36; John 12. 2.
ᶠch. 9. 10, 11; Lk. 15. 2.
ᵍPro. 8. 1, 32.
ʰPs. 81. 11-13; Is. 1. 2-5.
ⁱch. 12. 41, 42; Eze. 3. 6, 7.

siah. See on ch. 8 : 20. **Eating and drinking.** Jesus lived as men ordinarily lived, and gave attention to the social enjoyments of life. Thus, he attended the marriage at Cana in Galilee (John 2 : 1-11), and the feast at the house of Matthew, ch. 9 : 10-17. Yet they also found fault with him. They call him a *glutton*, a *wine-drinker*, a *friend of publicans and sinners*. The last clause suggests, however, their chief objection. He associated with the common people, eat with publicans and sinners, and proclaimed that he came not to call righteous men, but sinners, ch. 9 : 13. He was a friend not of their sins, but of their souls. How evident it was from the illustration here given, and the opposite modes of life of John the Baptist and Jesus, that the trouble was in the hearts of these fault-finders, who were determined to be satisfied with nothing.

But wisdom is, rather, *was,* **justified by her children,** or rather, according to the best text, *by her works,* the fruits and general effect of true wisdom in those who receive and practice it. In Luke 7 : 35 the correct text is, *by her children.* The meaning in both Gospels is substantially the same. Both point to results, ch. 7 : 18; John 8 : 39; 1 Cor. 2 : 6, 7. Jesus condemns the Jewish leaders, and approves of those who had accepted his doctrine. The former were *childish*, like petulant, peevish children; the latter were *child-like*, teachable, confiding, and faithful. The conduct of the former was condemned by that of the latter. The way is thus prepared for the fearful woes that follow.

20-24. WOES PRONOUNCED AGAINST THE CITIES OF GALILEE, where so great light had been enjoyed, yet misimproved. Only in Matthew. Because some of the expressions are found in the charge to the seventy disciples (Luke 10 : 13-15), we need not suppose that Matthew has merely in this chapter made a selection of our Savior's teachings, spoken at different times. The connections between the several parts of the discourse are too close for such a supposition. It was evidently spoken at one time and on one occasion. Some things were afterward repeated to the seventy; repetition was sometimes indulged in by Jesus, as indeed it is by all teachers.

20. **Then.** At that time. **To upbraid.** Chide, rebuke, expressing his disapprobation and holy indignation at their impenitence. *Mighty works.* Greek *dunameis*, wonderful works, miracles, the effect of supernatural power. On the words employed in Greek to express miracles, see Introduction to ch. 8. Jesus performed many miracles of which we have no special account, ch. 4 : 24; 8 : 16; 9 : 35.

21. **Chorazin** was a city only known from this passage and from Luke 10 : 13. Jerome informs us that it was situated on the shore of the Sea of Galilee, two miles from Capernaum. Some suppose it to be the modern *Tell Hum*, on the north-west shore of the lake; others suppose it to be the modern *Khorazy*, about three miles inland from Tell Hum. It has been suggested that after the latter was destroyed on the exposed coast, the inhabitants retired to a more secure spot, carrying with them the name of their home. **Bethsaida** is supposed to be the name of two towns, one on the east, and the other on the west, of the lake. The name, which means *a house of fishing*, or *fishery*, could easily be applied to more than one place, especially where fishing was so common a business. The Bethsaida on the north-eastern border of the lake is referred to in Luke 9 : 10; Mark 6 : 32; 8 : 22. The one mentioned here was on the west side near Capernaum, the birthplace of Andrew, Peter, and Philip, Luke 10: 13; John 1 : 44; 12 : 21.

A.D. 29. MATTHEW XI. 157

were done in you had been done in Tyre and Sidon, they would have repented long ago ᵏ in sackcloth
22 and ashes. But I say unto you, ˡ It shall be more tolerable for Tyre and Sidon at the day of judg-
23 ment than for you. And thou, ᵐ Capernaum, ⁿ which art exalted unto heaven, shalt be brought down to hell; for if the mighty works, which have

ᵏ Jon. 3. 7, 8.
ˡ ch. 10. 15; Lk. 12. 47, 48; Heb. 10. 26–31.
ᵐ ch. 4. 13.
ⁿ Is. 14. 13, 15; Lam. 2. 1; Am. 9. 2; Lk. 14. 11.

Tyre and Sidon were the two principal cities of Phœnicia on the coast of the Mediterranean Sea. Sidon, one of the most ancient cities of the world, is believed to be founded by Zidon, the eldest son of Canaan, Gen. 10 : 15; 49 : 13. Tyre, about twenty miles south, was of later date, but grew in importance, and gained an ascendency over Sidon, and became the commercial emporium of Phœnicia. They were the subjects of prophecy, and of the divine judgments, under Nebuchadnezzar and Alexander, Isa. ch. 23; Ezek. chs. 26–28; 29 : 18. On account of gross idolatry and wickedness, the inhabitants of Tyre are represented as filled with pride and luxury, and all the sins attending prosperity and great wealth. The cities that grew up on the ruins of the ancient ones existed in the time of our Savior, Acts 12 : 20; 21 : 3, 7; 27 : 3. Sidon, now called Saida, contains about five thousand inhabitants, and is spoken of as dirty and full of ruins. Tyre, now called Sur, is at present a poor town, and has a population of about three thousand.
Long ago. In ancient times. The inhabitants of those ancient cities would have repented, and thus would have escaped the fearful judgments which came upon them. **Sackcloth and ashes.** It was customary in the east for mourners to wear a garment of coarse black cloth, commonly made of hair, and made to hang on the body like a sack, Gen. 37 : 34; 1 Kings 21 : 27; Jon. 3 : 5. To sit in ashes (Luke 10 : 13) was a token of grief and mourning (Job 2 : 8), as was also strewing them upon the head, 2 Sam. 13 : 19. These would have been the external symbols of their sorrow and patience, Jon. 3 : 8.
22. **But.** Not only is their sin less than yours, because they enjoyed less light and fewer advantages than you, but also at the day of judgment their punishment will be more endurable than yours. The greater the light, the greater the guilt and the greater the punishment. See on ch. 10 : 15.
23. **Capernaum.** On the north-western coast of the Sea of Galilee. See on ch. 4 : 13. **Exalted unto heaven.** Exalted in privilege as the residence of Christ. The Lord from *heaven* had come and dwelt there, thus raising it in honor and privileges to the very heavens, ch. 9 : 1. According to the oldest manuscripts, this passage should read, "And thou, Capernaum! shalt thou be exalted to heaven? Nay, thou shalt go down to the under-world." In view of the distinction and the privileges of my residence in thee shalt thou be exalted to heaven? Nay, on account of thy misimprovement of them, thou shalt, etc. **Hell.** Not *Gehenna*, the place of punishment for the wicked, but *Hades*, the abode of the dead, the world of departed spirits, and may be translated *the under-world*. On Gehenna see ch. 5 : 22. *Hades* in the Greek has the same signification as *Sheol* in the Hebrew, both representing the region of the departed. As *Sheol* in the Old Testament is represented figuratively as *beneath* (Isa. 14 : 9; Ezek. 31 : 17; Amos 9 : 2), so is *Hades* in the New Testament. Thus in this passage it is represented as the *depth below* in contrast to *heaven*, as the *height above*. Compare Rom. 10 : 6, 7; Phil. 2 : 10; Rev. 5 : 3, 13. *Under-world* thus corresponds with the scriptural conception of this abode. *Hades* occurs ten times in the New Testament, namely, Matt. 11 : 23; 16 : 18; Luke 10 : 15; 16 : 18; Acts 2 : 27, 31; Rev. 1 : 18; 6 : 8; 20 : 13, 14. It occurs also in 1 Cor. 15 : 55, in the text from which the common version was translated, and is there rendered *grave*. The true text reads *death* in both clauses of the verse. *Heaven* and the *under-world* here stand in contrast, the one representing height of privileges and blessings, and the other the depth of woe and desolation. See further on ch. 16 : 18.

been done in thee, had been done °in Sodom, it
24 would have remained until this day. But I say
unto you, ᵖ That it shall be more tolerable for the
land of Sodom in the day of judgment, than for
thee.
25 ᵠ At that time Jesus answered and said, I thank
thee, O Father, Lord of heaven and earth, because

° Ge. 13. 13; 19. 24, 25.
ᵖ ch. 10. 15; 12. 36.

ᵠ Lk. 10. 21, 22; Ps. 8. 2; Phil. 2. 10, 11; John 1. 18.

As the privileges of Capernaum had been greater than those of other cities in Galilee, so is her guilt represented as greater, by being compared, not with Tyre and Sidon, but with **Sodom,** the residence of Lot, and probably the chief of the wicked cities of the plain. **Remained unto this day.** Jesus thus shows that his knowledge extends not merely to actual but also to supposed circumstances. He knew that the inhabitants of Sodom would have repented, and their city remained, if they had enjoyed the privilege which had been granted to Capernaum. And here we may get a glimpse of the harmonious and eternal relation between the divine purposes and God's foreknowledge. The two are coexistent and coextensive. To suppose imperfection in either is to detract from the character of God. But neither compel men to a course of action. God's purpose was, that Sodom should enjoy only the preaching of Lot, and Capernaum the residence, the preaching, and works of Jesus. He knew that the former city, with the blessings and privileges of the latter, would have been saved from destruction. Yet it did not alter his purpose. Sodom enjoyed enough light to condemn her. She sinned freely, and thus brought upon herself her own destruction. Divine sovereignty is strikingly brought to view in the remarkable prayer that follows, vers. 25–27.

24. Sodom is described by Jude (ver. 7) as "suffering the vengeance of eternal fire;" yet so much less the light, and hence her guilt, than that of Capernaum, that her punishment will be proportionally less and more endurable. "It is a remarkable fact, that the very names and ruins of these three cities on the lake of Gennesareth have utterly disappeared, and their locality is a matter of dispute among travelers; while even that of Sodom and Gomorrah is pointed out on the shores of the Dead Sea."— DR. SCHAFF.

25–27. DIVINE SOVEREIGNTY IN THE DISPENSATION OF THE GOSPEL gratefully acknowledged and asserted. Only in Matthew.

25. **At that time.** On that occasion, when he had been considering the wicked conduct of that generation, and pronouncing woes upon the most highly favored cities of Galilee. The position of the prayer of Jesus is so natural, and the connection so close, that it is hardly necessary to consider even a brief pause in the discourse. He repeated it after the return of the seventy, Luke 10 : 21, 22. **Jesus answered.** The word *answer* is often used in Scripture as a kind of response to some words, circumstance, or occasion that precedes. Thus, the unbelief of the scribes, lawyers, and leaders of the people (vers. 16–24), and the eagerness of the common people to receive him (ver. 12), gave him occasion to thank the Father for the wisdom displayed in the bestowment of Gospel blessings. See ch. 22 : 1; John 2 : 18; 5 : 17, as illustrative of this use of the word. **Father** intimates the close relation existing between him and the Father. He uses it on four other occasions, this being the first recorded instance. See John 11 : 41; 12 : 28; 17 : 1; Luke 23 : 34. **Lord of heaven and earth.** The absolute sovereign. How appropriate thus to designate his Father, when he was about to speak specially of his sovereignty, as one who works all things after the counsel of his own will, Eph. 1 : 11. It should be remarked that Jesus addresses God as Father, but never as *his* Lord. **I thank thee.** The verb in the original is of broad signification, including both praise and acknowledgment: I praise thee and acknowledge to thee the wisdom and justice of thy doings. **Because thou hast hid.** *That thou didst hide*, conceal these things, concerning the Father, the Son, and the kingdom of heaven. **From the wise and prudent.** The wise and discerning, intelligent, in

thou hast hid these things from the wise and prudent, and hast revealed them unto babes. Even so,
27 Father: for so it seemed good in thy sight. All things are delivered unto me of my Father; and no man knoweth the Son, but the Father; neither knoweth any man the Father, save the Son, and *he* to whomsoever the Son will reveal *him*.
28 *ʳ* Come unto me, *ˢ* all *ye* that labor and are heavy

ʳ Is. 45. 22; 55. 1-3; John 7. 37; Ac. 16. 31. ch. 23. 4; Ps. 38. 4; Lk. 18. 13; Ro. 7. 22-25.

their own estimation and in the estimation of the world. Wise and discerning in regard to worldly matters and human learning, and many of them in the *letter*, though not in the *spirit*, of the law. **To babes.** Babes in knowledge and simplicity; so considered by the world, and also by themselves; the humble, having a teachable spirit, and feeling their need of heavenly wisdom. They are "the poor in spirit" (ch. 5 : 3), "the little ones" (ch. 10 : 42), the believing followers of Jesus. Jesus thanks the Father that Gospel blessings had been thus bestowed. It was a rebuke and just punishment to pride and worldly wisdom, humbling to man and honoring to God, 1 Cor. 1 : 26-29; 2 : 6-8. The *hiding* was the withholding of his grace, a righteous judgment upon a proud and self-righteous generation; the *revealing* was the making known of spiritual truths by his words and grace, an act of infinite compassion and of unmerited and undeserved favor, ch. 16 : 17; 1 Cor. 2 : 9-14.

26. **Even so.** A simple affirmation, and should be translated *yea*, as the word is translated verse 9, and elsewhere. **For.** Rather, *that*. **Seemed good.** Thy good will, purpose, or pleasure. The word in the original includes the ideas both of sovereign choice and benevolence, Eph. 1 : 9; Phil. 2 : 13. This verse is closely connected with the last, and presents the highest cause of our Savior's thanksgiving. Its meaning may be thus expressed: Yea, I do thank thee, O Father! that such was thy good pleasure. It is good and right, just and best.

27. Jesus now addresses his hearers again, presenting himself as the revealer of the Father, his close and intimate relation to him, and his own sovereignty. **All things** in heaven and on earth (ch. 28 : 18) were committed by the Father to Christ as a mediator. He is head over all things to the church (Eph. 1 : 22), and the Judge of the living and the dead, John 5 : 22, 27; Acts 10 : 42. **No man knoweth.** No one *knoweth fully* (for this is the meaning of the verb) the Son but the Father, neither can any one know fully the Father but the Son. **Will reveal him.** *Is pleased to reveal* him by his word and by the Spirit. Christ, as the Revealer of the Father, is also a sovereign, and exercises his good pleasure, ver. 26. The Son and the Father are equally incomprehensible and omniscient.

It has been often remarked that the spirit and form of expression in this verse are the same as those of the discourses given in the Gospel according to John. It is thus an incidental evidence of the credibility of the fourth Gospel. It is a taste, a glimpse of those high and sublime truths which formed the subject of many of the discourses of Jesus, and which John alone records.

28-30. A GRACIOUS INVITATION TO THOSE GROANING UNDER SPIRITUAL BONDAGE to come to him for rest. Jesus thus exercises his own sovereign good pleasure in inviting sinners to come to him by repentance and humble submission. It was a practical illustration of the poor having the Gospel preached to them, ver. 5. Found only in Matthew.

28. **Ye that labor.** That toil, struggle, work hard, voluntarily. **Heavy laden.** Burdened, loaded down beyond your strength, and that, too, by others. We have here the active and passive sides of human misery. Many of those who perceived the spiritual import of the law were toiling hard to keep it, and were weighed down by its requirements, as well as by a sense of their shortcomings and of their condemnation. The law, with its strict requirements and its ceremonies, was indeed a burden, Acts 15 : 10. An additional burden was imposed by the scribes and Pharisees through their traditions, ch. 23 : 4. So the figures may

29 laden, ¹ and I will give you rest. Take my yoke upon you, ᵘ and learn of me; for I am meek and ᵛ lowly in heart: ʷ and ye shall find rest unto your 30 souls: ˣ for my yoke is easy, ʸ and my burden is light.

¹ Ps. 31. 6; Heb. 4. 3, 9.
ᵘ Lk. 10. 39; John 13. 15; Eph. 4. 20, 21; Phil. 2. 5; 1 Pet. 2. 21; 1 John 2. 6.

in general be applied to those of any age who are groaning over a sense of sin, Ps. 38 : 4. They toil in vain to meet the divine requirements, and are weighed down beneath the sense of guilt. The holy law of God, with its just condemnation, is like a crushing load to their souls. To such Jesus says, **Come unto me,** literally, *Hither to me.* Though Jesus exercises his good pleasure in specially inviting this class of persons, yet it is the duty of all who have not come to him to be of this class, conscious of their spiritual poverty and of their need of a Savior. **I will give you rest.** *I* is emphatic. In contrast to yourselves, seeking in vain for relief, to the law which thunders condemnation, to your teachers who bind heavy burdens upon you, *I* will give you rest, cause you to cease from this unrequiting toil, and relieve you of this crushing burden. You shall have inward peace.

29. **Take my yoke.** Instead of the yoke of sin, of Satan, the world, false teachers, formality, and legal bondage, Gal. 5 : 1. Christ has his yoke, his requirements and ordinances. A *yoke* is an emblem of subjection and service, Jer. 27 : 8; Lam. 3 : 27. To take his yoke is to become subject to him, to make his will and law supreme, to submit to his authority and to all his commands and ordinances. Obedience is a mark of discipleship. **Learn of me.** Rather, *Learn from me,* from my teaching and from my example. Jesus bore his yoke for us both as our Redeemer and our Exemplar. From him we must learn to endure self-denial, and to take up and bear our cross. And especially are we to learn from him meekness and lowliness of heart. **For I am meek,** etc. We are to become like Christ. He was **meek,** kind, gentle, and forgiving, and **lowly in heart,** humble, condescending, and compassionate. Jesus, by these traits, comes down to our lowly condition, and is thus fitted to be our teacher, as to his authority, precepts, and example. "There is, as Olshausen suggests, an essential difference between humility of heart, which Christ possessed in the highest degree, from *free* choice and condescending *love* and *compassion,* and poverty of spirit (ch. 5 : 3), which can not be predicated of him, but only of penitent *sinners,* conscious of their own unworthiness, and longing for salvation." —DR. SCHAFF, *Lange's Com.* How did Jesus contrast with the scribes and Pharisees, who were proud and hypocritical. **Rest unto,** rather, *for* your **souls.** Compare Jer. 6 : 16. Relief from spiritual burdens and distresses; inward peace; resting of the soul on Jesus. The rest is not bodily rest, but soul rest, without which there can be no true enjoyment.

30. A general and final reason for taking his yoke upon them. **For my yoke is easy,** mild and gentle. Man was made to be subject to God. In that subjection he finds his highest freedom. To be in a state of sin is bondage, but to be in a state of holiness is perfect freedom. In that state alone can we fulfill the laws of God, which are the laws of our highest nature. This holiness is to be obtained only through Christ, and just in proportion as man is holy, just in the same proportion is Christ's yoke easy and his burden light. In man's sanctified and perfect state, so harmonious will be the natural workings and desires of his heart with the will and command of Christ that there will be no friction, no feeling of a yoke, no conscious bearing of a burden, 1 John 5 : 3.

REMARKS.

1. Christ was ever busy; so we should toil on, not weary in well-doing, ver. 1.
2. Our work on earth may not cease with our active labors; in trials and afflictions we may be called to suffer, like John in prison, the will of God, ver. 2; 1 Pet. 4 : 19.
3. It is our duty to study the evidences, and to be fully satisfied that Jesus is the Christ, ver. 3; 1 Pet. 1 : 10, 11.
4. The proofs of the Messiahship of Jesus, from miracles, fulfillment of prophecy, and the preaching of the Gospel,

Jesus vindicates the disciples in plucking corn on the Sabbath, and himself in healing a man with a withered hand.

^v ch. 12. 19, 20; Is. 42. 1–4; Phil. 2. 7, 8.
^w Jer. 6. 16.
^x 1 John 5. 3.
^y Phil. 4. 13.

XII. AT that time ^v Jesus went on the sabbath day

are unanswerable and constantly increasing, vers. 4, 5; John 14 : 12; Rev. 19 : 10; Matt. 24 : 14.

5. The miracles of Jesus were types of the spiritual deliverances he brings to the soul, ver. 5; Ps. 146 : 8; Isa. 35 : 5–6; 61 : 1.

6. Let us not be offended with Jesus, because prophecy is slowly fulfilled and his cause slowly advances, or because sin abounds and judgment is delayed from coming upon the wicked, ver. 6; 2 Pet. 3 : 9, 10.

7. Beware of flattery. Jesus spoke words of warning, reproof, and encouragement to John through his disciples, but waited their departure before speaking of him in the highest terms. How unlike the world, who praise to the face but traduce behind the back, vers. 7–14; Luke 7 : 24.

8. How poor an account of Gospel blessings can many give who attend upon the preaching of the word, vers. 7–9; Heb. 5 : 11, 12.

9. How exalted and responsible the position of the Christian minister, who is not only more than a prophet, but even greater than John himself, ver. 11; Eph. 3 : 8.

10. Only the earnest and whole-hearted enter into the kingdom of heaven. Strive to enter in through the strait gate, ver. 12; Luke 13 : 24.

11. All the prophets and the law until John unite in their testimony that Jesus is the Christ, vers. 13, 14; Acts 10 : 43.

12. Religious cavilers are fickle and childish in their opposition to Christ, his cause, his ministers, and people, and the arrangements of his grace and providence, vers. 16–19.

13. The same objections essentially are raised against divine truth now as in the days of John and Christ. The law is too severe; the Gospel too lax, vers. 18, 19; 1 Cor. 1 : 23.

14. The children of wisdom sanction the divine arrangements, having learned their fitness and necessity by happy experience. "First, the law, then the Gospel; first, death, then life; first, penitence and sorrow, then joy; first, the Baptist, then Christ."—LANGE. Ver. 19; 1 Cor. 1 : 24; Rom. 1 : 16.

15. A day of judgment and future punishment are plainly taught in our Savior's woes against the cities of Galilee, vers. 22, 24.

16. There will be degrees of punishment in the future world according to the light and privileges enjoyed, and the unbelief and ingratitude manifested in this life, vers. 21–24; ch. 5 : 21, 22; Luke 12 : 47, 48; Rom. 2 : 12.

17. Even while the sinner is living, the woe that seals his everlasting doom may be pronounced upon him, vers. 21–24; 2 Pet. 2 : 6, 12–17.

18. Many now living will experience a more dreadful doom than that not only of Tyre, Sidon, and Sodom, but even of Capernaum, ver. 24; Jude 7, 11–13.

19. Nations receive their punishment in this world; individuals in the next, vers. 21–24.

20. The humble, teachable, and childlike are fitted for the reception of the Gospel; while the proud, the self-confident, and the worldly wise are totally unfitted, vers. 25, 26; 1 Cor. 1 : 21; 1 Tim. 6 : 20; Isa. 28 : 9.

21. God has the best and wisest reasons for all his dealings with men, ver. 26; Rom. 9 : 14, 19, 20; 11 : 22, 33, 34.

22. Correct views of God's character can only be learned from Christ, ver. 27; John 14 : 6.

23. The invitations of the Gospel are founded on the sovereignty of Christ, vers. 27, 28.

24. How gracious and condescending the calls of Jesus. None need be miserable. He gives rest to burdened souls, ver. 29; John 5 : 40.

25. The Gospel has its yoke; submission to the will of Christ and obedience to his word are essential to discipleship, ver. 29; John 14 : 23, 24.

26. Love makes the service of Jesus easy, light, and pleasant, ver. 30; Gen. 29 : 20; 2 Cor. 5 : 14.

CHAPTER XII.

In the preceding chapter, Matthew brings to view the opposition of the

through the corn; and his disciples were an hungered, and began to pluck the ears of corn, and 2 to eat. But when the Pharisees saw *it*, they said unto him, Behold, thy disciples do that which is not lawful to do upon the sabbath day. 3 But he said unto them, Have ye not read ᵃ what David did, when he was an hungered, and they that 4 were with him; how he entered into the house of God, and did eat ᵇ the showbread, which was not law-

ᵃ Mk. 2. 23-28; Lk. 6. 1-5; Deu. 23. 25.

ᵃ 1 Sam. 21. 3-6.

ᵇ Ex. 25. 30; Le. 24. 5-9.

scribes and Pharisees to John the Baptist and to Jesus. In this chapter, the opposition to Jesus is illustrated by special cases, and presented as increasing in intensity. Doctrines of the most momentous interest, miracles, fulfillment of prophecy, and his relation to his persecutors, to his relatives, and to his disciples are interwoven in the narrative.

1-8. THE DISCIPLES PLUCK THE EARS OF GRAIN ON THE SABBATH. The Pharisees censure them, which calls forth an answer from Jesus, in which he gives some lessons on the nature and object of the Sabbath, Mark 2 : 23-28 ; Luke 6 : 1-5.

1. At that time. A general expression, meaning at that season, about that time. Luke says that it was on "the second Sabbath after the first," or "second-first Sabbath," the meaning of which is doubtful, though generally regarded as the first Sabbath after the second day of the passover, or of unleavened bread; that is, the first of the seven Sabbaths, commonly reckoned between that day and Pentecost. See on Luke 6 : 1.

The Sabbath day. The Sabbath, the weekly day of rest. The name is derived from a Hebrew verb, signifying *to rest* from labor, *to cease* from action. The idea of *rest* was connected with its origin, Gen. 2 : 2, 3. It is generally supposed that the event here recorded occurred just after the second passover of our Savior's ministry. Compare John 5 : 1, and 6 : 1. The passover, A.D. 28, began March 29th; and the first day after the passover Sabbath, a sheaf of barley was usually presented as first-fruits, as that was the first grain reaped. **Through the corn.** The sown fields, the grain-fields. They passed through by a foot-path, which probably bounded the uninclosed grain-fields, the grain being in reach as they passed along. **Ears of corn.** Ears of grain. One word in the original, meaning ears of grain of any kind, especially wheat and barley, the common grains of Palestine. The disciples plucked ears of grain, rubbing them in their hand, thus separating the kernels from the ear, and ate them, Luke 6 : 1. The law allowed them to do this for appeasing hunger, but not to apply a sickle to another man's standing grain, Deut. 23 : 25. The custom still prevails in Palestine.

2. Not lawful—on the Sabbath. The Pharisees complain to Jesus of his disciples. By their traditions they had loaded this day of rest with grievous restrictions, raising the letter over the spirit, and even making formal acts usurp the place of spiritual observance. Among their many restrictions, plucking of ears of grain was forbidden. Hence not according to the law, but according to the traditions of the scribes, the disciples did that which was unlawful. The penalty for violating the Sabbath was death, Ex. 35 : 2 ; Num. 15 : 32-36.

3. Jesus replies by referring to what David did when he was hungry, from which it could be inferred what it was lawful for others to do under similar circumstances, 1 Sam. 21 : 1-6. Without at first objecting to the restrictions which pharisaical traditions had put on the Sabbath, Jesus shows by the example of David, whom all regarded as an eminent servant of God, that the letter of the law must give way to the law of necessity; and that hence it was lawful for them to do works of real necessity, such as appeasing hunger, on the Sabbath.

4. A statement of what David and his men did. They entered into **the house of God**, into the tabernacle which was then located at Nob, a place probably a little north of Jerusalem, and ate of the hallowed bread, which it was not lawful for any but the priests to eat. **The**

A.D. 29. MATTHEW XII. 163

ful for him to eat, neither for them which were with
5 him, ᶜ but only for the priests? Or have ye not read
in the ᵈ Law, how that on the sabbath days the
priests in the temple profane the sabbath, and are
6 blameless? But I say unto you, That in this place
7 is ᵉ one greater than the temple. But if ye had
known what *this* meaneth, ᶠ 'I will have mercy,
and not sacrifice,' ye would not have condemned

ᶜ Ex. 29. 32, 33;
Le. 8. 31.
ᵈ Num. 28. 9, 10;
John 7. 22, 23.
ᵉ vers. 41, 42; 2
Chr. 6. 18; Hag.
2. 7, 9.
ᶠ ch. 9. 13.

---

showbread. Literally the bread *set before, set out, exhibited* on a table in the holy place. It was *set before* Jehovah (Ex. 25 : 30), and probably symbolized God's presence with his people, as their sustenance, strength, and support. It consisted of twelve loaves, which were changed every Sabbath, the old being eaten by the priests, Lev. 24 : 5–9.

SHOWBREAD.

It would also seem from 1 Sam. 21 : 6, that, the bread having just been changed, David and his men partook of it on the Sabbath.

5. A second argument in which Jesus strikes a blow against a mere literal and formal exposition and application of the Sabbath-law. The appeal is now made to the law itself, whereby it is shown that its letter is violated by its own directions. **Profane the Sabbath.** Violate the regulations of the Sabbath. The priests were more busily engaged than on any other day, being required to offer double offerings, and to place on the table in the holy place hot showbread, hence just baked, Num. 28 : 9, 10; 1 Sam. 21 : 6. The argument is: All work can not be absolutely forbidden on the Sabbath; for the priests are required by the law itself to offer sacrifices, and to do work in the temple, and are **blameless,** because they act under the divine command and in the service of the temple. The work necessary to the religious observance of the day is therefore not only allowable, but also a duty.

6. Jesus clinches the argument. If the priests in the temple service violate the letter of the law and are guiltless, much more may my disciples, who have grown hungry in my service, since ye behold in me something greater than the temple. **One greater than the temple.** According to the latest critical authorities, *greater* should be in the neuter gender, *something greater, a greater thing,* or simply, *a greater* than the temple. The *neuter* may refer to his own *body,* which he styles a temple, John 2 : 21. For as God was present among his people in the temple, so in a higher and nobler sense was he more immediately present in the body of Jesus, in his incarnation. The Word became flesh and dwelt among us, John 1 : 14. His disciples were indeed a holy priesthood in his service, 1 Pet. 2 : 5. Alford refers the greater than the temple to the Son of Man, *the true temple of God.*

7. Jesus presents a third argument, drawn from the prophet Hosea (Hos. 6 : 6), by which he shows that his disciples had acted according to the spirit of the law, while they, the Pharisees, had violated the spirit by their strict adherence to the mere letter. **I will have mercy,** etc. I desire mercy. I desire not the mere external observance, *sacrifice* in the letter, but *mercy,* the inward outgushing of kindness and love, in doing good to the needy, which is the true sacrifice in spirit and of the heart. Compare the same quotation in ch. 9 : 13. See 1 Cor. 13 : 1–3; Heb. 10 : 5–9. The external sacrifice is worthless without the internal, and where the two come in conflict, the former must give way to the latter, sacrifice to mercy. Compare Ps. 51 : 16, 17. Jesus declares that if they had understood the meaning of this divine requirement, they would not have condemned the **guiltless,** the *blameless,* the word in the original being the same as that so rendered in verse 5. The

MATTHEW XII. A.D. 29.

8 the guiltless. For the Son of man is *Lord even of the sabbath day.
9 ʰAnd when he was departed thence, he went
10 into their synagogue: and, behold, there was a man which had *his* hand withered. And they asked him, saying, ⁱIs it lawful to heal on the sabbath days?
11 ᵏ that they might accuse him. And he said unto

* Mk. 2. 27, 28; John 5. 17, 18.
ʰ Mk. 3. 1–6; Lk. 6. 6–11.
ⁱ Lk. 13. 14; 14. 3; John 9. 16.
ᵏ Lk. 11. 53, 54; John 8. 4–6.

---

scripture cuts both ways. On the one hand, they would have seen that his disciples were blameless in doing what they did, when they were hungry in his service; and on the other, they would themselves have been led to the exercise of mercy, and withheld their condemnation. On the one hand, the disciples are vindicated as having acted according to the spirit of the law; and on the other, the Pharisees are condemned for showing a want of mercy in their close adherence to the letter.

It is worthy of notice that Jesus thus far draws his arguments from the example of a king and of priests, and from the words of a prophet of the old dispensation, all especially applicable in his case, since he himself is king, priest, and prophet in his spiritual kingdom. A good preparation also to his argument from himself, as Son of Man.

Mark (ch. 2 : 27) inserts here a fourth argument: "The Sabbath was made for man, and not man for the Sabbath;" it was made for the benefit and happiness of man; man is not a mere machine, made for a mechanical observance of the Sabbath.

8. The final and crowning argument in the reply of Jesus. **Son of Man.** The Messiah, as "God manifested in the flesh." See on ch. 8 : 20. **Lord** is emphatic. As mediator, redeemer, and sovereign, he is emphatically the lord of the Sabbath. It is right, therefore, for him to direct, and for his disciples to labor in his service on the Sabbath, John 5 : 17, 18. He was its lord, as Dr. Brown remarks (*Lange's Com.*), not to abolish it—for that would be strange lordship after saying that it was made or instituted for man—but to *own* it, *interpret* it, *preside over* it, and *ennoble* it, by merging it into the Lord's day (Rev. 1 : 10), breathing into it a liberty, spirituality, and love necessarily unknown before, and conforming it more nearly to the Sabbath rest of the people of God, Heb. 4 : 9, 10.

9–13. **Jesus heals a withered hand on the Sabbath.** By precept, example, and miracle Jesus gives a further exposition of the law of the Sabbath. See Mark 3 : 1–5 ; Luke 6 : 6–11. This occasioned more intense opposition, and more directly toward himself.

9. Matthew, more intent on the connection of thought, uses the general phrase, **departed thence,** *passed on from thence*, and at once relates the miracle, while Luke, more intent on the chronological order, says, it occurred on another Sabbath, probably the next following. **Their synagogue.** Of the Jews, especially where these opponents, the Pharisees, attended. The place is not mentioned. Probably in Galilee, and most probably in Capernaum.

10. **His hand withered.** The disease was the drying up or the pining away of the hand, with a loss of the power of motion, similar to that with which Jeroboam was afflicted, 1 Kings 13 : 4–6. It may have been caused by paralysis, or by a defect in receiving nourishment from the body. It was regarded as incurable. Luke informs us that it was his right hand, Luke 6 : 6. **And they,** the scribes and Pharisees (ver. 2 ; Luke 6 : 7), **ask him.** According to Mark and Luke, they were watching him to see if he would heal on the Sabbath. They wished to entrap him. Possibly they became impatient, and, wishing to hasten the action of our Lord, or at least convict him of heresy, they ask him, Is it lawful to heal on the Sabbath ? Or, knowing their thoughts, he may have commanded the man to arise and stand forth in the midst (Luke 6 : 8), when, seeing his intention to perform the miracle, they asked the question. Their object was to **accuse him** before the local judges, who were doubtless present, and probably identical with the rulers of the synagogue, ver. 14.

11, 12. Jesus replies by a pointed question, which was really an appeal to and an argument upon their own prac-

them, What man shall there be among you, that shall have one sheep, and ¹if it fall into a pit on the sabbath day, will he not lay hold on it, and
12 lift *it* out? ᵐ How much then is a man better than a sheep! Wherefore it is lawful to do well on the
13 sabbath days. Then saith he to the man, Stretch forth thine hand. And he stretched *it* forth; and it was restored whole, like as the other.

The Pharisees' conspiracy against Jesus; his retirement, by which a signal prophecy is fulfilled.

14 Then ⁿ the Pharisees went out, and held a council [*or*, took council] against him, how they might de-

¹ Deu. 22. 4.

ᵐ ch. 6. 26.

ⁿ ch. 27. 1; John 10. 39; 11. 53.

---

tice, to show that it was lawful to heal upon the Sabbath. There was not a man among them that would not, on the Sabbath, lay hold and lift out a sheep of his own from a pit or cistern, dug in the earth for the purpose of water. **How much then is a man better than a sheep?** The argument is from the less to the greater, conclusive, and condemnatory of the inconsistency of the Pharisees in applying a rule publicly to Jesus which they did not apply privately to themselves. They made an exception in favor of a dumb animal; much more should they allow Jesus to make an exception in favor of healing a diseased man. A man's life and happiness were surely far more important than those of a sheep. The Jews, in their later traditions, and, as some suppose, on account of these very words of Christ, forbid raising a sheep from a pit on the Sabbath, declaring it to be lawful only to give necessary food, and straw to lie upon, or to lay planks for it to come out of the pit. According to Mark and Luke, Jesus also asks, "Whether it was lawful on the Sabbath to do good or to do evil? to save life or to destroy it?" Convicted by their own consciences that it was lawful to do good, they were silent, Mark 3:4. Jesus concludes from their own practice, and from the obvious nature of the Sabbath, which was designed for the good of man, that it is lawful to **do well**, to do good, on that day, and hence to do this act of mercy, and heal the withered hand of the man who was now standing in their midst. Compare the same argument substantially applied on other occasions, Luke 13 : 14–17; 14 : 2–6.

13. Jesus proceeds at once and performs the miracle. He does it, however, without any bodily effort on his part. His adversaries, therefore, could not accuse him of laboring on the Sabbath. Some suppose that the healing was performed without uttering a word, and that Jesus commanded the man to stretch forth his hand, as an evidence of its being fully restored. It is better, however, to suppose that the healing took place immediately upon Jesus's uttering the command and the man making the effort to obey. The faith of the man is thus brought into its natural relation to his obedience and his cure. It is also in harmony with the declaration which follows, **it was restored whole**, as the other hand. How remarkably does the strong faith of the man contrast with the unbelief and hatred of the scribes and Pharisees! The man thus practically acknowledges the power and authority of Jesus, preferring him as a religious guide to the scribes and Pharisees. Jesus also gives in the miracle a practical evidence of his authority, not only over diseases, but as the Lord of the Sabbath, and of the correctness of his doctrine and practice in regard to that day.

14–21. THE CONSEQUENT CONSPIRACY to destroy Jesus; HIS RETIREMENT, yet ceaseless, quiet working, by which a SIGNAL PROPHECY IS FULFILLED. Mark 3 : 6–12.

The Pharisees were baffled not only with his arguments, but also with the fact that, by performing the miracle without outward action, he had deprived them of all legal ground of objection. They therefore went out and **held a council,** took counsel against him, conferring one with another, and with

15 stroy him. But when Jesus knew *it*, ᵒ he withdrew
himself from thence. ᵖ And great multitudes fol-
16 lowed him; and he healed them all, and ᑫ charged
17 them that they should not make him known: that
it might be fulfilled which was spoken by Esaias the
18 prophet, saying, ʳ 'Behold my servant, whom I have
chosen; my beloved, ˢ in whom my soul is well
pleased: I will put my spirit upon him, and he
19 shall show judgment to the Gentiles. He shall
not strive, nor cry; neither shall any man hear his

ᵒ Mk. 3. 7, 8; Lk. 4. 29–31; John 7, 1; 10. 39, 40; 11, 53, 54.
ᵖ ch. 19. 2.
ᑫ ch. 9. 30; Mk. 3 12.
ʳ Is. 42. 1–4.
ˢ ch. 3. 17; 17. 5.

the Herodians (Mark 3:6), how they might destroy him. This is the first mention of counsel, consultation, or organized effort to put Jesus to death. The enmity of the Pharisees now began to take definite, organized shape, and the greatness of it is shown by their willingness to unite with the court-party of Herod in an organized movement against Jesus.

15. **But when Jesus knew it.** Rather, *But Jesus knowing it*, an act of his omniscience. He knew what was in their hearts, and their plottings to take his life. **He withdrew** from Capernaum, or the town or city, where he had just performed the miracle, and indeed from the cities of Galilee generally, to the shores of the lake of Gennesaret, Mark 3:7. For his hour had not yet come to suffer and die. So he also withdrew in other instances, when threatened with violence, John 7:1; 10:39, 40; 11:54. **Great multitudes,** according to Mark (3:7, 8), from Galilee, Judea, Jerusalem, Idumea, from beyond Jordan and about Tyre and Sidon, followed him. It was not from the common people, but from the scribes and Pharisees that he withdrew. **Healed them all.** All the sick among them. All the multitude were whole when the sick were healed.

16. **He charged them,** earnestly, strictly, with the idea of a severe rebuke in case of disobedience, not to **make him known.** The opposition of the Pharisees was sufficiently aroused; he would not have it increased at present by the reports of the multitude, and especially of those who were healed. He would make his retirement as perfect as possible.

17. Matthew states that this was a fulfillment of prophecy, which he freely quotes from Isa. 42:1–4, giving the sense rather than the exact rendering of every word. As an inspired man, he gives the mind and meaning of the Spirit. He was writing his Gospel specially for Jews; he therefore frequently appeals to ancient prophecies, showing their fulfillment in Jesus. See on ch. 1:22. In this instance it was very signal and pointed. The withdrawal of Jesus from observation, his gentleness and meekness, his quiet and noiseless ministry, and his spirituality, were directly opposed to Jewish ideas of the Messiah, but answered exactly to the prediction of Isaiah.

18. **My servant.** The word thus translated admits of the idea of *son* as well as *servant*, and is also applied to Christ, in Acts 3:13, 26, and 4:27, 30. Though a son, he took upon himself the form of a servant, Phil. 2:7. He was indeed a servant of Jehovah in the highest and most honorable sense. There seems to be in this portion of the prediction a direct allusion to the descent of the Spirit upon him at his baptism, and to the words, "This is my beloved Son," etc., uttered from heaven then and at his transfiguration. **He shall show judgment,** etc. Some refer these words to final judgment and to Jesus as Judge. It however suits the prophecy and the context better to take the word *judgment* in a Hebraistic sense, of *law, statutes*, the *true religion* as made known in the Gospel. Compare Deut. 32:4; Jer. 22:15; Luke 11:42. He shall *make known* the principles of truth and righteousness, *declare* the true religion, its laws, ordinances, institutions, to the Gentiles. This he did through his followers, who preached the gospel to Gentiles as well as Jews, Eph. 2:17. Many Gentiles, however, doubtless heard him (Mark 3:7, 8); some we know with profit, ch. 8:10; 15:28.

19. His quiet, noiseless, unostentatious ministry foretold. Here begins

20 voice in the streets. A bruised reed shall he not break, and smoking flax shall he not quench, till he
21 send forth judgment unto victory. ¹ 'And in his name shall the Gentiles trust.'

¹ Ro. 15. 12; Isa. 11. 10.

Healing of a demoniac; accusation of casting out devils by Beelzebub, and the answer of Jesus.

22 ᵃ THEN was brought unto him one possessed

ᵃ Lk. 11. 14–23; ch. 9. 32; Mk. 3. 11.

that part of the prophecy to whose fulfillment Matthew now specially refers. **He shall not strive.** He shall not wrangle, quarrel, contend. Had he seen fit, he could have headed a strong popular party, been proclaimed king, excited insurrection. Instead of this, he withdrew from violence, and from scenes and places where tumults might have been excited. **Nor cry** in a noisy, turbulent manner. He shall not be clamorous like a man of strife. He shall not wrangle nor clamor; or, to extend the figure, he shall not light nor utter the battle-cry. Nor shall any man **hear his voice in the streets,** in uttering angry words, in sounding the alarm, in noisy contentions, or in rallying his followers in sedition. He shall not only be modest and peaceful in his conduct and bearing, but also in the extension of his kingdom, which shall partake of a like spirit and nature.

20. **A bruised reed,** cane or calamus, a plant with a jointed, hollow stalk, growing in wet ground, frail, easily shaken and broken. The reed here is *bruised, broken together*, but not entirely broken off. **The smoking flax.** The smoking lamp-wick, which was made of flax. The bruised reed represents the weak, oppressed, and afflicted, especially those burdened with sin and broken in spirit. The smoking flax, the lamp-wick not burning but merely smoking, represents the spiritual life almost extinguished and ready to die, Rev. 3: 2. Jesus was gentle and compassionate. He did not **break** the reed already nearly broken off. He did not carry on the work of destruction and crush it, entirely break it, but dealt tenderly with the broken-hearted, the humble, the penitent, and the afflicted. Neither did he **quench** or extinguish the feeblest beginnings, or the smallest spark of grace in the soul, but rather cherished it and supplied it with grace as with oil. Compare Isa. 61: 1–3. Alford says on this verse, "A proverbial expression for 'He will not crush the contrite heart, nor extinguish the slightest spark of repentant feeling in the sinner.'" His disciples, too, were but babes in spiritual knowledge and experience. He would in retirement strengthen their graces, which could not yet well endure greater opposition from the religious and political leaders of the people. The prophecy had a striking fulfillment in them.

Judgment unto victory. Shall make the principles of truth and righteousness successful and victorious, in individual believers and in the world. This successful issue is to be brought about in the mild, gentle, and spiritual manner just described. Not by might nor by power, but by the Spirit of the Lord, Zech. 4: 6. Not by meat, drink, and ceremonies, but by righteousness, peace, and joy in the Holy Spirit, Rom. 14: 17. Not by military power or physical compulsion; for his kingdom is not of this world; if it was, then would his servants fight, John 18: 36. He conquers and rules in the heart by the Spirit and by love, 1 John 4: 19; 1 Cor. 2: 13–16.

21. An abbreviation and paraphrase of Isa. 42: 4. The words in the original prophecy, *The isles shall wait on thy law*, are equivalent to **In his name shall the Gentiles trust;** for *isles* means *distant nations, Gentiles*, and to wait on his law is indeed to trust in his name, hopefully. *Hope* is a better translation than *trust*. Compare Rom. 15: 12. Hoping for his instruction and guidance. There is no article before *Gentiles* in the original. The mild and gentle sway of Jesus shall extend, and nations, remote as well as near, Gentiles in general, shall hope in him as their Redeemer.

22–37. CASTING OUT A DEMON, WHICH LED TO THE CHARGE OF CONFEDERACY WITH BEELZEBUB, AND THE DISCOURSE OF JESUS THEREON. The increasing en

with a devil, blind, and dumb: and he healed him, insomuch that ˣ the blind and dumb both spake and saw.

ˣ Is. 32. 3, 4.

23 And all the people were amazed, and said, ʸ Is
24 not this the son of David? ᶻ But when the Pharisees heard *it*, they said, This *fellow* doth not cast out devils, but by ᵃ Beelzebub, the prince of the devils.

ʸ ch. 21. 9; 22. 43; John 7.40-42.
ᶻ Mk. 3. 22-30; Lk. 11. 15.
ᵃ ver. 27; 2 Ki. 1. 3.

25 And Jesus ᵇ knew their thoughts, and said unto them, ᶜ Every kingdom divided against itself is brought to desolation; and every city or house di-

ᵇ ch. 9. 4.
ᶜ Is. 19. 2, 3; Gal. 5. 15.

---

mity of the Jews is exhibited, Mark 3 : 19-30; compare Luke 11 : 14-23.

22. **Then.** This is to be taken indefinitely. *In that period*, while Jesus was quietly doing his work and avoiding notoriety. **One possessed with a devil,** a demon **blind and dumb.** Blindness and dumbness are here connected with, and were probably occasioned by, demoniacal possession, like that recorded in ch. 9 : 32. This is the only instance recorded of possession of a demon and blindness together. By comparing these with the account of the deaf man in Mark 7 : 32-35, we may see the distinction between diseases connected and occasioned by demons and those that are not. See also on 4 : 24. **He healed him,** so that the blind and dumb both spoke and saw. This was a great miracle in itself, being a complicated disease. The special object of recording it here seems to be to show its effect in arousing and developing the hatred of the Pharisees, and to give Christ's discourse to them.

23. **All the people,** all the multitudes, **were amazed,** filled with wonder and astonishment, so as to be in a measure *beside themselves*. Their astonishment was aroused by witnessing not only his healing a disease so complicated and desperate, but especially his power over the demon that possessed the man and occasioned the disease. **Is not this,** etc.? Rather, Is this the son of David, the Messiah? See on ch. 9 : 27. The form of the question in the original is one of doubt and surprise, of belief contending with unbelief. They were staggered at witnessing such power. Jesus, in his quiet and unassuming manner, was altogether different from their ideas of the Messiah; yet did he not show the power and give a striking evidence of the Messiah? They could neither affirm directly nor deny. In their excited, amazed, and confused state of mind, they ask a question implying strong conviction, yet remaining doubt.

24. **The Pharisees.** They were scribes, as Mark informs us (ch. 3 : 22), who had come down from Jerusalem; they had probably come to Galilee to watch the movements of Jesus. They heard the question of the multitude; possibly it was propounded to them. **This fellow.** This one, this man. There is nothing necessarily contemptuous in the original. **Beelzebub.** *Beelzebul*, a name applied to Satan (ver. 26), and immediately explained as **prince of devils,** chief, ruler, presider over demons, ch. 9 : 34. He is also called "prince of this world" (John 12: 31 ; 14: 30; 16 : 11), and "prince of the power of the air," Eph. 2 : 2. See further on ch. 10 : 25. The Pharisees were compelled to acknowledge superhuman power; but in their hatred they would not acknowledge it as the power of God. They choose, therefore, the fearful alternative of ascribing it to the powers of darkness, and alleging that he was in league with the Devil, the prince of demons.

25. **Knew their thoughts.** The Pharisees had said this, not in the hearing of Jesus, but to some of the multitude. But Jesus knew their words and their thoughts, their malignant feelings, intentions, and purposes, Luke 11 : 15, 17. He replies to the infamous charge, first by showing its absurdity. Satan would not fight against himself, and destroy his own power and kingdom. A kingdom must have unity, or it will be destroyed. If it is divided against itself, rent by internal strifes, it will, such a state of things continuing, be brought to desolation. So of any **city,** or

A.D. 29.   MATTHEW XII.   169

26 vided against itself shall not stand: and if Satan cast out Satan, he is divided against himself; how
27 shall then his kingdom stand? And if I by Beelzebub cast out devils, ^d by whom do your children cast *them* out? therefore they shall be your judges.
28 But if I cast out devils by the Spirit of God, then

^d Mk. 9. 38, 39; Ac. 19. 13–16.

---

house, family; it can not **stand,** be made to stand, or be established. A kingdom, city, or house, thus divided, would indeed be arrayed against its own existence, and hence must fall.
26. So **if Satan cast out Satan,** if I, as a representative of Satan, or if Satan through me, cast out demons, the representatives of Satan in men, then he is **divided against himself,** he is destroying his own power; then the kingdom of darkness has lost its unity against the kingdom of light. Satan is opposing and fighting against himself. It is here recognized that Satan has a kingdom, but being a usurper, he is never called a king. Hatred and strife indeed prevail in his kingdom, but there is among the devil and all his subjects a unity in their enmity to God and men, and neither he nor they will deliver any from their cruel tyranny. Should Satan turn against himself, he would lose his distinctive character, and be for God and man, and not against them.
27. Jesus proceeds to a second argument, derived from a similar power, which the disciples of the Pharisees professed to exercise, by which their base charge is made to recoil upon themselves. **Your children.** Not the Apostles; for they professed to derive their power from Jesus, and the Pharisees would naturally refer their power to the same agency as that of their Master. But rather the disciples of the scribes and Pharisees, the Jewish exorcists, who pretended to expel evil spirits by certain incantations, prayers, and ceremonies. The terms *father* and *children* were applied respectively to teachers and pupils. See 2 Kings 2 : 3, 12; 13 : 14. Doubtless some of their own children professed to exercise this power. In Acts 19 : 13–17 we have an account of some of these exorcists at Ephesus, among whom were the seven *sons* of one Sceva, a Jewish chief priest. From Josephus (*Antiq.* viii. 2, 5, and *Jewish War*, vii. 6, 3) we also learn that there were among the Jews persons who professed to cast out demons by the use of a certain root, and by certain formulas and incantations, which were ascribed to Solomon as their author. The language of Jesus does not necessarily imply that they really did cast them out. The argument is: Your children profess to cast out demons as well as I; why ascribe my power to Satanic influence and not theirs? If I cast out demons by Beelzebul, do not your own disciples and exorcists also? They therefore shall be **your judges,** shall convict you of injustice and maliciousness in ascribing to me collusion with Satan, when you ascribe no such thing to them.
28. Having shown the absurdity of their charge, and their inconsistency and maliciousness in making it, Jesus now presses home the only remaining alternative, that he cast out demons through the Spirit of God. **Spirit of God.** These words are emphatic in the original. But if I through the Spirit of God cast, etc. Luke says (ch. 11 : 20), But if I with the *finger of God,* etc. Not through an influence merely, but through the personal Spirit* that was in him, his own personal divinity. Since it is evident that I do not cast out demons through the prince of demons, therefore I must cast them out through the king of heaven; and if so, then the kingdom of God (see on ch. 3 : 2) **is come unto**

---

* Some suppose the third person of the Godhead is here meant, in support of which view they quote John 3 : 34. To me, however, it seems that the reference is made rather to the absolute Spirit of him who is Spirit (John 4 : 26), irrespective of the persons in the divine nature. This accords with the corresponding phrase in Luke, "finger of God," the actual power of God himself, without distinct reference to the person of the Godhead exercising it. Compare Exod. 8 : 19. If, however, it be asked, Through what person of that absolute Spirit did Jesus cast them out? it must be answered emphatically, Through the Second Person. Jesus performed miracles through his own divine power, John 2 : 11; 15 : 24; Matt. 10 : 1.

29 * the kingdom of God is come unto you. ᶠ Or else how can one enter into a strong man's house, and spoil his goods, except he first bind the strong man? 30 and then ᵍ he will spoil his house. ʰ He that is not with me is against me; and he that gathereth not with me scattereth abroad.

31 Wherefore I say unto you, ⁱAll manner of sin and blasphemy shall be forgiven unto men: but the blasphemy *against* the *Holy* Ghost shall not be for-

ᵉ ch. 3, 2; Dan. 2. 44; 7. 14; Lk. 1. 33; 17. 20, 21; Col. 1. 13.
ᶠ Lk. 11. 21-23.
ᵍ 1 John 3. 8; 4. 4.
ʰ ch. 6. 24; Jos. 24. 15; Mk. 9. 40; 2 Cor. 6, 15, 16.
ⁱ Mk. 3. 28, 29; 1 John 1. 7-9.

you, or rather is come near to you, or upon you, with probably an idea of suddenness and surprise. Jesus cast out devils with a word, not by incantations, roots, and ceremonies, as the exorcists professed to do. The Pharisees were compelled to acknowledge a superhuman power, and by the argument of Jesus could not escape the conclusion that it was through the Spirit of God himself. Such manifestations of God's power and presence were an evidence of the presence of the Messiah's kingdom on earth, however sudden and surprising it might be to them. This reference to the Spirit of God prepares the way for speaking on blasphemy against the Holy Spirit.

29. Jesus gives another illustration which still further clinches the conclusion he had arrived at, and showing from the nature of the case that he was the opposer of Satan and superior to him and all his hosts. **Or else.** Simply, *or; else* not being in the original. **Strong man.** Not *strong one*, referring to Satan, as some have supposed, but *strong man*, referring to what occurs among men. The illustration is drawn from life. A strong man's house is entered and plundered, not by himself or friends, but by an enemy, who is stronger than he, who first binds him, and then spoils his goods, Luke 11: 21, 22. So the casting out of demons by Jesus proves that he is an enemy of the Devil, and superior to him. **Spoil his goods,** his instruments, tools, agents. Thus Jesus did in casting out demons. The only conclusion then was, that Satan himself was overpowered and conquered, cast out and judged, John 12: 31; 16: 11; Luke 10: 18.

30. This conflict existing between Jesus and Satan, between the kingdom of light and the kingdom of darkness, Jesus now states that there can be no neutrality, that **he that is not with me is against me.** This suited the various classes of his hearers, many of whom were either secret enemies, or undecided and wavering or timid friends. There can be no middle ground. **Gathereth not—scattereth abroad.** An allusion to harvesting. Christ and his disciples gather in the harvest of souls, while all who gather not with them, like ravagers of fields, scatter the harvest abroad from Christ. He that does not take part with Christ must take part with Satan. The converse of this saying is true (Mark 9: 40; Luke 9: 50); for since there is no neutrality in religion, he that is not really against Christ is for him. See further on Mark 9: 40.

31. Jesus, having shown by an irresistible course of argument that he cast out demons by the power of his own indwelling divinity, and that the Pharisees in opposing him were themselves of the kingdom of darkness, now as a faithful teacher warns them against blaspheming the Holy Spirit, which they were in danger of committing. **I say unto you.** A solemn and authoritative expression often used by our Savior when he was about to utter a momentous truth, or to reveal some new fact to men, ch. 5: 20, 28, 34; 6: 2; 18: 10, etc. The declaration which follows was most solemn, and contained a truth never before revealed: *Therefore I,* the Messiah, as my miracles abundantly prove me to be, *say unto you,* etc. **Blasphemy.** The word thus translated primarily means speaking evil, reviling, slandering. Among the heathen, speaking evil of gods was common as well as of men, and but little thought of. But among the Jews, reviling the one true God was regarded as a terrible and capital crime. Hence the word in Scripture, when applied to God, took upon itself the stronger meaning of *blasphemy,* the speaking irreverently and impiously to God, or of God, or of sacred things. As reviling a fellow-

man presupposes a malicious purpose, so blasphemy presupposes an impious intention to detract from the glory of God, and to alienate the minds of others from the love and reverence of God. Wherever it is spoken of in Scripture, it is also connected with oral utterance. An idea of this sin may be gained from Lev. 24 : 10–16, where the son of an Israelitish woman blasphemed the name of Jehovah, vented against him abuse and imprecations, and he was stoned to death. It was a most heinous sin, and indeed amounted to treason under the theocracy. Another instance of blasphemy is recorded in 2 Kings 18 : 28–35; 19 : 6, where Rabshakeh maliciously reviled Jehovah and his perfections, putting him on a level with the gods of the surrounding nations, and endeavored to lessen the reverence and trust of the Jews in him as the one true living God, 2 Kings 19 : 4. Thus also in Rev. 16 : 10, 11, when the fifth angel had poured his cup on the throne of the beast, his kingdom was darkened, and they gnawed their tongues and *blasphemed*, in their rage gave vent to the most malicious and impious reproaches against the God of heaven, because of their pains and sores.

We may conceive of a gradation of blasphemy in this passage, the highest being that against the Holy Spirit, as God convicting, renewing, and sanctifying. Next to this is that against the Son, as God manifested in the flesh in the work of redemption. And lower still against the Father, as God, the great original source of love and mercy, or, as Whedon styles him, the original *background* of Deity. And lowest of all, speaking reproachfully of sacred things, 1 Tim. 6 : 1; Tit. 2 : 5. Jesus declares that all sin and blasphemy, except the blasphemy against the Holy Spirit, shall be forgiven; that is, upon repentance; they are pardonable, and all shall be forgiven in different individuals.

What, then, is **blasphemy against the Holy Spirit?** It can not be mere continued opposition to the Gospel, obstinate impenitence, or final unbelief; for this is not specific enough; and besides, on the same principle that this is regarded unpardonable, every sin might be styled unpardonable if the individual continues to indulge in it. The sin, however, was of a special kind, and seems to have been willfully maligning and vilifying the Holy Spirit. This seems evident from the context. The Pharisees had attributed the power of Jesus to his being in colleague with Satan, and had used the contemptuous and opprobrious term, Beelzebul, and had also said, "He hath an unclean spirit," Mark 3 : 30. They were guilty in this of blasphemy against the Son, and especially his divine nature. He warns them, therefore, that but a step further and their sin would be unpardonable. The sin, however, implies a *state of heart*, malignant and willful opposition to the Spirit. Thus the Pharisees, surrounded with abundant evidence that Jesus was the Son of God, exercised a malignant and willful opposition to him, ver. 28. Their abusive language, under these circumstances, an index of the malignity within, was blasphemy against the Son. So in regard to blaspheming against the Spirit, there must be a knowledge and a full intention. It can be committed therefore only where a person is surrounded with the evident manifestations of the Spirit, and under his influence; where he knows and is convicted that it is the Spirit, and yet in his opposition he maliciously and willfully maligns and traduces the Spirit. Compare 1 Tim. 1 : 13, where we learn that Saul of Tarsus, the *blasphemer*, obtained mercy because he did it ignorantly in unbelief. The sin is more aggravated than grieving the Spirit, Eph. 4 : 30; it is the extreme and highest form of resisting the Spirit, Acts 7 : 51. It is without doubt the sin unto death (1 John 5 : 15), and, in an aggravated form, is referred to in Heb. 10 : 29 as doing despite unto the Spirit of grace. Compare Heb. 6 : 4–8 ; 2 Tim. 3 : 8; Jude 4, 12, 13.

Since God comes to the hearts of men only as the Holy Spirit, sins against the Spirit are the most heinous, being the most directly against God, and blasphemy against him the extreme of all sin. It is an insult which always oversteps that line between God's patience and his wrath, which results in incorrigible hardness of heart and in the departure of the Spirit forever. Hence it is a sin which both from its nature and the consequent final departure of the Spirit can never **be forgiven.** Omit, **unto men.**

32. This verse is explanatory of the preceding verse; the statement is repeated with emphasis, and blasphemy against the Spirit compared with that against the Son of Man. It was the more necessary to bring these two kinds

32 given unto men. And whosoever ᵏ speaketh a word against the Son of man, ˡ it shall be forgiven him: but whosoever speaketh against the Holy Ghost, it shall not be forgiven him, neither in this world, neither in the *world* to come.

33 Either make the tree good, and ᵐ his fruit good; or else make the tree corrupt, and his fruit corrupt:

34 for ⁿ the tree is known by *his* fruit. O ᵒ generation of vipers, ᵖ how can ye, being evil, speak good

ᵏ ch. 11. 19; 13. 55; John 7. 12, 52.
ˡ Lk. 23. 34; Ac. 3. 14, 15, 19; 1 Tim. 1. 13.
ᵐ ch. 7. 16–20; John 15. 4–7.
ⁿ Jam. 3. 12.
ᵒ ch. 3. 7.
ᵖ 1 Sam. 24. 13; Is. 32. 6; Jam. 3. 5 8.

---

of blasphemy into prominence since they are especially connected with the new dispensation. **Speaketh a word —speaketh against,** that is, blasphemously. The language here is to be interpreted by the preceding verse, and evidently refers to blasphemy. It must be borne in mind that the word translated *blaspheme,* primarily means *to speak evil of,* to rail at, to slander. And it is worthy of notice that this sin against the Spirit is always connected with speaking, oral utterance—that malignity which finds vent in blasphemous language. **Son of Man.** The Messiah, the second person of the Trinity, vailed in human flesh and in humiliation, Phil. 2: 6–8; see ch. 8: 20. His divine character might be more easily overlooked than after his resurrection. Blasphemy against him was therefore less heinous than now. But the same is true of blasphemy against the Spirit; for his power was also less manifest before the day of Pentecost than since. As the truth then uttered was intended not merely for that particular occasion, but for the whole gospel dispensation, we must regard it as referring to Christ and the Holy Spirit, the second and third persons of the Godhead.

The reason why blasphemy against the Spirit is greater than that against the Son, must be found in the closer relation of the Spirit to man in bringing truth to the heart, in conviction and in regeneration. Yet since this truth presents Christ, it is difficult to conceive how an individual can commit blasphemy against the Holy Spirit without committing blasphemy also against the Son. If the latter suggestion be true, then we get a glimpse at the fact that blasphemy against the Holy Spirit, though the great fatal and unpardonable crime, is generally complicated with other sins, is the result of some previous course of sin, and is inseparably connected with willful malignity and obduracy of heart.

Neither in this world, etc. The phrases, *this world,* and the *world to come,* generally signified, among the Jews, before and after the Messiah, and hence the idea conveyed to the Jewish mind by the language of Jesus was, that he who committed this sin against the Spirit shall *never* be forgiven. The New Testament idea of the phrases, however, is equivalent to the *present* and the *future life,* time and eternity. See Mark 10: 30; Luke 20: 34, 35; Tit. 2: 12. Whether we take the Jewish or the Gospel idea, the conclusion is the same, namely, that which is so clearly expressed in Mark 3: 29, "Hath never forgiveness, but is in danger of eternal damnation."

33. Jesus, having shown the fallacy and absurdity of their wicked charge, and warned them of blaspheming against the Holy Spirit, admonishes them by enforcing the well-known principle that profession and practice should agree. Truth here is indeed a two-edged sword, cutting both ways, in reference to Jesus and in reference to the Pharisees. Do not pretend to be righteous when your charges against me are so fallacious and wicked; see that your own hearts and characters are good, and then will your fruits be good; be honest and consistent, one thing or the other, both in profession and practice. And in regard to me, exercise the same honesty and consistency: either admit that my good works have a good origin, or else show that both the origin and works are bad. **For the tree,** the heart, the character, the man, **is known by his fruit,** by his works, by his conversation, conduct, and practice. See on ch. 7: 16–20.

34. Jesus now addresses the Pharisees, pointedly indicating their character which had been implied by his previous discourse. They are **a generation of**

things? ᑫ for out of the abundance of the heart the 35 mouth speaketh. ʳ A good man out of the good treasure of the heart bringeth forth good things: and an evil man out of the evil treasure bringeth 36 forth evil things. But I say unto you, That ˢ every idle word that men shall speak, they shall give ac- 37 count thereof in the day of judgment. For by thy words thou shalt be ᵗ justified, and by thy words thou shalt be condemned.

ᑫ ch. 15. 18, 19.
ʳ ch. 13. 52; Ps. 37. 30, 31; Col. 4. 6.
ˢ Ecc. 12. 14; 1 Tim. 5. 13.

ᵗ Pro. 13. 3; Ro. 10. 10; Jam. 2. 21-25.

The Pharisees demand a sign; the reply of Jesus.

38 ᵘ Then certain of the scribes and of the Pharisees

ᵘ Lk. 11. 16, 29-32.

---

vipers, brood of vipers, deceitful and malignant persons; hypocritical, and holding pernicious doctrines and principles; "the poison of asps was under their lips," and hence by their doctrines, influence, and slandering words, they were poisoning the minds of the people, and prejudicing them against the Messiah. They were evidently of the *seed of the serpent* (Gen. 3 : 15), and in their natures opposed to Christ, the *seed of the woman*. The merciful Redeemer is compelled in faithfulness to use the same designation as did John. See on ch. 3 : 7. **How can ye?** It is impossible that ye being **evil,** malignant, wicked, and depraved in heart, and full of hatred to Christ and the truth, should **speak good things;** for out of the **abundance,** the overflowing of **the heart,** the inward dispositions and feelings, whether good or bad, the mouth speaketh. Language is the overflowing of the soul, and naturally indicates its state and condition, ch. 15 : 18; Rom. 10 : 9; 2 Cor. 4 : 13.
35. The truth just announced is further illustrated both in regard to good and bad men. **A good man.** Rather, *The good man;* so also *the evil man.* *Of the heart* is not in the original, according to the best manuscripts; it is simply, **out of the good treasure.** *Treasure* means *stores,* any thing laid up, be it good or bad, and here refers to inner, spiritual stores, the feelings, thoughts, purposes of the soul. **Bringeth forth.** Rather, *sendeth forth.* The idea is that of sending forth out of the abundant treasures of inner dispositions and feelings good or bad things. This movement may be both voluntary and involuntary. Among the evil things must be included all deceit and hypocrisy.

36. **I say unto you.** Jesus most solemnly asserts the relation of words to the judgment. This was fitted to deepen the impressions he had already made, and to remove the objections of any who might suppose that he had laid too much stress upon the mere words of men. **Idle word.** Every morally useless word; unprofitable, trifling, or foolish talk. Men are accountable for not only blasphemous, but also for vain and trifling words. If they must give an account for the latter in the day of judgment, how much more for those which are of a more pernicious or of a blasphemous character? Any word, speech, or discourse, not morally injurious, and useful in its tendency to the heart, mind, or body, is not *idle.*
37. Explanatory of the preceding verse. **By thy words.** Rather, *from* thy words, as the source from which the decisions at the judgment shall be derived. The words of men are the index of their hearts; and, taken as a whole, an index of their characters and lives. This is as true of hypocrites as of others, for their hypocritical discourses will show their hypocrisy. Careless and thoughtless words (ver. 36) also reveal the real state of the heart, coming forth as they do from its abundance. See James 3 : 2-12. Judgment according to *words* does not exclude that according to *deeds.* The two are harmonious, and lap on each other; and both are included in "the things done in the body," 2 Cor. 5 : 10. *Words,* as the utterance of the soul, are inseparably connected with the works of the individual, and indeed form an important part of his works. Both the acts and words of men will at last also agree in their testimony for or against them, ch. 25 : 31-46. **Justified.**

answered, saying, Master, we would see a sign from 39 thee. But he answered and said unto them, An evil and ˣ adulterous generation seeketh after a sign; and there shall no sign be given to it, but the 40 sign of the prophet Jonas: ʸ for as Jonas was three days and three nights in the whale's belly; so shall

ˣ ch. 16. 4; Is. 57. 3; Mk. 8. 38; Jam. 4. 4.
ʸ Jon. 1. 17.

Shown to be righteous. **Condemned.** Shown to be wicked.

38–45. THE PHARISEES DEMAND A SIGN. Jesus replies that NO SIGN BUT THAT OF THE PROPHET JONAH shall be given them. He reaffirms their great wickedness, foretells their final condemnation and fearful ruin; compare Luke 11 : 16, 24–26, 29–32.

38. That this demand followed immediately the preceding discourse seems evident from the words, **Then, answered him.** See on ch. 11 : 25. In Luke 11 : 15, 16, those who made this demand were different persons from those who had charged him with casting out demons through Beelzebul; and they did it tempting him. **Master.** Teacher. So he was called by the multitude, as well as by the disciples. The Pharisees fall in with others, and thus address him, hypocritically indeed, possibly to flatter, possibly in a tone which indicated a vein of irony, but with the design of attaining their own wicked ends. **We would see.** The original is stronger, expressing a decided choice, which really amounted to a demand. We wish, desire, or choose to see **a sign.** Miracles were called *signs* (see introduction to ch. 8), but the sign here demanded was *from heaven;* compare Luke 11 : 16. A sign from heaven is what we desire, not merely one on earth, or possibly from hell. Many of the ancient prophets had given such signs, Moses (Ex. 9 : 22–24 ; 16 : 4), Joshua (Josh. 10 : 12), Samuel (1 Sam 7 : 9, 10 ; 12 : 16–18), Elijah (1 Kings 18 : 36–38 ; 2 Kings 1 : 10), Isaiah (Isa. 38 : 8). If prophets gave them, surely, they might reason, the Messiah should give them. That they expected something of the kind is evident from the frequent demands for a sign from heaven, ch. 16 : 1; Luke 11 : 29; John 6 : 30, 31. This expectation may also have been strengthened by Daniel's prophecy (Dan. 7 : 13) of the glorious coming of the Messiah, to the fulfillment of which Jesus himself refers when he speaks of "the sign of the Son of Man in heaven," ch. 24 : 30. Though he refused these demands, his life was remarkable for such signs; at his birth (ch. 2 : 2; Luke 2 : 13, 14), baptism (ch. 3 : 16, 17), transfiguration (ch. 17 : 5), while discoursing to certain Greeks (John 12 : 28), on the cross (ch. 27 : 45), at his resurrection (ch. 28 : 2–4), and ascension, Acts 1 : 9–11. They were having signs from heaven and other evidences enough. Jesus could not consistently yield to their dictation, nor pass by their caviling spirit without reproof. Hence the answer which follows.

39. An evil and adulterous generation. A wicked and unbelieving, faithless people. A perverse and apostate race. In the Old Testament God is represented as the husband of his chosen people, and hence idolatry and unfaithfulness on the part of the latter are represented as spiritual adultery, Ex. 34 : 15. In their departure from God, in their rejection of Jesus, the God incarnate, their true husband, and in their spiritual idolatry (see Ezek. 14 : 3), they were indeed an *adulterous, faithless* generation. **No sign be given.** No sign to them. His signs were not for such insolent cavillers and blasphemous opposers. Yet there would be one sign given them, the greatest of all miracles, namely, his resurrection, which they could not attribute to Beelzebul, and which they would find it impossible by any argument to meet, ch. 28 : 11–15. **But the sign of the prophet Jonah.** As if to remind them that all the prophets did not give signs from heaven. Here was one with a sign from beneath. So the Son of Man shall give a similar one; one of which that of the prophet Jonah was a type.

40. In the whale's belly. In the belly of a huge fish or sea-monster. The language does not necessarily refer to a whale, but to any great fish. The objection that the whale seldom enters the Mediterranean Sea, and that its throat is too small to swallow a man, is thus set aside. The white shark has often been found in the Mediterranean,

the Son of man be three days and three **nights in**
41 the heart of the earth. The men of Nineveh shall rise in judgment with this generation, and shall condemn it; because they repented at the preaching of Jonas; and, behold, a greater than Jonas *is* here.
42 ᵃ The queen of the south shall rise up in the judgment with this generation, and shall condemn it: for she came from the uttermost parts of the earth to hear ᵃ the wisdom of Solomon; and, behold, ᵇ a greater than Solomon *is* here.

ᵃ 1 Ki. 10. 1-13; 2 Chr. 9. 1.

ᵃ 1 Ki. 3. 9-12; 4. 29-34; 10. 23, 24.
ᵇ Is. 9. 6, 7; 11. 1-3; 1 Cor. 1. 24; Col. 2. 3.

---

sometimes measuring sixty feet in length. This fish has been known to swallow a man entire. **Three days and three nights.** According to the Jewish mode of reckoning time, the odd parts of a day were reckoned as a whole of a day and night. Jesus died and was buried on Friday afternoon, and rose on Sunday morning; the time intervening was one whole day and parts of two days, which were reckoned as three whole days and nights, 1 Sam. 30 : 12, 13. **Heart of the earth.** The rock in which was the sepulchre of Jesus may be styled heart of the earth, yet a deeper meaning seems to be demanded, both from the phrase itself and its parallel in the case of Jonah. The underworld (Greek, *Hades;* Hebrew, *Sheol*), the place of departed spirits, answers better to the belly of the fish, and to the heart of the earth, than to the sepulchre which was on the surface of the earth. Jonah also uses the language, "Out of the belly of hell," that is, Hebrew "Sheol," the underworld, or place of the dead, Jon. 2 : 2. Moreover, the soul of Jesus, the real Son of Man, did not go merely to the tomb in the rock, but, according to the declaration of Jesus on the cross, to paradise (Luke 23 : 43), that part of the underworld assigned to the departed spirits of the righteous. Compare Acts 2 : 27, 31; Eph. 4 : 9. It must be borne in mind that such popular expressions as heart of the earth, underworld, paradise, can not decide the locality of the world of departed spirits, or of that portion of it assigned to the righteous dead. See article by the author on "The Righteous Dead between Death and the Resurrection," *Christian Review,* April No., 1862.

It may also be noted that Jonah came forth from the sea-monster to preach to the Ninevites; Jesus from the heart of the earth, to send forth the Gospel to every creature. Jonah prophesied a destruction in forty days; Jerusalem was destroyed after about forty years.

41. Reference to Jonah leads Jesus to contrast that generation of religious formalists with Ninevites, whom they despised as heathen and Gentile sinners. **Men,** without the article; inhabitants of that proud and wicked city of Nineveh, **shall rise up at the judgment,** in company with this generation, for trial at the bar of the Judge, and shall condemn it by their example, as it shall be remembered and there recounted. They will be witnesses to the unreasonableness of the impenitence of this generation, and will condemn its wicked unbelief; for they repented at the preaching of Jonah, who only made them a transient visit, and performed no miracles; and behold, this generation reject **a greater than Jonah,** the preaching and Gospel of the Messiah, with the Messiah himself. See Jonah 3 : 5, 10. Jonah preached to the Ninevites about B.C. 840. Their city was finally destroyed about B.C. 606.

42. **The queen,** etc. Rather, *A queen of the south,* referring more specially to her character, a heathen queen, a mere barbarian. The queen of Sheba, 1 Kings 10 : 1. *Sheba* is supposed to be the southern part of the Arabian peninsula, Arabia Felix, which abounded in spices, gold, precious stones. It is called here **the uttermost parts of the earth,** the extremes or ends of the earth, a Greek and also a Hebrew phrase, denoting a great distance. See Jer. 6 : 20, where Sheba is called "a far country." The Arabians call this queen Balkis. Josephus, however, represents her as a queen of Egypt and Ethiopia, with which modern Abyssinian tradition agrees, the latter calling her Maqueda, and supposing her to have embraced the Jewish religion in Jerusalem. She was more probably from Ara-

MATTHEW XII.

43 ᶜWhen the unclean spirit is gone out of a man, ᵈhe walketh through dry places, seeking rest, and
44 findeth none. Then he saith, I will return into ᵉmy house from whence I came out; and when he is come, ᶠhe findeth *it* empty, swept, and garnished.
45 Then goeth he, and taketh with himself seven other spirits more wicked than himself, and they enter in and dwell there; ᵍand the last *state* of that man is worse than the first. Even so shall it be also unto this ʰwicked generation.

ᶜ Lk. 11. 24.
ᵈ Job. 1. 7; 1 Pet. 5. 8.
ᵉ ver. 29.
ᶠ ch. 13. 20–22; Ps. 81. 11, 12; 1 John 2. 19.
ᵍ Heb. 6. 4–8; 10. 26–31; Jude 10–13.
ʰ ch. 21. 38–41; 23. 29–36.

---

bia Felix, which was bounded east by the Persian Gulf, south by the ocean between Africa and India, and west by the Red Sea. Sheba was a tract of this country near the southern extremity of the Red Sea, not far from the present Adan. **Wisdom,** etc. The contrast is between her treatment of Solomon's wisdom, and their treatment of the Messiah and his wisdom. She *came* and was filled with admiration; they did not come to Jesus, but he came to them, not as a mere man, but as a divine teacher, speaking as never man spake; yet they despised both him and his wisdom, which were greater than Solomon. Her example, and her presence at the judgment, will condemn their blindness of mind and hardness of heart.

43. Jesus illustrates and foretells the final and fearful condition of this apostate race by a reference to a return of demoniacal possessions, which, doubtless, sometimes occurred. When a demon goes out of a man voluntarily, or through supernatural influence, he passes through **dry places,** unwatered, desert places, such places being represented as the abodes and haunts of evil spirits, Isa. 13: 21, 22; 34: 14; Rev. 18: 2. So the later Jews thought, as appears from the Apocrypha, Tobit 8: 3; Baruch 4: 35. The wanderings of demoniacs through desert places (compare ch. 8: 28) would strengthen this opinion, and forms an argument that demons do really prefer scenes of barrenness, desolation, and woe. **Seeking rest and findeth none.** Restless and discontented, he wanders in misery, seeking in vain for repose.

44. **My house,** my previous abode, the body and soul of the man I once possessed. And coming he finds it **empty, swept,** and *garnished,* or set in order, that is, for his use. He finds it empty of the Spirit and good influences, swept and clean of all impressions and hinderances to his entrance, and set in order for his use and occupancy.

45. **Then,** finding his abode in readiness, he goes forth in search of a strong reinforcement, so that he may hold his house more securely and permanently. **Seven.** A round, full number. It may mean the definite number, *seven;* or, as it is often used, it may refer to an indefinite number, *several.* **More wicked.** Some evil spirits are more wicked than others. **Worse than the first.** This last state or condition is at least seven times worse. A relapse is generally worse than the first sickness. So, doubtless, some of his hearers could refer to cases like the one here described, of a return of demons after real or apparent cure, by Jewish exorcists, with fearful aggravations, a hopeless, fatal issue. So moral, spiritual relapses are more aggravated and fearful than the first stages of sin. **So shall it be unto this generation.** This was true historically of the Jewish race. Their last state, after their rejection of Christ, was far worse than their first, whatever we may regard that to have been. Their conduct, before their final destruction by the Romans, was like that of persons possessed with demons, and wrought up to the last degree of madness. The application is true, whether we refer to their first state: 1st. To the period before the Babylonish captivity, when the people were plagued with idolatry, but which was extinguished by that captivity. The emptying, sweeping, and setting in order may then aptly refer to Pharisaic hypocrisy and formalism, which paved the way for a worse idolatry of heart, and a more willful and aggravated un-

The mother and brethren of Jesus seek to speak with him.

46 WHILE he yet talked to the people, ⁱ behold, *his* mother and ʲ his brethren stood without, desiring to
47 speak with him. Then one said unto him, Behold, thy mother and thy brethren stand without, desiring
48 to speak with thee. But he answered and said unto him that told him, Who is my mother? and

¹ Mk. 3. 31–35; Lk. 8. 19–21.
ʲ ch. 13. 55; Mk. 6. 3; John 2. 12; 7. 3, 5; Ac. 1. 14; 1 Cor. 9. 5; Gal. 1. 19.

faithfulness and opposition to God. Or, 2d. To the reformation of that generation, under the preaching of John, when even Pharisees came to his baptism. The intervening period would be the ministry of Jesus, and the emptying, etc., the increasing hostility of the people, ending in their rejection of the Messiah. Or, 3d. To the very many cases of demoniacal possessions of that generation. This supposes that these possessions were especially permitted, in order that Jesus might openly demonstrate his power over the kingdom of darkness; and that he so thoroughly manifested this power, that for the time being that generation was freed from such possessions; but in their increased wickedness in rejecting Jesus and the Gospel, they were permitted, as a people, to be possessed and urged on by demons to utter and irretrievable ruin. Or, *finally*, to their first sins and departures from God, from which there may have been repeated reformations, but ending in their final rejection of Christ and his Gospel, with irrecoverable ruin both in this world and the next. The last state of that generation was indeed worse than the first. Their course was downward and their end terrible, both in the exhibitors of their depravity and in the severity of their punishment.

46–50. HIS MOTHER AND BROTHERS seek to SPEAK with him. He improves the opportunity of showing WHO ARE, IN THE TRUEST AND HIGHEST SENSE, HIS MOTHER AND HIS BRETHREN, Mark 3 : 31–35; Luke 8 : 19–21.

46. **While he was yet speaking to the people.** To the multitudes. See Mark 3 : 31. He was probably speaking in the open air at or near Capernaum. **His brethren.** The presumption is, that these were his brothers, the children younger than himself, of Joseph and Mary. They must be so regarded, unless it be shown to the contrary, or some valid objection established against such a view. Some have regarded them as the children of Joseph by a former marriage. Others take the word *brothers* in the wider Oriental sense to mean near relations, kinsmen, Gen. 14 : 8. See further on ch. 13 : 55, 56. While Jesus was thus plainly preaching, they **stood,** were standing, without, **desiring,** seeking, to speak with him. They could not come near him on account of the multitude (Luke 8 : 19), which was so great and so eager to hear him that he and his disciples had not had time to eat bread, Mark 3 : 20. On account of this continuous teaching his relatives had experienced great anxiety, and had gone to lay hold of him, saying, He is beside himself, Mark 3 : 21. All this accomplished nothing. Now his mother and brothers, his nearest and dearest relatives, seek to get a hearing. They not only feared that he might injure himself by overwork and fasting, but they also trembled at the dangers to which he was exposing himself by such plain admonitions. They, doubtless, wished to caution him, get him away from the multitude and the present excitement, and shield him from the assaults or machinations of those whose enmity he had just embittered by his discourse.

47. This verse should be omitted according to the highest critical authorities. It was probably inserted here from Mark 3 : 32; Luke 8 : 20, on which see.

48. Jesus improves the occasion to call attention to a higher and a spiritual relationship, and hence he asks, **Who is my mother?** etc. It should be noticed that this was said, not to his mother and brethren, but to the multitude, to him and to others who had just announced the presence of his mother. See verse 47 and Mark 3 : 32. There was nothing contemptuous in this lan

49 who are my brethren? And he stretched forth his hand toward his disciples, and said, Behold, 50 my mother and my brethren! For *k* whosoever shall do the will of my Father which is in heaven, the same is my brother, and sister, and mother.

k ch. 7. 21; John 15. 14; Ro. 8. 29; 2 Cor. 5. 16; Gal. 6. 15; Col. 3. 11; Heb. 2. 11-16.

guage. Jesus did not despise human relationships, but only esteemed the spiritual the more.

49. He then looked around on those who sat about him (Mark 3: 33), and **stretched forth his hand toward his disciples** with an affectionate regard, and to point out those who were his followers, and especially his constant attendants, he says, **Behold my mother and my brethren,** these are my nearest and dearest kindred, and their claims upon me are superior to that of any earthly friends.

50. Jesus explains himself, and at the same time shows a reason for his assertion. **Whosoever shall do the will,** etc. They only are his true disciples who do the will of his Father in heaven; and, by so doing, they show their spiritual relationship to his Father, and consequently to him. And this condition extends on into the future, *whosoever shall do the will*. **Brother and sister** may both be included in the plural *brethren*, vers. 47, 48. **And mother.** A climax, the nearest relationship that any human being can hold to me. Even beyond my beloved and highly-favored mother, according to the flesh, is the nearness and dearness of that relationship which exists between me and my followers. Or we may view the enumeration here as a uniting and concentrating human relationships in one, to express and symbolize the higher spiritual relation between Jesus and his disciples. Jesus does not introduce the word *father*, for he had no human father, and he never speaks of any but God as his Father.

Jesus thus refused, or at least delayed, speaking to his mother and brothers. It was thus a silent reproof to them; and the whole forms a decisive argument against that popish superstition which makes Mary, the mother of Jesus, an object of worship. Compare ch. 2: 11; Luke 2: 49; John 2: 4.

REMARKS.

1. The followers of Christ may be called to suffer hunger and want, together with the reproaches and fault-findings of their enemies. Let them commit their cases to Jesus, who will defend their cause, vers. 1-8; ch. 9: 1-17.

2. They who are most destitute of true godliness are often the most tenacious of the forms of the law and of traditions, ver. 2; ch. 23: 23, 24; 2 Tim. 3: 5.

3. We must not sacrifice the spirit to the letter, inward piety to external forms; and especially must we beware of uncommanded observances, ver. 2; Isa. 1: 12.

4. Jesus has taught us the right use of the Sabbath, that it is in harmony with the fourth commandment to do deeds of necessity and mercy, and to perform all the labor that public and private worship require, vers. 4-12.

5. Religious services are an essential part of Sabbath observance, ver. 5; Lev. 19: 30; 26: 2.

6. The Sabbath was made for man, given him at creation, when in a state of innocence (Gen. 2: 3), continued as a merciful provision in his fallen state (Gen. 8: 10-12; Ex. 16: 23-26; Job 1: 6; 2: 1), confirmed under the law (Ex. 20: 8), and bequeathed by the Lord of the Sabbath himself at his resurrection, in its greatest and highest glory, as the Christian Sabbath or Lord's Day under the Gospel, ver. 8; John 20: 1, 19, 26; Acts 20: 7; 1 Cor. 16: 2; Rev. 1: 10.

7. "Christ is Lord of, being himself the personal Sabbath or rest; all that leads to him and is done in him is Sabbath observance; all that leads from him is Sabbath-breaking."—LANGE. Vers. 3-12.

8. "Our whole life should be a Sabbath devoted to the Lord, a type of the eternal Sabbath in the world to come."—LISCO. Vers. 3-12; Heb. 4: 9.

9. Men often condemn in others things like to what they do themselves; and especially do the wicked, in their fault-finding with Christians, often condemn their own deeds, vers. 5, 11; Rom. 2: 1-4.

10. How many care more for their

cattle, and the preservation of their property, than they do for the spiritual and temporal good of their fellow-men, vers. 10, 11; ch. 8: 34.

11. The greater the success of the Gospel, and the clearer the evidences of its divine origin, the greater will be the opposition of its enemies, vers. 14, 24; ch. 2 : 16; John 5 : 16; 10 : 31; 11 : 47-50.

12. The Christian is to be prudent as well as bold and courageous. He is not to expose his life needlessly, but should withdraw himself from danger when he can do so without injury to Christ and his cause, ver. 15; Luke 4 : 30; John 7: 1; 10 : 39; 11 : 54.

13. When the Christian withdraws himself from danger, he must not from usefulness. His withdrawal may result in doing greater good to others, ver. 15; Mark 3 : 7-11; John 10 : 40, 41; Rom. 12 : 21.

14. The Christian in his life and in doing good should be like Jesus, active and persevering, earnest and affectionate, meek and lowly, kind, compassionate, and condescending, vers. 18-20; Phil. 2: 5.

15. A love of strife is inconsistent with the spirit of Christ, ver. 19; 1 Pet. 2 : 23; Rom. 8 : 9; Gal. 5 : 19-23; 2 Tim. 2 : 24, 25.

16. Christ will not extinguish the smallest beginning of spiritual life, but will nourish it and carry on the good work unto completeness, ver. 20; Phil. 1 : 6.

17. The feeblest and the most lowly may come to Jesus, ver. 20; ch. 11: 28-30.

18. Christ is kind and gentle to the penitent; sympathizing and compassionate to the tried and afflicted, ver. 20; Heb. 4 : 15, 16.

19. Christ will carry on the great designs of redemption to the complete discomfiture of his foes, and to the salvation of all them that trust in him, vers. 18-21; Isa. 43 : 13, 19, 20; Rev. 14 : 6-13; 21 : 2-4.

20. Infidels and opposers of Christ will ascribe his works and the success of his Gospel to any other cause rather than the true one, ver. 24.

21. Ascribing the work of God to the devil is peculiarly offensive to God and dangerous to men, vers. 24-31.

22. Men should be careful of their treatment of the Spirit, for he only brings the kingdom of God to our hearts, ver. 28.

23. There are two opposing kingdoms in this world, of Christ and of the Devil, vers 26-28.

24. Jesus, who cast out demons, will at last cast out the devil and his angels, vers. 22, 29; Rev 20 : 1-3.

25. There can be no neutrals in these kingdoms. We must be either for Christ or against him, ver. 30; ch. 6 : 24.

26. Christians should seek unity in faith, practice, and in the promulgation of the truth. Let them learn a lesson from the kingdom of darkness, which will not divide against itself, so as to destroy itself, ver. 26; John 17: 17, 20-23.

27. Men should especially beware of all blasphemy, since even the lowest tends to the highest, which can never be forgiven, vers. 31, 32.

28. They who have blasphemed against the Holy Spirit are entirely forsaken by the Spirit, ver. 32.

29. The Holy Spirit is a personality, and in the highest and fullest sense God, since blasphemy against him is the most heinous sin, ver. 32.

30. There can be no probation after death; the final state of every man is determined in the present life, ver. 32; Eccle. 11 : 3; Luke 16 : 26; John 9 : 4; Gal. 6 : 7; Heb. 9 : 27.

31. The nature and hearts of men are depraved, not merely their acts, ver. 33; Jer. 17 : 9; Rom. 3 : 9-20.

32. Our chief concern should be with our hearts, not merely with our acts, vers. 33-35.

33. We do not inherit the Spirit of God by natural descent. A change of heart is necessary to doing the will of God, ver. 34; John 3 : 5; 8 : 44.

34. By our fruits are we known in this life, and by them, without any possibility of mistake, shall we be known and judged at the last great day, vers. 33, 36, 37; Luke 19 : 22; Eccle. 12 : 14; Rom. 2 : 16; Jude 15.

35. Many profess unbelief from want of evidence, and others are seeking greater evidence, when that which God has given them is all sufficient, ver. 38; 1 Cor. 1 : 22.

36. A certain preparation of heart is necessary to a right perception of the evidences of Christ and Gospel, ver. 39; ch. 13 : 14-16; Luke 24 : 25, 45; 1 Cor. 1 : 24.

37. Wicked men often think there are no evidences to Gospel truth, because they are too blind to see them, ver. 39.

38. The resurrection of Christ was the

Seven parables illustrating the mysteries of the kingdom of God.

XIII. THE same day went Jesus out of the house, 2 ¹and sat by the sea side. And great multitudes were gathered together unto him; so that ᵐ he went into a ship, and sat; and the whole multitude stood on the shore.

¹ Mk. 4. 1-20; Lk. 8. 4-15.
ᵐ Lk. 5. 3.

---

greatest of his miracles, and the crowning evidence of his divine mission, ver. 40; 1 Cor. 15 : 12-18.

39. "Many from the remotest regions of the earth, who, by some faint report of the Gospel, have been led to inquire after Christ and his salvation, will rise up against unbelievers of this age and nation."—SCOTT. Vers. 41, 42; ch. 8 : 11, 12.

40. Resisting the influences of the Spirit and the impressions of truth, opposing the Gospel and its evidences, or tending to a mere outward reformation to a neglect of an inward change, will tend to greater hardness of heart and blindness of mind, and will put the soul more and more into the power of the Devil, vers. 43-45; ch. 23 : 15; 2 Pet. 2 : 21, 22; 2 Tim. 3 : 13.

41. Love for our nearest friends must not stand in the way of duty, ver. 48; ch. 10 : 37.

42. How great the love of Jesus for his disciples! The very weakest share an affection beyond any earthly love, vers. 46-50; Isa. 49 : 15.

43. How great, too, the honor of being a disciple of Jesus! ver. 49; Rom. 8 : 17.

44. "All obedient disciples are near akin to Jesus Christ. They wear his name, bear his image, have his nature, are of his family."—MATTHEW HENRY. Ver. 50.

45. If we would enjoy this love and this honor, we must do the will of our Heavenly Father, ver. 50; ch. 7 : 21; John 15 : 14.

CHAPTER XIII.

1-52. SEVEN PARABLES CONCERNING THE KINGDOM OF GOD; the first four spoken to the multitude by the sea-side, and the last three to the disciples in the house. As in chapters eight and nine we have specimens of the miracles of Jesus, so here we have samples of his parables. The former were selected from a large number without regard to chronological order, the latter were all spoken on the same day. The Sermon on the Mount presents a specimen of our Savior's direct, plain, and early teaching, when he spake without parables, or mainly so; this chapter exhibits not only a specimen but also the beginning of his parabolic teaching (vers. 10, 34), after the malice of the Pharisees had been considerably aroused and developed into determined opposition, and it had begun to take shape and to manifest itself in organized action. The seven parables here given illustrate the kingdom of God in its inner life and outer manifestations from the first sowing of Gospel seed to its final consummation.

1, 2. JESUS GOES TO THE SEA-SIDE, Mark 4 : 1, 2.

1. **The same day.** On *that day*, when the circumstances, related in the latter part of chapter twelve, occurred. It was on the day that the Pharisees charged him with casting out demons through Beelzebul, the prince of demons, and also demanded a sign from heaven, that Jesus changed his mode of teaching. **Out of the house.** Probably out of the house where he resided at Capernaum, which is styled "his own city," ch. 9 : 1. **Sat by the sea-side.** On the shore of the sea of Galilee. Sitting was the usual posture for teaching, ch. 5 : 1. Here, indeed, according to Mark, he began to teach, Mark 4 : 1.

2. **Great multitudes,** crowds, masses of people, seeing him in a posture of teaching, gather unto him, so that he found it convenient to enter into a **ship,** the small vessel or fish'ing *boat* that was usually there for transporting passengers, or perhaps one that was usually used by Jesus and his disciples, ch. 8 : 23; 9 : 1; Mark 3 : 9; 4 : 36; Luke 5 : 3. **The shore.** The beach, a low, flat shore, where all the multitude could stand while listening to Jesus. A level beach runs along the edge of the lake.

3 And he spake many things unto them in parables, saying, Behold, a sower went forth to sow.

3–9. THE SOWER. The various receptions that men give to the word of God. The causes and consequences, Mark 4 : 2–9; Luke 8: 4–8.

3. He spake many things—in parables, of which those that follow are specimens. It was not the design of the Spirit that the Evangelists should give a complete history of either the acts or discourses of Jesus. Matthew, we must believe, was divinely directed in selecting from the parables of that day those which would be of permanent value and of general interest.

Parable is derived from the Greek noun thus translated, which comes from a verb meaning *to throw beside, to compare.* Hence a parable in the most general sense is a *placing beside* or *together*, a *comparing*, and may apply to any illustration from analogy, a comparison, similitude, allegory, figurative or poetical discourse, dark saying, or proverb, Num. 23 : 7; Job 27 : 1; Ps. 49 : 4; 78 : 2; Matt. 13 : 35. In Luke 4 : 23 it is properly translated *proverb.* In a more restricted sense the word denotes an illustration of moral and religious truth drawn from events which take place among mankind. The narrative, or discourse, may be fictitious; but it must be within the limits of probability, else it becomes a fable. Teaching by parables was common in the east, especially among the Jews, 2 Sam. 12 : 1–14; Isa. 5 : 1–5; Ezek. 19 : 1–9.

THE PARABLES OF CHRIST were of the more restricted kind, and deserve special notice. *First,* they were not *fables.* Fables illustrate human character and conduct; the parables of Christ illustrate moral and spiritual truths. Fables are founded on the supposed words and acts of brutes or inanimate things; the parables of Christ were all founded on common and familiar incidents in nature and human experience, and all drawn, with one exception, from the present world. None of them was even necessarily fictitious. Jesus, with his omniscience, had no need to resort to fiction, when all events connected with the present and future world were known to him. What need of fiction when *facts* were at his hand? Compare the fables of Jotham (Judges 9 : 8–15) and Joash (2 Kings 14 : 9) with any of the parables of Christ. *Second,* they were not proverbs. Proverbs are brief, sententious sayings, often enigmatical, commonly including or implying some simile or comparison, but sometimes merely stating in a pithy manner the result of human experience and observation. The parables of Christ were more extended, illustrating truth neither obscurely nor briefly, but plainly and in detail. In general, it may be said that parables are expanded proverbs, and many proverbs are concentrated parables. Christ could have reduced each of his parables to a proverb and expanded some of his proverbs to parables. Compare the proverbs, "Physician, heal thyself" (Luke 4 : 23), "A prophet is not without honor, save in his own country and in his own house" (ch. 13 : 57), with the parable of the Wicked Husbandmen, ch. 21 : 33–44. Yet many a proverb expanded would be a fable or an allegory. *Third,* neither were they *Allegories.* Dr. Trench has well remarked that "the parable differs from the allegory in form rather than in essence." The allegory bears to the parable a relation similar to that which the metaphor bears to the simile or comparison. Thus "that man is a fox," is a metaphor; but "that man is like a fox," is a simile, or comparison. So "I am the true vine, etc." (John 15 : 1–8) is an allegory; but "the kingdom of heaven is like to a grain of mustard seed," etc., is a parable. In the parable one thing is *compared with* another; the thing representing and the thing represented are kept separate, and stand side by side; but in the allegory the two are united and mingled together, and the former is really invested with the attributes and powers of the latter. Thus, the allegory is self-interpreting; at least the interpretation is contained within itself. Bunyan's imaginary Christian is invested with the attributes and powers of the real one, and thus the signification is mingled with the fictitious narrative. But the parable, strictly speaking, contains in itself only the types, which illustrate something without and running parallel with them. Thus, in the parables of Christ, the

4 And when he sowed, some *seeds* fell by the way side,
5 and the fowls came and devoured them up. Some fell upon ⁿstony places, where they had not much earth: and forthwith they sprung up, because they
6 had no deepness of earth: and when the sun was up, they were °scorched; and because they had no
7 root, they withered away. And some fell among thorns; and the thorns sprung up, and choked
8 them. But other fell into good ground, and brought forth fruit, some ᵖan hundredfold, some

ⁿ Ezek. 11. 19; 36. 26.
° Jam. 1. 11; Rev. 7. 16.

ᵖ Ge. 26. 12.

various facts in human observation and experience are made to illustrate and typify great moral and spiritual facts and truths, which are always kept separate, and yet are always parallel. The latter are compared with the former. Compare the allegories of Christ in John 10: 1-16; 15: 1-8 with his parables in this chapter; or the parable in Isa. 5: 1-7 with the allegory in Ps. 80: 8-16.

The parables of Christ were thus the illustrations of spiritual things by an analogy of facts and incidents in everyday life and human experience. Their design (vers. 10-16) and the right mode of expounding them (vers. 18-23) will appear as we proceed.

Behold, a sower. Rather, *Behold, the sower,* representing the whole class of sowers. His hearers had often beheld the sower going forth to sow. Possibly one was near them in a neighboring field, to whom Jesus directed their attention, and thus made his parable the more striking and impressive.

4. By the wayside. "The ordinary roads or paths in the east lead often along the edge of the fields, which are uninclosed. . . . Hence, as the sower scatters his seed, some of it is liable to fall beyond the plowed portion, on the hard, beaten ground which forms the wayside."—DR. HACKETT's *Illustrations of Scripture,* page 176. **Fowls.** The birds, such as the lark and the sparrow.

5. Stony places. Rocky places; not where stones were numerous, for the soil might be rich and deep; but where a thin soil slightly covered a rocky surface. It would be, therefore, soon warmed and soon parched. The seed would spring up quickly, and there being no chance for the plant to root downward, its whole vitality would tend upward.

6. Sun was up. The hot oriental sun soon scorched them with its beams, evaporating their vital juices, and having no root, they withered away for want of needful moisture, Luke 8: 6.

7. Among thorns. Rather, *upon thorns,* upon soil where the roots of thorns yet remained, not having been carefully extirpated. These came up and **choked,** strangled, stifled the grain by pressing upon it, overtopping it, shading it, and exhausting the soil, and thus "it yielded no fruit," Mark 4: 7. "Every one who has been in Palestine must have been struck with the number of thorny shrubs and plants that abound there. The traveler finds them in his path, go where he may. Many of them are small, but some grow as high as a man's head."—HACKETT's *Scripture Illustrations,* p. 134.

8. Into good ground. Rather, *upon good ground,* upon rich, deep soil; neither hard and beaten, nor rocky, nor infested with thorns, but well prepared for receiving the seed. **A hundredfold.** An abundant harvest. Thus Isaac, when sojourning in the land of the Philistines, is said to have sowed and "received in the same year a hundred-fold," Gen. 26: 12. Herodotus mentions two hundred-fold as a common return in the plain of Babylon, and sometimes three. Large portions of Palestine were anciently very fertile in grain, as they might now be under proper cultivation. "It has been judged that a single plain, that of Esdraelon, between the hills of Samaria on the south, and the last ridges of Lebanon on the north, would yield grain enough, if properly cultivated, to support the entire population at present within the ancient limits of the Holy Land."—Dr. HACKETT's *Scriptural Illustrations,* p. 150. "The parable about sowing has here its

A.D. 28. MATTHEW XIII. 183

9 sixtyfold, some thirtyfold. ⁹ Who hath ears to
hear, let him hear.
10 And the disciples came, and said unto him, Why
11 speakest thou unto them in parables? He answered and said unto them, Because ʳ it is given
unto you to know the ˢ mysteries of the kingdom of
12 heaven, but to them it is not given. ᵗ For whosoever hath to him shall be given, and he shall have

ᵍ ch. 11. 15.

ʳ ch. 11. 25, 26; 16. 17; Ps. 25. 14; 1 Cor. 2. 6–10; 1 John 2. 27.
ˢ 1 Cor. 2. 7; Eph. 1. 9; Col. 1. 26, 27.
ᵗ Mk. 4. 25.

---

illustration, even in its most minute details. Behold a sower *went forth to sow*. There is a nice and close adherence to actual life in this form of expression. The expression implies that the sower, in the days of our Savior, lived in a hamlet, or village, as all these farmers now do; that he did not sow near his own house, or in a garden fenced and walled, for such a field does not furnish all the basis of the parable. There are neither *roads*, nor thorns, nor stony places in such lots. He must go forth into the open country, as these have done, where there are no fences; where the path passes through the cultivated land; where thorns grow in clumps all around; where the rocks peep out in places through the scanty soil; and where also, hard by, are patches extremely fertile. Now here we have the whole four within a dozen rods of us. Our horses are actually trampling down the seeds which have fallen by this wayside, and larks and sparrows are busy in picking them up. That man, with his mattock, is digging about places where the rock is too near the surface for the plow, and much that is sown there will wither away. And not a few seeds have fallen among this *bellan*, and will be effectually choked by this most tangled of thorn bushes. But a large portion falls into really good ground, and four months hence will exhibit every variety of crop, up to the richest and heaviest that ever rejoices the heart even of an American farmer."
—Thomson, *The Land and the Book*, vol. i. p. 115.

9. A call to candid and solemn attention. He that can hear, let him attend seriously, and understand the important and solemn truths taught by this parable.

10–17. Jesus, in reply to his disciples, gives THE REASON FOR TEACHING IN PARABLES, Mark 4 : 10–12; Luke 8, 9, 10.

10. **The disciples.** Not only the twelve, but also those who believed on him as the Messiah, and attended on his instructions. Mark says, "They that were about him with the twelve asked him," **Why speakest thou—in parables?** The question implies that this was the first time that Jesus taught the multitude by parables. Before this he had addressed them in plain addresses, intermingled with occasional similitudes, as in the Sermon on the Mount. But now "without a parable spake he not unto them," ver. 34.

11. Jesus answers that he speaks in parables in order that the mysteries of the kingdom of heaven may be vailed to the careless and ill-designing, but illustrated to his believing followers. **Because it is given unto you.** Rather, *To you it is given*. By the sovereign will and good pleasure of God. Compare ver. 15, and the language in ch. 19 : 11; John 3 : 27; 19 : 11. *To you* is emphatic, and in contrast to **them.** *To them*, the hardened and evil-designing multitude, it was not given to know the mysteries of the Gospel and of Messiah's kingdom. To most it was never afterward given; some of them may have become followers of Jesus after the descent of the Spirit. **Mysteries.** Truths concerning the kingdom of Christ hitherto hidden, but now being revealed. See Rom. 16 : 25, 26; 1 Cor. 2 : 7, 8; 1 Tim. 3 : 16; Eph. 1 : 9, 10. On *kingdom of heaven*, see on ch. 3 : 2. Even what prophets had foretold was a mystery to the hard-hearted and worldly-minded multitude, 1 Cor. 2 : 14.

12. Jesus gives the principle on which the knowledge of the great and deep truths of the gospel dispensation is given or withheld. **To him that hath.** He who hears and understands; he who, having a teachable spirit, has already some knowledge of the Gospel and of Christ, and desires for more.

more abundance: but whosoever hath not, ^u from him shall be taken away even that he hath. Therefore speak I to them in parables: because they seeing see not; and hearing they hear not, neither do they understand. And in them is fulfilled the prophecy of Esaias, which saith, ^v 'By hearing ye shall hear, and shall not understand; and seeing ye shall see, and shall not perceive: for ^w this people's heart is waxed gross, and *their* ears ^x are dull

^u Is. 5. 4–7; Rev. 2. 5.
^v Is. 6. 9, 10; Eze. 12. 2; John 12. 40; Ac. 28. 26, 27; Ro. 11. 8; 2 Cor. 3. 14, 15.
^w Deu. 32. 15; Ps. 95. 8.
^x Heb. 5. 11; 2 Thess. 2. 10, 11.

This implies an experimental knowledge and a love for Christ. **Shall be given.** He shall have more knowledge. He shall have the means and facilities for the attainment and illustration of these truths, which he will gladly improve, and thus shall he have **abundance.** The main design of parables was doubtless to illustrate gospel truths to the humble and sincere followers of Jesus. But there was another design, which is immediately given. **Whosoever hath not.** He who has not a teachable spirit, and hence makes no use of the means and facilities he already has, neither loves Jesus nor desires to know his truth. Hence he has no experimental knowledge of Christ. **Even what he has.** The light, the means, and the knowledge which have been proffered him shall be withheld. Even that he "seemeth to have" (Luke 8 : 18), his mere speculative views and notions, shall become more confused and darkened. He who uses and improves the light he has shall obtain more light; but he who neglects to do it shall lose it altogether, and be condemned as an unprofitable servant, ch. 25 : 29, 30. "It is curiously true of any parable that *to him that hath*, namely, the key, *to him shall be given*, namely, the meaning. And the whole Gospel is a parable to him whose heart has not the key."—WHEDON.

13. The principle just laid down is, in this verse, applied to the multitude, "Therefore speak I **to them** in parables." In verse 16 it is applied to the disciples. **Because they seeing, see not.** They have faculties and opportunities, but they do not rightly use them. They do not perceive and understand the truths of the Gospel. Though they have moral and intellectual faculties, yet they are spiritually blind and deaf. They are thus of that class referred to in the latter part of the twelfth verse, *They have not*. Jesus therefore speaks to them in parables, **because** they are such, in order that the truths which they spurned and neglected might be hid from them. They are left to their own blindness and hardness of heart; in other words, to the consequences of their sins, which are the source of their blindness, prejudice, and ignorance.

14. Jesus affirms that in them is strikingly fulfilled a prophecy found in Isa. 6 : 9, 10. **In them is fulfilled.** A strong expression in the original: *Is being completely fulfilled*. This was a typical prophecy (see on ch. 1 : 22), applying first to the Jewish people of Isaiah's time, but more fully to the Jews in our Savior's time and under the Gospel dispensation. That hardness of heart, exhibited under the preaching of Isaiah, was but a type of that greater hardness of heart which would be shown by the unbelieving Jewish people in the rejection of Christ and his Gospel. Reference to the fulfillment of this prophecy, which was, and indeed is still, so complete under the Gospel, is also made in John 12 : 40; Acts 28 : 26, 27; Rom. 11 : 8. The language in these passages are "varied, so as to give prominence in some of them to that willful blindness which is a crime, and in others to that judicial blindness which is its punishment."—*Annotated Paragraph Bible.*

By hearing. *With the hearing*, with the sense of hearing, ye shall hear the words distinctly and clearly, but ye shall not understand their true meaning; and seeing, ye shall see clearly and distinctly their external form, but shall not perceive their hidden truths and their spiritual meaning. This spiritual deafness and blindness are sent upon them on account of sin.

15. The spiritual condition of the people further indicated prophetically. The quotation is in the language of the Septuagint version, being a slight variation, with the same essential meaning, of the

of hearing, and their eyes they have closed; lest at any time they should see with *their* eyes, and hear with *their* ears, and should understand with *their* heart, ʸ and should be converted, and I should heal 16 them.' ᶻ But blessed *are* your eyes, for they see: 17 and your ears, for they hear. For verily I say unto you, ᵃ That many prophets and righteous *men* have desired to see *those things* which ye see, and have

ʸ 2 Cor. 3. 16; 1 Thess. 1. 9.
ᶻ Lk. 10. 23, 24.

ᵃ Eph. 3. 5; Heb. 11. 13; 1 Pet. 1. 10-12.

Hebrew words of Isaiah. **For.** The reason of this fearful and fatal spiritual insensibility and blindness is about to be given. **Waxed gross.** Literally, *become fat;* a figure of great spiritual insensibility. **Dull of hearing.** Have heard heavily, with difficulty; spiritually dull. **Their eyes have they closed,** so as not to see. All these things have been voluntary on their part, and have all increased by their voluntary exercise. **Lest at any time.** Lest, perchance, they see, etc. It was, indeed, their own voluntary purpose not to see, hear, understand, turn, and be saved; but it was God's purpose, also, on account of their wickedness and hardness of heart. **Should be converted, and I should heal them.** Rather, *And turn, and I shall heal them.* In all this God did not take away their freedom. He was ready to heal them if they did but turn, which, however, they would not, and indeed could not do; for they were morally unable, because they were unwilling. Their moral inability was the result of their moral unwillingness, John 5 : 40. *Healed* of their spiritual malady, or, according to Mark (4 : 12), their sins *forgiven.* Hence, one of the reasons why our Savior spoke in parables was, that the truths of the Gospel might be vailed to those in whose spiritual condition the prophecy of Isaiah was so entirely fulfilled, and who were given over on account of their sins to hardness of heart and final destruction, 2 Cor. 4 : 3, 4.

16. In contrast to the spiritual blindness and insensibility of the unbelieving multitude, he congratulates his disciples on their spiritual perception. They were among the class who have and shall receive, and have abundance, ver. 12. **Blessed.** Happy. See on 5 : 3. Happy your eyes, for they see and perceive; and your ears, for they hear and apprehend the spiritual and glorious truths that are revealed by me. The disciples were indeed happy in contrast to the blinded scribes and Pharisees around them, who both hated and rejected the truth. These humble followers of Jesus, having teachable spirits, had received from him lessons of heavenly wisdom. And now, while parables only served to darken the minds of the haughty and self-righteous multitude, they cast new light into the minds of these truth-loving and truth-seeking disciples. They were like the pillar of the cloud and fire, which was darkness to the Egyptians but light to Israel, Ex. 14 : 20.

17. They were also happy in comparison to prophets and righteous men of old. **Many prophets and righteous men,** many of the most eminently pious men of the old dispensation, **have desired to see those things which ye see,** what ye are beholding, 1 Pet. 1 : 10; Job 19 : 23, 24; 2 Sam. 23 : 5; Isa. 52 : 7; and chs. 53 and 54. **And have not seen them.** Did not see them. They saw them not with their bodily eyes, and saw them but very dimly with the eyes of their soul. **And to hear those things,** etc. And to hear what ye hear (1 John 1 : 1), and heard not. They desired to hear Christ and the glorious things revealed by him. Such language as this could well be repeated by our Savior at another time, Luke 10 : 23, 24.

18–23. INTERPRETATION OF THE PARABLE OF THE SOWER. This is indeed a model interpretation, Mark 4 : 13. From this, and that of the Tares of the Field (vers. 36–43), we may learn how to interpret other parables. "It becomes us, therefore, in the two authoritative expositions here recorded for our learning, to observe not only what our Savior does, but what he leaves undone, the neglect of which has led to the excesses and absurdities of ultra-allegorical interpretation."—J. A. ALEXANDER. Mark 4 : 13–20; Luke 8 : 11–15.

18. It appears, from a comparison of

not seen *them;* and to hear *those things* which ye
18 hear, and have not heard *them.* ᵇ Hear ye therefore
19 the parable of the sower. When any one heareth
the word ᶜ of the kingdom, and understandeth *it*
not, then cometh ᵈ the wicked *one,* and ᵉ catcheth
away that which was sown in his heart. This is he
20 which received seed by the way side. But he that
received the seed into stony places, the same is he
that heareth the word, and anon ᶠ with joy receiveth
21 it; yet hath he not root in himself, but ᵍ dureth
for a while: ʰ for when tribulation or persecution

ᵇ Mk. 4. 14; Lk. 8 11.
ᶜ ch. 4. 23.
ᵈ 1 John 5. 18.
ᵉ 2 Cor. 4. 4; Jam. 1. 23, 24.
ᶠ Is. 54. 2; Eze. 34. 31. 32; John 5. 35.
ᵍ Hos. 6. 4; Gal. 5. 7; Heb. 10. 35-39.
ʰ Mk. 8. 34-36; Gal. 6. 12.

Mark 4 : 10 and Luke 8 : 9, that the disciples not only asked Jesus why he taught in parables, but also the meaning of this parable. The answer of the former question we have just considered; we now would attend to the latter. **Hear ye.** *You* who are of the class for whom parables are designed for the revealing and the illustration of truth, *you* who are so highly favored above the unbelieving multitude, and even above the most eminent saints of the past, hear and understand what the parable of the sower teaches. The **sower** represents the Son of Man (ver. 37), also his ministers and servants, ch. 25 : 45; 2 Cor. 5 : 20.

This parable divides the hearers of the Gospel into four classes: the thoughtless, the superficial and fickle, the worldly, and the truly pious.

19. **Heareth the word of the kingdom.** The truths of the Gospel. Luke (8 : 11) says, "The seed is the word of God." See 1 Pet. 1 : 23. **Understandeth it not.** He does not apprehend its spiritual meaning, and gives it no proper attention. These words represent the character of the wayside hearer as without spiritual understanding, thoughtless, careless, and stupid, Prov. 24 : 30-34. **The wicked one.** Rather, the evil one. Mark says, "Satan;" Luke, "Devil." **Catcheth away,** like the birds picking up the grain. Satan not only does this himself, but also through evil thoughts, desires, and lusts, and, indeed, by any thing which will attract the attention from the truths of the Gospel. **This is he that received.** *This is he that was sown;* or, *This was that sown,* etc. "The meaning is, This is the one whose case is represented by seed sown by the wayside."—CONANT. The fate of the seed is inseparable from the fate of the man; it can, therefore, truthfully represent the man.

20. **He that receiveth seed in stony places,** etc. The one sown on rocky places, etc. The seed in each of the four classes is made to represent the individual. This is the one whose case is represented by the seed sown on rocky places. **The same is he that heareth.** *This is he that heareth,* an emphatic expression, denoting more than the careless and indifferent hearing of the wayside. The same expression is also used in the original of the thorny ground and good ground hearers, vers. 21, 23. This one hears, indeed, but superficially. His emotions are easily aroused, but his heart beneath is hard and unaffected. There is no deep conviction of sin; no brokenness and contrition of spirit. He does not count the cost (Luke 14 : 25-33), but hearing the glad tidings, and thinking upon the pleasures and gains of salvation, **anon,** *immediately,* receives the word with joy.

21. **Yet hath not root in himself.** This characterizes the individual as superficial, rootless. He is wanting in the principles of true religion, humility, love, repentance, and faith. He is not "rooted and grounded in love" (Eph. 3 : 17). nor "rooted and built up" in Christ (Col. 2 : 7). He is destitute of that hidden life, that which "is hid with Christ in God," Col. 3 : 3. He therefore but **dureth for a while,** is only for a season, or temporary. He is superficial and fickle. As a disciple he is only a creature of excitement, carried away by the novelties, the pleasures, or the sentimental excitements of religion, and hence, as the excitement subsides, he himself changes and turns back.

ariseth because of the word, by and by ¹ he is of-
22 fended. ʲ He also that received seed ᵏ among the
thorns is he that heareth the word; and ˡ the care
of this world, and ᵐ the deceitfulness of riches, choke
23 the word, and he becometh unfruitful. But he
that received seed into the good ground is he that
heareth the word, ⁿ and understandeth *it;* which

¹ ch. 11. 6; 2 Tim. 1. 15.
ʲ ch. 19. 23; Mk. 10. 23; Lk. 18. 24. 25; 1 Tim. 6. 9; 2 Tim. 4. 10.
ᵏ Jer. 4. 8.
ˡ Lk. 10. 40–42; 21. 34; 1 John 2, 15, 16.

This is what Luke (8 : 13) describes as believing for a while, an emotional and apparent faith, not the believing with all the heart, Acts 8 : 37. **Tribulation.** Affliction, distress, including providential dealings and chastisements. **Persecution.** The word originally means *pursuit*, that is, of an enemy. The evils inflicted by enemies. Tribulation and persecution form what, according to Luke, is styled "the time of temptation." **By and by he is offended.** Rather, *Immediately*, as suddenly as he received the word at first, he taketh offense, becomes disaffected, his emotions are aroused in an opposite direction, and his profession is renounced. Thus, according to Luke, he "falls away" from a mere superficial religion and a false profession. As the hot sun causes the deeply-rooted plant to grow, while at the same time it withers the rootless grain on rocky places, so tribulation and persecution strengthen and develop the true child of God (Rom. 5 : 3; 8 : 28; 2 Cor. 4 : 17; Rev. 7 : 14), while they offend, discourage, and completely disaffect the false and superficial disciple, Hos. 9 : 16; 2 Tim. 4 : 10.

22. **He also that received seed among the thorns.** He sown among thorns, etc. His case is represented by the seed sown among thorns. His heart is like the plowed but illy prepared field, from which the thorn roots have not been entirely extirpated. He has conviction of sin, shows signs of sorrow and repentance, and passes through an experience similar to that often witnessed in true conversion. But the heart is divided, darling sins are secretly fostered, and the powers of the body and soul are not given up to Christ. He is not thoughtless, like the one of the first class, nor like the one of the second class does he fail to count the cost, and hence he does not participate in his false and fleeting joy. He hears, and hears seriously, has a conflict with the world, and fails to conquer. The cause is in a heart not consecrated to Jesus. **Cares of this world.** Anxious cares about worldly things, which divide the heart between God and the world, James 1 : 6–8. This may apply especially to the poor, whose struggles with poverty draw off the mind from God, but also to every one who is so unduly anxious about worldly things (ch. 6 : 25) as to prevent him from giving up himself to God, and casting his care on him, 1 Pet. 5 : 7. **Deceitfulness of riches,** in alluring the heart and leading it to exercise a false confidence in wealth, producing self-sufficiency and self-complacency. Hence he takes up with a false hope and a false profession. Luke adds, "The pleasures of this life," and Mark, "The lusts of other things," which are but the natural accompaniments of such a course, 1 Tim. 6 : 9, 10. These things **choke,** strangle the word, by their contact and pressure, so that it becomes unfruitful, or, as Luke has it, they "bring no fruit unto perfection," Prov. 11 : 28; Luke 21 : 34. **He becometh.** Rather, *it becometh*, referring to the seed, but of course representing the man. He may have much of the outward appearance of the disciple, and even apparent fruits; but these, not coming to perfection, are unfit for use, and as worthless as no fruit at all. In the sight of God he is really destitute of good works.

23. **But he that receiveth.** *The one sown,* whose case is represented by the seed sown on good ground. He *hears* the word attentively and rightly, and **understandeth,** apprehends its true spiritual import. According to Mark (4 : 20), this class "receive" the word, receive the truth, and act upon it; and Luke (8:15), they having heard, "in an honest and good heart, keep," or "hold fast the word and bring forth fruit with patience." Their hearts, like the good ground, are prepared for the

also ᵒ beareth fruit, and bringeth forth, some an hundredfold, some sixty, some thirty.

24 Another parable put he forth unto them, saying,

ᵐ ch. 19. 16-24; Job. 31. 24, 25; Ac. 5. 1-11.
ⁿ 1 Thess. 1. 5-7.

seed, ready to receive, understand, accept, and retain. All hearts are evil by nature, but in some there is a readiness, through the operations of the Spirit and the truth, to hear and accept the Gospel. It is heard not thoughtlessly (ver. 19), but seriously; received not superficially (vers. 20, 21), but it sinks deep into the heart; and accepted not partially (ver. 22), but fully with the whole heart. There is repentance and faith, a full surrender of the heart to Christ. While the soul acts freely, the Spirit works effectually in connection with the truth, and thus, without infringing upon the will, the heart is prepared by divine grace, John 5 : 40; 6 : 44; 16 : 8; 1 Cor. 2 : 14. **Beareth fruit.** In the original this is emphatically made a characteristic which distinguishes this class from the others. **Some a hundred-fold, some sixty, some thirty.** All of this class produce fruit, but in different degrees, in proportion to the natural endowments of the soul, the spiritual culture of the heart, the devotedness of the life and the faithfulness in the use of all Gospel means, graces, and blessings.

From our Savior's exposition of this parable we learn that, in expounding parables, we must avoid the two opposite extremes, the making of every minute point significant, on the one hand, and the overlooking some points which are really significant, on the other. The resemblance in the principal incidents is all that should be generally sought. First of all, seek carefully the grand design of the parable and its centre of comparison; and then, with the mind fixed on these, explain the principal parts accordingly, without giving too much prominence to minute particulars, which serve merely to complete the story. Avoid fanciful interpretations; beware of seeking resemblances which are foreign to the design of the parable. The interpretation must not be forced or far-fetched, but natural and easy. Beware, also, of founding a doctrine or a duty on single phrases or incidental circumstances. In seeking the *design* of a parable, particular attention must be given to its occasion, connection, introduction, and close. The *centre* of the comparison is that from which all parts of the parable extend in illustrating its grand design.

These principles may be briefly illustrated in the Parable of the Sower, as follows: The *general design* of parables is to illustrate the mysteries of the kingdom of God. The *particular design* of this parable is to illustrate the various receptions men give to the word of God; the causes and consequences are incidentally traced. The *centre* of the comparison is the receptivity of the ground to the seed with that of the heart to the word of God. All portions of the parable and its interpretation are in harmony with this grand design and central similitude. The sower is the Son of Man, or his representatives, his servants; the seed is the word of God; the ground, the hearts of men; the seed, with its results, as sown in the ground, the various classes of hearers. It can be seen that many resemblances might be affirmed which Jesus has not drawn. Thus, for example, from the *sower* as a *husbandman*, his *going forth*, the *time* and *manner* of his sowing, the *local position* of the wayside, and many other points too numerous to mention. But these would be foreign to the grand design, and very remotely connected, or not connected at all, with the centre of comparison. So, also, to refer the wayside hearer to thoughtless childhood; the stony ground, to ardent, superficial youth; and the thorny ground, to worldly-minded maturity, would be *fanciful* as well as unnatural. And, finally, to conclude that there are but three classes of fruit-bearing Christians, corresponding to the hundred-fold, the sixty and the thirty, each bearing no more and no less than the ratio of his class, would obviously be forced, and be founding a principle on *single phrases* and *incidental circumstances*.

21-30. THE PARABLE OF THE TARES. The principle for the treatment of the wicked under the administration of the Messiah. Found only in Matthew.

24. Another parable put he

A.D. 28. MATTHEW XIII. 189

25 The kingdom of heaven is likened unto a man which sowed good seed in his field: ᵖ but while men slept, ᵠ his enemy came and sowed tares among
26 the wheat, and went his way. But when the blade was sprung up, and brought forth fruit, then ap-
27 peared the tares also. So the servants of the householder came and said unto him, Sir, didst not thou sow good seed in thy field? From whence then
28 hath it tares? He said unto them, An enemy hath done this. The servants said unto him, Wilt thou

ᵒ Ps. 1. 1-3; 92. 13-15; John 15. 8, 16; Phil. 1. 11.
ᵖ Is. 56. 10.
ᵠ 2 Cor. 11. 13-15; Gal. 2. 4; Heb. 12. 15, 16; 1 Pet. 5. 8.

---

forth, laid or set before them for their careful consideration. The verb translated *put forth* is often used to express the setting or laying food before any one, Acts 16 : 34; 1 Cor. 10 : 27. This parable contained food indeed for the mind and heart. **The kingdom of heaven.** The reign, administration, or dispensation of the Messiah. **Is likened unto a man.** Is like the case of a man under the circumstances about to be detailed. *Good seed.* Wheat (ver. 30), clean, unmixed, and nutritious, in contrast to the poisonous, useless seed afterward sown by his enemy.

25. **While men slept.** Not his servants specially, but men generally. At the time when men usually sleep, that is, at night. **His enemy.** Doubtless, an ill-disposed and unfriendly neighbor. What he did was from malice. Similar acts of malice and revenge are practiced to this day. "Thus, in Ireland," says Trench, "I have known an out-going tenant, in spite at his eviction, to sow wild oats in the fields which he was leaving." **Sowed tares among the wheat.** Sowed in addition *darnel* or bastard wheat. That which the enemy sowed was not *tares*, which do not resemble wheat, and which is also useful as food for cattle, but *darnel*, a noxious plant, very common in the east, resembling wheat, and not only worthless, but intoxicating and poisonous. Its fruit is black, not yellow. "Except that the stock was not so high, it appeared otherwise precisely like wheat, just as the ears begin to show themselves and the kernels are swelling out into shape. . . . I collected some specimens of this deceitful weed, and have found, on showing them to friends, that they have mistaken them quite invariably for some species of grain,

such as wheat or barley."—DR. HACKETT's *Scripture Illustrations*, page 138. "The taste" of the grain "is bitter, and, when eaten separately, or even when diffused in ordinary bread, it causes dizziness, and often acts as a violent emetic. . . . In short, it is a strong soporific poison, and must be carefully winnowed and picked out of the wheat, grain by grain, before grinding, or the flour is not healthy."—DR. THOMSON. Having done the mischief, the enemy **went his way** as secretly and silently as he came.

26. **Then appeared the tares also.** While the blade was springing up and growing, all appeared alike; but when the time of producing fruit came, the tares or darnel were easily distinguished. So persons are known by their fruit.

27. **So the servants.** *And,* etc. It should be noted that Jesus makes no reference to these *servants* in his interpretation of the parable, vers. 36-40. They seem to be intended to represent no particular class of persons, but are rather introduced to fill up the parable, and for bringing out the truth taught by the answers of the householder to their questions. Yet the Bible student will be reminded of the disciples who asked, if they should command fire to come down from heaven upon the Samaritans who refused to entertain Jesus, Luke 9 : 54. **Didst not thou sow,** etc? Rather, didst thou not sow? The question has reference to the *sowing*, not to the *person* that sowed. It supposes an affirmative answer, and is thus preparatory to, and the ground of, the question that follows.

28. **An enemy.** Literally, *a hostile man*, his character as an *enemy* being made prominent. **Gather them up.** By weeding, pulling them up.

29 then that we go and gather them up? But he said, ʳ Nay; lest while ye gather up the tares, ye root up
30 also the wheat with them. Let ˢ both grow together until the harvest: and in the time of harvest I will say to the reapers, ᵗ Gather ye together first the tares, and bind them in bundles to burn them: but ᵘ gather the wheat into my barn.
31 Another parable put he forth unto them, saying, ᵛ The kingdom of heaven is like to a grain of mustard seed, which a man took, and sowed in his
32 field: which indeed is the least of all seeds: but

ʳ John 18. 36.
ˢ Mal. 3. 18; 4. 1, 2.

ᵗ ch. 25. 41; John 15. 6.
ᵘ ch. 3. 12.

ᵛ Ps. 72. 16–19; Is. 2. 2, 3; Mic. 4. 1, 2.

29. **Root up also the wheat.** Lest while you root up the tares or darnel you root up the wheat at the same time with them. This might happen from their close resemblance; but especially from the close connection and intertwining of their roots. "In those parts where the grain has *headed out* they (the tares) have done the same, and there a child can not mistake them for wheat or barley; but where both are less developed, the closest scrutiny will often fail to detect them. Even the farmers, who in this country generally *weed* their fields, do not attempt to separate the one from the other. They would not only mistake good grain for them, but very commonly the roots of the two are so intertwined that it is impossible to separate them without plucking up both. Both, therefore, must be left to *grow together* until the harvest."—Dr. Thomson.

Farmers among us sometimes pass through their grain-fields and cut off the tops of *cheat*, or American darnel, and thus clean their field without rooting up or injuring the wheat. But the householder does not intimate any such means. He would have all remain till harvest.

30. The harvest was the right time for separating the noxious weed from the grain. **Burn them.** The darnel is useless and injurious, and fit only to be burned. On account of the scarcity of wood in Palestine, even dried grass was used for fuel. See ch. 6: 30.

31, 32. Parable of the grain of mustard seed, Mark 4: 30–32. Compare Luke 13: 18, 19. The expansive power of truth.

31. Jesus had related two parables, in the first of which three fourths of the seed was unproductive, and in the second, a noxious plant was mingled with the growing wheat. Now he presents a brighter side, by relating two other parables. One small plant produces a tree. A little leaven leavens the whole lump. By the first he shows the expansive and accretive power of truth; by the second its assimilating and diffusive power. The first shows rather its *outward* workings; the second its *inward* influence. **Which a man took and sowed.** Literally, *Which a man taking* or *handling sowed.* Great minuteness and fullness in the description. There may be reference to the smallness of the seed, which required the most careful taking up and holding, lest it should be lost. **His field.** Luke (13: 19) says, "His garden." The word field in the original is the more general, and may include a "garden," that is, any place planted with herbs and trees.

32. **Least of all seeds.** This is popular, not scientific language. It was indeed the smallest of seed-grain used in Jewish husbandry, and, in proportion to the plant it produces, it was the smallest of all domestic garden seeds. In Jewish proverbial language it was also used to denote the smallest thing. See ch. 17: 20. It should, however, be noted that in the Greek the comparative is used here, as well as in the clause, **greatest among herbs:** *Less than all seeds; greater than the herbs.* The first is equivalent, or nearly so, to the superlative, since it obviously means *less than all* other *seeds*, hence *the least of all seeds*. The second is manifestly not so exactly expressed by *greatest*, etc.; for the growth of the mustard plant is described, though indeed an herb, yet becoming, when it is grown, greater than the herbs, **a tree,** so that the birds of

A.D. 28.   MATTHEW XIII.   191

ʷ when it is grown, it is the greatest among herbs, and becometh a tree, so that ˣ the birds of the air come and lodge in the branches thereof.   ʷ Ps. 80. 9–11; Pro. 4. 18.

the air may come and **lodge,** find shelter in its branches. Luke (13 : 19) says, it becomes "a great tree," of course in a comparative sense.

The mustard plant attains a considerable size in hot climates. Dr. Hackett, while riding across the plain of Akka, on the way to Carmel, examined an extensive field of this plant. "It was then in blossom, full grown, in some cases six, seven, and nine feet high, with a stem or trunk an inch or more in thickness, throwing out branches on every side. I was now satisfied in part. I felt that such a plant might well be called a tree, and, in comparison to the seed producing it, a great tree. But still the branches, or stems of the branches, were not very large, or, apparently, very strong. Can the birds, I said to myself, rest upon them? Are they not too slight and flexible? Will they not bend or break beneath the superadded weight? At that very instant, as I stood and revolved the thought, lo! one of the fowls of heaven stopped in his flight through the air, alighted down on one of the branches, which hardly moved beneath the shock, and then began, perched there before my eyes, to warble forth a strain of sweetest music. All my doubts were now charmed away."—*Scripture Illustrations*, page 132.

Dr. Royle, Art. "Sinapi," *Kitto's Encyc.*, supposes that Jesus refers to the mustard-tree, the *Khardal roomee*, or Turkish mustard, called by botanists *Salvadora Persica*, found in India, Arabia, and Syria, and grows abundantly, as he says, on the very shores of the sea of Galilee, where our Savior spake the parable of the mustard-seed. It is more natural, however, to suppose the mustard *plant* to be intended, since Jesus speaks of it as sowed in "a garden," (Luke), and by his language implies that it is an *herb*, that is, a garden-plant. The matter of wonder also is, not that a *tree*, but that a *plant* from so small a seed should grow to such a size.

The grand *design* of this parable is to show the expansive and growing power of the Gospel under the kingdom or reign of the Messiah. Its *centre of comparison* is between the power of growth as exhibited in the mustard-seed and that manifested in gospel truth. The grain of mustard represents the word of God, the truth; the man that sowed it, Christ or one of his servants; the field, the human heart; the seed in the soil becoming a plant, the individual believer. The idea of *growth* and of gradual development is vividly presented. A seed of gospel truth is lodged in the heart, a little word or a single idea. To human view it is indeed small, but it germinates into a new and growing life, begotten "with the word of truth," James 1 : 18. Thus it has pleased God "through the foolishness of preaching to save them that believe," 1 Cor. 1 : 21. The believer now grows in grace, his spiritual strength increases, his graces appear, and his powers are developed, going on from one degree of strength to another, till he becomes a full-grown man in Christ, Eph. 4 : 13. He has now the size, appearance, strength, and activities of a man. It may well be noted that the idea of growth involves not only internal development, but also accretion from without, through food, air, water, etc. So the Christian in his growth feeds upon the bread of life. The *birds of the air* are introduced to represent the strength and blessings of this matured and developed life. Christians, individually and collectively, are indeed a source of blessing and safety to the world, Gen. 18 : 23–33; Deut. 9 : 19, 20; Isa. 1 : 9.

But this parable may also be used to illustrate the power and growth of the Gospel generally in the hearts and lives of men. Jesus was indeed "the Word," the gospel seed, the babe at Bethlehem, the man of sorrows, despised of men, but planted of his own free will by his death, springing up in his resurrection, and bearing fruit in the thousands and the millions of his followers, John 12 : 24. This spiritual kingdom, beginning with himself, has been constantly augmenting. The Gospel from small beginnings has become extensive and powerful. See a prophecy of this kingdom in Dan. 2 : 44, 45; and compare Dan. 7 : 13, 14; Ezek. 17 : 22–24.

33 ʸ Another parable spake he unto them; The kingdom of heaven is like unto leaven, which a woman took, ᶻ and hid in three measures of meal, ᵃ till the whole was leavened.

ˣ Eze. 17. 23.
ʸ 1 Cor. 5. 6, 7.
ᶻ Ps. 119. 11; Lk. 2. 51.

---

33. THE PARABLE OF THE LEAVEN; compare Luke 13 : 20, 21. The assimilating power of truth.
33. **Leaven.** Yeast, sour dough. **Three measures.** The measure here meant was one third of an ephah; three measures, or an ephah, seems to have been the quantity commonly used for one baking. See Gen. 18 : 6; Jud. 6 : 9; 1 Sam. 1 : 24. Jerome says a *measure* is equal to a Roman *modius*, or about a peck and a half. **Meal.** Flour, fine meal; probably wheat flour.

In interpreting this parable, the question arises at the outset whether it is intended to illustrate the leavening power of gospel truth, or of false doctrine. Starting with the fact that leaven was forbidden at the passover, and in all offerings made by fire unto the Lord (Ex. 12 : 15; Lev. 2 : 11), and that it is generally used in Scripture in a bad sense, to symbolize evil (Luke 12 : 1 and 1 Cor. 5 : 7), some commentators refer this parable to the corruptions of doctrine and practice which have crept into the church, making the woman to represent the apostate church; exemplified very strikingly by the papacy. A fatal objection to this view is that Jesus says, *The kingdom of heaven* is like unto *leaven*. If leaven be error, then is it represented as overcoming the truth, and wholly leavening with corruption either the kingdom of the Messiah or its individual members, both of which are contrary to God's truth and to fact, ch. 16 : 18; John 10 : 27, 28. It may also be well to note that Paul calls the *bad* leaven the *old* leaven (1 Cor. 5 : 7), and that in offering the first fruits unto the Lord, the loaves were to be "baken with leaven" (Lev. 23 : 17), and offerings not burnt upon the altar, but eaten by the priests, might contain leaven, Lev. 7 : 13–16. The true state of the case seems to be, that leaven is a figure of diffusive and assimilating power, and although generally used in Scripture to represent that which is corrupt and evil, it may also be used to illustrate this power connected with truth.

The grand *design* of this parable therefore seems to be, the diffusive and assimilating power of the Gospel under the kingdom of the Messiah. The *centre* of comparison is between the pervasive power of leaven and that of gospel truth. The leaven represents the truth; the woman, the Holy Spirit; the meal, the human heart; the leaven pervading the three measures of meal, the individual Christian under the renewing and sanctifying influence of the Spirit. The three measures may aptly refer to *body*, *soul*, and *Spirit*, 1 Thess. 5 : 23. Thus, the Holy Spirit in connection with the truth begins the work of grace in the heart (James 1 : 18; John 16 : 8–11), and carries it on till the power of the whole man is pervaded by his influence, assimilated and fully subjected to Christ, John 17 : 17. And whereas it is said that the woman *took* and *hid* the leaven, so the inner principle of life comes from *without* (John 1 : 13), and the influence of the Spirit and truth in regeneration and sanctification is indeed hidden, silent and secret in its workings. Thus, as the parable of the mustard-seed illustrates the expansive power of truth by the principle of growth, that principle being in itself, this parable illustrates its pervading power by the principle of assimilation, that principle acting on a foreign mass till it is wholly pervaded and assimilated.

This parable may also illustrate this power of truth generally in Christ's kingdom. The meal in that case is the world, and the three measures may represent the world as inhabited by the descendants of the three sons of Noah. The leaven *taken* and *hid* in the meal, the kingdom of Christ as not of the world, but spiritual, a kingdom of truth, reigning in the hearts of its subject, coming not with "observation" but quietly pervading humanity, and drawing men to the truth, and conforming them to the image of Christ. This work is to go on till the *whole is leavened*, till the kingdom is completely triumphant, and the kingdom of the world becoming our Lord's and his Christ's, Rev. 11 : 15; Dan. 7 : 17.

34, 35. CONCLUSION OF THE PARA-

A.D. 28.　　　　　MATTHEW XIII.　　　　　193

34 ᵇ All these things spake Jesus unto the multitude in parables; and without a parable spake he not
35 unto them: that it might be fulfilled which was spoken by the prophet, saying, ᶜ 'I will open my mouth in parables; ᵈ I will utter things which have been kept secret from the foundation of the world.'
36 Then Jesus sent the multitude away, and went into the house. And his disciples came unto him, saying, ᵉ Declare unto us the parable of the tares of the field.
37 He answered and said unto them, ᶠ He that soweth
38 the good seed is ᵍ the Son of man; ʰ the field is the world; the good seed are ⁱ the children of the kingdom; but the tares are ʲ the children of the wicked

ᵃ Hos. 6. 3; Phil. 1. 6.
ᵇ Mk. 4. 33, 34.
ᶜ Ps. 78. 2.
ᵈ Ps. 49. 4; Ro. 16. 25, 26; Eph. 3. 9; Col. 1. 26.
ᵉ ch. 15. 15, 16.
ᶠ ver. 24.
ᵍ Dan. 7. 13; ch. 16. 13.
ʰ ch. 24. 14; 28. 19 –20; Mk. 16. 15; Lk. 24. 47; Ro. 10. 18.
ⁱ Ro. 8. 17; 1 Pet. 1. 23.

BLES SPOKEN TO THE MULTITUDES, Mark 4: 33, 34.

34. All these things. Concerning the kingdom of heaven. **Spake he not.** According to the highest critical authorities, **spake he nothing.** On this occasion he confined himself to parables in his instructions to the multitude (ver. 13), and according to Mark (4: 34), in private "he expounded all things to his disciples," of which we have two instances in this chapter. See vers. 10, 36.

35. Matthew points to a fulfillment of prophecy, Ps. 78: 2. The author of this Psalm (see its superscription) was Asaph, and called in 2 Chron. 29: 30 a *seer* or prophet. It is a typical prophecy (see on ch. 1: 23), the prophet himself being typical of Christ. Remember that the Spirit of Christ was in the prophets, 1 Pet. 1: 11. The history of Israel which he recounts was typical of higher mysteries in Christ's kingdom, as Paul also teaches, 1 Cor. 10: 6-11. **Kept secret.** Things *hidden*, unrevealed, the mysteries. **From the foundation of the world** is a free translation of the Hebrew *from of old*, meaning from the commencement of creation, or the beginning of human history. These eternal mysteries concerning Christ's kingdom and human history Jesus now propounds in parables.

36-43. INTERPRETATION OF THE PARABLE OF THE TARES. Only in Matt.

36. Then Jesus sent, etc. Rather, *Then leaving the multitudes he went*, etc. (correct text), showing that these parables were spoken on the same occasion. **The house.** Probably where he resided at Capernaum. **His disci-**ples. The twelve and others who acknowledged him as the Messiah. On a similar occasion Mark (4: 10) says, "they that were about him with the twelve." **Declare unto us.** Explain, unfold to us the meaning of the parable.

37. Jesus proceeds to interpret the parable. Its grand *design* is to show the principle by which the wicked are to be treated under the kingdom of Christ. This incidentally brings in the treatment of the righteous. Its *centre* of comparison is between the tares remaining with the wheat till harvest, and the wicked with the righteous till the end of the world. He that soweth the good seed is the **Son of Man;** the Messiah; human, though divine; and most important in this parable, *the Son* of *humanity*, in the highest sense, having an interest in the whole human race. See on ch. 8: 20. The sowing of the gospel seed by Christ's servants may be included, since they are his representatives.

38. The field is **the World.** The whole earth with its inhabitants; mankind. The field was not limited to the Jewish nation, but was co-extensive with the race. The **good seed,** as sowed and springing up, are the **children of the kingdom,** that is, subjects of the kingdom, the children of God, heirs of God and joint-heirs with Christ. Many interpreters suppose that this parable illustrates the mixed condition of righteous and wicked in the church of Christ. But this is evidently too limited a view. *The field is the world.* Jesus has no reference to his churches as such. His true followers constitute the subjects of his kingdom on earth.

39 *one;* ᵏ the enemy that sowed them is the devil; ˡ the harvest is the end of the world; and the reap-
40 ers are the angels. As therefore ᵐ the tares are gathered and burned in the fire; ⁿ so shall it be in
41 the end of this world. The Son of man shall send forth his angels, ᵒ and they shall gather out of his kingdom all things that offend, ᵖ and them which
42 do iniquity; ᵍ and shall cast them into a furnace of fire; ʳ there shall be wailing and gnashing of
43 teeth. ˢ Then shall the righteous shine forth as the

ʲ Ge. 3. 15; John 8. 44; Ac. 13. 10; 1 John 3. 8.
ᵏ ver. 25; Eph. 2. 2.
ˡ Joel 3. 13; Rev. 14. 15.
ᵐ ver. 49.
ⁿ Gal. 6. 7, 8.
ᵒ ch. 18. 7; Ro. 16. 17; 2 Pet. 2. 1, 2.
ᵖ Ro. 2. 6, 8, 9, 16; Rev. 21. 27.
ᵍ Rev. 19. 20; 20. 10.

His kingdom is *in* the world, though not *of* the world. The great Donatist controversy in the African church during the fourth and fifth centuries centered around this parable. The Catholics, represented by Augustine, opposed the strict discipline of the Donatists, claiming that this parable taught that the good and bad were to remain in the church to the end of the world, and hence that wicked men should be tolerated in the church. The Donatists, on the other hand, holding to strict church discipline and to the purity of the church from unworthy members so far as it was possible, truthfully replied, that the parable had no bearing on the controversy, for Christ himself declared *the field is* not the church, but *the world*. **The children of the wicked one,** or *of evil,* whether among the professed friends or enemies of Christ. See Appendix.

39. The enemy that sowed them is **the devil,** who is called in the preceding verse the wicked, or evil one. The word *devil* means *slanderer,* or *false accuser.* See on ch. 4: 1. In a sense he is the author of all sin and the dispenser of error, either personally or through his servants.

At this point Jesus passes over the proposal of the servants to pull up or weed out the tares, and the answer of the householder. The analogy, however, is so plain that it needs no comment. Besides, what immediately follows implies that the righteous and wicked are to be left in a mixed condition till the end of the world. The rooting out of the tares does not refer to the exclusion of the ungodly from any particular church (1 Cor. 5: 13), but to the extirpation of them from the world. Christ's kingdom is not one of worldly conquest, but of spiritual triumph. His servants are not to use carnal but spiritual weapons. They are not to be persecutors, destroyers, and avengers, but the messengers of peace. The essential principle of religious freedom or soul-liberty is here involved. Christ will attend to the rooting out of the wicked from the world. His followers must not undertake his work. "Vengeance is mine; I will repay, saith the Lord," Rom. 12: 19.

The **harvest** is the **end of the world,** the end of the present dispensation and of probationary time. The reapers are **angels;** the article should be omitted. *Angel* means *messenger,* and the word is here applied to spirits who are holy, and of a higher order than man, Ps. 8: 5. Compare ch. 25: 31.

40. **Gathered and burned; so shall it be,** etc. Not only shall the wicked be separated from the righteous, like the tares from the wheat, but like them they shall be burned.

41. The **Son of Man** is to be the Judge, John 5: 27. The **angels** are **his,** and they shall go forth as his official messengers to gather the wicked. **Out of his kingdom.** The world belongs to Christ (Ps. 2: 8, 9), and the dispensation of the Gospel bears a relation to every human being, Mark 16: 15. **All things that offend.** All stumbling-blocks, or causes of offense, whether of persons or things, Zeph. 1: 3. **And them that do iniquity,** not only that which causes iniquity, but them that practice it. There shall be a separation both of good and evil individuals and of good and evil things.

42. **Furnace of fire.** This represents the punishment of the wicked, which will consist of the most intolerable sufferings. **Wailing and gnashing of teeth** are the outward expressions of extreme anguish, denoting the extreme and unutterable distress of the wicked, ch. 25: 41.

A.D. 28.   MATTHEW XIII.   195

sun ᵗ in the kingdom of their Father. ᵘ Who hath ears to hear, let him hear.

44 Again, the kingdom of heaven is like unto ᵛ treasure hid in a field; the which when a man hath found, he hideth, and for joy thereof goeth and ʷ selleth all that he hath, and ˣ buyeth that field.

ᵗ ver. 50; ch. 8. 12.
* ch. 25. 34, 46; Dan. 12. 3; 1 Cor. 15. 41-54.
ᵗ ch. 26. 29; Lk. 22. 29; Jam. 2. 5.
ᵘ ver. 9.
ᵛ Pro. 2. 2-5; 16. 16.

43. **Then shall the righteous.** Then shall "the children of the kingdom" **shine forth as the sun,** as it breaks forth from a cloud, Dan. 12 : 3. They shall no longer sojourn, as it were, under a cloud, but shine forth inexpressibly glorious. **In the kingdom of their Father.** This is the heavenly garner, answering to the *barn* of the *wheat* in verse 30; the new heavens and the new earth wherein dwelleth righteousness, 2 Pet. 3 : 13. The expression is peculiar. It is *the kingdom of their Father*, that spoken of in 1 Cor. 15 : 24, at the consummation of all things. Attend then to these solemn truths, and act in view of them.

44. **The parable of the hidden treasure.** Found in Matthew only. How the kingdom of God must be valued, and an interest in it secured.

44. This parable, and the two that follow, were spoken to the disciples in the house after the explanation of the Tares. It will be found that while the four preceding parables were adapted to the promiscuous multitude, these were specially adapted to the disciples. **Again** is not found in the best manuscripts. It was not needed at the beginning of a new series of parables. **Treasure.** A treasure of gold, jewels, etc. **Hid in a field.** Hidden in the field. A treasure hidden in *the* field, was, as Lange suggests, one left there without any special owner. In the east, where the governments were despotic, and the country was subject to revolutions, invasions, and calamities of various kinds, the hiding of treasures was common, and so lost through the absence or the death of the owner, Job 3 : 21; Prov. 2 : 4; Jer. 41 : 8. **Which a man hath found.** A man, probably digging for some purpose in the field, found it. Dr. Thomson relates that some workmen, a few years ago, while digging in a garden in Sidon, found several copper pots containing a large quantity of ancient gold coin, which he supposes must have been buried during the reign of Alexander the Great, or immediately after. He also says, that while multitudes in the east are either secretly or openly searching for treasures, yet it is remarkable that they are always discovered accidentally. —*The Land and the Book*, vol. i. pp. 194-197. **He hideth it.** He conceals it; again hides the treasure, either by covering it again, or burying it elsewhere in the field. **For joy thereof.** For joy of the treasure; or, as some would have it, because of his joy, he goes and sells all that he has, and buys the field. Thus, according to Jewish law, he becomes the legal possessor both of the field and its treasure. Buying the field, and thus securing the treasure, rather than taking the treasure at once without purchasing the field, was an element of honesty on his part, and must have been so considered by the disciples. Jesus refers not to an unheard-of occurrence. To have discussed the absolute right of the transaction would have been foreign to our Savior's purpose, since the eagerness to obtain the treasure at any cost is the great point of comparison.

The grand *design* of the parable is to show the earnestness and self-sacrificing zeal necessary in obtaining heavenly treasures. The *centre* of comparison is found in the man obtaining the treasure by any trouble and at any cost, however great. The *field* represents the kingdom of heaven as it is received into the heart, 1 Cor. 3 : 21-23. *The treasure*, the blessings of that kingdom, salvation, eternal life. The *man* finding the treasure unexpectedly, represents the fortuitous discoverer of truth; one who stumbles, as it were, upon the truth, or to whom the truth comes with awakening or convincing power suddenly or unexpectedly. The woman of Samaria was a striking example of this class, John 4 : 28, 29. Compare also Isaiah's prophecy concerning the gospel being extended to the Gentiles, "I am sought of them that asked not for me; I am found of them

45 Again, the kingdom of heaven is like unto ʸ a
46 merchant man, ᶻ seeking goodly pearls: who, when he had found ᵃ one pearl of great price, went ᵇ and sold all that he had, and bought it.
47 Again, the kingdom of heaven is like unto a net, that was cast into the sea, and ᶜ gathered of every
48 kind; which, when it was full, they drew to shore,

ʷ ch. 19. 27, 28; Phil. 3. 7-9; Heb. 11. 24-26.
ᶻ Is. 55. 1; Rev. 3. 18.
ʸ ch. 16. 26.
ᵃ Ps. 4. 6, 7.
ᵇ Pro. 3. 13-18; 8. 10, 19; Eph. 3. 8; Col. 2. 3.

---

that sought me not," Isa. 65 : 1; Rom. 10 : 20. His hiding the treasure, selling all that he had, and buying the field, represents the giving up all, and receiving Christ and his kingdom into the heart. He has a receptive nature, he is in a prepared condition to receive the truth, and having discovered it, and appreciating its value, he seeks first the kingdom of God and his righteousness (ch. 6 : 33), and takes it by force, ch. 11 : 12. The suddenness and the greatness of the discovery arouses his whole emotional nature to its height, and he enters the kingdom with great joy.

It is also analogous with the parables of this chapter to interpret this as follows: The *field* is the world; the *man*, the Son of Man; the *treasure*, his chosen, believing people; *his selling all*, his becoming poor for our sake; his *buying the field*, the purchase of redemption by his death and blood, thus becoming the Savior of his people and the Judge of all, Ps. 2 : 8, 9; Phil. 2 : 9-11. The joy of the man, the joy set before him who endured the cross, Heb. 12 : 2.

45, 46. THE PARABLE OF THE PEARL OF GREAT PRICE. Found only in Matthew. How the kingdom of heaven must be sought.

45. **Merchant man.** A merchant, *merchantman* being now only used of a trading vessel, as distinguished from a ship-of-war. **Goodly pearls.** The pearl has from a most early period been esteemed as a precious stone, and used as an ornament. See on ch. 7 : 6. The merchant was in search of *goodly* pearls, not of inferior but of superior quality; not defective, but perfect.

46. **One pearl of great price.** This was very superior, and worth more than many other pearls which he had seen, though they may have been goodly of their kind. Almost fabulous prices were sometimes paid for pearls of unusual size and brilliancy.

The grand *design* of this parable is to show the earnestness and whole-heartedness with which salvation must be sought. Its *centre* of comparison is found in the merchant selling all he had and buying the pearl. The *merchant* represents the sincere inquirer after truth; the *goodly pearls*, wisdom, knowledge, philosophy, religious truth, things with which to satisfy the cravings of man's higher spiritual nature; *the pearl of great price*, the kingdom of God in the heart, which may be expressed by eternal life, or by the knowledge of God and of Jesus Christ, whom he has sent (John 17 : 3), or by Christ, who is to be received and formed in the heart, Col. 1 : 27. The selling all and buying the pearl represents giving up all to Christ, who takes up his abode in the heart and gives eternal life. Compare Prov. 2 : 3-8; 23 : 23; Rev. 3 : 18.

This and the preceding parable present two phases in men's reception of the Gospel. To some it comes unexpectedly; others, conscious of their own sinfulness and of the emptiness of earthly things, seek for the true good, and, guided by the Holy Spirit, find it in Christ. Mary, who had found the one thing needful, is an example of the latter class, Luke 10 : 41, 42.

Or this parable may be interpreted as follows: *Merchant*, is Christ; the *pearl of great price*, his chosen people; *selling all and buying it*, the laying aside of his glory, his humiliation and death upon the cross, by which redemption was secured.

47-49. THE PARABLE OF THE FISHING-NET. Found only in Matthew. Nominal professors shall be finally separated from the true, and punished.

47. **Net.** The word thus translated means a drag-net, a net of the largest size, and often of immense length, one thrown into the sea, and drawn to the shore. **Every kind.** Every sort or species of fish.

48. **Shore.** The flat, sandy beach or bank. **The good — the bad.** The choice and valuable; the maimed, putrid,

A.D. 28.   MATTHEW XIII.   197

and sat down, and gathered the good into vessels,   b ver. 44.
49 but cast the bad away. So shall it be at the end of   c ch. 22. 9, 10; 25. 1-4.
the world : d the angels shall come forth, and e sever   d ver. 39.
50 the wicked from among the just, f and shall cast   e ch. 22. 12-14; 25. 5-12, 32; 2 Thes.
them into the furnace of fire : there shall be wailing   1. 7-10; Rev. 20. 12-15.
and gnashing of teeth.
51 Jesus saith unto them, Have ye understood all   f ver. 42.

---

and worthless. So also may be included in the two classes the clean and the unclean, Lev. 11 : 9-11. This parable was very appropriate to his disciples, both because some of them had been fishermen, and because they were called to be fishers of men. Some suppose the parable founded on some actual occurrence, of which the disciples had knowledge, similar to that described in Luke 5 : 4-11. "Some must row the boat, some cast out the net, some on the shore pull the rope with all their strength, others throw stones and beat the water round the ends, to frighten the fish from escaping there; and, as it approaches the shore, every one is active in holding up the edges, drawing it to land, and seizing the fish. This is the net (the great drag-net) which gathered of every kind, and, when drawn to the shore, the fishermen sit down and gather the good into vessels and cast the bad away. I have watched this operation throughout a hundred times along the shore of the Mediterranean."—Dr. Thomson, *The Land and the Book*, vol. ii. p. 80.

49, 50. Jesus adds a partial interpretation, **So shall it be at the end of the world,** at the end of the present dispensation, at the final judgment. The grand *design* of the parable is to teach the final separation of false professors from the true, and their awful destruction. The *centre* of comparison is found in gathering the good into vessels and casting the bad away. *The net* represents the church, with its ministers, instrumentalities, and ordinances; the *sea,* the world, into which the gospel-net is cast; the *fish taken,* the members of churches, consisting of persons of all classes in society, and of all nations, including the truly pious, the deceived, and the hypocritical. The *shore* represents the shore of time, the limit of the gospel dispensation, when will occur the final judgment. The *good fish* are true Christians; the *bad* are false professors. When **the angels,** as represented in the parable of the tares (ver. 41), **shall sever the wicked from among the just.** It is noticeable that *fishermen* are not mentioned in the parable. It was not Christ's design to bring his ministering servants prominently into view in this connection. The *vessels* into which the good fish are gathered are the heavenly mansions (John 14 : 2), the kingdom prepared from the foundation of the world, ch. 25 : 34. *Casting the bad away* represents their everlasting destruction from the presence of the Lord (2 Thess. 1 : 9). The intensity of their sufferings is represented in verse 42, by the terrible figures, a furnace of fire, wailing and gnashing of teeth. A fitting close to this series of parables.

A re-examination of this parable, several years after the above was written, leads me to modify my former interpretation. It is *the kingdom of heaven* (ver. 47), or the gospel dispensation, which is represented by *the net.* Under its influence are all classes. It separates men into the bad and the good. The gospel proves a savor of death unto death, or of life unto life. It is thus preparing men for the judgment, when the final separation will be made. This parable and that of the tares are similar, and yet different. That principally illustrates the present intermixture of the good and bad; and teaches that we must not take the Judge's work into our own hands, and attempt to destroy the ungodly from the world. But in this the influence of the gospel upon men in this world is incidentally, and the final separation of the righteous and the wicked is principally, illustrated.

51-53. A GENERAL CONCLUSION OF THESE PARABLES, in which he exhorts his disciples to an intelligent and faithful use of the treasures of truth, following his example in their instructions. Only in Matthew.

51. **Have ye understood all these things?** Not only the parables which

these things? They say unto him, Yea, Lord. 52 Then said he unto them, Therefore every ᵍ scribe ʰ *which is* instructed unto the kingdom of heaven is like unto a man *that is* an householder which bringeth forth out of his treasure ⁱ *things* new and

ᵍ Ezra 7. 6.
ʰ Ecc. 12. 9–11; Col. 3. 16; 2 Tim. 3. 16, 17.
ⁱ John 13. 34; 1 John 2. 7, 8.

---

he had expounded in whole or in part, but also those which he had not expounded. **Yea, Lord.** They thought they understood them, and doubtless they did to a certain extent; but not so fully as afterward, under the enlightening influences of the Holy Spirit. They were to understand (ver. 11) and unfold them to men. The words, **Jesus saith unto them** and **Lord,** are wanting in the best manuscripts.

These seven parables had opened a broad field of practical religious truth before them. The opening parable was followed by two series of three each, the first series closing his parables to the multitude, the second spoken privately to his disciples, and connected with the first series by the interpretation of the tares. A close similarity has been noticed between the tares and the fishing-net, between the mustard-seed and the leaven, and between the hidden treasure and the pearl of great price. Four great channels of truth and thoughtful instruction are thus opened: First, The various classes of hearers and their different receptions of truth, the causes and consequences in this world (the sower). Second, The self-developing and growing power of truth, on the one hand, and its assimilating and subduing power, on the other, in individuals, communities, and the world (mustard-seed and leaven). Third, The supremacy of the truth, of Christ and the Gospel, over the whole moral, intellectual, and emotional being of his followers (the hidden treasure and pearl of great price). Fourth, The two great classes of persons in the world, their spiritual origin, the divine treatment toward the wicked in this world, resulting in their final destruction in another; and since the wicked are found even in the church, escaping the scrutiny of men, they shall be finally and surely separated and destroyed with the openly wicked at the day of judgment (the tares and fishing-net).

Some suppose that these seven parables present a bird's-eye view of the inner life of the church, from its first sowing to its final consummation. But all such attempts have been marked with inconsistencies and caprice. The main object of parables is not prophecy, but instruction; not to reveal the history, but the mysteries of Christ's kingdom. They indeed foretell, but foretelling is rather the means to the end; and only what is necessary to the instruction imparted.

52. **Therefore** connects this verse with the last, as a practical improvement: You say you understand all these things; well, then, consider your duties as scribes, instructed in the kingdom of heaven, and as I have taught you, so do ye teach others. This he enforces by the similitude of a householder. **Every scribe.** The Jewish scribe was a transcriber and interpreter of the law. The conception of scribe Jesus here transfers to religious teachers and disciples in his kingdom, ch. 23 : 2; John 9 : 28. **Instructed.** Literally, *discipled*, one converted to and taught in the truths and doctrines of Christ's kingdom. Every teacher or disciple thus taught is like a **householder,** a master of a house. Christ is the great householder (ch. 10 : 25; 13 : 27, 37); ministers as his ambassadors are especially householders under him. **His treasure.** From his *store*, of grain, provisions, supplies, etc. This represents the store of spiritual, experimental, and practical knowledge of gospel doctrines, duties, and ordinances. **New and old.** New and old supplies; products of this and former years. Thus the spiritually instructed teacher in the Gospel will bring forth truths of every kind adapted to every class of hearers. *Old* truths under the Law, *new* truths under the Gospel; *old* truths long familiar, *new* truths, not known before to the hearers; and *old* truths, as expressed in certain set forms, and hence in certain phases; *new*, that is, the same truths reproduced in new and living forms, and presented in a new light.

53. **Finished these parables.** These words afford an additional proof that the seven preceding parables were spoken at one time; and the words, de-

A.D. 28.   MATTHEW XIII.   199

53 old. And it came to pass, *that* when Jesus had finished these parables, he departed thence.

Jesus teaches, and is rejected, at Nazareth.

54 ᵏAND when he was come into his own country, ˡhe taught them in their synagogue, insomuch that they were astonished, and said, Whence hath this 55 *man* this wisdom, and *these* mighty works? Is not this the carpenter's son? ᵐIs not his mother called Mary; and ⁿhis brethren ᵒJames, and Joses, and 56 Simon, and Judas? and his sisters, are they not all with us? Whence then hath this *man* all these things?

ᵏ Mk. 6. 1–6; ch. 2. 23; Lk. 4. 16. 23.
ˡ Ps. 22. 22; 40. 9, 10.

ᵐ ch. 1. 18–20; Ac. 1. 14.
ⁿ ch. 12. 46; Mk. 3. 31; 6. 3; Lk. 8. 19; John 2. 12; 7. 3, 5, 10; 1 Cor. 9. 5.
ᵒ Mk. 15. 40; Gal. 1. 19.

---

parted thence, that they were spoken at one place. Leaving Capernaum, he crosses the Sea of Galilee (Mark 4 : 35), stills the tempest, heals the demoniacs at Gadara, returns, performs certain miracles, and goes to Nazareth.

54–58. JESUS REVISITS NAZARETH AND IS AGAIN REJECTED, Mark 6 : 1–6. Compare the account of his first rejection in Luke 4 : 16–29, just before his removal to Capernaum, ch. 4 : 13.

54. His own country. Nazareth and its vicinity, where he was brought up. See on ch. 2 : 23. **In their synagogue.** Synagogue means an *assembly*, *congregation*, and is applied to a religious gathering having certain religious powers (Acts 9 : 2; 13 : 43), and to the place where the Jews met for worship on ordinary occasions, ch. 6 : 2, 5; Luke 7 : 5. In this case it was doubtless both in their stated meeting, and also in the place built for their religious gatherings. See on ch. 4 : 23. Mark (6 : 2) says it was upon the Sabbath. How much in keeping with the compassion of Jesus to visit his townsmen again and preach to them the Gospel after their former ungrateful treatment! **Astonished.** Struck with amazement. They were amazed that their former humble townsman should speak in such a manner, and perform such miracles. Their wonder had, as is often the case, a hardening effect; they were jealous, envious, and offended, ver. 57; Acts 13 : 41. **Whence then hath,** etc.? They acknowledge his wisdom and his miracles, but by their questions imply that such wisdom and works looked suspicious in one of such humble condition and advantages. They would not accept them as his own, yet they could not account for them.

55, 56. The carpenter's son. Carpenter is here used in the widest sense, one who does all kinds of work in wood. The question is not one of contempt so much as of surprise; for the occupation of carpenter has always been regarded as among the most respectable manual employments. His old neighbors regarded Jesus not as inferior to themselves, but only as their equal. The evidences of his superiority excited his envy and wonder, and these evidences they would question and reason away.

His brethren, James and Joses, and Simon and Judas, and his sisters. Some suppose these to have been his *cousins;* others, that they were his *half-brothers,* children of Joseph by a former marriage; and others still, his *own brothers,* the younger children of Mary. The latter view is the correct one, which will appear from the following:

1. The brothers of Jesus are mentioned in the following passages: ch. 12 : 46, 47; 13 : 55, 56; Mark 3 : 31, 32; 6 : 3; Luke 8 : 19, 20; John 2 : 12; 7 : 3, 5, 10; Acts 1 : 14; 1 Cor. 9 : 5; Gal. 1 : 19.

2. There is nothing in the language or connection of any of these passages demanding that these persons should not be regarded as real literal brothers of Jesus. The presumption is therefore that they were.

3. It is not certain from the New Testament that Jesus had any cousins according to the flesh. John 19 : 25 is the only passage on which such an opinion can be grounded. *"His mother's sister"* evidently does not refer to Mary, the wife of Cleopas, for we can not suppose two Marys in one family without any other designation. By comparing Mark 15 : 40, the opinion of several eminent critics seems probable, that Salome is

57 And they ᵖ were offended in him. But Jesus said unto them, ۹ A prophet is not without honor, save ᵖ ch. 11. 6. ۹ Lk. 4. 21; John 4. 44.

meant. Yet this is uncertain in the light of ch. 27 : 55; for *many women were there.*
4. In every instance in the Gospels, except in John ch. 7, the brothers of Jesus are mentioned in connection with his mother; and since *mother* is taken in the literal sense, so *brothers* should be also. In ch. 12 : 50, the force of our Savior's declaration depends greatly on the fact that they were literally his brothers. To suppose them to be the sons of Alpheus, who is regarded the same as Cleopas (John 19 : 25), is to suppose them to have been among the apostles.
5. But this could not have been the case; for they did not believe in Jesus for some time after the appointment of the apostles, John 7 : 3, 5, 10. In Acts 1 : 14 they are distinguished from the apostles, and therefore could not have been of them. In Gal. 1 : 19, James, the Lord's brother, does not point necessarily to James the apostle; for that passage may mean, according to Dr. Schaff and others, "But no other of the apostles (besides Peter) did I see, only James, the Lord's brother." The names of our Lord's brothers were very common among the Jews, and therefore it is not strange that we find them among the children of Alpheus, and the apostles. We have even among the latter two Jameses, two Simons, and two Judases.
6. That they were children of Mary, and not of a former wife of Joseph, appears evident from the fact that with one exception they are always, in the Gospels, associated with her; and also that, if they were the elder children of Joseph, then Jesus would not be the heir to David's throne. It has been objected to this view that Jesus (John 19: 26), committed the keeping of his mother not to these brethren, but to the apostle John. It may be answered, that his brethren did not fully believe on him till after the resurrection; and that John, being the most intimate bosom friend of Jesus, could better take his place than any other person. We therefore conclude that the brothers and sisters here mentioned by the people of Nazareth were the younger children of Mary, the mother of Jesus. See on ch. 12 : 46. Thus, the perpetual virginity of the mother of Jesus, as held by many Protestants, and by the Catholic and Greek church as an article of faith, is without scriptural foundation. This view is very fully and clearly developed by Dr. Schaff, in *Lange's Commentary,* Matt. 13 : 53–58.

57. **Offended in him.** Rather, *at him,* as an occasion of dissatisfaction and dislike. The meaning is, They took offense at him, who in his humble birth and circumstances was in no way superior to themselves, and yet who seemed so far to excel them in wisdom and mighty works. They were too proud and envious to receive him as their teacher, much less to regard him as the Messiah. See on ch. 11 : 6. Jesus does not resent their treatment, but accounts for it by what seems to be a proverbial expression, **A prophet is not without honor,** etc. This contained a general truth, a fact in human experience, of which the treatment of Jesus in the present instance was an example. He had exercised before them his prophetical office, both in teaching and performing miracles, yet they reject him. They were so familiar with his earthly relations and circumstances that they were absorbed with these, and neglected to view him in his spiritual character, in his public acts, and in his divine authority. A stranger sees the public and spiritual acts of a prophet, and recognizes his heavenly character; but neighbors and acquaintances fix their thoughts upon his earthly relationships, to a partial or a total exclusion of his higher excellences, and thus come to a wrong conclusion. Prejudice, rejection, are the result. Somewhat similar to this language of Jesus are the proverbs, "Familiarity breeds contempt;" "Distance lends enchantment to the view." That Jesus as a *prophet* should receive such treatment, was highly unreasonable and wicked on the part of his former neighbors and acquaintances. His wisdom and his miracles should have overcome all prejudice and unbelief. **His own house.** His own family; those with whom he was brought up from childhood, John 7 : 3–5.

58. **He did not many mighty**

58 in his own country, and in his own house. And ʳ he did not many mighty works there because of their unbelief.

ʳ Mk. 6. 5, 6.

works, not many miracles. The reason of this was their **unbelief,** which was brought to view in the preceding verse. We are not to suppose that he refused to perform miracles. They were too proud and envious to recognize his power publicly by bringing their sick to him, and too unbelieving to expect cures even if they brought them. *Unbelief* was at the bottom; for had they believed, their pride, envy, prejudice, would have vanished. Bringing their sick to him would have been an evidence of faith in his power; hence we may conclude that but few brought them. Mark (6:5) notices the more intimate connection of faith with his miracles. "He could there do no mighty work." He had the power to perform miracles, but for moral reasons he could not exercise it. As he can not with propriety save without faith, so he could not heal without faith. There was not a physical, but a moral impracticability.

REMARKS.

1. Like Jesus, let us sow seed beside all waters; in the house, in the open air, by the sea-side, vers. 1–3; Eccl. 11 : 1.
2. Nature and human experience have in them many parables which we should use in the illustration of truth. Many earthly things are types and figures of the spiritual and heavenly, vers. 4–8; Heb. 8 : 5; 9 : 23. Compare Ezekiel's vision of a city and temple, Ezek. chs. 40–48, and John's vision of the new Jerusalem, Rev. chs. 21, 22.
3. While God makes truth sufficiently plain to those of a humble, teachable spirit, he gives opportunity for stumbling to those who will not come to the knowledge of the truth that they may be saved, ver. 11 ; 2 Thess. 2 : 10–12.
4. If we would have more light and grace, we must improve what we already have, ver. 12 ; Ps. 36 : 9 ; 1 John 2 : 10 ; Matt. 25 : 26–29.
5. He that receives the word of God only in its outward form is still in spiritual darkness, vers. 13, 14 ; Deut. 29 : 2–4 ; John 9 : 39–41 ; 2 Cor. 3 : 15, 16.
6. Hardness of heart is a fruit of sin, to which obstinate sinners are justly given over, ver. 15 ; Rom. 1 : 28–31 ; 2 Thess. 2 : 11, 12 ; 2 Tim. 3 : 13.
7. Happy are they who see and hear Christ in his word ; for they see in reality and fulfillment what prophets saw only in vision, vers. 16, 17 ; Prov. 8 : 3, 4 ; 1 John 1 : 1–4.
8. The Gospel should be preached to all classes of persons, though none will be savingly benefited but they who receive it in an honest and good heart. Let all take heed how they hear, vers. 19–23 ; Mark 16 : 15, 16.
9. However faithfully the Gospel may be preached, careless and thoughtless hearers grow harder and harder, and more and more under the influence of the devil, ver. 19 ; 2 Cor. 2 : 16 ; James 1 : 23, 24.
10. It is not enough that truth excites the feelings and arouses the emotion without taking possession of the whole heart, vers. 20, 21.
11. Joy is not always the best sign of conversion, ver. 20 ; ch. 7 : 20.
12. We must expect trials if we enter into the service of Christ, ver. 21 ; Mark 10 : 29, 30.
13. Many serious impressions and deep convictions are checked by the cares and the love of the world, ver. 22 ; ch. 19 : 22 ; 1 John 2 : 15–17 ; Rom. 8 : 13.
14. Where the word of God is understandingly and truly received into the heart, the soul is subjected and united to Christ and brings forth fruit to God, ver. 23 ; John 15 : 4, 7, 8 ; Ps. 126 : 6.
15. Christ never intended that his disciples should engage in religious persecutions, or that they should exterminate error by exterminating errorists, ver. 28–30 ; 2 Cor. 10 : 4.
16. God spares the wicked for the sake of the righteous who dwell among them, ver. 29 ; Gen. 18 : 26–32 ; Isa. 1 : 9.
17. The word of God is a living seed not returning unto him void, vers. 31, 32 ; Isa. 55 : 11 ; John 6 : 63.
18. In the work of the Lord we should not despise the day of small things, but rather expect great endings from small beginnings, vers. 31, 32 ; Isa. 41 : 14–16 ; 51 : 1–4 ; 60 : 22.
19. Christianity has a hidden power in renewing and transforming the charac-

Herod holds Jesus to be John the Baptist, whom he had put to death.

XIV. AT that time * Herod the tetrarch heard of the

* Mk. 6. 14, 21–29; Lk. 9. 7.

ter and lives of men, and the state and condition of the world, ver. 33 ; Ps. 119:11; Dan. 2:44, 45 ; Mark 4:26–29; 2 Cor. 3 : 18 ; 1 Pet. 1 : 3, 4.

20. The Gospel reveals to us mysteries which from eternity had been hid in God, ver. 35 ; Rom. 16 : 25, 26 ; 1 Cor. 2 : 9, 10 ; Col. 1 : 26.

21. The devil and his agents are ever busy in sowing error, and such is the natural soil of the human heart that they spring up without cultivation, vers. 25, 38 ; Acts 20 : 28–30 ; James 3 : 15.

22. Since error is often made to resemble the truth, as false professors do the true, it becomes us to take heed how and what we hear, ver. 38 ; Mark 4 : 24 ; 2 Cor. 9 : 13–15 ; Phil. 3 : 2 ; 2 Tim. 3 : 5.

23. The Gospel dispensation is to have an end, when every man's destiny is to be fixed according to his true character in the sight of God, vers. 39–43 ; ch. 24 : 30, 31 ; 2 Cor. 5 : 10 ; 2 Pet. 3 : 10 ; Rev. 22 : 11, 12.

24. The punishment of the wicked shall be unspeakably great, ver. 42; Nah. 1 : 6 ; Rev. 20 : 13–15.

25. The state of the righteous will be unspeakably glorious, ver. 43 ; 1 John 3 : 2 ; Rev. 22 : 5.

26. A discovery of the worth of the soul and the value of heavenly treasures will do us no good except we give up all to Christ, ver. 44 ; Luke 14 : 33.

27. Seeking salvation will avail nothing except we seek aright; none seek aright except with the whole heart ; and none with the whole heart except they value Christ above all things, vers. 45, 46 ; Job 28 : 12–18 ; Prov. 2 : 4, 5 ; Jer. 29 : 13 ; Phil. 3 : 7–9.

28. We must expect a mixture of evil with good in the churches of Christ, vers. 47, 48 ; John 6 : 70 ; 2 Pet. 2 : 1–3.

29. Churches should maintain a strict discipline, though they may not expect to free themselves entirely from unworthy members. Many of these can be certainly discovered only by the Searcher of hearts, ver. 47, 48 ; 1 Cor. 5 : 13 ; 2 Thess. 3 : 14, 15 ; Rev. 2 : 23.

30. Let not hypocrites and false professors think they are safe because they are among Christ's visible followers ; a final separation is to take place, vers. 49, 50 ; Job 27 : 8 ; Rev. 21 : 27.

31. Christ has set us an example of teaching by parables and illustrations, vers. 3, 52.

32. Ministers and all religious teachers should be learners at the feet of Jesus, making his word their own, and bringing forth newly-discovered truth with the old, according to the capacity and wants of their hearers, vers. 51, 52 ; Prov. 10 : 20, 21 ; Col. 3 : 16 ; 1 Tim. 4 : 14–16.

33. Like Jesus, we should bring the words of life to the unconverted of our own friends and neighbors, ver. 54.

34. Infidels and skeptics, like the inhabitants of Nazareth, seek to account for spiritual things by natural causes, and failing in this are offended with Christ, and reject him and his Gospel, vers. 55–57 ; Luke 2 : 34 ; Acts 17 : 18.

35. How great the condescension of Jesus, the Son of the Great Carpenter of the Universe (Heb. 3 : 4), in that he became the Son of Joseph, the humble carpenter of Nazareth, ver. 55 ; Phil. 2 : 6–8.

36. To judge of persons by their wealth, relatives, and outward circumstances, and not by their character and conduct, is a mark of pride, prejudice, and littleness of mind, ver. 57 ; John 7 : 41, 52.

37. Unbelief is the great obstacle in the way of personal salvation, and the conversion of the world, ver. 58 ; John 16 : 9.

CHAPTER XIV.

Matthew records the death of John the Baptist, and the consequent relation of Jesus to Herod; the withdrawal of Jesus and his miracles, exhibiting his power over the materials and elements of nature.

1, 2. THE EFFECT OF THE FAME OF JESUS ON HEROD, Mark 6 : 14–16 ; Luke 9 : 7–9.

1. **At that time.** A general expression, meaning, at that season or period, about that time. See 12 : 1. **Herod.** Herod Antipas, the son of Herod the Great, who slew the children at Bethlehem. See on ch. 2 : 22. When the

2 fame of Jesus, and said unto his servants, 'This is John the Baptist; he is risen from the dead; and therefore mighty works do show forth themselves in him.
3 "For Herod had laid hold on John, and bound him, and put *him* in prison for Herodias' sake, ʸ his brother Philip's wife. For John said unto him,

t ch. 16. 14.
u Mk.6.17-20; Lk. 3. 19, 20; ch. 4. 12.
v Lk. 3. 1.

kingdom of his father was divided between him and his brothers, Archelaus and Herod Philip, he received the title of **tetrarch,** a Greek word, meaning a *ruler of a fourth part*, and which became a common title for those who governed any part of a province, subject only to the Roman emperor. Hence, in general and popular language he was also styled "king." See ver. 9. His dominions comprised Galilee and Perea. See vers. 6, 11.

Heard the fame of Jesus. He heard of Jesus in connection with the preaching of the twelve, ch. 10 : 5; Mark 6 : 7, 12, 14; Luke 9 : 1, 6, 7. It is probable that Herod was residing at Machærus, a frontier fortress near the Dead Sea, between Perea and Arabia, where John the Baptist was in prison. This, in connection with his voluptuous life, and his murder of John, which must at least have startled his conscience and made him uneasy, will explain how Herod seems now to have heard of Jesus for the first time. If he had heard before of him, it produced no impression on his mind; but now the *fame* of Jesus, the report of his miracles and preaching, at once arrested his attention, and produced anxiety in a mind filled with superstition and tortured by a guilty conscience.

2. **His servants.** His attendants, ministers, courtiers. **He is risen from the dead.** Thus the guilty conscience of Herod led him to imagine. *Dead* refers not to a mere state or condition, but to persons in that state, *from among the dead*. Some suppose that Herod was a Sadducee, from comparing ch. 16 : 6 with Mark 8 : 15, and that his guilt and fears now made him a cowardly believer in the doctrine of the resurrection. Infidels and skeptics have been known to renounce their unbelief in times of danger. **Therefore.** On account of this, because he is risen. **Mighty works do show forth themselves in him.** Rather, *These powers work*, or, *are active, in him.* John did not work miracles (John 10 : 41); but now, Herod reasons, these powers of working them are active in his person on account of his rising from the dead. He imagines John as having come forth from the dead, which would have been a miracle, and as having acquired on account of it new spiritual and miraculous power, which he regards as in harmony with such a supposition. His fears may have been excited lest Jesus might become a political rival, or lest his superhuman power might be directed against him.

3–12. ACCOUNT OF THE IMPRISONMENT AND DEATH OF JOHN, Mark 6 : 17–29.

3. **For.** This is explanatory of what Matthew had just stated concerning Herod in reference to John. **For Herodias' sake.** "A princess was the foe of the latter Elijah, as Jezebel of the former."—BENGEL. Herodias was grand-daughter of Herod the Great, daughter of Aristobulus, and niece of Herod Antipas. **Brother Philip.** Not the tetrarch of Iturea (Luke 3 : 1), but another brother who lived in private life, having been disinherited by his father. He also was uncle to Herodias, whom he married. But she, preferring royalty, left him, and married Herod Antipas, who, to make way for her, divorced his own wife, the daughter of Aretas, king of Arabia, supposed to be the one mentioned by Paul in 2 Cor. 11 : 32.

4. **It is not lawful,** etc. For, *first,* she was the wife of Philip, who was still living; *second*, Herod's wife, the daughter of Aretas, was also living; *third*, by marriage Herodias was the sister-in-law of Herod, and by Jewish law a person was forbidden to marry his brother's wife, Lev. 18:16; 20 : 21. This incident strikingly illustrates the character of John as a consistent and faithful reprover and preacher of righteousness. He preached as plainly to those in kings' palaces as to the inhabitants of the wilderness.

5 ᵂ It is not lawful for thee to have her. And when he would have put him to death, he feared the multitude, ˣ because they counted him as a prophet.
6 But when Herod's ʸ birthday was kept, the daughter of Herodias danced before them, and pleased Herod.
7 Whereupon he promised with an oath to give her
8 whatsoever she would ask. And she, being before instructed of her mother, said ᶻ Give me here

ᵂ Le. 18. 16; 20. 21.
ˣ ch. 21. 26; Mk. 11. 30–32; Lk. 20. 6.
ʸ Ge. 40. 20.

ᶻ Pro. 29. 10.

5. **When he would have put him to death.** Or, rather, *desiring to put him to death.* Mark adds the interesting fact that at first John produced a deep impression on Herod's mind, who regarded him as a holy and just man, and, hearing him gladly, did many things, and saved his life from the malice of Herodias, Mark 6 : 19, 20. Matthew, passing this by in silence, states the changed condition of Herod's mind, when he was desirous of putting John to death, caused, doubtless, by the constant influence of Herodias, and by the truth, which hardens when it does not soften; and was now only prevented by the popularity of John with the multitude, who regarded him as a prophet. These two accounts are thus perfectly consistent, and throw light on each other. Josephus, probably being aware of no other grounds, gives only political reasons, that Herod was afraid lest John might raise a rebellion, and, to prevent any such mischief, he caused him to be imprisoned and put to death. There is no difficulty in supposing this also to be true; for Herod may have acted from a variety of motives, both political and private. He did fear on account of the popularity of John with the people, and he may have feared lest the people might be aroused against him through the influence of John, on account of his unlawful marriage. The reproof of John and the influence of the malicious Herodias were, however, the private and exciting grounds of his action.

6. **Birthday.** Birthday festivities or celebration, Gen. 40 : 20. This, from Mark 6 : 21, appears to have been given to the nobility of Galilee. It doubtless took place at Machærus, where John was imprisoned, and it is very probable that Herod was at this time engaged in the war which Aretas, king of Arabia, declared against him on account of the insult to his daughter. **Daughter of Herodias.** According to Josephus, her name was *Salome*, a daughter by Philip. She was afterward married to her uncle Philip, the tetrarch of Iturea, and then to her cousin Aristobulus. **Danced before them.** Danced in the midst, in the sight of all. This was, doubtless, a mimic or theatrical dance. It was, however, considered beneath the dignity of persons of rank and character to engage in this amusement, and hence her dancing before them all was a sacrifice of decency and maidenly decorum. But the voluptuous Herod, and those with him, all, quite likely, more or less intoxicated, were **pleased,** doubtless, with the skill and grace of her performance, and with the condescension of a princess in thus honoring the birthday of the king.

7. Herod considered the act of Salome as meriting a reward, and so enraptured was he that he not only made a rash promise, but also confirmed it by an oath. **Whatsoever she would** (*should*) **ask.** "Unto the half of my kingdom," Mark 6 : 23. Compare Esth. 5 : 3. The case of Herod is only one of many examples of eastern monarchs lavishing gifts on favorite dancers. Thevenot, who died in 1667, in his *Travels in Persia,* mentions a Shah Abbas who, being much intoxicated, was so pleased with a woman that danced before him, that he gave her a magnificent khan that yielded him a considerable revenue. But becoming sober, at the instance of his minister, he broke his promise, and obliged the dancer to be content with a sum of money. Such instances show the evils and dangers of sensual excitements, and of such sensual amusements.

8. **Being before instructed.** Rather, *Led on by, urged on by.* The fuller account of Mark (6 : 24, 25) is the best comment on this clause. There was no secret understanding between the mother and daughter; but the latter, going out to consult with her mother, was induced to ask for the head of John the

9 John Baptist's head in a charger. And ᵃ the king was sorry: nevertheless, ᵇ for the oath's sake, and them which sat with him at meat, he commanded
10 *it* to be given *her*. And he sent, ᶜ and beheaded
11 John in the prison. And his head was brought in a charger, and given to the damsel: and she

ᵃ ver. 1; Mk. 6. 14.
ᵇ Judg. 11. 30, 31, 39; Dan. 6. 14, 15.
ᶜ Lk. 9. 9.

Baptist. Perhaps Herodias had a deep design in having her daughter dance before Herod, hoping thereby to gratify her malice against John. If so, her highest anticipations were gratified. **Give me here.** In this place, on the spot, and hence without delay. The language implies haste. Herodias has at length got her opportunity for revenge, and she eagerly seizes it, and determines to accomplish her purpose while Herod is flush with wine, and before he has time to repent. **Charger.** *On a platter. Charger*, in old English, means a large dish; but now a horse used in battle. The Greek word originally meant a board; then, among other applications of the term, a wooden dish, and then a plate, dish, or platter of any material.

9. The king. Mark also styles Herod king. Though he had not received the official title of king, he is so called in a popular and general sense, and from courtesy. **Was sorry.** This is perfectly consistent with his having *desired* to put John to death. He had not purposed so to do. Now, when the crisis comes, and he is called upon to behead John, in fulfillment of a rash oath, he is *sorry;* for he knows it is wrong, and he fears lest the people, who regard John as a prophet, may cause him trouble. He may also have been concerned for his popularity among the people. **For the oath's sake and them,** etc. Rather, *For the sake,* or, *on account of the oath, and of them that reclined at table with him.* A twofold reason: he must perform his oath, and he must maintain his honor among his guests. Duelists and gamblers act upon a similar principle. He had, doubtless, some scruples of conscience in regard to his oath; he did not wish to be a perjurer, much less to be regarded as one; neither did he wish to be ridiculed as mean and fickle by his attendants and guests, who, doubtless, hated John, and applauded the king in the generous offer he had made. He was overcome through pride and shame. His oath was wicked, because it was uncalled for, and hence taking the Lord's name in vain (Ex. 20 : 7), and because no one has a right to pledge himself beforehand to do what may be wrong. Herod had placed himself in a dilemma to make a choice of two evils—to break a rash, wicked oath, or to commit murder. He should have chosen the former as the less of the two. Compare Lev. 5 : 4-6.

10. Beheaded John. By an executioner (Mark 6 : 27), a soldier of Herod. **In prison.** The narrative seems to imply that the prison was near at hand, and the execution performed at once. Hence that the feast was at Machærus. Some suppose it was at Tiberias, on the shore of the Sea of Galilee; but it would have taken at least two days for the execution of the sentence. Others suppose that it took place at Julias or Livias, another place of residence of Antipas, situate not far from Machærus, in the mountains on the eastern side of the Dead Sea. This is less objectionable. But Machærus is more in keeping with the ease and quickness of the execution. It was in the night, and, doubtless, late, before the promise of Herod was made, and all was accomplished, we should naturally suppose, by or before the morning's light. See verse 1. The execution by a soldier may be used as a circumstantial argument that he was now actually engaged in the war with Aretas. This could not have been many months after the message of John in prison to Jesus (ch. 11 : 2); the reply of Jesus, doubtless, invigorated his faith, preparing him for the last conflict and a martyr's death. He had been in prison about seventeen months, and it was about three years from the commencement of his ministry; for the Passover was at hand (John 6 : 4), the third of our Savior's ministry, when the report of John's death was brought to Jesus. He was probably beheaded in March or April, A.D. 29.

11. His head was brought, etc. The request was strictly carried out in every particular. The language implies

12 brought *it* to her mother. And his disciples came, and took up the body, and buried it; and went and told Jesus.

Jesus retires to a desert place, and feeds the multitude.

13 ᵈ WHEN Jesus heard *of it*, he departed thence by ship into a desert place apart. And when the people had heard *thereof*, they followed him on foot out of the cities.

14 And Jesus went forth, and saw a great multitude, and ᵉ was moved with compassion toward them, and he healed their sick.

ᵈ Mk. 6. 32; Lk. 9. 10; John 6. 1; ch. 10. 23; 12. 15.

ᵉ ch. 9. 36; John 11. 33–35; Heb. 4. 15.

---

that the head was brought while the feast lasted, given to this heartless dancing maid, and by her to her mother, who was the principal actor and the guiltiest party in this terrible tragedy. Not long after this Herod was totally defeated and his army destroyed by Aretas, which, according to Josephus, some of the Jews regarded as a punishment from God for putting John the Baptist to death. Jos. *Antiq.* xviii. 2. A little later he was banished to Lyons, in France, whither Herodias followed him, and then to Spain, where they died.

12. **His disciples.** The disciples of John, Mark 6 : 29. **Told Jesus.** Related to him the circumstances of his death and burial. They knew the confidence and love that had existed between John and Jesus; they tell him as a friend of their master, and as one who would sympathize with them. This is an incidental evidence that the reply of Jesus to John's question (ch. 11 : 2–6) had resulted in good, both to John and his disciples.

13–21. JESUS RETIRES, AND MIRACULOUSLY FEEDS THE MULTITUDE, Mark 6 : 30–44; Luke 9 : 10–17; John 6 : 1–14.

13. **He departed thence.** He retired, withdrew from thence, from the western side of the Sea of Galilee, and from the vicinity of Tiberias, the usual residence of Herod Antipas, to the north-eastern side, and, according to Luke 9 : 10, to a place called Bethsaida. According to Josephus (*Jewish Antiq.* xviii. 2, 1), Philip the tetrarch advanced this Bethsaida to the dignity of a city, and named it *Julias.* See on ch. 11 : 21. He withdrew on hearing of the death of John the Baptist; Luke (9 : 9) adds that Herod, on hearing his fame, desired to see him. We may well suppose that Herod heard of Jesus very soon after putting John to death, and that several days elapsed before the disciples of John came and told Jesus. About that time the twelve return from their mission, and Jesus invites them to retire with him and rest awhile, Mark 6 : 30, 31. Thus Jesus had a complex reason for withdrawing to a **desert place,** an uncultivated and uninhabited region, in the vicinity of Bethsaida, namely, the death of John, the desire of Herod, the weariness of his disciples. See on ch. 12 : 15. As the imprisonment of John marked an era in our Lord's ministry (ch. 4 : 12), so does also the death of John. Then Jesus began his ministry in Galilee; now he extends it beyond the Sea of Galilee, and northward to the region of Tyre and Sidon (ch. 15 : 21), and of Cæsarea Philippi (ch. 16 : 13).

By ship. By a transport or merchant *boat*, a general name for such vessels of every grade. See on 8 : 23. **The people.** Rather, *the multitudes;* they who had been attending on the preaching of Jesus, Mark 6 : 31–33. **On foot.** In opposition to going by *ship,* Jesus and his disciples passed over the sea by ship; the multitude passed around the sea by land on foot.

14. **Went forth.** From the ship. The multitude had run and arrived there before him, Mark 6 : 33. Prominent among the motives that had drawn them were his miracles in healing the sick, John 6 : 2. Seeing them, he had **compassion,** pity on them, and **healed their sick,** and taught them many things, Mark 6 : 34. Jesus then goes up into a mountain with his disciples, and the multitudes follow, John 6 : 3.

15 ᶠ And when it was evening, his disciples came to him, saying, This is a desert place, and the time is now past; send the multitude away, that they may go into the villages, and buy themselves victuals.
16 But Jesus said unto them, They need not depart;
17 give ye them to eat. And they say unto him, ᵍ We
18 have here but five loaves, and two fishes. He said,
19 Bring them hither to me. And he commanded the multitude to sit down on the grass, and took the five loaves, and the two fishes, and looking up to heaven, ʰ he blessed, and brake, and gave the loaves to *his* disciples, and the disciples to the multitude.

ᶠ Mk. 6. 35; Lk. 9. 12; John 6. 5.

ᵍ ch. 15. 33. 31; Num. 11. 21-23; 1 Ki. 17. 10-16; 2 Ki. 4. 1-7, 42-44.

ʰ ch. 15. 36; 1 Sam. 9. 13.

15. **Evening.** This was the *first* evening, the decline of the day, beginning with the ninth hour, about three o'clock in the afternoon; the *second* evening (ver. 23) began at sunset. These two evenings are recognized in the command to keep the Passover. The lamb was to be killed "in the evening," literally, *between the two evenings*, Ex. 12 : 6; Num. 9 : 3, 5. According to Josephus, the paschal lamb was regularly killed between the ninth and the eleventh hour. In some parts of our country evening is applied to the afternoon. **The time is now passed.** *The hour;* used in a general sense, the time for preaching, for dismissing the people, and preparing for the evening meal is already past. It is now late. "The day was now far spent, . . . and now the time is far passed" (Mark); "The day began to wear away" (Luke). **Send the multitude away.** Dismiss them; do not longer teach them to-day.

16. Jesus declares that there is no necessity for the multitude leaving them, and commands his disciples to give them to eat. The miracle afterward performed showed that there was no necessity, and the disciples did give them to eat. Some of the disciples ask Jesus if they shall go and buy two hundred pennies' (*denaries*, about thirty dollars) worth of bread, Mark 6 : 37. Philip, whom Jesus had, in the mean time, asked, in order to try his faith, "Whence shall we buy bread that these may eat?" declared that two hundred denaries' worth was not sufficient, John 6 : 5-7.

17. **We have here but five loaves and two fishes.** From John we learn that they were barley loaves, an inferior kind of food, and two small fishes; that a lad had them, and that it was Andrew who gave the information, John 6 : 8, 9. Loaves were usually made in the form of round cakes, of different sizes, and generally about a half an inch thick. The language of the four Evangelists clearly implies that this was all the food at that time upon the ground. Compare Luke 11 : 5.

19. **To sit down on the grass.** *To recline* or *lie down* on the grass, according to the customary posture of eating. Mark says that they reclined on the green grass, in companies or groups, by hundreds and by fifties. It was a *desert*, not because it was barren, but because it was uninhabited and uncultivated. Dr. Thomson supposes that Butaiha, lying south-west of Bethsaida, along the north-east shore of the Sea of Galilee, is the spot of this miracle. "This Butaiha," says he, "belonged to Bethsaida. At this extreme south-east corner of it the mountain shuts down upon the lake bleak and barren. It was, doubtless, desert then as now; for it was not capable of cultivation. In this little cove the ships (boats) were anchored. On this beautiful sward, at the base of the rocky hill, the people were seated." —*The Land and the Book*, vol. ii., p. 29.

Blessed. Blessed God, *praised* him for these provisions, and implored a blessing in their reception, Luke 9 : 16. John says, "He gave thanks." The latter is included in the former. The word *bless* in the original is applied not only to praising God for favors (Luke 1 : 64); but also to invoking God's blessing (Luke 2 : 34); also to God's conferring favors, Heb. 6 : 14; Acts 3 : 26. Dr. Alexander suggests that these three senses here meet in one. This was, doubtless, true as a matter of fact; for, as a man, Jesus praised God,

20 And they did all eat, and were filled: and they took up of the fragments that remained twelve baskets
21 full. ¹ And they that had eaten were about five thousand men, besides women and children.

¹ ch. 15. 32-38.

Jesus sends away his disciples by ship, and comes to them walking on the water.

22 ᵏ And straightway Jesus constrained his disciples

ᵏ Mk. 6. 45; John 6. 15.

---

and implored his blessing, while, as God, he granted it. **And brake.** The usual way of preparing the bread for eating. The Scriptures speak of breaking bread, but never of cutting it.
20. **Were filled.** The appetites of all were fully satisfied. **Fragments.** Broken pieces of bread. It is most natural to suppose that these had been distributed, or mostly so, and that they were gathered up from the ground where the companies had eaten. Thus, in connection with this miracle, Jesus taught a lesson of prudent economy, "Gather up the fragments that remain that nothing be lost," John 6: 12. They would also serve, while they lasted, to remind the disciples of the miracle. **Baskets.** The usual Jewish traveling basket. The number was twelve, the same as that of the apostles, and they were full; there thus remaining much more than the original five loaves, showing an actual increase of food, and not a supernatural restraining and satisfying of the appetite. Mark adds that a portion of the fishes were also gathered up.
21. **About five thousand men besides.** All the four Evangelists say that there were about five thousand *men;* Matthew adds, **women and children,** of whom there were, doubtless, many. It was customary then as now, in the east, for men to eat alone, and the women and children by themselves. On this occasion the men lay down in companies of hundreds and fifties, and could easily be numbered; the women and children probably sat around promiscuously. It is not extravagant to suppose eight or ten thousand in all. The multitude may have been increased by those who were going up to the Feast of the Passover, which was at hand, John 6: 4.

This is the only miracle described by all the Evangelists, and is, on that account, especially important, and deserving of the most careful study. Various attempts have been made to explain it away, by endeavoring to trace it to natural causes, and even supposing it originally a parable, but by mistake related as an actual occurrence! But all such attempts bear upon their face the absurd and ridiculous. All of the four narratives clearly convey the idea of miraculous, superhuman power. They do not tell how that power was exerted, or how the food was increased; but they do clearly tell us, that a few loaves and fishes, which a lad could carry in his basket, were increased so that thousands satisfied their hunger, and there remained at least twelve times more of fragments than of the original provisions. It is not necessary to suppose creative power; for, the laws and elements of the natural world being under the direction of Jesus, he could have brought together at his will all the elements constituting the bread. The power in the one case is as equally omnipotent as in the other. In the Old Testament we have similar exhibitions of divine power in giving the manna (Ex. 16: 4), and in multiplying the widow's oil, 2 Kings 4: 2-7.

In this miracle Jesus also exhibited himself as the bread of life. It was a sign, an external evidence, that as he gave them bread for their bodies, so could he give them spiritual bread for their souls. See the application and use which Jesus himself makes of it in John 6: 26-35, 48-58. Though the multitude were blind to this deep spiritual import and design, they felt the force of the miracle as an evidence of the Messiahship of Jesus, and they exclaim, "Of a truth this is the Prophet that cometh into the world," John 6: 14. Possibly a tradition, that the Messiah would rain manna from heaven, may also have had its influence in leading them to this conclusion.

22-33. JESUS WALKS ON THE SEA.

to get into a ship, and to go before him unto the
23 other side, while he sent the multitudes away. ¹ And
when he had sent the multitudes away, ᵐ he went
up into a mountain apart to pray. ⁿ And when the
24 evening was come, he was there alone: but the ship
was now in the midst of the sea, tossed with waves:
for the wind was contrary.
25 And in the fourth watch of the night Jesus went

¹ Mk. 6. 46.
ᵐ ch. 6. 6; 26. 36; Mk. 1. 35; Lk. 5. 16; 6. 12; 9. 28, 29; John 11. 41, 42.
ⁿ John 6. 16.

This was a three-fold miracle: Jesus walking on the sea; Peter, through his power, upon the water; and the wind subsiding at his will, Mark 6 : 45-52; John 6 : 15-21.

22. **Constrained his disciples.** He compelled or obliged them, by authoritative persuasion and command, to embark. They dreaded a night passage, and to leave him behind; but he insisted on their going. They may have been among the foremost with the multitude to make him king (John 6 : 15); and Jesus may have quietly thwarted their design by immediately constraining his disciples first to embark in **the ship** in which they came hither, and then dismissing the people. The distress of that night on the sea, and the miracle, were, doubtless, what they needed to humble and enlighten them. **Unto the other side.** To the western Bethsaida of Galilee, Mark 6 ; 45. As this Bethsaida was near Capernaum, John could well say (John 6 : 17) that they were going over the sea to Capernaum, or in the direction of Capernaum. Or they may have intended to have gone to both places.

23. **A mountain.** Rather, *The mountain* which was in that vicinity. See on ver. 19. **To pray.** His object was not rest, but prayer. He sought to be alone to commune with his Father. What was the burden of his prayer, we know not. Doubtless it was in regard to his kingdom: doubtless the events of that day and night, the disciples, the multitude, their desire to make him king, and his future labors, formed a part. **Evening was come.** The second evening (see ver. 15), beginning with sunset, from about six to nine o'clock.

24. **The ship was now in the midst of the sea.** At first they have a prospect of a quick and easy passage, but soon the tempest rises. While Jesus is alone, they are already in the midst of the sea, not necessarily in its centre, but out at sea, at some distance from land, in its middle portions. **Tossed.** Rather, *vexed, troubled,* or *tormented* by the waves; the waves beat against the bow of the vessel, hindering its progress; **for the wind was contrary,** adverse, blowing from a westerly direction.

25. **Fourth watch.** Between about three and six o'clock in the morning. According to the Roman custom the Jews now divided the night into four watches of about three hours each. See Mark 13 : 35. At an earlier period they had divided the night into three equal parts or watches, of about four hours each, called "the first watch" (Lam. 2 : 19), "the middle watch" (Jud. 7 : 19), "the morning watch," 1 Sam. 11 : 11. At this time, when Jesus was seen coming to them, they had rowed about twenty-five or thirty furlongs, more than half way across, John 6 : 19. **Walking on the sea.** In the original the accusative of motion, *walking over the sea* for the purpose of joining his disciples. In distinction from this we have in the next verse, *walking on the sea,* the genitive of the mere appearing on the sea. In the first, we have the general fact stated of his going to them, walking *over* the sea ; in the second, the particular fact as first discovered by the disciples, walking *on* the sea. The silly evasion of those who, to explain away the miracle, would read, "walking on the shore of the sea," is opposed alike to the grammatical structure and to the scope, form, and particular portions of the narrative. The seeing of a person walking on the shore surely would have been no reason of surprise, much less of terror. How Jesus could walk on the water we are not informed, whether he suspended the law of gravity in reference to himself, or counteracted the force of gravity by divine power, or made the waters solid beneath his feet. The second supposition to me seems the

26 unto them, walking on the sea. And when the disciples saw him ° walking on the sea, they were troubled, saying, ᴾ It is a spirit; and they cried out
27 for fear. But straightway Jesus spake unto them, saying, Be of good cheer; ᑫ it is I; be not afraid.
28 And Peter answered him and said, Lord, if it be
29 thou, bid me come unto thee on the water. And he said, Come. And when Peter was come down out of the ship, ʳ he walked on the water to go to
30 Jesus. But when he saw the wind boisterous, ˢ he was afraid; and beginning to sink, he cried, say-
31 ing, Lord, ᵗ save me! And immediately Jesus stretched forth *his* hand, and caught him, and said unto him, O thou of little faith, ᵘ wherefore didst
32 thou doubt? And when they were come into the

° Job 9. 8.
ᴾ Lk. 24. 37.

ᑫ Is. 41. 4, 10, 14; John 6. 20; 14. 1 -3.

ʳ ch. 17. 20; 21. 21.
ˢ Mk. 14. 38.
ᵗ ch. 8. 25; Ps. 69. 1
ᵘ Jam. 1. 6-8.

---

most plausible. It is enough, however, to know that he was divine, that the laws of nature were subject to his control, of which he could easily make a use wholly unknown to us.

26. Troubled. Agitated and greatly disturbed at the sight. **It is a spirit.** A *ghost* or *spectre;* an apparition. They supposed it impossible for any man to walk on the water. **Cried out for fear.** In terror they cry aloud, sending forth indistinct utterances, and incoherent exclamations.

27. Jesus at once speaks to them, bidding them to *take courage* and *fear not;* for *it is I*, or *I am he* whom you know as your Lord and Teacher. The familiar tones of his voice indicated who he was. Doubtless, too, being nearer to them, his general form might be distinguished.

28. The incident here related respecting Peter is recorded only by Matthew. It is in striking harmony with his character, as illustrated elsewhere, ch. 26: 33; John 18: 10; 21: 7. He was ardent, impulsive, sanguine, and confident. We should expect him to be the one first to speak. There seems to have been some ambition and vainglory in Peter when he said, **Bid me come,** etc. Not only would he out-do the other disciples, but, like Jesus, he would walk on the water.

29. Jesus answers, **Come.** Make a trial of your faith in me and in my power. Jesus knew that his courage and faith would fail him; but he saw that by permitting him to make the experiment he would be taught the importance of a faith which, surmounting all difficulties and dangers, fixes itself on Christ without wavering. **And when Peter,** etc. Rather, *Coming down from the ship, Peter walked on the water.* Peter actually walked on the water, upheld by the divine power of Jesus. **To go,** rather, *and came to Jesus,* according to the best text. As the apostles had performed other miracles through the power of Jesus, so now does Peter by the same power perform this.

30. But when, etc. Rather, *But seeing the wind.* The whole event occupied but a few moments. **Was afraid.** Was fearful, was affrighted. "As long as Peter looked to Jesus only, he rose by faith over the elements of nature; but as soon as he looked away from Jesus to the boisterous waves, he began to doubt, to despond, and to sink."—Dʀ. Sᴄʜᴀғғ, in *Lange's Com.* Both his courage and faith were impulsive. He descends from the ship all aglow with confidence; but how soon he sinks with the despairing cry, "Lord, save me."

31. Caught him. Jesus immediately seized him, or rather took hold of him. **Of little faith.** He had some faith, though it was small. See on ch. 8 : 26. **Didst thou doubt?** Turn in two directions, hesitate, waver, doubt. The same word is used in ch. 28: 17. It should be noted that Jesus reproves Peter for his weak faith, not for his bold proposal, nor his prompt compliance with the permission "to come."

32. And when they were come, etc. Rather, *When they had come up, or had entered into the ship.* Immedi-

33 ship, ˣ the wind ceased. Then they that were in the ship came and worshiped him, saying, Of a truth ʸ thou art the Son of God.
34 ᶻ And when they were gone over they came into
35 the land of Genessaret. And when the men of that place had knowledge of him, they sent out into all that country round about, and ᵃ brought
36 unto him all that were diseased; and besought him that they might only touch the hem of his garment: and ᵇ as many as touched were made perfectly whole.

ˣ Ps. 107. 29, 30.

ʸ ch. 16. 16; Mk. 1. 1; Lk. 1. 32; 4. 41; John 1. 49; 6. 69; 11. 27; Ac. 8. 37; 13. 32, 33; Ro. 1. 4.
ᶻ Mk. 6. 53.
ᵃ ch. 8. 16.
ᵇ ch. 9. 20, 21; Mk. 3. 10; Lk. 6. 19; Ac. 19. 11. 12.

ately upon their entering the ship the wind abated. John says (ch. 6 : 21), "Then they willingly received him into the ship." They had been affrighted, supposing him to be a ghost or spectre; but now recognizing him by his voice, they were, therefore, willing to take him into the ship, and ready to welcome him. The wind having ceased, and the sailing being fine, they were soon at the end of their voyage. "And immediately," says John, "they were at the land whither they were going."

33. **They that were in the ship.** The *sailors*, the *boatmen*, and perhaps some passengers, who are thus distinguished from the *disciples*, as the apostles are designated in vers. 15, 19, 22, 26. Compare ch. 8 : 27. **The Son of God.** In the original this title is without the article. *Thou art God's Son.* They acknowledge his divine nature and power, as proved by his control over the elements; and as such they worshiped him, paid him religious homage. See ch. 2 : 2 ; 4 : 3. These mariners more probably held the doctrine of one God. In the words, **Of a truth**, it seems implied that they had previously heard of his claim to Divine Sonship.

This miracle conveys spiritual truth which is applicable both to individual Christians and to the church of God.

34–36. JESUS VISITS THE LAND OF GENNESARET, where he performs many miracles, Mark 6 : 53–56.

34. **Land of Gennesaret.** A small district of country or plain on the western shore of the sea, about four miles long and two and a half broad, just south of Capernaum. Josephus graphically describes this beautiful plain: "Its nature is wonderful as well as its beauty; so fruitful is its soil that all sorts of trees can grow upon it, and all are accordingly cultivated there by the inhabitants; for the temper of the air suits every variety. Walnuts flourish luxuriantly ; so also do palm-trees ; and here are figs and olives. It produces grapes and figs ten months in the year, while the other varieties ripen the year round; for besides the good temperature of the air, it is also watered from a most fertilizing fountain, called Capernaum." The fine temperature may be accounted for by the fact that it is almost on a level with the sea, and is, therefore more than six hundred feet below the ocean. Gennesaret is probably a corruption of Chinnereth, the name of a fenced city and small district west of the sea, Josh. 19 : 35. It is supposed by some to be the ancient name of Tiberias. From it also the lake received one of its names. See on ch. 4 : 18.

35. **The men of that place.** The men inhabiting the plain, and especially those living or laboring in the vicinity where they landed. **Had knowledge of him.** Recognizing, knowing him. Capernaum, the residence of Jesus, being near at hand, they had had abundant opportunity of knowing his personal appearance. **Sent out into all that country.** They sent to the houses in all that region, all over the plain, and possibly beyond, and brought to him all that were diseased.

36. **Hem of his garment.** The fringe commanded to be worn as a badge of an Israelite, Num. 15 : 38. We have a vivid view of the faith of the people in his power to heal. As he is passing through that country, they ask that they may only touch the fringe of his garment, and as many as touched were made whole as an evidence of his power and their faith. They **touched,** and thus was kept before them the fact that Jesus

was the author of the healing, and at the same time their *touch* gave a practical manifestation of their faith. **Were made perfectly whole.** Rather, *were made whole;* they were restored to health. Mark (6 : 56) speaks of his visiting villages and cities in that vicinity at this time. And John (6 : 22-71) gives a discourse of Jesus at Capernaum on the true bread from heaven. We get a glimpse here of the many miracles performed by Jesus during his ministry. Compare chs. 4 : 24 ; 9 : 35.

REMARKS.

1. How many hear of the fame of Jesus, but, like Herod, reject him, ver. 1 ; Luke 13 : 31 ; 23 : 8–11.

2. In the case of Herod we have an illustration of the power of conscience. It condemned him and made him feel his guilt; his feelings of guilt arouse his superstition, and he imagines that John is risen from the dead, ver. 2 ; Job 15 : 20–23.

3. We have also an illustration of the progress of sin. Herod and Herodias are at first unlawfully married; at length they imbue their hands in innocent blood. Beware of tampering with sin, vers. 3–8 ; 2 Tim. 3 : 13 ; James 1 : 15.

4. In John we have an example of faithfulness. But he had the approval of conscience, of good men, and of God, vers. 3, 4 ; ch. 10 : 28 ; Rev. 2 : 13 ; 3 : 10–12.

5. The hearts of the wicked are worse than their lives. Herod would have put John to death long before, but for the fear of man and selfish consideration, ver. 5 ; Jer. 3 : 5 ; Gen. 31 : 7.

6. Worldly amusements are intoxicating, opening large avenues to vice and crime. Dancing led on Herod first to a rash oath and then to murder, ver. 6 ; Job 21 : 11–15.

7. In Herodias we have a noted example of the evil influence of a cunning and vicious woman, vers. 6–8 ; 1 Kings 21 : 25 ; Eccle. 7 : 26 ; Prov. 22 : 14.

8. In the daughter of Herodias we see the direful effect of the influence of a wicked mother. Educated in sin, and hardened to crime, she revolted not from being an accomplice in blood, ver. 8 ; 2 Chron. 23 : 3.

9. The commission of the greatest crime is sometimes less dreaded by the wicked than the rebukes of a good man. Herod could more easily imprison John and put him to death than endure his reproofs, ver. 8 ; Esth. 5 : 13.

10. Oaths and promises which may lead us to do wrong are rash and sinful. "God would rather have us break *our* word than *his* word."—GOSSNER. Vers. 7, 9 ; 1 Sam. 14 : 24–28 ; Eccle. 5 : 2.

11. The fear of man has led many, like Herod, into scenes of wickedness and to destruction, vers. 9, 10.

12. The reception of the head of John by Herodias and her daughter illustrates the cruel triumphing of persecutors over the martyred righteous of every age, ver. 11 ; Rev. 17 : 6.

When Pope Gregory XIII. heard of the St. Bartholomew's massacre, in 1572, he caused the city of Rome to be illuminated with bonfires, a *Te Deum* to be sung in the churches, and a medal to be struck in commemoration of the slaughter.

13. In all our trials, and especially at the death of friends, we should, like the disciples of John, go and tell Jesus, ver. 12 ; John 11 : 19–26, 32–35.

14. There are times when we may seek retirement, and refresh ourselves with a change of scenes and of labors, ver. 13.

15. They that seek Jesus shall not seek him in vain, ver. 14.

16. Jesus is far more compassionate than it is possible for his disciples to be, vers. 15, 16 ; ch. 15 : 23–28 ; Luke 18 : 39–42.

17. Jesus exercises a care over the bodily as well as the spiritual wants of men, vers. 16–21 ; ch. 15 : 32.

18. We should help the poor, and supply the bodily wants of men, as we have opportunity, and thereby we shall the better promote the welfare of their souls, vers. 16–21 ; Heb. 13 : 16.

19. We should obey the Christian law of benevolence, trusting in Christ for every necessary supply. He can make the desert teem with plenty, vers. 17, 19 ; 5 : 42 ; 1 Cor. 16 : 1, 2 ; Ps. 78 : 19–22 ; 107 : 33–37 ; Isa. 32 : 8.

20. This world indeed is a spiritual desert; but Christ is the living bread, and has abundant supplies for all, vers. 19–21 ; John 6 : 35.

21. Before partaking of food, we should give thanks to God and crave God's blessing upon it, ver. 19 ; ch. 15 : 36 ; Eph. 5 : 20 ; 1 Tim. 4 : 4.

22. Economy should be exercised both in temporal and spiritual things, ver. 20 ; ch. 7 : 6 ; 15 : 37.

A.D. 29.   MATTHEW XV.   213

Discourse on eating with unwashed hands.

XV. THEN ᶜcame to Jesus scribes and Pharisees, 2 which were of Jerusalem, saying, ᵈWhy do thy disciples transgress ᵉthe tradition of the elders? ᶠfor

ᶜ Mk. 7. 1.
ᵈ Mk. 7. 5.
ᵉ Col. 2. 8. 23.
ᶠ Lk. 11. 39, 40.

---

23. God's people are often constrained by his Providence to go into a way of trial, both to avoid spiritual evils and to receive spiritual good, ver. 22; Ps. 119: 67.

24. Jesus has himself set us an example of secret prayer, ver. 23; Luke 6: 12; 9: 28.

25. In times of temptation and trial we should be much in prayer. Jesus retires for prayer when the people would make him king, and continues till about three o'clock in the morning, vers. 23, 25; ch. 26: 36; Luke 22: 40.

26. If we are in the way of Christ's commandments, we should not fear danger, nor be discouraged with outward circumstances, vers. 22, 24-27; Rev. 3: 10.

27. Christ will in due time come to the relief of his afflicted followers who trust in him, ver. 25; Ps. 34: 15; Mark 6: 48; 1 Cor. 10: 13.

28. By laying aside our watch and declining in faith, we may fail to recognize the coming and presence of Jesus, ver. 26; Luke 24: 36-39.

29. The true disciple knows the Savior's voice, ver. 27; John 10: 2-4.

30. Whatever Christ bids us, we must do in faith on him alone, vers. 28-30; Phil. 4: 13.

31. Christ sometimes leaves his people awhile to show them their weakness and the folly of all self-dependence, ver. 30; ch. 8: 25; Ps. 69: 1, 2.

32. We should look for immediate answers of prayer, ver. 31; Dan. 9: 20-23; Isa. 65: 24.

33. Let us beware of having but little faith, notwithstanding all our blessed experiences of Christ and his love, ver. 31; ch. 16: 8-12.

34. Christ will in due time subdue all the storms of human passion against his people, and bring them into a quiet haven, ver. 32; Ps. 107: 29, 30; Phil. 3: 20, 21; Rev. 19: 1-4.

35. The miracles of Christ should convince men of his divine nature, ver. 33.

36. Christ is the Great Physician. He alone can make us whole, ver. 35, 36.

37. If the Galileans brought their friends to Jesus for bodily healing, surely we should bring ours for spiritual, ver. 35.

38. However earnestly we may strive to lead souls to Jesus, they must exercise personal faith in him for themselves, in order to secure salvation. "As many as touched were made whole," ver. 36.

CHAPTER XV.

Matthew now speaks further upon the relation of Jesus to the Pharisees, which he had already treated upon in the twelfth chapter. Withdrawing from their increasing opposition, Jesus visits the Gentile world, and performs a miracle upon a Gentile. Returning to the east side of the Sea of Galilee, he a second time miraculously feeds a multitude.

1-20. DISCOURSE ON EATING WITH UNWASHED HANDS, Mark 7: 1-23.

1. **Then came to Jesus.** When he was on the preaching tour recorded at the close of the last chapter, and in Mark 6: 56. Some suppose him to have been at Capernaum. The third passover of our Savior's ministry, which was close at hand when he fed the multitude (John 6: 4), was probably passed. He seems not to have attended the feast at Jerusalem. The **scribes** were generally Pharisees. See on ch. 5: 20. **Which were of Jerusalem.** Rather, *from Jerusalem.* Mark (7: 1) distinctly states that they "came from Jerusalem," and they probably belonged there. It is thought by some that they were a formal deputation, such as once visited John the Baptist, John 1: 19. But this is not necessarily implied. They appear to have come to watch Jesus and oppose his rising influence in Galilee.

2. **Tradition.** The oral law, which the Jews pretended was handed down from Moses, through Joshua, the judges, and the prophets. At the time of our Savior it was not reduced to writing. It was afterward compiled in the Mishna, or second law, and two commentaries were added, the Gemara of Jerusalem,

they wash not their hands when they eat bread.
3 But he answered and said unto them, ^g Why do ye also transgress the commandment of God by your
4 tradition? For God commanded, saying, ^h 'Honor thy father and mother: and, ⁱ He that curseth
5 father or mother, let him die the death.' ^k But

^g ch. 7. 3-5.
^h Ex. 20. 12; Le. 19. 3.
ⁱ Ex. 21. 17; Le. 20. 9; Deu. 27. 16; Pro. 20. 20; 30. 17.

and the Gemara of Babylon; and these three form the Talmuds of Jerusalem and Babylon. The Jews attached more importance to their traditions than even to their written law. The latter they compared to water, and also to salt; the former to wine, to pepper, and to fine spices. Thus they made the word of God of no effect through their traditions, Mark 7: 13. The Pharisees had charged Jesus with violating the written law (ch. 12 : 1-13); now they charge him with violating the tradition of the elders, than which in their estimation nothing could be more authoritative and binding. Still they come not out frankly and directly against him, but make their charge against his **disciples,** and consequently against him, as their teacher. See on ch. 9: 11, 14. **Elders.** Either the chiefs of the people as a class, to whom the traditions had been committed, and by whom sanctioned from generation to generation, including those then living; or, more probably, *the ancients,* the fathers of the nation, from whom they had been transmitted. Compare Gal. 1 : 14; Heb. 11 : 2. **For they wash not their hands.** Mark, who wrote his Gospel for Gentile readers, gives a particular account of the traditional usage in regard to washing before eating, Mark 7 : 3, 4. Matthew had no need to do this, as he was writing specially for Jewish readers, who understood these practices. The object of the washing was to remove any ceremonial defilement which may have been unknowingly contracted in the intercourse of life. So important was this regarded that the Talmud says, "He who eats bread with unwashen hands is as bad as if he were to commit fornication." The Rabbi Akiba was imprisoned, and having scarcely water sufficient to drink given him, preferred to die rather than to eat any thing with unwashen hands. **Eat bread.** *Bread,* being the principal article of food, is put for food in general, ver. 26; Luke 14: 1; John 6: 31.

3. Jesus meets the question fairly and frankly, and opposes human tradition by the divine law; the commandments and doctrines of men by the commandment of God. Notice the force of **also,** and of **your tradition,** as if he had said, I admit that my disciples transgress the tradition of the elders; but it is but *your tradition,* the precepts of human enactment, and only obligatory because you enjoin them; but you also transgress a law, even the commandment of God, the highest of all enactments, and that, too, for the sake of these mere human precepts, Mark 7 : 9. The interrogative form gives emphasis to the retort. **By your tradition.** This should be translated, *on account of,* or *for the sake of your tradition.* They set aside the word of God for the sake of their tradition, which they regarded as of greater worth and authority.

4. Jesus proceeds to maintain his charge against them. He selects a case where their tradition most plainly opposes the law of God, the filial feelings, the consciences and general customs of men. Their setting aside the fifth commandment was a most striking instance of raising human tradition over the word of God. **For God commanded.** Through Moses, Mark 7: 10. The oldest manuscripts and versions read, *For God said,* which corresponds exactly with the words *But ye say,* in the next verse, thus making the contrast perfect. The quotations are from the fifth commandment (Ex. 20 : 12), and the penalty for cursing or reviling a parent, Ex. 21 : 17. We have thus the testimony of Jesus to the divine origin not only of the decalogue, but also of the Mosaic law. Notice especially in Mark 7 : 9, 10, that what Moses *said* is equivalent to the *commandment* of God. **Curseth.** They who carry dishonoring of parents so far as *reviling* or *cursing* them. **Let him die the death.** There is a Hebraism in the original; an intensive expression, *let him end with death,* let him be executed, or more freely, *let him surely die.* The severity of the sentence showed the importance of the command, and the greatness of the sin in transgressing it.

ye say, Whosoever shall say to *his* father or *his* mother, ¹ *It is* a gift, by whatsoever thou mightest 6 be profited by me; and honor not his father or his mother, *he shall be free.* ᵐ Thus have ye made the commandment of God of none effect by your

ᵏ Ac. 4. 19; 5. 29.
ˡ Mark 7. 11, 12.
ᵐ Ps. 119. 126; Jer. 8. 8, 9; Hos. 4. 6; Mal. 2. 7, 9.

5, 6. Whosoever shall say. Rather, Whoever says, etc. *His*, before *father* and *mother*, should not be italicized. **It is a gift.** Devoted to God as an offering or sacrifice, ch. 5 : 23; 8 : 4; 23 : 18; Luke 21 : 1, 4. And even if a child should thus devote any thing to God in a moment of anger against a father or mother, the Jews held that it was binding. The word translated *gift* is here equivalent to the Hebrew *corban*, which means any thing brought near or presented to God, any sacrifice or religious offering, Mark 7 : 11. Even the mere pronouncing the word "corban" over one's property absolved him from the obligation of caring for his parents. **By whatsoever—profited by me.** Rather, *Whatsoever thou mightest be profited with from me.* The son addresses his parent. It is a gift, whatever assistance or support thou mightest derive from me; it is devoted to God, and therefore must not be used for any other purpose. But the worst feature was, that he was still allowed to use it for his own advantage, though not for the advantage of others. **And honor not his father or mother.** According to the majority of ancient critical authorities, this should read, *shall not honor his father and mother.* This is a strong negative assertion, and is what the Pharisees say, "Whoever says to his father or mother, It is a gift, etc., shall in no wise honor his father or his mother." The words of Jesus, recorded by Mark (7 : 12), is a good comment on this last clause, "And ye suffer him no more to do aught for his father or his mother." Treating a parent thus was indeed an act of dishonor, both in word and deed. If done in anger, it was in the spirit of cursing; and whether done in anger or not, the practical effect on a needy parent was the same as that of a wicked, cursing son; it was indeed a practical cursing. The saying of the Pharisees closes here, the words **he shall be free** being not in the original, and entirely unnecessary to complete the sense.

Commandment of God. The critical authorities are divided between *the commandment, the law,* and *the word.*—Dr. P. Schaff. *The word* is in the oldest manuscripts and versions.—Covenant. **Of none effect.** Ye made void, nullified, made of no effect the word or commandment of God. The language of Jesus implies that withholding any needed assistance or support from a parent, is breaking the fifth commandment; that the Pharisees admitted this; but rather *for the sake* of their tradition they made the word of God of no effect.

The same Pharisaic spirit was afterward exhibited among Christians, Acts 15 : 1, 5; Gal. 2 : 11–14; 5 : 2; Col. 2: 8. It showed itself in the latter part of the second century, in the dogma of baptismal regeneration, which in the third century gave rise to infant baptism in North-Africa; to infant communion, which continued in the western church till the twelfth century, and in the eastern church till the present day; and to pouring water upon, instead of immersing, those who were dangerously ill or near unto death. The same spirit has fostered infant baptism, and pouring and sprinkling, ever since. When, therefore, I am asked, Why do you transgress the traditional usages of the church in not baptizing infants? I may reply, But why do ye transgress the commandment of God for the sake of your traditions? For, by infant baptism, you set aside believers' baptism, and ye substituted sprinkling, or pouring, in place of immersion. Thus ye made the commandment of God of no effect for the sake of your tradition.

In the same spirit the democratic government of the church was changed into the monarchical; its ministry into a hierarchy, and an unconverted membership introduced; auricular confession, priestly absolution, homage paid to sacred relics, invocation of saints, worship of the Virgin Mary, celibacy of the clergy, and a host of other human doctrines and precepts were enjoined. And all of them with wonderful uniformity have the same effect, of annulling the commandments of God.

MATTHEW XV.

7 tradition. Ye ⁿ hypocrites, well did Esaias prophe-
8 sy of you, saying, ᵒ 'This people draweth nigh
unto me with their mouth, and honoreth me with
9 *their* lips; but their heart is far from me. But in
vain they do worship me, ᵖ teaching for doctrines
the commandments of men.'
10 ᵠ And he called the multitude, and said unto
11 them, Hear, and understand : ʳ not that which goeth
into the mouth defileth a man ; ˢ but that which
cometh out of the mouth, this defileth a man.
12 Then came his disciples, and said unto him,
Knowest thou that the Pharisees were offended,

ⁿ Mk. 7. 6.
ᵒ Is. 29. 13, Eze. 33. 31; Lk. 16. 15.
ᵖ Pro. 30. 5, 6; Col. 2. 18-22; Tit. 1. 14.
ᵠ Mk. 7. 14.
ʳ Ac. 10. 14, 15: Ro. 14. 14, 17, 20; 1 Tim. 4. 4, 5; Tit. 1. 15.
ˢ vers. 18-20; ch. 12. 34-37; Jam. 3. 5-8.

7. **Hypocrites.** Dissemblers, whose outward professions did not truly indicate their thoughts and feelings. They were from Jerusalem. "Rabbi Nathan says, If the hypocrites were divided into ten parts, nine would be found in Jerusalem, and one in the world beside."— STIER. **Well.** Rightly, aptly did Isaiah **prophesy of you.** This was a typical prophecy, including both those of Isaiah's day, and those in the day of our Savior. See on ch. 1 : 23.
8. This is a quotation from Isa. 29 : 13, not according to the exact language, but according to the sense of the Hebrew. **This people draweth,** etc. Simply, *This people honoreth me with their lips,* etc. *Draweth nigh with their mouth* is not found in the oldest and best manuscripts. They honor me with their professions, with their words and outward observances; but **their heart is far from me** in their aims, motives, and services. Thus were they hypocrites, as explained in the preceding verse.
9. **In vain.** *Empty* is all the honor you give me in your worship, teaching **for doctrines,** *as doctrines,* or *precepts,* the commandments of men. *Doctrines* refers to those things taught as binding upon the conscience, as obligatory. They thus acted the extreme part of hypocrites, in perverting the word of God, and raising mere human precepts to the position, and even above, the divine commands.
10. Jesus now turns away from those scribes and Pharisees who had come from Jerusalem, and addresses the multitude. **He called,** etc. Calling the attention of the multitude, and addressing them in particular. Many of them had doubtless heard the scathing rebuke and condemnation he had given the

Pharisees. **Hear, and understand.** Listen attentively, and understand my meaning. The Pharisees tell you of an imaginary defilement, and ye have heard also of a ceremonial defilement (Lev. 11 : 8, 26), but hear and understand in what real defilement consists.
11. **Not that which goeth into the mouth defileth.** It is not food that morally defileth a man; but wickedness in the heart, which comes out in false doctrines and wicked practices. They were in danger of supposing that there was something in the food forbidden as unclean, which would defile, not merely ceremonially, but also morally. This language of Jesus might at first sight seem to conflict with the Mosaic precepts. But things forbidden by the law could produce only a ceremonial defilement. This he does not deny. But he is speaking of real or moral defilement, and against imaginary defilement, according to the tradition of the elders, ver. 20. When the ceremonies of the law found their fulfillment in the death and sufferings of Jesus, the principle here laid down was of still more general application. Rom. 14 : 14.
12. **Then came his disciples.** Immediately after addressing the multitude, Jesus had probably gone into the house, Mark 7 : 17. The *disciples* were probably the twelve, for whom Peter soon after spoke as their representative, ver. 15. **Were offended.** Displeased, took offense. **This saying.** *The saying* which Jesus had just uttered in verse 11. The disciples were doubtless troubled that Jesus should have thus displeased men of such high standing as these scribes and Pharisees.
13. In reply, Jesus makes use of a parabolic figure derived from the vegetable

A.D. 29.   MATTHEW XV.   217

13 after they heard this saying? But he answered and said, *Every plant, which my heavenly Father
14 hath not planted, shall be rooted up. "Let them alone: *they be blind leaders of the blind. ʸAnd if the blind lead the blind, both shall fall into the ditch.
15 ᶻThen answered Peter and said unto him, De-
16 clare unto us this parable. And Jesus said, ᵃ Are
17 ye also yet without understanding? Do not ye yet understand, ᵇ that whatsoever entereth in at the mouth goeth into the belly, and is cast out into the
18 draught? But ᶜ those things which proceed out of the mouth come forth from the heart; and they
19 defile the man. ᵈ For out of the heart proceed evil thoughts, murders, adulteries, fornications, thefts,

ᵗ John 15. 2, 6; 1 Cor. 3. 12.
ᵘ 1 Tim. 6. 5.
ˣ ch. 23. 16; Is. 9. 16; Lk. 6. 39; John 3. 19.
ʸ Mic. 3. 6, 7.
ᶻ Mk. 7. 17.
ᵃ ch. 16. 9; Mk. 7. 18.

ᵇ 1 Cor. 6. 13.

ᶜ ch. 12. 34; Jam. 3. 6.
ᵈ Ge. 6. 5; 8. 21; Pro. 6. 14; Jer. 17. 9; Gal. 5. 19–21.

---

world, by which he teaches the utter extirpation of all mere human tradition. **Every plant.** Referring especially to the traditions and teachings of the Pharisees. **Heavenly Father hath not planted.** Which is not of divine origin. The figure may also apply to the false teachers themselves, so far as they shall be identified with their doctrines. They, as well as their doctrines, shall be rooted out from the world.

14. **Let them alone.** Leave them to themselves, let them go on, and have nothing to do with them. All that is necessary to their destruction is to let them alone. **Blind leaders,** etc. A proverbial expression. Spiritual deceivers and deceived. **Both fall into the ditch.** A *pit*, or *ditch*, which crosses their path, as an emblem of destruction. Thus, both these hypocritical guides and those deceived by them shall perish. They shall stumble, as now they are stumbling in taking offense at my doctrine, and fall into perdition.

15. Jesus, being in the house with his disciples (Mark 7: 17), Peter, in their behalf, speaks to him. **Answered.** This word implies something which had just transpired which occasioned the request of Peter. See ch. 11 : 25. **Declare.** Explain, expound. **Unto us.** Unto the disciples, for whom Peter acted as spokesman. **This parable.** The saying in verse 11. Compare Mark 7: 15-18. This saying was dark and enigmatical to Peter, and at the same time figurative. Peter, therefore, popularly styles it a parable.

16. **Also.** As well as the Pharisees. **Yet.** After so much instruction. **Without understanding.** Without comprehension; so lacking in common intelligence as not to perceive the meaning of my remark. This was a gentle rebuke, and intended to show them their spiritual ignorance. It also implies that what Jesus had said was perfectly plain and simple. Their difficulty may have arisen from their Jewish views in regard to clean and unclean meats. Peter was taught the lesson on a broader scale when Cornelius sent for him at Joppa, Acts 10 : 11-16.

17. **Yet** should be omitted, according to the highest critical authorities. **Understand.** Do you not perceive that food, received into the mouth, passes through the stomach and bowels, and is cast out into the privy, and therefore can not morally defile him? **Draught.** A place of sitting apart, a privy, drain, or sink.

18. But in contrast, those things that **proceed out of the mouth** in a *moral* sense, particularly *our words*, our sayings, commands, doctrines, etc. These come from the heart, where our purposes are formed. Out of the abundance of the heart the mouth speaketh, ch. 12 : 34. They defile **the man;** the man as having a soul, or moral nature. In the next verse he proceeds to state what these things are.

19. **Out of the heart.** The seat of moral intention and action. **Evil thoughts.** Not only wicked thoughts, but also wicked designs. From these, as so many germs in the heart, spring the dark catalogue of sins enumerated in this verse. We have here a striking evidence of innate depravity. **Adul-**

20 false witness, blasphemies: these are *the things* which defile a man: ᵉ but to eat with unwashen hands defileth not a man.   ᵉ ch. 23. 25, 26.

Jesus journeys to the region of Tyre and Sidon; a Canaanitish woman obtains the healing of her daughter.

21 ᶠ THEN Jesus went thence, and departed into the   ᶠ Mk. 7. 24.
22 coasts of Tyre and Sidon. And, behold, a woman of Canaan came out of the same coasts, and cried unto him, saying, Have mercy on me, O Lord,   ᵍ ch. 1. 1; 22. 42-45.
ᵍ thou Son of David; my daughter is grievously   ʰ Ge. 32. 24-30; 2 Cor. 12. 8.
23 vexed with a devil. ʰ But he answered her not a

teries. Breaking the marriage vow. **Fornications.** Violations of chastity by unmarried persons. **False witness.** False testimony, including lying of every kind. **Blasphemies.** Reviling God and sacred things, including, doubtless, the reviling of man. See ch. 12 : 31.

20. Jesus sums up what he had said. **These are the things,** such as I have mentioned, which **defile** the man, render him really, that is, *morally,* unclean. But to eat with **unwashen hands,** that in itself does not render the man unclean. Jesus speaks of such washings as had nothing to do with personal, but only with ceremonial cleanliness, according to the tradition of the elders. He would have his disciples wash as often as necessary; but not to suppose that it would make them clean in the sight of God. **A man.** In both instances in this verse this should be *the man,* as in verses 11, 18, including his higher spiritual nature, the soul.

21-28. THE JOURNEY OF JESUS TO THE REGIONS OF TYRE AND SIDON, AND THE CANAANITISH WOMAN, Mark 7 : 24-30.

21. **Then Jesus went thence.** More literally, *And Jesus, going forth from thence,* from the region of the plain of Gennesaret and Capernaum. **Departed into the coasts,** etc. More correctly, *Withdrew into the parts,* or *region of Tyre and Sidon.* Another illustration of the prophecy quoted in ch. 12 : 18-21. He withdrew from the organized opposition of the Pharisees, and from the cunning and watchful Herod, for the purpose also of making a visit to the Gentiles, thus foreshadowing the fact that the Gospel was intended for them as well as the Jews. He not only went to, but *into*

the region (ch. 2 : 22), or, according to Mark (7 : 24), *into the borders* of Tyre and Sidon, which were cities of Phœnicia, in the north-west part of Palestine, on the coast of the Mediterranean Sea. See on ch. 11 : 21. Thus he entered the frontier region, which joined upon Galilee. "I have the impression that it was to Sarepta he came, in the coasts of Tyre and Sidon, to visit, perhaps, the place where his great forerunner, Elijah, lived and wrought miracles; and that the woman of Canaan, whom Mark calls a Syro-Phœnician, belonged to the city of that poor widow with whom the prophet resided. He raised her son from death, 1 Kings 17 : 17-23. The Savior delivered this one's daughter from the power of the devil."—DR. THOMSON, *The Land and the Book,* vol. i. p. 232.

22. **A woman of Canaan.** The land was called Canaan from having been inhabited by the sons of Canaan, Gen. 10 : 15-19; Num. 13 : 29. That portion of country was called Phœnicia, and belonged to the Roman province of Syria, and had received a large admixture of Greeks as conquerors and settlers. This explains the language of Mark (7 : 26), who calls her a Greek and a Syro-Phœnician by nation. She was thus a heathen, and a native of that Phœnicia which belonged to Syria. **Came out of the same coasts.** More exactly, *coming out of those regions,* that district. **Cried unto him.** Called aloud. It appears from Mark 7 : 24 that Jesus entered into a house and would have no one know it; but he could not lie hid, for this woman came. Alford thinks that Mark's account commences with verse 25 of this chapter, and that this woman first cried to him by the way. Such a supposition

word. And his disciples came and besought him, saying, Send her away; ¹ for she crieth after us. 24 But he answered and said, ᵏ I am not sent but unto 25 the lost sheep of the house of Israel. Then came she and worshiped him, saying, Lord, help me. 26 But he answered and said, It is not meet to take 27 ˡ the children's bread, and cast *it* to ᵐ dogs. And she said, Truth, Lord: ⁿ yet ᵒ the dogs eat of the

ⁱ Ac. 16. 16–18.
ᵏ ch. 10. 5, 6; Ro. 15. 8.
ˡ Ro. 9. 4.
ᵐ ch. 7. 6; Phil. 3. 2.
ⁿ Ge. 32. 10; Job 40. 4, 5.
ᵒ Ro. 3. 29.

---

is certainly allowable, though not necessary. He may have gone into the house on his first arrival in that region. She had some knowledge of the Jewish religion, and also recognized Jesus as the Messiah; for she addresses him **Son of David,** a familiar name of the Messiah, ch. 9:27; 12:23. **Grievously vexed** *with a devil.* Literally, *badly demonized,* grievously possessed with a demon. See on ch. 4:24.

23. Jesus hears her cries in silence. We may suppose that Jesus now rises and goes forth from the house, and she continues her importunity. The disciples (the twelve) therefore beseech Jesus to **send her away,** *dismiss her,* that is, by granting her request, as is evident from our Savior's answer in the next verse. The reason given is, **for she crieth after us.** It was an annoyance; it would draw the attention of others to them, which Jesus seemed especially desirous to avoid. Their compassion also was, doubtless, aroused toward one so importunate and having so much confidence in his ability to cure. In the application of this Gentile, when the civil and religious leaders of the Jews were opposing him, we are reminded that the Jews were soon to be rejected and the Gentiles called.

24. **I am not sent,** etc. This reply does not contain a direct refusal to perform the miracle, but rather an intimation that it would be out of the ordinary course and object of his personal labors. This personal ministry was to be confined to the Jews, whom he speaks of as **lost sheep,** having wandered from and lost their true shepherd, ch. 10:6. "Yet even this was occasionally broken by such incidents as this. The 'fountain sealed' sometimes broke its banks in token of the rich floods of grace which should follow. See Rom. 15:8."
— ALFORD.

25. She now no longer cries after them, or at a distance, but comes near, and prostrates herself before him; probably while the conversation is going on between Jesus and his disciples. **Worshiped him.** *Bowed down to him,* as an act of reverence and homage. See on ch. 2:2. **Lord** is here the title denoting the most profound respect and reverence. See on ch. 8:2. Thus the Savior's dealings with her brought her to her knees in earnest pleadings, and, at the same time, made manifest her strong faith in his power.

26. Jesus would further manifest her faith, and also her humility, and therefore he replies, **It is not meet,** it is not good or proper to take away the children's bread, that designed for the children, as the Jews were called, and to cast it to the dogs, as the Gentiles were styled by the Jews. **Dogs.** Literally, *the little dogs,* the domestic dogs in the household that feed under the table, and not the wild and ferocious dogs which in flocks prowled through the street and about the country, Rev. 22:15. The tribes of Canaan, which remained in the land, were to be the servants, the domestic dogs, as it were, of Israel, Josh. 9:21; 1 Kings 9:20–22. In the use of this milder and domestic term we therefore see the kindness and compassion of Jesus. He gives her something to take hold of, if her faith and spiritual perception are sufficient.

27. The answer of the woman is a wonderful illustration of faith turning the most untoward circumstances to a good account. **Truth, Lord.** Rather, *Yea, Lord,* I admit all that thou hast said, that it is not good to take away the children's bread and give it to the dogs, of which I am indeed one; give me but the crumbs, for the little dogs do indeed eat these as they fall from their master's table. **Yet.** Not a correct translation of the original; rather, *for even,* or *for also,* introducing the reason for pressing her suit, based upon our Savior's own designation of

28 crumbs which fall from their master's table. Then Jesus answered and said unto her, O woman, great *is* thy faith: ᵖ be it unto thee even as thou wilt. ᵠ And her daughter was made whole from that very hour.

ᵖ ch. 8. 13; 9. 29, 30.
ᵠ Ps. 145. 19.

Jesus returns to the sea of Galilee, heals many, and again feeds a multitude.

29 ʳ AND Jesus departed from thence, and came nigh ˢ unto the sea of Galilee; and went up into a
30 mountain, and sat down there. ᵗ And great multitudes came unto him, having with them *those that were* lame, blind, dumb, maimed, and many others, and cast them down at Jesus' feet; and he healed

ʳ Mk. 7. 31.
ˢ ch. 4. 18.
ᵗ ch. 11. 5; Is. 35. 5, 6; Lk. 7. 22.

her, "For even the dogs," or "For the dogs also eat of the crumbs that fall from their master's table."

28. Great is thy faith. Others had overcome difficulties in coming to Jesus; but none had been so severely tried as she by an apparent unwillingness of Jesus himself. She thus showed herself to be of Israel by faith, though not by race. So, also, he commended the centurion's faith, ch. 8: 10. Both of these bright examples of faith were great in comparison with that of any of the more highly-favored Jews. **Be it unto thee.** Be it done to thee as thou wilt. **Was made whole.** Was healed. **From that very hour.** Rather, *From that hour*, from that time, from that moment. See on ch. 8: 13. Mark adds that, upon returning to her house, she found the demon gone out, and her daughter lying on the bed.

29-39. JESUS RETURNS TO THE SEA OF GALILEE AND FEEDS THE FOUR THOUSAND, Mark 7: 31-8: 9.

29. Jesus departed from thence. From the regions of Tyre and Sidon. According to the best critical authorities, Mark informs us that Jesus went from the borders of Tyre through Sidon, to the Sea of Galilee, through the midst of the borders of Decapolis, Mark 7: 31. Thus he traveled from Tyre northward to Sidon; then he appears to have crossed Lebanon by the great road to Cæsarea Philippi; and thence he passed through the northern portion of the Decapolis (ch. 4: 25), performing many miracles; and miraculously feeding the four thousand. **Nigh the sea,** etc. Near the Sea of Galilee. **A mountain.** *The* mountain, the high lands east of the Sea of Galilee. **Sat down there.** The usual posture for teaching, ch. 5: 1; possibly, also, to rest himself.

30. Great multitudes came to avail themselves of his healing power. As Matthew closes his account of our Savior's first circuit of Galilee by speaking of the numerous miracles he performed, ch. 4: 23-25; so does he close in a similar manner his account of our Savior's only visit, during his ministry, to the Gentile world. The Decapolis was largely inhabited by Gentiles, many of whom we may suppose to have been with the multitudes. **Lame, blind, dumb, maimed, and many others.** A great variety of diseases, four of which are named as specimens. Mark (7: 32) relates a cure of a deaf man with an impediment in his speech. The Greek word translated *maimed* means, strictly, *bent, crooked,* then more generally, *crippled* in the hands or feet. In Mark 9: 43 it is applied to the loss of a hand. It may here refer to persons whose limbs were so crippled by disease or wounds as to have lost all use of them. In the next verse it is said that the maimed were **made whole,** made *sound, healthy.* Thus there is a clear distinction between the lame and the maimed. **Cast them down.** They came with haste, and eager to have their sick healed. These words do not necessarily indicate any rudeness, nor any harshness, inconsistent with a proper care of the sick. They may be translated, *laid them down* in haste at his feet. **Healed them.** All that were brought.

31. Beholding these miracles, the people wondered, and **glorified the God**

31 them: insomuch that the multitude wondered, when they saw the dumb to speak, the maimed to be whole, the lame to walk, and the blind to see: and they glorified ᵘ the God of Israel.
32 ˣ Then Jesus called his disciples *unto him*, and said, I have compassion on the multitude, because they continue with me now three days, and have nothing to eat: and I will not send them away fasting, lest
33 they faint in the way. ʸ And his disciples say unto him, Whence should we have so much bread in the
34 wilderness, as to fill so great a multitude? And Jesus saith unto them, How many loaves have ye?
35 And they said, Seven, and a few little fishes. And he commanded the multitude to sit down on the
36 ground. And ᶻ he took the seven loaves and the

ᵘ Ps. 50. 10, 23; Mk. 2. 12.
ˣ ch. 9. 36; 14. 15–21; Mk. 8. 1.

ʸ 2 Ki. 4. 42, 44.

ᶻ ch. 14. 19.
ᵃ 1 Sam. 9. 13; Lk. 22. 19.

of Israel. The inhabitants of this district, being largely Gentile, were also largely heathen in their notions and religion. Hence, in witnessing these wonderful cures by this teacher of the God of Israel, they praise and extol the God of Israel.

32. Jesus now calls the twelve, and says, **I have compassion.** I am moved with pity for the multitude. The case was more urgent than on the former occasion (ch. 14 : 15), for they had continued with him *three days*—according to the Jewish mode of reckoning, parts of three days; the third day was now passing. **I will not send them away fasting.** I do not wish, or, I am unwilling to dismiss them without eating any thing. **Faint in the way.** Lest they become exhausted and entirely wearied out on their way home.

33. **Whence should we have**, etc. Whence should we have so many loaves in a wilderness, an uncultivated and uninhabited region, as to satisfy the appetite of so great a multitude? They could not have forgotten the feeding of the five thousand; yet they seemed not to have expected a repetition of the miracle. And why should they? For more than two years Jesus had exercised his ministry, attended everywhere with large multitudes, yet, thus far, only on one occasion had he miraculously fed them. The disciples were still babes in faith and knowledge, as is frequently illustrated in the Gospels, especially in regard to the death and the resurrection of Christ, Luke 24 : 25–27. Even putting the worst construction on their question, we find similar examples of a weak faith among God's people. The Israelites murmur immediately after their deliverance at the Red Sea (Exod. 15 : 24; 17 : 1–3); and even Moses showed unbelief when God was about to feed Israel with flesh in the wilderness, Num. 11 : 21–23. We can, therefore, see no reason, founded on this question, for supposing, with certain German interpreters, that this is only another account of the miracle recorded in ch. 14 : 15–21. The questions of Jesus in ch. 16 : 9, 10, show conclusively that there were two instances of miraculous feeding; and the two accounts show marked differences. The former appears to have been in the spring; the latter in the summer. That was in the vicinity of Bethsaida, north-east of the Sea of Galilee; this in Decapolis, and possibly some distance to the south-east. In the one, they were principally Jews from the western side of the Jordan, who had been with Jesus only one day; in the other, they are the mixed population of Decapolis, who had continued with him three days. Other differences, equally as marked, will appear as we proceed.

34. **Seven, and a few little fishes.** In the former miracle they had but five loaves and two fishes. They seem now to have suspected what Jesus was about to do: for they do not exclaim, as on the former occasion, "What are they among so many?" Their faith certainly had been benefited thereby, for not a word of doubt is expressed.

35, 36. **To sit down on the ground.** *To lie down*, according to oriental posture in eating. *On the ground*, instead of *on the grass*, in the

fishes, and ᵃ gave thanks, and brake *them*, ᵇ and gave to his disciples, and the disciples to the mul- 37 titude. And they did all eat, and were filled: ᶜ and they took up of the broken *meat* that was left seven 38 baskets full. And they that did eat were four thousand men, besides women and children. 39 ᵈ And he sent away the multitude, and took ship, and came into the coasts of Magdala.

ᵇ 1 Cor. 10. 31; 1 Tim. 4. 3, 4.
ᶜ 2 Kī. 4. 44.

ᵈ Mk. 8. 10.

former miracle. Dr. J. A. Alexander supposes it destitute of vegetation. He gave thanks and brake. See on ch. 14 : 19.

37. Broken meat. More correctly, *fragments that remained*, as in ch. 14 : 20; where we are also told the disciples, on the former occasion, took up twelve baskets instead of seven at this time. The kind of baskets were also entirely different. Those used then were the usual Jewish traveling basket; these now used were grain or provision baskets, and seem to have been much larger, as Paul was let down in one from the wall of Damascus. Thus the seven baskets of fragments may have equaled or exceeded the twelve baskets of the former miracle. See on ch. 16 : 9, 10.

38. Four thousand men. Instead of five thousand, on the former occasion. The women and children would doubtless raise the number to six or seven thousand. Thus we can get some idea of what the Evangelists mean when they speak of the great multitudes following Jesus. At the former miracle there must have been in all about nine thousand; in this, about seven. We should also notice that the larger multitude was fed by the smaller amount of provisions, which is also against the supposition that both accounts refer to the same miracle.

39. Took ship. Rather, *entered into the ship*, the one generally used by Jesus and his disciples (ch. 8 : 23; 9 : 1; 14 : 13, 22), or the one that generally crossed the lake at that point. **Coasts of Magdala.** The borders, the neighborhood of Magdala, or, as the oldest manuscripts read, *Magadan*. Magdala was situated on the west side of the Sea of Galilee, about three miles north of Tiberias, just south of the plain of Gennesaret. There is now a small village called Mejdel where the ancient town doubtless stood. Just south of it a line of high rocks overhangs the sea. It is probable that the place where Jesus landed was at the foot of these cliffs, toward Dalmanutha (Mark 8 : 10), a small village which probably lay about a mile south of Magdala. Magdala was also the birth-place of Mary Magdalene, from which she received her name, Luke 8 : 2.

REMARKS.

1. The Bible is the only rule of faith and practice, vers. 1–6; Isa. 8 : 20; John 5 : 39; Acts 17 : 11; Eph. 6 : 17; 1 John 4 : 6; 1 Tim. 1 : 4.

2. False religionists and formalists have ever been prone to rest their doctrines and practices on tradition rather than the word of God. The false doctrines and practices among professed Christians can be traced to the traditions and commandments of men. For example, Infant Baptism, in regard to which Professor Stuart says, "Comments, or plain and certain examples in the New Testament relative to it, I do not find;" adding, "nor, with my views of it, do I need them." "If any one asks me, 'Where is your text for baptizing children?' I reply that there is none."—HENRY WARD BEECHER. See *Origin of Infant Baptism, Christian Review*, 1861, pp. 33–57. See notes on ver. 6. Ver. 1–9; Isa. 29 : 13; Gal. 1 : 14; 2 : 14; 3 : 1; Col. 2 : 8, 20–23; 1 Pet. 1 : 18, 19.

3. God and not man has a right to add to his word, vers. 4–6; Deut. 4 : 2; 12 : 32; Prov. 30 : 6; Rev. 22 : 18, 19.

4. The first duty of a child, of whatever age, to his parents, is to honor them in word and deed. This can not be annulled or explained away by any artifice of man, vers. 4–6; Eph. 6 : 2, 3; Col. 3 : 20.

5. Hypocrites are especially abominable to God, vers. 7–9; Ezek. 33 : 31–33; Matt. 24 : 51; Tit. 1 : 16.

6. We should guard against formality in worship, since it is hypocrisy, ver. 8; 2 Tim. 3 : 5.

The Pharisees and Sadducees again ask a sign; Jesus warns his disciples against their teaching.

° ch. 12. 38; Mk. 8. 11; Lk. 11. 16; 12. 54–56; John 8. 6; 1 Cor. 1. 22.

XVI. THE ° Pharisees also with the Sadducees came,

---

7. Great carefulness in keeping the religious precepts and ordinances of men is an evidence of formality, and, when done knowingly, of hypocrisy, and is by no means pleasing to God, ver. 9; compare Isa. 1 : 12.

8. We should seek to understand the words of Christ, by careful attention and by imploring the guidance of the Spirit, vers. 10, 15; James 1 : 5.

9. Men are depraved by nature; the heart is the seat of sin, vers. 11, 18; Gen. 6 : 5; Ps. 14 : 1–3; Prov. 4 : 23; Jer. 17 : 9.

10. To take offense at kind and faithful reproof is an evidence of a wrong spirit, ver. 12; Prov. 9 : 8; 19 : 25.

11. Every error should be opposed; and, in due time, shall be rooted up, ver. 13; ch. 13 : 40–42; John 15 : 2.

12. Deceivers and the willingly deceived are often left to their own destruction, ver. 14; Isa. 9 : 16; Jer. 5 : 30, 31.

13. But none will be excused on account of the blindness of their teachers, ver. 14; Prov. 9 : 12; 1 John 4 : 1.

14. True purity depends on the state of the heart, vers. 17–20; Jer. 4 : 14; Rom. 14 : 17; 1 Cor. 8 : 8.

15. We should go first to God for cleansing, and not first to external ordinances, ver. 20; ch. 23 : 26; Ps. 51 : 7–10; Prov. 9 : 10; Acts 8 : 37.

16. Christ withdraws his Spirit from those who reject him, vers. 14, 21; Hos. 5 : 15; Acts 13 : 46.

17. In all our trials, whether for ourselves or others, we should go to Jesus. The cases of others we should make, as it were, our own, vers. 22, 25; ch. 14 : 12; Ex. 32 : 31, 32; Rom. 9 : 1–3.

18. In the Canaanitish woman we have an example of persevering, importunate prayer, ver. 23; Gen. 32 : 24–28; Matt. 26 : 39, 42, 44; Luke 18 : 3.

19. Those whom Christ intends to honor most he often tries the most, vers. 23–28; Heb. 11 ch.; 1 Pet. 1 : 7. Noted examples: Abraham, Joseph, David, Daniel, etc.

20. Under all circumstances we should exercise an unwavering faith in Christ, vers. 27, 28; Heb. 10 : 23; James 1 : 6; 1 Pet. 1 : 9.

21. We should come to God just as we are, poor sinners, in the exercise of humility, taking a low place at his feet, vers. 26, 27; Luke 15 : 18, 19; 18 : 13, 14; James 4 : 10.

22. Let us also learn the value and power of faith, ver. 28; Rom. 4 : 3; 5 : 1.

23. None need fear to come to Jesus, or to bring their friends to him, ver. 30; ch. 11 : 28–30; John 6 : 37; Isa. 35 : 5, 6; Heb. 4 : 16.

24. Jesus looks with compassion on those who are seeking for something to satisfy the longing of their souls, ver. 32; Isa. 55 : 1–3; 63 : 9; James 5 : 11.

25. Jesus exercises a care over his poor and needy followers, vers. 32–38; ch. 6 : 33; Ps. 37 : 25; 1 Pet. 5 : 7.

26. We see the truthful simplicity of Scripture. An impostor would, doubtless, have greatly increased the numbers fed the second time, and reduced the amount of provisions, quite likely, to a single loaf, vers. 33–38, compared with ch. 14 : 14–21.

27. God sometimes calls his people to special and unexpected labors; but when he does so, he provides means for accomplishing it. These are the loaves and the fishes, vers. 32–34; John 6 : 9; Acts 10 : 17–20.

28. God unites his power with human instrumentality in carrying forward his work in the world. Christ's power is exercised in connection with the bread, which he breaks, the disciples who distribute, and the multitude who recline upon the ground to receive, ver. 35, 36; Acts 27 : 23–26, 31, 32; Phil. 2 : 12.

See remarks on ch. 14 : 14–21.

CHAPTER XVI.

Matthew proceeds to relate the further opposition of the Pharisees, now combined with the Sadducees, against Jesus, and his warning against their doctrines. The Evangelist then turns to the relation of Christ to the apostles and to the church. Jesus reveals more clearly than before the doctrine of his sufferings and death and resurrection, and teaches the duty and necessity of self-denial.

and tempting desired him that he would show them 2 a sign from heaven. He answered and said unto them, When it is evening, ye say, *It will be* fair 3 weather; for the sky is red: and in the morning, *It will be* foul weather to-day; for the sky is red and lowering. O *ye* hypocrites, ye can discern the face of the sky; but can ye not *discern* ᶠ the signs of 4 the times? ᵍ A wicked and adulterous generation

ᶠ ch. 4. 23; 11. 5.
ᵍ ch. 12. 39, 40.

1–4. A SIGN FROM HEAVEN AGAIN REQUESTED. Mark 8: 10–12.

1. The Pharisees also with the Sadducees. Better, *And the Pharisees and Sadducees.* See on ch. 3: 7; and this chapter, verse 11. We get a view of the increasing opposition to Jesus from the fact that the Pharisees could unite with Sadducees, who were enemies and rivals, in tempting him. Nor does this seem strange, when we remember that they had on a previous occasion before counsel with the Herodians how they might destroy him, Mark 3: 6. See on ch. 12: 14. **Tempting.** Endeavoring to lead him to do something which they might use against him. They were unbelieving; their motives were wrong. **A sign from heaven.** They ask for a sign or miracle in the skies, and not a sign on the earth, such as his miracles were. "For in the Jewish superstition it was held that demons and false gods could give signs on earth, but only the true God signs from heaven."—ALFORD. That the Jews expected that the Messiah would give such signs, seems evident by their repeated requests, Matt. 12: 38, and Luke 11: 16; compare John 2: 18; 6: 30. His life was remarkable for such signs; but the Pharisees were blind and could not perceive the signs of the times. See on ch. 12: 38.

2, 3. Verse two, except **He answered and said unto them**, and the next verse, are wanting in some of the oldest and best manuscripts. They are, however, found substantially in Luke 12: 54–56. **Evening.** Doubtless the later evening of the Jews, just at sunset and before dark. **It will be fair weather.** There is but a single word here in the Greek answering very well to our exclamation, "Fine weather!" **Red.** Literally, *the color of fire;* flame-colored red. **Morning.** The word thus translated means the early morning, between daybreak and sun-rising. Compare Mark 1: 35; John 20: 1. **It will be,** etc. Another exclamation, consisting of two words in the original, and well expressed by *Foul weather to-day!* **Foul.** Stormy, cloudy, not fair. **Lowering.** Appearing gloomy, threatening. In these expressions we have the common and frequent observations upon the weather by the Jews of Palestine in our Savior's day. **O ye hypocrites.** This is not in the original, according to the best critical authorities. **Discern the face.** Ye can distinguish, or judge, from the looks or outward appearance of the sky. **Signs of the times.** The evidences that they were now living in the times of the Messiah, and that Jesus was he: *First,* the fulfillment of prophecy. The sceptre had departed from Judah and the lawgiver from between his feet, the government of the country being then in the hands of the Romans, which Jacob had foretold should not be till Shiloh, that is, the Messiah, should come, Gen. 49: 10. Daniel's seventy weeks of years was drawing to a close when the Messiah should appear, Dan. 9: 24–27. The predicted forerunner of the Messiah had come in the person of John the Baptist, ch. 3: 3; 11: 10–14. Prophecy concerning the Messiah was being fulfilled in the life of Jesus, as frequently noticed in this Gospel, chs. 1: 23; 2: 6, 15, 23; 4: 15–17; 8: 17; 12: 18–21; 13: 35. *Second,* wonderful heavenly phenomena: the star at his birth, the song of the angels, the descent of the Spirit upon him, and the voice from heaven at his baptism. And *third,* his wonderful miracles were evidences of his Messiahship. All these were signs of the times more convincing than any of the signs by which they were accustomed to judge very correctly of the weather. The interrogative form makes the expression the more emphatic, and implies that their spiritual want of discernment was truly astonishing.

4. In this verse we have in the origi-

A.D. 29.   MATTHEW XVI.   225

seeketh after a sign; and there shall no sign be given unto it, but the sign of the prophet Jonas. ᵇ And he left them, and departed.

5 AND ¹ when his disciples were come to the other
6 side, they had forgotten to take bread. Then Jesus said unto them, ᵏ Take heed and beware of the
7 leaven of the Pharisees and of the Sadducees. And they reasoned among themselves, saying, *It is* be-
8 cause we have taken no bread. *Which* ¹ when Jesus perceived, he said unto them, O ye of little faith,

ʰ Mk. 8. 13.
ⁱ Mk. 8. 14.
ᵏ ver. 12; Lk. 12. 1; 1 Cor. 5. 8.

ˡ Eze. 11. 5; John 2. 24, 25; Rev. 2. 23.

---

nal the exact words found in ch. 12 : 39, except that **prophet** before Jonah is omitted, according to the highest critical authorities. The repetition is not strange, since the class of persons and the occasion demanded the same answer. Possibly some of those were present who had then asked for a sign, and he reminds them that his determination is unchanged. See on ch. 12 : 39. After thus replying to them, Jesus stops not to explain the sign of Jonah, as in ch. 12:40; **but left them and departed.** They were unworthy, seeking occasion against him, and plotting to destroy him. This conversation took place on his arrival in the region of Magdala (ch. 15 : 39), or soon after, and now, leaving the unbelieving and evil-designing Pharisees and Sadducees, as well as the crafty Herod Antipas, he takes a ship and passes over again to the eastern side of the sea. See next verse and Mark 8 : 13.

5-12. JESUS WARNS HIS DISCIPLES AGAINST THE LEAVEN OF THE PHARISEES AND SADDUCEES, Mark 8 : 13-21.

5. **The other side.** Eastern side of the sea of Galilee, Mark 8: 13. **Had forgotten,** etc. Rather, *Forgot to take bread.* The disciples had not forgotten to take provision for their journey across the lake, for they had a loaf remaining after they were over (Mark 8 : 14); but after landing they forgot to take bread for their further journey into the region beyond.

6. We have an example here how Jesus improved the events of daily life for the spiritual advantage of his followers. Their neglect to provide provisions gave occasion for uttering in parabolic language a warning against the teaching of the Pharisees and Sadducees. **Leaven** is a figure of diffusive and assimilating power, generally, though not always, used in Scripture to represent that which is corrupt and evil. See on ch. 13 : 33. Here it denotes the pernicious teaching of the Pharisees and Sadducees, verse 13. Mark (8 : 15) omits *Sadducees* and adds, *the leaven of Herod.* The Herodians were more of a political party than a religious sect, and were doubtless for the most part Sadducean in religious sentiment, the wealthiest classes being Sadducees. It is not necessary to suppose, however, that *leaven of the Sadducees* and *leaven of Herod* are interchangeable phrases; for the teaching of all of these three classes was formal, worldly, and opposed to Christ and the truth. Indeed, leaven could be applied to any false religious teaching. The exhortation, **Take heed and beware,** carefully guard and watch against, implies that the disciples were more or less under the influence of this leaven. They came constantly in contact with the various Jewish sects and parties, and heard their opinions and utterances, which were adapted to affect their minds, which were still darkened with many carnal views and notions.

7. The minds of the disciples, being much absorbed in regard to their neglect in providing bread, and with the care of securing future provisions, they suppose at once that Jesus refers to material leaven, and suspect no spiritual meaning. His words suggest this thought to their minds; they speak of it, and so conclude. Yet the saying seemed somewhat dark to them. Was the leaven of the Pharisees unclean to them? Or would the Pharisees in their hatred and opposition put any thing in it injurious or poisonous? Or did Jesus wish them to have nothing to do with these malignant opposers? Such might have been their thoughts and reasonings.

8. Jesus rebukes them for their undue anxiety about bread. **Perceived.** Literally, *And Jesus knowing it.* He knew their thoughts and reasonings,

why reason ye among yourselves, because ye have
9 brought no bread? ᵐ Do ye not understand, neither remember the five loaves of the five thousand, and
10 how many baskets ye took up? ⁿ Neither the seven loaves of the four thousand, and how many baskets
11 ye took up? How is it that ye do not understand that I spake *it* not to you concerning bread, that ye should beware of the leaven of the Pharisees and of
12 the Sadducees? Then understood they how that he bade *them* not beware of the leaven of bread, but of ᵒ the doctrine of the Pharisees and of the Sadducees.

ᵐ ch. 14. 17-21;
John 6. 9.
ⁿ ch. 15. 34-38.

ᵒ ch. 15. 4-9.

Peter, in behalf of the twelve, confesses that Jesus is the Christ.

13 ᵖ WHEN Jesus came into the coasts of Cæsarea Philippi, he asked his disciples, saying, ᑫ Whom do

ᵖ Mk. 8. 27.
ᑫ Mk. 8. 27-29; Lk. 9. 18.

---

which showed that they had but **little faith.** Had they strong faith, they would not be reasoning about bread, and thus lose sight of the spiritual meaning of his recent caution. **Why reason ye,** etc. They had no cause of anxiety about provisions, as his miracles performed recently in that very region clearly showed.

9, 10. **Do ye not understand,** etc? Do ye not understand my language, and do you forget my two recent miracles in feeding large multitudes? Is there then any necessity for your anxiety about bread, and for interpreting my language in a literal sense? **Baskets.** In the original, the two kinds of baskets are distinguished here, as they are in the accounts of the miracles. In verse 9, it is the usual Jewish traveling basket, as in ch. 14 : 20 ; in verse 10 it is the grain or provision basket, as in ch. 15 : 37, which see. This shows the accuracy of the statement.

11. **How is it,** etc.? Since you know of these great miracles, and consequently of my power to provide provisions if necessary, how is it that you put such a low and literal sense on my language, and do not understand that I spake not of the material bread? **That ye should beware,** etc. According to the oldest and best manuscripts this should read, *But beware of the leaven,* etc.! Having asked the pointed question which implied that the dullness of their understanding was marvelous, he repeats his admonition, Beware of the leaven of the Pharisees and Sadducees. **Sadducees,** in this and the following verse, should be without the article, as in vers. 1 and 6. The Pharisees were the more numerous, as well as the leaders in this concerted and organized movement against Jesus.

12. Then the disciples understood that the leaven of which Jesus spoke was not the leaven of bread, but of doctrine or teaching. **Doctrine.** What is taught, the *instruction,* the *teaching* of the Pharisees and Sadducees. Their carnal and superficial expositions of the law, their worldly views of prophecy and the Messiah, their words in opposition to Jesus, their demand of a sign from heaven, their attributing his power to Beelzebub, were doubtless the teaching here specially meant. Of these the disciples were to beware, lest their minds and hearts should be affected by them. In the midst of the wonderful miracles and discourses of Jesus, such teaching betrayed a want of honesty, a *hypocrisy,* which is also styled *leaven* in Luke 12 : 1.

13-20. THE CONFESSION OF PETER IN BEHALF OF THE TWELVE THAT JESUS IS THE CHRIST, Mark 8 : 27-30 ; Luke 9 : 18-21. Here begins a new period in our Savior's ministry, the period of preparation for his last sufferings. He begins to prepare the minds of his disciples by clear views of himself and his church, and by distinct intimations of his sufferings.

13. Having passed up along the eastern shore of the Sea of Galilee, and healed a blind man at Bethsaida Julias (Mark 8 : 22), Jesus with his disciples proceed northward along the eastern bank of the Jordan. **Cæsarea Philippi.** A city three or four miles from

14 men say that I the Son of man am? And they said, Some *say that thou art* John the Baptist: some, Elias; and others Jeremias, or one of the prophets.
15 He saith unto them, But whom say ye that I am?
16 And Simon Peter answered and said, Thou art the

---

ancient Laish or Dan, situated at the southern ridge of Mount Hermon, upon the side of Mount Panium, adjacent to a cave from which gushes forth a large fountain, one of the sources of the Jordan. In Greece the worship of the Silvan Pan was associated with caves and grottos; and hence the Grecian settlers in Syria dedicated this spot to him and erected here a shrine, and named the city *Paneas*. It was rebuilt and enlarged by Philip the Tetrarch, brother of Herod Antipas, and named Cæsarea in honor of Tiberius Cæsar; and to distinguish it from Cæsarea on the Mediterranean, it was called Cæsarea Philippi, that is, Philip's Cæsarea. It was a beautiful city, in the midst of the most picturesque scenery, and surrounded with a rich and populous country. It was one of the residences of Philip. Agrippa II. (Acts 25 : 13) afterward embellished it, and called it *Neronias*, in honor of Nero. Both of these names have long been disused, and its ancient name under the Arabic form *Banias* is now applied to the small village of about forty huts, and the surrounding ruins, which mark its site.

The coasts. *The parts, region,* of Cæsarea Philippi. It is not certain that Jesus visited this city. Mark (8 : 27) says that Jesus went *into the villages of Cæsarea Philippi*, those which were dependent on it, and adjacent to it. **He asked his disciples.** While he was in this region visiting the cities. Mark (8 : 27) tells us that it was while they were in *the way*, and Luke (9 : 18) says that *he was alone praying*, and *his disciples were with him*. It was a fitting time and place for Jesus to draw forth from his disciples the truth which they had already learned, that *Jesus is the Christ*, and to teach them new truths in regard to his church and his sufferings. The design of the question was both to confirm them in the faith, and to prepare the way for further instruction. **Whom do men,** etc.? Who do men declare me, the Son of Man, to be? *Son of Man* was the name by which Jesus loved to designate himself as the Messiah. See on ch. 8 : 20. Some would translate, "Who do men declare me to be? The Son of Man?" But this does not suit the connection; for it would require a negative or affirmative answer. The oldest and best manuscripts, however, omit *me*, and read, *Who do men say (declare) the Son of Man to be?* Jesus would first of all call forth from them the views of the people generally, and then in contrast their views as his disciples.

14. We have here a vivid picture of the opinions, not of the scribes and Pharisees, and the ecclesiastical and political leaders of the Jews (ch. 12 : 24; John 7: 12), but of the people generally, Luke 9 : 18. They did not regard him as the Messiah, but intimately connected with him as a precursor or forerunner. Some, like Herod, thought him to be **John the Baptist** risen from the dead, ch. 14 : 2; some, **Elijah** who was to come, Mal. 4 : 5; others **Jeremiah,** who was regarded as the greatest of the prophets, and expected by some of the Jews as one of the Messiah's forerunners. See Apocrypha, Esdras 2 : 18. Others thought him one of the ancient prophets. Thus, some thought the living Elijah had appeared, while others thought one of the prophets had risen from the dead. The Jews held to the actual coming and bodily resurrection of these men, and not that the soul of any one of them had reappeared in the body of Jesus. Such were the views of the people in regard to Jesus. Yet his disciples and some persons of strong faith had recognized him as the Messiah, ch. 9 : 27 ; 15 : 22 ; John 4 : 42 ; 7 : 31.

15, 16. Jesus now turns to the twelve and asks their opinion of him. **Ye** is emphatic, and in contrast to the *men* whose views they had just answered. Ye have told me the confused and conflicting views of the multitude; *but ye, whom do ye say* or *declare me to be?*

Simon Peter. The full name of Peter is here given as it is found in the three catalogues of the apostles in Matthew, Mark, and Luke. See on ch. 10 : 2. He spoke as an apostle. Matthew also is about to relate the remarks

17 Christ, the Son of the living God. And Jesus answered and said unto him, blessed art thou, Simon Barjona; for flesh and blood hath not revealed *it*

r Deu. 5. 26.
s John 1. 42.
t Gal. 1. 11, 12, 16;
Eph. 2. 8.

of Jesus on the two names, vers. 17, 18. Peter evidently answers in behalf of the apostles, for Jesus addressed his question to them. They assent to his declaration of faith, for they make no other reply. The fact that they were disciples and apostles, implies that they had held that Jesus was the Christ. Compare John 1: 40-42; 6: 69, etc. Peter appears to have been the spokesman of the apostles, and to have acted somewhat like a chairman of a committee, or the foreman of a jury. See further on ch. 10: 2. **Thou art.** The language of firm conviction; not merely of united or individual opinion or belief; for he does not answer, *we say*, or *believe;* or, *I say*, or *believe that thou art;* but firmly, and with all the reverence becoming the announcement of so important a fact, **Thou art the Christ,** *the Messiah,* or *the Anointed,* as the word means, the one foretold by ancient prophets, and styled the Messiah or Anointed by David and Daniel, Ps. 2: 2; Dan. 9: 25. He was the Son of David, in whom was fulfilled all the types of *anointed* prophets, priests, and kings of the old dispensation. And to express the fullness of their faith in him as the Messiah, Peter adds, **The Son of the living God.** Not only human, but divine. Not Son of God in any inferior sense; but *the Son of God* in the highest sense, which could be asserted of no other being. God is here styled *living God,* not only because he is distinguished from dead idols, but also because he is the author of all life and existence, hence self-existent, eternal. *The Son* of the *living* God was one who partook of that living, self-existent, and eternal nature. In this confession we have thus brought to view the humanity and the divinity of Christ. "This was a view of the person of Christ quite distinct from the Jewish Messianic idea, which appears to have been (*Justin Mar. Dial.* p. 267), that he should be a man, born from men, but selected by God for the office on account of his eminent virtues."—ALFORD.

17. Jesus now in turn confesses Peter, and through him, as their representative or spokesman, all the apostles. **Blessed.** *Happy* art thou in thy relations and destiny, in this spiritual knowledge, and in the enjoyment of the divine favor. See on ch. 5: 3. **Simon Barjona.** A patronymic, Simon son of Jonah. In the Aramaic, the colloquial language of the Jews at that time, *bar* meant *son.* Simon is here reminded of his earthly state and parentage in contrast to his spiritual state, as Peter, an inspired apostle. So, also, when Jesus, after his resurrection, reminds Peter of his frailty by asking him thrice, *Lovest thou me?* he addresses him, *Simon son of Jonah,* John 21: 15-17. Some suppose that Jesus had special reference to the meaning of these names; to Simon, meaning *hearkening, obedient;* and to Barjona, the *son of a dove,* denoting harmlessness, or used as a symbol of the Holy Spirit. But it seems far-fetched and unnecessary to have recourse to any such interpretation. *Bar,* however, is used by Daniel (Dan. 7: 13) when he speaks of " the *Son* of Man;" and Jesus, as he doubtless spoke in the Aramaic at this time, had used *bar* in vers. 13, " the *Son* of Man," and Peter in verse 16, " the *Son* of the living God." *Bar-Jona* thus corresponds with *son* in the preceding verses. Its force may be thus given: " Your confession is true. I, the Son of Man, am indeed the Son of the living God; and so in turn I declare that thou, Simon son of Jonah, frail and fleshly by nature, art Peter, a spiritual stone and a representative of the truth thou hast uttered."

Flesh and blood. Human nature, man, as opposed to *my Father.* Compare Gal. 1: 16; Eph. 6: 12; 1 Cor. 15: 20. This knowledge had not come from man, nor from any human source, but had been revealed to him by the Father. See on ch. 11: 25. As Peter spoke in behalf of the twelve, so this answer of Jesus to Peter extended to them. They all, doubtless, shared with Peter in the unwavering conviction that Jesus was the Christ, the Son of the living God, and of all it could be said that the Father had revealed this fundamental truth to them. This was no new and sudden revelation; but it commenced with their discipleship, and grew with their growth, and strengthened with their strength,

unto thee, but ᵘ my Father which is in heaven.
18 And I say unto thee, That ˣ thou art Peter, and
ʸ upon this rock ᶻ I will build ᵃ my church; and
ᵇ the gates of hell shall not prevail against it.

ᵘ ch. 11. 25-27; John 6. 45; 1 Cor. 2. 10.
ˣ ch. 10. 2.
ʸ Ac. 4. 11.

John 1 : 12, 13, 41, 49; 6 : 69. Paul claims a similar divine teaching and inspiration, Gal. 1 : 1, 11, 12, 15, 16.

18. **And I say also.** Rather, *And I also*, etc. The emphasis is not upon *say*, but upon *I*. Peter had just confessed Christ; Jesus in turn confesses him. Thou hast said to me, Thou art the Christ, etc.; I also say to thee, Thou art Peter, etc. **Peter.** Meaning, literally, *a piece of rock, a stone*. This name was given to Peter when he first became a disciple (John 1 : 42); prophetically however, for Jesus said, "Thou *shalt be called* Cephas," etc.; but here he says, Thou *art* Peter. See on 4 : 18. In earthly descent, and as a frail man, he was Simon Bar-Jonah; but in Christ's spiritual kingdom, as an apostle, as acknowledging that Jesus was the Christ, the Son of the living God, and in his relation to the church, he was Peter, a stone, one of the foundation stones, Eph. 2 : 20; Rev. 21 : 14.

And on this rock. Great variety of interpretations have arisen among expositors as to what is meant by *this rock*. They may be stated as follows: 1. The term *rock* is referred to Peter with the idea of supremacy. This is the popish view, and presented by Baronius, Bellarmin, and Passaglia. 2. It is referred to Peter, as an apostle, in the office and work assigned to him. Peter is thus a rock, in a subordinate sense, to Christ, the foundation rock, on whom was laid, as a foundation stone, three thousand living stones on the day of Pentecost, and also Cornelius and his company, the first living stones of the Gentile church. Most of those who hold this view associate with Peter, more or less closely, his confession. Among the advocates of this view may be classed Hilary, Ambrose, Chrysostom, Cyril of Alexandria, Theodoret, and others of the fathers; Launoi and Dupin, of the Catholics; and from among Protestants, Bengel, Grotius, Le Clerc, Whitby, Doddridge, Bloomfield, Barnes, Ripley, Whedon, Nast, Olshausen, De Wette, Meyer, Alford, Lange, Schaff, and many others. Some, as Origen, apply the term to Peter, including the other apostles, and, indeed, all believers. 3. Others refer the term *rock* to the confession of Peter, namely, the Messiahship and divine Sonship of Jesus, embracing the whole personality of Christ, including his divine and human nature and work. This is alluded to in the preceding words, "Hath not revealed it," namely, this fact, my Messiahship and Sonship. The fathers named in the preceding class vary their interpretation, sometimes presenting this view. So Doddridge seems also to incline toward it. Among its advocates may be named Gregory the Great, Huss, Calvin (*Institutes*, b. 4, ch. 6, sec. 6), Luther, Scott, Febronius, Ewald, and others. Some include the faith of Peter, which grasped and gave forth this confession. 4. Others refer *this rock* to Christ, that is, to him in his personal office, so clearly brought out by the confession of Peter. The only difference between this and the last view is, that it makes the rock refer to a *person* rather than a *doctrine*, or, rather, that it carries it a step further downward to Christ, who is the foundation and the living embodiment of the doctrine. This view is advocated by Jerome, Augustine, in his later years, Fabricius, A. Clarke, Calovius, Dr. Wordsworth, J. A. Alexander, and others.

Whatever be the true interpretation, it is certain that the first view, the popish idea of Peter's supremacy, can never be scripturally maintained; to prove which it is necessary to show that there was a superiority of power conveyed to Peter alone, and that this power was to be transferred from him in succession upon the bishops of Rome. For, *first*, there is nothing here said or implied about a succession from Peter; and, moreover, the idea of such a succession is inconsistent with the figure of a foundation, which is one and unchanging, and not constantly renewed. *Second*. Admitting that *rock* is here applied to Peter, so is *Satan*, in verse 23. It was only the believing Peter who could be styled a *rock*, or even a *stone* (Peter); and when soon after, denying that Christ must suffer, he becomes a stone of offense and Satan (allied to the great adversary) to our Lord.

See ver. 23. *Third.* The other apostles were equally foundation stones with him, Eph. 2 : 20. *Fourth.* The same rights and privileges were bestowed on all the apostles. Compare verse 19 and ch. 18 : 18. *Fifth.* Paul's reproof of Peter, and his whole statement thereof, are fatal to the doctrine of Peter's supremacy, Gal. 2 : 7–14. *Sixth.* It is certain, from Peter's own language, that he knew nothing of any such supremacy. For, in his first epistle (5 : 1–3), he addresses the elders as *a fellow elder,* and exhorts not to be lords over the heritage, but examples to the flock; and, in chapter 2 : 4–6, he speaks of Christ as the chief corner-stone, and believers as living stones. *Seventh.* That Peter was ever bishop of Rome is without either scriptural or historical foundation. Thus, upon the supposition that rock here refers to Peter, the popish idea is a mere assumption. Neither can apostolic succession be supported from this passage; for nothing is said about a succession, which is also inconsistent with the nature and design of the apostolic office. See on ch. 10 : 2.

To me the fourth view seems the true one, namely, that Jesus by the words *this rock* meant himself, as the Christ, the Son of the living God. For, *First,* there is, in the original, a marked distinction between the masculine *petros* (Peter), which means, almost without exception, *a piece of rock* or *stone,* and the feminine *petra* (rock), which always means *rock.* Jesus spoke, doubtless, in the Aramaic, and it is quite probable that he used two words equivalent to the Greek words *petros* and *petra,* as *cephas,* meaning *stone,* and *cepha, rock.* Lightfoot, on this passage, says there is no reason why the Savior should not have used this very Greek word, since such Greek terms were then common among that people. But, supposing the Savior to have used a Syriac word, Lightfoot says (I give his language condensed), "I deny that he used the very same אבנא (keepho) here as in the other case. He either said *Cephas,* after the Greek manner, or with a Syriac formation. For how, I pray, could it have been understood, either by the disciples or by Peter himself, if in both cases he had used the same word? The Romanists allege in reply, *Petrum esse Petram.* But let them tell us why Matthew did not use the same word in Greek, if the Savior used the same in Syriac?"

In the Peshito Syriac version, however, the same word (keepho) is used in both instances, and it is the word everywhere used in that version as the proper name (*Cephas*) of the apostle. It is, however, used in that version for both *stone* and *rock.* Examples of the former are found in Luke 4 : 3; Matt. 4 : 3; 7 : 9; John 10 : 31. Examples of the other use is found in Matt. 27 : 51; 1 Cor. 10 : 4. In Matt. 27 : 60 it is found twice, the first meaning *rock,* the second *stone.** But whether Jesus used the same or different words, we must suppose that the inspired Matthew gave faithfully his meaning, and he says, "Thou art Peter (a stone), and upon this rock." He could have continued, with grammatical correctness, *and upon this stone.* The change, therefore, from *stone* to *rock* shows a change of idea; as *stone* applies to Peter, *rock* must at least apply to something more than Peter. What more natural than for Jesus to apply it to himself, the Christ, as just brought out in the confession of Peter. Peter, a stone, a piece of the rock; but Christ the rock itself. *Second,* the demonstrative *this* (*this* rock) naturally refers to some other one than Peter, whom Jesus was addressing. It is very unusual to apply it to the object of address. It accords with our Savior's manner of speaking, to refer it to himself. Thus, in ch. 21 : 44 he calls himself *this stone,* and in John 2 : 19–21 he calls his body *this temple.* Compare John 6 : 51, 58. *Third,* the figure of a rock is never applied in Scripture to a mere man; but is especially appropriated to God, or typically or prophetically to Christ, in the Old Testament (Deut. 32 : 4–37; 1 Sam. 2 : 2; 2 Sam. 22 : 2–47; 23 : 3; Ps. 18 : 2–46; 19 : 14; 28 : 1; 31 : 2, 3; 42 : 9; 61 : 2, 6, 7; 71 : 3; 73 : 26; 78 : 35; 89 : 26; 94 : 22; 95 : 1; Isa. 8 : 14; 17 : 10; 26 : 4; 30 : 29; 44 : 8; Heb. 1 : 12), and to Christ in the New, Rom. 9 : 33; 1 Cor. 10 : 4; 1 Pet. 2 : 8. This remarkable use of the figure affords a strong presumption against applying it here to

---

* In the Peshito version the following other words, of allied signification, are found: In one passage *ebhno* = Heb. אבן, 1 Peter 2 : 8, "*rock* of offense;" *Shungo,* for *massive rock* in its natural position, Matt. 7 : 24, 25; 13 : 5, 20; Luke 6 : 48; Mark 15 : 40, first clause, etc. Another word. Shegeepho, a steep rock or precipice. is used in Matt. 8 : 32; Mark 5 : 13; Luke 8 : 33.

Peter, or to his confession, and for applying it to Christ, since the figure is never applied in Scripture to mere abstract principles or doctrines. The disciples must have been familiar with this figurative application of rock, and when Peter proclaimed the Messiahship and divine Sonship of Jesus, what more natural than for Jesus to confirm the truth, and designate himself *this rock?* Peter was but the confessor; yet as believing and partaking of the Spirit of Christ, he was Peter, *stone,* a piece of the rock; but Christ was the embodiment of his confession, *the rock. Fourth,* this interpretation is in harmony with all the teachings of the New Testament, and especially with the relation between Christ and the apostles, and all believers, 1 Cor. 3 : 11 ; Eph. 2 : 20; 1 Pet. 2 : 4–8; Rev. 21 : 14. The objection that rhetorical taste and propriety are violated by mingling two figures, Christ the rock and Christ the builder, is of no force; for the two figures thus brought together beautifully illustrate a great fact in Christ's kingdom, and one taught in the word of God, namely, that Christ is both the foundation and the builder of his church.

My church. The Greek word *ekklesia,* translated church, is derived from its corresponding verb, *to call out, to convoke,* and means literally *the called out, a convocation, assembly, congregation.* All the earliest English versions translate it *congregation,* except that of Wickliffe (1384), which reads *church.* The Genevan version (1557) in a few instances, and the Bishops' Bible (1568) in all, except in Matt. 16 : 18 and Heb. 12 : 23, where *congregation* is retained, substituted *church* in place of *congregation* of previous versions; and in the revised and authorized version of 1611, *church* was substituted in all the passages in the New Testament. The word which was chosen by Christ for a special religious use in his kingdom deserves our careful study.

In its *classic or heathen usage* it meant a lawful assembly of qualified citizens of a free Greek city, especially of Athens, for the transaction of business; and, secondarily, any assembly convened for purposes of business. It involved the idea of a collection of *intelligent, rational agents,* assembled for the exercise of certain rights and prerogatives.

In the Septuagint (a Greek version of the Old Testament) it is found over seventy times as the translation of the Hebrew word *kahal,* which means *a coming together, an assembly, congregation, convocation.* It is mostly used to denote a regularly-called assembly of the Israelites for any, but especially religious purposes and business, Deut. 18 : 16; Judges 20 : 2 ; 21 : 8 ; 1 Kings 8 : 14 ; 1 Chron. 29 : 1 ; 2 Chron. 1 : 3, 5. It is also used to mean an assembly of persons for any purpose, 1 Sam. 19 : 20 (*company* of prophets); Ps. 26 : 5 ; 89 : 5 ("of saints," that is, *angels*). As in classic usage, so also in the Septuagint, it involved the idea of *intelligent* and *responsible agents,* being thus distinguished from the less noble Greek word *sunagōge,* and its equivalent Hebrew word *gnathah,* which are applied to *assemblies of both active and passive* agents, to *unconscious* and even *irrational* beings, Exod. 12 : 3, 19; Judges 14 : 8 (of *bees*), Ps. 68 : 30 (of *bulls*). The word *ekklesia* had been thus used with a religious import in the Septuagint for 250 years, when our Savior chose it for service in his kingdom.

In the New Testament it occurs 114 times, as follows:

1. It is used once in the usual classic sense of lawful *assembly for business,* Acts 19 : 39. 2. It is twice applied (a rare use of the word) to a tumultuous assembly, Acts 19 : 32, 41. 3. It occurs twice in the Jewish sense of *the congregation* convened for religious purposes, Acts 7 : 38 ; Heb. 2 : 12. 4. In all other cases it is applied to the followers of Christ. *First,* and more frequently, to a particular company of disciples, Acts 11 : 22 ; 1 Cor. 1 : 2, etc. Compare Acts 2 : 1, 41, 47. In this sense it is often used in the plural, Rom. 16 : 4 ; 1 Cor. 16 : 19 ; Gal. 1 : 2 ; Rev. 1 : 4. *Second,* it is applied to the collective body of discipleship wherever found, Gal. 1 : 13 ; Eph. 1 : 22 ; Col. 1 : 18 ; 1 Tim. 3 : 15 ; Heb. 12: 23. Christ uses the word twice, the only two times it is found in the Gospels, first in its general sense in this passage, and second in its particular sense in ch. 18 : 17.

In the New Testament, as in classic Greek and the Septuagint, it involves the idea of *conscious, active,* and *responsible agents.* It is never applied to a nation, a family, the eldership, a council, hierarchy, or to a house of worship (*robbers of churches,* Acts 19 : 37, correctly translated, is *robbers of temples*), but to the discipleship, either a local body or-

19 c And I will give unto thee the keys of the kingdom of heaven: and whatsoever d thou shalt bind on earth shall be bound in heaven: and whatsoever thou shalt loose on earth shall be loosed in heaven.

a Zec. 6. 12, 13; 1 Cor. 3. 9.
z Ac. 20. 28.
b Job 38. 17; Ps. 9. 13; 107. 18; Is.

ganized according to the rules of the Gospel, or the collective body of disciples. Neither is the word to be confounded with the more comprehensive term *kingdom of heaven*, of which the church is the external manifestation. See ch. 3: 2.

In this passage we have the first record of our Savior's use of the word, which he applies to his discipleship. To distinguish his own from the congregation of Israel, he says, **My church,** *my congregation.* See further on ch. 18: 17. It is worthy of notice that while Jesus speaks of the legislative power of an individual church in ch. 18: 17, he intimates no such power as exercised by his church in its collective capacity. Indeed, the church general, as an organization, is nowhere spoken of or implied in the New Testament. Hence, in Gal. 1: 22, it is not the *church* of Judea, but "the *churches* of Judea," etc. Compare 2 Cor. 8: 1; Rev. 1: 4.

The gates of hell, *of hades, the under-world,* the abode of departed spirits, without regard to their character and state of suffering. The portals of the realm of death. See on ch. 11: 23. The *gates*, the entrances into the realm of the departed, represent *death*, by which all enter there, and which is barred against their return. Compare Ps. 107: 18; Isa. 38: 10. "In these significant words, the Savior refers to his own near victory over 'the last enemy that shall be destroyed' (1 Cor. 15: 26); and to the assurance thereby given, that he was able to secure his church (the congregation of the faithful) unharmed of death (Heb. 2: 14). Compare his language (Rev. 1: 18), *I am alive for evermore, and have the keys of death and the under-world,* (as the words are arranged in all critical editions). The supposition, that by gates is meant an *aggressive* power, violates all propriety in the use of the figure. Gates are a *resisting* and *restraining*, but not an *aggressive* force."—Dr. Conant. Death shall not prevail against his church, neither by its *receptive* power as it opens like a yawning gulf to receive all; nor by its *destructive* power over the bodies of all as they enter; nor by its *retaining* power in keeping them in the realm of death; but they shall have a glorious resurrection. His church (*congregation*) shall continue to the end of time, notwithstanding death in its various forms of martyrdom and disease, and they shall ultimately be victorious.

19. **The keys.** These were symbols of power and authority. The steward of an ancient household often bore a key as a badge of his office. Oriental keys were generally of wood, often of so large size, and curved, as to be hung around the neck or on the shoulder. The figure is used in Isa. 22: 22 and Rev. 3: 7, to denote Christ's power and authority. Power and authority were thus conferred upon Peter and the rest of the apostles whom he represented. *Keys of the kingdom of heaven* naturally denote the means or instruments of access into that kingdom: the doctrines which Peter and the rest of the apostles were permitted to preach with divine authority. Compare Luke 11: 52. They spoke as inspired men and apostles of Jesus Christ. Whosoever received these doctrines should be admitted to the kingdom of heaven, and whoever rejected them should be excluded. This was remarkably fulfilled in Peter, who thus opened the kingdom of heaven to both the Jews and Gentiles, Acts chs. 2 and 10. See also Acts 8: 21; 13: 10, 46. This was of course a delegated power, enjoyed no longer than exercised in accordance with the divine will. Compare Gal. 2: 11-14.

Bind on earth—loose on earth, etc. The same power is bestowed on the rest of the apostles and the disciples generally, ch. 18: 18. To *bind* and *loose*, according to later Hebrew proverbial phraseology, means to *forbid* and *permit*, to declare a thing unlawful or lawful. This is something more than the keys, the power of opening and shutting as above explained; it is the power of declaring what is forbidden and permitted in regard to doctrine, practice, and discipline. Peter and the other apostles were thus empowered as inspired teachers and guides in the for

20 *Then charged he his disciples, that they should tell no man that he was ᶠJesus the Christ.

*38. 10; John 10. 27-30; Ro. 8. 33-39.
ᶜ Is. 22. 22.
ᵈ ch. 18. 18.
ᵉ Mk. 8. 30.
ᶠ John 20. 31.

Jesus foretells his death and resurrection; rebukes Peter, and teaches the necessity of self-denial.

21 From that time forth began Jesus ᵍ to show unto his disciples, how that he must go unto Jerusalem, and suffer many things of the elders and chief priests and scribes, and be killed, and be raised 22 again the third day. Then Peter took him, and began to rebuke him, saying, Be it far from thee,

ᵍ Mk. 8. 31; 9: 31; 10. 33; Lk. 9. 22; 24. 6, 7.

---

mation and discipline of the primitive churches. For examples of the exercise of this power see Acts 1 : 15-22; 5 : 3-10; 6 : 2-4; 11 : 1-18; 15 : 4-29. The power in this sense ceased with inspiration. In a subordinate sense, the power continues with the ministers of Christ, as his ambassadors and the proclaimers of his truth, and with the churches as the administrators of his laws in the regulation of their own affairs and in the exercise of discipline. Of course this power is valid only so far as exercised according to the will of Christ as expressed in his word. The New Testament, which has been given us by these inspired teachers, is our rule of faith and practice.

20. **Tell no man.** The time had not come for the public proclamation that he was the Messiah. He must suffer, die, rise from the dead, and the Spirit must come. The people were not yet ready for hearing this truth, neither were the disciples fully prepared for the work. Compare ch. 8 : 4; 9 : 30. **That he was Jesus the Christ.** According to the best manuscripts, *That he is the Christ.*

21-23. JESUS ANNOUNCES TO HIS DISCIPLES THE NECESSITY OF HIS DEATH AND RESURRECTION, and rebukes Peter for expressing his aversion to it, Mark 8 : 31-33; Luke 9 : 22.

21. **From that time.** Up to this time Jesus had taught them that he was the Christ; now he teaches them that he, the Christ, must suffer. Before he had given obscure intimations of both his sufferings (ch. 10 : 38; John 3 : 14) and his resurrection, ch. 12 : 40; John 2 : 19; but now he speaks plainly and teaches that it is necessary. The disciples, who held worldly views of the Messiah, needed instruction. They would thus be in a measure prepared for the event when it came, and afterward they would see the fulfillment of this prophecy, as well as those of ancient prophets, Isa. 53 : 4-10; Dan. 9 : 26. **Began Jesus to show.** He acts the part of a prophet in the highest sense. He *began* from this time to show the fact and the necessity of his sufferings, thus to correct their mistaken views. He continued afterward with further particulars, ch. 17 : 22, 23; 20 : 17-19. **Elders,** etc. The Sanhedrim, the highest ecclesiastical and civil court of the Jews. See on ch. 2 : 4. **Be killed.** Rather, *Be put to death.* See on ch. 17 : 23. Mark adds, that "he spake that saying openly."

22. Peter again appears as the spokesman of the twelve, showing his peculiar manner and temperament; for he evidently expresses their aversion to receiving what Jesus had just said concerning himself. **Then Peter took him.** He took him aside. **Began to rebuke him.** He only *began;* for Jesus interrupts him with one of his severest retorts. The scene is true to life. Extremes often meet in religious experience. The sudden transition from the bold and believing confessor of Christ to an unbelieving rebuker and adversary was consistent with Peter's impulsive and ardent temperament, and may have resulted from a certain vanity and pride, arising from the prominent position he had just taken in confessing Jesus, and the answer Jesus had given him in return.

Be it far from thee. Literally, *propitious to thee, merciful to thee,* a proverbial expression, an exclamation of aversion, and well expressed by the English translation, *Be it far from thee.* Peter, like the Jews generally, probably

23 Lord: this shall not be unto thee. But he turned, and said unto Peter, Get thee behind me, Satan: ʰ thou art an offense unto me: for thou savorest not the things that be of God, but those that be of men.

24 Then said Jesus unto his disciples, If any *man* will come after me, let him deny himself, and take
25 up his cross, and follow me. For ⁱ whosoever will save his life shall lose it: and whosoever will ᵏ lose
26 his life for my sake shall find it. For ˡ what is a man profited, ᵐ if he shall gain the whole world, and lose his own soul? or ⁿwhat shall a man give in

ʰ Ro. 8. 5–8; 1 Cor 2. 14.

ⁱ ch. 10. 39; Ac. 20. 23, 24; Rev. 12. 11.
ᵏ Gal. 2. 20; 6. 14;
Phil. 3. 10.
ˡ Job 2. 4.
ᵐ Lk. 12. 20; 16. 25.

---

thought that the Messiah would live forever, John 12 : 34.

23. Jesus turns about, looks upon his disciples (Mark 8 : 33), and says unto Peter, **Get thee behind me, Satan.** *Begone, out of my sight, Satan;* the same words as used by Jesus to Satan in the wilderness, ch. 4 : 10 ; Luke 4 : 8. Satan is here, as in every other place in the New Testament, the Hebrew proper name (meaning *adversary*) of the Devil. Satan was present with Peter, influencing him to evil. Compare Luke 22 : 3 ; Acts 5 : 3. Peter, in opposing what Jesus had said as if it was not true, was acting as a representative of Satan. He would have him be a worldly Messiah. Compare ch. 4 : 8, 9. **An offense unto me.** *A stumbling-block, a stone of offense,* an aggravation to me morally and religiously, exceedingly displeasing to God and to me. **Savorest not,** etc. *Thou art not of the mind of God, but of men.* Thou thinkest not the things of God, but the things of men. Compare Isa. 55 : 8. His views were carnal and not spiritual. He was thinking of a worldly kingdom, and not of a kingdom which is not of this world. His rebuke of Jesus was therefore in harmony with the views of men, and not with the designs of God.

24–28. JESUS TEACHES THE DUTY AND NECESSITY OF SELF-DENIAL ON THE PART OF HIS FOLLOWERS, Mark 8 : 34–9 : 1 ; Luke 9 : 23–27.

24. **Then said Jesus,** etc. This was said to the multitude as well as the disciples, Mark 8 : 31. He had just told his disciples that he must suffer; now he teaches them and the people that discipleship also involved sufferings and self-denials. If any one would be his follower, he must be willing to suffer, and also must expect to suffer. **Will come after me.** Purposes, determines to come after me as my follower or disciple. **Deny himself.** Renounce himself, abstaining from everything which stands in the way of duty. **Take up his cross.** A proverbial expression, denoting the self-denials and self-sacrifices, the inner and outer struggles pertaining to the Christian life; and also, doubtless, prophetic of his own ignominious death. See on ch. 10 : 38.

25. **Whosoever will save.** Whoever purposes or determines to save his natural or temporal life, makes this his great object and hence rejects me, shall lose his higher spiritual life. **Whosoever will lose.** Rather, *may lose.* Whosoever may lose his temporal life for my sake, making it only secondary and subservient to me, shall find eternal life. See on ch. 10 : 39.

26. **For what is a man.** According to the highest critical authorities, *For what will a man be*, etc. **Lose.** To bring loss upon one's self; to suffer loss or ruin as a penalty for a fault or crime; hence, *to forfeit his soul* by seeking the world and not following Jesus. The very spirit that Peter had manifested, if followed out, would result in the ruin of the soul. **Soul** is the word translated life in the preceding verse, and here denotes the higher spiritual, immortal nature of man. See on ch. 10 : 28, 39. It can not mean the life of the body; for a person must lose that, whether he gains the whole world or not; it must refer to the soul and its eternal life. **Give in exchange.** *Give as an exchange*, or as a ransom, as an equivalent. The meaning is, if a man forfeits his soul, what shall he give as an exchange, ransom, or equiva-

A.D. 29. MATTHEW XVI. 235

27 exchange for his soul? For ° the Son of man shall
come in the glory of his Father ᵖ with his angels;
ᵠ and then he shall reward every man according
28 to his works. Verily I say unto you, ʳ There be
some standing here which shall not ˢ taste of death,
ᵗ till they see the Son of man coming in his kingdom.

° Ps. 49. 7, 8.
° Mk. 8. 38.
ᵖ ch. 13. 41; 25. 31;
Dan. 7. 10; Zec. 14. 5; 2 Thes. 1. 7-10; Jude 14.
ᵠ ch. 10. 41, 42; 1 Cor. 3. 8; Rev. 2. 23.

lent for it? How can he redeem it? The interrogative form makes the statement the more emphatic. He can not possibly find an equivalent. The ruin will be irretrievable, and hence perpetual. Compare Ps. 49 : 7, 8.

27. **For.** This word introduces a most solemn reason for what he had just taught in the three preceding verses. There shall be a judgment; Jesus himself shall be the Judge, and every one shall be rewarded according to his works. **Shall come** is emphatic in the original. Jesus affirms with emphasis, that he, the Son of Man, now in humiliation, shall come. **In the glory of his Father.** In the majesty and splendor of his Father, John 17 : 5; Heb. 1 : 3; Matt. 24 : 30; 25 : 31. **According to his works.** According to his works as a manifestation of character, his whole course of conduct.

28. **Verily I say unto you.** A most solemn and authoritative declaration. See on 5 : 18. **Some standing here.** Of the twelve, and of the multitude, Mark 8 : 34. **Shall not taste of death.** A strong negative in the original, *Shall not die*, death being represented by the figure of a bitter cup or goblet. **See the Son of Man coming in his kingdom.** This is referred by different commentators : 1 To the Transfiguration. 2 To the Resurrection. 3 To the day of Pentecost. 4 To the destruction of Jerusalem. 5 To the progressive establishment of Christ's kingdom between the effusion of the Holy Spirit on the day of Pentecost and the destruction of Jerusalem. 6 To the second coming of Christ.

The great objection to any of these views is a want of comprehensiveness. See on ch. 10 : 23. It is a great principle in prophecy that it not only points to the final event itself, but also to the types of that event, thus including a series of events, all fulfilling one prediction. According to this principle, these words were fulfilled to his apostles and disciples in the resurrection, and to the Jewish nation in his providential coming at the destruction at Jerusalem which was a type of his final coming. The language according to Mark (9 : 1), "Till they have seen the kingdom of God come with power," and Luke (9 : 27), "Till they see the kingdom of God," may also include, in their fulfillment, the pentecostal season and the complete miraculous establishment of Christianity, Acts 4 : 25-30; 13 : 32-34, and Ps. 2 : 6.

We can hardly refer this prediction of Jesus to his transfiguration, which occurred only a few days after; for his language "*shall not taste of death till*," implies some distance of time, and not merely length of privilege. Compare also 2 Peter 1 : 15. So also it is not absolutely necessary to include the second coming to judgment in the fulfillment; yet the reference of Jesus to the judgment in verse 27, would naturally suggest that view. Thus some of those present saw Jesus as a king come in his kingdom, and in this they saw a type and earnest of his final coming. John (John 21 : 22), and probably Philip, survived the destruction of Jerusalem.

REMARKS.

1. Phariseeism and Sadduceeism have often joined hands in opposing Christ; thus have superstition and infidelity; formalism and skepticism; Unitarianism and Universalism, ver. 1.

2. Wicked men often repeat objections to Christ and the Gospel which have before been most fully answered, ver. 1 ; ch. 12 : 38-40.

3. Pharisaic and formal teachers understand earthly things better than spiritual. Many commentators are better expounders of the weather and science than of Scripture and religion, vers. 2, 3; Jer. 8 : 7-9.

4. We should watch the signs of the

The Transfiguration.

XVII. AND *after six days Jesus taketh Peter,

*Mk. 9. 1; Lk. 9. 27.
*Lk. 2. 26.

times in regard to the interests and progress of Christ's kingdom, ver. 3; Luke 12 : 54–56.

5. They that abuse the light and privileges given them shall have even these taken from them, ver. 4; ch. 13 : 12; Dan. 12 : 10; John 7 : 17.

6. We can not be too watchful against error and its silent, seductive, and corrupting influence, vers 6–12; 1 Cor. 5 : 6–8; 2 Tim. 2 : 17.

7. Men are very prone to misapprehend the word of God. Hence the need of the Spirit to enlighten and guide the mind into the truth, ver. 7; 2 Cor. 2 : 14.

8. Past experience of the power, love, and care of our Savior should lead us to exercise strong faith in him, vers. 8–10; Ps. 78 : 19–29.

9. Men are very prone to fall into the self-confidence of the Pharisees or into the skepticism of the Sadducees in regard to the future state, ver. 12.

10. We should seek to know what others think of Christ, so that we may correct their false views if they have them, and do them good, vers. 13, 14; John 1 : 45–49.

11. It is most important that we ourselves have correct views of Jesus, as the Christ, ver. 15; 1 Cor. 16 : 22; Gal. 1 : 8.

12. We should believe and confess Jesus as the Christ, the Son of the living God, without which we can not claim discipleship, ver. 16; Rom. 10 : 9, 10; 1 John 2 : 22, 23; 4 : 15; 5 : 10–12.

13. The doctrine of the human and divine Christ is divinely revealed; and in order properly to understand and believe it, we need to be taught of God, ver. 17; ch. 11 : 25–27.

14. Peter was indeed an important foundation-stone of the church, but Christ, his person and work, is the rock on which it is built, ver. 18; 1 Cor. 3 : 11; Eph. 2 : 20, etc.

15. The church is Christ's congregation of faithful followers, *called out* from the world. An unconverted membership is inconsistent in its very nature, ver. 18; Acts 2 : 47; Eph. 5 : 25–27; Col. 1 : 18.

16. The church is the only society on earth that shall really be indestructible, ver. 18; Eph. 1 : 22, 23; Rev. 18 : 2; 19 : 1–3.

17. Apostles, in making known and recording the will of God as they were taught by the Holy Spirit, and ministers of Christ in proclaiming it, allow or condemn on earth what is allowed or condemned in heaven, ver. 19; 1 Cor. 2 : 13; 2 Cor. 5 : 20.

18. Great prudence should be exercised in presenting truth at the right time and in the right way, ver. 20; ch. 7 : 6; Eccle. 12 : 11.

19. Professed disciples and true Christians may have mistaken views of many things in regard to divine truth, ver. 21; Acts 19 : 2; 1 Cor. 3 : 11–15.

20. Peter was indeed a poor, fallible man. The Church of Rome have imbibed the worldly, self-confident, and ambitious spirit which animated him when he proved to be Satan, and an offense to Jesus, vers. 22, 23.

21. Apostles, ministers, and churches can exercise the power of the keys only when they are of the mind of God, ver. 23; Gal. 2 : 11, 12.

22. Christ is the Lawgiver of his church. His word, and not our views and feelings, is the standard in matters of religion, vers. 21–23; ch. 7 : 24–27; 28 : 20.

23. Self-denial is essential to true Christian discipleship, ver. 24; ch. 10 : 38.

24. Religion must engage the powers and purposes of the soul, or we are lost forever, ver. 25; Luke 14 : 26–33.

25. The soul is of infinite value. If once lost, it can never be retrieved, ver. 26; Luke 9 : 25, 26; 12 : 16–21.

26. The second and final coming of Christ will be attended with glorious rewards to believers, and terrible punishment to unbelievers, ver. 27; ch. 25 : 46.

CHAPTER XVII.

By his transfiguration Jesus gives three of his chosen disciples a glimpse of his future glory. He points out John the Baptist as the Elijah that was to come. In the failure of his disciples in healing a demoniac, he teaches the necessity of a stronger faith, obtained through prayer and fasting. Predicts

James, and John his brother, and bringeth them up 2 into a high mountain apart; and was transfigured before them: and ʸ his face did shine as the sun, 3 and ᶻ his raiment was white as the light. And, behold, there appeared unto them Moses and ᵃ Elias

ᵗ ch. 10. 23; 24. 3, 27-31; 26. 64; Lk. 18. 8; 21. 27, 28.
ˣ Mk. 9. 2; Lk. 9. 28; ch. 26. 37;

again his death and resurrection; and teaches his relation, and hence that of his disciples, to the tribute for the temple service.

1–9. THE TRANSFIGURATION. Jesus miraculously presented to certain chosen ones of his disciples as a spiritual and glorified Savior, the Redeemer and Lawgiver of his people. An earnest of his future glory, and that of his followers, Mark 9 : 2–10; Luke 9 : 28–36.

1. After six days. Six days after the confession of Peter, related in the preceding chapter. Luke (9 : 28), counting the days of Peter's confession and of the transfiguration, says, "about eight days." **Taketh Peter, James, and John.** These were the three specially favored apostles, and the most intimate bosom friends of Jesus. They alone, of the apostles, saw Jesus raise the daughter of Jairus, Mark 5 : 35; they were the witnesses of his agony in the garden, ch. 26 : 37. Now they are chosen to behold his transfigured glory. Peter refers distinctly to this wondrous scene, 2 Peter 1 : 16–18. John, in a more general manner, says, "We beheld his glory," John 1 : 14. **Into a high mountain.** What mountain, is wisely concealed from us. Tradition says it was Mount Tabor, five miles east of Nazareth, but without foundation; for a fortified town stood on the summit of Tabor, and was garrisoned by the Romans in the time of Christ. The language, *bringeth them up into a high mountain apart*, means that Jesus brought them to the summit of the mountain, to a secluded, solitary place, and there they were alone by themselves. Besides, Jesus was more than fifty miles north of Tabor, in the region of Cæsarea Philippi; it does not appear that he returned to Galilee till after the transfiguration, Mark 9 : 30. It is quite probable that it was one of the summits of Hermon, in the vicinity of Cæsarea Philippi. Luke (9 : 28) says that Jesus went into the mountain to pray. Some suppose that the transfiguration occurred at night; for that was a common season with Jesus for prayer, and the disciples are described as "heavy with sleep," and not having descended the mountain till the next day, Luke 9 : 32, 37. The supposition is a very probable one.

2. Transfigured before them. He was changed in appearance. Luke (9 : 29), in place of *transfigured*, says, "the fashion (or *appearance*) of his countenance was altered," and that this occurred while he was praying. His divine nature shone forth, and its glory enveloped his person. **His raiment was white as the light.** Mark says (9 : 3), "His raiment became shining, exceeding white as snow, such as no fuller on earth can whiten." His raiment became like pure white light, resplendent as lightning. The three disciples were privileged to behold a glimpse of the future glory of Jesus (John 12 : 23; 17 : 1, 5; Rev. 1 : 13–16), and also of his true followers, John 17 : 22; Rom. 8 : 18; 2 Cor. 3 : 18; 1 John 3 : 2. They were thus being prepared for the sufferings of the Savior, and for their own sufferings; for his and for their resurrection and glory.

3. Moses and Elias. Moses, the representative of the law, and Elijah, of the prophets. Luke tells us that they "appeared in glory." The fact of their appearance is indicated as very marvellous by the word **Behold.** It is enough that the disciples knew them. It is idle to ask *how*, since many ways can be conceived how they came to this knowledge. Jesus may have saluted them by their names; or the conversation may have indicated them; or they may have known them intuitively through the Spirit, etc. In Moses, also, they saw in a glorious, visible form, a spirit of the just made perfect, and in Elijah, one in his glorified body. Elijah had been translated nine hundred years before, and Moses died more than fourteen hundred years before, on Mount Nebo, and the Lord "buried him in a valley, in the land of Moab, over against Beth-peor." There is no reason for believing that he had been raised from the dead. He may have appeared in a form assumed by angels on other occasions. This was not a mere

4 talking with him. Then answered Peter, and said unto Jesus, Lord, it is good for us to be here: if thou wilt, let us make here three tabernacles; one for thee, and one for Moses, and one for Elias.
5 ᵇ While he yet spake, behold, a bright cloud overshadowed them: and behold a voice out of the cloud, which said, ᶜ This is my beloved Son, ᵈ in whom I am well pleased; ᵉ hear ye him. ᶠ And when the disciples heard it, they fell on their face,
7 ᵍ and were sore afraid. And Jesus came and ʰ touched them, and said, Arise, and be not afraid.
8 And when they had lifted up their eyes, they saw no man, save Jesus only.

Mk. 5. 37; 2 Pet. 1. 18.
ʸ Ex. 34. 29; Rev. 10. 1.
ᶻ Dan. 7. 9.
ᵃ Mal. 4. 5.
ᵇ 2 Pet. 1. 17.
ᶜ ch. 3. 17; Lk. 3. 22; Ps. 2. 7.
ᵈ ch. 12. 18.
ᵉ Ac. 3. 22. 23; Heb. 12. 25, 26.
ᶠ 2 Pet. 1. 17, 18.
ᵍ Rev. 1. 17.
ʰ Dan. 8. 18; 9. 21; 10. 10, 18.

vision, but an *actual* appearance; for Luke (9 : 32) says that the disciples were heavy with sleep, but awaking, they saw Jesus in his glory, and the two men with him. The subject of conversation, as Luke (9 : 31) informs us, was concerning his *death*, "his decease (his *departure*), which he should accomplish at Jerusalem."

They speak of that of which the law and prophets had typified and foretold. "Moses, the Law, and Elias, the Prophets, are become one; and united with Jesus, the Gospel."—ORIGEN. The former are shown to be preparatory and subservient to the latter. Jesus, the greatest of all.

4. Peter again appears as spokesman, not of the twelve, but of the three. His **answering** was a response of his own feelings, in view of the circumstances around him. See on ch. 11 : 23. **It is good,** etc. Joy, a holy spiritual ecstasy, pervaded the souls of the disciples; but at the same time they were filled with awe and reverence—"*sore afraid,*" as Mark informs us; and knowing not what to say (Mark 9 : 6; Luke 9 : 33), Peter, in his bewilderment, proposes erecting three **tabernacles**, *booths,* or *tents.* According to some of the most ancient manuscripts, the reading here is, *I will make,* which is in harmony with Peter's self-confidence and ardent temperament. The *tabernacles,* which may be applied to any covered or shaded places, are doubtless here to be regarded as booths made of the branches and leaves of trees, such as could be made in that solitary retreat. Peter proposes three tabernacles, though six persons were present. He would have one for each of the glorious personages present, and he and his two fellow-disciples act as servants.

5. Two more wondrous events take place, the bright cloud and the voice, the account of each being introduced as extraordinary by the word **Behold.** The **bright cloud** was a symbol of the divine presence, as was the cloud over the tabernacle (Exod. 40 : 38), the cloud on Mount Sinai (Exod. 24 : 16, 17), and the cloud in Solomon's temple, 1 Kings 8 : 10, 11. Compare Exod. 16 : 10; Ezek. 10 : 4; Rev. 14 : 14. **Overshadowed them** with radiance and effulgent light. Who are meant by *them?* Some say Jesus, Moses, and Elijah; others, the disciples; and others, still more correctly, I think, all present. See Luke 9 : 34. **A voice** from God the Father, as in ch. 3 : 17. Here the divine testimony is attended with the command, **Hear ye him.** Attend to his instructions; hear and obey him as the Messiah, the Prophet, and Lawgiver of the Church. God would now speak through his Son, Heb. 1 : 1, 2. The disciples are in these occurrences favored with a sign from heaven. Compare 2 Pet. 1 : 16–18.

6, 7. **Fell on their face.** What they saw and heard overpowered them, prostrated them, filled them with awe and dread. But Jesus **touched** them, and they revived; their fears departed at his word. Compare Isaiah's overwhelming awe in his vision of the Lord of hosts (Isa. 6 : 5), the prostrating effect of a vision on Daniel and the touch of an angel (Dan. 10 : 9, 10), and John falling at the feet of the Savior as dead, who laid his hand upon him, Rev. 1 : 17. Also compare the falling of Saul of Tarsus to the earth, near Damascus, Acts 9 : 3, 4.

8. The disciples, restored, lift up their

9 And as they came down from the mountain, ¹ Jesus charged them, saying, Tell the vision to no man, until the Son of man be risen again from the dead.
10 And his disciples asked him, saying, ᵏ Why then say the scribes that Elias must first come? And
11 Jesus answered and said unto them, Elias truly shall
12 first come, and ˡ restore all things. ᵐ But I say unto you, that Elias is come already, and they knew

ᶦ ch. 16. 20, 21.
ᵏ ch. 11. 9-15; Mal. 4. 5; Mk. 9 11.
ˡ Mal. 4. 6; Lk. 1. 16, 17; 3. 3-14.
ᵐ ch. 11. 14; Mk. 9. 12, 13.

eyes and see **Jesus only**, the one foreshadowed, foretold, and testified to, by the law and prophets, and the one now to be heard and obeyed. The old dispensation is passing away; Jesus remains the same, yesterday, to-day, and forever.

9. **Tell the vision to no man.** By *vision* is not meant something unreal, but a *sight*, something actually seen. The same word in the original is used in Acts 7 : 31, and translated *sight*. That they actually *saw* is evident from Mark 9 : 9, and Luke 9 : 36. The time had not come for the announcement of what they had seen and heard. The minds of the people, and even of the other disciples, were not yet prepared for such revelations, either to receive or use them properly. Even these three privileged disciples were not yet prepared to announce the facts in their proper bearing. They still had carnal views of Christ, and did not yet understand about a crucified, risen, and glorified Redeemer. Hence the limitation, **until the Son of Man be risen again from the dead,** was not understood; for from Mark 9 : 10 we learn that they questioned one with another what *rising from the dead* should mean. **Be risen again.** Rather, *Is risen from,* etc.

10-13. JESUS ANSWERS THE QUESTION OF HIS DISCIPLES CONCERNING ELIJAH, Mark 9 : 11-13.

10. **Why then?** The short stay of Elijah with them, the secrecy of his visit, the prohibition of Jesus not to relate it at present, and his reference to rising from the dead (to them so mysterious, Mark 9 : 10) surprised them, and led to this question. **Scribes.** Jewish teachers, learned men in the Scriptures and the traditions. See on ch. 2 : 4. The scribes taught that Elijah would come personally, settle controverted questions, restore the theocracy, and prepare the people for the coming of the Messiah. The Jews still expect his coming. **First come.** Since he has just appeared after the advent of Jesus. The disciples seem to regard Mal. 3 : 1-4; 4 : 5, as having been just fulfilled on the Mount. In their reasoning on "rising from the dead," may they not have queried, Whether that did not mean another and greater coming, and that this appearance of Elijah was a precursor of it? However that may be, their minds were confused, and facts that had just occurred seemed to contradict the teachings of the scribes.

11. Jesus answers that Elijah indeed comes, and proceeds to correct false notions in regard to his person. **Elias truly shall first come.** Rather, *Elijah indeed comes.* The fact is merely asserted, without reference to the past or future. *First* is omitted by the best critical authorities. **Restores.** Rather, *Shall restore all things.* This is a brief summary of the prophecy concerning him, "He shall prepare the way before me;" "he shall turn the hearts of the fathers to the children," Mal. 3 : 1; 4 : 6. This he should begin to do (Luke 1 : 17), and this should be really done in the dispensation which he came to herald, Acts 3 : 21-23. He should thus reëstablish, reduce to order, and bring things to a proper religious state. He should be a reformer.

12. Jesus points to John the Baptist as the Elijah that was to come, and from his death gives a fresh intimation and illustration of his own. **Elias is come,** etc. Jesus implies that they were not to take the appearance of Elijah on the mount as the fulfillment of Malachi; but that he had already come in the person of one who had suffered. **They knew him not,** as the Elijah of prophecy, and the forerunner of the Messiah. **Done—listed.** *Did with him whatever they would.* Herod not alone was guilty of John's death; they who were with him at the feast (ch. 14 : 9) approved of his beheadal; the civil and ecclesiastical

him not, but ⁿ have done unto him whatsoever they listed. Likewise ᵒ shall also the Son of man suffer
13 of them. ᵖ Then the disciples understood that he spake unto them of John the Baptist.

ⁿ ch. 11. 2; 14. 3-10.
ᵒ ch. 16. 21.
ᵖ ch. 11. 14.

Healing of a demoniac.

14 ᑫ AND when they were come to the multitude, there came to him a *certain* man, kneeling down to
15 him, and saying, Lord, have mercy on my son: for he is lunatic, and sore vexed: for ofttimes he falleth
16 into the fire, and oft into the water. And I brought him to thy disciples, and they could not cure him.
17 Then Jesus answered and said, O faithless and perverse generation, ʳ how long shall I be with you! how long shall I suffer you! bring him hither to
18 me. And Jesus ˢ rebuked the devil; and he departed out of him: and the child was cured from that very hour.

ᑫ Mk. 9. 14; Lk. 9. 37.

ʳ Num. 14. 11, 27; Ps. 95. 10.
ˢ Lk. 4. 35, 36; Ac. 16. 18; 19. 13.

---

leaders of the people rejected him, and doubtless rejoiced in his imprisonment and death. See on ch. 11 : 14. So Jesus intimates that he **shall suffer,** *is about to suffer;* his suffering from the same classes, civil and ecclesiastical, Herod as well as others (Luke 23 : 11), is near at hand, and soon to commence.

13. The disciples then understood that Jesus spoke of John the Baptist, as the Elijah of Malachi's prophecy, who came in the power and spirit of Elijah, Luke 1 : 17. Elijah was the type, John the Baptist the antitype.

14–21. HEALING OF THE LUNATIC, POSSESSED WITH A DEMON, Mark 9 : 14–29; Luke 9 : 37–43.

14. When they were come. The next day after the transfiguration, Luke 9 : 37. **Kneeling down to him.** Did him homage with bended knees. Mark relates that Jesus found the scribes questioning with the disciples who had been left behind, and upon his asking what they questioned them, the man here referred to presented his petition.

15. Is a lunatic. One word, and that a verb in the original, *Is lunatic,* probably *epileptic.* See on ch. 4 : 24. **Sore vexed.** *Sorely afflicted.* He was possessed with a demon, a dumb and deaf spirit, which caused him to fall into the fire, and into the water, ver. 18; Mark 9 : 17, 22, 25. This was a severe case, like that related in ch. 12 : 22, though not quite as complicated.

16. Thy disciples. The nine apostles, among whom was Matthew himself. **Could not cure him.** On account of their weak faith, ver. 20. Jesus had given them power to cast out unclean spirits (ch. 10 : 1, 8), and doubtless they had exercised this power; but now they falter, and the enemies of truth triumph. Some have drawn an analogy between Israel turning to idolatry while Moses was absent in the mount, and the spiritual weakness of the disciples during our Lord's absence at his transfiguration. There was a striking contrast between Christ, transfigured on the mount, and the nine disciples below, unable to cast out a demon, humbled in the presence of the scribes and the multitude, and taunted by them.

17. Faithless and perverse generation. Unbelieving and perverted, Deut. 32 : 5, 20. This severe expostulation was addressed to all the disciples, with their weak faith, and indeed with no faith, to heal this one; the unbelieving multitude who were amazed to see Jesus (Mark 9 : 15), the father who acknowledged the weakness of his faith (Mark 9 : 22, 24), and the caviling scribes. **How long,** etc. ? This was not an exclamation of impatience of life, or of continuance with them; but of holy displeasure at their unbelief and hardness of heart. **Suffer you.** *Bear with you* in your perverseness and unbelief. Compare Exod. 32 : 19.

18. Rebuked him. Bade him come out of the child, Mark 9 : 25. Mark

19 Then came the disciples to Jesus apart, and said,
20 Why could we not cast him out? And Jesus said unto them, Because of your unbelief: for verily I say unto you, ᵗ If ye have faith as ᵘ a grain of mustard seed, ye shall say unto this mountain, Remove hence to yonder place; and it shall remove: and
21 ˣ nothing shall be impossible unto you. Howbeit ʸ this kind goeth not out but by prayer and fasting.

ᵗ ch. 21. 21; 1 Cor. 13. 2; Heb. 11. 32–38.
ᵘ ch. 13. 31, 32; Lk. 17. 6.
ˣ Mk. 9. 23.
ʸ ch. 12. 45.

Jesus again foretells his death and resurrection.

22 ᶻ AND while they abode in Galilee, Jesus said unto them, The Son of man shall be ᵃ betrayed into

ᶻ Mk. 9. 30; 8. 31.
ᵃ ch. 26. 16, 46.

gives a vivid description of the whole scene, the imploring father, the curious multitude, the terrible paroxysms of the child, the violent departure of the demon, leaving him as one dead, and his immediate restoration. **From that very hour.** Too strong for the original. Rather, *From that hour*, from that time.
19. **Jesus apart.** Mark informs us that this occurred in the house, privately, Mark 9 : 28. Luke omits this conversation entirely. Mark, whose account of the miracle is, as usual, the fullest, is here very brief, while Matthew, who is ever intent on giving the discourses of Jesus, is here the fullest. The question, **Why could not we**, etc.? implies that they had cast out demons on other occasions.
20. **Because of your unbelief.** Rather, *Because of your want of faith*, the absence of faith for the performing this miracle. According to some of the oldest manuscripts, this should read, *Because of your little faith*. Jesus at once intimates that they had not prayed and fasted sufficiently to exercise the faith necessary for casting out this demon. **A grain of mustard.** The smallest seed-grain used in Jewish husbandry. In proverbial language used to denote the smallest thing. See on ch. 13 : 32. As the mustard is used figuratively, so also may **mountain** be, though not necessarily. Compare Isa. 40 : 4; Zech. 4 : 7. It may denote great difficulties, formidable obstacles. Such shall be the power of any one who has faith, as a grain of mustard. See ch. 21 : 21. It must be borne in mind that true faith is exercised only according with the divine will, and hence only in the line of duty, 1 John 5 : 14. It is not caprice nor presumption. **Nothing shall be impossible** to him whose faith is in unison with the divine will. Jesus was speaking of faith connected with working miracles. Yet as the nature of faith is everywhere and in all ages the same, the spirit of the promise may be applied to all of Christ's servants and their work.

One can not fail to be reminded, as doubtless were the disciples, of the parable of the grain of mustard, and to think of faith as commencing with small beginnings and attaining a great growth, till every obstacle yields before it, and the greatest results are achieved.

21. **This kind;** of evil spirits. This implies that there are grades among demons, and that the one which had just been expelled was of the worse kind. The faith necessary to cast out such a demon could be obtained only by **prayer and fasting.** As yet the disciples were not accustomed to fast, ch. 9 : 14. But this verse is omitted in some of the best and oldest documents. Probably added by copyists from Mark 9 : 29.

22, 23. JESUS AGAIN FORETELLS HIS DEATH AND RESURRECTION, Mark 9 : 30–32; Luke 9 : 44, 45.

22. **While they abode in Galilee.** According to Mark 9 : 30, Jesus went from the region of Cæsarea Philippi, and passed through Galilee privately. The Greek verb translated *abode* has in it the idea of *returning*, and may be rendered, *again abode*. This was our Lord's last circuit through Galilee, and his last sojourn in that country. He made a flying trip through Samaria and Galilee a few months later, a little before his last sufferings, Luke 17 : 11. **Shall be betrayed.** Rather, *About to be delivered.* It was near at hand. Jesus here imparts the additional information to what he had given in ch. 16 : 21, that he should

23 the hands of men: ᵇ and they shall kill him, and the third day ᶜ he shall be raised again. And they were exceedingly sorry.

ᵇ Dan. 9. 26.
ᶜ Ps. 16. 10: John 2. 19.

Jesus miraculously provides for the sacred tribute.

24 AND ᵈ when they were come to Capernaum, they that received ᵉ tribute *money* came to Peter and said,
25 Doth not your master pay tribute ? ᶠ He saith, Yes. And when he was come into the house, Jesus preventeth him, saying, What thinkest thou, Simon ? of whom do the kings of the earth take custom or tri-
26 bute ? of their own children, or of strangers ? Peter saith unto him, Of strangers. Jesus saith unto him,

ᵈ Mk. 9. 33.
ᵉ Ex. 30. 13; 38. 26.
ᶠ ch. 22. 21; Ro. 13. 6, 7.

---

be delivered into the hands of men. It was thus not a repetition, but a gradual increase in revealing to his disciples the facts of his sufferings.
23. **Shall kill him.** In connection with his trial and judicial condemnation, it is better to say, *Will put him to death.* **Shall be raised again.** *Will rise again.* He will, through his divine power, rise from the dead, John 10 : 18. **Exceeding sorry.** The disciples saw that he really spoke of his death, though they did not fully understand his meaning, or how it could be (Mark and Luke), and they were very sorrowful, both because he should be so treated, and because their expectation of a temporal kingdom would thus meet with disappointment.
24-27. THE SACRED TRIBUTE-MONEY, the DISCOURSE of Jesus thereon, and his MIRACULOUS PROVISION for its payment. Related only by Matthew. Compare Mark 9 : 33.
24. It seems best to refer this to a time a little previous to John's account of our Savior's attendance at the Feast of the Tabernacles, to which he went up privately, John : 72-10 : 21. The feast, A. D. 29, began October 19th. It was now probably August or September.
Tribute-money. *The double drachma,* an Attic silver coin, equivalent to *the half-shekel,* and was worth about thirty cents. This was the temple tax. According to the Mosaic law (Exod. 30 : 13, 14), every male from twenty years old was to pay half a shekel yearly to the tabernacle, and afterward temple service, 2 Chron. 24 : 6. In both instances in this verse the original has the plural preceded by the definite article, *the double drachmas* or *the half-shekels.*

The article shows that it was the customary offering. The plural, in the first instance, refers to all the payments made to the receivers of this offering, and, in the second instance, to the payments made by an individual from year to year. The question, **Doth not your master ?** etc., shows that they expected an affirmative answer; yet it would seem to imply that the payment was not compulsory. It was due in the month of March, but it was not necessarily always paid at that time. If our chronological reckoning be correct, Jesus and Peter, and doubtless others, were in arrears. **Master.** Rather, *Teacher.*
25. Peter answers **Yes;** doubtless because he had known Jesus to pay it in former years. **Prevented him.** Rather, *anticipated him, spake first.* When the Bible was translated into English, to prevent meant to go before, to precede. The meaning here is, Jesus spoke first, before Peter said any thing. He then, as the Son of God, showed his divine knowledge of what had occurred between the tax-receivers and Peter. **Children.** Rather, *sons.* **Strangers.** Those who are not sons, not of their own families, other folks. Kings do not take tribute of their sons, but of their subjects.
26. Peter at once answers, **Of strangers;** of those out of their own families. Jesus draws the inference, **Then are the children** (*sons*) **free.** The argument is, Then am I, the Son of God, the Son of the great King of the temple, free from the obligation of paying tribute to the support of the temple worship. The temple was his Father's house, and therefore his own ; the money was for his Father's service ; he,

27 Then are the children free. Notwithstanding, ᵍ lest we should offend them, go thou to the sea, and cast a hook, and take up the fish that first cometh up; and when thou hast opened his mouth, thou shalt find a piece of money: ʰ that take, and give unto them for me and thee.

ᵍ Ro. 14. 13, 21; 15. 1–3; 1 Cor. 8. 13; 9. 19–22.

ʰ 2 Cor. 8. 9.

therefore, his Son and Representative, was the one to demand rather than pay it. Jesus asserts his Sonship and his superiority over the law and the temple, ch. 12 : 6, 8. He was a son in his own house, the temple, and not a servant. The question of Jesus was suited to remind Peter of his previous confession, "Thou art Christ, the Son of the living God" (ch. 16 : 16), and to show him that he had somewhat rashly answered in regard to the temple tax.

27. Although Jesus asserts his right to exemption from the temple tax, he, for prudential reasons, waives his right, and miraculously provides for the payment of both Peter's and his own. **Lest we should offend them.** Lest we should displease these tax-gatherers, and cause them to think that I disregard the worship of God, and thus give them occasion to reproach me. **Go thou to the sea,** etc. Jesus thus again shows his divine knowledge that the first fish that Peter should catch in the Sea of Galilee would have the money required. Miracles are the evidences of Christ's Messiahship and of his divine Sonship. This miracle was especially appropriate at this time; for while, by the payment of the tax, he waived the right of his Sonship, he at the same time asserted it by this remarkable display of his omniscience and miraculous power. **A piece of money.** Literally, *a stater*, an Attic silver coin, equivalent to a shekel, worth about sixty cents. At this time the double drachma, is said to have fallen into disuse in Palestine. It shows the great accuracy of Matthew in mentioning the stater, which was then current and of the same weight as the Hebrew shekel. Without doubt, Peter followed the direction of Jesus and obtained the promised money. It is not necessary to suppose the money created; it had been probably lost in the sea, and the miracle consisted in Christ's power over the fish in leading it to seize the money and then the hook. **For me and thee.** Notice Jesus does not say *for us*, putting himself on a par with Peter. The distinction of his Sonship is thus kept up. He was the only begotten Son; his disciples were indeed sons, but less intimately, and only mediately through him. Compare "*My* Father and *your* Father," John 20 : 17. The declaration, "Then are the sons free," applied especially to Jesus, though remotely it also applies to his disciples, who are the brethren of Jesus, and thus the sons of God.

REMARKS.

1. Jesus sees fit to give more intimate communion and greater revelations of himself to some of his followers than to others, in order to prepare them for trial and fit them for usefulness, ver. 1 ; Acts 9 : 15, 16; 2 Cor. 12 : 1–7.

2. The vailed glory of Jesus, which shone forth on the mount, is now unvailed at the right hand of God, ver. 2; Acts 9 : 3, 4 ; 2 Cor. 12 : 1–7.

3. The world of spirits is a reality ; disembodied spirits have a conscious existence, ver. 2; Job 26 : 5 (" The departed spirits tremble beneath the waters and their inhabitants"); Isa. 14 : 9–12; Luke 16 : 23; 23 : 42.

4. In Elijah we have a representation of those who shall be raised in glory, and especially of those who shall be changed at the second coming of Christ, ver. 2; 1 Cor. 15 : 51, 52; 1 Thess. 4 : 16, 17.

5. If foretastes of heaven are so glorious, what must heaven itself be ? If it was good to be on the mount, how good and blessed will it be to dwell with Jesus and the glorified forever! ver. 4.

6. The love of the Father for his Son is infinitely greater than the united love of all earthly parents of all time for their children. So is also his delight, ver. 5.

7. Jesus is the Prophet and Lawgiver of his people ; they are not to take any other as their guide, but follow human teachers only as they follow Christ, vers. 5–8; 1 Cor. 11 : 1.

8. No man in his present state can see

Jesus discourses in respect to the greatest in the kingdom of heaven.

[1] Mk. 9. 33; Lk. 9. 46; 22. 24; Ro. 12. 10; Phil. 2. 3.

XVIII. AT [1] the same time came the disciples unto

God and live; yet if Christ be with us, we must not fear to witness such displays of glory as he may think best to give us, vers. 7, 8; Exod. 33 : 20; Heb. 12 : 29; Rev. 1 : 17.

9. We should present truth in its proper order, and at proper times; milk for babes and strong meat for men, ver. 9; 1 Cor. 3 : 1, 2; John 16 : 12.

10. While we seek the aids of the learned to solve the difficulties of Scripture, we should especially apply to Christ for the guidance of his Spirit, ver. 10; John 16 : 13; James 1 : 5.

11. Formalists often hold to much that is true; but it is truth mingled with error, truth misunderstood and misapplied, vers. 10, 11; Luke 11 : 42.

12. We need to exercise caution in our interpretation of prophecy. It may be fulfilled in a way and at a time we little expect, vers. 12, 13; Luke 24 : 24–27.

13. Parents should feel a deep anxiety for those of their children who are spiritually under the power of Satan, and earnestly entreat Christ to come and save them, vers. 14, 15; Eph. 6 : 4.

14. The family relation affords some of our choicest comforts, and occasions some of our keenest sorrows, vers. 14–16; 2 Sam. 18 : 33; 1 Kings 1 : 48; Prov. 10 : 1.

15. The faithful labors and believing prayers of parents in behalf of their children shall not be in vain, vers. 17, 18, 20; Gen. 17 : 18, 20; James 5 : 16.

16. Unbelief may hinder us from doing what we might for Jesus, ver. 16, 17; Ps. 95 : 10; Phil. 4 : 13.

17. If Christ bears with our imperfections, we surely should bear with those of our brethren, ver. 17; 1 Pet. 3 : 8.

18. Christ may withhold from us success in winning souls, partly to humble us, and partly as a judgment upon sinners for their impenitence, vers. 19; Acts 28 : 23–27.

19. Our faith and our usefulness are to be increased by prayer and fasting, vers. 20, 21.

20. We are not permitted to behold the glories of Christ without beholding his sufferings, vers. 2, 22; 2 Tim. 2 : 12; 2 Cor. 12 : 7.

21. While we are very sorrowful over the death of Jesus, we should be especially sorrowful over our sins, which nailed him to the cross, ver. 23; Luke 23 : 28.

22. That which causes the people of God great sorrow will, in due time, be overruled for their good, ver. 23; Rom. 8 : 28.

23. We are to be subject to human government and obey its laws, if not contrary to the laws of God, vers. 24–27; ch. 22 : 21; Rom. 13 : 1–7.

24. Since Christ is a Son in his own house, and his disciples are his brethren, therefore are Christians free from the demands of the Jewish theocracy, vers. 25, 26; John 8 : 35, 36; Col. 2 : 14.

25. We should contribute our proportion toward supporting the Gospel, and extending its influence throughout the world, vers. 25–27; 2 Cor. 8 : 13, 14; 1 Cor. 16 : 1, 2.

26. To prevent a wrong construction being put on our actions, and to do the greater good, it may become us sometimes to act under protest, and not insist on our rights, but to forego our privileges, ver. 27; Rom. 14 : 13–15; 15 : 1–3; 2 Cor. 6 : 3; 11 : 7–9; Acts 16 : 3, and Gal. 2 : 3.

27. How great condescension does Christ show in paying the tribute, and how is his poverty manifest in having to perform a miracle to pay it, ver. 27; 2 Cor. 8 : 9.

CHAPTER XVIII.

In this chapter we have a discourse of Jesus to the twelve, occasioned by their question, "Who is the greatest in the kingdom of heaven?" It was spoken at Capernaum, and forms the last discourse, recorded by Matthew, of our Savior's ministry in Galilee. See ch. 19 : 1. The discourse and parables in Luke 17 : 20–18 : 14 may have been spoken in Galilee at a later period. It treats of the nature of true greatness in the Messiah's kingdom; of the terrible crime of the world for causes of offense against his followers; of the tender love and watchful care of his Father over them; of the Christian law for dealing with an offending brother; and of the Christian law of forgiveness toward the repenting offender.

A.D. 29.   MATTHEW XVIII.   245

Jesus, saying, Who is the greatest in the kingdom of heaven? And Jesus called [k] a little child unto him, and set him in the midst of them, and said, Verily I say unto you, [l] Except ye be converted, and become as little children, ye shall not enter into the

[k] ch. 19. 13, 14.
[l] Ps. 131. 2; John 3. 3-7; 1 Cor. 14. 20; 1 Pet. 2. 2.

1–6. THEY WHO ARE GREATEST IN CHRIST'S KINGDOM, Mark 9 : 33-42; Luke 9 : 46-50.

1. At the same time. More correctly, *At that time;* when Peter had returned from the sea-side, and had paid the sacred tribute, ch. 17 : 27. **The disciples.** The twelve, Mark 9 : 35. **Came—unto Jesus.** From Mark 9 : 33-35, it appears that they were at Capernaum, and in the house; that by the way they had disputed among themselves who was the greatest; that he asks them concerning the subject of their disputation, and they are silent, doubtless ashamed to confess the truth. But they soon break the silence by asking, according to Matthew, **Who is,** etc.? or, rather, *Who, then, is greatest,* etc.? We have here a good illustration of the manner in which the Evangelists may be shown to harmonize. What gave rise to this disputation we are not told. It is natural to refer to our Savior's address to Peter (ch. 16 : 17-19), and to the privilege granted the three disciples in witnessing his transfiguration, ch. 17 : 1. It is evident, from their disputing the point, that they did not understand Jesus, on either of these occasions, as pointing out Peter, or any of the disciples as the greatest. The *then,* in the question, "Who *then,* etc.," probably refers to something in the minds of the inquirers, occasioned by their dispute. **Greatest.** Literally, *Greater,* that is, than the rest in the kingdom of heaven; in effect, equal to *greatest.* The Greek comparative here is thus equivalent to the English superlative. Compare on ch. 11 : 11. The present tense is used, *Who then is,* implying that they regarded the Messiah's kingdom as commenced in the person of Jesus and his followers, and, at the same time, that they were looking forward to the highest honors and chief offices in his earthly government. The question, too, was somewhat different from that which they had discussed among themselves, "Which of *them* should be the greatest?" Luke 9 : 46. Doubtless, ashamed to present it in that light.

2. Jesus answers symbolically by calling a little child to him, and placing him in the midst of them. Mark adds the interesting item that he also folded it in his arms. The child was thus made a beautiful symbol of the true disciple who humbly, submissively, and confidently yields himself up to the Savior's will, guidance, and protection. Jesus thus taught them that his kingdom was spiritual, and that spiritual excellence, and not outward splendor, constituted true greatness in it. There is an interesting, though unreliable tradition, that this child was Ignatius, the martyr, pastor at Antioch from about 69 to 107 A.D.

3. **Be converted.** Rather, *Unless ye turn,* from a spirit of rivalry and worldly ambition, which has shown itself in your disputations and your desires after the highest offices in my kingdom, and **become as little children,** in simplicity, humility, docility, and obedience, ye can not enter, much less have preëminence in the kingdom of heaven. Little children are free from all worldly ambition. Those of the wise and ignorant, of the rich and poor, of princes and beggars, play together without feelings of distrust, jealousy, or rivalry. The verb translated *converted* should be translated *turn,* as it is in all other places in the New Testament. The idea is of *turning one's self* back from a course previously pursued. The compound form of this verb is, however, several times translated *convert* in our common version, as in ch. 13 : 15; Luke 22 : 32; Acts 3 : 19; James 5 : 19. Conversion and regeneration should be carefully distinguished. The soul is regenerated by an act of God; but a result of that work is a turning about, a conversion of the individual himself. In regeneration man is passive, but in conversion, under the influence of the Holy Spirit, he is active. The plural *children* shows that there was nothing particular in the child he set before them above other children.

4. Having explained the symbol of a child negatively, he now explains it positively. While failure to turn and

4 kingdom of heaven. ᵐ Whosoever therefore shall humble himself as this little child, the same is
5 greatest in the kingdom of heaven. And ⁿ whoso shall receive one such little child in my name re-
6 ceiveth me. ᵒ But whoso shall offend one of these little ones which believe in me, it were better for him that a millstone were hanged about his neck, and *that* he were drowned in the depth of the sea.

ᵐ ch. 20. 27; 23. 11, 12; Lk. 14. 11; Is. 57. 15; 1 Pet. 5. 5.
ⁿ ch. 10. 40-42; John 13. 20.
ᵒ Mk. 9. 42.

become like little children will prevent entering Christ's kingdom; humbling one's self like a little child will result not only in entering, but also in becoming the greatest in that kingdom. **Whosoever.** Jesus does not gratify their curiosity by telling who shall be the greatest; but he lays down the rule by which any one may become the greatest. Compare our Savior's reply to Nicodemus for a similar manner of teaching, John 3 : 2, 3; and 1 Cor. 14 : 20. **Shall humble himself.** The humility of the child is the chief point of comparison, from which spring its docility, obedience, submission, etc. Thus humility is a fundamental Christian grace, and inseparably connected with it, and springing from it are other Christian graces and virtues. It is to humility that Jesus would have his disciples turn from worldly ambition and pride. The Christian often needs thus to turn and become as a little child. He who completely divests himself of pride and ambition, and becomes entirely and fully permeated with humility, so that it pervades his whole being, as a **little child,** willing at all times and in all places to be just as little as he really is, the same is the greatest in Christ's kingdom. Compare Luke 18 : 14. *Greatest;* literally, *greater,* but equivalent, as in verse 1, to *greatest.* There are thus degrees of greatness in Christ's kingdom.

5. Jesus proceeds to show the nearness of his little ones to himself, the esteem and honor in which he holds them, and the exercise of love and fellowship which humility will excite in the hearts of others toward them. **Whoso receiveth;** cordially to his heart and fellowship. **One such little child.** Not an actual child, but one of these spiritual, humble ones; one truly regenerated and emptied of self, whether a child in years or not. He means not the one just described as *the greatest,* but one spiritually child-like, one of Christ's little ones, humble ones. The twelve, with the exception of Judas, belonged to these, Luke 9 : 48. **In my name.** On account of me, because he is my disciple, from love to me. This expresses the reason for receiving such little one. **Receiveth me.** Christ's disciples are his representatives and one with himself, ch. 10 : 40.

Just at this point Mark and Luke give a remark of John concerning a recent occurrence. Having found one who did not accompany the apostles casting out demons, they forbade him. This, according to Mark, called forth a reply from Jesus, disapproving of their conduct, embodying and developing all that is contained in the four following verses.

6. **Whoso shall offend.** Rather, *Whoever shall cause one of these little ones* —*to offend,* cause to fall into sin and error, cause him to become alienated from me. **One of these little ones.** Even one of my true and humble followers, ch. 10 : 42. What kind of little ones is explained by the words that follow, *that believe in me.* **It were better.** It would be profitable, well for him, and hence, better for him. **Millstone.** This was not the common hand-stone, which was turned by women (ch. 24 : 41); but the larger kind, which was turned by the ass, for the original literally means *an ass-millstone.* Or it may be more freely translated *upper millstone,* since this was the one turned, while the lower one remained stationary. The common hand upper millstone, being about two feet in diameter and a half foot thick, was well suited as an instrument of punishment for drowning criminals. When, therefore, our Savior speaks of the larger and heavier millstone being hanged about the neck, he uses the most forcible expression, and affirms in the strongest terms. Punishment by drowning was common among the Greeks and Ro-

A.D. 29.   MATTHEW XVIII.   247

7 Woe unto the world ᵖ because of offenses! for ᑫ it must needs be that offenses come; but ʳ woe to that man by whom the offense cometh!
8 ˢ Wherefore if thy hand or thy foot offend thee, cut them off, and cast *them* from thee: it is better for thee to enter into life halt or maimed, rather than having two hands or two feet, to be cast into ᵗ everlasting fire.
9 And if ᵘ thine eye offend thee, pluck it out and cast *it* from thee: it is better for thee to enter into life with one eye, ˣ rather than having two eyes to be cast into hell fire.
10 Take heed that ye despise not one of ʸ these little ones; for I say unto you, That in heaven ᶻ their angels do always ᵃ behold the face of ᵇ my Father

ᵖ 1 Sam 2. 17, 23, 24; 2 Sam. 12. 14; Ro. 2. 23, 24; 2 Pet. 2. 2.
ᑫ Lk. 17. 1.
ʳ ch. 13 41, 42; 26. 24; 2 Pet. 2. 3.
ˢ ch. 5. 29, 30; Deu. 13. 6-8.
ᵗ Mk. 9. 44.
ᵘ ch. 5. 28; Gal. 5. 24.
ˣ ch. 16. 26.
ʸ Ro. 14. 1-3. 13-15; 15. 1; Gal. 6. 1.
ᶻ Ps. 34, 7.
ᵃ Est. 1. 14; Lk. 1. 19.

---

mans, and the eastern nations, but not among the Jews. Execution by drowning is still practiced in the east. Doubtless, persons had been thus punished in the Sea of Galilee. Josephus records that the Galileans, at one time revolting from their commanders, drowned certain persons who were of Herod's party. (Joseph. *Antiq.* xiv. 15, 10).
Were drowned in the depth of the sea. A very strong and intense expression in the original. *Were drowned* means *were sunk* or *plunged into the sea;* drowning, of course, would be a necessary result. Dr. Conant truthfully and somewhat playfully remarks on this word, "If the man is *drowned*, the addition of the millstone is of no account; but makes a serious difference when he is plunged in deep water." *The depth* means *the high, open, deep sea*, in distinction from the shallow sea near the shore. Thus we have three words in the original brought together, "plunged into the sea," "the deep sea," and "the sea." It can not be better translated in English than by *plunged in the depth of the sea*.

7-9. CAUSES OF OFFENSE ARE FEARFULLY RUINOUS, AND SHOULD BY ALL MEANS BE AVOIDED, Mark 9: 43-50.

7. **Woe unto the world because of offenses;** rather, *for causes of offense*. Any occasion of sin or unbelief, or of falling, is a cause of offense. Compare Rom. 14 : 13, "an occasion to fall." Fearful retribution will be visited upon a wicked world for sins and errors produced among Christ's followers through artfulness and physical force. The errors and defects of Christians in faith and practice will also in turn have a terrible effect on the world in darkening their minds and hastening their destruction. **Offenses;** *causes of offense* must need come in a world of sinful men, when they act freely, where there is so much unbelief; they will necessarily lead others astray. **But woe to the man.** From the world he now descends to the individual, pronouncing a woe on the one through whom a cause of offense may come.

8, 9. Such being the fearful consequences of causes of offense on both the world and individuals, Jesus proceeds to exhort his disciples to avoid them at all hazards. **Hand, foot, eye,** the most valuable of our members, and often used proverbially to denote anything peculiarly dear and valuable; the dearest objects of our desires, the honors, possessions, or enjoyments we most prize. Should any of these cause us to offend, we must renounce and cast it from us, rather than, falling ourselves, and causing others to fall, we be lost. See further on ch. 5 : 29, 30, where *foot* is not mentioned, and the gradation is *eye* and then *hand*. **Halt,** or *lame* from the loss of a foot. **Maimed,** from the loss of a hand. **Everlasting fire, Hell fire.** Two ways of expressing the future punishment of the wicked. See on 5 : 22; 25 : 41.

10-14. WARNS THEM AGAINST DESPISING THESE LITTLE ONES. The esteem in which the humble followers of Jesus should be held. Found only in Matthew.

10. **Despise not.** Jesus warns them against the very beginning of causes of offenses in the mind. Beware how ye *look down upon* and *contemn* my humble and lowly followers. **These little**

11 which is in heaven. ᶜ For the Son of man is come to
12 save that which was lost. ᵈ How think ye? If a
man have an hundred sheep, and one of them be gone
astray, doth he not leave the ninety and nine and goeth into the mountains, and seeketh that which is

ᵇ ver. 14; John 20. 17; Heb. 2. 11.
ᶜ ch. 9, 12, 13; Lk. 15. 24; John 3. 17; 12. 47; 1 Tim. 1. 15.

---

ones; that believe in him, as in verse 6. The term is specially applicable to the poor, obscure, and humble followers of Jesus. **For I say unto you.** Jesus states the reason with authority, and reveals a fact which he alone could assert. See on 12 : 31. **In heaven their angels.** *Their angels in heaven,* who are their ministering spirits, Heb. 1: 14. In the Old Testament, angels are represented as guardians of God's people and nations (Ps. 34 : 7; Dan. 10 : 13, 20, 21); in the New, they are more particularly represented as guardians of individual believers. They rejoice at their repentance, Luke 15 : 10. They are ministering spirits for the heirs of salvation, Heb. 1 : 14. They bear such an intimate relation to them that they can be called *their angels,* as in this passage. From the expression in Acts 12 : 15, "It is his angel," it is evidently implied that those early disciples believed that individual Christians had their particular guardian and ministering angels. This was the opinion of the Jews, excepting the Sadducees, and of the Christian fathers. This is consistent with this passage, but not necessarily derived from it. Our Savior only reveals here the general fact that his followers have their angels, who are their attendants and guardians. Some suppose that by *their angels* are meant *the departed spirits* of the disciples in their heavenly state. But this is unnatural and far-fetched. Besides, *angels* in the original is never applied to spirits after death; and the present tense, and the connection, show that Jesus referred to the time when these humble followers were here on earth, and might be subject to contempt. **Always behold the face.** This is the fact which Jesus here emphatically states. Their angels are high in honor and privilege, and enjoy the divine presence and special favor. The highest officers in oriental courts are described as those who *see the king's face,* Esth. 1 : 4. So here it may mean that their angels are of the highest rank, or, on account of their relation to these little ones, enjoy the highest rank and honors, Rev. 1 : 4; 8 : 3, 4. In what high esteem, then, are these humble believers held in heaven, being under God's special providence, and guarded and ministered to by angels of the highest rank and dignity! Take heed, then, that ye despise them not. But since Christ is the Angel of his Presence in the highest sense, and thus acting as our Advocate and Intercessor at the right hand of God the Father, we may conceive of him as the great centre of angelic ministration and guardianship. By him heaven is indeed opened to the repenting and believing sinner, and the angels of God ascend and descend upon the Son of Man, John 1 : 51.

"Here is Jacob's ladder planted before our eyes: beneath are the little ones, then their angels, then the Son of Man in heaven, in whom alone man is exalted above the angels, who, as the great Angel of the Covenant, cometh from the presence and bosom of the Father to save those that are lost; and, above him again (ver. 14), the Father himself, and his good pleasure."—STIER.

11. They, too, are objects of Christ's saving mercy. These little ones have ministering angels who are in high honor before God, because Christ came to save them, and thus, through him, are the heirs of salvation. Here, then, is another reason for not despising the humble followers of Jesus, but for holding them in the highest esteem and affection. **That which was lost.** Lost from God and holiness, lost in sin; sinners. This verse is wanting in some of the best manuscripts. Many regard it as borrowed by copyists from Luke 19 : 10, where it is certainly genuine. If such is the case nothing is lost to Scripture as a whole. In the next two verses a further reason is added to that in ver. 10, from the case of the lost sheep.

12, 13. This parable is given more fully in Luke 15 : 3–6. **How think ye?** *What think ye?* as in ch. 21 : 28. What think ye in regard to what I am about to relate? What is your judgment? The question he asks must receive their affirmative answer; and his declaration in regard to the great joy of

13 gone astray? And if so be that he find it, verily I say unto you, ᵉ he rejoiceth more of that *sheep*, than of
14 the ninety and nine which went not astray. Even so it is not the will of your Father which is in heaven, ᶠ that one of these little ones should perish.

ᵈ Is. 53. 6; Lk. 15. 3–7.
ᵉ Mic. 7. 18; Lk. 15. 10, 23, 24.
ᶠ John 6. 39, 40; 10. 27–30; 17. 12; Ro. 8. 28–39; 1 Pet. 1. 3–5.

Method of dealing with an offending brother; the church's power in respect to discipline and prayer.

15 Moreover ᵍ if thy brother shall trespass against thee, go and tell him his fault between thee and him alone. If he shall hear thee, ʰ thou hast gained thy
16 brother. But if he will not hear *thee, then* take one or two more, that in ⁱ the mouth of two or three

ᵍ Le. 19. 17; Ps. 141. 5; Pro. 25. 9; Lk. 17. 3.
ʰ Jam. 5. 20; 1 Pet. 3. 1.
ⁱ Deu. 17. 6; 19. 15; John 8. 17; Heb. 10. 28.

the shepherd in finding his wandering, lost sheep must meet their hearty assent. **Doth he not leave, and goeth into the mountains.** Rather, *Doth he not leave the ninety and nine upon the mountains, and goeth*, etc. The mountain pastures were in many places very luxuriant, and often frequented by shepherds and their flocks. The interest of the shepherd in seeking the wandering sheep should not be lost sight of in this illustration. Thus Christ had come to seek and save the lost. It was natural that he should *rejoice more* over the one found. So Christ, the Good Shepherd, rejoices over the found ones; they are especially prized, and he will see that they are not lost again.

14. The application of the parable is different from that in Luke (15 : 6), this being spoken at a different time and for a different purpose. **Even so,** etc. *So it is not the will of your Father who is in heaven*, whose angels are appointed as guardians of these little ones, and whose Son came to save them (vers. 10, 11), *that* even *one* of them perish. The Son and ministering spirits are carrying out the will of God, who exercises this care over his children, so that none of them may be lost. Since it is the Father's will that not *one* of Christ's disciples perish, we must conclude that all of them shall be saved. We catch here the sentiment of the more positive declaration, *They shall* never perish, John 10 : 28. Hence the inference, Take heed that ye despise them not: for in so doing you act in opposition to the will of your heavenly Father.

15–20. MODE OF DEALING WITH AN OFFENDING BROTHER; first, privately; second, in the presence of a few; finally, before the church. The power of the church in such cases of discipline, and of effectual prayer. Only in Matthew.

15. Having cautioned his disciples against committing any offense against their brethren, he now instructs them how to act toward a brother who may sin against them. Their first step is to go to him privately, and their great object is to effect a reconciliation. **Shall trespass,** *shall sin.* Some ancient documents make the idea general by omitting **against thee.** The sin is made personal in ver. 21. **Go and tell,** *show his fault,* the wrong, make it plain to him. Not *reprove* or *rebuke* him; but *show* him, by kindly presenting the facts of the case. And do this in the most private manner, **between thee and him alone.** So that there shall be no motive of pride to induce the offender to make out a good case before others. Thus the aggrieved or injured brother is not to wait for the offender to come to him, but he is himself to go at once and strive kindly to win him. **Hear thee.** Listen to thee, so as to acknowledge his wrong and to act as a brother to thee. **Gained thy brother.** Recovered him to the path of obedience and duty; gained him to Christ and his cause, and to thee, from all of which he would be indeed lost if he should continue obstinately in his sinful course, ver. 17. Gained him, also, without further effort. Such treatment as this, performed in love, would, in most cases, reclaim the offender. Compare James 5 : 20.

16. But if the offender hears not, does not acquiesce in the statement of facts, acknowledge his fault, and return to duty, but perseveres in the wrong, then

17 witnesses every word may be established. And if he shall neglect to hear them, ^k tell *it* unto the church. But if he neglect to hear the church, let him be unto thee as an ^l heathen man and a publican.

^k Ac. 6. 1–3; 1 Cor. 6. 1–4.
^l Ezra 6. 21; Ro. 16. 17; 1 Cor. 5. 9–13; 2 Thes. 3.

a *second step* is to be taken. The object of this is also reconciliation, to gain his brother. **Take with thee one or two more, in the mouth of two or three.** According to some, the aggrieved brother, with the one or two more, would make the two or three witnesses. According to others, the offender, by acknowledging his fault, would make a third witness. It seems better to regard the *one or two* to be an indefinite phrase for a small number, and hence *two or three* are spoken of. The case is still to be conducted privately, in connection with two or three brethren, who shall strive to reclaim the brother, and, at the same time, be witnesses to the facts of the case. **Every word may be established.** That every declaration made, both by the offender and the offended, may be attested by witnesses, John 8 : 17; 2 Cor. 13 : 1. The supposition is, that the offending brother is the only one in the wrong. If the brother should be reclaimed, the case would end; but if he still perseveres in his course, there would be two or three witnesses to his persistency in the wrong. It is, indeed, very difficult to conceive how a truly Christian brother could fail to be reclaimed by such a mode of dealing, if carried out in love. The law of Moses enjoined a similar rule, Deut. 19 : 15.

17. If these efforts fail in gaining thy brother, a *third measure* is to be adopted. General publicity is still to be avoided; you are to tell it only to the church, to the company of believers with which the offender is connected, with the object still of restoring him to duty and effecting reconciliation. In all this you are to avoid giving cause of offense, and to labor in love. **Neglect to hear them.** Take no heed. The language becomes stronger than merely *not hear* of the preceding verse, implying something of obstinacy and indifference. **The church.** See on ch. 16 : 18. The term can not here be applied, as some have supposed, to the Jewish synagogue; for verses 18–20 show that it refers to a Christian, not a Jewish, community. Besides, the term is never applied to the synagogue. Neither does it refer to the officers of a church; for verses 19, 20 show that it refers to those gathered together in his name—a company of believers. Moreover, in no place in the New Testament is *church* applied to officers, elders, etc. They are represented as a part of the church, Acts 20 : 17. Compare Phil. 1 : 1. The term *church* here refers to the congregation of believers, the company of disciples, whether it be large or small, with which the offender is connected. The objection that no church was then fully organized is of no weight, since the directions here given by our Savior were intended for all future time. The disciples had previously heard Jesus speak of building his church (ch. 16 : 18). He had thus taught them that he was to have his congregation of faithful disciples in the world. They themselves formed the germ, the beginning under Christ, the head, of the first particular church, and from the use of the word *church* among the Jews, and doubtless from Jesus himself, they had a conception of its application and meaning.

If, however, the offender perseveres in his wrong—for it is here taken for granted that the church regards him as the offender, and advises him to retrace his steps—if after all this, he continues incorrigible, *then let him be to thee as a heathen and a publican*, let him bear no closer relation *to thee*, and consequently to the church, than you would permit to an open idolater. Exclusion from church-fellowship is implied in this language. Heathens and publicans were regarded by the Jews as excommunicated persons. It is impossible to conceive of a person with any grace in his heart being thus dealt with in kindness, in love, without being reclaimed. The legitimate conclusion is, that if he is not reclaimed under such treatment, he is not of them, and therefore should be put away from them. Yet neither the injured brother nor the church is to *hate* the excluded offender, as Jewish teachers taught (ch. 5 : 43), but treat him kindly (1 Cor. 5 : 11, and 2 Cor. 2 : 6, 7; 2 Thess. 3 : 14, 15), so that if possible he may be brought to repentance and salvation.

18 Verily I say unto you, ᵐ Whatsoever ye shall bind on earth shall be bound in heaven: and whatsoever ye shall loose on earth shall be loosed in heaven.

19 ⁿ Again I say unto you, That if two of you shall agree on earth, as touching any thing that they shall ask, ᵒ it shall be done for them of my Father which

20 is in heaven. For where two or three are gathered together in my name, ᵖ there am I in the midst of them.

6, 14, 15; 2 John 10.
ᵐ ch. 16. 19.
ⁿ Ac. 1. 14; 2. 1, 2:4 24-31; Jam. 5. 14-16.
ᵒ John 14. 13, 14; 1 John 3. 22.
ᵖ ch. 28. 20; John 20. 19-26; Rev. 21, 3.

On forgiveness; parable of the unmerciful servant.

21 Then came Peter to him, and said, Lord, how oft shall my brother sin against me, and I forgive him?

---

18. Verily, I say, etc. Jesus most solemnly and authoritatively asserts the power of the church. "For evidently, while verse 17 lays down the rule for the conduct of the church, verse 18 shows that the church is warranted in this conduct."—LANGE. **Ye,** the disciples who constitute the church spoken of in the preceding verse. The power and authority which was conferred on Peter (ch. 16 : 19) is here conferred upon the apostles and the disciples generally. Whatever they should do, according to Christ's directions and will, would be ratified in heaven. This is true of the church so far as she executes the laws and will of Christ. See on ch. 16 : 19.

19. Jesus makes another solemn and authoritative statement concerning the power of the church, and even of two or three of its members, in offering effectual prayer, so that he himself would be in the midst of them to bless and direct them. The church, possessing and exercising such power and privilege, would be well capable of exercising discipline according to the word and will of Christ. **That if two.** Christ takes the smallest number which can form a company; even two can make a company of believers. It is not necessary to suppose that Jesus here refers to a church of two, but rather to two of a church. But it is possible, under certain circumstances, for two or three (next verse) to form a church. It is essential that these **agree** concerning what they ask. There must be no offense, no alienation, but a true fellowship of soul and purpose. **Any thing they shall ask.** According to the divine will, 1 John 5 : 14. Spiritual fellowship with one another and with Jesus would insure entire submission to his will. Notice, **on earth** is contrasted with **in heaven,** as in the preceding verse. It is according to his will that the church should execute the laws and discipline of Christ; and as they need wisdom for this, they may expect all they need if they unitedly ask for it. It shall be given, even if only two thus ask for it.

20. **For,** etc. The truth reaffirmed, explained with the great reason: For Jesus is with them to bless and guide. **Two or three are gathered together in my name.** They are a company of my disciples, worshiping as a church or as members of a church may represent it in worship. **In my name;** in reference to me, and under my authority. They are thus united and agreed in acknowledging and acting under the authority of Jesus. They are thus gathered for his glory, and for attending to the things of his cause. **There am I in the midst of them.** By his power and spirit, ch. 28 : 20; Acts 18 : 10. Jesus is thus present to answer their prayers, and so direct all they do as to meet with the approbation of their heavenly Father. How superior was this to the Jewish notion that ten must be assembled in a synagogue to insure the Divine Presence and the answer of their prayers! According to the rabbins, "A smaller number God despises."

21–35. THE REPLY OF JESUS TO PETER'S QUESTION RESPECTING THE LIMIT OF FORGIVENESS, including the parable of THE TWO DEBTORS, or the Unmerciful Servant. Forgiveness is to be extended to the penitent without limit; we should ever be in the exercise of a forgiving temper. Only in Matthew.

21. **Then came Peter.** Our Savior's

22 ⁹ till seven times? Jesus saith unto him, I say not unto thee, Until seven times: ʳ but, Until seventy 23 times seven. Therefore is the kingdom of heaven likened unto a certain king, ˢ which would take ac- 24 count of his servants. And when he had begun to reckon, one was brought unto him, which

ᑫ Lk. 17. 3. 4.
ʳ ch. 6. 14, 15; Ps. 78. 38, 40; Mk. 11. 25; Ro. 12. 21; Eph. 4. 31, 32; Col 3. 13.
ˢ Rom. 14. 12; 2 Cor. 5. 10.

discourse concerning the treatment of private offenses (vers. 15–17) implied forgiveness if they "gained" their brother, either by a private interview, or by taking two or three witnesses, or by bringing the matter before the church. Peter did not as yet understand fully the nature of forgiveness, and hence was in doubt in regard to the extent of its exercise. He therefore asks, "How oft shall my brother sin against me, and I forgive him?" The Jewish rabbis limited forgiveness to three times, basing their view on Amos 1 : 3; 2 : 6; Job 33: 29, 30. Feeling that this number should be increased under the new law of love propounded by our Savior, Peter asks, **Till, until, seven times?** He doubtless limits the number of times to *seven*, as a sacred number closely connected, in the Scriptures, with forgiveness and retribution, Lev. 4 : 6; 16 : 14; 25 : 28; 26 : 18, 21, 24, 28; Ps. 79 : 12; Dan. 4 : 16; Rev. 15 : 1. Compare Prov. 24 : 16.

22. Jesus replies, placing no limit, **Seven times—Seventy times seven.** A contrast between a limited and an unlimited number of times. By *seventy times seven*, a general expression for a large, indefinite number, Jesus intended to teach that the times that forgiveness should be exercised by his disciples should be unlimited. Compare Gen. 4: 24. As often as a brother asks forgiveness we are to forgive him, ver. 33; Luke 17 : 4. If he fails to do so, we are to have a forgiving spirit, seeking to gain our brother (ver. 15), and should it prove necessary that he be excluded from the church, we are not to treat him with malice, but kindly and in love, 2 Thess. 3 : 15. Compare 1 Cor. 5 : 13, and 2 Cor. 2 : 6–10.

23. In order to illustrate the law of forgiveness under the new dispensation, how it may be violated, and the consequences of so doing, Jesus gives the parable of the UNMERCIFUL SERVANT. This is recorded by Matthew alone. **Therefore,** refers to the answer just given to Peter: *Because of this* law of unlimited forgiveness, which indeed requires a constant readiness to forgive, the kingdom of heaven in this respect **is likened,** is like to the case of a certain king, etc., to the circumstances about to be given. **Which would take account of.** Who desired, and hence determined, to make a *reckoning,* or *settlement,* with. Compare 2 Kings 12: 15; 22 : 7. **Servants.** His ministers or stewards; possibly the collectors of his revenue. In the despotic governments of the east, all, from the highest to the lowest, stood in a servile relation to the monarch. The large amount of indebtedness of one of these servants indicates a high official, rather than any common slave.

24. **When he begun.** Emphatic and significant. He had only *begun* to reckon. **One was brought unto him.** How natural and life-like the representation; he surely would never come of himself. **Ten thousand talents.** An immense sum, which he could never pay. A Hebrew talent was equal to three thousand shekels, or about $1500. An Attic talent is estimated at about $1170. A Syrian talent was about $225. The amount of this servant's indebtedness was about $15,000,-000, if Hebrew talents are intended; or about $11,700,000, if Attic; or about $2,-250,000, if Syrian. These calculations are based on the supposition that talents of silver are here meant, which is most probable. If they were talents of gold, the sum was perfectly enormous. Trench illustrates by comparing with other sums mentioned in Scripture. Thus, twenty-nine talents of gold were used in the construction of the tabernacle (Exod. 38 : 24); David prepared for the temple 3000 talents of gold, and the princes 5000 (1 Chron. 29 : 4–7); the Queen of Sheba presented Solomon 120 talents (1 Kings 10 : 10); the King of Assyria laid on Hezekiah 30 talents of gold (2 Kings 18 : 4); and in the extreme impoverishment to which the land was brought at last, one talent of gold was laid on it, after the death of Josiah, by the King of Egypt (2 Chron. 36 : 3).

A.D. 29. MATTHEW XVIII. 253

25 owed him ᵗ ten thousand talents. But forasmuch as he had not to pay, his lord commanded him ᵘ to be sold, and his wife, and children, and all that he
26 had, and payment to be made. The servant therefore fell down, and worshiped him, saying, Lord, have patience with me, and I will pay thee all.
27 Then the lord of that servant was moved with compassion, and loosed him, and forgave him the debt.
28 But the same servant went out, and found one of his fellow-servants, which owed him an hundred ˣ pence: and he laid hands on him, and took *him*
29 by the throat, saying, Pay me that thou owest. And
 . his fellow-servant fell down at his feet, and besought him, saying, Have patience with me, and I will pay
30 thee all. And he would not: but went and cast

ᵗ Ps. 19. 12; 40. 12.
ᵘ Le. 25. 39; 2 Ki. 4. 1; Ne. 5. 8.

ˣ ch. 20. 2.

At a later period, Haman promised 10,000 talents of silver to the Persian king, in compensation for the tribute of the whole Jewish people, should they be destroyed, expecting doubtless to reimburse himself from the spoils of the Jews.
25. Had not to pay. He had not means or power to pay; that is, he was not able to pay. **Commanded him to be sold,** etc. This was according to the laws of the Jews, and of many ancient nations. By the Mosaic law the servitude of a Hebrew was limited to six years, and in every case it terminated at the year of Jubilee, when liberty was proclaimed to all, Exod. 21 : 1; Deut. 15 : 12; Lev. 25 : 10, 39–41; 2 Kings 4 : 1; Amos 2 : 6. The scene, however, is probably not that of a Jewish, but of an oriental king, who had absolute power over the person and property of his subjects.
26. Worshiped. Falling down, he *prostrated* himself before him, and thus humbly did him reverence or homage. See on ch. 2 : 2. He first fell on his knees, and then bowed down to the ground. Compare 2 Kings 4 : 37. **I will pay thee all.** He promises an impossibility. The language is life-like, just what we should expect him to say in his extremity. It must therefore be interpreted not as the words of careful deliberation, but as the outburst of fear and anguish. It was an expression of readiness and determination to pay him all, if possible.
27. Loosed. Released from confinement and from prospective slavery.

Forgave him. This was more than he asked for; yet it was what he needed, for payment was impossible on his part. Thus his lord exercised the highest qualities of **compassion**.
28. One of his fellow-servants. This one probably occupied a lower station than himself; but being a servant of the same master, was a fellow-servant. **A hundred pence.** About fifteen dollars. How small a sum in comparison with ten thousand talents! *Pence* here represents a Roman silver coin, called the *denarius*. As we have no corresponding English coin, Dr. Conant very properly renders this passage, *a hundred denaries*, transferring the word with an English termination. See on ch. 20 : 2. **Took him by the throat.** Literally, *Seizing him, he choked him*. Exhibits his harsh, unmerciful spirit. The creditor was permitted, by Roman law, to seize his debtor by the throat and bring him before the tribunal. **Pay,** etc. The demand is peremptory. The highest critical authorities read, *Pay me, if thou owest aught.* But whether we adopt this or the common reading, the essential thought, as Dr. Conant suggests, is the same: *Pay me whatever thou owest.* It was a haughty demand of one determined to exact the utmost, not only of this one, but of all who owed him.
29. Fell down at his feet and besought him. Rather, *Fell down and besought him.* He humbled himself before his fellow-servant, in a manner similar to what that fellow-servant had done previously to his lord, or king. He makes the same promise, **Have pa-**

31 him into prison, till he should pay the debt. So when his fellow-servants saw what was done, they were very sorry, and came and told unto their lord
32 all that was done. Then his lord, after that he had called him, said unto him, O thou wicked servant, I forgave thee all that debt, because thou desiredst
33 me: shouldest not thou also have compassion on thy fellow-servant, ʸ even as I had pity on thee?
34 And his lord was wroth, and delivered him to the tormentors, till he should pay all that was due
35 unto him. ᶻ So likewise shall my heavenly Father do also unto you, if ye from your hearts forgive not every one his brother their trespasses.

ʸ Eph. 4. 32; Col 3, 13.

ᶻ ch. 6. 12, 14, 15; Pro. 21. 13; Jam. 2. 13.

---

tience, etc. All is omitted by the best authorities, but affects not the thought.

30. **He would not.** His ears were shut to his entreaties. He casts him **into prison,** which was not according to Mosaic law, but according to the laws of other nations. Here we have another reason for regarding the similitude of the parable, as that of a foreign despotism rather than of Jewish rule. "There is the climax of depravity, to be beggars with God and tyrants to our brethren."

31. **Very sorry.** From a fellow feeling and sympathy. How lifelike is this; and also the language in verse 34, *His lord was wroth.* Their feelings partook of sorrow, grief; his of wrath, indignation. Thus grief is becoming God's servants over the sin of others; but wrath is becoming him, for to him belongeth vengeance.

32. The language of the lord is that of severe reproof and condemnation. **Desiredst me.** Rather, *Besoughtest me.* An act of royal favor, of sovereign mercy.

33. An interrogative sentence, equivalent to a strong affirmative: Having thyself been an object of **compassion,** or pity, thou shouldst in like manner have exercised pity.

34. **The tormentors.** Not only was he to be imprisoned, but also tortured. The *tormentors* were not merely the prison-keepers, but those who had authority to examine and inflict tortures. Here, again, the scene is not Jewish, but foreign and Gentile. State criminals in eastern nations were sometimes subjected to scanty allowances, severe scourgings, rackings, loading with chains, or yokes of wood. Among the Romans the debtor could inflict on the creditor such tortures as loading him with chains, feeding on bread and water, etc. **Till he should pay all,** etc. This was equivalent to imprisonment and sufferings for life; for it was impossible for him to pay. This punishment was perpetual, and more severe and degraded than if he and his family had been sold into slavery. The king, as an absolute sovereign, recalls his act of forgiving the debt, and now punishes not only for the original debt, which he demands, but also for his unmerciful dealings toward his fellow-servant.

35. In this verse we have the key-note of the parable. True forgiveness is not merely *outward,* but *inward;* it must come **from the heart,** and presupposes a gracious state. If it comes not from your heart, then God will not forgive, but punish, as you deserve. With what measure ye mete, it shall be measured to you, ch. 6 : 14, 15; 7 : 2.

The grand *design* of this parable is to show the manner and the consequences of violating Christ's law of forgiveness under the Gospel dispensation. The *centre* of comparison is found in the treatment of the forgiven servant toward his supplicating fellow-servant. The *king* represents our **Heavenly Father;** the servant, his professed people. The *reckoning* is not the final judgment, but those times when God comes near to them by his Providence, by the terrors of the law or the admonitions of the Spirit, 2 Kings 20 : 1–6; 2 Sam. 12 : 1–7. Compare also the preaching of Jonah to the Ninevites, Jon. 3 : 4; and the barren fig-tree, Luke 13 : 7. The *one brought* to him, a professed believer, having a high trust, possibly a Judas; his *debt,* his sins. Sin is represented as a debt in the Lord's Prayer, ch. 6 : 12.

The greatness of his debt represents the great moral debt which every man owes to God; the exceeding sinfulness of sin and its vast amount, of thought, word, and act; and the impossibility of any one of himself ever discharging the debt. The *fellow-servant* represents a fellow-disciple; his *debt*, his trespass against him; its *smallness* shows how little are our trespasses against men compared with our sins against God.

The question here arises, Does this first servant represent a true child of God? And if so, does it teach that he can fall from grace and be finally lost? In answering these questions we must be careful, first, not to press the drapery and minor portions of the parable into an undue prominence; second, not to found a doctrine on a mere similitude, which is not taught elsewhere; third, not to interpret the figurative language of the parable in opposition to truths clearly taught without figure elsewhere in the Word of God. That no true child of God will ever so fall away as to be finally lost, is most clearly taught in Scripture. "I give unto them," says Jesus, "eternal life;" not a limited life of a few weeks, months, or years, but "*eternal* life; and they shall never perish; neither shall any one pluck them out of my hand." And again, "No one is able to pluck them out of my Father's hand," John 10 : 28, 29; 3 : 15; 6 : 30, 40; 17 : 11, 12; Rom. 8 : 1, 33–39; Col. 3 : 3, 4; 2 Tim. 1 : 12. Compare 1 Sam. 2 : 9; Isa. 49 : 14–16.

If a true child of God is meant by the first servant, then we must regard him as wandering from God and exercising an unchristian spirit. His being delivered to the tormentors, represents him as the backslider in heart filled with his own ways (Prov. 14 : 14), and chastened by the Almighty, Ps. 89 : 31–33. And as the imprisoned and tortured debtor would sometimes call forth the sympathy of his friends to raise the amount necessary to his release, so here we must view the chastened wanderer returning in penitence and looking to Jesus, who in his loving compassion cancels the debt with his own blood, and gives liberty to his afflicted child, 1 John 2 : 1, 2.

It seems better, however, to suppose a false professor to be intended, one who is entirely destitute of that spirit of love which must underlie all true forgiveness. The language of the parable favors this view. He *was brought*, an unwilling prisoner, to his lord; his prayer, "Have patience with me, and I *will pay thee all*," indicates fear and anguish, a want of proper conception of the greatness of his sins, and self-righteousness; and his going forth to seize a fellow-servant, and treating him without mercy, would also seem to prove that he knew nothing of forgiveness and mercy by practical experience. He was one of those of whom John speaks: "They went out from us, because they were not of us," 1 John 2 : 19. As a nominal disciple he professed to have been forgiven, and by his brethren was so regarded. And more. By some Providential dispensation we may also regard God as reckoning with him. He may be brought nigh to death by sickness; his sins rise up before him; he begs for mercy and life, and makes many fair promises. God listens and raises him up. But he goes forth the same unchanged person, forgets his vows, and by his harsh and unforgiving spirit, shows that he did not really receive what God offered to him—forgiveness through faith in Christ. God at length determines to bear with him no longer, and delivers him up to final condemnation, and to a punishment which can have no end. Thus, "he shall have judgment without mercy that hath showed no mercy," James 2 : 13. He who, like this servant, has not *the heart* to forgive, and therefore does not and will not from his heart forgive, must expect a like end and a like punishment. May this parable lead us to obey from the heart Christ's law of forgiveness, Eph. 4 : 32; 5 : 1, 2; Gal. 6 : 1.

Remarks.

1. The Christian must beware of pride and ambition, and of seeking after mere greatness and preëminence. Such a course leads to strife and contention, and is opposed alike to the will, example, and teaching of their Lord, ver. 1; Mark 9 : 33; Prov. 13 : 10; 2 Cor. 12 : 7; Jer. 45 : 5.

2. They who are contentious and overbearing, who strive after power and office, or use their professions for worldly gain, have reason to fear that they have never been renewed in the spirit of their minds, ver. 3; John 12 : 6; 13 : 6–16; 1 Tim. 6 : 3–5; 3 John 9–11.

3. Moral excellence and greatness is not contentious, but peaceful and love

ing, and should be diligently sought after and cultivated, vers. 2–4; ch. 5 : 19; 23 : 11, 12; 1 Tim. 6 : 9, 11.

4. Little children have many characteristics worthy of study and imitation, vers. 2–4; Mark 10 : 15; Ps. 131 : 1, 2.

5. Humility is essential to, and an evidence of, godliness, pleasing to God, and leads to true greatness, vers. 3, 4; Isa. 57 : 15; Luke 18 : 14; James 4 : 6, 10.

6. Christ sets us an example of humility, condescension, and love, in making the least and feeblest of his people representatives of himself, ver. 5; ch. 25 : 45.

7. It is better to lose our natural life than to cause a Christian to go astray, and thus injure his spiritual life, ver. 6; Luke 17 : 1; 2 Thess. 1 : 6; 1 Cor. 3 : 17.

8. The authors of error, and the promoter of heresies and wicked divisions, will meet with the more fearful punishment than those who have been destroyed by their wicked influence, ver. 7; Mal. 2 : 7–9.

9. Pride, contention, worldliness, and other causes of offense have led many to reject the Gospel, and perish, ver. 7; Rom. 2 : 24; 12 : 17, 18; 2 Tim. 2 : 24, 25.

10. Our dearest sins must be renounced and forsaken, and whatever separates between us and God, or we are lost forever, vers. 8, 9; Luke 17 : 33; Phil. 3 : 7–9.

11. We should not despise any followers of Christ because of their imperfections, humble circumstances and garb, since Jesus came to save them, and angels in heaven esteem them, and are not ashamed to minister to them, vers. 10, 11; Rom. 14 : 1–3, 10; 1 Cor. 8 : 9–11; Heb. 1 : 14.

12. God and holy angels rejoice in the salvation of sinners, vers. 12, 13; Luke 15 : 7, 22–24.

13. The patience and perseverance of our heavenly Father in seeking and saving the lost should call forth our admiration, gratitude, and love, vers. 12–14; Ezek. 34 : 11, 12, 16; Jer. 31 : 8, 20; Isa. 41 : 9.

14. God designs the full and final salvation of all his children, ver. 14; 1 Pet. 1 : 5–9.

15. We have no right to depart from Christ's law in treating with an offending brother, vers. 15–17; Isa. 8 : 20; John 14 : 23, 24.

16. How wise is Christ's rules of discipline! By privacy it guards the character of the offender, prevents the rising of pride, and fosters honesty and kindness; by seeking the aid of judicious brethren, it prevents haste and assures discretion; and, last of all, by appealing to the united wisdom of the church, nothing is left undone that should be done, vers. 15–17.

17. The encouragement for dealing with an offender according to Christ's directions are great, for thereby we may save him, ver. 15; Gal. 6 : 1; James 5 : 19, 20.

18. The individual church is Christ's only and highest ecclesiastical tribunal this side of death and the judgment, vers. 17, 18; Acts 1 : 23–26; 6 : 1–6; 13 : 1–3; 15 : 2, 22; 1 Cor. 5 : 3–5, 11–13; 6 : 1–5; 16 : 3; 2 Cor. 2 : 5–9; 8 : 19, 23.

19. The exclusion of a brother is the most solemn transaction that the church can do, and should be attended with prayer, vers. 17–19; 1 Cor. 5 : 4, 5.

20. While the united prayer of the smallest company shall be answered, disagreements in the largest company will prevent their prayers being heard, vers. 19, 20; John 16 : 23, 24; 1 Pet. 3 : 7.

21. Since God is so willing to forgive our sins against him, we should be ready to forgive the infinitely smaller offenses of our brethren, vers. 21–25; Eph. 4 : 32; Col. 3 : 12–15.

22. We must all give an account to God, vers. 23, 24; Rom. 2 : 16; 14 : 12; 2 Cor. 5 : 10; Gal. 6 : 7.

23. The unforgiving have neither the spirit of Christ, nor any claim to being his, nor any just expectation of his forgiveness, vers. 32–34; ch. 6 : 14; Rev. 13 : 10.

24. True Christians often suffer greatly for cherishing a malicious and unforgiving spirit, ver. 34; Ps. 89 : 30–33; Heb. 12 : 6, 11.

25. True forgiveness proceeds from the heart; false, from the lips, ver. 35.

CHAPTER XIX.

In this, and the chapter following it, we have Matthew's summary account of the last journey of Jesus to Jerusalem. Mark's account (ch. 10) is very similar. From a careful comparison of the accounts of Luke and John, we learn that soon after the discourse in the preceding chapter Jesus goes up to the Feast of the

Jesus goes beyond Jordan; he replies to the Pharisees' question respecting divorce.

XIX. AND it came to pass, ^a *that* when Jesus had finished these sayings, he departed from Galilee, and came into the coasts of Judæa beyond Jordan.
2 ^b And great multitudes followed him; and he healed them there.
3 ^c The Pharisees also came unto him, ^d tempting him, and saying unto him, ^e Is it lawful for a man

^a Mk. 10. 1; John 10. 40.

^b ch. 12. 15.

^c Mk. 10. 2.
^d ch. 16. 1.
^e ch. 5. 31, 32.

Tabernacles, which occurred on the 15th of Tishri, or October, John 7:2-10; Luke 9:51-10:16. For about two months he exercises his ministry in Judea (Luke 10:17-13:9); after which he attends the Feast of Dedication on the 25th of Chisleu, about the 20th of December, John 10:22-39. Then he goes beyond Jordan and exercises his ministry, probably about a month, in Perea (John 10:40; Luke 13:10-17:10); after which he goes to Bethany, probably early in February, and raises Lazarus, John 11:7. Compare Luke 13:22. After this he withdraws to a city called Ephraim, where he continued a few weeks with his disciples, John 11:54. From this point he makes a flying trip through Samaria and Galilee on his last journey to Jerusalem, Luke 17:11.

1, 2. JESUS FINALLY LEAVES GALILEE, AS A PLACE OF RESIDENCE, AND GOES TO THE EAST OF JORDAN, Mark 10:1; compare Luke 17:11-19.

1. **Finished these sayings.** Completed the instructions recorded in the preceding chapter. **Departed from Galilee.** It is possible that Matthew takes in at one view both departures of our Lord: that to the Feast of Tabernacles and that just previous to his last sufferings. The meaning then is that Jesus left Galilee, which had been the main scene of his ministry, no more to reside there, nor to exercise his ministry there, except as he should pass through on his last journey to Jerusalem, Luke 17:11. To his excursions and labors in Judea and Perea this verse may very briefly and incidentally refer. Thus we may have here the two extremities of a period which Matthew and Mark pass over. It is, however, more natural and probable that, after finishing the account of our Lord's Galilean ministry in the last chapter, the Evangelist passes to his last journey, without regard to intervening journeys. That six months of his ministry is silently passed over by Matthew and Mark, is quite generally admitted; and it seems better to place this lapse of time between the eighteenth and nineteenth chapters of Matthew than elsewhere. The reason of this omission by the first two Evangelists can only be conjectured. They trace the growing opposition to Jesus through the six months before the Feast of the Tabernacles. Luke, passing over that period with but slight references, traces the same opposition in the succeeding six months, and then the three Evangelists join in relating the result—the crucifixion of Jesus. See NEW HARMONY OF THE GOSPELS by the author, pp. 273-278, 287.

Jesus came into the coasts, rather, *borders,* the bordering territory of Judea **beyond,** *east* of the Jordan. The territory beyond the Jordan, east of Judea, was Perea, which was under Herod Antipas, who ruled over this province as well as Galilee. Mark, more particular than Matthew, says (10:1), correctly translated, "He cometh into the borders of Judea, and beyond the Jordan." He went to the frontiers of Judea, by the way of Perea, the region beyond Jordan, and not by the near route through Samaria. He visited and exercised his ministry both in Perea and Judea.

2. **He healed them there.** The sick which were brought to him. The multitudes having their sick healed, were indeed whole.

3-12. REPLY TO THE PHARISEES' QUESTION CONCERNING DIVORCE, Mark 10:2-12. This occurred in the Perean ministry of Jesus, just previous to his blessing little children, Luke 18:15.

3. The question here propounded to Jesus was one of dispute among Jewish teachers. Moses had directed (Deut. 24:1) that a man might put away his

4 to put away his wife for every cause? And he answered and said unto them, Have ye not read, ᶠ that He which made *them* at the beginning made them 5 male and female, and said, ᵍ 'For this cause shall a man leave father and mother, and shall cleave to his wife: and ʰ they twain shall be one flesh.' 6 Wherefore they are no more twain, but one flesh. ⁱ What therefore God hath joined together, let not man put asunder.

ᶠ Gen. 1. 27; 5. 2; Mal. 2. 15.
ᵍ Gen. 2. 21-24; Mk. 10. 5-9.
ʰ 1 Cor. 6. 16; 7. 2-4.
ⁱ Mal. 2. 14-16; Ro. 7. 2; 1 Cor. 7. 10-14.

wife by giving her a bill of divorcement, if she found "no favor in his sight, because he hath found uncleanness in her." The followers of Rabbi Hillel held that this meant that any thing that displeased her husband gave him a right to divorce her. But the followers of Rabbi Shammai held that "uncleanness" referred to unchastity, and therefore denied the right to divorce a wife except for adultery. **Pharisees.** Certain of this sect came to Jesus. The better translation is, *And there came to him Pharisees*. **Tempting him.** Having a wicked purpose to entice him and get him into difficulty. They commence a new mode of opposition. They had found fault with him for violating the law (12:2), and transgressing the tradition of the elders (15:2); had referred his power to Beelzebul (12:24), and had demanded a sign from heaven, 12:38; 16:1. But in every instance he had hurled back their objections with overwhelming power. Now they seek to entangle him in existing controversies on certain vexed questions, which it would be impossible to answer without displeasing one or another party. Notice this mode of attack continued in ch. 22:15-40. Very likely also they wished to call forth a condemnation of Herod Antipas in his married relationship, and thus insure to Jesus an end similar to that of John the Baptist. **For every cause.** That is, for any cause whatever. If he should answer in the affirmative, they could charge him with lax morality; if in the negative, with disregarding the authority of Moses.

4. But Jesus answers by appealing to the creation, thus showing what is the divine will in the matter. He argues, first, from what God *did;* second, from what he *said;* and then draws his irresistible conclusion in verse 6. **Have ye not read.** Jesus refers to the book of Genesis as of divine authority. Thus, from the declarations of Jesus we prove the inspiration of the Old Testament, Luke 24:27. **At the beginning.** *From the beginning*, the creation. **Made them male and female.** Or, *created them*, according to some excellent copies. They were made and designed one for the other. Thus God showed his will that man and woman should live together in the marriage state.

5. **And said.** What is here quoted was, according to Gen. 2:24, spoken by Adam. Adam, however, spoke prophetically, for the relation of father and mother did not yet exist. It was thus God, by inspiration, speaking through Adam. **For this cause.** Because Eve was taken out of Adam, and was bone of his bone and flesh of his flesh (Gen. 2:21-24), and hence because male and female were thus made. **Leave father and mother.** The relation between husband and wife is thus stronger and closer than that between parent and child. **Cleave.** Shall be joined unto and adhere. **The two** is not found in the original Hebrew, but is implied. It is, however, found in the Samaritan Pentateuch, and in the Septuagint version. **One flesh.** They two shall be united in the flesh, one being the part of the other. Compare 5:28. Thus, not only by the act of creation, but also by this prophetic declaration through Adam, did God show his will that man and woman should live in the marriage state.

6. The conclusion which Jesus now draws is manifest and irresistible. A relation which was made by God, and to which all other relations, even that of parent and child, must yield, can be severed only by him. **God hath joined together** the two, surely man has no right to put them asunder. God only has the right. The relation ceases at death; for the unity is based on **one**

7 They say unto him, *k* Why did Moses then command to give a writing of divorcement, and to put
8 her away? He saith unto them, Moses because of the hardness of your hearts suffered you to put away your wives: *l* but from the beginning it was not so.
9 *m* And I say unto you, Whosoever shall put away his wife, except *it be* for fornication, and shall marry another, committeth adultery; and whoso marrieth her which is put away doth commit adultery.
10 His disciples say unto him, *n* If the case of the

k ch. 5. 31; Deu 24. 1.

l Ge. 2. 24; 7. 7.
m ch. 5. 32; Mk. 10. 11; Lk. 16. 18; 1 Cor. 7. 10-13, 39; Rom. 7. 3.

n Pro. 21. 19.

---

flesh, their united relation in the flesh for this world, Ch. 22 : 30.

Although Jesus is discussing divorces and not polygamy, yet his language is also decisive against a man having more wives than one. *The two* are one flesh; they are no more *two*. God also creating the one woman for the one man showed also his will in this respect.

7. **Why did Moses, then, command?** These designing Pharisees now refer to Deut. 24 : 1, and suppose that they have got Jesus in a difficulty from which he can not extricate himself. They, however, misapprehended Moses. His object was to regulate, restrain, and diminish an evil that existed. What they called a command was really only a permission.

8. Jesus replies that Moses **suffered** them to put away their wives, but he did not *command* it. Neither did he suffer it in any such sense as to imply that God approved it as right; but he permitted it as the less of two evils, because of the hardness of your hearts. Such was the hardness and sinfulness of their hearts that they would have committed great sins, such as the murder of their wives. **But from the beginning,** etc. From the creation of the race it was not intended that man should put away his wife. Husband and wife were intended for each other. But unions were improperly formed and improperly dissolved. And such was the depravity of men, necessarily resulting in quarreling, putting away of wives, and kindred crimes, that this Mosaic regulation was made; which permitted, but regulated divorces, and thus restrained and lessened the evil, and prepared the way for bringing the race back to the true idea of marriage.

9. Jesus now instances the only just cause for divorce, **fornication,** here in the sense of adultery. This is consistent with our Savior's previous argument and conclusion; for the crime here referred to really *broke* the unity of the marriage state, and itself arose from the hardness of the heart. From comparing Mark 10 : 10, it would seem that Jesus now closed his conversation with the Pharisees, and spoke what follows to his disciples in the house. Jesus speaks with authority, *I say unto you,* as the lawgiver and expounder of the will of God. **Committeth adultery.** Because the unity of the marriage bond and state is not broken while both parties are living except by one act. The last clause, **and whoso marrieth,** etc., is omitted in the Improved version. Added probably by copyist from ch. 5 : 32.

In this age, when the laws on marriage and divorce are so lax, it becomes both churches and ministers to follow strictly the principles here laid down by our Lord. Christians should regard no one as really divorced except for the one cause.

10. **The case of the man—his wife.** Literally, *If the case of the man with the woman is so.* If the relation between man and woman in their married state is so, then **it is not good to marry.** If a man must live with his wife, whether she pleases him or not, then he better not marry at all. The disciples spoke with reference to things and society as they then existed, and under the influence of the teachings and practices of that wicked age. Accustomed to see wives divorced for various causes, they looked upon marriage which could not be sundered, except for the one cause mentioned, as almost intolerable. The application of this strict rule of our Savior, so far from making the marriage state intolerable, restores it to its original state and design, increases its happiness, and defends the wife as well as the husband.

11. Jesus replies that all can not re-

man be so with *his* wife, it is not good to marry.
11 But he said unto them, ° All *men* can not receive this
12 saying, save *they* to whom it is given. For there are some eunuchs, which were so born from *their* mother's womb: and there are some eunuchs, ᴾ which were made eunuchs of men: and ᵠ there be eunuchs, which have made themselves eunuchs for the kingdom of heaven's sake. He that is able to receive *it*, let him receive *it*.

° 1 Cor. 7. 2, 7, 9, 17.

ᴾ Is. 39. 7.
ᵠ 1 Cor. 7. 32–38; 9. 5. 15.

Jesus receives and blesses little children.

13 ʳ THEN were brought unto him little children, that he should put *his* hands on them, and pray.

ʳ Mk. 10. 13: Lk. 18. 15.

ceive **this saying** of yours, that it is not good to marry, except they to whom it is given; and then, in the next verse, he proceeds to enumerate certain just causes for remaining unmarried. **Given.** Either by God's providence in the natural constitution or in misfortune, or by divine illumination or direction. Some, indeed, may, under certain circumstances, be more useful in an unmarried state; some, in great dangers or great poverty, may think it not best to marry, 1 Cor. 7: 26. But while to some it is thus given to receive this doctrine, and to practice it without committing sin, to the great mass of the race it is not given. **All can not receive it.** Only persons of special classes are capable of acting upon it. Not to marry is contrary to both the natural and revealed law of God (Gen. 1: 28), to the wants and desires of men, and to the demands of the race, so that it may not become extinct. There are, therefore, only exceptional cases where men should not marry.

12. Jesus now states the three instances in which it is not given men to marry. **Eunuchs.** The word *eunuch* means a *bed-keeper*, and was applied to a class of persons who, in oriental countries, were subjected to a cruel and unnatural mutilation, and were employed as the keepers of oriental harems. The word here is extended not only to those incapacitated for the marriage state by nature, or the hand of man, but also to those voluntarily living unmarried. **So born;** as to be naturally unfit or averse to marriage. **Made, of men.** Eunuch properly so-called, made so by wicked men. **Made themselves, for the kingdom of heaven's sake.** Voluntarily abstaining from marriage for the sake of serving Christ's cause the better. Paul belonged to this class, 1 Cor. 7: 7. **Let him receive it.** He who is able to receive this doctrine, and practice it in the utmost purity of heart and life; in other words, he to whom it is given to receive it, and who is satisfied that he is an exception to the general rule of marriage, as laid down in the three cases of exemption just given, let him live unmarried.

Celibacy is thus an exceptional condition, and may be a misfortune, and only commendable when it is purely maintained for the glory of God and the advancement of Christ's kingdom. In only those to whom it is given of God is it desirable or commendable. The Romish church, in taking the matter out of God's hands, and enforcing celibacy on the whole class of clergy, without regard to their natural constitutions or their spiritual power, has misapplied the teachings of our Savior, committed a great wrong to God and man, and shown that she forms a part of the great apostasy, 1 Tim. 4: 3. The demoralizing results of this Romish dogma show that celibacy is not good nor safe except only when practiced according to the direction of our Lord. Not all the apostles were able to receive the doctrine and practice it, 1 Cor. 9: 5.

13–15. LITTLE CHILDREN, BROUGHT TO JESUS, ARE BLESSED BY HIM. Matthew, Mark, and Luke here unite in relating the same event for the first time since the Contention of the Disciples, in Matt. 18: 5; Mark 9: 37; and Luke 9: 48. See note at the beginning of the chapter, Mark 10: 13–16; Luke 18: 15–17.

14. **Little children.** Little boys and girls. The word in the original,

A.D. 30. MATTHEW XIX. 261

14 And the disciples rebuked them. But Jesus said, *Ps. 8. 2.
"Suffer little children, and forbid them not, to come
unto me: for ᵗ of such is the kingdom of heaven. ᵗ ch. 18. 3.

---

translated *little children*, is applied to different ages, as the following examples show: ch. 14 : 21; Mark 5 : 40, 41, translated "*damsel*;" Luke 1 : 59, 80; 2 : 40; John 4 : 49; 16 : 21. Luke says *infants* or *babes*. The word used by Luke is applied to the infancy of Jesus (Luke 2 : 12, 16), and also to the early childhood of Timothy. *From a child* thou hast known the Scriptures, 2 Tim. 3 : 15. They were evidently young children, of tender age. Jesus took them in his arms, Mark 10 : 16. They were **brought** to him, *borne* in the arms, or *led* by the hand. The verb in the original may be applied to either mode of bringing them. Who brought them, we are not told; probably the parents, relatives, or those who had charge of them.
Put his hands on them and pray. The object of their bringing them to Jesus, that he might bless them, or invoke the blessing of God upon them. Thus, Jacob put his hands upon the two sons of Joseph and blessed them, Gen. 48 : 14. It seems to have been common among the Jews to put their hands on persons when they prayed for them. "Hebrew mothers would be accustomed to seek in this manner a blessing for their children. The presidents of synagogues were also in the habit of putting their hands on children."—LANGE. Compare ch. 9 : 18. **The disciples rebuked them;** those who brought the children. They probably felt that the various duties of Jesus were too urgent for him to turn aside to bless little children. They may have been very much engaged in their conversation with Jesus, and did not wish to be interrupted, feeling that it was more important that they be instructed than that parents and friends be gratified in having their children blessed. They seem also to have thought it unsuitable for the little children to be brought to Jesus, either at this time or for this purpose, and hence Jesus replies, *Suffer the little children*, etc.
14. According to Mark, Jesus was *much displeased* at what the disciples had done. **Suffer little children.** Rather, *Suffer the little children*, that is, these little children that had been brought.

Jesus was pleased to have them come to him. The reason was, **for of such is the kingdom of heaven;** for to such as these belongs the kingdom of heaven. Who are meant by *such* is evident from ch. 18 : 6. *These little ones that believe in me;* of all those who have a child-like spirit, humble, teachable, submissive, and obedient. Such, indeed, are subjects and citizens of the Messiah's kingdom, which is commenced on earth and to be consummated in the world to come. They are entitled to the great blessings of Messiah's reign, both for time and eternity. Mark (10 : 15) and Luke (18 : 17) give an additional remark of Jesus, which shows, beyond all doubt, the symbolical reference of *children* to the child-like dispositions of the regenerated.
But, while Jesus referred generally to all true believers, as little ones in character, disposition, and conduct, he doubtless intended to convey a deep and important spiritual truth in regard to little children themselves; for if he made no reference to them, but only to believers, how could it be a reason for suffering little children to come to him, and forbidding them not. To me it seems that Jesus referred to little children in the following respects: *First*. As symbols of true believers, whether young or old, as just explained, and in ch. 18 : 2-6. They were the best symbols he could choose from the race, because, though depraved by nature through Adam, yet they were not guilty of actual transgression, and because of their humble and docile dispositions. Did Jesus use them as symbols? Surely, then, they should suffer them to come and receive his blessing. Hence, *Second*, as the most susceptible to the Gospel upon arriving to years of accountability. The age for arriving at this period varies in different individuals. A distinguished medical author says, "The seventh year, and the vicinity of each multiple of seven, is characterized by some great change in the human constitution. Thus, the seventh year is that of the second dentation, and the common belief fixes at that age the distinct perception of right and wrong." Children are easily led to Jesus. *Third*. In respect to the multitudes of little chil-

15 And ᵘ he laid *his* hands on them, and departed thence. — ᵘ Is. 40. 11.

dren who would enter into this kingdom on earth. Most enter into the kingdom in childhood and youth, and even of those who are converted in later years, the greater part trace their impressions to childhood. The most useful and devoted of Christ's followers have been those who, like Timothy, have *from a child* known the Scriptures. It would not be strange if some or all of these, whom Jesus blessed, were then impressed with the goodness and loveliness of Jesus, and that they early came to him by faith. These *lambs* of the flock, in every age of the Gospel dispensation, may most fittingly be included in the *such*, whose is the kingdom of heaven. The disciples, doubtless, thought the kingdom, with its deep and hidden truths, was especially intended for men of full age; but Jesus would correct their false notions, and have children also come to him, for the kingdom of heaven is, in a special sense, intended for and adapted to them. *Fourth.* That the kingdom of heaven, as consummated in glory, would be largely made up of children who died before coming to years of accountability. As their sinfulness is involuntary, so will also be their salvation. Since they were made sinners through Adam, and since Christ made an atonement for Adam's sin, we may reasonably conclude that those who die before committing actual transgression are saved by the blood of Jesus, and that they are regenerated by the Spirit as they enter the unseen world, and thus fitted for the kingdom of heaven. Compare Rom. 5 : 12–19. As a further argument for infant salvation, it may be remarked that the Bible addresses, not infants who are incapable of reason and choice, but persons who can reason, understand, and choose, and are thus accountable. And also that it lays great stress on the inability of knowing right from wrong, as distinguishing infants from adults, Deut. 1 : 39; Isa. 7 : 15, 16; Jonah 4 : 11; Heb. 5 : 14. Compare Gen. 2 : 17. Of all who have died probably not far from one half have been under five years of age. In view of the large proportion of infants thus saved, in the kingdom of glory, and in reference to them, our Savior could well say, "To such belongs the kingdom of heaven."

To infant baptism there is not the remotest reference. The passage can not be regarded either as an argument for it, an illustration of it, or as a kernel containing its germ. As well might we infer from it infant communion, or the perpetuity of circumcision. It is really an *argument* against infant baptism; for they were not brought for baptism, and they went away without baptism. The disciples evidently had no knowledge of such an institution; for we can not suppose they would have rebuked those who brought them, if they had been in the habit of baptizing such little children with the approval of Jesus. If Jesus had intended to institute infant baptism, when could he have had so fit a time as that? Yet he did not institute it. If his saying, "Of such is the kingdom of heaven," was not a sufficient reason for baptizing those children then, why should it be of infants now? The passage *illustrates* the spirit which Christians should exercise toward children. They should pray for them, instruct them, lead them to Jesus. It is a beautiful illustration of children coming to him by faith. The Scriptures do not speak of coming to him by baptism, but by faith. But how can it illustrate that which, according to Neander and other eminent church historians, was not an apostolic institution, and which is not recognized in the New Testament? As to the *germ* of infant baptism, baptismal regeneration was the kernel from which it and infant communion were developed. The notion of a magical charm, and a saving influence connected with the sacraments, gave rise to infant baptism in the North African Church in the third century. It was the development of error, not of truth. Nothing seems more far-fetched than to suppose a reference to an ordinance nowhere intimated in the New Testament, unknown and unpracticed in the apostolic churches, and, by its introducing an unconverted membership, opposed to the spiritual idea of the constitution of a gospel church. We should indeed welcome to baptism all those little children who have come to Jesus by faith; but even to the bap-

Answer to the inquiries of a rich young man.

16 ˣ AND, behold, one came and said unto him, ʸ Good Master, what good thing shall I do, that I may have
17 eternal life? And he said unto him, Why callest thou me good? ᶻ there is none good but one, *that is,* God. ᵃ But if thou wilt enter into life, keep the
18 commandments. He saith unto him, ᵇ Which? Jesus said, ᶜ 'Thou shalt do no murder, Thou shalt not commit adultery, Thou shalt not steal, ᵈ Thou
19 shalt not bear false witness, ᵉ Honor thy father and *thy* mother:' and, ᶠ 'Thou shalt love thy neighbor as

ˣ Mk. 10. 17; Lk. 18. 18.
ʸ Lk. 10. 25.
ᶻ Rom. 3. 9–12.
ᵃ Lc. 18. 5; Ro. 10. 5.
ᵇ Gal. 3. 10; Jam. 2. 10, 11.
ᶜ Ex. 20. 12–17; Deu. 5. 17.
ᵈ Le. 19. 18.
ᵉ 15. 4.
ᶠ Rom. 13. 9.

tism of these we can see no reference in this passage.

15. Laid his hands on them. In the act of blessing them; after which he **departed thence** to other places in that region; and directing his course toward Jerusalem, ch. 20, 17; Mark 10 : 32; Luke 18 : 31.

16–22. JESUS ANSWERS THE INQUIRIES OF THE RICH AND SELF-RIGHTEOUS YOUNG MAN, Mark 10 : 17–22; Luke 18 : 18–23.

16. Behold. Introduces something new, unexpected, and wonderful. **One came.** Mark says he came *running;* and Luke says he was a *ruler.* **Good master.** Simply, *Teacher,* the best critical authorities omitting *good.* Mark and Luke describe him as saying *Good Teacher.* He looked upon Jesus as a man of eminent virtues, and he wishes to know of him what work of merit he must do so as to attain to that goodness which insures eternal life. **What good thing shall I do?** etc.

17. Jesus replies that absolute goodness belongs not to man, but to God; the reply was adapted, on the one hand, to correct the false notion of the young man, who was expecting to arrive at absolute and meritorious goodness, and, on the other, to point him to God as the only source of goodness to man. **Why callest thou me good?** This should read, according to the oldest manuscripts and highest critical authorities, *Why dost thou ask me about good? One is the good;* that is, the absolutely good. This goodness, about which you inquire, belongs to God, not to man. Vain, therefore, is your thought of doing an absolutely good thing. In God is the true good for men. And then he asks (according to Mark and Luke), *Why callest thou me good?* since God is the only good, and you consider me but a virtuous man and eminent rabbi or teacher. Compare Rev. 15 : 4. "For thou only art holy."

Jesus then turns to the great end which the young man wished to attain, namely, *eternal life,* and says, **Keep the commandments.** These were the commandments of God, the absolutely good, and they pointed out the way of holiness, which is the way of God. Similarly he had answered the young lawyer, in regard to the commandments of the law, "This do and thou shalt live," Luke 10 : 28. The law was indeed intended to give life to all who should perfectly obey it, John 12 : 50; Rom. 7 : 10. It was fitted to Adam in his state of innocence, and to holy beings. It is fitted to show men that they are sinners, Rom. 7 : 7–9. As a wise physician, Jesus would first make this young man feel that he was sick, and hence he preaches to him the law. If he had come a sin-sick soul, he would have proclaimed the Gospel, ch. 11 : 28–30.

18, 19. **Which?** What commandments? He had kept the commandments of the law, as he supposed, and he little thought that Jesus would refer him back to them; he therefore asks, What ones he must still observe? Jesus replies by repeating a few from the decalogue, to show him that it is that code of laws to which he refers. He quotes mostly from the second table, the duties between man and man, because these are the more easily understood; the young man also may have laid less stress on these than the other commandments, and may have been remarkably deficient in honor to his parents and love to his neighbor, and then if he was wanting in performing his duty toward men, surely

MATTHEW XIX. A.D. 30.

20 thyself. The young man saith unto him, ᵍ All these things have I kept from my youth up: what lack I 21 yet? Jesus said unto him, If thou wilt be perfect, ʰ go *and* sell that thou hast, and give to the poor, and thou shalt have treasure in heaven: and come 22 *and* follow me. But when the young man heard that saying, ⁱ he went away sorrowful: ᵏ for he had great possessions.

ᶠ Ro. 3. 19. 20; 7. 9.
ʰ Lk. 12. 33; Ac. 2. 45; 4. 34, 35; 1 Tim. 6. 17-19.
ⁱ ch 6. 19-21.
ᵏ ch. 13. 22; 16. 26; Eze. 33. 31; Eph. 5. 5; Col. 3. 5.

he was lacking in his duties toward God, 1 John 4 : 20. **Do no murder.** *Thou shalt not kill.* Compare Deut. 4 : 42. The first five specimens here given are from Exod. 20 : 12-16. The last, which is from Lev. 19 : 18, is the second great commandment of God's universal law, ch. 22 : 39. **20. All these things have I kept.** Externally, in outward appearance, he had observed them; but he had no insight into the spiritual nature of the law, as exhibited in the Sermon on the Mount, or he would not have thus spoken. **From my youth up.** These words are not given by Matthew, but by Mark and Luke, according to the highest critical authorities. As he was still young, he must refer back to his early youth, his childhood. But though he was self-righteous, he felt a sense of need. All his strict external observances did not give him peace of mind. He therefore inquires, **What lack I yet?** He was, like Saul of Tarsus, sincere, earnest, circumspect, but intensely self-righteous, Phil. 3 : 4-6. Mark tells us that Jesus, beholding him, *loved* him.

21. **If thou wilt be perfect.** If thou desirest to have moral completeness, and lack nothing; if you would "be perfect, entire, wanting in nothing," James 1 : 4. See on ch. 5 : 48. **Go, sell that thou hast — come, follow me.** Jesus shows, by this single command, the weak point in the young man's character, and a fatal lack in his righteousness. He places before him a perfect standard, but not *such* as he desired. He wished to do those performances and observances which accorded with his proud and self-righteous spirit. Jesus places before him self-renunciation, a life of self-denial, and discipleship of the despised Nazarene. Thus we must understand the command; for not merely selling his earthly possessions would constitute perfection, or the complete circle of moral obligation.

The selling all that he had was but a type of giving up all for Christ. In his case it was made the test of love to God, and of the value he put on eternal life. In the spirit of love to God and man, he was to distribute to the poor, come and follow Jesus; Mark adds, "Take up the cross." The young man, in professing to keep the commandments, professed to love God supremely; yet Jesus shows him that he loved his possessions more than God; that he valued them above eternal life, and that he would break any or all of the commandments of God, rather than part with them. They were, in his case, his *idol;* and therefore they must be sacrificed.

The spirit of this command is required of every disciple, Luke 14 : 33. Jesus requires a full surrender of soul, body, talents, influence, property. He does not require us to sell our possessions, impoverish ourselves, and thus unsettle the social system; but he does require us, as his stewards, to use the world as not abusing it, and to give freely as we have the ability, Luke 12 : 33; 1 Tim. 6 : 17, 19. **Treasure in heaven.** In place of thy treasures on earth, ch. 6 : 19, 20.

22. Jesus had taken the young man at his word, and pointed him to a perfect standard, and by it showed him that, however moral and amiable he had been, he was lacking in the ground principles of righteousness. He **heard the saying** of Jesus, felt its force; but the requirement was too hard for him. He had great possessions, and his love for them was inordinate. He therefore goes away **sorrowful.** He has a struggle, but he can not give up the world. Thus his sorrow showed that Jesus had struck at the idol which stood in the place of God, and which must be renounced and forsaken, or salvation could not be attained. Had he renounced his love of wealth, had he gone forth to give up cheerfully his possessions to God and his cause, then as God restored to Abraham

Jesus discourses on riches, and on forsaking all for his sake.

23 Then said Jesus unto his disciples, Verily I say unto you, That ¹ a rich man shall hardly enter into
24 the kingdom of heaven. And again I say unto you, ᵐ It is easier for a camel to go through the eye of a needle, than for a rich man to enter into the king-
25 dom of God. When his disciples heard *it*, they were exceedingly amazed, saying, Who then can be

¹ Deu. 8. 10–18; Job 31. 24–28.

ᵐ ch. 6. 24; Jer. 13. 23.

Isaac, his son, whom he offered at his command, so Jesus might have said to this young man, "Take back thy possessions, and keep them for me; you have indeed obeyed, and given them to God in your heart; use them to his glory and in the extension of my kingdom." We have no further account of this young man. The words of our Savior may have taken root in after days. It seems pleasant to think that this one, whom Jesus loved, did afterward repent, and live a life of self-denial in his service. But, on the other hand, we can not rid ourselves of the thought that this was the decisive time in his existence, when, by his decision, he lost his soul.

23–30. JESUS DISCOURSES ON RICHES AND ON FORSAKING ALL FOR HIS SAKE. This was occasioned by the incident which had just occurred. The first part (vers. 23–26) centres about a reflection made by our Savior; the second (27–30), about the declaration and question of Peter, Mark 10 : 23–31; Luke 18 : 24–30.

23. **Verily, I say to you.** These words introduce a solemn and an authoritative declaration. **A rich man shall hardly enter,** etc. A rich man shall with the greatest difficulty become a subject, and attain to the blessings and honors of the new dispensation, here and hereafter. Wealth is so apt to produce self-indulgence and self-sufficiency, and lead those who have them to fix their hearts upon them and trust in them. Thus Jesus explained himself, according to Mark (10 : 24), "How hard is it for them that trust in riches to enter into the kingdom of God!" Thus it is not as a rich man that he can be saved, but only as he renounces his trust in them. "I understand you are very dangerously situated," said Mr. Cecil to a parishioner. "I am not aware of it," was the reply. "I thought you were not," rejoined Mr. Cecil, "and therefore I called on you: I hear you are getting rich; take care! for it is the road by which the devil leads thousands to destruction."

24. The extreme difficulty of a rich man entering Christ's kingdom is more emphatically expressed in strong proverbial language. **A camel—eye of a needle.** Instead of *camel*, some have supposed here a Greek word, meaning *anchor-rope*. This supposition, however, is entirely groundless. Others have asserted that *eye of a needle* was used to designate a low gate, through which a camel could not pass unless his load was taken off. The assertion is fanciful and precarious. Such explanations have been invented in order to get rid of the seeming difficulties connected with the plain meaning of this passage. The Koran uses the same figure, probably in imitation of this passage. The Arabs have a proverb of an elephant going through a needle's eye. Lightfoot refers to instances in the Talmud of similar proverbial expressions in regard to the elephant. In ch. 23 : 24 we have the figure of *swallowing a camel*. The passage, therefore, is in harmony with the oriental modes of conception and proverbial language. Compare also Jer. 13 : 23. It is a strong hyperbolical proverb, expressing the greatest conceivable difficulties, the greatest human impossibility of a rich man entering Christ's kingdom.

25. At so strong and striking an assertion well might the disciples be **exceedingly amazed. Who, then, can be saved?** This shows that our Savior's figure was a very strong one, and not the softened and enfeebled figures of some interpreters, referred to in the preceding verse. The disciples understood Jesus by his language to assert the impossibility of a rich man entering into his kingdom, and enjoying its blessings. They *generalized* the

26 saved? But Jesus beheld *them*, and said unto them, With men this is impossible; but ⁿ with God all things are possible.
27 ᵒ Then answered Peter and said unto him, Behold, ᵖ we have forsaken all, and followed thee;
28 what shall we have therefore? And Jesus said unto them, Verily I say unto you, That ye which have followed me, ᵠ in the regeneration ʳ when the

ⁿ Gen. 18. 14; Job 42. 2; Jer. 32. 17; Zec. 8. 6; Lk. 1. 37; 18. 27; 2 Cor. 3. 5; Phil. 4. 13.
ᵒ Mk. 10. 28; Lk. 18. 28.
ᵖ ch. 4. 18-22; Deu. 33. 9; Lk. 5. 11.
ᵠ Is. 65. 17; Ac. 3. 21; 2 Pet. 3. 13.

---

class of *the rich*, or of those who *trusted in riches*. They saw that the desire and love of riches were so common among men, and also the trust in them, both of those who had them and those who were striving to obtain them, as to seemingly render the Savior's declaration of almost universal application, and they exclaim, "Who, then, can be saved?" Their carnal views of a temporal kingdom doubtless made the declaration of Jesus the more amazing and difficult to their minds.

26. **But Jesus beheld them.** Rather, *But Jesus looking on them* with compassion, and to give greater force to what he was about to say. **With men, impossible.** It is a human impossibility. It is beyond human power for any to be saved, and especially those who are surrounded with the dangers and difficulties of wealth. **But with God all things are possible.** He can change the heart, and make the rich humble, believing, self-denying, and obedient; so that they shall trust in God rather than in their possessions, love him supremely, and, consecrating all to his service, act only as stewards. See Mark 9 : 23. The answer is general, *All things are possible*, thus including the conversion of the rich as well as the poor.

27. Peter now speaks in behalf of himself and the other apostles. His declaration, **We have forsaken all,** etc., was suggested by the command of Jesus to the young man, "Sell that thou hast, etc.," and his discourse on the difficulty of rich men attaining salvation; and his question, **What shall we have, therefore?** seems to refer to the promise of Jesus, "Thou shalt have treasure in heaven." Peter seems to expect they will have some great reward. As he thought upon the conditions of eternal life, as applied to this rich young man, he reflected that they had indeed complied with them. They had forsaken all, their homes, friends, and occupation, renounced the world and entered upon a life of self-denial, and had become disciples of Jesus and his constant attendants. None of them was rich; yet they had broken many fond ties, and made many great sacrifices. James and John, sons of Zebedee, had hired servants (Mark 1 : 20); Matthew was a man of some property, Luke 5 : 29. In the question, Peter seems to be looking too much after reward; he shows the influence of low views of a temporal kingdom; yet he asks it in so much faith, love, and devotion, that Jesus graciously answers it without reproof.

28. In his reply Jesus utters, first, a special promise to the twelve; second (verse 29), a general promise to all believers; and then (verse 30) intimates proverbially a fact in regard to the final distribution of rewards which would serve to arouse their zeal, faith, and humility, and at the same time check any wrong and worldly spirit.

Regeneration. Rather, *renovation*. The word thus translated is found only here and in Tit. 3 : 5. In the latter passage baptism is styled *the washing* or *bathing of regeneration*, an emblem of the new birth. The application of the word here is not to individuals, but to the general state of things in Christ's kingdom, and hence refers not to individual regeneration, but to a general renovation of the condition of men, and of the state of the world by the Gospel dispensation. Thus, a Greek writer uses this word to express the restored or renovated state of the earth after the flood; Josephus employs it to designate the renewed state of the Jewish nation after the captivity, and Cicero, the restoration of his dignity and fortune. So here the word naturally applies to that state of things which Jesus was accomplishing and would accomplish in his kingdom. Some join regeneration to what precedes, thus, *That ye who have followed*

Son of man shall sit in the throne of his glory, ᵗ ye also shall sit upon twelve thrones, judging the 29 twelve tribes of Israel. ᵘ And every one that hath forsaken houses, or brethren, or sisters, or father, or mother, or wife, or children, or lands, ᵛ for my name's sake, shall receive an hundred fold, and

ᵗ ch. 16. 27.
ˢ ch. 20. 21; Lk. 22. 28-30; 1 Cor. 6. 2, 3; 2 Tim. 2. 2. 12; Rev. 3. 21.
ᵘ ch. 10. 25; Mk. 10 29, 30; Lk. 18. 29, 30; Phil. 3. 8.

---

me in the renovation, in bringing in a new state of things. Others, however, more naturally, and more in accordance with the scope of the passage and scriptural usage, join *regeneration* to what follows, putting a comma after *followed me: That ye who have followed me, in the renovation when the Son of Man*, etc. In the new order of things, when the Son of Man shall sit on his throne of glory. It is not necessary to limit *renovation* to the new heavens and earth, or the completed glory of the new creation, 2 Pet. 3 : 13. It applies generally to Christ's kingdom and the order of things enjoyed under the Gospel dispensation, whether in this world or the world to come, Luke 18 : 30. The *renovation* had already commenced in that small company of Christ and his followers; it was accomplished, first of all, in the restored and glorified state of Jesus at his resurrection and ascension, which was a type and pledge of its accomplishment in all his followers, 1 Cor. 15 : 20-23. It began openly, aggressively, and in power among men at the pentecostal season, and has been going forward ever since; and it will be fully accomplished in the new heavens and earth, and in the complete and consummated glory of Christ's kingdom, Rom. 18 : 18-23; Acts 3 : 21; Rev. 21 : 5. Thus the promise of Jesus is a prophecy, which, like many of the prophecies of Scripture, has a progressive fulfillment. Compare on chs. 1 : 22, 23; 10 : 23; 16 : 28.
Shall sit in the throne of his glory; *on his throne of glory*, to which he ascended on the right hand of the Majesty on high (Eph. 4 : 8-10; Heb. 1 : 3; Acts 7 : 56; Phil. 2 : 9-11), where he shall sit till all enemies are put under his feet (1 Cor. 15 : 25); and on which also he shall judge the world, ch. 25 : 31. His throne of glory points to his glorified and exalted condition, and to his character and functions as conqueror, sovereign, and judge. Wherever he personally manifests his power and glory, and exercises his authority, he may be fittingly said to be on his throne of glory. Throne is an emblem of royal power (Gen. 41 : 40); and *to sit on a throne* is to rule, or exercise the powers of a monarch, Deut. 17 : 18.
Sit upon twelve thrones. The number of the apostles corresponded to that of the tribes of Israel. See on ch. 10 : 1. Jesus also speaks of twelve thrones, corresponding to the twelve offices; Judas lost his office, and Matthias was put in his place, Acts 1 : 20, 26. Christ shall sit on *his throne of glory;* they simply on *thrones*. They shall sit beside him, his assessors, partakers, indeed, of his power and glory. All believers share here his sufferings, and hereafter his glory, Rom. 8 : 17; 2 Tim. 2 : 12. The special dignity, power, and glory of the apostles, as the chief associates of Christ, are here represented, Rev. 21 : 12-14. Under him they exercise spiritual dominion. As inspired teachers, they are to be appealed to in matters of faith and practice; and, at the final judgment, condemnation or acquittal will be in accordance with the doctrines they were inspired to preach. **Judging the twelve tribes of Israel.** Coöperating with and approving his decisions. Believers generally are to have part in the judgment, 1 Cor. 6 : 2. The twelve apostles are to have a special part in judging the people of Israel. All the judgments on the Jewish people, and especially the destruction of Jerusalem, which is typical of the final judgment (ch. 24), may be said to be in accordance with the inspired truth given through the apostles. Compare on this passage Luke 22 : 28-30.

29. Jesus makes a general promise to all believers. **Every one.** Any one, whether an apostle or not. **Forsaken houses, or brethren,** etc. It has been remarked that the family relations are in the order in which they would be forsaken. **A hundred fold.** According to the highest critical authorities this should read *many times more*, or *manifold more*. He shall receive many times more real good in this world than all he renounced for the sake of Christ, ch. 5 :

30 shall inherit everlasting life. *But many that are first shall be last; and the last shall be* first.

ᵃ ch. 5. 11; 1 Pet. 4. 14.

5; 1 Cor. 3 : 20-23; 1 Tim. 4 : 8. Mark has (10 : 30) "a hundred fold now in this time, houses, and brethren, etc., with persecutions." In addition to this he shall inherit everlasting life. Thus the reward commences in this world, but has its great realization in the future world. See on Mark 10 : 29, 30.

30. Jesus announces in proverbial language a great fact in regard to the distribution of these rewards, which is illustrated by a parable in the next chapter. **First.** First in time of their calling, in their own estimation, and in the enjoyment of privileges and blessings. **Shall be last.** Last in receiving their rewards, in Christ's estimation, and in the scale of final joy and blessedness. Jesus would teach his disciples that God will exercise his sovereign pleasure, not, however, without good reasons, in the distribution of rewards. They must not ask, in the spirit of the hireling (verse 27), "What shall we have, therefore," since these rewards are not of merit, but of grace. They must not suppose that because they and others are first in the time of their calling into the kingdom, and in their privileges, that therefore they will be necessarily first in honors and rewards. They are to be faithful and earnest, committing themselves and their own final disposal to him whose right it is to dispense heavenly honors, and who will do it righteously and graciously, ch. 20 : 23; Rev. 3 : 21.

REMARKS.

1. As Pharisees tempted Christ, so will wicked and cunning men tempt his followers, and strive to perplex and embarrass them with doctrinal and practical difficulties, ver. 3; 2 Pet. 3 : 16.

2. In matters of religion our appeal should be to the Bible. Jesus appealed to the Old Testament as of divine authority, vers. 4, 5; John 5 : 39; 2 Tim. 3 : 16; 1 Cor. 2 : 13; 1 Thess. 2 : 13; 2 Pet. 3 : 2.

3. Marriage is an institution of divine origin, honorable in all, ministers as well as others, vers. 4-6; ch. 8 : 14; 1 Cor. 9 : 5; Heb. 13 : 4.

4. There is no relationship so close and intimate as that of husband and wife, vers. 5, 6; 1 Cor. 7 : 10, 11; Eph. 5 : 28-31.

5. Since the marriage relation is the closest of all earthly relationships, it should be entered in the fear of the Lord, and the parties entering it should be one in spirit. The Christian should, therefore, seek his companion for life from those who love Jesus, vers. 5, 6; 2 Cor. 6 : 14; 1 Cor. 7 : 39; 1 Pet. 3 : 7.

6. Many are found who misapply and pervert Scripture, or take advantage of the letter of the law to break its spirit, in order to ease their own consciences and defend themselves in a course of sin, ver. 7; ch. 15 : 3-6; ch. 12 : 10-12; 2 Pet. 3 : 16.

7. We must not conclude that a practice is right and meets with God's approval because he permits it for a time, ver. 8; Acts 17 : 30.

8. On account of the hardness and depravity of the heart God has given laws which would gradually do away with great moral social evils. Thus with divorces, polygamy, and slavery, ver. 8; ch. 7 : 12; Mal. 2 : 15, 16.

9. Human governments transgress the law of Christ if they grant divorces, except for one cause, ver. 9.

10. Christ's exposition of the law of marriage reinstates woman in her original rights. In heathen countries she has always been degraded, and generally treated as a slave. Among the Jews she was denied the right of divorcement, while she could be divorced for the most frivolous causes, vers. 8, 9.

11. While it is the duty of the mass of mankind to enter the marriage state, some, from peculiar circumstances, find it expedient and useful to live unmarried, vers. 10, 12; Gen. 1 : 28; 1 Tim. 4 : 3.

12. Christ's interest for little children should encourage us to bring them to him in faith and prayer and early instruction, vers. 13-15; Eph. 6 : 4.

13. Children should be encouraged to come to Jesus, who is displeased with any hindrances put in their way, ver. 14; Deut. 11 : 19; 1 Sam. 2 : 18; 3 : 10; Ps. 8 : 2; Prov. 8 : 17; Matt. 21 : 16.

14. Children who die in infancy are saved by virtue of Christ's sufferings and death, ver. 14; Rom. 5 : 12-19; 2 Sam. 12 : 23; 2 Kings 4 : 26.

A.D. 30.   MATTHEW XX.   269

Parable of the laborers in the vineyard.

XX. For ʸ the kingdom of heaven is like unto ᶻ a man *that is* a householder, which went out early in the morning to hire laborers into his vineyard.

ˣ ch. 8. 11, 12; 20. 16; 21. 31, 32; Lk. 13. 30; Ro. 9. 30–33.
ʸ ch. 3. 2; 5. 3, 10.
ᶻ ch. 9. 38; Is. 5. 1, 2; John 15. 1.

15. It is common for sinners to desire to do some good things to secure their salvation, ver. 16; John 6 : 28; Acts 2 : 37; Rom. 9 : 31, 32.

16. God is goodness in himself and the author of all good. Christ, being one with the Father, is also one with him in goodness, ver. 17; 1 Sam. 2 : 2; Ps. 36 : 9; 34 : 8; James 1 : 17; John 1 : 16–18.

17. The law of God is binding on us, and must either be satisfied in us or in Christ. We are condemned by the law unless justified through faith in Christ, vers. 17–19; Rom. 3 : 31; 5 : 1; 11 : 6; Gal. 2 : 16; Eph. 2 : 8, 9.

18. Through faith in Christ our natures are renewed by the Holy Spirit, and obedience to God becomes our delight, John 14 : 21; 15 : 14; Acts 15 : 9; James 2 : 17, 18; 1 John 3 : 3; 1 Cor. 6 : 9–11.

19. He who thinks he has kept the commands of God, is alike ignorant of himself, of God and his holy law, ver. 20; Luke 18 : 11, 12; Rom. 10 : 3; 7 : 9–11; Phil. 3 : 6. Compare 1 Cor. 8 : 2.

20. Perfection consists in a full surrender of all to Christ, a complete acquiescence of the human will in the divine, and an entire conformity of human acts to the divine requirement, ver. 21; ch. 5 : 48; Prov. 23 : 26; James 2 : 10; Phil. 3 : 7–10.

21. Many think they are willing to do any thing that God requires of them in order to be saved, yet when told to forsake all, they are unwilling to do it, ver. 22; 2 Tim. 4 : 10.

22. The poor should not envy the rich, but rather rejoice that they are not exposed to the dangers and temptations of wealth, ver. 23; Deut. 31 : 20; 32 : 15; Matt. 13 : 22; 1 Tim. 6 : 8, 9; James 5 : 1–3.

23. The great danger of riches is the love and confidence which men place upon them, vers. 23, 24; 1 Tim. 6 : 10.

24. The rich should feel that they are intrusted with their Lord's money, and should exercise great liberality toward the poor and in support of the Gospel. By thus doing riches will be a blessing indeed, vers. 21–24; ch. 6 : 19, 20; Luke 12 : 33.

25. We should rejoice that the salvation of all, whether rich or poor, which was impossible with men, is rendered possible through Jesus Christ, ver. 26; Rom. 8 : 3, 4.

26. It is a great privilege to live under the Gospel dispensation, and to enjoy its renovating power both here and hereafter, ver. 28; Jer. 31 : 31–34; 1 Cor. 2 : 7–10; 1 John 3 : 1, 2.

27. Christians are to enjoy with Christ the highest honors of heaven, vers. 28, 29; Rom. 8 : 17; Rev. 3 : 21.

28. If we give up all to Christ, we shall receive Christ and all things in return, ver. 29; Rom. 8 : 32; 1 Cor. 3 : 21–23.

CHAPTER XX.

This chapter continues and completes Matthew's account of the last journey to Jerusalem.

1–16. PARABLE OF THE LABORERS IN THE VINEYARD. Many first shall be last, and the last first. God will distribute his rewards of grace according to his own good pleasure. Recorded by Matthew only.

1. **For,** connects this with the last verse of the preceding chapter. Peter, after affirming that they, the twelve, had forsaken all and followed Jesus, had asked, "What shall we have therefor?" Jesus replied first in reference to the twelve (ver. 28), and secondly in reference to all believers (ver. 29), and then announces, in proverbial language, a great fact in regard to the final distribution of these rewards, "But many that are first shall be last, and the last shall be first." *For,* to illustrate this maxim, the kingdom of heaven, in respect to its final rewards, **is like unto a man,** etc., is like the case of a householder, is like the circumstances about to be narrated. **A householder.** A head or master of a family. **Early in the morning.** At dawn, before the sunrising. Morier, in his *Second Journey through Persia* (page 265), mentions a custom like that alluded to in this parable. "Here," speaking of the market-place at Hamadam, "we observed every morning, before the sun rose, that a numerous band of peasants

2 And when he had agreed with the laborers for a
3 penny a day, he sent them into his vineyard. And
  he went out about the third hour, and saw others
4 standing idle in the market-place, and said unto
  them, Go ye also into the vineyard, and whatsoever
  is right I will give you. And they went their way.
5 Again he went out about the sixth and ninth hour,
6 and did likewise. And about the eleventh hour he
  went out, and found others standing idle, and saith
7 unto them, ^a Why stand ye here all the day idle?
  They say unto him, Because no man hath hired us.
  He saith unto them, Go ye also into the vineyard;
8 and ^b whatsoever is right, *that* shall ye receive. So
  ^c when even was come, the lord of the vineyard
  saith unto his steward, ^d Call the laborers, and give
  them *their* hire, beginning from the last unto the

^a Acts 17. 21; Heb. 6. 12.

^b Eph. 6. 8; Heb. 6. 10.
^c ch. 25. 19; 2 Cor. 5. 10.
^d ch. 25. 19, 32, 34.

were collected, with spades in their hands, waiting, as they informed us, to be hired for the day, to work in the surrounding fields. This custom forcibly struck me as a most happy illustration of our Savior's parable of the laborers in the vineyard, particularly when, passing by the same place late in the day, we still found others standing idle, and remembered his words, *Why stand ye here all the day idle?* as most applicable to their situation; for, in putting the very same question to them, they answered, *Because no man hath hired us.*"

2. **For a penny a day.** A denárius or denáry; about fifteen cents a day, which was liberal wages at that time. About

two thirds of a Roman denárius was the daily pay of a Roman soldier. Polybius (ii. 15) says that the charge for a day's entertainment in the inns of Cisalpine Gaul (northern Italy) was one half of an as, which was equal to one twentieth of a denáry.

3, 4. **About the third hour.** About nine o'clock, when the market-place would be full of people. The Jews, as well as the Greeks and Romans, divided the working day, between sunrise and sunset, into twelve hours, which of course varied with the length of the day, at different seasons. The longest day in Palestine is fourteen hours and twelve minutes; the shortest, nine hours and forty-eight minutes. The hour on the longest day was thus seventy-one minutes; on the shortest, forty-nine minutes. **Whatsoever is right I will give you.** He agreed to pay these, and indeed all the laborers, with this difference: The first were to receive a stipulated sum; the others, depending on the justice of the householder, were to receive a sum which should be considered just and right. The last, according to the best reading, received no promise (see ver. 7).

5. **Sixth and ninth hour.** At midday, and about three in the afternoon.

6, 7. **The eleventh hour.** About one hour before sunset. **Why stand ye . . . idle?** The question implies that there is enough to do, and a call to labor; the answer implies a readiness to labor. The last clause, **And whatsoever is right,** etc., is omitted by the highest critical authorities. The simple command, **Go ye also into the vineyard,** implies an agreement of some equitable reward for their services; and especially as they had just said that "No man had hired them."

8. **Evening.** At the setting of the sun. **This steward.** This overseer, or agent, to whom was intrusted the affairs of his household. **Their hire.** The wages which he had been instructed to give. It was according to the Mosaic

9 first. And when they came that *were hired* about the eleventh hour, they received every man a penny.
10 But when the first came, they supposed that they should have received more; and they likewise re-
11 ceived every man a penny. And when they had received *it*, they murmured against the good man of
12 the house, saying, These last have wrought *but* one hour, and thou hast made them equal unto us, which have borne the burden and heat of the day.
13 But he answered one of them and said, Friend, I do thee no wrong: didst not thou agree with me for a
14 penny? Take *that* thine *is*, and go thy way: I will
15 give unto this last, even as unto thee. *c* Is it not lawful for me to do what I will with mine own?

c Dan. 4. 32, 37; John 17. 2; Ro. 9. 15-24.

---

law that hired laborers should be paid at the close of each day. "Thou shalt give him his hire, neither shall the sun go down upon it" (Deut. 24:15); "The wages of him that is hired shall not abide with thee all night till morning," Lev. 19:13. The parable indicates that it was the practice in our Savior's day, as it is now in the east, of ending work at sunset, and paying wages daily.

9, 10. All receive a denary. The contrast is made between those of the eleventh hour and the first, because the most striking, the most natural, and the best adapted to bring out our Savior's meaning. **Supposed that—received more.** Seeing such great liberality toward the last, the first supposed that they should also be sharers, and thus receive more than the stipulated sum. **Every man a penny.** Very similar was the dealing of Ananus, probably the Annas of the New Testament, who, a few years later, paid the workmen employed in repairing the temple a day's wages, though they had labored only a single hour. Josephus, *Antiq.* xx. 9, 7.

11, 12. **They murmured against.** They grumbled, and showed sullen discontent. This portion of the parable seems to be introduced more especially to bring out the answer of the householder, and must not be pressed too far in the interpretation. **The good man of the house.** The householder, *goodman* being an old English appellation of the master of a house, or householder. **Have wrought.** Some take this to mean, *have tarried;* but the idea of active labor is better, *have wrought, have worked.* Ruth 2:19. **Borne the burden and heat of the day.** *Borne the burden of*

the day, that is, the whole day's toil, *and the burning heat,* the intense heat of the sun, and of the burning east wind, coming at midday from the Arabian desert; from all of which they were exempt who labored during only the closing hour.

13. **Friend.** The word thus translated is used in the New Testament only by Matthew. It was indeed a kind and friendly term, but was applied to strangers and indifferent persons as well as to companions and acquaintances. Thus, according to many, it is found in ch. 11:16, meaning *comrades,* or *fellows.* In ch. 22:12 it is applied to the guest who had not on the wedding garment; and in ch. 26:50, by Jesus to Judas, when in the act of betrayal. It is equivalent here to *My good man,* and shows that the rebuke that follows was spoken in kindness. The other and more general word for *friend (philos)* always implies affection and regard. **I do thee no wrong.** I do thee no injustice; for I give you all that I agreed.

14. **Take that is thine.** Take what belongs to thee; I deal with thee justly, and I will be generous and liberal, and **give unto this last** even as to thee.

15. **Is it not lawful?** My property is my own, and it is right and proper for me to do with it as I please. You have, therefore, no reason to complain of my generosity. **Is thine eye evil,** etc. Art thou *envious* because I act kindly? Dost thou *look grudgingly* on what others receive as a free gift above what they could claim as their due, when no wrong is done to thee? On *evil eye,* compare Prov. 28:22; also, Deut. 15:9; 1 Sam. 18:9; Prov. 23:6; Mark 7:22.

16. This verse, and ch. 19:30, con-

16 ᶠ Is thine eye evil, because I am good? ᵍ So the last shall be first, and the first last: ʰ for many be called, but few chosen

ᶠ ch. 6. 23; Deu. 15. 9; Pro. 23. 6.
ᵍ ch. 19. 30.

tains the design and lesson of the parable. It is important that we bear this in mind in interpreting this parable, which is only second to the Unjust Steward, both in regard to the difficulties which beset it and the number of explanations offered. By so doing we shall avoid many of these difficulties, and also the necessity of considering many explanations which are far-fetched and entirely needless. It seems evident that its grand *design* is to illustrate a great fact under the Gospel dispensation, namely, that many who are first in the order of their calling will be last in their final rewards. It should be noted that the last verse of the preceding chapter does not say "*All*," but "*Many* that are first shall be last, and the last first." The *centre* of comparison is found in the sovereign distribution of the rewards among the laborers. The *householder* represents God; the laborers who were hired, his believing people; his *vineyard*, his kingdom; the *market-place*, the world; men *standing idle*, sinners; the householder going forth *to hire* them, God seeking his laborers, and not they him, "You have not chosen me, but I have chosen you" (John 15: 16); the various *hours* of day, the different periods of life (compare Jer. 7: 25); the *evening*, the close of the present dispensation or state of things; the *steward*, Christ; the *gathering* of the laborers to *pay* them, the judgment; the *penny*, or denary, everlasting life. See ch. 19: 29; John 17: 2, 3.

Some suppose that the *penny* represents the temporal good, and the favor of the householder, the eternal good, and that the first hired received only the former, while the others received the latter. But such a supposition is altogether improbable; for the penny was paid at the close of the day, which represents the reward given at the close of life, or at the judgment, while temporal rewards are all received in this life. And then these first had truly labored, they had borne the burden and heat of the day, they had not been negligent, they were not condemned for slothfulness or unfaithfulness; they thus represented true disciples; and finally, the householder did not withhold from the one and give to the others, for he says, "I will give unto these last even as unto thee." But it may be asked, How can everlasting life, which is a free gift of grace, be represented as *hire, wages*, or *reward?* It may be answered that there is a reward of *grace*, as well of *merit*; that God makes himself a debtor of grace by his free promise and covenant; and that everlasting life is given for what Christ has done. It is thus constantly represented by Christ and his apostles as a *reward*, ch. 5: 12; Luke 6: 23, 35; John 4: 36; 1 Cor. 3: 8, 14; Heb. 10: 35; 2 John 8.

That every man received a penny may represent, in a certain sense, an equality in the final rewards: all believers will enter upon the full enjoyment of everlasting life. Yet this is not inconsistent with the doctrine elsewhere taught, that there will be degrees in glory, ch. 25: 20–23; 1 Cor. 3: 15; 2 Cor. 5: 10. Everlasting life will itself vary, according as each one is prepared to receive and enjoy it. All will be filled with joy and life, but their spiritual capacities will differ; the development which they have received spiritually in this world will vary. The five cities (Luke 19: 16–19) will be as much to him that has gained five pounds as ten cities to him that has gained the ten pounds.

Great difficulty has been experienced in explaining the *murmurings* of those first hired. How can the righteous be said, at the last great day, to murmur against God? Doubtless they will find many causes of surprise, but also of joy and admiration, and especially of submission and thankfulness. It would seem that the murmuring language of these workmen was especially introduced in order to bring out more strikingly the *underlying reason* for giving unto the last even as unto the first, namely, the *righteous and absolute sovereignty* of God in the disposal of his favors. His acts will be according to his own good pleasure, and founded in righteousness. "Is it not lawful for me to do what I will with my own? Is thine eye evil because I am good?" At the same time this portion of the parable was adapted to check any tendency to a

Jesus a third time foretells his sufferings, death, and resurrection.

17 ¹ AND Jesus going up to Jerusalem took the twelve disciples apart in the way, and said unto
18 them, ᵏ Behold, we go up to Jerusalem; and the Son of man shall be betrayed unto the chief priests and unto the scribes; and they shall condemn him

ʰ ch. 22. 14; Acts 9. 15; 2 Thes. 2 13, 14; Jam. 1. 23-25.

ⁱ Mk. 10. 32; Lk. 18-31.
ᵏ ch. 16. 21.

---

self-righteous and mercenary spirit, such as might be suggested by Peter's question, which led to this discourse, "Behold, we have forsaken all and followed thee; *what shall we have therefore?*" ch. 19 : 27. The rewards will be of *grace*, and so distributed as to afford no one any ground of boasting, or of self-righteous satisfaction. Such a spirit will vitiate the longest and most laborious service, and will lessen the final reward and the divine favor. Compare Rom. 4 : 1-4; and a similar difficulty in Luke 15 : 25-32.

In closing the parable, Jesus reiterates, **So the last shall be first, and the first last.** Many first in order of calling shall be last in their rewards, shall fall behind and occupy a less honored position than others, while many called last will be advanced and more highly honored. It was a distinguishing favor for the householder to both pay the last first, and also to pay them the same amount. So God's distinguishing grace will be exercised and manifested toward certain called later in life, than toward some others called earlier. So also in regard to different periods in the gospel dispensation. Thus, Paul, called last to be an apostle, will doubtless be among the first in the rewards. To the Jews the Gospel was first preached before it was to the Gentiles, yet doubtless many Gentiles will receive the highest honors, while many believing Jews will receive the lowest.

And in harmony with the teaching of this parable, and as a reason for such a final disposal of rewards, Jesus adds, **For many are called, but few chosen.** In the exercise of his sovereign pleasure, God calls many into his kingdom, but chooses only a few to enjoy its highest honors and benefits. Compare Acts 9 : 15. Since all the laborers in the parable, the first and the last, represent true believers, it seems more natural to understand the terms *called* and *chosen* as referring also to true believers. See ch. 22 : 14, where this proverbial declaration has a different and wider reference. The figure may be derived from the practice of *choosing* men from those *called* out for war, Josh. 8 : 3; Judg. 7 : 7. But some of the best manuscripts omit this clause.

17-19. JESUS FORETELLS, THE THIRD TIME AND MORE FULLY, HIS SUFFERINGS, DEATH, AND RESURRECTION, Mark 10 : 32-34; Luke 18 : 31-34.

17. **Going up to Jerusalem.** He had now actually commenced his last journey to Jerusalem. They were going up to attend the Feast of the Passover. Mark tells us that, as Jesus was going before them, his disciples were amazed, and as they followed him were afraid, doubtless on account of his boldness and eagerness to go up to Jerusalem, the seat of his bitterest foes, and where they were counselling to destroy him, John 11 : 53-57. Jerusalem is about four thousand feet higher than the valley of the Jordan. It could well be said, he was *going up* to Jerusalem. To have predicted his approaching sufferings just as he was nearing or entering Judea, would also be most timely. **Took the twelve disciples apart in the way, and said,** etc. This should read, according to the best critical authorities, *Took the twelve apart, and in the way said to them.* He took them apart from others, who were journeying with them, and as they traveled on toward Jerusalem he communicated the solemn facts concerning his sufferings and death, which were near at hand.

18. He had first announced to his disciples his death and resurrection after the confession of Peter (ch. 16 : 21); then the second time after his transfiguration (ch. 17 : 22, 23); and now the third time he announces it as about to take place. He commences this solemn communication with **Behold,** by which he would call the particular attention of his disciples to what he was about to

19 to death, ¹ and shall deliver him to the Gentiles to mock, and to scourge, and to crucify *him:* and the third day he shall rise again.

¹ ch. 27. 2, 27-31; Ps. 22. 7, 8; Is. 50. 5, 6; 53. 3, 5.

Request of the mother of the sons of Zebedee, and our Lord's reply.

20 ᵐ THEN came to him ⁿ the mother of Zebedee's children with her sons, worshiping *him*, and desir-

ᵐ Mk. 10. 35.
ⁿ ch. 4. 21.

foretell. **Go up to Jerusalem.** See on preceding verse. Jerusalem was also morally elevated, John 2 : 13 ; 7 : 8 ; 11 : 55. **Shall be betrayed.** *Will be delivered*, with evil intent, into the hands of the chief priests and scribes. "This word" (*to deliver up*) "is used by classic writers in cases of actual treachery."—DR. CONANT, on ch. 10 : 4. In the next verse it is translated *shall deliver* him to the Gentiles. Thus we have a two-fold *delivering up*, or betrayal, first, by one of his own followers ; second, by the highest ecclesiastical and civil court of his own nation. **Chief priests and scribes.** The Sanhedrim. See on ch. 2 : 4. **Condemn him to death.** The Sanhedrim could pass sentence of death, but the Roman governor alone had the power of executing the sentence.

19. **Gentiles.** The Greek word for *Gentiles* literally means *nations*, that is, *all nations* besides the Jews, and very nearly equivalent to our *heathen*. It here referred particularly to the Romans, to Pilate, and the Roman soldiers, ch. 27 : 2, 27. **To mock and to scourge,** etc. Better, *To mock, and scourge, and crucify.* For this purpose they would deliver him to the Gentiles. Crucifixion properly commenced with scourging, yet in our Savior's case, through the petulance of the brutal soldiery, he was also *mocked*. Thus these three verbs describe what Pilate and his soldiers should do to him. This is the first time that Jesus had told his disciples of the mode of his death, by crucifixion; and Matthew alone records that he foretold it at this time. **Shall rise again.** As on the two former announcements of his death, he foretells his resurrection. This was a gleam of light which shone up beyond the intervening darkness. Without his resurrection, his death would have been in vain, 1 Cor. 15 : 12-18. Several ancient manuscripts read, *will be raised*, by which the power of God, in his restoration to life, is exhibited in contrast with the sufferings and death inflicted by men.

Luke (18 : 34) adds, "They understood none of these things;" they may have regarded his language as figurative of great obstacles and difficulties in setting up a temporal kingdom. Or his words may have been to them dark and parabolic sayings, which they did not attempt to understand, much less did they desire to understand in their literal sense.

20-28. THE AMBITIOUS REQUEST OF THE MOTHER OF THE SONS OF ZEBEDEE, AND THE REPLY OF JESUS. The jealous emulation of the ten other apostles is excited, which leads Jesus to explain how distinction can only be attained in his kingdom, Mark 10 : 35-45.

20. **The mother of Zebedee's children.** Rather, *The mother of the sons of Zebedee.* From comparing ch. 27 : 55, 56 with Mark 15 : 40 ; 16 : 1, it appears that her name was Salome. The sons were James and John, Mark 10 : 35. According to Mark, the sons came making the request for themselves, which is in entire harmony with Matthew, who says that the mother of the sons of Zebedee came **with her sons.** They asked, through their mother, and with their mother. " Probably the two brethren had directed this request *through their mother*, because they remembered the rebuke which had followed their former contention about precedence," ch. 18 : 1-3 ; Mark 9 : 33-37.—ALFORD. They too understood the power of woman in making a request. Compare 1 Kings 1 : 16 ; Esth. 5 : 2 ; 7 : 3-7 ; Matt. 14 : 6-8. **Worshiping him.** *Bowing down* to the earth with profound reverence. See on ch. 2 : 2. **Desiring a certain thing.** Rather, *Asking something.* She did something more than *desire ;* she *asked*, possibly by her falling down before him and by her gestures, but more probably by words, Mark 10 : 35. She asked not now the great and definite thing for which she and her sons were seeking, but *some-*

21 ing a certain thing of him. And he said unto her, What wilt thou? She saith unto him, °Grant that these my two sons ᵖ may sit, the one on thy right hand, and the other on the left, in thy kingdom.
22 But Jesus answered and said, Ye know not what ye ask. Are ye able to drink of ᑫ the cup that I shall drink of, and to be baptized with ʳ the baptism that I am baptized with? They say unto him, We are able.

° Ro. 12. 10; Phil. 2. 3.
ᵖ ch. 19. 28.

ᑫ ch. 26. 39, 42; John 18. 11.
ʳ Lk. 12. 50; Ps. 42. 7.

---

thing general, which would prepare the way for, and thus include what she was about to ask. She would obtain his willingness, and possibly his promise, to do whatever she should request. Compare 1 Kings 2: 20.

21. **Grant.** *Command*, as the Greek word is translated in ch. 4: 3. So also it is translated *bid* in Luke 10: 40. She would have him authoritatively *say*, or *command*, as the Messianic king, that her two sons should occupy the two highest places of honor in his kingdom. It was a very inappropriate request, made at a very inappropriate time. It showed that they did not understand what Jesus had just told them in regard to his sufferings and death, Luke 18: 34. The promise made to the twelve, in ch. 19: 28, probably suggested the idea of making the request. **Thy right hand—the left.** The first and second positions of honor. Josephus (*Antiq.* vi. 11, 9) speaks of Jonathan sitting on the right hand of Saul, and Abner, the captain of the host, sitting on the left. These were the highest, and next to the highest, places of honor in eastern royal courts. So, also, in the Sanhedrim, the vice-president sat on the right hand of the president, and the referee, or third officer of rank, on the left. **In thy kingdom,** which they expected would immediately appear, Luke 19: 11. Little did they think that Jesus would soon be crucified, with robbers on *his right and left hand*. How keenly must John have been reminded of their ambitious request as he stood before the cross, John 19: 26.

22. **Ye know not what ye ask.** You know not what these high positions of honor are, or the trials and sufferings necessarily connected with attaining them. They did not understand the spiritual nature of his kingdom and of the sufferings which must precede its honors. **Drink the cup.** The cup of suffering, especially of internal suffering, ch. 26: 39; John 18: 11. The cup is a common figure in the Bible, sometimes representing joy (Ps. 16: 5; 23: 5; 116: 13); and sometimes sorrow, Ps. 11: 6; 75: 8; Isa. 51: 17; Jer. 25: 15; Rev. 16: 19.

And to be baptized with the baptism that I am baptized with. According to the oldest manuscripts and versions, and the highest critical authorities, these words do not belong to either this or the following verse, but to Mark 10: 38, 39. It was probably inserted here by some copyist to make it conform with Mark's account. The reference is not to the ordinance of baptism, but to the overwhelming suffering which Jesus was about to endure. The Greek word *baptizo* means *immerse, plunge, dip,* and figuratively, *whelm* or *overwhelm.* See ch. 3: 6. In the Greek, and, indeed, in all languages, may be found such expressions as these: Plunged in affliction, immersed in suffering, overwhelmed with sorrow. Compare such scriptural expressions for calamities and suffering as, "All thy waves and billows have gone over me" (Ps. 42: 7); "I am come into deep waters, where the floods overflow me (Ps. 69: 2); "We went through fire and through water," 66: 12. The idea of our Savior's language is, Can ye endure the overwhelming sufferings that I shall endure? Thus, Dr. E. Robinson (*Lexicon of the New Testament*, under *baptizo*), referring to this passage, explains, "Can ye endure to be overwhelmed with sufferings like those which I must endure?" See *Calmet Dict.* As the *cup* which is to be drunk refers more especially to internal sorrow, so the *baptism,* which completely surrounds and covers over, refers more especially to the external sufferings of persecution and crucifixion, or martyrdom, though not excluding, but rather embodying, the mental anguish connected with them.

We are able. James and John, to whom the questions of Jesus had just

23 And he saith unto them, *Ye shall drink indeed of my cup, and be baptized with the baptism that I am baptized with: but to sit on my right hand and on my left, is not mine to ᵗ give, but it *shall be given to them* for whom it is prepared of my Father.
24 ᵘAnd when the ten heard *it*, they were moved with
25 indignation against the two brethren. But Jesus called them *unto him*, and said, Ye know that the princes of the Gentiles exercise dominion over them, and they that are great exercise authority upon them.

* Ac. 12. 2; Ro. 8. 17; 2 Cor. 1. 7; 2 Tim 2. 11, 12, Rev. 1. 9.
ᵗ ch. 25. 34; Heb. 11. 16.
ᵘ Pro. 13 10; 1 Cor. 13. 4; Phil. 2. 3; Jam. 3. 14 , 16; 1 Pet. 5. 5.

been addressed, now speak for themselves, showing, on the one hand, a willingness and courage to encounter difficulties and endure sufferings, and, on the other, a small conception of what those sufferings were. Doubtless they thought of those which would necessarily arise in assuming kingly power. They were truly Sons of Thunder (Mark 3 : 17), and may have felt ready for war and fighting under Jesus against his enemies. Had the position of the two robbers crucified on either side of Jesus arisen to their view, and been offered them, how would they have shrunk from it.

23. Ye shall drink. Ye shall indeed be called to pass through such suffering as I shall endure. They endured not the same but similar sufferings. James was the first martyr among the apostles, slain with the sword by Herod, A.D. 44, Acts 12 : 2. John was the last survivor of the twelve, and by his long life of trials and persecutions for Christ's sake more than equaled the suffering of actual martyrdom. He was scourged by the Jews (Acts 5 : 40), banished by the Roman emperor to Patmos. Such facts show what hatred and persecution he must have endured. The *cup* and the *baptism* find their fulfillment in these, without having recourse to the traditions that at one time he was plunged into a cask of boiling oil, by which he was refreshed instead of destroyed, and at another, that he drank a cup of poison without injury.

Is not mine to give, but it shall be given, etc. Rather, *Is not mine to give, but it is for those for whom it has been prepared*, etc. It has already been decided, even from the foundation of the world (ch. 25 : 34; Eph. 1 : 4), who shall enjoy these honors. It was not for Jesus to bestow them then, nor to change the arrangements already made.

Neither did it become him to inform them whether it was assigned to them or to others; for it had been prepared according to the principles of the divine government, in which God's sovereignty and man's free agency harmonize. According to those principles, they who enjoyed those honors should also partake of his sufferings (vers. 26–28; 2 Tim. 2 : 12); and, according to them, Jesus, who was one with the Father, should also dispose of the honors of his kingdom, John 5 : 19–23; Luke 22 : 29; Rev. 3 : 21. A very ancient and common interpretation is to take *but* in the sense of *except*, "It is not mine to give, *except* to those for whom it is prepared of my Father." But this can not be philologically sustained.

24. The ten. The ten other apostles, among whom was Matthew himself. We have in this a proof of his humility and truthfulness. **They were moved with indignation.** *They were indignant;* or, better, *They were much displeased*, as the verb is translated in Mark 10 : 14, 41. The same emulation which prompted the request of the two now arouses the displeasure of the ten, and needed correcting.

25. Called them. They were at least a little apart from Jesus while they were indulging in their angry feelings. **Princes of the Gentiles.** The rulers of the heathen nations. See on ver. 19. **Exercise dominion.** Literally, *Lord it over them.* **They that are great.** Their great men, their nobles. **Exercise authority.** The verb in the original is somewhat stronger than the one in the preceding clause. They exercise their authority arbitrarily. Both verbs, however, represent the power which rulers were accustomed to exercise over their subjects. **Them.** The Gentiles.

26. Not be so. In his kingdom his

26 But ˣ it shall not be so among you: but ʸ whosoever will be great among you, let him be your minister; ᶻ and whosoever will be chief among you, let
27
28 him be your servant: ᵃ even as the ᵇ Son of man came not to be ministered unto, ᶜ but to minister, and ᵈ to give his life a ransom ᵉ for many.

ˣ ch. 23. 8-12; Lk. 14. 7-11; 1 Pet. 5. 3.
ʸ Mk. 9. 33-35.
ᶻ ch. 18. 4.
ᵃ John 13. 4-17.
ᵇ Phil. 2. 4-8.
ᶜ Lk. 22. 27; John 13. 14.
ᵈ Is. 53. 10, 11; Dan. 9. 24-26; John 10. 15; 11. 51, 52; Ro. 3. 24

Healing of two blind men near Jericho.

29 ᶠ AND as they departed from Jericho, a great

ministers and great ones were not to exercise civil power or authority over their brethren; neither were they to lord it over God's heritage, 1 Pet. 5 : 3. They were not to seek after greatness by exercising power and authority, but through eminent services and self-denials. **Whosoever will be great.** Whoever would become preëminent among you. In humility let him engage in a service of love and in doing good to others. **Your minister.** A waiter, an attendant, one who ministers to you. The word in the original was applied to one who served or waited on another, principally at table, and who was not a slave. It was afterward applied, among Christians, officially to *deacons*, 1 Tim. 3 : 8. Dr. Conant, in speaking of its use in the New Testament, says, "One who *ministers* to another, or others; either in waiting on guests at table (John 2 : 5, 9; compare the verb in Luke 22 : 27); or as a distributor of alms (compare the use of the noun and verb in Acts 6 : 1, 2); or as a magistrate in administering justice (Rom. 13 : 4); or as an attendant on a person of a sovereign to execute his commands (Matt. 22 : 13); or as one who furthers or promotes a thing (*minister of sin*, Gal. 2 : 17); or as a religious teacher, dispensing knowledge of saving truth (1 Cor. 3 : 5)." Jesus teaches that they that would become great must in humility engage in a service of love and in doing good to others.

27. Whosoever will be chief. Whoever would be *first* among you. The two disciples had sought the first and second honors of his kingdom; he now points out the way to become *great* and *first* among his followers. **Your servant.** The word here translated *servant* was the usual name of a *bondman* or *slave*, and was thus a stronger word than that translated *minister* in the preceding verse, denoting a humbler service. Though it was generally applied to involuntary service, it is often applied, as here, to that which is voluntary, Rom. 6 : 16; Eph. 6 : 6; 2 Pet. 1 : 1. He who would be first, let him engage in the humblest service, and in the most self-denying labors.

28. Jesus illustrates and enforces this precept and principle by his own example. He, the King of his kingdom, the Head of the church, the Elder Brother, voluntarily entered upon the greatest humiliation and the most humble and self-denying service, Phil. 2 : 7-11. **Son of Man.** The Messiah. See on ch. 8 : 20. **Came—to minister.** He took the *form of a servant* when he came to save men (Phil. 2 : 7); he came to serve or wait on others. Compare John 13 : 4, 5. It was true of his whole life that he ministered to others. But, in addition, at its close he **gave his life a ransom,** his ministration to and for others extended even to the giving up of life, it culminated in becoming *obedient unto death,* Phil. 2 : 8. A *ransom* was the price paid to redeem one from death (Exod. 21 : 30) or from slavery, Lev. 25 : 51. Men were slaves of sins, dead in trespasses and sin, and condemned to eternal death. Christ came to *give* his life (John 10 : 18), which was not forfeited by sin, a ransom **for,** *in the stead,* of many. He gave his life in their place as a substitute. His death was a substitution for their death. **Many.** The multitude of the redeemed, Rev. 5 : 9; 7 : 4, 9. *Many* is in contrast with the one life which he gave, Rom. 5 : 15, 17, 19. Here those are referred to who shall enjoy the efficacy of the ransom, who shall be actually redeemed, ch. 26 : 28. In 1 Tim. 2 : 6, *ransom for all* (in behalf of all), the relation of Christ's atonement and death to all men, its sufficiency and its free offer to all, is presented, Rom. 5 : 18.

30 multitude followed him. And, behold, ^g two blind men sitting by the way side, when they heard that Jesus passed by, cried out, saying, Have mercy on

—26; Ep. 1. 7; 1 Tim. 2. 6; Tit. 2. 14; 1 Pet. 1. 18, 19.

29–34. JESUS HEALS TWO BLIND MEN NEAR JERICHO, Mark 10 : 46–52; Luke 18 : 35–43.

29. **Jericho** signifies "the fragrant place," and was a city of Benjamin (Josh. 18 : 21), situated about eighteen miles north-east of Jerusalem, and seven miles west of the Jordan. It was founded probably after the destruction of Sodom, called "the city of palm-trees" (Deut. 34 : 3), and famous for its roses and balsam. It was the first city in Canaan taken and destroyed by Joshua (Josh. 6 : 24–26), rebuilt five hundred years afterward by Hiel, (1 Kings 16 : 34), and became distinguished for its school of the prophets, and as the residence of Elisha, 2 Kings 2 : 18. Meanwhile, a new Jericho appears to have been built on a neighboring site, Judg. 3 : 13; 2 Sam. 10 : 5; Josephus, *Bell. Jud.* iv. 8 : 2, 3. From Josephus and 2 Kings 2 : 19–22, we infer that the ancient city stood near Elisha's fountain, supposed to be the one now named Ain-es-Sultan, the plain around which is now strewn with ancient ruins and rubbish. Nearly two miles south of this fountain, and near the place where the road from Jerusalem enters the plain, and on the banks of Wady Kelt, stood the modern city, which Herod the Great adorned with splendid palaces and buildings. Ancient ruins now mark its site. It lies on the direct route from Perea to Jerusalem. Jericho was second in importance only to Jerusalem, of the cities of Israel; and was the residence of a chief publican, Zaccheus (Luke 19 : 1), on account of the balsam trade. Dr. Robinson found only a single palm-tree remaining of the city of the palms, and even that is said now to be gone. Nearly the whole plain is now waste and desolate, though the soil is good. Rihah, a poor, miserable Arab village of about two hundred inhabitants, now stands on the plain, and is about a mile and a half nearer the Jordan than either the ancient or later Jericho.

Departed from Jericho. *Was going out of Jericho.* With this agrees Mark; but Luke says (18 : 35), *As he was come nigh unto Jericho.* This is one of the most difficult points in harmonizing the Evangelists. Did we know the full particulars, all would be plain. Some little circumstances not related might remove all apparent discrepancies. In our ignorance of the details of our Savior's visit at Jericho, we may present several ways which the learned have proposed for harmonizing Luke with Matthew and Mark: 1. There was an *old* and a *new* Jericho. Jesus may have been leaving one and approaching the other. The first two Evangelists may describe the former act, while Luke describes the latter. 2. There may have been two miracles, one just before entering the city, and one as he was leaving it, Luke mentioning the former and Mark the latter; and Matthew describing both under one account. 3. One of the blind men may have besought Jesus on his entering the city, but for some reason was not answered; but at the departure of Jesus, on the following morning, with a companion he may have renewed the appeal, when they both obtained a cure. 4. Jesus may have remained several days at Jericho, during which time he would naturally visit points of interest in the vicinity. Compare Mark's language, "They came to Jericho." The miracle, therefore, might have been performed, not when he was finally leaving Jericho, but when he was *occasionally* going *out of* and returning *to* Jericho. 5. The Greek verb in Luke, rendered *to come nigh*, may signify *to be near.* See Septuagint, 1 Kings 21 : 2; Deut. 21 : 3; Jer. 23 : 23; Ruth 2 : 20; 2 Sam. 19 : 42. Thus, the language of Luke may mean, while he was *yet near* the city, including the idea expressed by Matthew and Mark. No one need stumble on an apparent discrepancy like this when we can conceive of so many ways of explaining it. The second and fifth explanations are, however, the least satisfactory. But see Clark's Harmony, § 129.

A great multitude. Jericho would be full of people who were going up to Jerusalem to attend the Feast of the Passover. The number would be greatly increased by those coming from Galilee by the way of Perea, to avoid passing through Samaria.

30. **Two blind men.** Mark and

31 us, O Lord, *thou* son of David! And the multitude rebuked them, because they should hold their peace. ʰ But they cried the more, saying, Have
32 mercy on us, O ⁱ Lord, *thou* son of David! And Jesus stood still, and called them, and said, What
33 will ye that I shall do unto you? They say unto
34 him, Lord, that our eyes may be opened. ᵏ So Jesus had compassion *on them*, and touched their eyes; and immediately their eyes received sight, and they followed him.

* ch. 26. 28; Ro. 5. 15-19; Heb. 9, 28.
ᶠ Mk. 10. 46; Lk. 18. 35.
ᵍ ch. 9. 27-31.
ʰ Gen. 32. 26; Lk. 18. 1; Col. 4. 2; 1 Thes. 5. 17.
ⁱ Ps. 119. 18; Eph. 1. 17-19.
ᵏ ch. 15. 32.

Luke speak only of one. But the two includes the one, and the one does not exclude the two. See a similar case of the demoniacs of Gadara, ch. 8 : 28. One of them, Bartimeus, was perhaps the more prominent individual, and generally known. Thus we may suppose Mark and Luke to narrate the miracle performed on him, while they pass unnoticed that performed on the other, who may have been a person of no prominence, and scarcely known, or perhaps an entire stranger in that vicinity. Matthew, who was present with Jesus on that journey, speaks of the two just as the scene appeared to him as an eye-witness. **Jesus passed by.** The great prophet of Galilee, the miracle-worker, whose name had become familiar to the sick and afflicted of Palestine. **Son of David.** The royal descendant of David, and the successor to his throne; the Messiah, ch. 22 : 42. See on ch. 9 : 27. **Rebuked them.** Admonished them sternly that they should be silent. **Because they should,** etc. Rather, *That they might hold their peace.* They would not have Jesus annoyed or interrupted in his journey, nor did they care to be disturbed with the cries of these two poor blind men. They did not, probably, object to the title *Son of David*, for they were doubtless the same in part who themselves soon after applied it to him, ch. 21 : 9. **They cried the more.** The rebuke of the multitude only aroused their earnestness, for they believed that Jesus would be willing to heal them. It was a trial of their faith. They saw the difficulties of their situation, and faith in the ability and willingness of Jesus to open their eyes excited them to surmount every barrier, and to cry "Have mercy on us," etc. A good illustration of the sinner seeking of Jesus the salvation of his soul.

32, 33. **Jesus stood still** at the believing and importunate cry of these blind suppliants. He publicly recognizes the title, Son of David, as applied to himself. He now asks what they desire him to do. They had asked a general petition; he would now call forth their particular and special request. Faith brings to Jesus particular objects of desire. Thus they ask that their eyes may be opened.

34. **So Jesus had compassion,** etc. Rather, *And Jesus, moved with compassion, touched their eyes.* His pity was excited; their faith was sufficient (Mark 7 : 52; Luke 18 : 42); and yearning over them with complaisant compassion, he touched their eyes and they received sight. **Followed him.** Mark adds, "In the way;" and Luke, "Glorifying God." Thus we may suppose them going on with the joyous multitude in their festive journey, ascending through that wild and desolate region between Jericho and Jerusalem.

REMARKS.

1. Christ calls upon sinners to enter and to labor in his kingdom, vers. 1, 3, 5; Jer. 7 : 25; Prov. 8 : 1-16; Rev. 22 : 16, 17.
2. Whoever labors for Christ will get his wages, vers. 1, 4, 8, 9; Ps. 19 : 11; Matt. 6 : 33; Heb. 6 : 10; 1 Cor. 3 : 14, 15; Rev. 22 : 12.
3. He is an idler in God's service, and a slave to sin, who has not repented and believed on Christ, ver 4; Prov. 19 : 15; Ezek. 16 : 49; John 6 : 28, 29; 8 : 24.
4. There can be no excuse for idleness when there is so much to do in Christ's kingdom and service, ver. 6; Eccle. 9 : 10; John 9 : 4; Eph. 5 : 16; Col. 3 : 12-14; 4 : 5; 2 Thess. 3 : 11, 12.
5. Let us beware of a hireling spirit in

Christ's service, and of doing his work grudgingly, vers. 10–12; 2 Cor. 8 : 12; 9 : 6, 7; Eph. 6 : 5, 6.

6. Christ at the judgment will take into account not merely the *time*, but also the manner and quality of our service, vers. 10, 12; Luke 19 : 16–19; Rom. 2 : 6, 7.

7. Christ is a righteous sovereign, and will dispense his rewards of free grace according to his own good pleasure, with injustice to none, vers. 13–15; Ps. 19 : 9; 145 : 17; Jer. 12 : 1; 1 John 2 : 1; Rev. 4 : 11; 16 : 17.

8. We should not murmur at the dispensations of grace and Providence, nor envy the position of others in Christ's kingdom, vers. 13–15; 1 Cor. 10 : 10; Phil. 4 : 11–13; 1 Tim. 6 : 6.

9. Many who are first in advantages are the last to be converted. And many Christians who are first in privileges in this world will, in the world to come, fall below their less privileged brethren, ver. 16.

10. Christ chooses from among his followers those who shall perform special work and enjoy special honors, ver. 16; Acts 9 : 15; 10 : 41.

11. It is possible for sinners to be saved at any period of life; but this should not lead them to put off repentance till old age. Notice that no one was called to labor after the eleventh hour, vers. 1–16.

12. How wonderful the grace and compassion of Jesus, and his willingness to suffer, as exhibited by his going up to Jerusalem when he knew what was to befall him there, vers. 17–19; Luke 12 : 50; John 12 : 27, 28; Rom. 5 : 6.

13. Prejudice and a false education may prevent us from understanding the teachings of Scripture. We need the enlightening influence of the Spirit to fully understand the plainest doctrines of the Gospel, vers. 17–19; Luke 18 : 34; 24 : 45; John 12 : 16; 16 : 13.

14. Parents often, through ignorance and pride, seek places of worldly distinction for their children, which, if obtained, would prove very injurious to their souls, ver. 20.

15. Christians are too prone to be actuated with a spirit of worldly ambition. This spirit was thrice strikingly exhibited in the case of the disciples, vers. 21, 22, 24; ch. 18 : 1; Luke 22 : 24.

16. If we seek the highest places in Christ's kingdom, we must count the cost, knowing that they are attained only through the deepest humility and suffering, vers. 22, 23; Acts 14 : 22; Rom. 8 : 17; 2 Tim. 2 : 11, 12; 2 Cor. 1 : 5–7; Col. 1 : 24.

17. An ambitious and domineering spirit is unbecoming the church of Christ, and should not be exercised among its membership, ver. 25; John 13 : 13–17; Rom. 12 : 10; 2 Cor. 1 : 24; James 3 : 1; 1 Pet. 5 : 3–5; 3 John 9.

18. Humility is a foundation grace, and is necessary to true usefulness, vers. 26, 27; Luke 18, 14; 1 Pet. 5 : 5.

19. Christ's sufferings and death were vicarious or substitutional, ver. 28; Isa. 53 : 10, 11; Dan. 9 : 24–26; John 10 : 11; 2 Cor. 5 : 21; Gal. 3 : 13, 14; Tit. 2 : 14; Heb. 9 : 28; Rev. 5 : 9.

20. Sinners are blinded by sin. They do not spiritually discern Jesus or his truth, ver. 30; Jer. 5 : 21; John 1 : 5; 1 Cor. 2 : 14; 2 Cor. 3 : 15; 4 : 6.

21. Sinners should call on Jesus to open their blind eyes, ver. 30; Ps. 119 : 18; Isa. 42 : 7; Luke 4 : 18; John 8 : 12; 9 : 39; 2 Cor. 3 : 14; Rev. 3 : 18.

22. Sinners should improve present opportunities while Jesus is yet graciously near, and before their blindness becomes forever fixed, ver. 30; Isa. 55 : 6; Ps. 60 : 3; Isa. 44 : 18; Acts 28 : 25–27.

23. They who are seeking spiritual sight will meet with obstacles and opposition from the world; but this should only excite them to greater importunity, lest they fail of a cure, ver. 31; Luke 11 : 5–10; Acts 2 : 40.

24. The sinner has no plea but mercy for the sake of Jesus, ver. 31; Luke 18 : 13.

25. The compassion of Jesus is infinite. He pauses, as it were, to attend to the importunate cry of the sinner, ver. 32; Mark 10 : 49.

26. The seeker after Jesus, as well as the Christian, should come to him with definite requests, vers. 32, 33; Acts 8 : 22; Phil. 4 : 6.

27. Jesus will open the eyes of the blind as they send up the prayer of faith, ver. 34; ch. 21, 22; Isa. 29 : 18, 19; Acts 9 : 11, 18.

28. They who are made to spiritually see will follow Jesus, ver. 34; Luke 14 : 27; John 15 : 14.

Our Lord's public entry into Jerusalem.

XXI. AND ¹ when they drew nigh unto Jerusalem, and were come to Bethphage, unto ᵐ the mount of

¹ Mk. 11. 1; Lk. 19. 29; John 12. 12.
ᵐ Zec. 14. 4.

CHAPTER XXI.

With this chapter Matthew begins his account of the last public ministry of Jesus at Jerusalem, and the winding up of his prophetic ministry on earth. The six days, corresponding remarkably with the six days of creation, whose history is about to be narrated form an era in all time and eternity; "a world was re-created, and the last fearful efforts of the rulers of its darkness met, quelled, and triumphed over for evermore."

1-11. THE TRIUMPHAL ENTRY OF JESUS INTO JERUSALEM, Mark 11 : 1-11; Luke 19 : 29-44; John 12 : 1, 12-19.

1. And when. John says, "Jesus, six days before the Passover, came to Bethany." The *six days* may include, or exclude, both the day of his arrival at Bethany and the day of the paschal supper; or it may include one and exclude the other. It accords better with later Greek usage to include the former and exclude the latter. It was six days *before* the Passover. The Passover began with the evening closing the fourteenth—that is, the fifteenth—day of Abib (Exod. 12 : 2; 13 : 4; Lev. 23 : 5, 6), or Nisan, as the month was afterward called (Esth. 3 : 7). Six days before would, therefore, be the ninth; and as Jesus was crucified on Friday, the day which began with the paschal supper, his arrival at Bethany must have been on the Saturday previous. We can not suppose, however, that Jesus and his company would have traveled from Jericho on the Jewish Sabbath. We must, therefore, conclude that they performed their journey on Friday. It is possible that they were too late to arrive at Jerusalem before the Sabbath, which began at sunset on Friday; and that, therefore, they tarried near the Mount of Olives, and observed the day quietly in their tents. At the same time Jesus could have gone to Bethany, arriving there at sunset, or a little after, on Friday evening, and, after spending the Sabbath with Mary, Martha, and Lazarus, could have rejoined the company on Sunday, and with them entered Jerusalem.

Unto Jerusalem. The goal of their journey, on their route from Jericho. On Jerusalem, see on ch. 2 : 1. **Bethphage.** Mark and Luke say, "To Bethphage and Bethany," implying that the two places were near to each other. The former name means the *place of figs;* the latter, according to some, *the place of dates;* but according to others, *the place of sorrow.* The site of Bethphage is unknown. According to Mark (11 : 1), where the places seem to be named from west to east, Bethphage would appear to be between Jerusalem and Bethany. But according to Luke (19 : 29), Bethphage would seem to have been reached before Bethany in the journey from Jericho, and hence a little east of Bethany. Hence it is better to suppose that the direct route from Jericho passed through Bethphage, and not through Bethany, a little south and west of the latter; so that those traveling from Jericho would come to Bethphage first, and would turn off from thence to Bethany, if they should desire to visit that place. See further, on this verse and the next.

The Mount of Olives. Literally, *The Mount of the Olives*, being descriptive of the olive trees which grew thereon. Olive trees still grow there, but less thickly than of old. Compare 2 Sam. 15 : 30; Neh. 8 : 15; Ezek. 11 : 23; Zech. 14 : 4. It is also called Olivet (Acts 1 : 12), a place set with olives, an olive-yard. This mount is the high ridge east of Jerusalem, and parallel to the city, and separated from it by the valley of the Kidron. The top is notched with three summits, the middle one of which is the highest, being about 2600 feet above the Mediterranean, 560 feet above the bed of the Kidron, 200 feet above the highest part of the city, and about half a mile from the city wall. The southern summit, which is lower than the other two, is called the "Mount of Offense," and also "Mount of Corruption," because Solomon and some of the later kings defiled it by idolatrous worship. Three paths lead over the Mount of Olives, the middle one directly to Bethany, which is situated on the eastern slope. The one further to the south passes a little to the right of that village, and is the road to Jericho. Geth-

2 Olives, then sent Jesus two disciples, saying unto them, Go into the village over against you, and straightway ye shall find an ass tied, and a colt
3 with her: loose *them*, and bring *them* unto me. And if any *man* say aught unto you, ye shall say, The Lord hath need of them; and straightway he will
4 send them. All this was done, that it might be fulfilled which was spoken by the prophet, saying,

---

semane lay just at the western foot of Olivet.
Jesus sent two disciples. Who we are not informed. Compare Mark 14 : 13 and Luke 22 : 8. Sunday morning had come. The company prepare to enter Jerusalem. They are increased by a great multitude, who had come up to the feast, and had heard that Jesus was coming to Jerusalem, John 12 : 9-12.
2. **The village over against you.** Bethphage. About one third of a mile west of Bethany, and about two hundred yards to the south of the road, is an ancient site. It is separated from Bethany by a low ridge and a deep glen. If this site marks the position of Bethphage, then Jesus, on gaining the top of this low ridge, was just opposite to that place, and could say, "Go into the village over against you."—J. L. PORTER, *Alexander's Kitto's Cyclo.*
An ass tied, and a colt with her. The other Evangelists speak only of the colt, and Mark and Luke add, "Whereon never man sat," a fact which especially showed its fitness for a religious use, being ceremonially pure and unblemished, Deut. 21 : 3. The colt only was needed, and the ass would naturally follow. The other Evangelists do, therefore, no violence to truth in speaking only of the colt. Matthew has occasion to speak of both the ass and colt, as he is about to show a remarkable fulfillment of prophecy, wherein both animals are mentioned.
3. **Say aught unto you.** Make any objection, or ask you why you loose the ass and colt. Thus, according to Mark, "Certain of those that stood there," and according to Luke, "The owners thereof," did question them when they were loosing the colt. The owners may have been a man and his sons, the members of a family, to whom the ass and colt belonged. **The Lord hath need.** *Lord* may refer to the Lord Jehovah, or to Jesus as the King Messiah. Compare Mark 1 : 3; 5 : 19; 13 : 20. The two meanings really unite in Jesus; he was both Jehovah and Christ. Compare Acts 2 : 36. What the owners would understand by the expression is another question from what was the full meaning in the mind of Jesus. They most probably understood that Jesus, as the Messiah, wanted the beasts for a temporary use in the Lord's service. They were, probably, acquainted with Jesus, and quite likely joined the multitude in shouting, Hosanna to the Son of David. Their friendliness to him, and their willingness to accommodate him, is evident from the declaration of Jesus, **"And straightway he will send them."** All this was divinely arranged. Jesus knew that he was perfectly welcome to the use of these animals. As the King, Messiah, he could claim their service. Compare 1 Sam. 8 : 16. As Jehovah, they were his, Ps. 50 : 10. The singular number *he* refers to any one who might say aught, and really decides nothing, as to whether the animals were owned by one or more. Practically, all difficulty is solved by supposing a man and his sons, or family, as interested in the property.
4. Matthew and John refer to the event as a fulfillment of prophecy, which reveals a marked characteristic of the Gospel of the former. See on ch. 12 : 17. Jesus did this in order that prophecy might be fulfilled; but back of prophecy there was a reason for what he did. The time had come for him to claim and receive Messianic honors, and this he could not well do on foot in a procession. He therefore rides in triumph. The act itself, riding in triumph into Jerusalem on a colt of an ass, was significant, appropriate, and suited to the nature of Christ's kingdom. The horse was an animal of pride and war, the ass of humility and peace. Thus Jesus publicly claimed and received honors as the Messiah; yet not as a proud,

A.D. 30. MATTHEW XXI. 283

5 ⁿ 'Tell ye the daughter of Sion, Behold, thy King cometh unto thee, meek, and sitting upon an ass, and a colt the foal of an ass.'
6 ᵒ And the disciples went, and did as Jesus
7 commanded them, and brought the ass, and the colt, and ᵖ put on them their clothes, and they set

ⁿ Ps. 2. 6; Jer. 23. 5; Zec. 9. 9; Matt. 11. 29.

ᵒ Mk. 11. 4.

ᵖ 2 Ki. 9. 13.

worldly monarch, but as the Prince of Peace. His meekness and lowliness in thus entering Jerusalem was in harmony with the nature of his kingdom, and inconsistent with the views of some rationalistic interpreters, that Jesus really designed to head a military movement, and, delivering the Jews from the Roman yoke, become a temporal monarch. How unfounded the last supposition is, appears from the facts that the multitude was without arms, and that the Roman authorities failed to take any notice of the triumphal procession as in any degree wrong or disloyal. Many of the ancient interpreters symbolized the ass and the colt. Thus, Justin Martyr makes the former to represent Judaism under the law; and the latter, untamed heathenism. Chrysostom, and others likewise, make the ass, accustomed to burdens, a symbol of the synagogue under the yoke of the law, and the colt of the Gentiles, as untamed and unclean before Christ sat upon them and sanctified them. Lange suggests the contrast between the old theocracy and the young church. But such allegorizing speculations should be cautiously received. **By the prophet.** *Through the prophet,* Zechariah, 9: 9. The fulfillment of this prophecy did not occur to the disciples at the time; but they understood it as fulfilled in Jesus after he was glorified, John 12: 16. The language of the prophet is quoted freely, and such portions of it as was now most manifestly fulfilled. With the first clause of this quotation compare Isa. 62: 11.

5. **Daughter of Zion.** Zion was that part of Jerusalem where David, and the kings after him, dwelt. Zion here represents Jerusalem and its inhabitants. Spiritually, it represented the pious part of the Jewish people. **Meek and sitting,** etc. Rather, *Meek and mounted on an ass.* His meekness and gentleness is shown by his being mounted on an animal used, not in war, but in the peaceful pursuits of life. **And a colt.** More exactly, *And upon a colt;* which is explanatory of the clause preceding, showing what the ass was on which he rode, and might be rendered, *Yea,* upon a colt, etc. **A foal of an ass.** Literally, *The son of a beast of burden.* The ass is here described by its use as a bearer of burdens, and was doubtless thus characterized to mark the more clearly the condescension of Jesus in riding upon its colt. He rode not upon the horse, which the Scriptures invariably associate with the idea of war (Ex. 15: 21; Ps. 76: 6; Prov. 21: 31; Jer. 8: 6); nor upon the king's mule (1 Kings 1: 33, 38, 44); but upon the humble, laboring ass. Not upon one which had been kept for the use of royalty; but upon a colt of one which was used in hard labor, and for the carrying of burdens. The ass, however, was used by persons of the highest rank, Judges 5: 10; 10: 4. Besides, the kings of Israel were forbidden to multiply horses to themselves, Deut. 17: 16.

6. **The disciples went and did,** etc. Mark (11: 4–6) relates in detail their going and obtaining the colt.
7. **Put on them their clothes.** In place of saddles the disciples cast upon them their outer garments or mantles. **They set him thereon.** According to the oldest manuscripts, and highest critical authorities, *He sat thereon.* Both animals are mentioned. Matthew speaks in a general and no uncommon way, putting the whole for a part. It is a foolish cavil to make the Evangelist say that Jesus rode them both at once. He may possibly have ridden them alternately; but this is not the necessary or probable meaning of the words. Mark and Luke are more explicit in speaking of the colt alone. Whether the ass followed by natural instinct, or was led by one of the disciples, Jesus equally directed both animals, and both were intended for his use, and were in his service. The one he actually rode; the other formed a royal relay, but was not probably needed in the short journey of less than two miles into Jerusalem.

8. **A very great multitude.** Rather, *Most of the multitude,* in contrast to

8 *him* thereon. And a very great multitude spread their garments in the way; 9 others cut down branches from the trees, and strewed *them* in the 9 way. And the multitudes that went before, and that followed, cried, saying, ʳ Hosanna to the son of David! ˢ Blessed *is* he that cometh in the name of the Lord! Hosanna in the highest!
10 ᵗ And when he was come into Jerusalem, all the

ᑫ Le. 23. 40; John 12. 13.

ʳ Ps. 118. 24–26.
ˢ ch. 23. 39.

ᵗ Mk. 11. 15; Lk. 19. 45; John 2. 13, 15.

---

the *others* who strewed the branches of palm-trees in the way, John 12 : 13; Mark 11 : 8. As the disciples had spread their outer garments on the beasts, so the multitude spread theirs in the way. This was a royal honor, 2 Kings 9 : 13. Robinson mentions an instance which he saw in Bethlehem, when the people spread their garments under the feet of the English consul, whose aid they were imploring. The palm branches were symbols of joy and victory, Lev. 23 : 40; Rev. 7 : 9.

9. **That went before and that followed.** Probably they who had come out from Jerusalem to meet him went before him, and the company who had come with him from Jericho followed behind him. The shouts of welcome and of praise doubtless began with the disciples around Jesus, and was caught by the multitude before and behind. Compare Mark 11 : 9; Luke 19 : 37. **Hosanna.** The first two words of Ps. 118 : 25. A Hebrew phrase of two words, meaning *save now*, and used in triumphant acclamation and joyful greeting. It is here an expression of joy and of triumphant gratulation, including an invocation of blessings on Jesus, the royal descendant of David, the King-Messiah. Compare 1 Kings 1 : 34. **Son of David.** The Messiah. See on ch. 9 : 27. **Blessed is he,** etc. From Ps. 118 : 25, 26, which were prophetical of the Messiah, and came to be applied to him by the Jews. He was the one that was to come, ch. 11 : 3. Compare Heb. 10 : 37. The multitude, very like, uttered these words responsively, interspersed with Hosannas. **Blessed,** *favored* of God with divine and royal honors. **In the name.** By the authority, and as the Messiah (the anointed) of Jehovah. **Hosanna in the highest.** Variously understood to mean in the highest strains, or in the highest regions, that is, heaven. The latter may mean ratified by God in heaven, or repeated by angels in heaven. The general idea is: Let our hosannas be in the highest degree realized, responded to, and ratified in heaven. The 118th Psalm, according to Jewish tradition, was one of the psalms sung at the Passover. Luke (19 : 37) informs us that this took place just at the descent of the Mount of Olives, that is, just as he began to descend the mount.

It is probable that thus early all the open ground near the city, including the sides of Olivet, were being occupied with the tents and temporary structures of the multitude, who were assembling from all parts of the country to celebrate the Passover. Josephus speaks of the number of paschal lambs slain as 256,500, and, estimating twelve persons to each lamb, we have about three millions in attendance. Joseph. *Jewish War,* vi. 9, 3. See on ch. 26 : 25.

According to Luke and John (12 : 17, 18), the people met Jesus with these royal honors, boldly and enthusiastically, because of the miracles they had seen, and especially because of the raising of Lazarus. Luke also adds that the Pharisees wished Jesus to rebuke the applause; and also that Jesus, when he came near and beheld the city, wept over it. He probably came by the road over the southern summit of the Mount of Olives. He proceeded in the descent till he came to the spot where, it is said by travelers, the whole city would burst into view. While the multitude continue to shout his honors, he now weeps over the wicked and unbelieving city.

10. **All the city was moved.** *The whole city.* The mass of the people living in Jerusalem. The excitement was great; it spread and became general. The people who had come out of the city to meet Jesus were composed mostly of those who had come up to the feast, John 12 : 13. The question, **Who is this?** was one of surprise, not necessarily implying ignorance, for Jesus was

A.D. 30.   MATTHEW XXI.   285

11 city was moved, saying, Who is this? And the multitude said, " This is Jesus, ˣ the prophet of Nazareth of Galilee.

" ch. 16. 13, 14; Lk. 7. 16.
ˣ ch. 2. 23; John 6. 14; 7. 40; 9. 17.

The cleansing of the temple; the curse of the barren fig-tree.

12 ʸ And Jesus went into the temple of God, and cast out all them that sold and bought in the

ʸ Mk. 11. 15; Lk. 19. 45; John 2. 13–17.

known in Jerusalem. Compare 1 Sam. 17 : 55, 58. But he had heretofore entered the city quietly and on foot; now on an ass and in a triumphal procession. Notice the contrast between the question and the acclamations of the entering multitude. The people of the city share but little in their enthusiasm. There may have been something of scorn mingled with wonder.

11. **This is Jesus, the prophet of Nazareth.** According to the oldest manuscripts, *This is the prophet Jesus, from Nazareth of Galilee.* The multitude do not call him Messiah, or king, but prophet, in their answer to the people of Jerusalem. They had been announcing him as the Messiah, and this the people had heard. The question was, Who is this, thus coming in triumph, and proclaimed as the Son of David, the Messiah? And the answer distinguishes him by his name, character, and the like. He is the prophet Jesus, so well known, from Nazareth of Galilee. See verse 46; Mark 6 : 15; Luke 7 : 16; 24 : 19. There was, perhaps, some provincial and local pride in the answer.

Mark here adds that Jesus entered the temple, and, having looked around on all things, the evening being come, he went out to Bethany with the twelve. Compare John 12 : 36. Here, too, should come in John's account of certain Greeks who desired to see Jesus, John 12 : 20–36. It should not be overlooked that on this very day of his triumphal entrance into Jerusalem, the tenth of Nisan, the paschal lamb was set apart for its offering on the fourteenth, Exod. 12 : 3. Thus may we not behold in the events of the day the setting apart of Jesus the great and true paschal lamb, preparatory to his sacrifice?

12–17. JESUS IN THE TEMPLE: CASTS OUT THE TRAFFICKERS, performs miracles, and defends the children in their joyful acclamations, Mark 11 : 12–19; Luke 19 : 45, 46.

12. John relates a similar cleansing of the temple at the first Passover of our Lord's ministry, three years before this, John 2 : 14–17. It was appropriate that Jesus should thus exercise his power as the Messiah, especially at the opening and at the close of his public ministry. It betrays great folly to suppose the one related by John to be identical with that related by the other Evangelists. There certainly would have been no unfitness in Jesus cleansing the temple often instead of only twice. The reason why the first three Evangelists omitted the first cleansing, is doubtless found in the fact that it took place before the opening of his Galilean ministry, which forms the principal subject of their Gospels. John, however, gives an account of it, because he supplemented the other Gospels, and gives principally the Judean ministry of Jesus, paying special attention to that portion of his ministry in Judea before the imprisonment of John, and the commencement of his ministry in Galilee.

From Matthew's account, it would seem that the cleansing of the temple took place on the day of our Savior's triumphal entry into the city, and with it the general account of Luke would seem to agree. But Mark is very explicit, in relating that upon that day Jesus went into the temple and looked around on all things, and it being evening, he went to Bethany, and that the next day he returned, cursing the fig-tree on his way, and drove out the traders from the temple. There is no great objection to supposing that Jesus drove them out on the afternoon of his public entry; and that, finding others there the following day, he repeated the act. Yet I do not consider such a supposition really necessary. Matthew often groups together things, such as miracles, discourses, and circumstances, without strict regard to chronological order. Thus here, in verses 12–22 he groups together certain notable deeds of Jesus; and then, with verse 23, begins to relate his teaching. But Mark,

temple, and overthrew the tables of the ² money-changers, and the seats of them that sold ᵃ doves;

¹ Deu. 14. 24–26.
ᵃ Le. 1. 14.

going more into detail in relating the doings of Jesus, describes the expulsion of the traffickers in the order of time.

Temple of God. The word here translated temple, denotes _sacred_, a sacred, consecrated place, and is applied to the whole sacred inclosure of courts and buildings, including the temple in its strict and proper sense, which is expressed by another word in such passages as ch. 23 : 35 ; 27 : 51. The temple stood on a rocky eminence, the hill Moriah, on the eastern part of the city, north-east of Zion, from which it was separated by a valley. Here, it seems, that Abraham was about to offer up Isaac (Gen. 22 : 1, 2), and David interceded for his people at the threshing-floor of Araunah, 2 Sam. 24 : 16–25 ; 2 Chron. 3 : 1. On three sides of this hill walls of huge stone were built up from the bottom, and filled in with cells, or earth, so as to form a large area on which to erect the temple. These walls remain to this day, and in some places, toward the south, are still sixty feet in height. The first temple was built by Solomon, commenced B.C. 1011, and finished B.C. 1004; and was burned down B.C. 588. The second temple was commenced under Zerubbabel B.C. 534, and completed under Ezra B.C. 516. The temple of Herod, which might indeed be styled the third temple, since it was the rebuilding and enlarging of the second, was commenced about fifteen years before the birth of Jesus—about B.C. 20 of our common era, and in a year and a half the temple proper was finished by priests and Levites. The out-buildings and courts required eight years. But some building operations continued long after in progress, and to these the Jews had reference when they said, "Forty-and-six years was this temple in building, John 2 : 20. According to Josephus, the whole sacred inclosure was a half-mile in circumference. Many ancient copies omit _of God_.

The temple proper consisted of two parts ; the holy of holies, containing the ark, the lid of which was the mercy-seat ; and the holy place, a vail separating it from the holy of holies, where were the golden candlestick, the table of show-bread, and the altar of incense. Before the door of the temple stood the great brazen altar of burnt offerings, and around the temple was a court or inclosure, into which none but priests might enter. Descending twelve steps was another court, inclosing the former, called the court of Israel, into which none but male Jews might enter, and in front of the court of women. Around these and lower still, was the large outer court, inclosing the whole, paved with variegated stone, and called by some the Court of the Gentiles, where Jews and Gentiles might resort, and where were exposed for sale animals and things necessary for the sacrifices and worship of the temple. On the south side of this outer court was a synagogue, where religious services were performed. Here the Jewish doctors might be questioned, and their decisions were heard (Luke 2 : 46); here Jesus taught, and his disciples daily attended with one accord, Acts 2 : 46. Thus each inner inclosure rose as in terraces, above the outer ; and the temple proper was situated on the highest point, toward the north-western corner of the square, and could be seen from the city above the surrounding inclosures.

The front of the temple was on the eastern side, where was its principal entrance, facing the Mount of Olives. It was built of white marble, and stones of stupendous size, some of them twenty-five cubits long, eight cubits high, and twelve cubits thick.

Cast out all them that sold and bought. In the court of the Gentiles was the temple-market, where animals, oil, wine, and other things necessary for sacrifices and temple worship, were sold. This was a convenience for those who came to worship. But what was intended at first for an accommodation became a source of gain and extortion, of noise and confusion. Jesus casts out these profane intruders ; they were doubtless filled with awe before him. His moral power and spiritual authority, as the Messiah, ruled them into submission, and they flee before him. "Jerome regards this expulsion of a multitude by one humble individual as the most wonderful of the miracles, and supposes that a flame and starry ray darted from the eyes of the Savior, and that the majesty of the Godhead was radiant in his countenance."—P. SCHAFF, D.D.

13 and said unto them, It is written, ᵇ 'My house shall be called the house of prayer; ᶜ but ye have made it a den of thieves.'

14 ᵈ And the blind and the lame came to him in the temple; and he healed them.

15 And when the chief priests and scribes saw the wonderful things that he did, and the children crying in the temple, and saying, Hosanna to the

ᵇ Is. 56. 7.
ᶜ Jer. 7. 11; Mk. 11. 17; Lk. 19. 46.
ᵈ Is. 35. 5; Acts 3. 1, 9.

Money-changers. These changed at a premium, often a very exorbitant one, the current coin of the day, which was regarded as profane, for the Jewish half-shekel, the yearly temple tribute. See on ch. 17: 24. Some made donations to the treasury (Luke 21 : 1, 2); and others who came to the Passover probably paid their tribute, which became due in the month Adar, answering to parts of February and March. The Jews of Palestine, and especially those who were dispersed abroad, were under the necessity of exchanging the Greek and Roman coin, which they used for the common purposes of trade, but not for their sacred purposes. Money-changers were a convenience and a necessity; but they were dishonest in their exactions, practiced extortion, and violated the law, Deut. 23 : 19, 20. Jesus overturned also the seats of the sellers of **doves.** The poor were allowed to offer doves in sacrifice, instead of a lamb, Lev. 5 : 7; 12 : 8; 14 : 22; Luke 2 : 24.

13. **And said.** A new sentence commences here, *And he said.* **It is written.** Jesus appeals to the Holy Scriptures as of divine authority. He quotes freely Isa. 56 : 7 and Jer. 7 : 11, and unites them together, doing no injustice to their meaning. **My house.** The temple is represented as God's earthly dwelling-place. **House of prayer.** Mark (11 : 17) adds the quotation, "for all nations;" for Gentiles as well as Jews. Prayer is a principal part of worship, 1 Kings 8 : 33, 35, 38, etc.

Ye have made it a den of thieves. More correctly, *Ye make it a den of robbers.* In contrast to *a house of prayer* is *a den*, cave, or cavern, where robbers often resort, *a den of robbers.* The word here translated thieves means robbers, those who seize what does not belong to them, openly and by violence, and is stronger than the Greek word for thief, which means one who takes what is another's, by fraud, and in secret. The latter word is always translated thief, in our common version; but the former is unfortunately translated thief eleven times, and correctly, robber, only four times, John 10 : 1, 8; 18 : 40; 2 Cor. 11 : 26. These two words are used together in John 10 : 1, 10, where their meanings may be compared. Jesus thus rebukes their open dishonesty and extortion, which presents a marked difference from his former cleansing the temple, when he reproved the unbecoming introduction of worldly business, John 2 : 16. This court, where Gentiles might pray, they had turned into a place of dishonest gain and open fraud.

Thus began to be fulfilled the prophecy of Malachi (3 : 1–3). Jesus, the Lord Messiah, suddenly came into his temple, and began the work of purification. According to the prophecy of John the Baptist (ch. 3 : 12), his "fan was in his hand," and he wielded it in separating the precious from the vile, and in reforming the abuses of his house. Compare Isa. 4 : 2–4.

14. Jesus now exercises his power as the Messiah in working miracles in the temple. Having driven out the profane intruders from the court of the Gentiles, he very appropriately turns it into a proper use, and performs deeds of mercy. Such deeds were surely equally becoming the temple as the Sabbath, ch. 12 : 12. All was peace and quiet; men could worship God, the diseased could come for healing, and little children could shout forth his praise.

15. **And the chief priests.** Rather, *But the chief priests.* Matthew turns to notice the conduct of the chief priests and scribes, the leading members of the Sanhedrim, in striking contrast to the hearty and enthusiastic expressions of the multitude, echoed by the children. **Wonderful things.** Literally, *the wonders*, which he did in the temple, such as casting out the profane traffickers, the healing the lame and blind, and exercising his power as the great Reformer, the Messiah. **Hosanna,** etc. See on verse

16 son of David; they were sore displeased, and said unto him, Hearest thou what these say? And Jesus saith unto them, Yea; have ye never read, ᵉ ' Out of the mouth of babes and sucklings thou hast 17 perfected praise'? ᶠ And he left them, and went out of the city into ᵍ Bethany; and he lodged there. 18 ʰ Now in the morning as he returned into the

ᵉ Ps. 8. 2; 1 Cor. 1. 27-29.
ᶠ Jer. 6. 8; Hos. 9. 12.
ᵍ Mk. 11. 11; John 11. 18.
ʰ Mk. 11. 12; Heb. 4. 15.

9. **Sore displeased.** They were indignant, much displeased with what they saw and heard. They saw that Jesus was assuming something like Messianic authority, that his miracles would tend to confirm it in the minds of the people, and indeed that the children echoed but the sentiments of his followers, and many of the people. They hated the light, and were especially displeased that children should be its propagators.

16. **Hearest thou what these say?** Dost thou hear these children greeting thee with their joyful and prayerful acclamations as the Son of David, the Messiah? They would indeed disapprove of fully grown people thus bestowing on him divine and royal honors, as the Pharisees did on his triumphal entry (Luke 19 : 39); but especially so in children, whom they regarded as too young and incompetent for such utterances.

Yea, I hear them, and approve what they do, and indeed it is according to the declaration of Scripture. **Have ye never read?** The quotation is from Ps. 8:2. This Psalm is elsewhere quoted in the New Testament, and applied to Christ, 1 Cor. 15:27; Heb. 2:6. It had a deep typical fulfillment in Christ, as the highest and greatest representative of perfect human nature. See on ch. 1 : 23. **Babes and sucklings.** The first of these should be referred to young children in distinction from nursing babes, the meaning of the second word. Such is the plain meaning of the Psalmist in the Hebrew. God was glorified by young and infant voices. **Perfected praise.** This should be translated, *Thou hast prepared praise,* as the verb is translated in Heb. 10 : 5: "A body hast thou *prepared* for me." The quotation is from the Septuagint version, and hence we have *praise* for the Hebrew *strength,* which also means, sometimes, *glory, praise,* Ps. 29 : 1; Isa. 12 : 2. What the Psalmist says is ordained out of the mouth of babes and sucklings is surely the strength of utterance and of praise.

God was glorified by them. The meaning, therefore, of the original Hebrew and the Greek quotation is the same—the latter really explanatory of the former. The idea is, If, as the Scriptures declare, God has prepared praise for himself from the mouth of children, surely you should not be displeased with these children, nor should I rebuke them for their hosanna to the Son of David, the Messiah, God's representative.

17. **Bethany** signifies, according to some, *place of dates,* but according to others, *house of the afflicted,* and was a village two miles south-east of Jerusalem. It is closely associated with the last days of our Savior's life. Here he raised Lazarus; here he spent the nights of the passion-week, visiting the houses of Martha and Mary and of Simon. It is now known by the name *El-Azariyeh,* derived from Lazarus, a miserable village, of some twenty families, situated on the eastern slope of Olivet, about a mile from the summit. Jesus went forth from Jerusalem, which at this time was full of people, and passed the night with his friends at Bethany. This is supposed to be the visit to Bethany mentioned in Mark 11 : 11, just after his triumphal entry into Jerusalem. If so, then it seems to be mentioned to introduce the cursing of the fig-tree the following morning. If, however, Monday night be meant, following the cleansing of the temple, then the Evangelist goes back to relate what occurred on the morning of that day, implying that he had spent the previous night out of the city. And then he goes on to notice the cursing and the withering of the fig-tree, the first of which occurred one day, and the second the next day, Mark 11 : 12, 14, 20. This instance shows how Matthew often arranges his facts according to their relations, rather than according to their chronological order.

18–22. THE CURSE OF THE BARREN FIG-TREE, Mark 11 : 12–14, 20–26.

18. **In the morning.** The early morn-

19 city, he hungered. ⁱ And when he saw a fig-tree in the way, he came to it, ᵏ and found nothing thereon, but leaves only, and said unto it, ˡ Let no fruit grow

ⁱ Mk. 11. 13.
ᵏ Lk. 13. 6-9; Jno. 15. 2, 6; 2 Tim. 3. 5; Tit. 1. 16.

ing, between daybreak and sunrise. This was the morning after his triumphal entry, Mark 11:12. Some suppose that he had passed the night in the open air, in solitude and prayer; and that hence he was hungry. He probably did not take breakfast at Bethany. His leaving at so early an hour showed the ardor with which he returned to his work at Jerusalem. He had a work of God to perform (John 9:4); he must exhibit his Messianic power and authority over the inanimate creation and in the realm of nature, as he was about to exercise it over the bodies and souls of men in the temple. He hungered; it was real hunger. It was but following the inclination of his appetite to go to the fig-tree, which, by its leaves, gave signs of fruit, though he knew no fruit was thereon. But such was the divine plan. His hungering was a part of his humiliation. Thus he became perfect through sufferings, and able to sympathize with his followers in every trial. But since the tree was fruitless, he found food in doing the will of his Father, John 4:34.

19. **A fig-tree.** Literally, *one fig-tree*, a single or solitary one. The expression, however, according to later Hebrew and Aramæan usage, is equivalent to *a fig-tree*. It was doubtless alone, as it is spoken of as **in the way,** *by the roadside*, its branches probably extending over the beaten path. The fig-tree was one of the most common and valuable trees of Palestine, and was a symbol of peace and plenty, 1 Kings 4:25. Its fruit begins to appear before the leaves, and without any visible blossoms. The Bible never speaks of its blossoms, though it has them hidden in the corolla. The passage in Hab. 3:17 should read, "Although the fig-tree should not bear," instead of "blossom." The early fig ripened in June, the summer fig in August, and a later fig sometimes hung upon the trees all winter. The fresh fruit is shaped like a pear, and whether fresh or dried, is greatly prized.

Nothing thereon but leaves only. Having leaves, it was natural to expect fruit of some size, since the fruit begins to form before the leaves are put forth. But he found the leaves premature and unnatural; for Mark says, "The time of figs was not yet," that is, "it was not the time or season of figs." By its leaves it gave promise of what it had not. And the curse that follows was pronounced upon it not merely because it was barren, but because it had leaves and yet was barren; its signs were false, its appearance deceptive. It was thus an emblem of the hypocrite, and particularly of the Jewish people, with their high professions, their show of ritual and formal worship, without the fruits of righteousness, Jer. 2:21; Luke 13:6-9. The Jews, indeed, alone, among the nations, professed to be the worshipers of Jehovah, but they were barren of fruit.

Let no fruit grow. Skeptics have caviled at the destruction of property. But the fig-tree was by the wayside, and probably the property of no one. It belonged, however, to Jesus, in the highest sense, and he could do as he pleased with his own, ch. 20:15. It was barren, and worse than useless; for it might mock the hungry traveler as it had him. It grew, existed, and was destroyed, that the work and glory of God might be manifested through it (John 9: 2-4), that Jesus might show his power as the Messiah over the material world, and that the faith of his disciples might be strengthened, and they prepared for the trials and work before them, John 11:4, 15. Jesus knew what he was about to do; all the circumstances occurred according to the divine arrangement. The fig-tree, and its destruction, may also be regarded as a symbol of the spiritual condition and end of the Jewish nation, and of hypocrites in general. The only other destruction of property connected with our Lord's ministry were the swine. See on ch. 8:32. It is worthy of notice that he symbolized his judgments on the disobedient and unfruitful with only *one* miracle, and that on a senseless tree; while in numberless miracles for the good of men, he showed forth the mercies and blessings of his salvation. Compare the parable of the fig-tree, Luke 13:6; and notice the fact that it is only the fruitless or barren fig-tree that is brought prominently forward in the New Testament, in these two in-

on thee henceforward forever. And presently the
20 fig tree withered away. ᵐ And when the disciples
saw *it*, they marveled, saying, How soon is the fig-
21 tree withered away! Jesus answered and said unto
them, Verily I say unto you, ⁿ If ye have faith, and
ᵒ doubt not, ye shall not only do this *which is done*
to the fig-tree, ᵖ but also if ye shall say unto this
mountain, Be thou removed, and be thou cast into
22 the sea; it shall be done. And ᑫ all things, whatsoever ye shall ask in prayer, believing, ye shall receive.

¹ Heb. 6. 8.
ᵐ Mk. 11. 20.

ⁿ ch. 17. 20.
ᵒ Jam. 1. 6.
ᵖ 1 Cor. 13. 2.
ᑫ ch. 7. 7; Mk. 11. 24; Lk. 11. 9; John 14. 13; 15. 7; Jam. 5. 16; 1 Jno. 3. 22; 5. 14, 15.

The authority of Jesus questioned; his question in reply, respecting the authority of John the Baptist; parable of the two sons.

23 ʳ AND when he was come into the temple, the

ʳ Mk. 11. 27; Lk. 20. 1.

stances, and in each used as a symbol of evil.
Presently—withered. So soon as the curse was pronounced, it began to wither; the sap immediately ceased to flow, and the withering soon began to appear.
20. **When the disciples saw it.** From Mark 11 : 12, 20, we learn that this was the next morning after the cursing. Jesus cursed the fig-tree on Monday morning; they saw it on Tuesday morning, as Mark says, "dried up from the roots." In rapid and vivid discourse days, and even weeks, are sometimes passed over unnoticed. Matthew was intent on telling the fact rather than marking definitely the time of each part of the fact.
How soon is the fig-tree! This should be translated either, *How soon the fig-tree withered away!* or, *How did the fig-tree immediately wither away!* The latter is supported by the larger number of scholars, and agrees best with the context. They were surprised at the suddenness of the withering, and in wonder they inquire, How came it to pass? Jesus answers in a manner best suited to profit them.
21. **If ye have faith.** Jesus answered that it is by faith that such and even greater miracles are performed. The kind of faith is that which is free from *doubt;* they must **doubt not.** He thus uses this miracle to strengthen their faith and prepare them for the trials before them. **This mountain.** Probably the Mount of Olives, over which they were passing. It is implied that Jesus could have removed this mountain as well as dried up the fig-tree. Compare Zech. 14 : 4. **The sea.** This is a general expression, the Dead Sea, the Sea of Galilee, or the Mediterranean Sea, being several miles distant. The exercise of faith in miracles, as well as in prayer, must be in accordance with the will of God. Indeed, true faith is so in harmony with that will that it really asks nothing contrary to it. The mountain may symbolize any great and apparently insurmountable difficulty. Faith is also attended with works, James 2 : 18. And by works the man of faith often in a measure answers his own prayers. He meets these mountains of difficulties with an earnest, active faith, and they disappear before him while he labors on. See on ch. 17 : 20.
22. **All things whatever ye shall ask in prayer.** This promise is to prayers of faith; these are inspired by God, and hence will be according to his will (1 John 5 : 14), and in the name of Christ (John 14 : 13), and will be answered either in kind or in equivalent, 2 Cor. 12 : 8, 9. The promise is not to the presumptuous, the arrogant and self-confident, but to those who exercise simple and childlike faith in their heavenly Father, with entire submission to his all-wise and infinitely benevolent will, ch. 18 : 4. The faith required is unwavering confidence in the power, love, and wisdom of God.
23–27. THE AUTHORITY OF JESUS QUESTIONED BY THE SANHEDRIM. He replies by questioning them in regard to the authority of John the Baptist, after

chief priests and the elders of the people came unto him as he was teaching, and "said, By what authority doest thou these things? and who gave thee 24 this authority? And Jesus answered and said unto them, 'I also will ask you one thing, which if ye tell me, I in likewise will tell you by what authority 25 I do these things. "The baptism of John, whence was it? from heaven, or of men? *And they reasoned with themselves, saying, If we shall say, From heaven; he will say unto us, Why did ye not then

* Ex. 2. 14; Ac. 4. 7; 7. 27.
t Pro. 26. 4, 5; Col. 4. 6.
u ch. 3. 1-6.
x Pro. 12. 5; 1 Jno. 3. 20.

which he speaks three parables, in which he pictures forth the disobedience, the fearful guilt, and the terrible doom of the Jewish people, Mark 11 : 27-33; Luke 20: 1-8.

23. **When he was come.** On Tuesday morning, just after the disciples had noticed the withered fig-tree, Mark 11 : 1, 12, 19, 20, 27. **The chief priest and the elders.** Mark and Luke add, *the scribes.* Thus, members of the three classes composing the Sanhedrim, or the highest ecclesiastical council of the Jews, approach Jesus. In reference to these classes, see on ch. 2 : 4. They were evidently the leading members of the Sanhedrim, though it does not appear that they came as an official and formal deputation, similar to that which had been sent to John the Baptist, John 1 : 19-28. **By what authority?** Not only *by what*, but also *by what kind* of authority, divine or human, the authority of the Messiah, or of a mere prophet or teacher. **These things.** His whole course of conduct, cleansing the temple, performing miracles and teachings. **Who gave thee?** Who, with authority, gave thee this authority? The Sanhedrim authorized teachers in the temple, and tried false prophets, but Jesus had not been authorized by them. Hence their two questions. The Mosaic law had given directions for the discovery, rejection, and death of false prophets (Deut. 13 : 1-5; 18 : 20-22); these questions in themselves were therefore entirely proper, for any Jews, and especially for the members of the Sanhedrim to ask. John had asked a somewhat similar question, ch. 11 : 3. But they now ask with wrong motives, wishing to entrap him and find occasion to destroy him (Luke 19 : 47), and to draw forth some such declaration as that he was the Son of God, and charge him with blasphemy, ch. 26 : 64, 65. The questions were also really needless; for the works and doctrines of Jesus were evidences that he was the Messiah, and that he came from God, John 3 : 2; 10 : 24, 25, 37, 38; 12 : 37. Jesus therefore was not called upon under such circumstances to answer their questions. We have here the first direct assault of the authorities of the temple and of the great Jewish council upon Jesus.

24. Jesus might have appealed to the raising of Lazarus, and his other miracles; but since these Jewish rulers came with wicked designs, and were not even deserving an answer, he adopts a different mode of reply, one which both answers and confounds them. The reference to John, whom Jesus had declared to be his forerunner (the Elijah that was to come, ch. 11 : 14), and by whom he had been baptized, was indeed a suggestive answer that he was from God, the Messiah, since John had declared him so to be, John 1 : 26, 29, 32-34. At the same time he defeats their designs, and extorts from them an unwilling and hypocritical confession that they are unable and incompetent to judge.

25. **The baptism of John.** The whole ministration of John, of which baptism formed a very prominent part. **From heaven, or of men.** Did John act by the authority of God, or by his own? Was he a true prophet or a false one? **They reasoned with themselves.** According to the best critical authorities, *they reasoned among* themselves; they consulted and deliberated as to what answer they should give, and what might be the effect of the different replies which suggested themselves. **Why did ye not then believe him?** Why did ye not become his followers and believe when he testified of me as the Messiah? They saw that to acknowledge John as a true prophet would be to condemn themselves for rejecting not

26 believe him? But if we shall say, Of men; we fear
27 the people; ʸ for all hold John as a prophet. And they answered Jesus, and said, ᶻ We can not tell. And he said unto them, Neither tell I you by what authority I do these things.
28 But what think ye? A *certain* man had two sons; and he came to the first, and said, Son, go work to-
29 day in my vineyard. He answered and said, I will
30 not: but afterward he repented, and went. And he came to the second, and said likewise. And he
31 answered and said, ᵃ I *go*, sir: and went not. Whether of them twain ᵇ did the will of *his* father? ᶜ They say unto him, The first. Jesus saith unto them, ᵈ Verily I say unto you, That the publicans and the harlots go into the kingdom of God before

ʸ ch. 14. 5; Mk. 6. 20; Lk. 20. 6; John 10. 41.
ᶻ ch. 15. 14; 16. 3.

ᵃ Is. 29. 13; Tit. 1. 16; Jam. 1. 22.
ᵇ ch. 7. 21; Ez. 33. 31.
ᶜ 2 Sam. 12. 7; Job 15. 6.
ᵈ ch. 9. 9; Lk. 7. 29. 50; Ro. 9. 30 –33.

only John, but also Jesus, whom John had proclaimed to be the Christ.

26. If, however, they said *of men*, they feared **the people**, the indignation of the multitude, Luke 20: 6. **Hold John as a prophet;** regarded him as a divinely commissioned religious teacher, ch. 14: 5; Luke 7: 29.

27. **We can not tell.** Rather, *We do not know*. Their answer was insincere, and their confession of ignorance hypocritical. **Neither tell I you.** One of our Savior's brief replies, replete with meaning. If you are unable or unwilling to judge of John and his teaching, you are equally so in regard to me. If you will not believe his testimony, you will not believe mine. If you dare not deny his divine commission, you should acknowledge mine. Your real unwillingness to acknowledge, according to the convictions of your own consciences, that John was a true prophet, clothed in a hypocritical answer, merits from me a corresponding unwillingness to give you any more evidence in regard to myself than that you already have.

28–32. PARABLE OF THE TWO SONS. Recorded only by Matthew. Doing the will of God consists in hearty and true obedience.

28. Having silenced the members of the Jewish Sanhedrim, Jesus now speaks three parables, by which he shows their great guilt, their severe punishment, and their final rejection as a people. **But what think ye?** You express no opinion as to whether John's baptism was from heaven or of men; *but what think ye* of what I am about to relate? **Two sons.** The same as in the parable of the Prodigal Son, though they are not, as there, specially distinguished as the older and younger.

29. **Repented.** He *regretted* what he had done, *changed his purpose*, and **went**. The word translated *repent* here and in ver. 32, is not the more common one (see ch. 3: 2), being found only in three other places in the New Testament, ch. 27: 3; 2 Cor. 7: 8; Heb. 7: 21. An adjective derived from it is found in Rom. 11: 29; 2 Cor. 7: 10. It properly expresses an *after care, concern*, or *anxiety* for something done, which may be felt where there is no inward radical change, as in the remorse of Judas (ch. 27: 3), as well as where there is true repentance. To the command of the father, this son had given a blunt and rude reply, a flat refusal. But he afterward *went*. In this place, the word evidently expresses a regret for what he had done, and a change of purpose which is connected with a change of conduct.

30. **The second.** According to the highest critical authorities, *the other*. It is evident that no stress is to be laid on the order of the calling. **I go, sir.** Rather, *I will, sir*. *I* is emphatic in the original, expressing a great willingness to obey in contrast to the disobedience of his brother. It was also a polite reply, with a *sir;* but his heart was not in it, for he **went not**.

31. **Whether of them twain,** etc. Which of the two did his father's will? They answer, **The first.** Not fully, nor perfectly; for he was at first rebellious, but in that he finally obeyed, and

32 you. For *John came unto you in the way of righteousness, and ʲ ye believed him not; ᵍ but the publicans and the harlots believed him: and ye, when ye had seen it, ʰ repented not afterward, that ye might believe him.

*ch. 3. 1-8.
ʲ ch. 11. 18.
ᵍ Lk. 3. 12, 13.
ʰ Ps. 81. 11, 12; Zec. 7. 11, 12.
ⁱ 2 Tim. 2. 25.

The parable of the vineyard let out to wicked husbandmen.

33 ⁱ HEAR another parable: There was a certain householder, ᵏ which planted a vineyard, and hedged

ᵏ Mk. 12. 1; Lk. 20. 9; Ps. 80. 8-11; S. Song 8. 11; Is. 5. 1-4; Jer. 2. 21.

in comparison to the conduct of his brother. According to another Greek reading of considerable authority, they answer, *the latter, the tardier one*, he who in his compliance was behind the prompt, professed obedience of the other. It is thus descriptive of his character.

This parable is followed by its interpretation, or rather its application to the Jews. Its *grand design* was to show that doing God's will consisted in hearty obedience. Its centre of comparison is found positively, in that the first son *went*, and negatively, in that the other *went not*. The *man*, in the parable, represents God; the *two sons*, two classes among the Jews, or, in a more general application, two classes among men. The *first*, the openly irreligious, the immoral and vicious, such as publicans and harlots; the *other son*, those who professed to obey God and yet did not, such as the scribes and Pharisees; the *vineyard*, the kingdom of God. The command, *Go work*, represents what God requires of men, and was binding on both classes of the Jews. *To-day* represents the present life and present duty.

Let us now follow Jesus in the application. He commences with a solemn and authoritative declaration as a divine Teacher. **Verily I say unto you. Publicans** (see on ch. 5 : 46) **and harlots**, the openly irreligious, the unjust, immoral, and vicious, had said to the requirements of God, both by their words and deeds, *I will not*. Yet Jesus declares that they go into the kingdom of God *before you*, scribes and Pharisees, though you make such high pretensions to godliness. The language implies that the door of the kingdom was still open to them, but that as a class they would not enter.

32. Jesus gives a reason for his declaration by referring to their conduct toward John the Baptist and his preaching. John came in **the way of righte-** **ousness,** in the right way, the way of God's commandments, the very way you profess to follow; he came in this way, walking in it himself and preaching it to you; he came in this way as my forerunner, and called on you to prepare for my coming by repentance and obedience. Compare ch. 22 : 16 ; Acts 13 : 10 ; 2 Pet. 2 : 5. Though you professed to be in this way and ready to walk in it, yet you **believed him not,** ch. 3 : 7-9. But the publicans and harlots, who had been openly irreligious and had refused to obey God, afterward **believed** John, accepted him as a true teacher, repented and obeyed God, Luke 7 : 29, 30. And ye, when ye had **seen it,** the conversion of these notorious sinners, attended with so great a reformation of life, **repented not afterward,** rather, *did not even repent afterward*, **that ye might believe him.** The word translated *repent* is the same as that in verse 29, and expresses here that state of mind which borders on and results in true repentance and faith. Thus Jesus condemns them; or rather brings upon them their own self-condemnation. They had acknowledged that the first son had done his father's will, while the other had not; and by this application of the parable Jesus made them condemn themselves for not doing the will of God, and approve of the publicans and harlots who believed John, for doing it. They had acknowledged that doing God's will consists in hearty obedience, and by so doing they justified the publicans and condemned themselves.

The parable may have a wider application. The two classes are found in every age under the Gospel dispensation.

33-44. THE PARABLE OF THE WICKED HUSBANDMEN, Mark 12 : 1-11 ; Luke 20 : 9-18. The fearful guilt and the terrible doom of the Jewish people.

33. **Hear another parable.** Consider attentively another parable, which

it round about, and digged a wine-press in it, and built a tower, and let it out to husbandmen, and 34 ¹ went into a far country; and when the time of the fruit drew near, ᵐ he sent his servants to the husbandmen, ⁿ that they might receive the fruits of it.

ᶦ ch. 25. 14, 15.
ᵐ 2 Ki. 17. 13, 14;
Jer. 25. 3–7.
ⁿ S. Song 8. 11, 12.

---

will not only show further your guilt, but also your punishment. While Matthew and Mark relate this parable as addressed to the scribes, chief priests, and elders (ver. 23; Mark 11 : 27), Luke relates it as spoken to the people (Luke 20 : 9); but in ver. 19 he implies that the chief priest and scribes also heard it. Thus we have here one of the many beautiful illustrations of the diversity and harmony in the independent accounts of the same thing by the different evangelists. The scribes, chief priests, and elders, with the people, were his auditors. It was specially intended for the former; but he also intended that the people should hear it, for it was a matter of great interest to them. The Evangelists relate it, according to their different stand-points. **A certain householder.** *Certain* should be omitted according to the highest authorities. A head, or master of a family. **A vineyard.** A simile often used in Scripture, Ps. 80 : 8–16; Isa. 27 : 2–7. See especially Isa. 5 : 1–7, which bears a close resemblance to this parable. The Jews planted their *vineyards* most commonly on the sides of hills or mountains, 2 Chron. 26 : 10; Jer. 31 : 5. **Hedged it round about.** Put a hedge about it, fenced it in with a thick row of thorn-bushes. Sometimes a vineyard was surrounded with both a hedge and a wall, Isa. 5 : 5. **A wine-press.** Consisting of an upper vat for treading the grapes, and a lower vat for receiving the juice. The *winefat* in Mark 12 : 1 is this lower receptacle. Dr. Hackett (*Illustrations of Scripture*, p. 165) thus describes the wine-press as ordinarily used at the present day: "A hollow place, usually a rock, is scooped out, considerably deeper at one end than the other. The grapes are put into this trough, and two or more persons, with naked feet and legs, descend into it, where they jump up and down, crushing the fruit as they trample on it, while to enliven their labor they often sing at the same time. The juice flows into the lower part of the excavation. . . . . The place for treading out the grapes is sometimes dug in the ground, lined, probably, with a coating of stone or brick. The expression in Matt. 21 : 33, *and he digged a wine-press* in his vineyard, may allude to such an excavation. . . . Dr. Robinson describes a wine-press which he saw at Hebleh, near the site of Antipatris (Acts 23 : 31), which was hewn out of a rock and divided into two parts. The upper and more shallow part was the place where the grapes were put, the lower and deeper one was the place for receiving the liquor pressed out of them. It was the work, no doubt, of the ancient Hebrews or Philistines."
A tower. A watch-tower from which the whole vineyard and its surroundings might be seen. In it a watchman kept guard against thieves, especially during the season of ripe grapes. Watch-towers are still common in Palestine, built of stone, circular in shape, though sometimes square, and generally fifteen or twenty feet high, yet occasionally rising to forty or fifty feet. "Those which I examined had a small door near the ground, and a level space on the top, where a man could sit and command a view of the plantation."—Dr. HACKETT, *Scrip. Illus.*, p. 172. Compare Luke 14 : 28. **Let it out to husbandmen.** From Sol. Song 8 : 11, and Isa. 7 : 23, we may infer that a most valuable vineyard of a thousand vines yielded a rent of a thousand shekels of silver, or about five hundred dollars. In this instance the husbandmen were to give a portion of the fruits as the rent, Luke 20 : 10. Vineyards were very productive, but required great labor and care in digging, planting, propping, pruning, gathering grapes, and making wine. **Went into a far country.** Rather, *went to another country.* Nothing is said whether it was far or near. Luke adds, "for a long time."
34. **The time of the fruit,** etc. The season of fruits, the vintage, drew near. The general vintage was in September. The "first ripe grapes" were gathered somewhat earlier, Num. 13 : 20. **The fruits of it.** More correctly, *His fruits;* the fruit that belong to him as rent.
35, 36. The husbandmen treated the

35 ⁿ And the husbandmen took his servants, and ᵖ beat one, and ᵠ killed another, and stoned another.
36 Again, he sent other servants more than the first:
37 and they did unto them likewise. But last of all ʳ he sent unto them his son, saying, They will reverence my son.
38 But when the husbandmen saw the son, they said among themselves, ˢ This is the heir; ᵗ come, let us kill him, and let us seize on his inheritance.
39 ᵘ And they caught him,ˣ and cast *him* out of
40 the vineyard, and slew *him*. When the lord therefore of the vineyard cometh, ʸ what will he do unto those husbandmen ?
41 ᶻ They say unto him, ᵃ He will miserably destroy those wicked men, ᵇ and will let out *his* vineyard unto other husbandmen, which shall render him the fruits in their seasons.

ⁿ 2 Chr. 24. 21; Heb. 11. 36, 37; 1 Thes. 2. 15.
ᵖ Jer. 37. 15; 38. 6.
ᵠ Jer. 26. 20-23.
ʳ ch. 3. 17.
ˢ Ps. 2. 2-8; Heb. 1. 2.
ᵗ ch. 2. 13-16; 26. 3; 27. 1; Jno. 11. 53; Ac. 4. 27.
ᵘ ch. 26. 50-57; Jno. 18. 12; 19. 16-18; Ac. 2. 23.
ˣ Heb. 13. 11-13.
ʸ Heb. 10. 29.
ᶻ Lk. 20. 16.
ᵃ Is. 5. 5-7; Lk. 21. 24; Heb. 2. 3.
ᵇ ch. 8. 11; Lk. 13. 28, 29; Ac. 13. 46-48; 15. 7; 18.

servants worse and worse. One they **beat,** another they **killed,** another they **stoned** to death ; stoning being a more atrocious way of killing, ch. 23 : 37. A large number of servants were then sent, but they were treated in like manner. Mark is more particular in describing this gradation. The first servant "they *beat*, and sent away empty;" at another "they cast stones, and wounded him in the head, and sent him away shamefully handled;" another "they killed;" and many others, "beating some, and killing some," Mark 12 : 2-5.

37. **But last of all,** etc. Rather, *And last. And afterward he sent to them his son.* According to Mark (12 : 6), it was his only son, "Having yet therefore one son, his well-beloved, he sent him also last unto them." **Will reverence.** Will so respect and revere my son as to heed what he says, and pay their rent.

38, 39. **The heir.** The one to whom the vineyard would at length belong, as an inheritance or patrimony. **Come, let us kill him.** Compare the very similar language of the sons of Jacob concerning their brother Joseph, Gen. 38 : 20. **Seize on his inheritance.** According to the highest critical authorities, *and have his inheritance.* So Mark (12 : 7), "And the inheritance shall be ours." And Luke (20 : 14), "That the inheritance may be ours." When the only son and heir was destroyed, they thought to hold the inheritance as their own. This parable presents an extreme case. It is not necessary to regard it unlife-like or fictitious. Doubtless his hearers could recall similar agreements violently broken. In the unsettled state of the country, we can conceive that an atrocious case, as the one here presented, could have happened.

40, 41. The parable is completed by a question of Jesus, and the answer of the rulers. They are thus made to pass sentence upon themselves. According to the most natural construction of Mark and Luke, Jesus seems to answer the question himself. It is not impossible, however, to regard the answer even in them as given by some of the hearers, namely, the chief-priests and elders, and to suppose, *they say unto him,* omitted. But it seems better to suppose that Jesus repeated the answer, to give it emphasis and his approval. And as he repeated it, the people seemed to have caught the meaning of the parable, for, according to Luke (20 : 16), they exclaimed, *God forbid!* or rather, May it not be! Far be it! Let it never happen ! **He will miserably destroy,** etc.; or wretchedly destroy those wretches; that is, he will utterly destroy them. Compare Isa. 5 : 4, 5.

The *grand design* of this parable was to shadow forth the rejection of the Jewish people on account of their rejecting the prophets of the Lord, and especially the Messiah. Verses 33-37 referred to the past; verse 38 and onward was prophetic. The *centre of comparison* is found in the ungrateful and cruel treatment of the servants and son, on the one hand; and the righteous judgment visited on the husbandmen, on the other. The *householder* represents God the Father; the *husbandmen*, the Jewish people, as is evident from verse 43, "The kingdom of God shall be taken from you, and given to a nation bringing forth the fruits in their seasons." The chief priests and Pharisees, being both the civil and religious leaders, representatives and rulers of the people, could very truly regard the parable as against them, ver. 45; Mark 12 : 12; Luke 20 : 19. The *vineyard* can not here represent, as in Isa. 5 : 1, the Jewish people, for they are already represented by the husbandmen; but rather, the religious blessings and privileges intrusted to them as a people; the *true religion* as revealed in the word of God, Rom. 9 : 4, 5.

The minute details in regard to the vineyard need not be pressed closely. The *planting* may be said to have occurred under Moses and Joshua, Ps. 80 : 8. The *hedge*, "the middle wall of partition" between Jews and Gentiles, Eph. 2 : 14. It has been noted by commentators that Palestine is geographically hedged around, east by the river Jordan, south by the desert and mountainous country of Idumea, west by the Mediterranean, and north by the mountains of Lebanon. Compare Ps. 125 : 2; Zech. 2 : 5. The *wine-press* may represent the services, ordinances, and ceremonies in which the people could engage for the glory of God and their own spiritual advantage; the *tower*, the office of the watchman, Isa. 62 : 6. The *letting it out to husbandmen* may refer to the solemn covenants between God and the people, as at the giving of the law, Ex. 20 : 19; 24 : 7, 8. The householder *going to another country* can also be used to represent the withholdment of such open revelations as upon Sinai, and the speaking face to face with Moses, Deut. 34 : 10-12. The *fruit* represents the wise improvement of their gifts and blessings, the bringing to God not only the service of their lips, but also their hearts (Isa. 5 : 4; 29 : 13); the tithes, offerings, prayers, and labors, Mal. 3 : 8-10; Rom. 7 : 4.

The *servants* sent by the householder represent the prophets. A period of about three hundred and eight years intervened between the death of Moses and the call of Samuel to be a prophet. Though there were prophets during the Judges, yet the more conspicuous prophets began with Samuel, continuing till Malachi, and ending with John the Baptist, ch. 11 : 13. The treatment they received accords well with the language of the parable. Thus, the children of Israel preferred a king to Samuel in his old age, 1 Sam. 8 : 6-8 ; 12 : 12, 13. Elijah was persecuted by Ahab, 1 Kings 18 : 10-12. Isaiah, according to Jewish tradition, was sawn asunder by King Manasseh. Zechariah, the son of Jehoiada, was stoned to death, 2 Chron. 24 : 20-22. Jeremiah was imprisoned (Jer. 37 : 15), and, according to tradition, was stoned by the exiles in Egypt. Compare also 1 Kings 22 : 26-28 ; 2 Chron. 36 : 16; Neh. 9 : 26; Matt. 28 : 37; Acts 7 : 52; Heb. 11 : 36-38.

The *son* represents Christ, who was sent after a long series of revelations and prophets, Heb. 1 : 1, 2. He is the only-begotten and well-beloved Son, the Son of God in the highest sense, ch. 3 : 17; John 1 : 14; Heb. 1 : 3-9. He is the "*heir* of all things," Heb. 1 : 2. Thus, in parabolic language, Jesus answers the question of the chief-priests and elders, in ver. 23. He had done "these things" by the authority of the Son. The language of the householder, *They will reverence my son*, presents the human side, as it would seem to men, to intelligent creatures who had no knowledge of the future. It was their duty to reverence the Son of God. It was reasonable to suppose that they would have reverenced their long-expected Messiah. God's foreknowledge of their wicked conduct did not affect their freedom and their duty. They acted without compulsion. The *killing of the son* points to the crucifixion, ch. 27 : 35; Acts 3 : 13-15. And as the son was *cast out of the vineyard*, so Jesus "suffered without the gate," Heb. 13 : 12, 13; Matt. 27 : 32, 33. Compare 1 Kings 21 : 13 ; Acts 7 : 58. The *reason* for killing the son, *that the inheritance may be ours* (Luke 20 : 14), must not be pressed too closely. The very nature of sin is robbery; the sinner robs God, and would usurp his place and authority. So the Jewish people, in rejecting Christ, wanted their own way, and were determined to have it. They were robbers, murderers, and usurpers. John 11 : 47-53 throws light on their feelings and motives a little time before uttering this parable. They feared lest *all* should *believe on him*, and they would lose their power and position; they also feared, or professed to fear, lest the people should make him king, and the *Romans come and take away* their *place* and *nation*.

Thus far the parable represents the patience and forbearance of God in send-

42 Jesus saith unto them, ᶜ Did ye never read in the Scriptures, 'The stone which the builders rejected, the same is become the head of the corner: this is the Lord's doing, and it is marvelous in our eyes'?
43 Therefore say I unto you, ᵈ The kingdom of God ᵉ shall be taken from you, and given to a nation
44 bringing forth the fruits thereof. And whosoever ᶠ shall fall on this stone shall be broken; ᵍ but on whomsoever it shall fall, it will grind him to powder.

6; 28. 28; Ro. ch. 9. to ch. 11.
ᶜ Ps. 118. 22, 23; Is. 28. 16.
ᵈ ch. 3. 2; 12. 28.
ᵉ ch. 8. 11, 12; Ac. 13. 46–48.
ᶠ Lk. 20. 18; Is. 8. 14, 15.
ᵍ Ps. 2. 9; Is. 60. 12; Dan. 2. 34, 35, 44.

ing his servants, the prophets, and last, his Son. What more could he have done? Isa. 5: 3, 4. After receiving such ungrateful and cruel treatment from their hands, what was left but to punish? Isa. 5: 5, 6.
The coming of the Lord of the vineyard, and the *miserable destruction* of these husbandmen, represent the coming of God in judgment upon the Jewish nation, in the destruction of Jerusalem, when "their house was left unto them desolate" (Luke 13: 35), and they suffered "tribulation such as had not been since the beginning of the world," ch. 24: 21, 22. At Jerusalem alone, it is said, 1,100,000 perished by sword, famine, and pestilence. Besides, 97,000 were sold as slaves, and vast multitudes perished in other parts of Judea. See also ch. 23: 34–36. The *letting out* the *vineyard to other husbandmen* represents the rejection of the Jews, and the calling of the Gentiles, Rom. 9: 30, 31; 11: 9, 10.
42. Jesus further rivets the application of the parable by quoting an ancient prophecy. **Did ye never read,** etc. You surely have read. **The Scriptures.** The inspired writings embraced in the Old Testament; these could well be called, in distinction from all others, the *Scriptures, the writings.* The quotation is made from Ps. 118: 22, and in the words of the Septuagint version. The Jews applied this same to the Messiah; from it (vers. 25, 26) the multitude had derived their hosannas, at the public entry of Jesus into Jerusalem, ch. 21: 9. As the multitude had applied this Psalm to Jesus, so Jesus now applies it to himself as the Christ. **The stone,** in the figurative language of prophecy, was Christ. This is regarded as a typical prophecy, some referring its typical fulfillment to David, who was disallowed and rejected by Saul and the ruling men of the nation, and yet was chosen to be the king of Israel; others refer it to Zerubbabel (Zech. 3: 8, 9; 4: 7); and others still to Mordecai; its special and complete fulfillment was in Christ. See on ch. 1: 22, 23. **The builders** are the Jews. **Rejected.** More correctly, *disallowed;* they did not allow the claims of Jesus. **The head of the corner.** The head-stone, or corner-stone; the stone that lies at the foundation of the building, where the two walls come together, binding them firmly, and giving the building its strength and support. Thus, Christ is the support of the spiritual building, the "holy temple in the Lord," Eph. 2: 20–22; 1 Cor. 3: 11. Though the Jews rejected Jesus, yet God had made him the head-stone of the spiritual temple. He should triumph over all their unbelief, malice, and opposition. **This is the Lord's doing.** *This thing is from the Lord,* that the stone which was disallowed should become the head of the corner, and is **marvellous,** *wonderful,* in our eyes. Compare Acts 4: 11, and 1 Pet. 2: 6, 7, where this prophecy is quoted with a similar application.
43. **Therefore,** as you builders reject the head-stone of the corner, you yourselves shall be rejected; which shows that the parable just related is applicable to you. **The kingdom of God;** the privileges and blessings of the Messiah's administration. **Given to a nation,** etc. A race of people different from you, "a holy nation, a people for a possession" (1 Pet. 2: 9), the community of believers. You Jews shall be rejected as a people, and the blessings of the Gospel shall be extended to the Gentiles, among whom shall be found a people who **shall bring forth** spiritual **fruits** unto God, Acts 15: 14.
44. Jesus adds another word of terrible warning, still using and applying the figure of a stone. **Whosoever shall**

45 And when the chief priests and Pharisees had heard his parables, [b] they perceived that he spake
46 of them. But when they sought to lay hands on him, they feared the multitude, because [i] they took him for a prophet.

[b] Lk. 11. 45; John 8. 9.

[i] Lk. 7. 16; John 7. 40.

fall on this stone; he that makes it a stone of stumbling, that takes offense at Christ, **shall be broken,** shall suffer accordingly, Isa. 8 : 14, 15; Luke 2 : 34. Thus, the Jews already had taken offense at Jesus in his humiliation, and were suffering hardness of heart, and all of the direful consequences of unbelief. But, as a person in a fall may only so break his limbs as to recover, so to many of these Jews there was yet hope. Some, however, were doubtless so broken as to be beyond hope and recovery. **On whomsoever it shall fall.** They who shall continue to oppose and neglect him, on them his vengeance shall fall. The weight of his power and indignation shall fall on all such as continue to stumble and take offense at him, resulting in their most fearful destruction. **Grind him to powder.** The verb, which generally means to *winnow*, has here the idea of *scattering in minute fragments*, making chaff of him, crush him to pieces, grind him to powder. It shall break him in pieces, and he shall become "like the chaff of the summer threshing-floors," Dan. 2 : 35, 44, 45. Such was the ruin of the hardened Jews after Christ's exaltation; and such will be the destruction of all the finally impenitent. Thus, Jesus presents himself in four aspects under the figure of a stone: 1, a *rejected* or *disallowed stone*; 2, the *headstone of the corner*; 3, a *stumbling-stone*; and, lastly, *the stone of retribution*.

45, 46. THE EFFECT OF THE PARABLES ON THE CHIEF PRIESTS AND PHARISEES. They had already resolved to kill Jesus (John 11 : 53), and now, perceiving these parables had direct reference to them, they were enraged, and would have put their resolution into immediate execution had it not been for fear of the people. **Perceived he spake of them.** They saw that their secret and evil designs were brought to light, that they themselves were condemned and threatened with overwhelming ruin. **They sought to lay hands on him.** In order to kill him, as the Scriptures and Jesus in this parable had foretold. But they feared the **multitude,** the common people. Multitudes were now gathered from all parts to celebrate the Passover. **Took him for a prophet.** They held or regarded him as a prophet, a divinely-commissioned teacher (see on ch. 11 : 9); so common was this feeling that the Pharisees said, "Behold, the world is gone after him," John 12 : 19.

REMARKS.

1. Jesus is omniscient and knows all things in regard to events, persons, and things, vers. 1, 2; John 2 : 24, 25; 16 : 30; 21 : 17.
2. We should promptly obey Jesus, and cheerfully give whatever we possess, if he require it, vers. 2, 3, 6; Isa. 1 : 19; Acts 4 : 19, 20, 32.
3. No person, animal, or thing is so mean or humble as not to be received, employed, or required in Christ's service, ver. 3; Num. 22 : 28-33; 1 Cor. 1 : 26-29.
4. The fulfillment of the old Testament prophecies in Jesus proves that he was the Christ, ver. 4; Luke 24 : 44; Acts 3 : 23, 24; 10 : 43.
5. Since Jesus was meek and lowly even in his triumphal entrance into Jerusalem, pride, avarice, and ambition are unbecoming his followers under any circumstances, ver. 5; Phil. 2 : 3-5; Eph. 4 : 1, 2; James 3 : 13-18.
6. We should do our part in honoring Jesus, our Prophet and King, thankful to engage in any service, however humble, vers. 7-11; Isa. 52 : 7; Zeph. 3 : 14-20; Acts 20 : 19.
7. Many who would with the multitude shout hosannas to Jesus, would also with the multitude cry, Crucify him, ver. 9; ch. 27 : 20-23.
8. A community may be greatly moved with the presence of Jesus, and yet not be savingly benefited; but only hardened for destruction, vers. 10, 11; Luke 19 : 41-44; Hos. 4 : 6.
9. Whenever we visit the city or town, we should rather seek the house of God than the places of amusement, ver. 12; Ps. 65 : 4; 84 : 1, 2; 122 : 1.

The parable of the Marriage of the King's Son.

XXII. AND Jesus answered [k] and spake unto them

[k] Lk. 14. 16; Rev. 19. 7-9.

---

10. The followers of Christ should manifest great zeal in removing every thing erroneous and injurious from his house and worship. They should do it wisely, in the name of Christ, and according to his word, ver. 12; 1 Tim. 3 : 15; Rev. 2 : 20.

11. God's house is emphatically a house of prayer, and any thing inconsistent with prayer is unbecoming it, or his people, ver. 13; Jer. 7 : 8-11; 1 Cor. 3 : 16, 17.

12. Deeds of mercy, saving sinners, and strengthening Christians, are especially becoming God's house, ver. 14; Luke 18 : 10, 13, 14.

13. Children should love and honor Jesus, and join in speaking and singing his praise. Cold and formal professors may be displeased, and unbelievers and sceptics may criticise and ridicule, but the true, warm-hearted Christian will rejoice, ver. 16.

14. It is not enough that we have an outward profession and an appearance of fruitfulness, but we must *bear* fruit, if we would meet our Lord's approval, vers. 18, 19; Gen. 3 : 7, 11; Matt. 7 : 20-23.

15. The curse of Christ will rest on all who shall fail to bring forth fruit to him, vers. 19, 20; ch. 23 : 25-28; 1 Cor. 16 : 22.

16. The miracles of Jesus should strengthen our faith and encourage our prayers, since he is our Intercessor, and through him we can do all things, vers. 21, 22; John 14 : 12-14; Phil. 4 : 13; Heb. 7 : 25.

17. The servants of Christ must expect opposition, and that their authority will be questioned by the enemies of truth, ver. 23; John 15 : 20.

18. Analogical arguments and interrogative answers to the cavils of sceptics are often the most effectual, ver. 24.

19. Formalists and wicked opposers of Christ will feign ignorance and lie rather than injure their popularity, or confess the truth which they dislike, vers. 25, 26.

20. They who do not honestly seek after the truth must expect to be left in error, ver. 27; ch. 13 : 12; Ps. 35 : 9-14; Isa. 19 : 15, 16.

21. Openly wicked men are often converted, while those who are externally moral, and profess high regard for religious things, continue in disobedience, and are lost, vers. 20 : 32; Luke 18 : 10-14.

22. Many who profess to obey God are in heart most disobedient, vers. 30, 32; Jer. 3 : 10; Rom. 2 : 17, 24; 10 : 3.

23. How great the patience and mercy of God in sending so many messengers to men with so many warnings, invitations, and promises, vers. 33-37; Heb. 1 : 1, 2; Jer. 7 : 25.

24. The greater the privileges, if unimproved, the greater the guilt, and the more awful the condemnation, vers. 40, 41; ch. 23 : 34-38; Luke 12 : 45-48.

25. They who obstinately reject the offers and privileges of the Gospel shall have them forever taken from them, vers. 41, 43; Prov. 1 : 24-32.

26. Let those to whom Christ has become a stone of stumbling beware lest he become a stone of condemnation and unutterable ruin, ver. 44; Luke 2 : 34; 2 Cor. 2 : 16.

27. A far more terrible doom awaits wicked men and nations under the Gospel than under the law, vers. 43, 44; Heb. 10 : 28, 29.

CHAPTER XXII.

1-14. PARABLE OF THE MARRIAGE OF THE KING'S SON. Or, Parable of the Royal Marriage and the Wedding Garment. Recorded only by Matthew. This parable is supposed by some to be the same as that of the Great Supper recorded in Luke 14 : 16-24. An examination of the two will show that they were different in time, place, occasion, and design. That in Luke was spoken earlier in our Savior's ministry, in the house of a Pharisee, occasioned by the remark of a guest, who, putting a wrong interpretation on the words of Jesus, supposed him to refer to the great opening festival of Messiah's kingdom, when he, as a Jew, would be certainly admitted; and the parable in reply was designed to correct the false views which he held in common with the Jews generally, showing that comparatively few of those who presumed upon the enjoyment of the Messiah's kingdom would

2 again by parables, and said, ¹ The kingdom of heaven is like unto a certain king, ᵐ which made a marriage for his son; ⁿ and sent forth his servants to call them that were bidden to the wedding: ᵒ and
4 they would not come. ᵖ Again, he sent forth other servants, saying, Tell them which are bidden, Behold, ᑫ I have prepared my dinner: my oxen and *my* fatlings *are* killed, and all things *are* ready:
5 ʳ come unto the marriage. ˢ But they made light of *it*, and went their ways, ᵗ one to his farm, another
6 to his merchandise: and ᵘ the remnant took his servants, and entreated *them* spitefully, and slew

¹ ch. 3. 2.
ᵐ Pro. 9. 1-6; Is 25. 6; 55. 1.
ⁿ Lk. 14. 17.
ᵒ John 5. 40.
ᵖ Ne. 9. 17; Ps. 86. 5.

ᑫ John 6. 50, 58.

ʳ 2 Cor. 6. 1.
ˢ Gen. 25. 34; Ps. 106. 24.
ᵗ Lk. 14. 18-20.
ᵘ John 15. 19, 20; 16. 2, 3.

really be prepared to receive and value it when offered to them. But this parable in Matthew was spoken in the temple only a few days before the crucifixion, occasioned by the hostility of the scribes, chief-priests, and elders, and their demand as to his authority (ch. 21 : 15, 23, 46), and was designed to show the terrible judgments which should come upon the Jewish people on account of their rejection of the Messiah, and the final punishment of mere nominal professors. This also was a royal marriage feast, and hence has the additional figure of a wedding garment; that was merely a great supper. In this the guests treat the invitation with the utmost contempt and insolence, and are destroyed for their conduct; in that the invited guests show at least enough courtesy to excuse themselves, and are debarred from tasting the supper. This is severer, and relates more especially to the judgment of the Jewish people as the rejecters of Christ; that is milder, and relates more especially to the graciousness of the Gospel's invitations. Each was peculiarly adapted to the respective occasions and to the feelings manifested by the Jewish leaders.

1. Jesus answered. The word *answer* is often used in Scripture as a kind of response, where no question is asked, to some words, circumstances, or occasion that precedes. Here it refers to the two last verses of the preceding chapter, where we have an account of the conduct of the chief priests and Pharisees, which *occasioned* or caused Jesus to *respond* in an additional parable. **By parables.** *In parables.* The parabolic mode of teaching is expressed in general terms by the plural *parables*, ch. 13 : 3, 10; Mark 3 : 23; 12 : 1.

2. The kingdom of heaven. The reign of Messiah in the Gospel dispensation, in respect to open rejecters and mere nominal professors, is **like** the case of a **certain king. A marriage.** Not merely the act of uniting the two parties in matrimony, but all the arrangements of the occasion, including the festivities. The marriage festival commonly lasted seven days, Gen. 29 : 27; Judg. 14 : 17, 18.

3. To call them that were bidden. According to an oriental custom, those who had been previously invited are now summoned at the beginning of the festivities. Compare Esth. 5 : 8; 6 : 14. The first call having been given, so that they might have time to prepare, it was now expected that they would be in readiness to go. **They would not come.** In this refusal they show not only their disrespect, but also their disloyalty to their sovereign. Compare Esth. 1 : 12, 16, 17.

4. Sent forth other servants. This strikingly shows the graciousness and leniency of the king. Instead of bringing punishment at once upon those that were bidden, for their contempt, he endeavors to remove any misunderstanding, barrier, or difficulty, which may have been in their way, and gives them an opportunity to retrace their steps, and come to the marriage. He sends forth other servants to tell them, in the most explicit language, that the preparations are made, and all things are ready. **Dinner.** The mid-day meal, the opening meal of the marriage festivities. **Fatlings.** The smaller and younger animals fatted for slaughter.

5, 6. The treatment these servants received at the hands of those bidden. Two classes of rejecters of the king's in-

7 them. But when the king heard *thereof*, he was wroth: and he sent forth ˣ his armies, and destroyed
8 those murderers, and burned up their city. Then saith he to his servants, The wedding is ready, but
9 they which were bidden were not ʸ worthy. ᶻ Go ye therefore into the highways, and as many as ye shall
10 find, bid to the marriage. So those servants went out into the highways, and ᵃ gathered together all as many as they found, both bad and good: and the wedding was furnished with guests.
11 ᵇ And when the king came in to see the guests, ᶜ he saw there a man ᵈ which had not on a wedding gar-
12 ment: and he saith unto him, Friend, ᵉ how camest thou in hither not having a wedding garment?

ˣ Dan. 9. 26; Lk. 19. 27, 42-44; 21. 21-24.
ʸ Ac. 13. 46; Rev. 3. 4.
ᶻ Pro. 1. 20-23; Is. 55. 1-3; Mk. 16. 15, 16; Rev. 22. 17.
ᵃ ch. 13. 47, 48; John 10. 16.
ᵇ ch. 25. 31, 32.
ᶜ 1 Cor. 4. 5; Heb. 4. 12, 13; Rev. 2. 23.
ᵈ Zec. 3. 3, 4; Lk. 15. 22; Ro. 3. 22; Eph. 4. 24; Rev. 19. 8.
ᵉ ch. 5. 20.

vitation are here given—*first*, those who slighted the invitations; *second*, those who persecuted and murdered his servants. The first class are again divided, one to his farm, another to his merchandise. **They made light of it.** They treated the invitation of the king, and the words of the servants, with indifference and disregard. They showed a disloyal and rebellious spirit. **Went their ways.** Rather, *Went away*. Their disregard and indifference was especially shown by their going away to attend to their own private affairs, just at the time when the king's invitations were urgent, and his business required haste. Compare 2 Chron. 30: 1, 10. **The remnant.** *The rest*, the second class, who were open and violent opposers. **Took his servants.** Laid hold of them, laid violent hands on them. **Entreated them spitefully.** Abused and ill-treated them. They went on in their deeds of violence till, reaching the climax of their crime, they **slew them.** Thus their rebellion becomes open; they are guilty of disloyalty, murder, and treason.

7. The severe punishment the king brings on these rebels and murderers. The king **was wroth,** both on account of their unmerciful treatment and cruel murder of his servants, and the insult, rebellion, and treason thereby committed. The crime he rightfully regards as done against himself. Compare 2 Sam. 10: 2-6. He therefore destroyed both them and their city.

8-10. **Not worthy.** Not specially because they were murderers, but because they did not accept of the king's invitation. Compare Luke 14: 18-20, 24.

Underlying their terrible crimes was the spirit of rebellion. **The highways.** *The forks of the roads*, where the roads from the country came together, and the people from the country would come in from different directions. **Gathered together—both bad and good.** Persons of all classes and conditions. Instead of **the wedding**, a preferable reading is, *the bridal hall*, etc.

11, 12. The second portion of the parable, the man without the wedding garment, here begins. **To see the guests.** Rather, *To view the guests*. *Guests* means those reclining at table. They were doubtless arranged on their couches, at the tables, when the king entered to view the company. **Wedding garment.** A garment suited for the occasion, and also expressly intended for it. The important point here is not *how* he might have obtained a wedding garment, but that he ought to have had it. It was necessary to the enjoyment of the feast, and expected of all, and he alone was without it. To allow him to explain his failure in not having on the proper costume, the king says to him, **Friend,** my good man (see ch. 20: 13), **how camest thou in hither, not having a wedding garment? And he was speechless;** he was silenced, convicted of his folly, saw that the fault was entirely his own, and could say nothing, not even offer a shadow of an excuse. He had not a word to say of poverty, haste, and hurry in coming, or inability from any cause. It is evident that he was guilty of base neglect, and of contempt toward the king himself. It is probable that the guests had garments furnished them, gathered as they

13 ᶠ And he was speechless. Then said the king to the servants, ᵍ Bind him hand and foot, and take him away, and cast *him* ʰ into outer darkness; there

ᶠ Ro. 3. 19.
ᵍ Zeph. 1. 7, 8.
ʰ ch. 8. 12; 2 Pet. 2. 4, 17.

were from the thoroughfares of the city, and brought with great haste to the wedding. This would have been no great task on the part of the king, since the treasures of the wealthy consisted largely of changes of raiment, Job 27 : 16; James 5 : 2; see also on ch. 6 : 19. Horace says that Lucullus, a Roman who lived a little before the Christian era, on examining his wardrobe, found that he had five thousand mantles. And Chardin, who traveled in the east in the seventeenth century, says that the king of Persia gave away an infinite number of garments. It is also a modern custom in the east, to furnish garments on marriage, festive, and other occasions. At the royal marriage of Sultan Mahmoud, a number of years ago, every guest had made for him, at the expense of the sultan, a wedding garment. No one, however dignified his station, was permitted to enter into the presence-chamber of that sovereign without a change of raiment. Travelers relate similar customs in Persia. Chardin mentions a vizier who lost his life for not appearing before his sovereign, a Persian king, in a robe that had been sent him for the purpose. Since eastern manners change so little, it is likely that such customs existed in the days of our Savior, and long before. Circumstantial evidence may also be derived from such passages as Gen. 45 : 22; 1 Sam. 18 : 4; 2 Kings 10 : 22; Esth. 6 : 8; Dan. 5 : 7; Rev. 3 : 5; 6 : 11.

13. The guest, being thus inexcusable, and guilty of neglect of plain duty, of great impropriety on such an occasion, and of contempt toward his sovereign, is summarily punished. **To his servants.** To his *attendants*. These were his ministering and personal attendants, the officers who attended him and executed his will. They are to be distinguished from his *servants*, mentioned in the preceding verses. **Bind him hand and foot.** As criminals were bound for punishment; it was also a part of the punishment. **Take him away,** according to the best critical authorities, should be omitted. **Outer darkness.** The darkness outside the royal banqueting house, which was brilliantly illuminated. His chagrin, shame, and anguish are expressed by the outward signs of **weeping and gnashing of teeth.** See on ch. 8 : 12.

This being a *complex* parable, consisting of the royal marriage and the wedding garment, it has a complex design and a double centre of comparison. Its grand design was to show the rejection of the Jewish people and the destruction of Jerusalem, on account of their rejection of Christ, and also the final punishment of all mere nominal professors. Its centres of comparison are found in the destruction of the city of those rejecters and murderers, and in the casting forth into outer darkness of the man without the wedding garment. The first portion of the parable bears some resemblance to Prov. 9 : 1–6; the second portion to Zeph. 1 : 7, 8.

The *king* represents God the Father; the *son*, Jesus Christ the Son of God; the *marriage*, the marriage supper of the Lamb (Rev. 19 : 7–9), the full and complete union of Christ and his congregated people in glory. The crowning blessings of the Gospel are frequently set forth in Scripture under the figure of a marriage, Ps. 45 : 6–15; Isa. 61 : 10; 62 : 5; Hos. 2 : 19, 20; 2 Cor. 11 : 2; Eph. 5 : 25–27, 32.

Those *bidden to the wedding* were the Jewish people, ch. 10 : 5, 6; John 4 : 22; Acts 13 : 46. The *first* invitation, which is implied, was given by John the Baptist and the prophets who foretold the coming of Christ (Acts 3 : 22–24). This parable belongs entirely to the new dispensation, and therefore can extend back into the old only as it was foretold or announced. The *second* invitation, or the *summons* to the wedding by the servants, was the preaching of the glad tidings by the twelve and the seventy (Luke 9 : 1, 2 ; 10 : 1) before the crucifixion; the *refusal to come* represents the Jews, especially the scribes, chief-priests, and Pharisees, as the political and religious representatives and leaders of the people, rejecting Christ and salvation, John 5 : 40. The *third and last invitation* represents the preachers of the Gospel to the Jews after the resurrection. The announcement (ver. 4), *I have prepared my dinner; my oxen*

14 shall be weeping and gnashing of teeth. many are called, but few *are* chosen. ¹ For ¹ ch. 7. 14; 20. 16.

---

and the fatlings are killed, etc., shows an advancement in the divine preparation: Christ offering himself a sacrifice for sin, dying, rising, ascending, and the Holy Spirit descending in power. Compare John 6: 51-58; Acts 2: 38, 39; 3: 26. The unbelieving Jews who rejected this invitation are represented under *two classes:* first, those who were *indifferent*, like Demas, loving this present world, and so absorbed in it as to have but little thought about God and religion; second, the open opposers of Christ and the persecutors of his disciples. Thus, they cast Peter and John into prison (Acts 4 : 3); then the apostles (Acts 5 : 18); then the disciples generally, both men and women, Acts 8 : 3. They scourged some (Acts 5 : 40; 16 : 22) and slew others, as Stephen and James, Acts 7 : 58; 12 : 2. This last invitation continued about thirty five years.

The *city* of *these murderers* (ver. 7) represents Jerusalem; the *armies*, the Roman armies under Titus Vespasian, who utterly destroyed the city and the temple, A.D. 70. See on ch. 21 : 41, *last paragraph*. They are called *his armies*, because they were God's messengers of wrath against that devoted city. God often uses the wicked to execute his judgments, Jer. 25 : 9; Joel 2 : 25.

The Jews had shown themselves *not worthy* (Acts 13 : 46), by their rejection of the Gospel, and their opposition to Christ and his cause, culminating in cruel persecution. They are rejected, their city destroyed, and those that remain are scattered, and the Gospel is offered to the Gentiles. Thus, the servants are commanded to *go forth into the highways*, the thoroughfares of the world, to the Gentiles, the heathen world. *The bad and good* represent men of all descriptions; the best as well as the worst men need the Gospel, and all are welcome to it. It was by *accepting* the invitation that the wedding was *furnished with guests*.

The *man without the wedding garment* represents the mere nominal professor; the *wedding garment* is the righteousness which is obtained through faith (Phil. 3 : 9), which is professed in baptism (Gal. 3 : 27; compare Eph. 4 : 23, 24), and which is indispensable to entering and enjoying the kingdom of glory, Heb. 12 : 14. "The fine linen is the righteousness of the saints," Rev. 19 : 8. Compare Isa. 61 : 10.

The *questioning this man* without the wedding garment, by the king, represents the judgment coming home to each individual heart, 2 Cor. 5 : 10. And here may be a reason why one individual is made to represent a class, in order that the application might be the more pointed and personal. As he was *speechless*, so shall nominal professors be without excuse and struck dumb in the presence of their Judge. Righteousness was a free gift; their guilt will consist in not accepting it from the heart. This man, coming in his own dress, represents them clothed in and trusting in their own righteousness. This was a warning to scribes and Pharisees, to Judas, and to all who had the form of godliness without the power.

As *he was cast forth*, so shall nominal Christians be excluded from heaven. The *servants*, or *ministering attendants* (ver. 13), represent the angels who "shall gather out of his kingdom all that offend, and them that do iniquity," ch. 13 : 41, 49. The *binding him hand and foot* points to their perfectly helpless and disgraceful condition. The *casting forth* is their banishment from the presence of the Lord (2 Thess. 1 : 9); the *outer darkness*, the blackness of darkness forever (Jude 13); the *weeping and gnashing of teeth*, the misery of the lost soul, arising from despair, remorse, and the wrath of a holy God.

14. In closing, Jesus utters one of his solemn proverbial sayings. **For.** Such is the solemn fact under the Gospel dispensation, which is in harmony with the teaching of this parable, and indeed renders its narration necessary. **Many are called**, referring to verses 3 and 9, and including Jews and Gentiles, all who are invited to receive the blessings of the Gospel. **Few are chosen.** This is to be explained in harmony with the parable. But few enjoy the benefits of the Gospel by accepting its provisions. All indeed is of sovereign grace, and of a sovereign purpose; but the human side in accepting the invitation is prominent in the parable. See on ch. 20 : 16,

Concerning the payment of tribute to Cæsar.

15 ᵏ THEN went the Pharisees, and took counsel
16 ˡ how they might entangle him in *his* talk. And they sent out unto him their disciples with the Herodians, saying, ᵐ Master, we know that thou art true, and teachest the way of God in truth, neither carest thou for any *man:* for thou regardest not the
17 person of men. Tell us therefore, What thinkest thou? Is it lawful to give tribute unto ⁿ Cæsar, or

ᵏ Mk. 12. 13; Lk. 20. 20; Ps. 2. 2.
ˡ Ps. 56. 5, 6; Heb. 12. 3.
ᵐ Ps. 5. 9; Gal. 6. 7.

ⁿ Lk. 2. 1; John 19. 12, 15; Ac. 17. 7; 25. 8.

15–22. THE REPLY OF JESUS TO THE PHARISEES AND HERODIANS, CONCERNING THE LAWFULNESS OF PAYING TRIBUTE TO CÆSAR, Mark 12: 13–17; Luke 20: 20–26.

The Jewish rulers having been worsted in their direct attempt to silence Jesus, and being greatly enraged by his rebukes and threatenings, and being restrained from laying hands on him for fear of the people, now strive to unite all parties opposed to him, and in various ways endeavor to draw from him something which might afford a civil or ecclesiastical accusation against him, or at least might destroy his popularity and influence with the people.

15. Then went the Pharisees, etc. The Pharisees were the leaders of the opposition, and probably formed the principal ones of those who had just questioned the authority of Jesus. **How they might entangle him in his talk.** How they might *ensnare* or *entrap him with a word.* Compare 1 Sam. 28: 9; Prov. 6: 2. **In his talk.** More exactly translated, *with a word*, the Pharisees supposing that he must necessarily entrap himself by answering either *yes* or *no* to their question in verse 17. "Not in *discourse* in general; but with specific reference to the artfully devised question in verse 17, to which it seemed he could answer neither yes nor no, without fatally involving himself in his relations either to the government or the people."
—DR. CONANT, *Revision of Matthew*.

16. Their disciples. To carry out their plan, the Pharisaic rulers could not come themselves to Jesus, for they were known; they therefore sent their disciples, their pupils and followers, young and unknown persons. Compare Acts 22: 3. **Herodians.** This class is referred to by name only in this passage, and in Mark 3: 6; 12: 13. The Herodians appear to have been a political rather than a religious party, though, as it is supposed, mostly Sadducees in religious sentiment. They were partisans of the Herodian family, and consequently of the Roman dominion over the country, which was odious to the Jews generally. They may be regarded also as the friends and partisans of Herod Antipas, tetrarch of Galilee and Perea, and hence Galileans, and belonging to the same province with Jesus, whose testimony might be of great importance. Herod was desirous of obtaining the title of king from the Roman emperor; and if his friends could rid Palestine of one who opposed Roman dominion and aspired to be king of the Jews, it might work to the advantage of Herod. Thus, while the Pharisees hated and opposed the Herodians, they hated Jesus so much more that they could unite with them in their opposition to him. The Herodians, on the contrary, united with the Pharisees more from political and selfish motives.

Master, we know, etc. *Teacher, we know.* They affirm what is true, but hypocritically. Nicodemus used similar language, but sincerely. Luke says the chief priests and scribes "sent forth spies, who should feign themselves just men, that they might take hold of his words," Luke 20: 20. They pretended to acknowledge Jesus to be all that he claimed, and to be ready to abide by his decisions, since they would be absolutely true and just, independent of the influence and authority of men. They came to Jesus not as Pharisees, nor Herodians, but as just men, hoping by their words to hide their character, and flatter Jesus, and lead him into an unguarded position. **Neither carest;** for the censure or applause of any. **Thou regardest not;** thou art perfectly impartial. **The way of God.** The way which God has marked out for men to walk in before him, Ps. 27: 11.

17. Tell us, therefore, what

A.D. 30. MATTHEW XXII. 305

18 not? But Jesus ° perceived their wickedness, and ° ch. 16. 8.
19 said, ᵖ Why tempt ye me, *ye* hypocrites? Show me ᵖ Pro. 15. 11.
   the tribute money. And they brought unto him ᑫ a ᑫ ch. 18. 28; 20. 2.
20 penny. And he saith unto them, Whose *is* this im-
21 age and superscription? They say unto him, Cæsar's. ʳ ch. 17. 25-27; Ro.
   Then saith he unto them, ʳ Render therefore unto   13. 7.

---

thinkest thou. What are thy thoughts and opinion on this much disputed point? Tell us, and settle the question, for we have determined to submit it to thy judgment. **Is it lawful,** for us as Jews, as the chosen people of God, Luke 20: 22. The question is not whether it was advisable, but whether it was *lawful* for them, who acknowledged God as their king. **To give tribute.** The poll-tax imposed on all males from fourteen, and females from twelve to sixty-five. **Cæsar.** The family name of Julius Cæsar, the first Roman emperor, and applied to his successors, whether of his family or not, as a designation of their office, and a representation of Roman power. The *Cæsar* then reigning was the Emperor Tiberius. **Or not?** The question was so put as to require, as they thought, the answer, either *yes* or *no.* They would rather have him answer in the negative, for then they would "deliver him into the power and authority of the governor" as a seditious person, Luke 20: 20. But if he answered in the affirmative, then they would accuse him before the people as opposed to the law of God. The Herodians, as friends of Herod, and hence of the Roman supremacy, were in favor of paying tribute. The Pharisees generally espoused the popular Jewish sentiment, that paying tribute to a foreign power was a badge of servitude, and even contrary to the law of Moses. Thus Judas, the Gaulonite (Acts 5: 35), had raised an insurrection in opposition to levying this tax, holding that it was unlawful, and even rebellion against God for the Jews to pay tribute and submit to a foreign power. These sentiments were extensively promulgated; and the Jewish people, who were very restless under the Roman yoke, quite generally espoused, or sympathized in them. This was, however, a fanatical view of the law, since the Jews were nowhere forbidden to pay tribute to a foreign conqueror. They were only forbidden to set a stranger over them as king, Deut. 17: 15. They had, at diffe-

rent times, paid heavy tribute to Syria and Babylon.

18. **Perceived their wickedness.** Rather, *knowing their wickedness,* their evil disposition, their malicious artifice. **Why tempt ye me?** Why entice me to say something which you can use against me? Why do you try to draw me into a snare, so as to entrap me? **Hypocrites;** dissemblers, pretenders, assuming a character that does not belong to you.

19. **Tribute money.** *The current coin of the taxation,* the money in which civil taxes were paid. **A penny.** *A denary,* a Roman silver coin, worth about fifteen cents. See on ch. 18: 28; and wood-cut, ch. 20: 2. It was a current maxim of Jewish teachers, that "wherever a king's coin is current, there his sovereignty is acknowledged." It was an evidence of the Roman dominion over the land, that Roman currency was used; and, by using it, the Jews in fact acknowledged their subjection to the Roman power.

20. **Image and superscription.** The *image* was probably the likeness of the Roman emperor, Tiberius Cæsar. The *inscription* was the motto of the coin, the title of the emperor, declarative of his sovereignty.

21. **Cæsar's.** They thus acknowledged that they were peacefully submitting to his government, and enjoying his protection. **Render.** *Pay off.* The idea is not *rendering* a *gift,* but rendering what is *due.* **The things that are Cæsar's.** Render to Cæsar whatever is due to him, what rightfully belongs to him; if you are under his government, obey him and pay him fully for his protection, so long as you violate no divine obligation. He does not discuss a political question, nor the right or wrong of Roman supremacy; but taking their condition as it really was, the Roman power peacefully acknowledged and its protection enjoyed, he teaches that they should pay toward its support, and render to it whatever was rightfully its due. Paul expands

Cæsar the things which are Cæsar's; ᵗ and unto God
22 the things that are God's. When they had heard
these words, they marveled; and left him, and went
their way.

ᵗ ch. 4. 10; Dan. 3. 16–18; 6. 10–13; Ac. 5. 29.

Concerning the Resurrection.

23 ᵗ THE same day came to him the Sadducees,
ᵘ which say that there is no resurrection, and asked
24 him, saying, Master, ˣ Moses said, 'If a man die,
having no children, his brother shall marry his wife,

ᵗ Mk. 12. 18; Lk. 20. 27.
ᵘ Ac. 23. 8; 1 Cor. 15. 12–14; 2 Tim. 2. 18.
ˣ Deu. 25. 5–10.

---

this idea in Rom. 13 : 1–7. **The things that are God's.** And since in the highest sense you are under God's government, preserved, protected, and supported by him, render to him whatever is due to him as your God and King—your obedience and the whole circle of religious duty. The two precepts are in harmony, and the one really flowing out of the other. As love to our neighbor is in harmony with, and flows from, love to God, so rendering all rightful obedience to human government is in harmony with, and springs from, discharging our full obligation to God, 1 Tim. 2 : 1, 2; 1 Pet. 2 : 13–16. " Man is the coinage, and bears the image of God, Gen. 1 : 27; 9 : 6; Acts 17 : 29; James 3 : 9. . . . We owe, then, *ourselves* to God; and this solemn duty is implied, of going ourselves to him, with all that we have and are. The answer also gives them the real reason why they were now under subjection to Cæsar, namely, because they had fallen from their allegiance to God," 2 Chron. 12 : 5–8.—ALFORD.

22. **Marveled.** They wondered at a reply so unexpected, so apt and true, and at his wisdom in escaping their snare. He maintained both the rights of government and the rights of God, and in such a manner that neither party could accuse him. The wisdom of his reply may well command our admiration. He laid down a great moral principle, which is applicable in every age of the world, and which, if properly carried out, will conduce to the highest good of man and to the glory of God.

23–33. THE REPLY OF JESUS TO THE SADDUCEES CONCERNING THE RESURRECTION, Mark 12 : 18–27; Luke 20 : 27–40. The attack of the Sadducees was less artful and insidious than that of the Pharisees and Herodians. Their question was most frivolous, and their design seems to have been to throw contempt not merely on the doctrine of the resurrection, which they denied, but especially upon Jesus, by any answer he might give.

23. **The same day;** on which Jesus battled and silenced the Pharisees and Herodians. **The Sadducees.** There being no article in the original, it should read simply, *Sadducees.* See on ch. 3 : 7. The Sadducees believed that the soul perished with the body, and hence that there **is no resurrection** of the dead, and denied the doctrine of a future state and of spiritual existence, such as angels and spirits, Acts 23 : 8. The word *resurrection*, as used in this and the following verses, appears to have a somewhat broader signification than merely rising from the dead, including not only the life that ensues, but also the life of the soul previous to the reunion of soul and body. Thus it is very nearly equivalent to future life, the rising from the dead being the central hinge around which that life turns. Compare the language of Mark 12 : 23, "In the resurrection, therefore, when they shall rise."

24. **Master.** *Teacher.* They also approach him with apparent regard for his authority as a religious teacher. **Moses said.** Rejecting all human tradition, they acknowledged the authority of Moses. The law which they cite is found in Deut. 25 : 5, 6, and was designed to prevent any family in Israel from becoming extinct. The case here stated was probably a fictitious one, and taking for granted that, if there was a resurrection, the present relations of life must continue in the future state, they thought to show from the law the manifest absurdity of the doctrine. It may have been a favorite argument of the Sadducees with the Pharisees, and is an illustration of their manner of opposing the doctrine.

25–27. **Now there were with us.**

25 and raise up seed unto his brother.' Now there were with us seven brethren : and the first, when he had married a wife, deceased ; and, having no issue,
26 left his wife unto his brother : likewise the second
27 also, and the third, unto the seventh : and last of
28 all the woman died also. Therefore in the resurrection whose wife shall she be of the seven ? For they all had her.
29 Jesus answered and said unto them, ʸ Ye do err, ᶻ not knowing the Scriptures, ⁿ nor the power of God.
30 For in the resurrection they neither marry, nor are given in marriage, but ᵇ are as the angels of God in

ʸ Ps. 17. 15; 49. 14, 15; Is. 26. 19; Dan. 12. 2; Hos. 13. 14.
ᶻ Ps. 119. 130; Jno. 5. 39; 20. 9; Ro. 15. 4.
ⁿ Ge. 18. 14; Jer. 32. 17; Phil. 3. 21.
ᵇ 1 John 3. 2; Rev. 5. 9-11.

The Sadducees state the case as if it had actually occurred among them. It may have been a long disputed case, never before fully solved. Some suppose it founded on the apocryphal book of Tobit 3 : 8. **Having no issue.** Having no seed.
28. **In the resurrection.** In the resurrection state or life; the state of being into which the resurrection issues. **Whose wife should she be?** The Pharisees appear to have held that the relationships of this life would continue in the future state. And with no other conception of the doctrine the Sadducees foresaw a certain conflict between these seven brothers. All, then, can not have her, but only one; yet none has a claim upon her above the rest. Whose wife, then ? They see here, as they suppose, an insurmountable difficulty to supposing a resurrection life. It would be a state of confusion, with interests and relationships which could never be justly settled. And besides, as this case grew out of a Mosaic enactment, it was evident, as they thought, that Moses never intended to reveal a resurrection and a future life. Their object was not to have their question solved, but rather to puzzle Jesus, or to draw forth some expression which they could use against him. They could not expect him to deny the resurrection; for he had raised Lazarus from the dead, and had repeatedly inculcated the doctrine. He was doubtless known to side with the Pharisees in this respect. But they hoped to bring him into conflict with the law of Moses, or induce him to utter that which they could construe into blasphemy, or turn into ridicule.
29. Jesus answers them quite differently from what they expected. He does not so much notice the question as the underlying error that suggested it. He first shows their mistake through ignorance, and then expounds a passage in point from the law. **Ye do err.** You go astray, you wander through your twofold ignorance of Scripture and the power of God. **Not knowing the Scriptures.** Not understanding the Scriptures in their deep spiritual import, especially in regard to a future existence. **Nor the power of God**, which can and will remove all obstacles in the way of a future life, as taught in his word. Since God is omnipotent, the dead can be raised; and they will be raised, since he has so taught us in his word. The same two-fold ignorance and unbelief lie at the foundation of the principal objections to the resurrection at the present day, Acts 26 : 8; Rom. 4 : 17; 1 Cor. 6 : 14; 15 : 34.
30. **In the resurrection.** In that state ushered in by the resurrection. The reference is to the resurrection state of the righteous, Luke 20 : 35. The Jew, as one of God's chosen people, would look forward to the future condition of the righteous. **Neither marry.** With reference to males. **Given in marriage.** With reference to females, who, among the Jews, were given in marriage by their fathers. **Are as the angels of God.** Not constituted for the marriage relation. Their existence, relations, and state will be similar to those of the angels ; not earthly, sensual, and mortal, but heavenly, spiritual, and immortal. "Neither can they die any more ; for they are equal unto the angels, and are the children (*sons*) of God," Luke 20 : 36. They are not dependent on the marriage relation for the preservation of their species, but are themselves immor-

31 heaven. But as touching the resurrection of the dead, have ye not read that which was spoken unto
32 you by God, saying, ^c 'I am the God of Abraham, and the God of Isaac, and the God of Jacob?' God
33 is not the God of the dead, but of the living. And when the multitude heard *this*, ^d they were astonished at his doctrine.

^c Ex. 3. 6, 16; Ac. 7. 32; Heb. 11. 16

^d ch. 7. 28.

---

tal. As the righteous will be as the angels, the wicked will be as the fallen angels, or demons.

31. Touching the resurrection of the dead. Concerning the resurrection. The future life which the Sadducees were making to hinge on the resurrection. The *dead* here refers not merely to the bodies of those who have died, but to their disembodied spirits—with reference, indeed, to their being reunited to their bodies and raised. The Hebrew had a distinct word, *rapha*, which refers to that part of man which survives death, and was a distinct name for that separate existence, Job 26 : 5; Ps. 88 : 10; Prov. 2 : 18; 9 : 18; 21 : 16; Isa. 14 : 9; 26 : 14, 19. **Have ye not read** that spoken by God, which is a proof of the resurrection and of the whole future state which it implies? Jesus appeals to Moses, Exodus 3 : 6, inasmuch as they had just drawn their argument from Moses. Some affirm, and others deny, that the Sadducees rejected all the other parts of the Holy Scriptures but the five books of Moses. The true statement seems to be, that they rejected all tradition, and received only the written law, and that they held that the five books of Moses should be greatly preferred above the rest of the Old Testament, and regarded as the only ultimate standard of appeal for all doctrine. We thus see another reason why Jesus appeals to Moses, since they regarded his writings of the highest authority. He, however, implies, according to Luke, that he might have appealed to the strong testimonies of other Scripture (Isa. 26 : 19; Ezek. 36 : 1-14; Dan. 12 : 2): "*Even* Moses showed," Luke 20 : 37.

32. I am the God of Abraham, etc. The living and eternal God, bearing a personal relation, as the living God, to Abraham and to Isaac and to Jacob, which supposes that those patriarchs were still bearing a living and personal relation to him as his servants, and also implies he will not suffer them always to remain under the power of the grave, but will, in due time, raise them to a glorified life. Jehovah is the **I am,** the ever faithful, the unchangeable, the living and eternal God. He was the personal God of the patriarchs. That he continued this personal relation implies their continued existence. Since he declares, "*I am* the God of Abraham," etc., their God absolutely and without reference to time, that is, eternally, their immortality is implied. And since he was the God of their whole existence, body and soul, it is implied that, though the relation between their bodies and souls be suspended for a time, they will be reunited ere long in an endless existence.

Not the God of the dead. Dead is here used in the sense of the Sadducees, *extinct*. God is not the God of the extinct, of a non-existence. He can bear no relations to a nonentity. **But of the living.** Of those who continue to live. The souls of the patriarchs, that which was essentially theirs, were still living; their bodies, the less important part, had indeed died, yet still existed in matter, and the fact that Jehovah was God of the living was a pledge that this suspension of bodily existence was only temporary. The additional idea of a covenant-keeping God is fitting here, since "*I am the God,*" etc., may briefly express the blessing pertaining to a covenant relation to God. Compare Deut. 26 : 16; Isa. 41 : 10; Zech. 13 : 9; Heb. 11 : 16. All of the blessings and promises of God connected with this covenant relation can be enjoyed only by the living, and the full enjoyment must be in connection with their most perfect life and highest state of being, their glorified and immortal bodily existence.

33. Astonished at his doctrine. *At his teaching*, which had thrown such a flood of light on the doctrine of the resurrection and a future life, and which had brought out so clearly the deep meaning of Scripture in support of the

The two Great Commandments.

34 * BUT when the Pharisees had heard that he had put the Sadducees to silence, they were gathered to-
35 gether. Then one of them, *which was* ᶠ a lawyer, ask-
36 ed *him a question*, tempting him, and saying, Master,
37 which is the great commandment in the law? Jesus said unto him, ᵍ 'Thou shalt love the Lord thy God ʰ with all thy heart, and with all thy soul, and with

ᵉ Mk. 12. 28.

ᶠ Lk. 10. 25, 26.

ᵍ Deu. 6. 5; 10. 12; 30. 6.

doctrine. The multitude probably had confused notions of the resurrection. The Pharisees supposed it would be some way connected with the coming of the Messiah. The easy manner in which Jesus had solved the question of the Sadducees, removing all absurdity, supporting the resurrection by a citation from one of the books of Moses, astonished all. The argument also carried conviction; for one of the Pharisees, a scribe, said, "Teacher, thou hast well said," and the Sadducees, put to confusion and silenced, "no longer dared to ask him any question," Luke 20 : 39, 40.

34–40. JESUS REPLIES TO A PHARISEE CONCERNING THE GREAT COMMANDMENT IN THE LAW, Mark 12 : 28–34. Compare Luke 10 : 25–29.

34. **When the Pharisees heard.** The Pharisees would gladly have seen Jesus ensnared by the Sadducees; but the latter had been so thoroughly routed and put to silence that it caused much excitement and pleasant emotion among the Pharisees, who **gathered together,** *collected together in the same place.*

35. But, however much they might approve of the victory won for the doctrine of the resurrection, they did not intend giving up their efforts to entangle Jesus. One of them, **a lawyer,** one skilled in the law, a teacher and interpreter of the divine law, asked, **tempting him,** as spokesman for the Pharisaic party; who, from wrong motives, still hoped that he might say something which they considered wrong, and which could be used against him. There does not appear to have been that maliciousness, either in the question or in the one asking it, as in the former attack in regard to tribute. Indeed, Mark (12 : 28) presents this lawyer as one of the scribes who had heard and approved of the answer of Jesus to the Sadducees. Privately he may have desired to hear the opinion of Jesus. But though he is thus favorably presented by Mark, he was the spokesman of the Pharisees, who were anxious to find some means to destroy him.

36. **Which is the great commandment?** Literally, *What kind of commandment?* or, *What commandment is great?* There appears to be a reference both to the greatness and the quality of the commandment. The scribes made numerous distinctions and classifications of the law, dividing the commandments, six hundred and thirteen in number, into greater and less, rather giving preference to the letter than the spirit, and to the ceremonial rather than the moral. The Jewish doctors were by no means agreed as to which precept was preëminent, some contending for the law of sacrifices, others for that of circumcision, others for that of meats, washing, phylacteries, etc. As a rule among them, the law of the Sabbath was to give way to the law of circumcision. **In the law,** of Moses. See on ch. 5 : 19.

37. Jesus answers by giving the great law of love, first, to God; second, to men. He gives not any one precept of the decalogue, but a comprehensive summary found in Deut. 6 : 5 and Lev. 19 : 18. **The Lord thy God.** Jehovah is God, whatever be the desires of men. The fact that he is *their* God should call forth their supreme love. **With all thy heart.** With all thy desires, feelings, and affections. **With all thy soul.** With all thy sentiments, passions, and vital bodily powers. **With all thy mind.** With thy whole will and intellectual powers. Whatever be the distinction between *heart, soul,* and *mind,* the three combined are equivalent to the whole man with all his powers and affections. Thou shalt love God supremely.

38. **This is the first and great.** The true order of these words, according to the highest critical authorities, is, *This is the great and first.* This involved

38 all thy mind.' This is the first and great commandment. 39 And the second *is* like unto it, ¹ ' Thou shalt 40 love thy neighbor as thyself.' ᵏ On these two commandments hang all the Law and the Prophets.

ʰ Ps. 103. 1.
ⁱ Le. 19. 18; Lk. 10. 27; Ro. 13. 9, 10; Gal. 5. 14; Jam. 2. 8.
ᵏ ch. 7. 12; 1 Tim. 1. 5; 1 John 4. 19-21.

The Christ the Son of David.

41 ˡ WHILE the Pharisees were gathered together, 42 Jesus asked them, saying, ᵐ What think ye of Christ? whose son is he? They say unto him,

ˡ Mk. 12. 35; Lk. 20. 41.
ᵐ ch. 16. 13-17.

---

the most direct answer to the question of the scribe; for the command just cited was *great*. But it was also *the great and first* command in its nature, order, rank, and importance, involving a principle which lies at the foundation of all goodness and every proper affection.

39. And the second, etc. Rather, *And a second is like unto it.* There is a second similar to the first, and of like nature with it, and hence a second great command. As the first command is a summary of the first table of the law, of the duties we owe to God; so the second is a summary of the second table, the duties we owe to men. Supreme love to God involves indirectly proper love to our fellow-men; and a right love toward men presupposes and springs from true love to God, Rom. 13 : 9; 1 John 4 : 20, 21. The two commands are thus alike in nature, springing from the same source, yet they are distinct. **Thy neighbor.** Thy fellow-man. See Luke 10 : 29-37. **As thyself.** The Scriptures forbid *selfishness*, but not *self-love*. Self-love is an original principle in our nature, and, though the Scriptures do not command it, they take for granted and imply that men ought to exercise a proper love for themselves. The command here is the inner life and principle of the golden rule. " God loves me as he loves thee; and thee as he does me; therefore I ought to love thee, my neighbor, as myself; and thou me as thyself; for our love ought to correspond to God's love."—BENGEL. This answer of Jesus showed the Pharisees that their conduct toward him was a transgression of this law of love.

40. On these two—hang; as a door on its hinges; upon these the law and the prophets depend; these are fundamental precepts, from which all others spring, and which compromise all others. **All the law and the prophets.** According to the best ancient authorities this should read, *The whole law, and also the prophets.* The lawyer had asked what command was great in the law. Jesus answers, The great law of love, remarking that on it hung the law, and adding, "and also the prophets," showing that it was a fundamental principle, not only in the law, but in all Scripture. See on ch. 5 : 17 and 7 : 12. Jesus thus showed not only what commands were great, but what were the greatest; and also what must be the nature of any command in order to be great, that it must involve in some degree and be in harmony with the principle of love. Compare 1 Cor. 13 : 1-13. Mark relates that the scribe or lawyer, on hearing this reply, expressed his full approbation, and that Jesus said to him, " Thou art not far from the kingdom of God."

41-46. Jesus confounds and silences the Pharisees with A QUESTION CONCERNING THE PARENTAGE OF THE CHRIST, Mark 12 : 35-37; Luke 20 : 41-44. He had been acting on the defensive; but now he turns to the offensive, and convicts the scribes and Pharisees with ignorance and false views of the Messiah, which opens the way for his terrible denunciations against them in the next chapter. They had disputed his claims as a spiritual Messiah, and, by repeated efforts, had vainly tried to prove him a base pretender; he now turns and shows the incongruity of their view of a worldly Messiah with the prophetic idea of him.

42. What think ye of Christ? Not merely *of*, but *concerning the Christ;* the Messiah whom you are expecting? *The Christ,* or *the Messiah,* was at that time the title of an office, and was not applied to Jesus as a name while he was on earth. See on ch. 1 : 1. The question of Jesus related to the parentage of the Messiah, the *Anointed One.* **Whose son is he?** Of whom is he the son, the

43 ᵒ *The son of* David. He saith unto them, How then
44 doth David ᵒ in spirit call him Lord, saying, ᵖ 'The Lord said unto my Lord, Sit thou on my right hand,
45 till I make thine enemies thy footstool?' If David
46 then call him Lord, ᑫ how is he his son? ʳ And no man was able to answer him a word. ˢ Neither durst any *man* from that day forth ask him any more *questions*.

ᵒ ch. 1. 1; 21. 9.
ᵒ 2 Sam. 23. 2.
ᵖ Ps. 110. 1; Ac. 2. 34; 1 Cor. 15. 25; Heb. 10. 12, 13; Rev. 3. 21.
ᑫ Ro. 1. 3, 4.
ʳ Lk. 14. 6.
ˢ Mk. 12. 34; Lk. 20. 40.

---

descendant? **Of David.** "Son of David" was a common title of the Messiah. See on ch. 9 : 27.
43. **How, then?** In what sense, or on what ground? What does David mean? **In spirit.** *By* the guidance of *the Holy Spirit*. **Call him Lord.** Apply to him the reverential and solemn title of Lord. If the Messiah is only a descendant of David, a mere man, as you suppose, how, then, does David solemnly entitle him Lord, thus addressing him as his superior? **Saying.** In Ps. 110 : 1. This passage is said to be more frequently quoted or referred to in the New Testament than any other in the Old Testament. The psalm from which it is quoted was written by David, after Zion became the seat of the theocracy (2 Sam. 6 : 16, 17), and not long after the promises made to David in 2 Sam. 7 : 11–16 and 1 Chron. 17 : 9–14. The application of the psalm, and of the language here quoted, to the Messiah, is taken for granted by Jesus, is silently acknowledged by the Pharisees, and was the common interpretation among the Jews at the time of Christ and long after.
44. **The Lord.** Jehovah. **To my Lord.** The Messiah, as the Jews understood the words to refer, and as our Savior applied them. Thus David spoke of the Messiah as his Lord, his superior and sovereign. **On my right hand.** On the throne beside me, not merely as a position of honor, but as a partner of my sovereignty and power. Ps. 110 : 2, 3. See on ch. 20, 21. **Till I make,** etc. According to the highest critical authorities, *Till I put thine enemies under thy feet,* implying utter and ignominious defeat, and the most abject submission. The foot was often put on the neck of the vanquished, Josh. 10 : 24, 25; Ps. 47 : 3. *Till* does not limit the time of his reign, but only carries the thought to a certain point, without going beyond it. Compare Gen. 28 : 15; Ps. 112 : 8. Paul, in 1 Cor. 15 : 24–28, reveals to us some things that shall take place after Christ has totally subjugated his enemies under his feet.
45. **How is he his son?** If David called him Lord, thus acknowledging him as his superior and sovereign, in what sense or on what ground is he his son, and hence his inferior? The question can only be answered by acknowledging the divinity and humanity of Christ. It is thus answered in Rom. 1 : 3, 4.
46. **No man was able to answer him a word.** In their worldly views of the Messiah they did not perceive his divinity. Hence no one could answer. If the scribes had understood the true idea of the Messiah, they could have said, As man, he is David's son; but as God, David's Lord. And so thoroughly entangled and discomfited were they that from that time they durst not enter into debate with him and question him any more. They felt their inferiority and dare not risk another defeat. This closes his earthly debate with these his enemies.

REMARKS.

1. The provisions of the Gospel are rich, royal, and abundant, and its invitations to men are most honorable, earnest, and condescending, vers. 2–4; Prov. 9 : 1–6; Isa. 55 : 1–3; Rev. 22 : 17.
2. If sinners perish, it will be because they would not come to the Gospel feast, ver. 3; Prov. 9 : 12; Isa. 50 : 2, 3; John 3 : 20; 5 : 40; 6 : 37.
3. It is the duty of sinners, as subjects of the King of heaven, to obey. They have no right to be lost, vers. 2–4; ch. 25 : 26–28; Acts 17 : 30.
4. Indifference to the calls of God, and turning the attention from them to the affairs and pursuits of this life, is to make light of Christ and the Gospel, ver. 5; Prov. 1 : 22; Acts 24 : 25; Heb. 2 : 3.

5. The spirit of neglect and of trifling with the Gospel, if carried out positively, will result in open opposition and persecution, ver. 6; Rom. 10 : 21; 1 Thess. 2 : 15.

6. Rejecting the invitations of the Gospel is contempt toward God, the Son of God, his messengers, and the Gospel feast itself, and highly dishonoring to the rejecters themselves, vers. 3–6; Acts 13 : 41; Rom. 2 : 4.

7. The destruction of Jerusalem is a type of the fearful judgments which will come upon those who refuse to accept the Gospel, ver. 7; 1 Thess. 2 : 16; Prov. 1 : 24–31.

8. They who reject the Gospel prove themselves unworthy of everlasting life, ver. 8; ch. 10 : 13, 37, 38; Acts 13 : 46.

9. Many of the poor, needy, and little favored will be saved, while others, more highly favored, rich, and haughty, will be lost, vers. 9, 10; 1 Pet. 5 : 5, 6.

10. It is not enough to come outwardly to Christ; there must be repentance, faith, and holiness of life, ver. 11; Isa. 61 : 10; 2 Cor. 5 : 3; Phil. 3 : 9; Col. 3 : 10, 12; Rev. 16 : 15; 19 : 8.

11. God will at last try the characters of men, when the finally impenitent, whether nominal professors or open rejecters, will be without excuse, ver. 12, 13; Rom. 1 : 20; 3 : 19; 2 Thess. 1 : 8–10.

12. While those who are saved are indebted to the riches of electing grace, those who perish owe their destruction wholly to themselves, ver. 14; Luke 12 : 47; 1 Cor. 1 : 27–29; Gal. 6 : 8; 1 Pet. 1 : 2.

13. How great the opposition of the wicked to Christ, which will lead enemies to unite in conspiring against him, to play the hypocrite and act as his friends, to acknowledge the truth and his true character with evil intent, vers. 15, 16; Ps. 2 : 2; 12 : 2; 55 : 21.

14. Hypocrisy and deceit in religion will not escape the detection of Christ, nor his withering curse, ver. 18; Isa. 29 : 15, 16; Heb. 4 : 13.

15. Let us beware of partial views of truth and duty, failing neither to recognize our duties to government nor to God, ver. 16, 17; Dan. 6 : 3, 10.

16. The distinction made by Jesus between duties to God and to government shows that the two are in harmony, yet not to be mingled together. The church and state should be distinct yet harmonious, ver. 21; Rom. 13 : 7; 1 Pet. 2 : 13–17.

17. Civil government is an ordinance of God, and all of its lawful requirements ought to be obeyed. The best citizen will make the best Christian, ver. 21; Rom. 13 : 1–5; Acts 4 : 19; Dan. 4 : 27; 3 : 16–18.

18. Beware of imaginary difficulties in the doctrine of a future life, and of drawing certain conclusions in respect to it from analogies of the present life, vers. 23–28; 1 Cor. 15 : 39–41, 51–54; 1 John 3 : 2.

19. Thorough and experimental knowledge of Scripture, and just conceptions of the power of God, is a preventive of error in regard to the doctrines of revealed truth, ver. 29; Job 26 : 14; Ps. 62 : 11; John 5 : 39; Acts 17 : 11; 26 : 8; 1 Cor. 1 : 25; 2 Tim. 3 : 15.

20. Christ and the Scriptures clearly teach the existence of angels, ver. 30; ch. 13 : 41; 24 : 31, 36; Ps. 8 : 5; Heb. 2 : 7, 9.

21. We may reason analogically from the condition of angels in regard to our future state, ver. 30; Jud. 13 : 17–20; 2 Sam. 14 : 20; Ps. 103 : 20; Heb. 12 : 22; Rev. 12 : 7; 22 : 8, 9.

22. There is to be a resurrection of the body from the dead, ver. 31; John 5 : 28, 29; 1 Thess. 4 : 16, 17.

23. There is a conscious existence between death and the resurrection, vers. 31, 32; Job 19 : 26, 27, the Hebrew of which is clearly and correctly rendered by Dr. Conant, *Without my flesh I shall see God*, that is, separated from my body, in my disembodied state after death. Luke 16 : 22, 23; 23 : 43; 2 Cor. 5 : 8; Phil. 1 : 21–23.

24. The resurrection is so important in man's future existence, and essential to his glorified state, that the Scriptures associate it with his whole future life and immortality. "Without the body man has not his whole full life."—NAST. Vers. 31, 32; Luke 20 : 36; Rom. 8 : 11, 23; 2 Cor. 5 : 4; 2 Tim. 1 : 10.

25. In the establishment and defense of any doctrine, our first appeal should be to Scripture, vers. 31, 32; Isa. 8 : 20.

26. Seek not the mere letter of Scripture, but its deep spiritual meaning, ver. 32; John 16 : 13; 1 Cor. 2 : 10–16; 2 Cor. 3 : 6.

27. The essence of true religion is holy love, vers. 38–40; Rom. 5 : 5; 13 : 8, 10; 1 Cor. 13 : 1–3, 13; 1 John 4 : 21.

28. What think you concerning the Christ? of his nature, character, work?

The last public discourse of Jesus to the Jews; warnings and woes against the Scribes and Pharisees.

XXIII. THEN spake Jesus to the multitude, and
2 to his disciples, saying, 'The scribes and the Pharisees sit in Moses' seat: all therefore whatsoever they
3 bid you observe, *that* observe and do; but do not ye after their works: for " they say, and do not.

t Ne. 8. 4-8; Mal. 2. 7; Mk. 12. 38; Lk. 20. 45.
u Ro. 2. 19-24; 2 Tim. 3. 5; Tit. 1. 16.

What is he to thee? ver. 42; ch. 21: 42-44; 1 Cor. 1: 23, 24; Heb. 12: 2, 3.
29. Jesus recognized the Old Testament Scriptures as written by inspiration of God, vers. 31, 40, 43; Luke 24: 25-27.
30. The doctrine of Christ's humanity and divinity is taught in Scripture, and explains difficulties which would be otherwise insuperable, vers. 43-45; ch. 1: 23; John 1: 1, 14; Phil. 2: 6; 1 Tim. 2: 5; Heb. 2: 14-17.
31. Many wonder at the wisdom of Christ, and feel the force of his doctrines, without being savingly benefited, vers. 22, 23, 46; Acts 13: 41.

CHAPTER XXIII.

1-39. WARNINGS AGAINST THE EXAMPLE OF THE SCRIBES AND PHARISEES, AND WOES AGAINST THEM. This last public discourse of Jesus to the Jews is found only in this Gospel. A trace of it is, however, found in Mark 12: 38-40 and Luke 20: 45-47. Compare Luke 11: 42-52; 13: 34, 35, from which it will be seen that Jesus now utters more publicly, fully, and comprehensively what he had said on previous occasions. It is a final and closing summary of all his woes against the scribes and Pharisees. It is worthy of notice that the first recorded public discourse of Jesus begins with beatitudes, and his last ends with woes.

This discourse consists of three parts: *First*, A warning against imitating the example of the scribes and Pharisees, vers. 1-12. *Second*, Eight woes (*seven*, according to the oldest manuscripts and versions; see on verse 14) against them on account of their hypocrisy and wickedness, vers. 13-36. *Third*, A tender lamentation over the doomed city of Jerusalem, vers. 37-39.

1. **Then.** After he had completely baffled the scribes and Pharisees. Turning from them, he addressed **the multitude** and **his disciples.** Luke says, "In the audience of all the people, he said unto his disciples"—a good illustration of stating the same thing with great precision.

2. **The scribes and Pharisees.** The reference is not to individuals, but to classes; the *scribes* representing the class of men educated for the purpose of preserving and expounding the sacred books, and the *Pharisees*, the most numerous and influential sect among the Jews, the moralists and legalists of the age. See on ch. 2: 4, and 3: 7. **Sit in Moses' seat.** *Sat down*, or *seated themselves in Moses' seat.* It is implied that, having sat down, they continue to sit. They occupied that position, though they had no rightful claim to it. Moses occupied his *own seat* as lawgiver, expounder of the law, and judge. They who afterward sat in *his seat*, did so in the two last respects. For an account of Moses' seat, and of those who sat with him, see Exod. 18: 13, 24-26; Num. 11: 16; Deut. 16: 18; 17: 8-10. The Sanhedrim, made up largely of scribes and Pharisees, in their spirit expounded the law and acted as judges. The language of Jesus shows the great influence of the scribes and Pharisees among the Jews. They were the leaders in expounding and executing the law. In the synagogue, in the Sanhedrim, and other Jewish councils, theirs were the prevailing ideas. They thus occupied a relation to the Jews similar to that once held by Moses. *Sitting* was the usual posture in teaching and judging.

3. **All—bid you observe.** All they bid you out of the law of Moses, or by the authority of Moses, whose seat they occupy. That the meaning is thus limited, and does not include their traditions, is evident from the denunciations which follow, and from ch. 15: 3. **Therefore** is emphatic. Since they occupy Moses' seat, *therefore do and observe* all they bid you upon his authority. The contrast between their teaching and life is the prominent idea: **they say, and do not. Do not ye,** etc. Do not

4 ˣ For they bind heavy burdens and grievous to be borne, and lay *them* on men's shoulders; but they *themselves* will not move them with one of their fin-
5 gers. But ʸ all their works they do for to be seen of men. ᶻ They make broad their phylacteries, and
6 enlarge the borders of their garments, ᵃ and love

ˣ Lk. 11. 46; Ac. 15. 10; Gal. 6. 13.
ʸ ch. 6. 1, 2, 5, 16.
ᶻ Num. 15. 38; Deu. 6. 8; 22. 12; Pro. 3. 3.
ᵃ Mk 12. 38, 39; Lk. 11. 43; 14. 7

imitate their example, contradicting your precepts and professions by your life. What *their works* are, may be learned from verses 4–7. Their characteristics are described as four-fold: (1) They live contrary to the truths they preach, ver. 3. (2) They are severe toward others, but lax toward themselves, ver. 4. (3) Their ruling motive is to appear righteous before men, ver. 5. (4) Their ruling passion is the love of popular respect, veneration, and applause, vers. 6, 7. Jesus takes it for granted that their false interpretations of the law and their unscriptural traditions are of no binding force.

4. **For they bind,** as wood into a mass, or other things into bales. Jesus shows how they said, and did not. **Heavy burdens.** By their interpretations of the law, they placed oppressive rites and observances upon the people. They rigidly explained the letter rather than the spirit. They made the law thus both heavy, oppressive, and **grievous to be borne,** irksome, and intolerable. The language is especially applicable to their interpretations of the law. In addition, it may be applied to their traditional requirements, which were even more burdensome and intolerable. **They will not move them.** Much less will they *bear* them. **One of their fingers.** Much less will they take them with the hand, and place them upon *their own shoulders.* They make not the slightest attempt to give the law a true spiritual obedience, Acts 15:10; Rom. 2:17–23; Gal. 6:13.

5. Having pointed out the contradiction between their teaching and their practice, Jesus now tells what is their great ruling motive in all the works they perform, namely, **to be seen of man.**

Phylacteries, *keepers,* derived from a Greek word, signifying *to keep* safely. They are small boxes, generally an inch and a half square, made of parchment or leather, containing slips of parchment on which were written Exod. 13:2–10; 11–16; Deut. 6:4–9; 13–22, and bound with a long strap, one upon the left arm and the other upon the forehead, signifying that the law should be both in the heart and in the head. They were worn while at prayer, and probably began to be used after the exile, as a literal and mechanical observance of Exod. 13:9; Deut. 6:8. They were probably regarded at first as reminders and as aiders in keeping the law. Afterward they came to be regarded as charms and a defense against evil spirits. They are still in use among the Jews. The scribes and Pharisees made **broad,** enlarged their phylacteries, so as to be more conspicuous and visible at a greater distance, and thus to indicate more emphatically, and to a larger number, that they were engaged in prayer, or in holy meditation.

Enlarge the borders of their garments. Rather, *Enlarge the fringes* of their garments, ch. 9:20. The Jews were commanded to wear fringes of blue in the borders of their garments, Num. 15:38. These distinguished their dress, as circumcision their bodies, indicating to others and reminding them that they were God's people. They were especially intended to remind them of "all the commandments of the Lord," Num. 15:32–40, especially verse 39. Blue was a symbol of *faithfulness* to God's covenant. The scribes and Pharisees enlarged the fringes of their garments to indicate their greater piety and faithfulness to God.

6. **Uppermost rooms at feasts.** *Rooms* is here in the obsolete sense of *place, position,* the uppermost *places* at feasts. Literally, *the first reclining place at feasts,* the most honorable position, which was the middle place of the couch on which they reclined at table. Compare Luke 14:7–10. **Chief seats of the synagogues.** The first seats,

PHYLACTERY.

the uppermost rooms at feasts, and the chief seats
7 in the synagogues, and greetings in the markets,
8 and to be called of men, [b] Rabbi, Rabbi. [c] But be
not ye called Rabbi: for [d] one is your Master, *even*
9 Christ; and all ye are brethren. And [e] call no *man*
your father upon the earth: [f] for one is your Father,

−11; 20. 46; Ro.
12. 10; 3 John 9.
[b] John 1. 38.
[c] Jam. 3. 1; 2 Cor.
1. 24; 4. 5; 1
Pet. 5. 3.
[d] ch. 10. 25; John
13. 13, 14.

the foremost row, nearest the reading-desk and the ark where the sacred books were kept. See on ch. 4: 23. They loved positions of honor.

7. They also loved reverential salutations, titles of honor, and praise of men. **Greetings.** Deferential and complimentary salutations. **Market-places.** The chief places of public concourse. **Rabbi.** Literally, my master; a title of great respect given to a teacher. It is derived from a verb signifying *to become great, distinguished.* The title was employed in the Jewish schools under a three-fold form: *Rab*, the great, master, doctor; *Rabbi*, my master, a more honorable title; *Rabboni*, my great master, the most honorable of all. The title *Rabbi* was conferred with imposing ceremony, and the laying on of hands by the delegates of the Sanhedrim. A table book was presented to the recipient of the honor, a symbol of his diligence in study, and a key, which was afterward worn as a badge of honor, implying power and authority to teach others. It was not merely a literary but also an ecclesiastical honor. The teachings of the Rabbins were with authority, and most highly regarded; their words were as the words of God. The Pharisaic teachers loved to be publicly accosted with the salutations paid to men of eminent learning, and hailed with the title of Rabbi. They loved the honor and the authority in religious matters which such a title implied.

8. **But be not ye,** my disciples, **called Rabbi.** Be not like the Pharisees in this respect. Do not assume nor favor such a title. The reason is twofold: **One is your master,** *Teacher;* **all ye are brethren.** All ye are the children of God, and thus enjoy a fraternal equality; no one of you having an authority in religious matters over the rest. Peter's authority was only equal to that of his brethren, 1 Pet. 5: 1. **Christ** should be omitted here, according to the highest critical authorities. Jesus condemns the assumption of spiritual authority over the faith and practice of their fellow-disciples, as infringing on his rights as *the Teacher* of his followers, and on their rights as brethren. Any title which thus implies or assumes an authority which rightfully belongs to Christ, or which trespasses upon the fraternal relations of Christians, as brethren, is here forbidden. Hence *Doctor of Divinity* is opposed and rejected by some, as the Christian equivalent to the Jewish *Rabbi*. The former, however, is a literary honor, and does not imply any superior spiritual authority as a teacher, nor does it impress people generally with any such idea. Neither, as a mere literary honor, is there necessarily any infringement upon, or inconsistency with, the fraternal relation existing between Christian brethren. That it does sometimes engender pride, self-conceit, a sense of superiority, and envy, is, however, true, and thus our Savior's injunction is doubtless often transgressed, not so much by the title as by the spirit which covets and abuses the title. This prohibition is to be understood in spirit and not merely in the letter. It indeed prohibits Christians from wearing the honorary and ecclesiastical titles of the Jewish schools; Saul of Tarsus left these all behind when he embraced Christianity; and it equally prohibits all like ecclesiastical distinctions and titles among Christians which have been imposed by a worldly hierarchy, such as the perversion of the terms priest, bishop, and their application to the ministry, with that of archbishop, etc. But, that we must not be too fastidious about mere titles, appears from the next verse, where Jesus forbids the title of *father;* yet Paul speaks of himself as the father of the Corinthians (1 Cor. 4: 15); and applies to both Timothy and Titus the appellation of *son* (1 Tim. 1: 2; Tit. 1: 4); and Peter does the same to Mark, 1 Pet. 5: 13. The mere title is comparatively nothing, if the proud, ambitious, and authoritative spirit, which Jesus condemned, is wanting, being neither assumed nor implied.

9. **Your father upon the earth.** Call not, or name not, any your father

10 which is in heaven. Neither be ye called masters:
11 for one is your Master, *even* Christ. But ᵍ he that
12 is greatest among you shall be your servant. ʰ And whosoever shall exalt himself shall be abased; ⁱ and he that shall humble himself shall be exalted.
13 But ᵏ woe unto you, scribes and Pharisees, hypo-

ᵉ Job. 32. 21, 22.
ᶠ ch. 6. 8, 9; Mal. 1. 6; 1 John 3. 1.
ᵍ ch. 20. 26, 27; Mk. 9. 35.
ʰ Pro. 16. 18, 19; 29. 23.
ⁱ ch. 18. 4; Job 22.

on the earth. Compare 2 Kings 2 : 12; 6 : 21. *Father* was another title given to a teacher, implying that paternal wisdom and authority which should command childlike submission, confidence, and obedience. **One is your Father.** God only is your Father in this high and supreme sense. By the spirit of adoption, Christians can cry, Abba, Father, Rom. 8 : 15. To make any one a supreme authority in matters of religion is to rob God. This command is manifestly not broken by applying the term father to either our natural or spiritual parents; but it is broken wherever that reliance or submission is given to a fellow-man, whether with or without the title, which belongs to our Father in heaven. As striking examples of its transgression, both in letter and spirit, may be instanced the practical application of the term patriarch in the eastern churches, and especially that of pope (which signifies father) of the Romish Church. "The worst corruption is calling any man *father;* that is, to honor in any man an absolute spiritual authority." —LANGE. Notice that Jesus makes a contrast between *on the earth* and *in heaven.*
10. **Neither be called masters.** Rather, *Neither be ye called leaders.* The word translated *masters* means *leaders* or *guides.* It is found nowhere else in the New Testament, and implies more than rabbi. "The rabbi was the teacher in the synagogue. The leader was the head of a whole section, the guide who might be followed by many rabbins."—HEUBNER. Thus, the Corinthians were divided between Paul, Apollos, Cephas, and Christ, 1 Cor. 1 : 12. This command is broken by being lords over God's heritage (1 Pet. 5 : 3), by exercising authority over and controlling the ministry as a bishop, archbishop, or pope, by heading an erroneous party or a heretical sect. Notice that Jesus forbids calling any one *father,* or being called *leader.* **One is your master, even Christ.** Rather, *One is your leader, the Christ.*
Some suppose that the three persons of the Godhead are intended by the three titles, Teacher, Father, Leader; the first referring to the Holy Spirit, the second to the Father, the third to the Son. The interpretation seems to me somewhat fanciful. I should rather refer the first to Christ, as the Teacher and Lawgiver of his church.
11. Jesus points out the greatest in his kingdom. **But he that is greatest.** Literally, *But the greater among you,* which is about equivalent to the English expression, *greatest among you.* Jesus may here be contrasting true greatness not only with high Jewish positions, but also with high Jewish titles. *Rab* means *great,* ver. 7. But the greatest among Christ's followers are not to be those exercising outward authority and wearing titles, but those who shall be servants of their brethren through their abundant labors and sacrifices, ch. 18 : 4; 20 : 26. It is not enough to style one's self *a servant;* for the pope styles himself "servant of servants," yet violates the whole preceding command of Jesus.
12. Jesus states the principle by which exaltation or abasement is insured. **Exalt himself.** Like the scribes and Pharisees. **Shall be abased.** By the divine condemnation. **Shall humble himself.** Before God, and as a servant of his brethren. **Exalted.** By the divine favor, and the honor that comes from God. Somewhat similar to this is Ezek. 21 : 26, "Exalt him that is low, and abase him that is high;" and the rabbinical sentiment, "My abasement is my exaltation, and my exaltation my abasement." The maxim which Jesus announced on this and several other occasions (Luke 14 : 11; 18 : 14) is, however, superior to all similar ones, as a universal principle of God's government, and as embracing man's agency in his exaltation or abasement: "Shall exalt *himself;* shall humble *himself,*" Prov. 16 : 18.
13. We now come to the SECOND PORTION of this discourse (13 : 36), where Jesus turns for the last time, to the

crites! for ye shut up the kingdom of heaven against men: for ye neither go in *yourselves*, ¹ neither suffer 14 ye them that are entering to go in. Woe unto you, scribes and Pharisees, hypocrites! ᵐ for ye devour widows' houses, and for a pretense make long prayer. Therefore ye shall receive the greater 15 damnation. Woe unto you, scribes and Pharisees, hypocrites! for ye compass sea and land to make

29; Ps. 138. 6; Pro. 15. 33; Lk. 18. 14.
ᵏ Lk. 11. 52; John 7. 46-52; Ac. 4. 17, 18; 5. 28. 40.
ˡ 1 Thes. 2. 15, 16.
ᵐ Mk. 12. 40; Lk. 20. 47; see also 2 Tim. 3. 6; Tit. 1. 11.

---

scribes and Pharisees, and utters against them his most terrible woes, "summing up," as Alexander remarks, "at the close of his prophetic ministry, all that he had said against them during its previous course." It will prove a profitable exercise to contrast these woes with the beatitudes in ch. 5 : 3-11.

Woe. Here an exclamation of righteous indignation, implying impending calamities and most terrible judgments upon the guilty. The scribes and Pharisees are held up in their true character, as **hypocrites,** religious dissemblers, assuming a character for piety and virtue that did not belong to them. The several woes reveal the following characteristics of these hypocrites: (1) They shut up the kingdom of heaven against others, ver. 13. (2) They made religion a cloak for the grossest iniquity, ver. 14. (3) They showed a party proselyting zeal, resulting not in the good but ruin of their converts, ver. 15. (4) They misguided the people in regard to practical duties and doctrines, shutting out God from their view, vers. 16-22. (5) They sacrificed the essentials of the law to the minutest ceremonial observances, vers. 23, 24. (6) They attended only to an external and apparent righteousness, and neglected the inward cleansing of the heart, vers. 25, 26. (7) They affected great piety before men, while they knew the deceit, falsehood, and secret wickedness within, vers. 27, 28. (8) They professed great veneration for the martyred and pious dead, while in principle and practice they followed their murderers, vers. 29-32.

For ye shut up the kingdom of heaven. *Because ye shut,* etc. The kingdom of the Messiah is here represented as a palace or temple; they shut its doors in the face of the people—before them, in their presence. They shut the kingdom, first, by their example, which was weighty, in the sight of the people: **For ye neither go in;** second, by their opposition to Jesus, their false interpretations of the law, and false doctrines: **Neither suffer,** etc., ch. 12 : 24; John 9 : 34. Compare Luke 11 : 52.

14. According to some Greek manuscripts, this is the first woe, and should be verse 13—verse 13 being changed to verse 14. But the oldest manuscripts and versions omit this verse altogether, and hence it is supposed by the best scholars to have been inserted by some transcriber from Mark 12 : 40 and Luke 20 : 47.

Devour widows' houses. *Because ye devour,* etc. Like cunning yet ferocious beasts, they devoured the substance of widows, who were the most defenceless of the poor, and the most deserving of sympathy and kindness. *Houses* is here used for *possessions, property.* They influenced widows to give them of their property, as an act of piety, or to bequeath it to them. As spiritual advisers, and sometimes as the executor of their wills and the guardian of their children, they could rob widows of their property. Pious women were accustomed to contribute to the support of religious teachers, Luke 8 : 2, 3. **For a pretense, make long prayers.** For a show, praying long. As a pretext. They made religion a mask in order to gain the confidence and the property of even the most helpless. Some of the rabbins would pray nine hours a day. **Greater damnation.** A more abundant condemnation, implying a most terrible punishment as a consequence. For the double sin of hypocrisy and fraudulent injustice, they should meet a terrible doom.

15. **Ye compass sea and land.** Ye make the most strenuous, and all sorts of efforts. A proverbial expression similar to our "leaving no stone unturned." The proselyting zeal of the Jews was notorious in that age. **Proselyte.** A convert from heathenism to

one ⁿ proselyte; and when he is made, ye make him twofold more the child of hell than yourselves.

16 Woe unto you, ᵒ *ye* blind guides, which say, ᵖ Whosoever shall swear by the temple, it is nothing; but whosoever shall swear by the gold of the temple,
17 ᵠ he is a debtor! *Ye* fools and blind; for whether is greater, the gold, ʳ or the temple that sanctifieth the gold?
18 And, Whosoever shall swear by the altar, it is nothing; but whosoever sweareth by the gift that is upon it, he is guilty [*or*, bound].
19 *Ye* fools and blind: for whether *is* greater, the gift, or ˢ the
20 altar that sanctifieth the gift? Whoso therefore shall swear by the altar, sweareth by it, and by all
21 things thereon. And whoso shall swear by the temple, sweareth by it, and by ᵗ him that dwelleth
22 therein. And he that shall swear by heaven, sweareth by ᵘ the throne of God, and by him that sitteth thereon.

ⁿ Ac. 2. 10; 6. 5; 13. 43.
ᵒ ch. 15. 14: Is. 56. 10, 11; John 9. 39-41.
ᵖ ch. 5. 33, 34; Jam. 5. 12.
ᵠ Ezk. 33. 31; 2 Pet. 2. 3.
ʳ Ex. 30. 29.

ˢ Ex. 29. 37.

ᵗ 1 Ki. 8. 13; 2 Chr. 6. 2; Ps. 26. 8; 132. 14.

ᵘ ch. 5. 34; Ps. 11. 4; Ac. 7. 49.

Judaism. A Gentile, who, submitting to the whole Mosaic law, was incorporated into Israel. The later rabbins have distinguished between *proselytes of righteousness*, those who had submitted to circumcision and to the whole law, and thus become full Israelites, and *proselytes of the gate*, those who had so far renounced heathenism as to worship the one true God, and practice morality. But in the days of our Savior, and still later, no male could become a proselyte without submitting to circumcision. A freewill sacrifice was offered. After the destruction of the temple, and probably as early as the second or third century, the baptism of proselytes was practiced as one of the initiatory rites.
Two-fold more the child of hell. Two-fold more belonging to hell as their proper place or portion. Twice as wicked. They were made proselytes not so much to Judaism as to Pharisaism. They were not converted from heathen vices and depravity, but, in addition to these, were taught Pharisaic wickedness and hypocrisy.
16. **Blind guides.** As is shown by their misguiding the people in reference to oaths. They made distinctions in these between those that were binding and those which might be violated, keeping in view their own selfish ends. **It is nothing.** It is no oath in reality, only in appearance; it is not binding. **The gold of the temple.** Some refer this to the golden ornaments and utensils of the temple; it is better to refer it, with others, to the golden treasure of the temple. It was for their own interests to raise the temple treasure into an uncommon sacredness and prominence. **He is a debtor;** to fulfill his oath; he is bound by it.
17. **Fools and blind.** Stupid and wanting discernment. **For whether is greater,** etc. The gold of the temple would have no sacredness above any other gold were it not for its relation to the temple; hence the absurdity of raising it in its sacredness above the temple.
18. **The gift.** The sacrifices and oblations on the altar. **He is guilty.** In the original the same as in verse 16, and should be translated, *He is a debtor*, or, *He is bound*.
19. The same reasoning as in verse 17. **Sanctifieth the gift.** Gives it its sacredness.
20-22. Jesus shows that an oath by the altar involved all things thereon; and one by the temple, all things therein, and him who dwelt therein. The simple assertion of the truth in regard to oaths here and in ch. 5 : 34-36, was enough to show how futile were all the Pharisaical distinctions in regard to them. Every oath has reference to God, since an oath in its essence, nature, and significance, is a declaration as before God, an appeal to him to witness what is asserted. An oath by the altar, the temple, or heaven, was really an oath by

A.D. 30. MATTHEW XXIII. 319

23 Woe unto you, scribes and Pharisees, hypocrites!
ˣ for ye pay tithe of mint and anise and cummin,
and ʸ have omitted the weightier *matters* of the law,
judgment, mercy, and faith: these ought ye to have
24 done, and not to leave the other undone. *Ye* blind
guides, ᶻ which strain at a gnat, and swallow a
25 camel. Woe unto you, scribes and Pharisees, hypocrites! ᵃ for ye make clean the outside of the cup
and of the platter, but within they are full of extortion and excess. *Thou* blind Pharisee, ᵇ cleanse
26 first that *which is* within the cup and platter, that

ˣ Lk. 11. 42.

ʸ ch. 9. 13: 12. 7;
1 Sam. 15. 22;
Hos. 6. 6; Mic.
6. 8.

ᶻ John 18. 28, 40.

ᵃ Mk. 7. 4; Lk. 11.
39.

ᵇ Is. 55. 7; Jer. 4.
14; 13. 27; Eze.
18. 31; Heb. 10.
22.

God himself, to whom these stood sacredly related. See on ch. 5 ᵗ 34–36.
23. Ye pay tithe. Ye pay a tenth part to the priests and Levites for the service of God. "Of the yearly products of the land, the first fruits were first deducted; out of the rest, the tenth part was taken for the Levites, Num. 18 : 21; of the nine remaining parts, another tenth part is to be taken and brought to Jerusalem, and there eaten by the owners, Deut. 12 : 6; though this second tithe was every third year distributed to the poor, Deut. 14 : 28."—PROF. BUSH on Lev. 27 : 30. The Mosaic law did not define strictly what things were subject to the tithe, but extended it generally to vegetables and animals, Lev. 27 : 30–32. The Jewish canons applied the law to every thing that was eatable in the field, embracing the smallest garden-herbs and aromatic plants. Hence, tithe was paid of the **mint,** garden or spear-mint; the **anise,** the fragrant plant called by us *dill,* and resembling caraway; and the **cummin,** a fragrant plant something like fennel, Isa. 28 : 25,27.
The weightier matters. The weightier, the more important things of the law, three of which he notices. **Judgment.** The distinguishing between right and wrong; the determining according to the principles of right and law, Luke 12 : 57. **Mercy.** Kindness, compassion to the needy. See on ch. 9 : 13. **Faith;** not merely in its active exercise outwardly, but in its internal existence in the soul, and in the state of the heart. *Trust* manifested in *faithfulness,* or *fidelity* to God, and the piety he requires. Compare Mic. 6 : 8; Hos. 12 : 6. **These ought ye to have done.** These great moral requirements ought to have been observed; the internal and spiritual observance of the law ought to have been specially regarded.

And at the same time the smaller matters of the law should not be neglected. Jesus censured the Pharisees not for strictly keeping the latter, but for connecting with this a neglect of the former, which in themselves were the more important. This is pithily put in the proverbial language of the following verse.
24. Strain at. *Strain out.* At was probably a typographical error for *out,* in the first edition of our common version. The **gnat** and **camel** are put for the smallest and largest animals, and both unclean, Lev. 11 : 4, 21–24, 41, 42. The Jews strained their wine carefully, so as to avoid drinking any unclean insect. But while they *strained out the gnat,* in their close attention to the ceremonies and the letter of the law, they *swallowed the camel,* one of the largest of animals, and unclean also, in overlooking the weightier matters, and neglecting to observe the spirit of the law. The language is hyperbolical and proverbial, but strongly expressive of their hypocritical strictness in external matters, and their wicked unfaithfulness in things spiritual. In this we have also an additional illustration of their misguiding the people, and hence Jesus appropriately repeated the appellation, **Blind guides.**
25. Ye make clean the outside. They cleanse the outside of the cup and platter, the drink and the food within are unclean and most impure. You attend to mere outside righteousness, while your cups and platters are full of **extortion,** *rapacity,* robbery, unrighteous gain, and of **excess,** incontinence, inabstinence. The cup and platter, which they were so careful to cleanse, were full of the fruits of their own secret dishonesty and vicious indulgence.
26. Blind Pharisee. Willfully

27 the outside of them may be clean also. Woe unto you, scribes and Pharisees, hypocrites! ᵉ for ye are like unto whited sepulchres, which indeed appear beautiful outward, ᵈ but are within full of dead
28 *men's* bones, and of all uncleanness. Even so ᵉ ye also outwardly appear righteous unto men, but within ye are full of hypocrisy and iniquity.
29 ᶠ Woe unto you, scribes and Pharisees, hypocrites! Because ye build the tombs of the prophets, and
30 garnish the sepulchres of the righteous; and say, If we had been in the days of our fathers, we would not have been partakers with them in ᵍ the blood
31 of the prophets. Wherefore ye be witnesses unto yourselves, that ʰ ye are the children of them which
32 killed the prophets. ⁱ Fill ye up then the measure

ᶜ Is. 58. 1, 2; Lk. 11. 44; Ac. 23. 3.
ᵈ Ps. 5. 9.

ᵉ 1 Sam. 16. 7; Jer. 17. 9. 10.

ᶠ Lk. 11. 47, 48.

ᵍ 2 Chr. 36. 15, 16; Jer. 2. 30.
ʰ Ac. 7. 51. 52: 1 Thes. 2. 15.
ⁱ Ge. 15. 16; Dan. 8. 23; 1 Thes. 2. 16.

blind. **Cleanse first that within.** The cleansing of the inside is of the first importance, for only thus may the outside become clean. It is necessary to attend to internal purification in order to insure external. The latter is nothing without the former.

27, 28. **Ye are like unto whited sepulchres.** The Jews whitewashed their graves once a year, on the fifteenth of Adar (the last month of the year), so that persons might not pass over them and be rendered unclean. A person who touched a grave was unclean seven days. Num. 19 ; 16. The custom of whitewashing sepulchres still continues in Palestine. "I have been in places where this is repeated very often. The graves are kept clean and white as snow, a very striking emblem of those painted hypocrites, the Pharisees, beautiful without, but full of dead men's bones and all uncleanness within."—DR. THOMSON. The Pharisees were really sepulchres of loathsome impurity; their religion was but whitewash.

29. **Tombs—sepulchres.** Rather, *Sepulchres—tombs.* Both words, in the original, are used in the New Testament for burial-houses or places, which, among the Jews, were natural or artificial chambers in the rock or earth. The former expresses the more general idea of burial-house or sepulchre; the latter, originally meaning *memorial*, then *monument*, and then a *burial-house*, often carries along with the last meaning the idea of a monument, a memorial, as in this passage, **garnish**, or *adorn the tombs*, the monumental burial-houses of the righteous. Jesus does not condemn the mere fact that the Pharisees built the sepulchres and adorned the tombs of the martyrs of preceding ages. By thus doing they recognized and bore testimony to the goodness and fidelity of righteous men of old. All this would have been well had they not been base hypocrites, and manifesting a tendency to creature worship directly opposed in doctrine and practice to those old prophets, and in sympathy with their murderers.

30. **And say.** By building and adorning the sepulchres; by their extolling the eminent piety of the prophets, and by confidently affirming that they were better than their fathers, and that they would not have been partakers in their crimes. They thus condemned their fathers for the murder of the prophets, which, in their own case, amounted to a self-condemnation.

31. **Ye be witnesses to yourselves that ye are the children,** etc. By your words you are witnesses to yourselves that you are the sons of persecutors and murderers. And by not following the teachings of the prophets, and by rejecting the Messiah whom they foretold, and in resembling your fathers in disposition and life, you give evidence to yourselves that you are their sons or descendants *spiritually* as well as naturally. Or, ye bear witness to yourselves that you are the sons of a wicked and degenerate ancestry, and nothing that they did will be too bad for you to do.

32. **Fill ye up their.** Jesus gives them over to their wicked course, bidding them do what he foresaw they would fully accomplish. **Measure of** iniquity, persecution, etc. As you are

33 of your fathers. *Ye* serpents, *ye* [k] generation of vipers, [l] how can ye escape the damnation of hell? 34 [m] Wherefore, behold, I send unto you [n] prophets, and wise men, and [o] scribes: and [p] *some* of them ye shall kill and crucify; and [q] *some* of them shall ye scourge in your synagogues, and persecute *them* 35 from city to city: [r] that upon you may come all the righteous blood shed upon the earth, [s] from the blood of righteous Abel unto [t] the blood of Zacha-

[k] ch. 3. 7.
[l] Heb. 2. 3; 10. 29; 12. 25.
[m] ch. 10. 16; 28. 19, 20; Lk. 11. 49; Ac. 1. 8.
[n] Ac. 11. 27; 13. 1.
[o] ch. 13. 52.
[p] Ac. 5. 40; 7. 58, 59; 12. 2; 14. 19.
[q] ch. 10. 17, 18; Ac. 22. 19; 2 Cor. 11. 24, 25.

---

the descendants of such a wicked ancestry, and you knowingly and willfully partake of their spirit and works, though hypocritically professing the opposite, go on as you will, and fill up the measure of iniquity, crucifying the Messiah, and persecuting and killing his followers, Acts 7 : 51-53. They filled up their measure of punishment also, vers. 34-38; 1 Thess. 2 : 14-16.

33. Being the descendants of such an ancestry, and so like them, Jesus addresses them accordingly. **Serpents.** Representing their cunning and depraved character, their hurtful and poisonous influence. **Generation of vipers.** *Offspring, brood of vipers.* They were the brood of viperous parentage, and all of the old serpent, the devil, Gen. 3 : 1; John 8 : 44; Rev. 12 : 9. John had also discovered their true character, and had thus addressed them. See on ch. 3 : 7. **How can ye escape?** A question equal to a strong affirmation, that it was impossible for them to escape. **Damnation.** *Condemnation, judgment,* including both the condemnation and the execution of the sentence.

34. Having pronounced upon them these terrible words, and declared the certainty of their eternal ruin, Jesus proceeds to tell how they would fill up the measure of their fathers by committing their deeds, and even forming a climax of all preceding generations in respect to their sins, guilt, and punishment.

Wherefore. Since such is your character, and you imitate your father's. You shall have opportunity to show your malignant wickedness. **I send unto you.** I send them as messengers of salvation; but in the end they will prove swift witnesses of destruction against you on account of your treatment of them. Notice that on a former occasion, *the wisdom of God* is represented as thus speaking, Luke 11 : 49. Jesus was himself, indeed, the wisdom of God, the sender of prophets, and the great Prophet of prophets. This is not really a quotation. There may be a general allusion to 2 Chron. 24 : 18-22. **Prophets.** The apostles, ch. 10 : 5, 6; the seventy, Luke 10 : 1; and other preachers of the Gospel. See on ch. 10 : 41. **Wise men.** Men deeply versed in divine things, such as Stephen, Acts 6 : 5, 10. **Scribes.** Those who are true scribes of the law and of the kingdom, ch. 13 : 52. These three united in the Apostle Paul. **Some of them ye shall kill,** etc. You shall inflict upon them all manner of indignities, even unto the most cruel death. **Crucify** doubtless refers to his own death, as well as to some of his disciples, who doubtless suffered crucifixion before the destruction of Jerusalem. The Acts of the Apostles is a general witness to the sufferings of Christians at the hands of the Jews, Acts 5 : 40; 7 : 59; 8 : 3; 12 : 2; 13 : 50; 14 : 19, etc.

35. **That upon you.** The idea is not merely that this is to be *the consequence,* but that it enters into the divine *design. That* is equivalent to *in order that.* It was the design of God that this generation should be, as it were, the focus of the world's wickedness and punishment. **The righteous blood.** The blood of innocent and righteous persons, Lam. 4 : 13. The punishment for shedding it. Compare ch. 27 : 25. **Abel—Zacharias.** Abel was the first righteous martyr, and the first recorded in the Bible, and Zachariah, the son of Jehoiada, is the last one recorded, according to the Jewish arrangement of the Old Testament, 2 Chron. 24 : 20-22.

Son of Barachias. It has been a matter of great dispute who this Zacharias was, since the one to whom the language seems to refer is called "son of Jehoiada the priest," 2 Chron. 24 : 20. Chrysostom speaks of an ancient opinion which held that it was the prophet Ze-

rias son of Barachias, whom ye slew between the
36 temple and the altar. Verily I say unto you, " All
these things shall come upon this generation.
37 ˣ O Jerusalem, Jerusalem, ʸ *thou* that killest the
prophets, ᶻ and stonest them which are sent unto
thee, ᵃ how often would I have gathered thy children together, ᵇ even as a hen gathereth her chick-
38 ens ᶜ under *her* wings; ᵈ and ye would not! Behold,
39 ᵉ your house is left unto you desolate. For I say
unto you, ᶠ Ye shall not see me henceforth, till ye
shall say, ᵍ Blessed *is* he that cometh in the name of
the Lord.

ʳ Rev. 18. 24.
ˢ Ge. 4. 8; 1 John 3. 12.
ᵗ 2 Chr. 24. 20, 21.
ᵘ ch. 24. 34.
ˣ Jer. 6. 8; Lk. 13. 31, 35.
ʸ ver. 30.
ᶻ 2 Chr. 24. 21.
ᵃ Jer. 6. 16, 17; 11. 7, 8; Zec. 1, 4.
ᵇ Deu. 32. 11, 12.
ᶜ Ps. 17. 8; 91. 4.
ᵈ Pro. 1. 24–31; Is. 1. 2.
ᵉ 2 Chr. 7. 20, 21; Jer. 22. 5.

chariah, the son of Berachiah. Origen and others refer it to Zacharias, the father of John the Baptist, who, according to a mere legend, was slain in the temple. Others suppose that the Zachariah, the son of Baruch, is meant, who, according to Josephus (*Jewish War*, b. iv. 5, 4), was slain in the temple just'before the destruction of Jerusalem. Others suppose that "son of Barachias" was inserted by some transcriber who mistook this Zachariah for the prophet Zechariah, Zech. 1 : 1. It is better, however, to explain, either by supposing that Zachariah was the son of Barachiah and grandson of Jehoiada, the former, perhaps, dying before the latter; or that Jehoiada, according to a not uncommon custom among the Jews, had two names, just as Azariah was called also Uzziah, 2 Kings 15 : 1; 2 Chron. 26 : 1. **Between the temple and the altar.** In the court of the priests, between the temple proper, the sanctuary, and the altar of burnt-offering. See on ch. 21 : 12.

36. **This generation.** About forty years from this time Jerusalem was destroyed. It was, therefore, within the lifetime of many then living.

37. Jesus now turns from the utterance of terrible woes to a TENDER LAMENTATION over the doomed city of Jerusalem, the representative of the Jewish race and theocracy. **Jerusalem,** the personification of the Jewish race in its then present and past history. **Killest the prophets.** Their sins, which call forth both lamentation and vengeance. The present tense is used in vivid discourse. At a single glance Jesus saw their whole history, in which the persecution of prophets was common, and often repeated. As a race, they were the murderers of the prophets, and the stoners of the messengers of God. **How often would I.** As a hen gathers her brood under her wings in maternal love, and *for* safety *and* protection against birds of prey, or any thing that may injure them. Hens are now very common in Palestine. **Children.** The inhabitants; the Jewish people. **Ye would not.** Their sins were voluntary. They were free moral agents. Freedom of the will is in harmony with God's sovereignty and divine decrees.

38. **Your house.** Your temple, left by the Messiah, forsaken by God, no longer his house, but *yours*. Its destruction and desolation is vividly spoken of as present. Jesus was about leaving it. Compare ch. 21 : 13; 2 Chron. 6 : 2; Ps. 26 : 8. Some suppose, by *your house*, that reference is made to the city, their dwelling-place, Ps. 69 : 25.

39. **Ye shall not see me henceforth.** He now closed his public ministry among them. They saw him no more in his Messianic ministration and work. After his resurrection he appeared, not to all the people, but to chosen witnesses, Acts 10 : 41. **Blessed is he.** Acknowledging him to be the Messiah, as the multitude had done in his triumphal entry into Jerusalem, ch. 21 : 9. Ye shall not enjoy my presence among you again till ye are ready to receive me and acknowledge that I am the Messiah. Jesus knew that generation would not do it, and hence the opening language of this verse: **For I say unto you.** He was the only salvation of the people, the only safety of the city and temple. His leaving them was their certain and utter destruction. But while his language implied the destruction of the city and temple, and the scattering of

the Jews, it pointed forward over a long period to the general conversion of the Jewish people in the last days, when their descendants should acknowledge him. Hos. 3 : 5; Zech. 12 : 10; Rom. 11 : 25–28.

At this point Mark (12 : 41–44) and Luke (21 : 1–4) relate the incident of the widow's mite. Here, also, many insert the request of the Greek proselytes, John 12 : 20–36, though it is better to put it after his triumphal entry on Sunday. See AUTHOR'S HARMONY, p. 271, § 140.

REMARKS.

1. We are to respect the office of a religious teacher, and follow his instruction so far as it is in accordance with truth, vers. 2, 3; Mal. 2 : 7; Acts 23 : 4, 5.

2. We must not follow the man instead of the truth he teaches; neither must we reject the truth because of the unworthiness of the one who utters it, ver. 3; 1 Cor. 11 : 1; Gal. 1 : 8–10.

3. Ministers and all religious teachers should beware lest their works contradict their teachings, ver. 3; ch. 21 : 30; Rom. 2 : 21; Tit. 1 : 16.

4. The true character of men is to be learned from their conduct rather than from their words merely, ver. 3; ch. 7 : 15–21.

5. Legalists and false teachers impose upon men heavy burdens, and grievous to be borne; but, in contrast, the yoke of Christ is easy and his burden is light, ver. 4; ch. 11 : 28–30; Acts 15 : 10, 28, 29; Gal. 5 : 1.

6. A religion that seeks a mere outward appearance, and has for its motive the applause of men, is not only destitute of the power of godliness, but an enemy to it and its graces, ver. 5–7; ch. 6 : 1, 5, 16; 2 Tim. 3 : 2–5; 2 Pet. 2 : 3; 3 John 9.

7. A love of human honors and flattering titles is unbecoming a follower of Jesus, vers. 8–11; Phil. 2 : 5; 1 Pet. 5 : 5; 1 John 2 : 15.

8. We must beware of usurping Christ's position in the church, or assuming an authority that does not belong to us, ver. 8–10; 2 Cor. 1 : 24; James 3 : 1; 1 Pet. 5 : 3.

9. We should seek for greatness, honor, glory, and immortality, but only in the spirit and through the service of humility, ver. 11, 12; Rom. 2 : 7; 1 Cor. 14 : 12; 1 Pet. 5 : 5, 6.

10. We should expose the errors and hypocrisy of false teachers, especially if they are persons of great influence, with boldness mingled with humility, and by the word of God, without assuming the authority of him who knew what was in man, and who is himself the Judge of men, vers. 13–33; Isa. 8 : 20; Gal. 1 : 8, 9; 1 John 4 : 1; 2 Pet. 2 : 1–3; 2 John 10.

11. Teachers of a worldly and formal Christianity stay away from Christ themselves, and by their outward observances, and often by their opposition to evangelical religion, keep others from coming, ver. 13; Luke 11 : 52; John 9 : 22; Rom. 10 : 2–4.

12. They who defraud others, and cover over their characters by a show of religion, evince a desperate depravity, and expose themselves to a most desperate punishment, ver. 14; Isa. 10 : 1, 2; Mic. 3 : 1–3.

13. While we should seek to win souls to Christ, and to the whole truth, we should beware of that proselyting zeal which is wholly absorbed in and seeks the interests of a mere party, ver. 15; 1 Cor. 1 : 12, 13; James 5 : 20.

14. We should beware how we in any way attempt to lessen obligation, or to nullify a promise, for in so doing we shall be guilty of double sin, vers. 16–22; Ps. 15 : 2–5.

15. Since even the mildest oath has reference to God, we should use great simplicity of language. A simple promise should have to us the sacredness of an oath, vers. 20–22; ch. 5 : 34–37.

16. Careful attention to outward observances with neglect of internal duty is an evidence that men are deceivers or deceived, vers. 23, 24; ch. 5 : 7; 9 : 13; Hos. 4 : 1; Rom. 16 : 18; 2 Cor. 11 : 13–15.

17. No external performances can stand in the place of moral and spiritual service, vers. 23, 24; Luke 18 : 11–14.

18. "Let us seek to be pure in heart, if we would be vessels sanctified and made meet for the Master's use," vers. 25, 26; ch. 5 : 8; Heb. 12 : 14; James 4 : 8.

19. "The heart may be a temple of God or a grave; a heaven or a hell."— STIER. Vers. 27, 28; ch. 12 : 35; Eccle. 9 : 3; Jer. 17 : 9; Rom. 3 : 12–16; 1 Cor. 3 : 16.

20. They who are satisfied to *appear* what they *should* be, are *inwardly* what they *should* not be, vers. 25–28; ch. 6 : 1; 7 : 21; 25 : 5–12.

21. How valuable must religion be which men are at so much trouble to counterfeit, vers. 13–29; 1 Tim. 4 : 8.

Christ foretells the destruction of Jerusalem and his second coming.

XXIV. AND ^h Jesus went out, and departed from the temple : and his disciples came to *him* for to

^f Hos. 3. 4, 5.
^g Ps. 118. 26; Zec. 12. 10; Ro. 11. 25, 26; 2 Cor. 3. 14-18.
^h Mk. 13. 1; Lk. 21. 5.

22. The glorification of martyrs may be carried so far as to amount to creature-worship, manifesting principles and a spirit directly opposed to that of the martyrs themselves, ver. 29-32; John 8 : 39, 40.

23. The most fearful denunciations of divine wrath is consistent with the tenderest compassion, vers. 34-38; Luke 19 : 41-44.

24. While we may rejoice in our great religious privileges, let us see to it that they prove blessings indeed to our souls, and not means for filling up our measure of iniquity, vers. 34-36; 2 Chron. 36 : 16; Acts 7 : 51; 1 Thess. 2 : 16.

25. Men often suffer the temporal consequences of the sins of their fathers; but are only punished for their own sins, vers. 34-36; Exod. 20 : 5; Prov. 9 : 12; Ezek. 18 : 20.

26. Nations are punished in this world. A race or nation may be treasuring up wrath for ages, and may make the guilt of the past their own through their personal sins in transgressing the concentrated light of the past and present, and may thus justly receive the accumulated judgment which God visits upon them, vers. 35, 36; 2 Kings 17 : 13-18.

27. If men perish, it is because they will not come to Christ and be saved, ver. 37; Ps. 81 : 11, 12; John 5 : 40.

28. God often mingles promises of mercy with announcements of judgments, ver. 39; Isa. 30 : 12-20; Jer. 30 : 3, 4; and many similar examples in the prophets.

CHAPTER XXIV.

Jesus, having closed his ministry to the people, continues it with his disciples. In this and the following chapter we have a remarkable prophetical discourse, which has been variously explained and justly considered one of the most important and difficult in the New Testament. However interpreted, every unprejudiced reader must admit that four important events are distinctly foretold : The destruction of the temple and Jerusalem by the Romans; the second coming of Christ; the end of the world, or the present dispensation; and the final judgment. The great point of difficulty is to understand the relation of the several portions of this prophecy to these topics, and their relation to one another. Some hold that they are successively presented, and that the transitions from one to another can all be clearly marked. They are not, however, agreed as to where the transitions are. Others suppose a blending of topics, in which the destruction of Jerusalem is made typical of the end of the world, and that this, like many of the prophecies of the Old Testament, has successive fulfillments. See on ch. 1 : 22, 23. These points will be more particularly considered in the notes that follow. In order to get a view of the whole discourse, I suggest the following synopsis :

I. The Occasion of the Inquiry and Discourse. Jesus leaves the temple and foretells its destruction, ch. 24 : 1, 2.

II. The Inquiry. Threefold.
1. When will these things be? 2. What is the sign of thy coming ; and (3) of the end of the world? Ver. 3.

III. The Reply, ver. 4 to ch. 25 : 46.
1. Caution against expecting his coming before the Gospel is preached in all the world, vers. 4-14. This includes cautions:
   a. Against being deceived by false Christs, vers. 4, 5.
   b. Against being troubled about wars and calamities, which are only the *beginning* of sorrows, and not the end, vers 6-8.
   c. Against being offended in persecution, vers. 9, 10.
   d. Against being led astray by false prophets, vers. 11, 12.
   e. Against not enduring to the end, ver. 13.

2. The destruction of Jerusalem, with directions as to what they should then do, and a caution against expecting him then, vers. 15-25.
   a. The abomination of desolation betokening the destruction of Jerusalem and the temple, ver. 15.
   b. The disciples are instructed to make a precipitate flight, vers. 16-18.
   c. The unparalleled judgments of that time, vers. 19, 21.

2 show him the buildings of the temple. And Jesus said unto them, See ye not all these things? verily I say unto you, ¹ There shall not be left here one stone upon another, that shall not be thrown down.
3 And as he sat upon the mount of Olives, ᵏ the

¹ 1 Ki. 9. 7, 8; Jer. 26. 18; Mic. 3. 12; Lk. 19. 44.
ᵏ Mk. 13. 3.

d. Those days shortened for the sake of believers, ver. 22.
e. Caution against the Christs of the day, for they will be but pretenders, vers. 23–25.
3. Caution against expecting him to come as he was then, in his humiliation, in his retiring and unassuming manner, or as an earthly prince, since his coming would be conspicuous as the lightning of heaven, vers. 26–28.
4. The *signs* and the *time* of his coming, vers. 29–31.
a. Terrific phenomena and changes in nature immediately after the Jewish people have endured their full measure of suffering, ver. 29.
b. The sign and appearance of the Son of Man on the clouds of heaven, ver. 30.
5. The attendant circumstances of his coming, vers. 31. The angels sounding the trumpet and gathering together God's elect.
6. Returning somewhat in his discourse, he teaches them, by a reference to the fig-tree, to judge of the time which, in a certain sense, would be in that generation, and more certain than the established order of nature, vers. 32–35.
7. But the time of his coming is known neither to men nor angels, but only to the Father. It would be sudden and unexpected, vers. 36–41.
8. Watchfulness enforced, ver. 42 ff.
a. By a case of burglary, vers. 42–44.
b. By a household servant, ver. 45–51.
c. By the ten virgins, ch. 25 : 1–13.
d. By the talents, ch. 25 : 14–30.
9. The coming judgment, 25 : 31–46.
1. **Jesus went out,** etc., rather, according to the best text, *Jesus went out from the temple* (Mark 12 : 41), *and was going on his way,* toward the mount of Olives and Bethany.
1. **His disciples.** The twelve. From Mark (13 : 1) we learn that one of them spoke for the rest, probably Peter. It was now Tuesday, April 4th, toward evening. **Buildings of the temple.** The whole temple edifice. See on ch. 21 : 12. The lamentation over Jerusalem, and the denunciation against her (ch. 23 : 37, 38), may have led his disciples to turn his attention to the magnificence of the temple, as if to plead for its preservation. Josephus (*The Jewish War*, v. 5, 6) describes the temple as built of white marble, its face to the east covered over with plates of gold, appearing in the distance like a mountain covered with snow, with its gilding dazzling as the rays of the sun. Some of its stones were forty-five cubits long, five high, and six broad. Mark says (13 : 1), "What manner of stones and what buildings are here;" Luke (21 : 5) says, "Goodly (beautiful) stones."
2. **See ye not,** etc. The question was intended to fix their attention and prepare them for what he was about to say. **There shall not be left one stone upon another.** This was fulfilled forty years afterward. Josephus relates that Titus tried in vain to save the temple. The Jews themselves first set fire to the porticoes of the temple; after which one of the Roman soldiers, without any command, threw a burning firebrand into the golden window, and soon the holy house was in flames. Titus ordered the fire to be extinguished, but his command was not obeyed. The soldiers were furious, and nothing could restrain them. Thus, even against the will of Cæsar, the temple was completely destroyed, and the prophecy was fulfilled. After the city was taken, Titus gave orders to demolish the entire city and temple, except three towers and part of the western wall. The rest of the wall was laid so completely even with the ground by those who dug it up from the foundation that there was nothing left to make those believe that came thither that it had ever been inhabited (Josephus, *Jew. War*, vi. 4, 5–7; vii. 1). Later still, Terentius Rufus, an officer in the army of Titus, ordered the site of the temple to be furrowed with a plowshare. Thus nothing was left but parts of the massive foundations, which still remain, Mic. 3 : 12.
3. **Mount of Olives.** From which they had a fine view of Jerusalem and the temple. See on ch. 21 : 1. He was retiring to Bethany over the Mount. It is a

28

disciples came unto him privately, saying, ¹ Tell us, when shall these things be? and what *shall be* the sign of thy coming, and of the end of the world?
4 And Jesus answered and said unto them, ᵐ Take
5 heed that no man deceive you. For ⁿ many shall

¹ 1 Thes. 5. 1; Ac. 1. 7.
ᵐ Eph. 5. 6; Col. 2. 8, 18; 2 Thes. 2. 3; 1 John 4. 1.
ⁿ Jer. 14. 14; 23. 21, 25; John 5.

---

remarkable fact that the siege of Jerusalem began on this mount, and at the Passover, the time of this prophecy (Joseph. *Jewish War*, v. 2. 3; vi. 9. 3). **The disciples.** Peter, James and John, and Andrew, Mark 13 : 3. The rest of the twelve probably came after them, and heard the discourse. Or, possibly, the four asked for the rest, or were the only earnest inquirers. **These things.** The destruction of the temple and the judgments of God upon Jerusalem and the Jews, ch. 23 : 36-38. **Thy coming.** His second coming. The disciples seem to have associated his coming with the destruction of the temple which Jesus had foretold, for, while they ask the *time* of *these things*, they only ask the *sign* of his coming. They probably expected that, after destroying his enemies, he would establish a magnificent and religious kingdom, Luke 24 : 21; Acts 1 : 6. **The end of the world.** The end of the present state of things. "It should be kept in mind that when the end of the world is spoken of in the New Testament the term *aion*, the present dispensation or order of things, is used, and not *kosmos*, the planetary system, the created universe."—SCHAFF. The sign of the end of the world is connected with that of his coming. The disciples evidently expected his coming when these judgments should befall their nation, and that then the existing state of things would come to an end. Matthew alone specifies these three questions. Mark (13 : 4) and Luke (21 : 7) unite them in "these things," which also shows how closely they were associated together in the minds of the disciples. Jesus in reply wisely says nothing about a temporal kingdom, but describes more minutely the destruction of Jerusalem, the signs and manner of his second glorious coming, and the final judgment, which should usher in a heavenly kingdom and the full enjoyments of an endless life.

4-14. JESUS BEGINS HIS REPLY to their questions by CAUTIONING THEM AGAINST EXPECTING HIM BEFORE THE GOSPEL IS PREACHED IN ALL THE WORLD.

4. In this and the following verse Jesus cautions them against false Christs. A false Christ is one who assumes to take the place or act the part of the Messiah. **That no man deceive you.** Lest any one lead you astray.

MODERN JERUSALEM FROM THE MOUNT OF OLIVES.

come in my name, saying, I am Christ; °and shall
6 deceive many. And ye shall hear of wars and rumors of wars. P See that ye be not troubled: for all *these things* must come to pass; q but the end is
7 not yet. For r nation shall rise against nation, and kingdom against kingdom: and there shall be s famines, and pestilences, and t earthquakes, in divers

43; Ac. 5. 36, 37.
° ver. 11.
p Ps. 27. 1-3; 46. 1-3; John 14. 1, 27; 2 Thes. 2. 2.
q Dan. 9. 24-27.
r 2 Chr. 15. 6; Is. 19. 2; Hag. 2. 22; Zec. 14. 13.
s Ac. 11. 28.
t Hag. 2. 21-23.

---

5. **In my name.** Not in the name of Jesus, but of the Messiah, claiming to be him, or to represent him. There were many such. Josephus, a Jew not converted to Christianity, but an eye-witness of the calamities attending the destruction of Jerusalem, and, to a considerable extent, an actor in them, has, in his account of the Jewish War, given a striking comment, and delineated the wonderful fulfillment of the first portion of this chapter. He speaks of the land being overrun with magicians, seducers, and impostors, who drew the people after them into the wilderness, promising to show them signs and wonders. Thus, Theudas, not the one mentioned Acts 5 : 36, but a later one, persuaded a large body of people to follow him to the Jordan, promising to divide the river, as Elijah and Elisha had done of old. But he was taken prisoner before arriving there, and beheaded. An Egyptian also pretended to be a prophet (Acts 21 : 38), and deluded thirty thousand men. (Joseph. *Antiq.* xx. 5, 1; 8. 6; *Jewish War*, ii. 13. 4, 5.) After the destruction of Jerusalem, Bar Cochba and Jonathan appeared, and almost every age since has witnessed false Christs.

6. In this and two verses that follow Jesus cautions them against being troubled with wars and various calamities which should come upon the earth and the Jewish nation, supposing them to be indicative of the end, when they were but the beginning of sorrows. **Hear of wars and rumors of wars.** These wars must be such as to be a terror to Christians, threatening their nation and their homes. The *wars* are to be regarded as certain and actual to them. But the *rumors of wars* would naturally be exaggerated, confused, and frightful, and hence more terrible than war itself. There were numerous agitations and insurrections in the Roman empire previous to the destruction of Jerusalem, in which much blood was shed. Also in Rome itself four emperors, Nero, Galba, Otho, and Vitellius, came to violent deaths in eighteen months. Alford refers to the *three threats of war against the Jews* by Caligula, Claudius, and Nero.

See that ye, etc. *Take heed, be not troubled.* The reason is given: such things must take place, but the end of the world is not yet. Some suppose *end of tribulations* is here meant; but it is more natural to refer it to the end of the world, or the present state of things, since that is one of the main points of his discourse. When it is remembered how often Christians have regarded wars and great national commotions as signs of the coming of Christ and the end of the world, it may be seen how wise and necessary this caution of our Savior: These things must take place; they are in the divine plan, but the end is not yet; therefore be not troubled, but patient, hopeful, and tranquil.

7. **Nation shall rise against nation, and kingdom,** etc. Race against race, and kingdom against kingdom. In the preceding verse, Jesus says they shall *hear*; now he states what will certainly take place. There shall be great national struggles, and political revolutions. "There were serious disturbances (1), which gave rise to the complaint against and deposition of Flaccus, and Philo's work against him (A.D. 38), in which the Jews as a nation were the especial objects of persecution; (2) at Seleucia, about the same time (Josephus, *Antiq.* xviii. 9. 8, 9), in which more than fifty thousand Jews were killed; (3) at Jamnia, a city on the coast of Judea, near Joppa. Many other such national tumults are recorded by Josephus."—ALFORD. The reference here, however, must not be confined merely to the Jewish people.

Famines. Historians speak of several famines, in different parts of the world, which happened in the reign of Claudius (A.D. 41-54), one of which was

8 places. ᵘ All these *are* the beginning of sorrows.
9 ˣ Then shall they deliver you up to be afflicted, and shall kill you: and ye shall be hated of all nations
10 for my name's sake. And then shall many ʸ be offended, and shall betray one another, and shall hate
11 one another. And ᶻ many false prophets shall rise,
12 and ᵃ shall deceive many. ᵇ And because iniquity shall abound, the love of many shall wax cold.

ᵘ Deu. 28. 59.
ˣ Dan. 11.33; John 15. 20: 16 2; Ac. 4. 2, 3; 7. 59; 1 Pet. 4. 16; Rev. 2. 10, 13.
ʸ ch. 11. 6; 13. 57; 2 Tim. 1. 15; 4. 10, 16.
ᶻ Ac. 20. 29.
ᵃ ver. 24; 1 Tim. 4. 1.

---

particularly severe in Judea, about A.D. 44–47, Acts 11 : 28; Joseph. *Antiq.* xx. 2. 5; 5. 2. Suetonius and Tacitus speak of famines about this time. There was also a famine in Judea in the third year of Nero's reign. **Pestilences.** A common attendant of famine, and often produced by it. One at Rome in the autumn of A.D. 65, which carried off 30,000 persons. The oldest and best manuscripts omit *pestilences* here. It is found, however, in Luke 21 : 11. **Earthquakes.** A great earthquake occurred in Crete about A.D. 46; at Rome in 51; in Phrygia in 53; at Laodicea in 60; in Campania in 58; at Jerusalem in 67 (Joseph. *Jewish War*, iv. 4. 5). Pompeii was visited with two disastrous earthquakes about 63.

8. **The beginning of sorrows.** Not the end, as too many will be ready to imagine, but the beginning of *throes* or *pangs*. The death-pangs of the present state and the birth-pangs of Christ's glorious kingdom, Acts 3 : 21; Rom. 8: 18–23.

9. In this and the next verse Jesus foretells the severe persecutions which shall befall his disciples, when many shall be offended. Being forewarned, they would be forearmed against being offended. **Then.** At that time, or during that period just referred to. **To be afflicted.** Scourging, imprisonment, etc. The apostles were imprisoned and scourged, Acts 5 : 18, 40. So also Paul and Silas, Acts, 16 : 23, 24. **Kill you.** Some of you. Stephen was stoned (Acts 7 : 59); James was killed by Herod, Acts 12 : 2. Indeed, most of the apostles suffered martyrdom. Nero (A.D. 64) persecuted Christians, putting them to death with the most fearful tortures. **Hated of all nations.** "Concerning this sect, we know that everywhere it is spoken against," Acts 28 : 22; see also 1 Pet. 2 : 12; 3 : 16; 4 : 14. Christians have been hated and persecuted beyond the adherents of any other sect. **For my name's sake.** On account of their attachment to me, and because they bear my name. Here do we see the reason of Christians being so universally hated, not only in every age, but also in the apostolic age, when philosophers were pushing free inquiry and deriding popular superstition, and at the same time the doctrines of Moses were extensively propagated among the Gentiles. Christians proclaimed Christ the only Savior, and all other religions as of no avail. The numerous religions of heathenism acknowledged one another as standing on a common level. The Christian, however, demanded the renunciation of these, and faith in Christ. Hence he was regarded as an enemy of the gods and of men, and was hated by all.

10. **Offended.** They counted not the cost; and hence in persecution they became disaffected toward the cause they had embraced, and left it, ch. 13 : 21; 1 John 2 : 19. They who thus apostatize from a professed attachment to Christ would **betray** their brethren. Tacitus relates that, in the persecution under Nero, many were convicted by the testimony of persons from among themselves. **Hate one another.** The direct opposite of Christ's command to love one another, which was to be a mark of discipleship, John 13 : 34, 35.

11. Jesus also foretells and cautions them against **many false prophets,** who should arise and lead many astray. The Epistles give abundant evidence of the many false teachers who arose in the apostolic age; and, if then, how much more in the ages succeeding, Rom. 16 : 17 ; 2 Cor. 11 : 13; Gal. 1 : 7; 1 Tim. 1: 6, 20; 2 Tim. 3 : 17, 18; 1 John 2 : 18; 4 : 1; Jude 3, 4; Rev. 2 : 14, 20; see also Acts 20 : 30.

12. In this and the next verse Jesus forewarns them of the love of many waxing cold, and of the necessity of remaining faithful unto the end. **Ini-**

13 ᶜ But he that shall endure unto the end, the same
14 shall be saved. And this ᵈ Gospel of the kingdom
ᵉ shall be preached in all the world for a witness
unto all nations; and then shall the end come.
15 ᶠ When ye therefore shall see the abomination of

ᵇ 2 Tim. 3. 1-5.
ᶜ ch. 10. 22; Heb. 3. 6, 14.
ᵈ ch. 4. 23; 9. 35.
ᵉ ch. 28. 19; Ac. 1. 8; Ro. 16. 25, 26.
ᶠ Mk. 13. 14; Lk. 21. 20.

quity shall abound. On account of lawlessness and wickedness, both out of the church and in the church, the love of *the many* will become cold. A very large proportion of the professors of Christianity would degenerate in their love. This would be the natural result of the increase of heresies and general wickedness, Gal. 3 : 1; 2 Tim. 1 : 15; 2 Pet. 2 : 22; 1 John 2 : 18; Rev. 2 : 4; 3 : 15.

13. **Unto the end.** He who remains faithful unto the end of life, which is practically the end of the world to the individual. The persevering and enduring to the end evidently refers to spiritual fidelity in opposition to the defection of false professors; and the salvation is not merely one from temporal trials, but from sin and spiritual foes. It is, however, worthy of notice that not a single Christian, so far as is known, perished in the destruction of Jerusalem. They escaped to Pella, beyond the Jordan, where they remained in safety till after the fall of the city. Their deliverance, then, may indeed be taken as an illustration and type of the deliverance of all God's people at the end of the world and the judgment.

14. **Gospel of the kingdom.** The good news of the Messiah's reign or dispensation. **Preached in all the world.** This was really the case, so far as the world was then known, in the apostolic age, and before the destruction of Jerusalem, Rom. 10 : 18; 15 : 24; Col. 1 : 6, 23; 2 Tim. 4 : 17. So before the end of this dispensation the Gospel shall be made known to all nations. " The universal promulgation of the Gospel is the true sign of the end, both in the (narrow and restricted) sense in which the disciples put the question, and in the (wider and universal) sense which, in the Savior's mind, it really involved."— JUDGE JONES. "The *apostasy of the latter days*, and the *universal dispersion of missions*, are the two great signs of the end drawing near."—ALFORD. **For a witness.** For a testimony of the Messiah to all nations, in order that men everywhere might believe and be saved. **Then shall the end come.** The end of the world, of the Gospel dispensation, of which the destruction of Jerusalem and the end of the Jewish state were typical.

15-25. Jesus now proceeds to speak more definitely of the DESTRUCTION OF JERUSALEM, and to answer the first question of the disciples, with directions to his disciples as to what they shall then do, and with a caution, or hint, that THEY ARE NOT TO EXPECT THE SECOND COMING OF CHRIST AT THAT TIME.

15. **Abomination of desolation.** Spoken of through Daniel the Prophet, Dan. 9 : 27; compare Dan. 11 : 31; 12 : 11. These words were supposed by the Alexandrine Jews to refer to an idol statue of Jupiter Olympius, erected in the temple by Antiochus Epiphanes (B.C. 168), when for three years and a half the Jews were deprived of their civil and religious liberties. See Apocrypha, 1 Macc. 1 : 54; 6 : 7; 2 Macc. 6 : 2. Josephus (*Antiq.* x. 11. 7) seems to refer this prophecy to the destruction of Jerusalem. The *abomination* in the original Hebrew refers to things unclean and revolting, and especially to objects of abhorrence connected with idols and idolatry. The *desolation* is especially applied to the wasting devastations of war. The *abomination of desolation* thus naturally refers to the profanations connected with the devastations of heathen conquest, and points unmistakably to the destruction of Jerusalem and the temple by Titus. But what particular thing or event in this destruction is here meant? Some refer it to the eagles, which the Romans carried as standards, worshiped as idols, and hence were an abomination to the Jews. The standards in the hands of the Roman legions besieging the holy city foreshadowed its conquest and destruction. This view is supported by the fact that the Roman army under Cestius Gallus, after taking a portion of the city A.D. 66, withdrew, and thus gave time to the Christians to escape before the city was closely invested by Vespasian A.D. 68. The expression of Luke (21 : 20), who wrote especially for Gentile readers, also favors it: "When ye shall see

desolation, spoken of by ᵍ Daniel the prophet, stand
in the holy place, (ʰ whoso readeth, let him under-
16 stand): then ⁱ let them which be in Judea flee into
17 the mountains : ᵏ let him which is on the housetop
not come down to take any thing out of his house:
18 neither let him which is in the field return back to
take his clothes.

ᵍ Dan. 9. 27; 11. 31: 12. 11.
ʰ Dan. 9. 23, 25; Rev. 1. 3.
ⁱ Prov. 22. 3.
ᵏ Lk. 17. 31, 32.

Jerusalem compassed with armies, then know that the desolation thereof is nigh." Others, however, think that "the abomination of desolation" points especially to the murders committed in the temple by the party of the zealots, who occupied it at the very time that the Roman general, Cestius, approached the city and assaulted it. Such pollutions and tragedies in the temple must have deeply impressed Jewish Christians, and, in connection with the threatening armies and conquest of the Romans, must have deepened the conviction that the end of the city and its temple was nigh. Still, we think that the language more especially refers to this first approach and attack of the idolatrous Roman armies, with their idolatrous ensigns, ready to desolate Jerusalem. See on ver. 29.
Daniel the Prophet. Jesus thus testifies to the authenticity of the prophecy of Daniel, and also applies the prediction here quoted to his own times. **Stand in the holy place.** Some think this to mean the whole of Palestine; but this is too general. Nor is it necessary to limit it to the temple, but it may be properly applied to the holy city and its precincts. Compare ch. 4 : 5.
Whoso readeth, let him understand. Let him that readeth consider, give heed to it, and note it. A parenthetical clause, uttered probably by our Savior, being an admonition to any who should read this prediction of Daniel. Compare the words of the angel to Daniel, "Know and understand," Dan. 9: 25. Many suppose the clause to be thrown in by the Evangelist, intimating the near approach of this sign. But why should Mark also use the same language, if it was not a part of the discourse of Jesus? Mark 13 : 14. The omission by Luke (21 : 20) may be explained by the fact that he was writing for Gentile readers, giving a brief synopsis of the discourse, and that he gives the admonitory and significant clause,

"Then know that the desolation thereof is nigh."
16. In this, and the four following verses, the disciples are instructed to make a precipitate flight **then**, when they should see this abomination in the holy place. **Them which be in Judea.** In the country, towns, and cities of Judea. **Mountains.** The mountainous regions and highlands, where there were caves affording a safe retreat. By a singular providence, the Roman general Cestius, after taking a portion of the city, with good prospects of capturing the whole, withdrew without any apparently good reason. This gave the Christians an opportunity to escape, which they did, over the mountainous region to Pella, and other places east of the Jordan, where the country was at peace with the Romans. Pella was on the northern border of Perea. According to Eusebius, the historian, the Christians were divinely directed to flee thither.
17. They were to flee with all possible haste, and not descend into their houses to collect their goods. **Housetop.** Literally, *Upon the house.* The houses in Palestine were flat-roofed, and communicated with each other, so that a person might proceed to the city walls and escape without coming down into the street. Persons would naturally go to the house-top to view an invading army. Jesus, however, may have referred to escaping by a stairway leading from the court to the roof, without entering the house. The admonition is not against *coming down*, but against coming down *to take any thing out of his house.* The stairway landed "outside the house, but within the exterior court. It would not be either agreeable or safe to have the stairs land outside the inclosure altogether, and it is rarely done, except in mountain villages, and where roofs are but little used."—Dr. Thomson, *The Land and the Book*, vol. i. p. 52.
18. **To take his clothes,** or garments; or, according to several high cri-

19 And ¹ woe unto them that are with child, and to
20 them that give suck in those days! But pray ye
that your flight be not in the winter, neither on the
21 sabbath day. For ᵐ then shall be great tribulation,
such as was not since the beginning of the world to
22 this time, no, nor ever shall be. And except those
days should be shortened, there should no flesh be
saved : ⁿ but for the elect's sake those days shall be
shortened.

¹ Lk. 23. 29.

ᵐ Dan. 9. 26; 12. 1; Zec. 11. 8, 9; 14. 2, 3.

ⁿ Is. 65. 8, 9; Zec. 13. 8. 9; Ro. 11. 25–31.

tical authorities, *garment*, the cloak, which one dressed for the field would only need for a journey. He must escape at once without his full dress, or his garments at home.

19. Woe unto them—with child, etc. Both Jewish and Christian females. The sufferings of both would be greatly increased. Flight would be far more difficult, or impossible.

20. But pray ye. Thus he would teach them their entire dependence upon God, and the necessity of prayer for the facilities and alleviating circumstances desirable in their flight. **Winter.** When storms were frequent, and roads were bad; a season unfavorable for traveling, and especially for a hasty flight. Dr. Thomson says that it is not easy to exaggerate the hardships, and even dangers, which traveling parties encounter at this season of the year. Heavy falls of snow often occur. The final siege took place in the spring and summer. **Sabbath-day.** The grammatical construction is indefinite, *In winter nor on a Sabbath*. The former presented *natural* impediments to their flight, the latter *legal*. The gates of the cities were shut on the Sabbath, Neh. 13 : 19. It was also unlawful to travel on the Sabbath, Exod. 16 : 29. A Sabbath-day's journey was two thousand cubits, or about five furlongs. Escape would be the more easily detected, or prevented, by the Jews on the Sabbath. Many, too, might have scruples about traveling from a superstitious reverence for the Jewish Sabbath.

21. Jesus foretells the unparalleled judgments and sufferings of the time. **Great tribulation.** Great affliction, distress. According to Josephus, eleven hundred thousand perished during the siege at Jerusalem by the sword, pestilence, and famine. The city was full of people, attending the Passover festival, when the last siege under Titus commenced. Thousands had come from remote parts of the earth, not only to attend the festival, but to assist in the defense of their religion, country, liberties, city, and temple. Ninety thousand were taken prisoners, and sold into perpetual bondage. Besides, during the entire war nearly three hundred thousand Jews perished elsewhere, in addition to a vast multitude who died in caves, woods, common sewers, banishment, and various ways, of whom no computation could be made. **Since the beginning of the world.** The sufferings and distress of the Jews for so short a time (the last siege lasted five months), and so confined a space, exceeds any thing in the known history of the world. The prediction in Deut. 28: 53–57 was literally fulfilled. The language of Josephus is noteworthy: "I shall, therefore, speak my mind here at once briefly, that neither did any other city ever suffer such miseries, nor did any age ever breed a generation more fruitful in wickedness than was this, from the beginning of the world." And again : "The multitude of those that therein perished exceeded all the destructions that either men or God ever brought upon the world." (*Jewish War*, v. 10. 5; and vi. 9. 4.)

22. Jesus intimates that **those days** of judgment and distress shall be shortened for the sake of those among the Jews who were and should be his chosen followers. **No flesh be saved.** No one of the Jewish nation. The whole nation would have perished. **For the elect's sake.** For the sake of those whom God had chosen from among the Jews to be his people. **Those days shall be shortened.** The time from the first siege under Cestius to the destruction of the city by Titus was four years. The final siege lasted only about five months. It commenced in April, A.D. 70. The daily sacrifice ceased for want of priests to offer it on the twenty-third of

23 ᵒThen if any man shall say unto you, Lo, here is
24 Christ, or there; believe it not. For ᵖthere shall arise false Christs, and false prophets, and shall show great signs and wonders; insomuch that, ᵠif it were possible, they shall deceive the very elect.
25, 26 Behold, ʳI have told you before. Wherefore, if

ᵒ Lk. 17. 23.
ᵖ vers. 5, 11; Deu. 13. 1, 2; Rev. 13. 13.
ᵠ John 6. 37; 10. 28, 29; Ro. 8. 28-30; 2 Tim. 2. 19; 1 Pet. 1. 5.
ʳ John 16. 1-4.

June, and from that day to the fourteenth of July the last death-struggle took place. Then followed plunder and destruction, till the whole city was reduced to ashes, except the three great towers on the western wall. Titus recognized divine help in taking the city, and confessed, "We have indeed had God for our assistant in this war, and it was no other than God who ejected the Jews out of these fortifications; for what could the hands of men or any machines do toward overthrowing these towers?" (Josephus, *Jewish War*, vi. 9. 1.) Alford, and others, notice several things which may be regarded as providential causes in shortening the siege: (1) Herod Agrippa had begun to fortify the walls of Jerusalem, and make them, as Josephus says, "too strong for all human power to demolish;" but was stopped by orders from Claudius, A.D. 42 or 43. (2) The Jews, being divided into factions among themselves, had totally neglected to prepare to withstand a siege. (3) The magazines of grain and other provisions, which, according to Josephus, "would have been sufficient for a siege of many years," were burnt just before the arrival of Titus. (4) Titus arrived suddenly, and the Jews voluntarily abandoned parts of the fortification." (Josephus, *Antiq.* xix. 7. 2; *Jewish War*, v. 1. 4; vi. 8. 4.)

23. In this verse, and the two that follow, Jesus cautions his disciples against false Christs and false prophets which shall arise in those days. **Then.** At the time of these sufferings, or immediately after. **Lo, here is Christ.** Rather, *the Christ*, the Messiah. He was not to come in this manner, ver. 27. Neither was he then to come personally, vers. 29, 30. There was danger of some Jewish Christians expecting that Christ might come to deliver the city from destruction. But, at the most, there would be only an invisible and impersonal coming then, which would be in judgments upon the unbelieving race and their wicked city.

24. Jesus now asserts that there will be **false Christs,** those who pretend to be the Messiah; and **false prophets,** false teachers, who should **show great signs and wonders,** work false miracles. They would, like Simon Magus (Acts 8 : 10), lead many to regard them as illustrious instruments of God's power. **If possible,** which, it is implied, is not, John 10 : 28, 29. **Deceive the very elect.** Lead them astray; seduce them from Christ and the truth. Compare Acts 21 : 38; 2 Thess. 2 : 9-12; 1 John 2 : 18; Rev. 16 : 13, 14.

These impostors were numerous before and after the destruction of the city. Felix, A.D. 53-60, put down false prophets and false Messiahs. According to Josephus, they persuaded many "to follow them into the wilderness, and pretended that they would exhibit manifest wonders and signs, that should be wrought by the providence of God." They "deluded the people under pretence of divine inspiration." So, also, during the siege a great number of false prophets proclaimed that the people "should wait deliverance from God;" and, just before the burning of the temple, one of them made a public proclamation that "God commanded them to get upon the temple, and that they should receive miraculous signs of deliverance." (Joseph. *Antiq.* xx. 8. 6; *Jewish War*, ii. 13. 4; vi. 5. 2.) And long after this, about A.D. 135, a false Messiah arose, who called himself Bar Cochevas, or son of a star, from the star prophesied by Balaam. He performed tricks of legerdemain, deluded multitudes, among whom were three of the greatest rabbis, and raised an insurrection against the Roman government, which was put down with great bloodshed.

25. **I have told you before.** To be forewarned was to be forearmed. As I have affectionately exercised the caution to foretell this danger, so do you exercise a like caution in guarding against it.

they shall say unto you, Behold, he is in the desert; go not forth: Behold, *he is* in the secret chambers;
27 believe *it* not. *ᵗ For as the lightning cometh out of the east, and shineth even unto the west; so shall
28 also ᵗ the coming of the Son of man be. "For wheresoever the carcass is, there will the eagles be gathered together.
29 ˣ Immediately after the tribulation of those days

ˢ Lk. 17. 24.
ᵗ ch. 25. 31.
ᵘ Job 39. 30; Lk. 17. 37.
ˣ Is. 13. 10; Dan. 7. 11, 12.

26–28. JESUS REVEALS SOMETHING OF THE MANNER OF HIS COMING, which is to be neither in an unassuming way, nor yet as an earthly prince, but most conspicuous, like the lightning of heaven.

26. He is in the desert. Like John the Baptist in the wilderness; his second coming would not be like his first. He would not then be found, as he often had been, in the desert. False Christs would indeed be found there, drawing multitudes after them. **In the secret chambers.** In the retired part of some house, with his confidential friends, ready soon to make his appearance. He is to be found neither in ascetic and monastic life, nor in the abodes of wealth and luxury. Several impostors, according to Josephus, assembled their followers in the wilderness (see Acts 21 : 38); and one false prophet enticed a multitude into the chambers of the temple, where six thousand perished. Such examples illustrate what did take place, not only before, but after the destruction of the city.

27. For as the lightning—so the coming of the Son of Man. His coming will not be from the earth, but from heaven; not manifested only in a certain place, but everywhere conspicuous, like the lightning, which "cometh from the east and shineth even unto the west." It shall be sudden, unmistakable, and so public that every eye can see him. Rev. 1 : 7.

28. For wherever the carcass is. A proverbial expression, especially applicable to what he had just said, containing much truth in a nutshell. The eagles, or carrion vultures, which were usually included by the ancients among eagles, would quickly scent the corrupt carcass and gather around to devour it. The precise application has, however, been much discussed. (1) It may mean that, wherever the carcass of Judaism shall be found, there will be found the false Christs and prophets foretold in verses 23–26. Or (2) there will be the Roman armies and ministers of vengeance, as at the destruction of Jerusalem, and frequently in the history of the Jews since that event. Or (3) as surely as the vultures gather around the carcass, so surely and unmistakably will the Son of Man come to judgment. Some, modifying this last view, understand by "eagles" the angels who shall gather out of his kingdom all things that offend and those that do iniquity, ch. 13 : 41. The third view is most natural in this connection. So also in Luke 17 : 37 it is preferable. It is, however, not unlikely that Jesus uttered this language here with great pregnant meaning, designing more than a single application, and that thus it is proper to apply it in the several ways just mentioned; and that it has been verified frequently in Jewish history, and will be especially in the history of the world at the second coming of Christ.

29–31. JESUS NOW FORETELLS THE SIGNS AND THE TIME OF HIS COMING.

29. Tribulation of those days. This refers to not only the afflictions at the time of the destruction of Jerusalem, but to all flowing out of that event, *those days* extending till "the fullness of the Gentiles come in." In verse 21 he has spoken especially of the distress and affliction connected immediately with the destruction of Jerusalem; now he passes on and also includes the trials connected with the dispersion of the Jews. Thus, about A.D. 135 (see on ver. 24), Jerusalem was captured again, in consequence of an insurrection under Bar Cochevas, which brought most terrible sufferings upon the Jews, who were utterly driven out from the land of their fathers. A temple of Jupiter was then erected on the site of the Lord's house. Afterward, A.D. 635, the mosque of Omar was built upon the same site. If we may conceive of Daniel's prophecy, concerning the abomination that made

y shall the sun be darkened, and the moon shall not give her light, and the stars shall fall from heaven, and the powers of the heavens shall be shaken.

30 ᶻ And then shall appear the sign of the Son of man in heaven: ᵃ and then shall all the tribes of the earth mourn: ᵇ and they shall see the Son of man coming in the clouds of heaven with power and great glory.

31 ᶜ And he shall send his angels with a great sound of a trumpet, ᵈ and they shall gather together his elect from the four winds, from one end of heaven to the other.

32 Now learn ᵉ a parable of the fig-tree; When his

y Joel 2. 10, 30, 31; Am. 5. 20; 8. 9.

z Dan. 7. 13, 14.
a Zec. 12. 10-12.
b ch. 16. 27, 28; Is. 26. 21; Ac. 1. 11; 2 Thes. 1. 7, 8; Jude 14.
c ch. 13. 41; 1 Cor. 15. 52; 1 Thes. 4. 16.
d Ps. 50. 3-5; 2 Thes. 2. 1.

e Lk. 21. 29.

---

desolate, having repeated fulfillments, we might place its final reference to this last event, and also suppose it to mark the commencement of his periods of 1260, 1290, and 1335 years. The distress of the Jews still continues, and Jerusalem is still trodden under foot by the Gentiles. **Immediately** is plain and easily understood according to this view; but it has afforded, and always will, great difficulty to those who limit those days to the destruction of Jerusalem.

The sun be darkened and the moon, etc. This language may be taken figuratively to mean great calamities and revolutions among the nations of the earth, after the manner of Hebrew prophecies, Isa. 13 : 10; Ezek. 32 : 7; Joel 3 : 15. It is doubtful, however, whether all of these, and similar passages from the Old Testament, are to be taken figuratively. It is better to take this language of our Lord literally, especially as what follows in regard to his coming must be taken literally. See on next verse. The meaning is, that terrific phenomena and changes in nature shall occur immediately after the Jewish people shall have endured their full measure of suffering. There shall be darkness, as during the crucifixion of our Savior (ch. 27 : 45) and in the plague of Egypt (Exod. 10 : 22, 23); appearances of falling stars, or the shooting of meteors; and the powers and forces of nature, the elements of the heavens, shall be agitated and convulsed like the waves of the sea. Compare 2 Pet. 3 : 12; Rev. 21 : 1.

30. Jesus here speaks of the sign and appearance at his second coming. The coming of Christ is spoken of elsewhere as actual and visible, Acts 1 : 9, 11; 1 Thess. 4 : 16; 2 Thess. 1 : 8; 2 Pet. 3 : 10, 12; Jude 14; Rev. 1 : 7. In harmony with these plain declarations of Scripture, this passage should be taken literally. **Sign of the Son of Man.** The manifestation of light and glory just preceding his visible appearance. **Tribes of the earth.** Not the Jews merely, but all nations, shall **mourn,** wail with terror and anguish. **Coming in the clouds.** As he ascended, Acts 1 : 9. Not merely in ordinary clouds, but such as anciently attended the divine presence, Exod. 16 : 10; 19 : 18; Dan. 7 : 13. **With power,** with the actual possession of it; **and great glory,** a visible display of his power and majesty, Ps. 68 ; 17.

31. Jesus foretells the attendant circumstances of his coming.

Great sound of a trumpet. As at the giving of the law, when the trumpet sounded exceeding loud (Exod. 19 : 16; 20 : 18; Heb. 12 : 18-21) to call the people together to receive the law. Trumpets were sounded for public gatherings, Num. 10 : 1-10; Jud. 3 : 27; Joel 2 : 1, 15. Angels are described as attending Christ at his coming and active at the judgment, ch. 13 : 41, 49. They shall gather **his elect,** his chosen followers, to him, 2 Thess. 2 : 1; 1 Thess. 4 : 16, 17. **From the four winds,** etc. From every quarter, and from the remotest places under heaven, Deut. 4 : 32; Ezek. 37 : 9. The gathering of the elect will be for safety, for the enjoyment of Christ's presence, and for glorious rewards. Then will follow the gathering of the wicked for punishment. Compare Rev. 20 : 4, 5, 12-15.

32-35. Jesus, having dwelt more particularly upon the signs of the destruction of Jerusalem, his second coming and the

branch is yet tender, and putteth forth leaves, ye 33 know that summer *is* nigh: so likewise ye, when ye shall see all these things, know ᶠ that it is 34 near, *even* at the doors. Verily I say unto you, ᵍ This generation shall not pass, till all these things 35 be fulfilled. ʰ Heaven and earth shall pass away, ⁱ but my words shall not pass away.

ᶠ Jam. 5. 9.
ᵍ ch. 23. 36; Lk. 21. 32.
ʰ Lk. 21. 33; Heb. 1. 11.
ⁱ Num. 23. 19; Is. 40. 8.

end of the world, now approaches more directly THE TIME OF THESE GREAT EVENTS, especially his second coming. Returning somewhat in his discourse, he teaches them to judge FROM THE FIG-TREE OF THE TIME, WHICH, IN A CERTAIN SENSE, WOULD BE IN THAT GENERATION, and more certain than the established order of nature.

32. **Now learn a parable of,** etc. Rather, from the fig-tree learn the parable which illustrates the circumstances and signs preceding these great events; learn the illustration which the fig-tree affords. Fig-trees abounded on the Mount of Olives, where Jesus was now discoursing. "On my first arrival in the southern part of Syria, near the end of March, most of the fruit-trees were clothed with foliage and in blossom. The fig-tree, on the contrary, was much behind them in this respect; for the leaves of this tree do not make their appearance till comparatively late in the season. . . . As the spring is so far advanced before the leaves of the fig-tree begin to appear (the early fruit, indeed, comes first), a person may be sure when he beholds this sign that summer is at hand."—Dr. HACKETT, *Illustrations of Scripture,* p. 141. See on ch. 21:19.

33. **Ye shall see all these things.** Those signs which he had told them in his discourse, particularly those described, verses 7, 8, 15. **It is near.** Especially the destruction of Jerusalem, foretold in ch. 23; 36-38, and referred to by the words *these things* in the third verse of this chapter. The illustration applies also to the coming of Christ and the end of the world. If they, or his followers, to whom he spoke through them, should observe the signs described in verses 29, 30, then they would know that his coming and the end are at hand.

34. **This generation.** That present generation. **All these things.** The *these things* of verse 3, connected with the destruction of Jerusalem. *All these things* are in contrast to *that day* in ver. 36, which refers exclusively to the coming of Christ. Thus Jesus passes, in verses 34, 36, from one event to the other, the former being typical of the latter.

Another explanation makes *this generation* to mean those who know and observe these signs, the generation of his followers who shall be living when these signs occur. In which case it could apply to both the fall of Jerusalem as a type, and Christ's coming to judgment as an antitype.

Others maintain that, according to Hellenistic Greek, *this generation* may mean *this race,* or *family of people.* According to which view our Savior says, This race or Jewish people shall not pass away till all these things just foretold be accomplished. The first view is preferable. The destruction of Jerusalem occurred about forty years afterward, within the lifetime of many then living. If, however, we give a double or extended meaning to *these things,* we must give a corresponding extended meaning to *this generation.* **Be fulfilled.** Are accomplished or done. To say with some, "Are in course of fulfillment, or begin to be fulfilled," is grammatically incorrect.

35. Jesus had just announced the preceding declaration with the authoritative and solemn clause, "Verily, I say unto you." He now affirms most emphatically that his words shall be certainly accomplished. **Heaven and earth shall pass away.** Even these which have been so generally regarded as firm and unchangeable, Ps. 89:37; Jer. 33:25. Even these shall be changed, and give place to the new heaven and new earth, 2 Pet. 3:11-13. **My words,** in general, and what I have spoken at this time. **Shall not pass away.** Can not at any time prove to be false, or fail of their accomplishment. They are infallible, and more certain than th · established order of nature, Isa. 40:8; 51:6; 1 Pet. 1:24, 25.

36-41. THE TIME OF HIS COMING

36 ᵏ But of that day and hour knoweth no *man*, no, not the angels of heaven, ˡ but my Father only.
37 But, ᵐ as the days of Noe *were*, so shall also the coming of the Son of man be.
38 ⁿ For as in the days that were before the flood they were eating and drinking, marrying and giving in marriage, until the
39 day that Noe entered into the ark, and knew not until the flood came, and took them all away; so shall
40 also the coming of the Son of man be. ᵒ Then shall two be in the field; the one shall be taken, and the
41 other left. Two *women shall be* grinding at the mill; the one shall be taken, and the other left.

ᵏ ch. 25. 13; Ac. 1. 7; 1 Thes. 5. 2.
ˡ Zec. 14. 7.
ᵐ Ge. 6. 3-5.
ⁿ Lk. 17. 26.

ᵒ Lk. 17. 34; 1 Cor. 4. 5.

KNOWN ONLY TO THE FATHER. He would come suddenly and unexpectedly.
36. But of that day. Emphatic, and in contrast to *these things* in verse 34. The exact time of his coming. **Knoweth no man.** *Knoweth no one.* Mark (13 : 32) adds, *Neither the Son.* Jesus spoke in respect to his human nature. As a man he increased in wisdom and acquired knowledge (Luke 2 : 52), and was ignorant of the exact time of his coming. **My Father only.** God only knew the time, and hence Jesus could have known it only in his divinity. This verse is a strong statement that the time was kept a profound secret in the counsels of God. See on Mark 13 : 32.
37. **But.** Though the time is unknown, yet it will come suddenly and unexpectedly upon the inhabitants of the earth. **As the days of Noah.** A parallel between the days of the flood and those of the coming of Christ. The latter shall be as the former. See the same illustration in Luke 17 : 26-30. See also 2 Pet. 2 : 4-10; 3 : 5, 6.
38. **For.** Explanatory. The idea of the preceding verse is expanded and explained in this and the three succeeding verses. **Eating and drinking.** They were living in apparent security, unconscious of the calamities that awaited them. **Marrying,** etc. Forming new connections in life, and expecting a posterity. The words do not necessarily imply open and notorious wickedness, but a perfect security, not anticipating their sudden and terrible doom.
39. **So shall also the coming.** It shall be sudden and unexpected. Some apply this whole description to the destruction of Jerusalem. But it can not be said that it came thus suddenly and unexpectedly upon its inhabitants.
40. **Two in the field.** Engaged as in the days of Noah in their ordinary occupation. **One shall be taken.** One of the elect shall be taken by the angels and borne to the presence of Christ and the company of the redeemed. The other is left to be borne at length to the company of the wicked at the left hand of Christ. See verse 31. The suddenness of his coming is thus illustrated in this and the next verse.
41. **Two women grinding at the mill.** Grain was ground by a hand-mill,

HAND-MILL.

and generally by women. "The proverb of our Savior is true to life, for *women only* grind. I can not recall an instance in which men were at the mill."—Dr. Thomson, *The Land and the Book*, vol. ii. p. 295. "In the court of one of the houses of this village (Jenin, on the border of the plain of Esdraelon) I saw two young women, sitting on the ground, engaged in this mode of grinding. The mill consisted of two stones, the upper one circular, the lower one partly so, with a projection on one side, two or three inches long, slanting downward, and scooped out so as to carry off the meal. The lower stone had an iron pivot (I

42 ᵖ Watch therefore: ᵍ for ye know not what hour
43 your Lord doth come. ʳ But know this, that if the goodman of the house had known in what watch the thief would come, he would have watched, and would not have suffered his house to be broken up.
44 Therefore be ye also ready: for in such an hour as
45 ye think not the Son of man cometh. Who then is a faithful and wise servant, whom his lord hath made ruler over his household, to give them meat in due
46 season? Blessed is that servant, whom his lord
47 when he cometh shall find so doing. Verily 1 say unto you, That he shall make him ruler over all his

ᵖ ch. 25. 13; Mk. 13. 33; Lk. 12. 35-38; 21. 36; 1 Thes. 5. 6; 1 Pet. 4. 7.
ᵍ ver. 36.
ʳ Lk. 12. 39-44.

think it was) extending from its centre through a hole in the centre of the upper stone. An upright handle was fixed in a socket near the edge of the upper stone, and both the women, taking hold of this handle, whirled the stone round and round with great rapidity. One of them every now and then dropped a handful of grain into the hole at the centre of the upper stone. . . . At an earlier stage of my journey, at Pompeii in Italy, I had seen a pair of millstones entirely similar to these in the east. They were in the house known among the ruins there as the house of the baker, occupying, in all probability, the very spot where they stood on the day when the eruption of Vesuvius buried that ill-fated city."—Dr. Hackett, *Illustrations of Scripture*, p. 86.

42 to ch. 25: 30. Jesus proceeds to enforce watchfulness, by illustrations and parables drawn from daily life and experience.

42. **Watch.** Be awake and on your guard against danger. **Ye know not what hour.** Rather, *What day*, according to the oldest and best manuscripts. The more exact term *hour* is found in verse 44. Ignorance of the time of his coming is the reason given for watchfulness. The same reason will apply to death and the judgments which are coming on the earth. We should watch, since we know not their time.

43. Jesus illustrates the necessity of constant readiness and watchfulness by a case of theft. **Good-man of the house.** Master of the house, or householder, as in ch. 20: 11. The head of the family is intended. **What watch.** The night was divided by the later Jews into four watches, by the earlier into three. See on ch. 14: 25. **Broken up.** Literally, *Dug through*. Eastern houses were built of stone or clay. The word shows how houses were often plundered, by stealthily opening a passage through the wall. It became, however, to be applied to any mode of forcing an entrance, and hence may here be rendered *broken through*.

44. **Therefore be ye also ready.** As, like the householder, you know not the time, so be always ready: for, as he knew not the time of the thief's coming, so ye know not when the Son of Man will come. As after death comes the judgment, and as at death we pass into the state of retribution, so death is virtually to individuals what the coming of Christ will be to those then living. To all the exhortation may, therefore, be given.

45 Jesus still further enforces watchfulness and a constant readiness for his coming by the parabolic case of a servant left in charge of his master's house. He had used this illustration on a previous occasion, Luke 24: 42. **Who is a faithful?** Rather, *Who is the faithful*, etc.? The interrogative form makes the sentence the stronger, and leads every hearer and reader to more reflection, and to a personal application. **Hath made ruler.** Rather, *Whom his lord*, when he left, *set over his household*. He had placed him over his household to provide **meat**, that is, *food*. This language especially illustrates the duties and responsibilities of the apostles and all ministers of the Gospel, 2 Tim. 2: 15; 2 Pet. 5: 2-4.

46. **Blessed.** *Happy.* See on ch 5: 3. **So doing.** Discharging his duties faithfully.

47. **Ruler over all his goods.** As a reward of faithfulness, he pro-

48 goods. But and if that evil servant shall say in his
49 heart, *ᵃ* My lord delayeth his coming; and shall begin to smite *his* fellow servants, and to eat and drink
50 with the drunken; the lord of that servant shall come in a day when he looketh not for *him*, and in
51 an hour that he is not aware of, and shall cut him asunder, and appoint *him* his portion ᵗ with the hypocrites: ᵘ there shall be weeping and gnashing of teeth.

ᵃ Ecc. 8. 11; 2 Pet. 3. 3-5.

ᵗ Job 8. 11-14; 20. 4-7.
ᵘ ch. 8. 12; 25. 30.

motes him to a high post of honor, just as Potiphar made Joseph head-steward in his house (Gen. 39 : 4), and a little later Pharaoh set him over all the land of Egypt, Gen. 41 : 39–41. Compare Gen. 24 : 2. Such shall be the reward of the faithful pastor and teacher. Compare ch. 25 : 21; Rev. 2 : 26; 3 : 21.

48. In contrast to the faithful and wise servant, Jesus contrasts an evil servant, **evil** both in heart and act. **Say in his heart.** This wickedness commences in his heart, and shows itself in unbelief and presumption, then in overbearance and oppression, in gluttony and dissipation.

49. **Smite his fellow-servants.** Every hierarchy has persecuted the disciples of Jesus. Formal Christianity has ever been proud, insolent, and oppressive. It is the glory of Baptists that they have always held to the rights of conscience, and hence have never been persecutors.

50. But Christ shall come suddenly and unexpectedly to popes, priests, to unfaithful leaders and their followers, and bring upon them swift and terrible destruction.

51. **Cut him asunder.** Cutting in two, or sawing asunder, was a terrible punishment inflicted on great criminals, 1 Sam. 15 : 33; Dan. 2 : 5; 3 : 29; Heb. 11 : 37. Figuratively it expresses sudden and terrible punishment. That it does not express annihilation or extinction of being, is evident from what follows, "Appoint him his portion with hypocrites and unbelievers; there shall be weeping and gnashing of teeth." **With hypocrites.** He had been a hypocrite, assuming a false zeal, and making pretensions to what he was not. Hypocrites are the most odious sinners in the sight of God. **Gnashing of teeth.** Denotes extreme anguish. See on ch. 8 : 12.

REMARKS.

1. Earthly temples, however costly, are of no religious worth without spiritual worship. They are doomed if the Lord has departed from them, vers. 1, 2; 1 Sam. 4 : 21; Jer. 7 : 3, 4, 14.

2. We should guard against false leaders, and trust only in Jesus as the true Messiah, vers. 4, 5, 23, 24; Jer. 29 : 8, 9; Acts 20 : 30; Eph. 5 : 6; Col. 2 : 8; 2 Thess. 2 : 3.

3. National convulsions, conflicts, and disasters, while they are the beginning of sorrows to the wicked, are instrumental in advancing, purifying, and consummating Christ's kingdom, vers. 6–8; Hag. 2 : 6, 7; Rom. 8 : 19–23.

4. Persecutions, defections from the faith, false teachers, and decrease of love amid abounding iniquity, are to be expected, and should lead us to trust in Christ, and persevere unto the end, vers. 9–13; Heb. 10 : 39; James 5 : 7–11; 1 Pet. 4 : 12, 13; Rev. 2 : 10.

5. The Gospel, if received, is a witness of the power of God unto salvation; but if rejected, it is a witness of the righteousness and justice of God in final condemnation, ver. 14; Mark 16 : 16; Acts 10 : 36; 2 Cor. 2 : 16; 1 John 5 : 9–12.

6. We should mark in history the abomination of desolation and the destruction of Jerusalem, and behold in them a testimony to the truth of Christ, vers. 15; Rev. 1 : 3.

7. We should live in constant readiness, so that if called to escape dangers which may threaten Christians or the church, we may do so at once, vers. 16–18; Gen. 19 : 17; Prov. 22 : 3; Luke 17 : 31, 32.

8. It is right to pray that the seasons and the weather may be favorable to us in all Christian enterprises and undertakings, ver. 20; James 5 : 17, 18.

9. The judgments of nations in this world foreshadows the judgment of in-

Parables inculcating watchful preparation and watchful activity.

XXV. ˣ THEN shall ʸ the kingdom of heaven be likened unto ten ᶻ virgins, which took their lamps,

ˣ ch. 24. 44–51.
ʸ ch. 3. 2.
ᶻ Ps. 45. 14.

dividuals in the world to come, vers. 16–21.

10. Christians are the salt of the earth, on whose account the calamities of men and nations are limited and restrained, ver. 22; Gen. 18 : 23–33; Isa. 1 : 9.

11. We are not to believe a teacher merely because he can produce great phenomena. The sorcery of ancient times, the witchcraft and spiritualism of modern days, have done this, vers. 23, 24; Lev. 19 : 31; 20 : 6; Isa. 8 : 19, 20; Acts 8 : 9–12; 13 : 8; 1 John 4 : 1.

12. Our only safety is in Christ. So surely as the eagles gather to devour their prey, so surely shall judgment come upon the wicked, whatever their plans and combinations, vers. 25–28; Prov. 11 : 21; 16 : 5; 2 Pet. 3 : 4–7.

13. Though heaven and earth be visited with fearful phenomena, foreboding the coming of Christ, yet, amid the sorrows of the nations, Christians may rejoice and feel secure, vers. 29–31; Luke 21 : 28; 2 Tim. 2 : 19.

14. Let us be as wise in perceiving the signs of the spiritual world as of the natural, and be prepared for the coming of the Lord either in death, judgments, or the clouds of heaven, vers. 32, 33; ch. 16 : 1–3.

15. Nothing can be more certain than the coming of Christ, and the fulfillment of his word, vers. 34, 35; Isa. 54 : 10; Luke 16 : 17; 1 Pet. 2 : 24, 25; 2 Pet. 1 : 19; 3 : 9, 10.

16. It is best for us to be ignorant of the time both of our death and of Christ's coming, ver. 36; Acts 1 : 7.

17. The coming of Christ will be a time of separating the righteous from the wicked, a day joyous to the former but terrible to the latter, vers. 39–41; 1 Thess. 4 : 17; 5 : 1–3; 2 Thess. 1 : 7–10.

18. Watchfulness is a trait of a faithful and wise disciple; slothfulness of a worldly and formal professor, vers. 42–47; 1 Cor. 6 : 20; 1 Thess. 5 : 5–7.

19. Fidelity to the Master will be gloriously rewarded, ver. 47; Rev. 2 : 7, 11, 17, 26–28; 3 : 5, 12, 21.

20. Let us beware of the secret and common persuasion that God will not soon call us to an account, ver. 49; Eccle. 8 : 11; 2 Pet. 3 : 3, 4.

21. The false professor shall meet with a terrible doom, especially if he has held high positions of trust or office, vers. 49–51; ch. 22 : 13.

CHAPTER XXV.

1–13. Jesus enforces the necessity of CONSTANT READINESS for his second coming, by the PARABLE OF THE TEN VIRGINS. Found in Matthew only.

1. **Then.** When the Son of Man comes, of which Jesus had just been discoursing in the preceding chapter. **The kingdom of heaven.** The reign or administration of the Messiah, in relation to his professed followers, shall be likened to the circumstances about to be related. **Ten Virgins.** Ten maidens. *Ten* was a common and favorite number among the Jews. There were ten commandments. The tabernacle had ten curtains. The Jewish harp had ten strings. Ten men living in one place were necessary to form a congregation in a synagogue. Ten lamps or torches were the usual number in a marriage procession. **Took their lamps.** See on ch. 5 : 15. The need of these arose from the fact that the marriage ceremonies, including the bridal procession, on account of the heat of the day, took place at night. **Went forth to meet the bridegroom.** When, according to the custom of the age and country, the bridegroom was returning with his bride from her father's house to his own, where the nuptials were to be performed. The virgins were to meet them and join the procession, and thus enter in with the bridal company to the marriage. "It was the custom in the land of Ishmael," says Rabbi Solomi as quoted by Wetstein, "to bring the bride from the house of her father to that of her husband in the night time; and there were about ten staffs; upon the top of each was a brazen dish containing rags, oil, and pitch, and this being kindled formed blazing torches, which were carried before the bride." Trench also quotes the

2 and went forth to meet ᵃ the bridegroom. ᵇ And
3 five of them were wise, and five *were* foolish. They
that *were* foolish took their lamps, and ᶜ took no oil
4 with them: but the wise ᵈ took oil in their vessels
5 with their lamps. ᵉ While the bridegroom tarried,
6 ᶠ they all slumbered and slept. And ᵍ at midnight
ʰ there was a cry made, ⁱ Behold, the bridegroom
7 cometh; ᵏ go ye out to meet him. Then all those
8 virgins arose, and ˡ trimmed their lamps. And the
foolish said unto the wise, ᵐ Give us of your oil;
9 ⁿ for our lamps are gone out. But the wise answered, saying, *Not so;* ᵒ lest there be not enough for us
and you: but go ye rather to them that sell, and
10 buy for yourselves. And ᵖ while they went to buy,
ᵠ the bridegroom came; ʳ and they that were ready

ᵃ John 3. 29; Eph. 5. 25-32; Rev. 19. 7; 21. 2, 9.
ᵇ ch. 13. 47; 22. 10.
ᶜ ch. 23. 25; Is. 48. 1, 2; Eze. 33. 31.
ᵈ Ro. 8. 9; 2 Cor. 1. 22; 1 John 2. 27.
ᵉ ch. 24. 48.
ᶠ 1 Thes. 5. 6-8.
ᵍ 1 Thes. 5. 1-3; Rev. 16. 15.
ʰ ch. 24. 31; John 5. 28, 29; 1 Thes. 4. 16.
ⁱ 2 Thes. 1. 7-10.
ᵏ Am. 4. 12; 2 Cor. 5. 10.
ˡ Lk. 12. 35, 36; 2. Pet. 3. 14.

---

following extract from Hughes's *Travels in Sicily*, etc. (vol. ii. p. 20), which will serve to illustrate the custom brought to view in the parable: "We went to view the nocturnal procession which always accompanies the bridegroom in escorting his betrothed spouse from the paternal roof to that of her future husband. This consisted of nearly one hundred of the first persons in Joannina, with a great crowd of torch-bearers and a band of music. After having received the lady, they returned, but were joined by an equal number of ladies, who paid this compliment to the bride." The virgins in the parable were doubtless young female friends of both the bride and bridegroom.

2. **Wise.** Discreet, prudent. **Foolish.** Stupid, lacking in discretion and prudence. The names are rightly applied; for the one class showed a wise foresight; the other a foolish stupidity. Compare ch. 7: 24, 26. The best text names the **foolish** first. So ver. 3 should begin, *For the foolish*, introducing a reason.

3, 4. These verses present an important part of the parable. The foolish were more intent on their lamps; the wise on their oil. These *torch-lamps* needed to be often replenished from their vessels. **Oil.** The word in the original means *olive-oil*, that being regarded the best for lamps by the Hebrews, and commonly used for that and other purposes.

5, 6. **Slumbered.** Nodded, became drowsy, and **slept** or fell asleep. There was nothing wrong in this, provided they were in readiness for the bridegroom. The wise fell asleep with preparation, oil in their vessels; the foolish, having commenced wrong, thoughtlessly fell asleep without preparation. **At midnight.** He came upon them suddenly as a thief. It was a bad time for the foolish virgins to procure oil; indeed it was no time for them, as it afterward appears. **A cry made.** Doubtless by the heralds that were sent before the procession. The announcement, according to the best critical authorities, should be, **Behold the bridegroom!** *Cometh* should be omitted.

7, 8. **Trimmed their lamps.** Put in order, prepared or trimmed their lamps, by pouring on fresh oil, and clearing the wick of the excrescences that prevented a clear flame. The latter is supposed to have been done by a sharp-pointed wire attached to the lamp, as still seen in the bronze lamps found in sepulchres. All the virgins arose and prepared their lamps; but the foolish, finding that their lamps needed fresh oil, asked for a supply from the wise. **Gone out.** Rather, *Are going out.* The wick is cleared and put in readiness; but alas! the flame burns dimly, and is even now going out for want of oil.

9. **Not so; lest there be**, etc. According to the best critical authorities, this should read, *Not so! there will not be enough for us and you.* The answer was an emphatic refusal, *Not so, by no means*, and shows earnestness and the necessity of haste. The wise had only enough oil for themselves; the foolish, to obtain it, must do as the wise had previously done, **buy** for themselves.

10. But it was too late to make the needed preparation; the bridegroom

went in with him to the marriage: and ⁰ the door was shut. Afterward came also the other virgins, saying, ᵖ Lord, Lord, open to us. But he answered and said, Verily I say unto you, ᵠ I know you not.

ⁿ Ps. 49. 7.
ᵒ Job 8. 13, 14; Lk. 8. 11-14, 18.
ᵖ Eze. 11. 14, 16.
ᵠ Is. 55. 6.

came, and the **ready** entered in with him to the marriage festivities. **And the door was shut.** All that could participate in the marriage were now admitted; the door was shut against all others, including all who, through negligence, had failed to be present and enter with the bridegroom.

This portion of the parable is strikingly illustrated as follows, by Mr. Ward, in his View of the Hindoos: "At a Hindoo marriage, the procession of which I saw some years ago, the bridegroom came from a distance, and the bride lived at Serampore, to which place the bridegroom was to come by water. After waiting two or three hours, at length, near midnight, it was announced, as if in the very words of Scripture, 'Behold, the bridegroom cometh; go ye out to meet him.' All the persons employed now lighted their lamps, and ran with them in their hands to fill up their stations in the procession; some of them had lost their lights, and were unprepared; but it was then too late to seek them, and the cavalcade moved forward to the house of the bride, at which place the company entered a large and splendidly illuminated area, before the house, covered with an awning, where a great multitude of friends, dressed in their best apparel, were seated upon mats. The bridegroom was carried in the arms of a friend, and placed in a superb seat in the midst of the company, where he sat a short time, and then went into the house, the door of which was immediately shut and guarded by sepoys. I and others expostulated with the doorkeepers, but in vain. Never was I so struck with our Lord's beautiful parable as at that moment. *And the door was shut.*"

11, 12. The foolish virgins should have known that now admittance was impossible; but they remain *foolish* still, and come and seek for entrance. As those well acquainted, as expected guests, and as virgins wishing to do him honor, they address him **Lord;** and in their earnestness and importunity, they repeat the appellation. But he answers, **I know you not;** I know you not as mine; I do not recognize you, and I do not acknowledge you, as my guests.

The *grand design* of this parable is to show the necessity of being ever *prepared* for the second coming of Christ. It is especially necessary to keep this thought prominent to a right understanding of the parable. Its *centre of comparison* is found in the wise virgins having provided themselves with oil, which the foolish had neglected to do. The *bridegroom* represents Christ. The *bride* is not mentioned in the parable, and hence it is evident that Jesus did not intend to bring that figure into the comparison at this time. The *coming* of the bridegroom is the second coming of Christ, ch. 24: 42-44. The *marriage* is the marriage-supper of the Lamb, Rev. 19: 7-9. The *virgins* are the professed followers of Christ, who shall be living on the earth at that time. The *wise* are *true* disciples; the *foolish*, the *mere professed* disciples, ch. 7: 21. The *kingdom of heaven* being *likened* to these virgins, shows what will take place among the followers of Christ, under his kingdom or administration, at his second coming.

The *oil* is the Holy Spirit, in his enlightening and sanctifying influence, "the unction," or "anointing from the Holy One" (1 John 2: 20, 27); or more generally, the grace of God in the heart, the inward principle of spiritual life. *Oil* is a Scripture symbol of the Holy Spirit, Zech. 2: 2, 11-14; Acts 10: 38; 2 Cor. 1: 21; Heb. 1: 9. The *lamps* represent the outward profession (ch. 5: 14-16; 1 Tim. 6: 12); the *vessels*, the body which in believers is an earthen vessel containing the Gospel treasure, and a temple of the Holy Spirit, 1 Cor. 3: 16; 2 Cor. 4: 7; 1 Thess. 4: 4. Thus the *wise* made a *true* profession, the direct effect of the Holy Spirit's work within; they presented their bodies a living sacrifice, holy and well pleasing to God, Rom. 12: 1. The *foolish* made a *false* profession, the result of wrong principles or excitements within; they had a form of godliness, but not the power, 2 Tim. 3: 5.

The *bridegroom tarrying* represents the delay of Christ in coming, and may have

13 ᵠ Watch therefore, for ye know neither the day ᵛ Rev. 22. 12, 20. ʳ Lk. 12, 37.
nor the hour wherein the Son of man cometh. ˢ Ge. 7. 16; Lk. 13. 25; Heb. 3. 19.
14 ʸ For *the kingdom of heaven is* ᶻ as a man traveling

been intended to intimate that it would be delayed beyond the expected time. The *slumbering and sleeping* of the virgins very happily illustrates the peaceful confidence of the truly prepared and waiting disciples on the one hand, and the false security and stupidity of the mere nominal and unprepared professor on the other. It may also be an intimation that Christians will very generally cease to look for and expect the second coming of Christ, Luke 18 : 8. His coming at *midnight* may represent the suddenness of his coming (1 Thess. 5 : 2; 2 Pet. 3 : 10); and the *cry*, "the voice of the archangel and the trump of God," 1 Thess. 4 : 16.

The *trimming of their lamps* represents Christians setting themselves in order for the immediate coming of their Lord. The *wise* and true professor already prepared will put himself at once in order through the influences of the Spirit; but the *foolish* and false professor will find his light going out, his hopes and his outward manifestations of piety expiring, and in his dismay will discover that he lacks the Holy Spirit and the principle of inner life, Luke 21 : 26.

The *refusal* of the wise virgins to give the *foolish* of *their oil* may be an intimation that no one will have more grace than he needs himself, that religion is a personal matter, and each one must be wise for himself, Prov. 9 : 12. This portion of the parable must, however, be interpreted cautiously. There is here some drapery. The answer of the wise virgins and the going of the foolish virgins to buy oil, till in and prepare the way, for presenting the bridegroom as coming and the door as shut. The answer, *Go to them that sell, and buy* must mean, Go to God, and through the appointed means and way obtain the Spirit and his blessings of a new heart and life. This, however, they were too late to obtain.

Only those who were *ready* entered in with the bridegroom, so the truly prepared disciple shall enter in with the Lord into the enjoyment of the glories of heaven. The shutting of the door, compare Gen. 7 : 16; Rev. 3 : 7, represents heaven as then closed against all mere nominal professors, Rev. 21 : 7, 8.

And as the bridegroom said to the foolish virgins, *I know you not*, so at his second coming Christ will not acknowledge the mere professor as his disciple, however great or many his pretensions may have been, ch. 7 : 22, 23. This parable may, in a secondary sense, be applied to death and the personal preparations for it; since death, as surely as the second coming closes the season of preparation for heaven. The true believer then departs to be with Christ (Phil. 1 : 23), while the victim of false hopes and professions becomes alarmed and anxious for the help of others; but often when it is too late.

13. This verse forms the connecting link between this and the following parable. It both enforces the lesson taught by the parable of the Ten Virgins, and prepares the way for that of the Talents. **Watch therefore.** Be prepared; be in constant readiness, so that you may be like the wise virgins. But be not only vigilant in *preparation* and *readiness*, but also in *activity* and *faithful labors* which will be enforced in the parable about to be spoken, 1 Pet. 4 : 7; Heb. 10 : 24, 25. **For ye know neither the day nor the hour!** Such is the true reading, according to the highest critical authorities, *wherein the Son of Man cometh* not being found in the oldest manuscripts and versions. The *day* and *hour*, however, refer to the coming of Christ, ch. 24 : 44; 25 : 31.

14–30. THE PARABLE OF THE TALENTS. Related only by Matthew. In the former parable, Jesus enforced upon his disciples the duty of watchful preparation; in this, of watchful activity, in view of his second coming and the judgment.

This parable is very similar to that in Luke 19 : 11–27, yet distinct from it in time, place, occasion, design, and structure. They can not therefore be, as some have supposed, identical. That in Luke was spoken to the multitude during the last journey of Jesus to Jerusalem, probably while he was at the house of Zaccheus, in order to correct the view of those who "thought that the kingdom of God should immediately appear," to enforce the duty of patiently waiting and actively working for him,

into a far country, *who* called his own servants, and
15 delivered unto them his goods. And unto one he gave ᵃ five ᵇ talents, to another two, and to another one; ᶜ to every man according to his several ability;
16 and straightway took his journey. Then he that had received the five talents ᵈ went and traded with the
17 same, and made *them* other five talents. And likewise he that *had received* two, ᵉ he also gained other
18 two. But he that had received one went and digged
19 in the earth, ᶠ and hid his lord's money. After a long time the lord of those servants cometh, ᵍ and
20 reckoneth with them. And so he that had received five talents came and brought other five talents, saying, Lord, thou deliveredst unto me five talents: behold, ʰ I have gained beside them five talents

ᵗ ch. 7. 21-23; Heb. 12. 17.
ᵘ Ps. 5. 5; Hab. 1. 13; John 9. 31; 2 Tim. 2. 19.
ˣ ch. 24. 42-44; 1 Cor. 16. 13; 1 Pet. 5. 8; Rev. 16. 15.
ʸ Mk. 13. 34; Lk. 19. 12-26.
ᶻ ch. 21. 33.
ᵃ Ro. 12. 6-8; 1 Cor. 12. 7-11; 1 Pet. 4. 10.
ᵇ ch. 18. 24.
ᶜ Ro. 12. 6-8; 1 Cor. 12. 7-11, 29; Eph. 4. 11.
ᵈ 1 Cor. 9. 16-23; 1 Tim. 6. 17, 18; 3 John 5-8.

and to shadow forth the fearful destruction which would come upon the Jews for rejecting the Messiah. This in Matthew was spoken to the disciples, possibly to only four of the twelve, Peter, James, John, and Andrew (Mark 13: 3); on the Mount of Olives, the third day before the crucifixion (ch. 26 : 2), and was intended to enforce the duty of laboring faithfully for Christ and bringing forth fruit in proportion to the capacities and opportunities given. Other differences are readily seen on comparing the two parables, such as, a wealthy private individual, three servants, and different amounts distributed, in this; a king, ten servants, and the same amount given to each, in that.

14. For the kingdom of heaven, etc. Literally, *For as a man going abroad called his servants.* Though it does not state what is compared to the man who went abroad, yet the meaning is plain. *For* connects this parable with the exhortation in the preceding verse to *watch*. This parable presents reasons for watchfulness additional to those given in that of the Ten Virgins. As both the preceding verse and parable related to the coming of the Son of Man, so does also this. With the same general idea different scholars insert, *the kingdom of heaven, the Son of Man, he is,* and *it is,* and some omit all insertion. The meaning is, For the Son of Man is as a man going abroad, etc.; or, For as a man going abroad and returning deals with his servants, so shall the Son of Man deal with his professed followers at his second coming. **Traveling into a far country.** *Going abroad,* or *to another country,* implying nothing in regard to distance, whether far or near. See ch. 21 : 33. **Servants.** The slaves of antiquity were frequently trained to various kinds of business, and intrusted with money and other property with which they traded in their master's behalf. **His goods.** His property in hand, of which we are told in the next verse.

15. Talents. A Hebrew talent was worth about $1500. See ch. 18: 24. **According to his several ability.** According to his own ability, or power, for business or trafficking. **Took his journey.** *Went abroad;* the same verb as in verse 14.

16, 17. Went and traded. Two of the servants labor faithfully and diligently in their master's behalf; which is as important a feature of this parable as the waiting in readiness was of that of the Ten Virgins. **Other five talents—other two talents.** Not only did they receive, but they also improved what they received, according to their respective business ability.

18. Hid his lord's money. He neither improved his own ability nor the property intrusted to him. It was his *lord's* money; he had no right to bury it in the earth; it was given him for trading. Slothfulness also in not using his business ability was unfaithfulness to his master.

19. The man who went abroad now appears in his official and authoritative character, as **lord,** an absolute master, and **reckoneth,** or makes a settlement with his servants. See ch. 18 : 23.

20. I have gained beside them

21 more. His lord said unto him, ¹ Well done, *thou good and faithful servant: thou hast been faithful over a few things,* ʲ I will make thee ruler over many
22 things: enter thou into ᵏ the joy of thy Lord. He also that had received two talents came and said, Lord, thou deliveredst unto me two talents: behold,
23 I have gained two other talents beside them. His lord said unto him, ¹ Well done, good and faithful servant: thou hast been faithful over a few things, I will make thee ruler over many things: enter thou
24 into the joy of thy lord. Then he which had received the one talent came and said, ᵐ Lord, ⁿ I knew thee that thou art a hard man, reaping where thou hast not sown, and gathering where thou hast
25 not strewed: and I was afraid, and went and hid thy talent in the earth: lo, *there* thou hast *that is*
26 thine. His lord answered and said unto him, *Thou* wicked and slothful servant, thou knewest that I reap where I sowed not, and gather where I have

ᵉ Ecc. 11. 1-6; 2 Cor. 8. 12; Eph. 5. 16; Heb. 6. 10.
ᶠ Pro. 18. 9; 26. 13-16; Hag. 1. 2-4.
ᵍ Ro. 14. 11, 12; 2 Cor. 5. 10.
ʰ 1 Cor. 15. 10; Col. 1. 29.
ⁱ 1 Cor. 4. 5; 2 Cor. 10. 18.
ʲ ch. 10. 40-42; 24. 47; Lk. 12. 44; 22. 29, 30; Rev. 21. 7.
ᵏ Ps. 16. 11; John 14. 3; 17. 24; 2 Tim. 2. 12; Heb. 12. 2; 1 Pet. 1. 8; Rev. 7. 17.
ˡ ver. 21.
ᵐ ch. 26. 49; Lk. 6. 46.
ⁿ Mal. 3. 14, 15; Job 21. 14-16.

---

five, etc.; other five talents besides them, in addition and by means of them.
21-23. **Well done.** An exclamation of commendation and praise. *Good! right well! well done!* **Over a few things.** Over a little. **Make thee ruler over many things.** I will appoint or set thee over much. Mark the contrast. If the talents intrusted to them were a *little*, what must have been the *much?* **Enter thou into the joy,** etc. Participate in my joy and share with me my pleasure. It is thought by many that the figure here is that of a master making a great feast, and inviting his servants who had proved faithful to enter in to its enjoyment. Such occasions were sometimes signalized by giving freedom to those servants who sat down with their master. The joy here seems to be that which was connected with his possessions and the honor and higher positions to which they were to be raised. Notice also that the same words of approval are made to the servant who had gained the two talents as to him that had gained the five, showing that it was not the amount that they had gained, but their *fidelity* which pleased their master.
24, 25. **A hard man.** Stern, harsh, 1 Sam. 25: 3. **Reaping where thou,** etc. Over-exacting; exacting more than thou oughtest, and more than thy servants are able to perform. **Gathering where thou hast not strewed;** where thou hast not scattered, that is, the seed. Some take it to mean *scatter abroad* grain to the wind, that is, to *winnow*, Ezek. 5: 2, 10, 12. But it was the straw and chaff that was scattered and not the grain; for winnowing was usually done by tossing up the mingled broken straw, chaff, and grain against the wind with a fork, by which the grain fell to the ground and the rest was dispersed. This clause, by clothing the idea of the clause before it in a new garb, gives it emphasis and new force. The seed is now not *sown* and now not *scattered;* a harvest, however, is now *reaped* and now *gathered* into the barn. **And I was afraid.** Yet he is not now afraid to speak insolently to his master. His fear was evidently put on, a base counterfeit. He was slothful and lacked the disposition to work. **Lo, there thou hast that is thine.** Lo, thou hast thine own. He adds falsehood to hypocrisy; for his skill, labor, and time were his master's, as well as the money.
26, 27. **Wicked.** In contrast to the *good* servants; and shown by his insulting language, his hypocrisy and his want of regard for his master's interests. **Slothful.** Opposed to the *faithful* servants, and shown by his idleness and hiding the talent in the earth. **Thou knewest that,** etc. This is a question of surprise and displeasure, and should be so punctuated. Thou knewest all

27 not strewed: Thou oughtest therefore to have put my money to the exchangers; and *then* at my coming I should have received mine own with usury.
28 Take therefore the talent from him, and give *it*
29 unto him which hath ten talents. ᵒFor unto every one that hath shall be given, and he shall have abundance: but from him that hath not ᵖ shall be taken away even that which he hath. And cast ye
30 the unprofitable servant ᑫ into outer darkness: there shall be weeping and gnashing of teeth.

ᵒ ch. 13. 12; Mk. 4. 25; Lk. 8. 18; 19. 26; John 15. 2.
ᵖ ch. 21. 41; Rev. 2. 5.
ᑫ ch. 8. 12; 24. 51; Lk. 14. 34, 35; John 15. 6.

this, didst thou? Then surely thou oughtest to have been diligent; thou art self-condemned, Luke 19:22. **To the exchangers.** To the bankers, who exchanged money, and received money on deposit at interest. **Mine own with usury;** the interest which the bankers allowed on deposited money. This thou couldst have done with no exertion on thy part, and no risk to thyself; thou art therefore utterly without excuse. *Usury* meant lawful interest when our translation of the Bible was made.

29. The same principle as that presented in ch. 13:12. **For unto every one that hath;** by a wise use of his ability and opportunities, **shall be given** greater opportunities and means. **Have abundance.** He shall be made to abound, Heb. 6:7. But he that **hath not,** by not improving his opportunities according to his ability, and having no disposition to do so. **Shall be taken away.** Even the opportunities and means of gain shall be taken from him, 1 Sam. 15:17-19, 28.

30. The servant is presented in a new light, **unprofitable,** to his master, to others, and to himself. **Outer darkness.** The darkness without the banqueting house, the figure being that of a feast, where he shall give vent to his chagrin and anguish by **weeping and gnashing of teeth.** See on ch. 8:12. As the good and faithful servants were welcomed to joy, so the wicked, slothful, and unprofitable servant was plunged into sorrow.

The *grand design* of this parable was to enforce watchful activity in the service of Christ, thereby bringing forth fruit corresponding to the ability and opportunity enjoyed. It enforces the duty of doing with our might whatever our hands find to do (Eccles. 9:10), and of working while it is day, John 10:4. That of the ten virgins taught us the necessity of the *inner life* of godliness, and of *waiting* in calm confidence for the coming of our Lord; this brings to view the necessity of the *outer* life, and of being prepared by active and faithful service. The two parables may thus be regarded as counterparts, and explanatory of each other. The former by no means teaches idleness and a dead faith, nor the latter, human dependence and salvation by works. The *centre of comparison* is found in the use which the servants made of their lord's money.

The *man* who went abroad represents Christ, who has indeed gone to *another country*, even the heavenly, John 14:2; 16:28; Acts 1:9-11. *His own servants* are the professed followers of Christ. The *goods* which were delivered to the servants, represent the *trust in general* which Christ has committed to his followers; and the *talents* the trust in *particular*, as given to individuals. *Talents* can not mean *ability;* for they were given according to each man's ability; nor *saving grace,* for one at least had it not. They evidently represent the blessings, opportunities, and privileges which Christ intrusts to his followers, 1 Pet. 4:7-11. It should also be remembered here that the *ability*, the powers and capacities of men, is also the gift of God. Compare John 3:27; James 1:17. As *different amounts* were intrusted to the servants according to their ability, so does Christ intrust to his followers blessings and opportunities corresponding to their individual powers and capacities. The *servants trading* with their talents, represent the Christian engaged in active Christian duty, according to his opportunity and capacity. The *one who hid* his lord's money, represents the nominal professor neglecting to use his ability in improving the blessings of the Gospel.

The *coming of the lord* is the second

346 MATTHEW XXV. A.D. 30.

Graphic scene of the final judgment.

31 ʳ WHEN the Son of man shall come in his glory, and all the holy angels with him, then shall he sit

ʳ ch. 16. 27; 19. 28; Dan. 7. 13, 14; Zec. 14. 5; Mk. 8. 33; Ac. 1. 11; 1 Thes. 4.

coming of Christ. And as it is said that *after a long time* he came, so is it here intimated that a long time would intervene between Christ's ascension and his return, 2 Thess. 2: 2. The whole period between the ascension and second coming of Christ is thus brought to view in the parable. The *reckoning* represents the judgment, Eccles. 12 : 14; 2 Thess. 1 : 7-10; Heb. 9 : 27; Rev. 20 : 12.

As the two good and faithful servants met with the approval of their lord, so will true Christians receive the approval of Christ for their fidelity in his service, vers. 34-36. The contrast between a *few things*, or *little* and *many things*, or *much*, is an intimation of the enlarged powers and opportunities and blessings of Christ's followers in their glorified state, 1 Cor. 15 : 52-54; 1 John 3 : 2; Rev. 20: 6; 21 : 3, 4; 22 : 3-5. *The joy of the lord* represents the joy of Christ's fully consummated and glorified kingdom (Heb. 12 : 2), into which his followers shall enter, not as "servants," but "friends" (John 15 : 15), sharing with him as heirs, "heirs of God and joint-heirs with Christ" (Rom. 8 : 17), and as kings reigning with him forever, Rev. 3 : 21; 22 : 5. And inasmuch as the lord uttered the same words of approval to each of his faithful servants, so shall believers be at last rewarded according to their improvement of Gospel blessings (2 Cor. 5 : 10); and each shall receive according to the measure of his enlarged and developed ability.

The *account rendered* by the servant with *one talent* represents the nominal professor, as without love for Christ, having a wrong estimate of his character and service, and as hypocritical, slothful, wicked, and unprofitable; and doing only what he thought necessary to escape punishment. The *reply* of his lord shows that false professors will be self-condemned, and victims of their own folly. As he ought to have put his lord's money to the exchangers, so false professors will see at the judgment that, according to their own confessions, they ought to have made at least an ordinary improvement of their blessings and opportunities. Here *exchangers* are variously interpreted to mean believers in general, strong and leading Christians, the machinery of religious and charitable societies, etc. But this part of the parable should not be pressed. It is clearly taught that neglect to improve the talent was injustice toward his master. The *taking of the talent from him* represents the false professor at last deprived of all privileges, opportunities, and blessings, and his *being cast forth into outer darkness* represents the everlasting punishment which shall be executed upon hypocrites and unbelievers, vers. 41, 46.

The *giving* the one talent to him that had ten talents illustrates the confidence which Christ will at last exercise in his faithful followers, who will have even those trusts which would have been confided to others had they not proved unfaithful and unprofitable. Compare Luke 16 : 10.

31-46. JESUS CLOSES HIS DISCOURSE BY A GRAPHIC DESCRIPTION OF THE FINAL JUDGMENT. In the two preceding parables he had illustrated the condition and the recompense of professed disciples at his second coming. Now he proceeds to describe the final judgment of all men. This is not a parable; for it presents literally and distinctly "the Son of Man," and not a parabolic character of husbandman, householder, or the like. It indeed likens the Son of Man to a shepherd in verses 32 and 33, but it immediately presents him in his literal capacity of "King." The whole description abounds with living imagery, but without any intimation of a parabolic similitude. It does not *liken* the kingdom of heaven or the judgment to any thing, but describes the latter in language not to be misunderstood. See on verse 1, and on ch. 13 : 3.

31. **When.** Rather, *And when.* Jesus proceeds to speak further of his second coming, and of the scenes which will follow. **Come in his glory.** His second and glorious coming, to which Jesus had referred in ch. 24 : 30, 31. **Shall he sit.** As a King and Judge. Christ is Lawgiver, King, and Judge, and thus combines every power and attribute of government. **Throne of his glory.** The throne of his eternal kingdom and of infinite majesty, the throne

32 upon *the throne of his glory: and ᵗbefore him shall be gathered all nations : and ᵘhe shall separate them one from another, as a shepherd divideth *his*
33 sheep from the goats : and he shall set ᵛthe sheep on his ʷright hand, but the goats on the left.
34 Then shall the King say unto them on his right hand, Come, ye blessed of my Father, ˣinherit the kingdom ʸprepared for you from the foundation of
35 the world : ᶻfor I was an hungered, and ye gave me meat : I was thirsty, and ye gave me drink : ᵃI was
36 a stranger, and ye took me in : ᵇnaked, and ye clothed me : I was sick, and ye visited me : ᶜI was

16; 2 Thes. 1. 7; Jude 14 ; Rev. 1. 7.
ᵛ Rev. 3. 21; 20. 11.
ᵗ Ro. 14. 10-12 ; 2 Cor. 5. 10; Rev. 20. 12.
ᵘ ch. 13. 42, 43, 49; Eze. 20. 38; 34. 17, 20 ; Mal. 3. 18.
ᵛ Ps. 95. 7; John 10. 26-28.
ʷ Ps. 45. 9; 110. 1; Eph. 1. 20.
ˣ Ro. 8. 17; 1 Pet.

of his glorious power and righteous judgment, Rev. 20 : 11-13; Phil. 2 : 10, 11.

32. **All nations.** *All the nations.* The whole world. The people of every tribe and of all ages. The judgment is of individuals, as is evident from all that follows. **He shall separate.** He shall divide them one from another. All mankind are in character divided into two classes. So shall they actually be divided at the judgment. **As a shepherd.** This brief parabolic language is itself an evidence that the whole passage is not a parable. That which illustrates, and that illustrated, can not both be parabolic. **Sheep—goats.** Sheep, being gentle and docile, are made to represent the righteous; while goats, being stubborn and unteachable, represent the wicked. Compare Rom. 2 : 7, 8, where these two classes are briefly described by their characteristics. Sheep and goats pastured together in ancient times (Gen. 30 : 33), as they still do in Palestine. The language seems to indicate that the righteous and wicked will continue together in the world till the judgment.

33. **He.** The Son of Man. The *sheep* and *goats*, which follow, show that the passage is partly figurative. The verse partakes more of the nature of the allegory than of the parable. See on ch. 13 : 3. The **right hand** was the position of honor and approbation. The **left hand** was the less honored position (see on ch. 20 : 21), and, in this case, indicative of disapprobation and approaching evil.

34. **The King.** Christ will come in royal dignity and power, Rom. 14 : 9; Rev. 19 : 16. As King of kings he combines in himself all power—legislative, executive, and judicial. He is the King who judges and executes, John 5 : 22,

23, 27; Acts 17 : 31; 2 Cor. 5 : 10. Only in this instance does Jesus style himself a king. **Blessed of my Father.** As regenerated and sanctified by the Spirit, delivered from the curse of the law, heirs of God, loved and chosen by the Father, Eph. 1 : 3; 2 Thess. 2 : 13, 14 ; 1 Pet. 1 : 2-5. **Inherit.** As heirs of God and joint-heirs of Christ, Rom. 8 : 17. This idea is the more striking with the kind invitation, **Come**, literally, *hither, come hither.* Compare on ch. 4 : 19- **Kingdom.** The state and place of glory. **Prepared for you,** as my chosen people. "Therefore elect men are not chosen in place of the angels, who sinned."—BENGEL. **From the foundation of the world.** From the beginning of the world, from eternity. Compare John 17 : 24; Eph. 1 : 4, 5 ; 1 Pet. 1 : 20.

35. **For.** The reason why they are thus gloriously rewarded. By their fruits are they known; by the deeds done in the body are they judged. By their deeds of love they had shown their love to Christ, and their *faith* working by love, Gal. 5 : 6; 1 John 3 : 10-12. Love is the fulfilling of the law, and the greatest grace, ch. 22 : 37-40; Rom. 13 : 8-10 ; 1 Cor. 13 : 13 ; Gal. 5 : 14. The King enumerates not what they had *said*, but what they had *done*, James 1 : 22-24. And these deeds were charity, hospitality, beneficence, visitation, sympathy, and attention. They required self-denial, and the sacrifice of time, property, and ease. Compare James 1 : 27. **Gave me meat.** Rather, *Gave me to eat.* **A stranger.** One of another country, a foreigner. **Took me in;** to your home, and as one of your family.

36. **Visited me;** so as to look after me, and render me assistance. The enu-

37 in prison, and ye came unto me. Then shall the righteous answer him, saying, Lord, ^d when saw we thee an hungered, and fed *thee?* or thirsty, and
38 gave *thee* drink? When saw we thee a stranger,
39 and took *thee* in? or naked, and clothed *thee?* Or when saw we thee sick, or in prison, and came unto
40 thee? And the King shall answer and say unto them, Verily I say unto you, ^e Inasmuch as ye have done *it* unto one of the least of these ^f my brethren, ^g ye have done *it* unto me.
41 Then shall he say also unto them on the left hand, ^h Depart from me, ⁱ ye cursed, ^j into everlasting fire,
42 prepared for ^k the devil and his angels: ^l for I was an hungered, and ye gave me no meat: I was thirsty,
43 and ye gave me no drink: I was a stranger, and ye took me not in: naked, and ye clothed me not:
44 sick, and in prison, and ye visited me not. Then shall they also answer him, saying, Lord, ^m when saw we thee an hungered, or athirst, or a stranger, or naked, or sick, or in prison, and did not minister
45 unto thee? Then shall he answer them, saying, Verily I say unto you, ⁿ Inasmuch as ye did *it* not

1. 4, 9; 3. 9; Rev. 21. 7.
^y ch. 20. 23; Mk. 10. 40; 1 Cor. 2. 9; Eph. 1. 3, 4; Heb. 11. 16.
^z Is. 58. 7; Eze. 18. 7; Jam. 1. 27.
^a Heb. 13. 2; 3 John 5.
^b Jam. 2. 14-16.
^c 2 Tim 1. 16; Heb. 13. 3.
^d ch. 6. 3; 1 Chron. 29. 14.
^e ch. 10. 42; Pro. 14. 31; 19. 17; Mk. 9. 41; Heb. 6. 10.
^f ch. 12. 49, 50; 28. 10; Heb. 2. 11-15.
^g ch. 18. 5; Ac. 9. 4, 5; Eph. 5. 30.
^h ch. 7. 23; Ps. 6. 8; Lk. 13. 27; 2 Thes. 1. 9.
ⁱ Gal. 3. 10; Heb. 6. 8.
^j ch. 13. 40, 42; Mk. 9. 43-48; Rev. 14. 11.

meration of sufferings are from the less to the greater. **Came unto me;** to sympathize with me, and relieve my necessities.

37-39. The righteous are represented as replying with modest self-forgetfulness and self-renunciation. We are not to suppose this will be the actual language of the righteous at the judgment. The scene is thus vividly and dramatically presented in order to illustrate the great truth, that as they had treated his brethren they had treated him. At the same time it truthfully portrays the modesty and humility of the righteous, who absorbed and lost, as it were, in the glory and work of their Lord, exclaim, "Not unto us, O Lord; not unto us, but unto thy name give glory," Ps. 115: 1.

40. **The least—my brethren.** The least of his followers, and especially of his messengers, who have preached the Gospel, ch. 12: 49; 28: 10; Heb. 2: 11, 12. **Done it unto me.** His ministers, and indeed all his followers in the world are his representatives. He shares with them trials, afflictions, and persecutions, and they with him, ch. 10: 40; Prov. 19: 17; Heb. 4: 15; 1 Pet. 4: 13. Not even the gift of a cup of cold water will be forgotten, ch. 10: 42.

41. **Ye cursed.** *Accursed* on account of their sins. The difference of the language to the wicked from that to the righteous (verse 34) is marked, and deserves notice. *Of my Father*, is not appended to *cursed*. The wicked are condemned *by* God, but they are not *his* in the full sense that the righteous are. "The everlasting fire" is **prepared** not for *you*, but for *the devil and his angels*, or *demons*. See on ch. 4: 24. There is an election unto life, but not unto death. It also appears from Rev. 20: 10-13 that the Devil will first be cast into hell, after that the wicked. Neither is it here added, prepared *from the foundation of the world*. Neither devils, nor any portion of men, were set off and appointed from eternity as reprobates. **Everlasting fire.** By this is implied the intensity and eternity of the punishment.

42, 43. Let it be noticed that only sins of omission are mentioned here. Men need only neglect the great salvation to insure their eternal ruin, Heb. 2: 3.

44. **They also.** Their reply, in some respects similar to that of the righteous, is opposite in spirit and meaning. Their self-righteousness in striving to vindicate themselves is vividly presented. **Minister.** *Wait upon, serve.* "As if they would always have been ready to

to one of the least of these, ye did *it* not to me. 46 And ᵒ these shall go away into everlasting punishment: ᵖ but the righteous into life eternal.

ᵏ 2 Pet. 2. 4; Jude 6; Rev. 20. 10.
ˡ Am. 6. 6; 1 John 3. 17.
ᵐ Lk. 10. 29.

serve him. But there is nothing of the spirit of love in their assumed readiness; only in the spirit of servitude they would have waited on him, had they seen him."—LANGE.

46. Everlasting punishment — life eternal. *Everlasting* and *eternal* are the translations of the same word, and should have been both translated *everlasting*. The misery of the wicked will be as enduring and endless as the blessedness of the righteous. The word thus translated (*aionios*) is used in the New Testament 71 times, of which 3 refer to the long indefinite past (Rom. 16: 25; 2 Tim. 1 : 9; Tit. 1 : 2), 2 to complete eternity without beginning or end, once of God, and once of the Spirit, which was in Christ (Rom. 16 : 26; Heb. 9 : 14), 51 to the future happiness of the righteous, 7 to the future misery of the wicked, and in the remaining 8 instances it involves the idea of an unending future, Luke 16 : 9; 2 Cor. 4 : 18; 2 Thess. 2 : 16; 1 Tim. 6 : 16; Philem. 15; Heb. 13 : 20; 2 Pet. 1 : 11; Rev. 14 : 6. It is the most expressive of endless duration of any single term in the Greek language.

The *punishment* is not annihilation; for (1) the word so translated (*kolasis*) involves the idea of suffering and not of annihilation. It is used twice in the New Testament, here, and in 1 John 4 : 18, where it is rightly translated *torment*, "Fear hath *torment*." The verb from which it is derived is used twice (Acts 4 : 21; 2 Pet. 2 : 9), and both cases expresses punitive suffering. (2) The connecting and explanatory words, *everlasting fire*, *everlasting* punishment, are decisive against annihilation. To speak of everlasting annihilation is an absurdity. The everlasting punishment is the everlasting fire, where "they shall be tormented day and night, forever and ever," Rev. 20 : 10. It is the unquenchable fire, where "their worm dieth not, and the fire is not quenched," Mark 9 : 44. **Life eternal.** This is the opposite of everlasting punishment, or spiritual and eternal death. It is not merely existence, but unending blessed existence—the whole being in spiritual harmony and intimate union with God forever, with all of the blessed and glorious results. "Eternal life" in this passage is explained by the preceding invitation (ver. 34), "Inherit the kingdom prepared for you." Compare also ch. 19 : 16, 21; John 5 : 24; 17 : 2, 3; Rom. 8 : 6.

REMARKS.

1. An outward profession is important, but not enough; an inward spiritual life is essential to salvation, vers. 1–4; Jer. 8 : 4–9; 2 Cor. 13 : 5; 1 John 2: 19, 20.

2. Let us be wise, exercising foresight in regard to the future, and living in constant readiness for eternity, vers. 3. 4; ch. 7 : 21–27; 1 Tim. 6 : 11, 12.

3. The true and the false professor may not be distinguished now, the calm confidence of the one from the false security of the other; but the time is coming when the distinction will be clear, both to themselves and others, vers. 5–12; Ps. 5 : 5; Prov. 1 : 29–33; Mal. 3 : 18; 2 Tim. 2 : 19.

4. The foolish professor depends on the church, its external ordinances, and seeks from these what should be sought of God, vers. 8, 9; Isa. 55 : 1, 6; Acts 4 : 12; Rev. 22 : 11.

5. Preparation for another world is an individual work. No one can do it for another, vers. 8–10; Ps. 49 : 7; Prov. 9 : 12; Rom. 14 : 12.

6. Let us watch and be ever ready to enter into the marriage supper of the Lamb; when the door is shut, it will be too late, vers. 10–12; Luke 13 : 25; 2 Cor. 6 : 2; 1 Thess. 5 : 6; Heb. 3 : 18, 19; Rev. 22 : 11.

7. God has bestowed upon men a diversity of talents according to his own sovereign will and pleasure, yet in accordance with every man's ability, ver. 15; 1 Cor. 12 : 4–11; Rom. 12 : 6–8.

8. Our talents may be largely increased. Even those who have but few may turn them to a good account, vers. 16, 17; Prov. 8 : 19–21.

9. Our fidelity, and not the number of our talents, will determine our final reward, vers. 21, 23; 1 Cor. 4 : 2; 2 Cor. 8 : 12; 10 : 18; 2 John 8; Rev. 3 : 21.

10. Simple neglect will insure our condemnation, vers. 24–28; Heb. 2 : 3.

11. Self-righteousness, pretension to superior knowledge, and fault-finding

Jesus announces his crucifixion; the Jewish rulers conspire against him.

XXVI. AND it came to pass, when Jesus had finished all these sayings, he said unto his disciples,
2 [q] Ye know that after two days is *the feast of* the passover, and the Son of man [r] is betrayed to be crucified.

[q] Pro. 14. 31; 17. 5; Zec. 2. 8; Ac. 9. 5; Heb. 4. 15.
[r] Dan. 12. 2; Lk. 16. 26; John 5. 29; Ro. 2. 7, etc.; 2 Thes. 1. 9; Rev. 21. 8.
[p] ch. 13. 43; John 3. 15, 16, 36; Ro. 5. 21; 6. 23.

with God, are signs of the slothful servant, vers. 24, 25; Job. 21 : 15; Prov. 26 : 12, 16; Mal. 1 : 13.

12. The wicked, at last, will be self-condemned, vers. 26, 27; Rom. 2 : 1-3.

13. He that brings forth no fruit unto God is absolutely unprofitable, and fit only to be cast away, ver. 30; ch. 3 : 12; John 15 : 6.

14. Christ is the judge of the world, vers. 31, 32; John 5 : 22, 27; Acts 10 : 42; 17 : 31.

15. In view of the solemn assemblage and separation at the judgment-seat, let us inquire to which company do we belong, vers. 32, 33; ch. 13 : 41, 49.

16. The least believer is a child of God and a representative of Jesus in the world, vers. 40, 45; ch. 10 : 40-42; Luke 14 : 12-14; Rom. 12 : 5, 16; 1 Pet. 4 : 9-11.

17. The spirit we possess toward Christ will be manifested toward his followers, vers. 34-45; 1 John 3 : 14; 4 : 20.

18. We are justified by faith alone, yet it is a faith productive of good deeds, and which works by love, vers. 31-36; Rom. 5 : 1; Eph. 2 : 8, 9; Gal. 5 : 6; James 2 : 14, 22.

19. Union with Christ on earth will insure union with him in heaven; disunion, banishment forever, vers. 34, 41; Isa. 1 : 28; John 15 : 2-6; 1 John 1 : 3; Rev. 21 : 7.

20. Life and death are placed before us. According to our lives on earth will be our condition throughout eternity, ver. 46; Rom. 2 : 6-10; 2 Thess. 1 : 7-10.

CHAPTER XXVI.

With the last chapter Matthew closes his account of the *prophetical* ministry of Christ. In this and the next following he proceeds to the *sacrificial* work of Christ, which he narrates somewhat more fully than either of the other evangelists.

1, 2. JESUS FINALLY AND DEFINITELY ANNOUNCES HIS CRUCIFIXION. Found only in Matthew.

1. **Finished all these sayings.** Of the last two chapters. Turning from the scenes of his glory, and of the final judgment, Jesus directs the minds of his disciples to his humiliation and sufferings. The prophetic description of the former was well fitted to sustain the disciples while witnessing the latter. **His disciples.** The twelve.

2. **After two days is the feast of the Passover.** Rather, *After two days comes the Passover.* The Jews reckoned the day as beginning at sunset. This was probably spoken on Wednesday (April 5th), either after sunset of Tuesday or the following morning.

The *Passover* was instituted in commemoration of God's sparing the Hebrews when he destroyed the first-born of the Egyptians. On the tenth day of the month Abib (Exod. 13 : 4), or, as it was afterward called, Nisan (Esth. 3 : 7), answering most nearly to our month of April, a male lamb or kid, without blemish, was selected. On the fourteenth day of Nisan, it was slain in the temple, between the two evenings of three and six o'clock. In the evening, the beginning of the fifteenth day, the paschal supper was eaten by not less than ten nor more than twenty persons. Bitter herbs and unleavened bread were to be eaten with it, and all was done originally with haste, standing, with loins girt, their feet shod, and their staff in hand. With the paschal supper began the feast of unleavened bread, which lasted seven days. See Exod. 12 : 1-20; Lev. 23 : 5-8; Num. 9 : 1-5. The Jewish year was reckoned from this month, and John marks the various stages of Christ's public ministry by the Passover, John 2 : 13, 23; 4 : 45; 5 : 1; 6 : 4; 11 : 55.

In the New Testament, the word *passover* is applied to the paschal lamb (Mark 14 : 12; Luke 22 : 7); to *the paschal supper*, including the lamb (ch. 26 : 17;

A.D. 30.   MATTHEW XXVI.   351

3   *Then assembled together the chief priests, and
the scribes, and the elders of the people, unto the
palace of the high-priest, who was called Caiaphas;
4 and consulted that they might take Jesus by subtil-

q Mk. 14. 1; Lk.
22. 1; John 13. 1.
r ch. 17. 22.
s Ps. 2. 2; John 11.
47; Ac. 4. 25.

Mark 14 : 12, 14; Luke 22 : 11, 15; Heb. 11 : 28); and to the *paschal festival* of unleavened bread, Luke 2 : 41; 22 : 1; John 2 : 13; 6 : 4, etc. In Mark 14 : 1, the whole is specified by *the passover and the feast of unleavened bread*. Here the word refers more properly to the whole festival. For farther on the Passover see on ver. 20.
  Is betrayed. Literally, *given up, delivered* into the power of another. The word in the original does not necessarily imply an act of treachery; but is sometimes so applied by classic writers. Jesus now for the first time foretells the exact time of his crucifixion, and that he shall be delivered up into the power of others for this purpose.
  3–5. THE JEWISH AUTHORITIES CONSPIRE TO KILL JESUS, Mark 14 : 1, 2; Luke 22 : 1, 2.
  3. **Then.** Two days before the Passover, ver. 2. While Jesus is foretelling with certainty his death, the Jewish Sanhedrim are plotting in uncertainty. **Chief priest, scribes, elders.** *Scribes* should be omitted, according to the highest critical authorities. The Sanhedrim, the highest court of the Jews. See on ch. 2 : 4. **Unto the palace of the high-priest.** Not *palace*, but *court;* the inclosed square, under the open sky, around which the house was built. Thus, in ver. 69 the same court

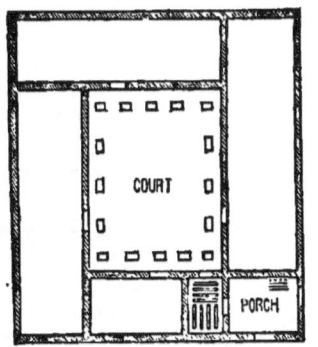

is meant where Peter was sitting "without in the court," not "without in the palace," which would be absurd. So, also, the same court or inclosed space is meant in Luke 22 : 55, where it is said that they "kindled a fire in the midst of *the hall*," that is, "*the court*." The usual meeting-place of the Sanhedrim was an apartment in one of the courts of the temple, called Gazeth, at the south-east corner of the court of Israel. In cases of emergency, or, as in this case, where great secrecy was desired, it sat at the house of the high-priest, who was generally president of the court.
  The **High-Priest** was the head of the priesthood and of all religious affairs. Aaron was the first high-priest (Exod. 28 : 1–38), and the office continued in his family about fifteen centuries; but Herod, and the Roman governors after him, changed the incumbents at pleasure, so much so that the office became almost annual. Compare John 11 : 51, where it is said that Caiaphas was high-priest *that year*.
  Caiaphas. Joseph Caiaphas was high-priest about nine years, during the whole procuratorship of Pontius Pilate, but was deposed by the Proconsul Vitellius soon after the removal of Pilate. He was son-in-law to Annas, who had been formerly the high-priest, and who still exerted great influence as father-in-law of Caiaphas, and is thought by some to have shared the office with him; the latter as actual high-priest, the former as president of the Sanhedrim, or else that Annas acted as the vicar or deputy of Caiaphas. Compare Luke 3 : 2; John 18 : 13, 19, 24; Acts 4 : 6.
  4. **Consulted.** They consulted together. **Subtilty.** *Craft, artifice.* Jesus had overcome them in argument and in his teaching, both before and in the view of the people. They were afraid to undertake it openly, lest he should be rescued by the people, or they should be still more humiliated by him in the presence of the people. **Kill him.** Put him to death as an official act.
  5. **Not on the feast-day.** Rather, *Not at the feast*, the whole festival of seven days, during which time the vast multitude, amounting sometimes to two millions, were gathered at Jerusalem,

5 ty, and kill *him*. But they said, 'Not on the feast day, lest there be an uproar among the people. ᵗ Pro. 19. 21.

The Supper and Anointing at Bethany.

6 ᵘ NOW when Jesus was in ᵛ Bethany, in the house
7 of Simon the leper, there came unto him a woman having an alabaster box of very precious ointment,

ᵘ Mk. 14. 3; John 11. 1, 2; 12. 3.
ᵛ ch. 21. 17; Ex. 30. 23, 33.

They were afraid of an **uproar** or *tumult* among the people; they say nothing of the sacredness of the feast. They hoped to carry out their plans the better after the feast, when the people had gone. But this determination of the Sanhedrim was changed by the treacherous proposal of Judas, as will be presently related.

6-13. THE SUPPER AND THE ANOINTING AT BETHANY, Mark 14 : 3-9; John 12 : 2-8. The three evangelists evidently relate the same event, with merely the variations of independent narrators. The anointing related in Luke 7 : 36-50 is altogether different from this in time, place, and circumstances. That took place much earlier, in Galilee, probably in the vicinity of Nain; this at Bethany, just before the crucifixion. The one at the house of Simon the Pharisee; the other at the house of Simon the leper. That both were named Simon is not strange in a country where that name was very common. There were even two Simons among the apostles, ch. 10 : 2, 4.

6. **In Bethany.** See on ch. 21 : 17. The time of this supper has been much discussed. From John 12 : 1 it appears that Jesus came to Bethany six days before the Passover, on Friday, about sunset (see on ch. 21 : 1), and from Luke 21 : 37 we learn that during the week Jesus was wont to spend the days in the city, and the nights at or near Bethany. Hence, the supper might have occurred upon any one of these evenings. According to John, it seems more natural to place it about twenty-four hours after his arrival, on the evening of Saturday, a common time for suppers. But, according to Matthew and Mark, it would seem that it could not have occurred earlier than two days before the Passover. They both relate the supper as the occasion which led to the treachery of Judas. The language in ver. 14, *then went Judas*, connects his visit to the chief priests immediately with the supper. As the Sanhedrim had, two days before the Passover, probably Wednesday morning, resolved not to put Jesus to death till after the feast, this visit of Judas must have occurred later on Wednesday, or early on Thursday. The supper, then, might have taken place on the evening of Tuesday, after his final discourses in the temple, and on the Mount of Olives, or on Wednesday evening, after spending the day in retirement in Bethany. The latter seems the more natural conclusion, when we remember how much Jesus did on Tuesday, and that Wednesday appears to have been spent in quiet among his friends. Yet the language, *From that time*, etc., in ver. 14, seems to imply a longer time than a part of a day, and would rather incline us to the supposition that the supper occurred Tuesday evening. This, however, is one of the points that will never be certainly settled in this world.

Simon the leper. Who had probably been healed by Jesus. He was, perhaps, a relative of Lazarus, and a near neighbor, or both families may have occupied the same house. Hence, Martha serves and Lazarus is a guest, John 12 : 2. One tradition makes him the father of Lazarus, another the husband of Martha. This is, however, all uncertain.

7. **A woman.** John calls her Mary, the well-known sister of Martha and Lazarus. Matthew and Mark speak indefinitely, as they make no special reference to the family of Lazarus. The same characteristics are here observable as in the incident recorded in Luke 10 : 38, 41. Martha serves; Mary comes in to be by her Lord, and to show her devotion to him.

Alabaster. A variety of gypsum, white and semi-transparent, very costly, and used for making vases and vials for ointments. It was considered by the ancients the best for preserving them. Layard found vases of white alabaster among the ruins of Nineveh, which were used for holding ointments or cosmetics.

8 and poured it on his head, as he sat *at meat*. ˣ But ˣ John 12. 4, 5.
when his disciples saw *it*, they had indignation,
9 saying, To what purpose *is* this waste ? For this
ointment might have been sold for much, and given
10 to the poor. When Jesus understood *it*, he said ʸ ch. 25. 35–40;
unto them, Why trouble ye the woman ? for she Deu. 15. 11; John 12. 8.
11 hath wrought a good work upon me. ʸ For ye have ᶻ see ch. 18. 20; 28.
the poor always with you ; but ᶻ me ye have not al- 20; John 13. 33;
12 ways. For in that she hath poured this ointment 14. 19; 16. 5, 28; 17. 11.
13 on my body, ᵃ she did *it* for my burial. Verily I ᵃ 2 Chr. 16. 14.

The general shape of these boxes or vases was large at the bottom, with a long, narrow neck. It was probably the neck of the flask which the woman broke (Mark 14 : 3), an act expressive of her feelings that she would devote it all to her Lord, reserving nothing for herself. **Ointment.** This was pure spikenard, nard of the finest quality (Mark 14 : 3); an aromatic oil or ointment, probably produced from the *jatamansi* plant in India. The quantity was a pound, John 12 : 3. **Very precious.** Very costly. **Poured it on his head.** A distinction conferred on guests of honor, Luke 7 : 46. John says she anointed his *feet*. She anointed both his head and feet, which was the very highest honor. There is no contradiction, but only variety of statement between the Evangelists. Matthew and Mark notice only the first act, anointing the head; John dwells upon the final and longest, and on her part the most humble and devoted act, the anointing the feet and wiping them with her hair. See on ver. 12. **As he sat.** As he reclined at table on a couch.

8. His disciples. *The disciples.* Mark says, *There were some;* but John, pointing out the leader and instigator, says, *One of his disciples, Judas Iscariot.* We have here a beautiful illustration of the independent and truthful statement of the three Evangelists. Judas probably suggested it; others caught up and repeated it. **Had indignation.** Were displeased. They had the feeling of disapprobation, bordering on resentment.

9. For this ointment. Simply, *For this. Ointment* is omitted by all the highest and best authorities. **Sold for much.** Mark, *For more than three hundred pence* or *denaries;* that is, forty-five dollars. **Given to the poor.** Under ordinary circumstances a good reason, and, doubtless, uttered honestly by all except Judas, who desired the money for his own use rather than for the benefit of the poor, John 12 : 6.

10. When Jesus understood—Why trouble ye the woman ? Rather, *And Jesus knowing it,* etc. The murmuring was against the woman, and the reproof was intended for her, probably administered to her by Judas, but not intended to be heard by Jesus, who was the recipient of such honor. The disapprobation of the disciples would naturally trouble and confuse her. But, Jesus knowing their complainings, and the avaricious and thievish spirit of Judas, takes up her defense. **Wrought a good work.** A work distinguished for its moral beauty, fitness, and grace; literally, a *beautiful* work. He goes on in the next two verses to show why it was such a work.

11. The poor always—me not always. They would ever have opportunities of doing good to the poor; but their opportunity to honor him would be short, and soon gone. The next verse shows that such an opportunity would never again occur.

12. Poured this ointment on my body. Indicating how profusely she had poured it forth. Although the Evangelist had only spoken of anointing the head, his language here seems to intimate that more than that had been anointed. See on ver. 7. **She did it for my burial.** *To prepare me for burial,* to anoint and embalm my body as if it were already dead, and thus prepare it for the sepulchre. This anointing was not only a symbol of what was about to take place, but was an act performed with definite reference to his death. The language seems to imply a *motive* on the part of Mary; she seems to have had a presentiment, a knowledge beyond his disciples of his approaching death. Her act of love and of faith

say unto you, Wheresoever this Gospel shall be preached in the whole world, *there* shall also this, that this woman hath done, be told ᵇ for a memorial of her.

ᵇ 1 Sam. 2. 30.

Judas engages to betray Jesus.

14 ᶜ THEN one of the twelve, called ᵈ Judas Iscariot, went unto the chief priests, and said *unto them*,
15 ᵉ What will ye give me, and I will deliver him unto

ᶜ Mk. 14. 10; Lk. 22. 3; John 13. 2, 30.
ᵈ ch. 10. 4.
ᵉ ch. 27. 3; Zec. 11. 12, 13.

stands out in striking contrast to the avarice of Judas, and the murmurings of the others.

13. Jesus proceeds to confer upon her one of the greatest honors ever bestowed upon a mortal. **Verily,** etc. A solemn and authoritative assertion. See on ch. 5 : 18. **This Gospel.** The glad tidings of salvation through a dying and living Savior, which he commanded to be preached to every creature, Mark 16 : 15. **For a memorial of her.** Her deed shall be immortal; it shall be held in everlasting remembrance, and hence she shall, on account of it, be everywhere spoken of. It is remarkable that Matthew and Mark, who give this prophecy, do not give her name, but John, who gives her name, omits the prophecy. But her *deed* was the great thing; again, she was *one* in the world's history, the only one in regard to whom Jesus made such a promise; but her name, Mary, was common, and designated many. Yet John, in giving the account, and revealing the fact that the woman was Mary, the sister of Martha, still farther contributes toward making the knowledge of her deed and person commensurate with the preaching of the Gospel. Alford sees in this prophecy a distinct reference to the *written records* in which this event should be related.

14-16. JUDAS ENGAGES WITH THE CHIEF PRIESTS TO BETRAY JESUS, Mark 14 : 10, 11; Luke 22 : 3-6.

14. **Then.** This closely connects this act of Judas with the supper, and with what had just transpired. The words of Jesus were counter to his own, and, in connection with the high honor bestowed upon Mary, were a severe reproof to him. He must have felt that, in the eyes of Jesus, and, indeed, of the others, he stood in insignificant contrast to the devoted Mary. Stung with the transactions and the words of the hour, his evil nature was aroused to thoughts both of abandoning the cause of Jesus, and of treachery. With a heart unrenewed he had not only been captivated with an idea of an earthly kingdom, but a spiritual reign and a suffering Savior were also repulsive. He could not perceive spiritual truth. Hence the humiliation of Jesus, his prophecies concerning his death, his denunciation of the Jewish hierarchy, all ran counter to his feelings and spirit. He saw no prospect of worldly power, and his hopes of gain died with the anointing at Bethany, and the approving declaration of Jesus, that it was anticipatory of his burial. Turning away from Jesus and his cause with resentment and disappointment, he seeks to satisfy his avarice by selling him to his enemies. See on ch. 27 : 3. **Iscariot.** *Man of Karioth*, probably native of Karioth of Judah. See on ch. 10 : 4.

15. **What will ye give?** The question reveals the ruling passion of Judas. His offer was received with joy by the chief priests. Luke says, "They were glad;" they thought that now they could apprehend him privately, without causing a tumult among the people. **They covenanted with him.** Literally, *They placed*, that is, in a balance; hence, *They weighed out to him*. Others translate, *They appointed*, or *fixed upon*, the price for him. It is thought that the language of Mark (14 : 11), "They promised to give him money," and of Luke (22 : 5), "They covenanted to give him money," favor the latter. But in ch. 27 : 3 we learn that Judas had been paid. The first translation makes Matthew's account the more complete. The money could have been weighed out to him at this time, and laid aside, or placed in the hands of another, to be given him when he fulfilled his engagement. **Thirty pieces of silver.** Thirty silver shekels, the price of the life of a slave (Exod. 21 : 32), commonly estimated at

A.D. 30.	MATTHEW XXVI.	355

you? And they covenanted with him for ᶠ thirty
16 pieces of silver. And from that time he sought opportunity to betray him.

Jesus celebrates the Passover, and points out the traitor.

17 ᵍ NOW the first *day* of the *feast of* unleavened bread the disciples came to Jesus, saying unto him, Where wilt thou that we prepare for thee to
18 eat the passover? And he said, Go into the city to such a man, and say unto him, The Master saith, ʰ My time is at hand; I will keep the passover at
19 thy house with my disciples. And the disciples did as Jesus had appointed them; ⁱ and they made ready the passover.

ᶠ comp. ch. 27. 9; Ex. 21. 32.

ᵍ Mk. 14. 12; Lk. 22. 7; Ex. 12. 6, 18-20.

ʰ John 12. 23; 13. 1.

ⁱ Ex. 12. 4-10.

---

about fifteen dollars. They were probably sacred shekels, heavier than the common shekel, and hence paid by weight. The amount fixed upon shows the contempt of the Sanhedrim toward their victim, and the avarice of Judas, 1 Tim. 6 : 10. Thus also was prophecy fulfilled, Zech. 11 : 12. See also ch. 27 : 9, 10.
16. **From that time.** For one, possibly, for nearly two days. The expression more naturally implies the longer rather than the shorter time. See on ver. 6. **Sought opportunity;** to deliver him quietly into their hands; "in the absence of the multitude," Luke 22 : 6; "how he might conveniently betray him," Mark 14 : 11. **Betray him.** Deliver him up into their power, answering to the *deliver him unto you* of ver. 15. See on ver. 2.
17-25. PREPARATION AND CELEBRATION OF THE PASSOVER. JESUS POINTS OUT THE TRAITOR, Mark 14 : 12-21; Luke 22 : 7-30; John 13 : 1-30.
17. **The first day of the feast of unleavened bread.** The day when the paschal lamb was killed, Mark 14 : 12; Luke 22 : 7. Hence the 14th of Nisan, occurring this year on Thursday, April 6th, Exod. 12 : 18. This in popular language was the first day of the Passover, although the feast did not strictly begin till the fifteenth. Hence Josephus speaks of the feast of unleavened bread lasting eight days. On the 14th, the leaven was removed and the unleavened bread took its place. Compare Num. 28 : 16, 17. It is evident from this verse and the references given, that Jesus observed the Paschal Supper at the regular time, and not an anticipatory meal, as some suppose, twenty-four hours before the usual time. See a discussion of this question in the HARMONY OF THE GOSPELS by the author, throughout ¿ 159. **Where;** etc. The point of this question refers to the *place* of the supper, and only incidentally to the preparation of the paschal lamb.
18. **Go into the city.** From Bethany where they now were, into Jerusalem, where only the paschal supper could be eaten. Hence, since the destruction of Jerusalem and of the temple where only the paschal lamb was slain, the Jews omit eating the lamb, and confine themselves to the usual feast of unleavened bread, which followed the supper. According to Luke (22 : 8) the duty enjoined in this command was specially intrusted to Peter and John. **Such a man.** Jesus does not mention him by name, or if he does, his disciples do not know him; for his place was to be found by following a man bearing a pitcher of water, Mark 14 : 13, 14; Luke 22 : 10. **The Master.** *The Teacher.* Probably a disciple of Jesus. Possibly some previous understanding existed between them; but more probably the man had prepared the room in advance, as was common at that season, for the use of any who might need it, and Jesus by his omniscience knew it. Some very plausibly suppose that Jesus concealed the place and the name of the individual, so as to prevent Judas from executing his purpose before the proper time. **My time;** of suffering and death, John 13 : 1. It is not probable that either the householder or his disciples fully understood his meaning. They doubtless thought of his time of keep-

20 ᵏ Now when the even was come, he sat down with
21 the twelve. And as they did eat, he said, ˡ Verily
I say unto you, that one of you shall betray me.
22 And they were exceeding sorrowful, and began every
23 one of them to say unto him, Lord, is it I? And

ᵏ Mk. 14. 17; Lk. 22. 14.
ˡ John 6. 70, 71; 13. 21.

---

ing the Passover. But identical with that was the time of Jesus our Passover, 1 Cor. 5 : 7.

19. **The disciples did,** etc. They went into the city, found the man as *directed*, and a large upper room furnished and ready, Mark 14 : 15. The man may have prepared it, and reserved it under a deep divine impression. **Made ready the Passover.** Had the lamb slain in the temple, its blood sprinkled at the foot of the altar, and its fat burned thereon, the bitter herbs, the bread and wine prepared.

20. **The even was come.** The evening which commenced Friday, the 15th of Nisan. **He sat down.** *He reclined at table*, according to the custom of eating, with the left hand resting upon the couch, which was usually higher than the low table. The whole service was originally performed standing, but reclining was adopted after the Israelites possessed Canaan, symbolizing the rest God had given them. Sundry additions were afterward added. According to the Talmud, compiled in the third century from earlier traditions, four cups of the common red wine of the country, usually mingled with one fourth part of water, were drunk during the meal, and marked its progress. The first, as they reclined at table in connection with an invocation and blessing upon the day and the wine, corresponding with the cup mentioned in Luke 22 : 17. Then followed washing of hands, the bringing in of unleavened bread, bitter herbs, the roasted lamb, and a sauce or fruit-paste. The master of the feast then blessed God for the fruit of the earth and gave the explanation respecting the Passover prescribed in Exod. 12 : 26, 27. Psalms 113, 114 were then sung, and the second cup was drunk. Then each kind of food was blessed and eaten, the paschal lamb being eaten last. A third cup of thanksgiving, called the cup of blessing (compare 1 Cor. 10 : 16), for deliverance from Egypt was drunk. Psalms 115-118 were sung and the fourth cup drunk, closing the celebration. Sometimes Psalms 120-137 were sung or repeated, followed by a fifth cup.

We may presume that Jesus observed the more ancient manner of celebrating the Passover, rather than that of the later Jewish traditions. We have no evidence that he used more than one cup at the Passover, Luke 22 : 17, 18. Before the drinking of this cup, the contention among the twelve (Luke 22 : 24-30) probably occurred, and the washing of the disciples' feet (John 13 : 1-20) immediately after. The paschal supper is continued; the traitor is pointed out, who withdraws, and then the Lord's Supper is instituted.

The Passover was both commemorative and typical in its nature and design. It commemorated the deliverance from the destroying angel in Egypt, and typified the greater deliverance through Christ, "the lamb of God that taketh away the sin of the world." At this very feast "Christ our passover was sacrificed for us," 1 Cor. 5 : 7.

21. **As they did eat;** the Passover, after the washing of the disciples' feet, John 13 : 11, 18. Luke (22 : 19-23) gives an account of the institution of the Lord's Supper before that of pointing out the traitor; the latter is but a passing notice; the position of the former was probably decided by the mention of the first cup of wine. Both Matthew and Mark place the supper afterward. **Shall betray me.** One of you will deliver me up into the power of my enemies.

22. **Exceeding sorrowful.** Greatly distressed at this terrible announcement. **Began every one.** *Each one* (Judas of course excepted), in anxiety and amazement began to ask, "Lord, is it I?"

23. From the full account of John, we learn that Peter beckoned to John, who was leaning on Jesus' breast, requesting him to ask privately, who it was of whom he spoke. John did so, and Jesus gave him a sign by which he might know the traitor, namely, he to whom he should give a sop or morsel. **He that dippeth his hand with me.**

A.D. 30.   MATTHEW XXVI.   357

he answered and said, ^m He that dippeth *his* hand
24 with me in the dish, the same shall betray me. The
Son of man goeth ⁿ as it is written of him: but
° woe unto that man by whom the Son of man is
betrayed! It had been good for that man if he
25 had not been born. Then Judas, which betrayed
him, answered and said, Master, is it I? He said
unto them, Thou hast said.

Jesus institutes the Lord's Supper.

26 ^p AND as they were eating, Jesus took bread, and

^m Ps. 41. 9; Lk. 22. 21; John 13. 18.
ⁿ Ge. 3. 15; Ps. 22; Is. ch. 53; Dan. 9. 26.
^o ch. 27. 3–5; John 17. 12; Ac. 1. 16–20.
^p Mk. 14. 22; Lk. 22. 19; 1 Cor. 11. 23–25.

More exactly, *He that dipped*, etc. Persons often expressed their affection to others by presenting them with dipped bread, etc. Hence this act of Jesus might easily be misunderstood. The right hand was used at the table, instead of spoons and forks; the hands being washed before and after eating. We may suppose the answer recorded by Mark (14 : 20) to have been first given; then the sign to John, while the several disciples continued to ask, "Is it I." Having dipped his hand in the dish with Judas and given him the sop, he replies, "He that dipped," etc. **In the dish.** Of sauce prepared of dates, figs, and seasoning, which was of brick color, representing the clay and brick of Egypt. Into this they dipped their bread and bitter herbs. This pertained to the Passover, from which it is evident the Lord's Supper had not commenced. One dish may have been used, but more probably there were several. Judas was probably near Jesus, using the same dish. The language in Mark 14 : 18, 20, seems to imply this. The replies of our Saviour seem to have been better understood by Judas than by the others; for when Judas went out, no one appears to have understood the intent of our Lord's language to him, John 13 : 28, 29. The object of Jesus was not to expose the traitor, but to give him all necessary warning against committing so terrible a crime.

24. **Goeth as it is written.** The Messiah goeth in the path of humiliation and suffering to death, as it is written of him in such prophecies as Isa. 53 : 4–12; Dan. 9 : 26; Zech. 12 : 10; 13 : 7. **Woe unto that man.** Though his death was according to God's purpose, and foretold by ancient prophets, yet his betrayer and murderers were without excuse, Acts 2 : 22–24. The woe upon the traitor points him out as an object both of pity and of wrath. The terrible consequences of his guilt are unutterable: it were good if he had never had an existence. His very being will be a curse to him. The original is peculiar, *It were good for him, if that man had not been born.* As in the whole transaction, so here the language is pointed in respect to Judas, yet general and somewhat indefinite as to the other disciples.

25. **Then Judas.** Rather, *And Judas.* Following this and other things recorded by the other evangelists, Judas last of all, from a sense of guilt and lest he should be considered *that man,* the betrayer, with feigned sorrow, yet doubtless somewhat troubled, asks, **Master,** or *Rabbi, is it I?* Notice, while the others address him *Lord,* ver. 22, Judas, colder and more formal, calls him *Rabbi,* an honorary title of a Jewish teacher or doctor. **Thou hast said.** The object of the verb, according to Hebrew idiom, is understood, *Thou hast said it,* it is as thou hast said; a form of an affirmative answer common among the Jews. Matthew alone records the question of Judas and the reply of Jesus. Jesus may have spoken in an undertone, since his reply seems to have been heard only by Judas himself, John 13 : 28. His evil nature is thoroughly aroused when he finds that Jesus not only knows his treachery, but plainly tells him of it. Satan takes possession of the heart prepared to receive him, and Judas in bitterness hastens forth from the company where he can feel no longer at home into the congenial darkness without, to execute his treacherous plan, John 13 : 27–30. Hence he was not present at the institution of the Lord's Supper. See ver. 23.

26–30. INSTITUTION OF THE LORD'S SUPPER, Mark 14 : 22–26 ; Luke 22 :

blessed *it*, and brake *it*, and gave *it* to the disciples, 27 and said, Take, eat; this is my body. And he took

19, 20. The supplemental character of John's Gospel explains his silence in regard to the institution of this ordinance. Its fourth account, though wanting in the fourth Gospel, is supplied by Paul in 1 Cor. 11 : 23–26.

26. **As they were eating.** This is in harmony with the supposition that Judas was not present at the supper. See on vers. 23, 25, and John 13 : 30. The time here indicated was probably very soon after.

These words show that the supper was instituted while they still reclined at the Passover table; but they do not teach that the Lord's Supper was grafted on the Passover, or sprang out from it. The supper was not instituted at the Passover because it was in any way connected with it, but because the Passover night immediately preceding his sufferings was the best and fittest time for its institution. It was entirely distinct, a new ordinance of the new dispensation. The Passover was sacrificial, the Lord's Supper is not; Christ has been offered once for all. The former was national and observed by families, the latter is intrusted to the church, and is emphatically a church ordinance. The one was commemorative of a temporal deliverance, yet pointing to the great Paschal Sacrifice of Christ; the other commemorates what Christ in his sufferings and death has done for his followers, yet points to him as a living Savior, absent for a time, but who will come again without sin unto salvation.

Took bread. Took *a loaf* or thin cake of unleavened bread, which was before him. The *one loaf* points to the one body of Christ which has been offered up, and to the *oneness* of his followers with him, forming "one loaf, one body," 1 Cor. 10 : 16, 17. **Blessed it.** *It* is not in the original. He blessed God and invoked the divine blessing; Luke and Paul say, *he gave thanks.* The two verbs explain each other and amount to the same thing. The giving thanks was blessing God, and both were a blessing of the bread and a setting it apart to a sacred use. Compare ch. 14 : 19 and note, and John 6 : 11. **Brake.** This represented his body broken on the cross, the wounds and sufferings of death. Hence *breaking* of the bread is essential to the true idea. Cutting it is a perversion. The ordinance was even called, "the breaking of bread," Acts 2 : 42. **Gave to the disciples.** The Apostles were the representatives of that one body the church; hence they alone partook, because it was an ordinance of that one body. The Lord's Supper is a church ordinance, 1 Cor. 11 : 20, 33. **Take, eat.** Signifying not only that Jesus is himself the spiritual bread to them, but also that they in receiving and eating it accept of him and his atonement by faith. Thus we commune in this ordinance with Christ, and through Christ we indirectly commune with one another, 1 Cor. 10 : 16, 17. The language, *Take, eat*, as well as, *Drink ye all*, seems to imply that Jesus did not himself partake. Indeed, the whole account is in harmony with such a view. There really could be no significance in Jesus partaking of that which represented his own body and blood. They were offered for others; he himself needed no offering.

This is my body. Luke adds, "which is given for you; this do in remembrance of me." Not literally *my body*; for Jesus was present in his body, and the broken bread was visibly not a part of it. So also in Paul's account, who declares that he received it from the Lord, and is therefore of the highest authority. Jesus says, "This cup is the New Testament in my blood," 1 Cor. 11 : 25; so also Luke 22 : 20. If this broken bread was literally Christ's body, then "This cup," etc. means, This material cup, (not the wine in it), is the actual New Testament or covenant. The latter so evidently demands a figurative or symbolic meaning that Maldonatus, the Jesuit commentator, could meet the difficulty only by impiously setting himself up against the inspired penman, and declaring that Christ never uttered these words. The verb *is*, in the expression, *This is my body*, upon which papists have laid so much stress in advocating the doctrine of transubstantiation, belongs only to the Greek translation of our Savior's language, though it was implied in Aramaic, the language in which our Savior spoke. Similar ex-

the cup, and gave thanks, and gave *it* to them, say-

pressions are, however, found in all languages, and with no doubtful meaning. Thus, Joseph in explaining the dream of Pharaoh says, "The seven good kine are seven years," Gen. 41 : 26. They signified or represented seven years. So also "The good seed are the children of the kingdom" (ch. 13 : 38); "that rock was Christ" (1 Cor. 10 : 4]); "Agar is Mount Sinai" (Gal. 4 : 25), and many similar expressions. So also Jesus calls himself a door (John 10 : 9), a vine (John 15 : 1), a star (Rev. 22 : 16). He also spoke of the temple of his body, John 2 : 19, 21. No one would for a moment take such language literally, but emblematically. So the bread represents his body, is an emblem of it. Or, turning our minds from the verb to the two things compared, we may say that as Christ is spiritually and figuratively a door, a star, a vine, or a temple, so his body is figuratively and spiritually the bread of life. Thus, in this part of the ordinance Christ is represented as the sustenance of his people. The doctrine of transubstantiation, therefore, finds no basis in this passage; it is contrary to its plain meaning as well as to common sense.

27. **A cup.** Including the wine which it contained. Probably the wine mixed with water, used at the Passover. "The common wine of Palestine is of red color. Such was the wine used at the sacrament, as it would seem both from the nature of the case and from the declaration, This is my blood."— L. COLEMAN, D.D. Some hold that it was unfermented wine, since nothing fermented was permitted at the feast. But of this there is wanting proof. The Jews in Palestine now use fermented wine at the feast, but if any wine is found to be running into acetous fermentation, it is removed. Dr. C. V. A. Van Dyck, who has resided for more than a quarter of a century in Syria, says (*Bibliotheca Sacra*, vol. xxvi. p. 170): "In Syria, and as far as I can learn in all the East, there is no wine preserved unfermented; . . . . they could not keep grape-juice or raisin-water unfermented, if they would; it would become either wine or vinegar in a few days, or go into the putrefactive fermentation. . . . At the Passover, only fermented wine is used. As I said before, there is no other, and therefore they have no idea of any other." Dr. Van Dyck is decided in the opinion that such a thing as unfermented wine never has been known in Syria.

According to the highest critical authorities, this should read *a cup*. But whether we have the definite or indefinite article, we must beware of falling into the error of supposing that it was one of the Passover cups. The wine was doubtless that used at the passover; but it was a cup of a new ordinance and of a new dispensation. We must not suppose that Jesus slavishly followed the tradition of the elders in celebrating the Passover.

Gave thanks. The same act as performed over the bread. He praised God for it, set it apart to a sacred use, thereby blessing it. Hence it is called the *cup of blessing*, 1 Cor. 10 : 16. From the Greek verb, *eucharisteo*, to give thanks, the ordinance has been called *the eucharist*. So also it has been called the *communion*, because in it there is a communion or partaking emblematically of the body and blood of Christ, 1 Cor. 10: 16, 17. The latter name is objectionable, because it conveys mere Christian fellowship too prominently to most minds. The former conveys too solely the idea of a thank-offering. Better call it by the names inspiration has given, either *The breaking of bread* (Acts 2 : 46), or, better still, the more comprehensive title, *The Lord's Supper* (1 Cor. 11 : 20), to which latter title the former seems to have given way. The Romish names *Mass*, and *High Mass*, the latter being sung or chanted, is without any scriptural foundation or authority.

Drink ye all, etc. That is, *Drink all ye of it.* Mark adds, "They all drank of it." The *all* is noticeable, as connected with the cup only; the fact may be used against the popish custom of withholding the cup from the people. The Apostles were the representatives of the church; the entire membership of the church are, therefore, to drink of the cup. As has been remarked by Bengel, "If one kind were sufficient, it is the cup that should be used. The Scripture thus speaks, foreseeing (Gal. 3 : 8) what Rome would do." In receiving the cup we signify our faith in the efficacy of that blood which cleanseth from all sin, the acceptance of the atonement

28 ing, Drink ye all of it; for this is my blood of the New Testament, which is shed for many for the re-
29 mission of sins. But ᑫ I say unto you, I will not drink henceforth of this fruit of the vine, ʳ until that day when I drink it new with you in my Fa-

ᑫ Mk. 14. 25; Lk. 22. 18.
ʳ Ac. 10. 41.

---

made and the redemption procured. And as blood stood for life (Lev. 17: 11, 14), so we by faith receive Christ as our life, his life as our life. For a beautiful illustration, see the language of our Savior in John 6 : 53-58.

28. For. The reason is now given for receiving the cup. **This is my blood.** This represents and is an emblem of my blood. **Of the New Testament,** or, *my blood of the covenant,* of the Gospel dispensation (the conditions, promises, and pledges of salvation), Jer. 31 : 31 ; Heb. 8 : 7-13. In contrast to the blood of the old dispensation, of which that of the Passover, of course, formed a part. The blood of the old covenant was the blood of lambs, calves, goats, and bulls, Exod. 24 : 8; Heb. 9 : 18-22. The blood of the new covenant is the blood of Christ, of which the wine of the cup is an emblem, Heb. 9 : 11, 12, 24-26. As the former covenant was made, dedicated, and its blessings secured by the blood of beasts, so the latter was procured and established, and its blessings secured to all believers through the blood of Christ. The former by *types,* the latter by the *reality;* but both by the shedding of blood. In receiving the cup, therefore, we openly accept this covenant.

Which is shed. Though before his sufferings, yet Jesus, by anticipation, speaks of it as virtually accomplished. **For many.** Great multitudes. In this place, in connection with the Lord's Supper, *many* are those to whom his blood is rendered efficacious through faith. The relation of Christ's atonement to all men is presented in 1 Tim. 2 : 6, and similar passages. See on ch. 20 : 28. Thus, the wine poured forth represents Christ's death as substitutionary *for many,* in their behalf, in their stead. **The remission of sins.** Omit the article. In order to forgiveness of sins. *Remission of sins* is the freeing of one from the guilt and consequences of sin, hence pardon, forgiveness. Christ's death was, therefore, a sacrifice, propitiatory and expiatory in its nature. Compare Isa. 53 : 5; Rom. 3 : 24, 25; Eph. 1 : 7.

29. I will not drink henceforth. Emphatic, *I will in nowise,* etc. These words he had uttered at the Passover, Luke 22 : 16, 18. He repeats them at the Supper. They are not inconsistent with the supposition that Jesus himself did not partake of the bread and wine of the supper. See on ver. 26. Instead of saying definitely *this cup,* he says generally, *this fruit of the vine.* He had just previously drank of it for the last time with them; now he takes the cup, gives thanks, hands it to them, commanding all to drink, saying that from this time onward he will not drink it till he drinks it with them, fresh and of a different kind, in the kingdom of his Father. *This fruit of the vine,* however, includes the cup, and must have referred to the wine in it as a beverage. Hence it is worthy of notice that, though he had said, *This is my blood,* he yet speaks generally of the wine as *this fruit* of the vine. No change had taken place.

The phrase also affords an argument against the use of the various forms of domestic and adulterated wines at the Lord's Supper. It should be *the fruit of the vine.* Whether it better be fermented, or unfermented, is a question worthy of attention. Although there is no proof that unfermented wine was used at the Passover (see on ver. 27), yet it was more in accordance with its spirit and nature, as the feast of *unleavened* bread. And in the Lord's Supper unfermented wine is in the truest and most literal sense *the fruit of the vine,* and answers to the idea of *freshness* implied in *new,* immediately following. Such considerations, together with the present state of society, and of the temperance question, incline me to prefer unfermented wine at the Lord's table.

New. The word in the original conveys not only the idea of *freshness,* but also of a *new kind,* and of *superior excellence.* Thus, *this fruit,* etc., and *new,* are in contrast. Jesus will not drink of the earthly beverage, which is an emblem of his death, though also of the life of his people; but he will drink of that which is the result of his death, and which all

A.D. 30. MATTHEW XXVI. 361

30 ther's kingdom. ^l And when they had sung an hymn, they went out into the mount of Olives.

The scattering of the disciples and Peter's denial foretold.

31 THEN saith Jesus unto them, ^t All ye shall ^u be

^l Mk. 14. 26; Eph. 5. 19; Col. 3. 16.

^t Mk. 14. 37; John 13. 36-38; John 16. 32.
^u ch. 11. 6.

---

his followers shall share with him; not of the earthly type, but of the heavenly reality. Thus, the new wine points to the felicity of the glorified state, the bliss of eternal life, which shall be enjoyed and celebrated at the marriage supper of the Lamb. The cup points to the life given for his people; the new wine, to that glorified life obtained for them, Rev. 19 : 6-9; 22 : 2.

This verse also shows that the ordinance not only looks back to the death of Christ, but also forward to the establishment of his glorified kingdom. Paul more exactly defines its future limit and prospect by the words, *till he come*, 1 Cor. 11 : 26. The ordinance is thus confined to the church during the absence of the Lord. It is an ordinance of the earth, not of heaven. When he comes to be present with his glorified people, they will have the reality, and will not need the emblems, either to remind them or to aid their faith. Jesus probably now utters that memorable discourse and prayer recorded by John in ch. 14-17.

30. Sung a hymn. A fitting close of the supper. This is the only recorded instance of singing by Jesus and his disciples. After an ordinance emblematical of his complete and perfect work, and after his consoling discourse and affectionate prayer, in all of which he seems to have viewed the work in its full accomplishment, he could well sing with his disciples a hymn of praise. In the original, a single word is used, literally *having hymned, having sung hymns*, or *praise*, or *psalms*, the word by no means limiting it to a single hymn, or composition. It is very commonly supposed that they sung or chanted Psalms 115-118, which were said to be used at the close of the Passover. Of this, however, we have no means of determining. The ordinance is one of mingled solemnity and joy.

This is a fitting place to refer to the relation between the two ordinances Christ has intrusted to his church. In order of time, Baptism first, the Lord's Supper after. See on the various passages relating to baptism. In relation to individuals and churches, baptism is the initial rite, the Lord's Supper the memorial, covenanting, and communing rite of those initiated by baptism. The former to individuals separately, and but once; the latter to individuals assembled in church relations, and oft-repeated. The one is a profession of faith, a putting on Christ; the other the renewed vows and confession of the soul in Christ, and living on Christ. Again, baptism points to our burial into Christ's death; the Lord's Supper, to our living by Christ's life. The former is a symbol of our new birth; the latter, of the sustenance of our new life. The one shows how we are made one in Christ; the other, how we are continued one in him. Thus, in whatever way we may view these ordinances, the former precedes the latter. Baptism is in its nature and in its divine arrangement a prerequisite to the Lord's Supper. Faith, or a regenerate state, which is presupposed by baptism, and an orderly walk (2 Thess. 3 : 6) are also prerequisites.

The Mount of Olives. See on ch. 21 : 1. Jesus passes out of the city, down the deep gorge on the eastern side, crosses the Kedron, about where a small bridge now spans the dry channel, to a grove at the foot of the Mount of Olives, named Gethsemane, where he was wont to resort with his disciples, Luke 22 : 39; John 18 : 2. He goes thither to enter upon his sufferings, and to be betrayed to his enemies.

31-35. THE SCATTERING OF THE DISCIPLES AND PETER'S DENIAL FORETOLD, Mark 14 : 27-31; Luke 22 : 39; John 18 : 1. Compare Luke 22 : 31-38 and John 13 : 31-38. It is very commonly supposed that these four accounts refer to the same conversation. It seems very difficult to reduce them to any sort of harmony. The circumstances and time seem to be different. The scene in Matthew and Mark is on their going out to the Mount of Olives; that in Luke and John while they were still in the upper room. It seems more natural and

362　　　　　　MATTHEW XXVI.　　　　A.D. 30.

offended because of me this night; for it is written,
x 'I will smite the shepherd, and the sheep of the
32 flock shall be scattered abroad.' But after y I am
risen again, z I will go before you into Galilee.
33 Peter answered and said unto him, Though all
men shall be offended because of thee, a yet will I
34 never be offended. Jesus said unto them, b Verily
I say unto thee, That this night, before the cock

x Zec. 13. 7.
y ch. 16. 21; 20. 19.
z ch. 28. 7. 10, 16; Mk. 14. 28; 16. 7; John 21. 1.
a Ps. 17. 5; Pro 28. 26; Phil. 2. 3.
b Mk. 14. 30; Lk. 22. 34; John 13. 38.

in perfect harmony with the four narratives to suppose that Jesus twice intimated Peter's denial; the first after the departure of Judas, related by Luke and John, and the second an hour or two afterward, as they were going to the Mount of Olives, related by Matthew and Mark. See author's HARMONY on § 169.

31. **Then.** As they went out. **All ye.** The eleven apostles. **Offended because of me.** Literally, *Offended in me;* not *at me*, but *in me*, as the occasion or ground of their disaffection and doubt, so far as to desert him, ver. 56. **For it is written.** In Zech. 13 : 7. The quotation which follows conforms quite closely to the Septuagint version of the Old Testament, and expresses the thought of the original Hebrew. Jesus quotes this prophecy, thereby intimating that a suffering Messiah was in accordance with the purposes of God, and that in connection with it his followers should be scattered. He quoted it also for their sake; doubtless they pondered it during those days of darkness. **I will smite.** God is said to smite Jesus, since he both permitted and purposed it; he gave him to be smitten, John 3 : 16; Acts 2 : 23. **The shepherd.** The Messiah, the great shepherd of the sheep (Heb. 13 : 20), spoken of immediately after as *my fellow* (Zech. 13 : 7), a fellow-ruler, the king of kings, and an equal, Phil. 2 : 6. In Zech. 11 : 8–13, it was foretold that he should be rejected and sold, and in 12 : 10, that he should be pierced. **Shall be scattered.** A strong and authoritative assertion. Their scattering implied that they were offended in him, disaffected in their faith, discipleship, and thoughts of him, Luke 24 : 21.

32. **I will go before.** As a shepherd. In accordance with the remainder of the verse in Zechariah, "And I will turn mine hand upon the little ones." It does not imply that he would not appear to them previous to meeting them in Galilee; but rather that, rising before their return thither, he would again collect the flock, and go before them to Galilee, ch. 28 : 7, 10; Luke 24 : 33–36. For the fulfillment of this promise see ch. 28 : 16; John 21 : 1; 1 Cor. 15 : 6.

33. **Peter answered.** Impulsive and self-confident, Peter is the first to speak. He speaks not now, as frequently, as spokesman of the apostles, but for himself, arrogating a courage and devotion above his associates. **Though all men.** Omit *men*. Notice the strength of his self-reliant assertion, *Though all* (the rest), or even more strongly, *all* (every one) *should be offended*. Jesus had said, *this night;* but he asserts, *I will* **never** *be offended*. Peter had been before warned of his defection and denial, Luke 22 : 31-34. The second warning arouses him to the strongest assertion. His self-sufficiency and arrogance found an antidote in his fall, and seem to have been alluded to by Jesus after his resurrection, at the Sea of Galilee, "Simon, son of Jonas, lovest thou me *more than these?*" John 21 : 2.

34. Jesus replies with the solemn and authoritative beginning, "Verily, I say unto you." **This night.** As in verse 31, and in opposition to the *I will never* of Peter. **Before the cock crow.** *A cock*, etc. So in the other Gospels the indefinite article is used, which is in harmony with the supposed scarcity of this fowl. Fowls are very abundant in the east at the present day. Later Jewish writers affirm, though not always consistent with themselves, that the inhabitants of Jerusalem, and the priests everywhere, were forbidden to keep fowls, because they scratched up unclean worms. But even if this were so, the Roman residents, over whom the Jews could exercise no power, might keep them. Mark says, "Before the cock crow twice." The first about midnight; the second about three o'clock. The latter more generally marked time, and

A.D. 30.   MATTHEW XXVI.   363

35 crow, thou shalt deny me thrice. Peter said unto him, ᵉ Though I should die with thee, yet will I not deny thee. Likewise also said all the disciples.

ᵉ Pro. 28. 14; 1 Cor. 10. 12.

The agony in Gethsemane.

36 ᵈ THEN cometh Jesus with them unto a place called Gethsemane, and saith unto the disciples, Sit 37 ye here, while I go ᵉ and pray yonder. And he took with him ᶠ Peter and the two sons of Zebedee, and

ᵈ Mk. 14. 32; Lk. 22. 39; John 18. 1.
ᵉ Heb. 5. 7.
ᶠ ch. 4. 21; 17. 1.

was the one meant when only one cock crowing, as here, was mentioned. The expression, therefore, means the same in both Gospels. **Deny me.** Deny that I am your Lord and Teacher, and that you are, or ever have been, my disciple; disown me. **Thrice.** Emphatic in the original, *thrice deny me*. Thus, he who exalted himself the highest should be abased the lowest.

35. This reply of Jesus leads Peter to make a still stronger assertion, that he would die with him rather than deny him. In this Peter showed his strong self-will and self-confidence. The rest of the disciples catch his spirit and words, and join in like declarations. Such warnings should have put Peter and the other apostles on their guard, and led them to depend humbly on God; but they seem to have had the opposite effect of arousing their spiritual pride, and a dependence on their own will and strength.

36-46. THE AGONY OF JESUS IN GETHSEMANE, Mark 14 : 32-42; Luke 22 : 40-46; John 18 : 1.

36. **Then cometh he.** The incident just related occurred while they were on their way to the Mount of Olives, ver. 30. **A place called Gethsemane.** This was a *garden*, an orchard, or oliveyard, according to John, where he was wont to retire, Luke 22 : 39. *Gethsemane* means "*olive-press*," a name seemingly prophetic of Christ's agony, where he trod the wine-press alone (Isa. 63 : 3), without the city, Rev. 14 : 20. It was just across the brook Kedron, about one halfmile east from Jerusalem, at the foot of the Mount of Olives. The modern garden without doubt occupies the same site, or a portion of it, possibly somewhat smaller, being an inclosure of about one third of an acre, and surrounded by a low wall. In it are eight venerable olive-trees, still green and productive, but so decayed that heaps of stone are piled up against their trunks to keep them from being blown down. They were standing at the Saracenic conquest of Jerusalem, A.D. 636, since the sultan receives a tax on them, fixed at that time. But as all the trees around Jerusalem were cut down by Titus at the destruction of Jerusalem (Josephus, *Jewish War*, vi. 1, 1), these olive-trees probably sprang from the roots of those standing in the days of our Lord. Thomson (*Land and Book*, ii. 284) thinks that the ancient Gethsemane was situated in a secluded vale, several hundred yards to the north-east of the modern one. There is much evidence, however, in support of the present locality. **The disciples.** Really only eight, as the event showed, three being selected to go further with him. **Pray.** In regard to his sufferings, ver. 39. **Yonder.** A little further on, probably in a more secluded part of the garden, in a shady retreat. Luke says, "About a stone's throw;" that is, from a sling. Luke makes no mention of the separation of the three; the stone's cast would seem to accord better with the distance from the eight than the "*forward a little*" (Mark 14 : 35) from the three. It was now probably between eleven and twelve o'clock at night, and within two days of the full moon.

37. **Peter and the two sons of Zebedee.** Peter, James, and John (Mark 14 : 33), who witnessed his transfiguration (ch. 17 : 1), are selected to be witnesses of, and sympathizers in, his great humiliation and agony in the garden. The former scene was a preparative for the latter. He who had professed such an undying attachment to Jesus, and the two who would sit on his right and left hand, and said they were able to drink of his cup, ch. 20 : 20-23. **Began to be sorrowful.** Here commenced the passion, or sufferings of Jesus, in the limited sense. **Very heavy.** Deeply dejected, burdened in

38 began to be sorrowful and very heavy. Then saith he unto them, ᵍ My soul is exceeding sorrowful, even unto death: tarry ye here, and ʰ watch with
39 me. And he went a little farther, and fell on his face, and ⁱ prayed, saying, ᵏ O my Father, ˡ if it be possible, ᵐ let this cup pass from me: nevertheless
40 ⁿ not as I will, but as thou *wilt*. And he cometh unto the disciples, ᵒ and findeth them asleep; and saith unto Peter, What! could ye not watch with

ᵍ Ps. 69. 20; Is. 53. 3; John 12. 27.
ʰ Lam. 1. 12.
ⁱ Mk. 14. 36; Lk. 22. 42; Heb. 5. 7.
ᵏ John 12. 27.
ˡ Heb. 2. 10, 18; 9. 16, 22, 23.
ᵐ ch. 20. 22.
ⁿ ch. 6. 10; John 5. 30; 6. 38; Phil. 2. 8; Heb. 5. 8.
ᵒ Lk. 9. 32.

spirit. According to some, the word expresses the sorrow of loneliness, which presses like a weight of lead upon the soul. **38. Then saith he.** The beginning of his anguish has just been stated. Another step in his overwhelming agony is now brought to view. **My soul.** Jesus had a human soul; and this was the scene of his agony. His emotional nature was overwhelmed with sorrow. **Exceeding sorrowful.** Literally, *environed with grief*, shut in, with sorrow on every side. This was in view of the connection of his sufferings and death with sin. **Even unto death.** The extremest intensity; deathly; a little more would be death itself. Compare Ps. 18: 4, 5; 55: 4; Jon. 4: 9. This language points to sufferings in his human nature. He had been before troubled in the anticipation of his sufferings (John 12: 27), now he is overwhelmed with the sufferings themselves. A body and soul untainted, and unmarred by sin, must have been capable of endurance far beyond any of our sinful race. This endurance must have been far greatly increased by the connection of the divine with the human. Hence the *sorrow unto death* was beyond any thing that ever has, or could be, experienced in this world by any one of our fallen race. It was beyond all human conception. He was suffering for sinners, in their place. He made their case, as it were, his own. The horror and woe of the lost, and the pangs of hell, were taking hold upon him, so far as it was possible in his state of innocence. **Watch with me.** Keep awake to keep me company, and act as a guard. The principal idea is that of companionship and sympathy. In great dangers it is a comfort to know that friends are near us and vigilant, even though unable to help us.
39. Went a little further. Mark says, "Went forward a little." Thus, there were three companies: the eight, the three, and the one. As the highpriest entered the holy of holies alone, so Jesus must suffer alone. The disciples were probably as near to him as they could bear. The glory of the transfiguration doubtless fitted the three to be nearer than the rest. **Fell on his face and prayed.** Luke says he "kneeled down." Doubtless he knelt first, and, as his agony increased, fell forward, as Mark says, "on the ground." The posture was indicative of his extreme humiliation and anguish. **My Father.** He prays as the Son. **If it be possible**; that God's glory be respected and displayed, and the world's salvation be secured without this suffering. **This cup.** This bitter cup of anguish. *Cup* is a common figure of Scripture, sometimes representing joy (Ps. 16: 5; 23: 5; 116: 13), and sometimes sorrow, Ps. 11: 6; 75: 8; Isa. 51: 17; Jer. 25: 15; Rev. 16: 9. Not the cup of death, but of present overwhelming anguish; for to suppose him overwhelmed with the dread of death, and praying for its removal, is contrary to the spirit he had ever manifested toward it, and to all his declarations and prayers concerning it, John 12: 27, 28; chs. 14–17. **Not as I will.** Not my will, but thine be done. Wonderful faith and resignation combined! The will of Jesus, who was both priest and victim, is swallowed up in the divine will. **As thou wilt** was his rule, not only of action, but also of will. The words of the prayer vary slightly in the different Evangelists, but with the same import.
40. The disciples. The three. **Findeth them asleep.** Luke says they were asleep from sorrow. **Saith unto Peter.** He who had been foremost in his professions and promises. **What.** Not found in the original. Literally, *So could ye not*, or *could ye not then;* were ye so unable, not strong enough? The

41 me one hour? ᵖ Watch and pray, that ye enter not into temptation. ᑫ The spirit indeed *is* willing, but the flesh *is* weak.

42 He went away again the second time, and prayed, saying, O my Father, if this cup may not pass away

43 from me, except I drink it, thy will be done. And he came and found them asleep again: for their eyes were heavy.

44 And he left them, and went away again, and prayed ʳ the third time, saying the same words.

45 Then cometh he to his disciples, and saith unto them, Sleep on now, and take *your* rest: behold, ˢ the hour is at hand, and the Son of man is betray-

ᵖ Mk. 14. 38; Lk. 22. 40. 46; Eph. 6. 18.
ᑫ Ro. 7. 18-25; Gal. 5. 16, 17, 24.

ʳ Lk. 18. 1; 2 Cor. 12. 8.

ˢ ver. 2; Jno. 17. 1.

---

expression was one of mingled reproof and pity. **One hour.** An indefinite short time, ch. 9 : 22; 15 : 28; 17 : 18. Some find here an intimation of the length of the agony of Gethsemane.

41. Jesus reënjoins watchfulness, with the addition of prayer, with special reference to themselves, that they might not fall under the power of temptation. Their hour of trial was at hand, and they needed both to watch and also pray, for they needed strength and grace. The motive of the former injunction was sympathy with him; that of this is their personal preservation and safety.
Spirit—flesh. Your higher spiritual nature is willing, but your lower animal nature is feeble, worn, and tired, yielding to the exhaustive weariness of anxiety and sorrow. This was a kind apology for their slumbering, yet, at the same time, an incentive for immediate watchfulness and prayer; for the weaker their flesh, the more they needed divine help, and to be on their guard. Alford and some others suppose Jesus referred to himself also: "At that moment he was giving as high and preëminent example of its truth as the disciples were affording a low and ignoble one. He in the willingness of the spirit—yielding himself to the Father's will to suffer and die, but weighed down by the weakness of the flesh; they having professed, and really *having* a willing spirit to suffer with him, but, even in the one hour's watching, overcome by the burden of drowsiness." The idea is beautiful and truthful, but the connection rather confines the application to the disciples.

42. **If this cup may not pass.** *Cup* should be omitted, according to the highest critical authorities. *If this can not pass.* The Father has heard him; and, according to *as thou wilt,* the present agony must be endured. Hence submission is the prominent idea of the second prayer.

43. Returning a second time, Jesus finds them sleeping; **for their eyes were heavy,** weighed down, burdened with drowsiness. This implies that they were not in a deep but in a drowsy sleep. Mark adds that "they knew not what to answer him."

44. **The third time.** The repetition shows the intensity and continuance of the agony. Luke vividly describes it: "His sweat was as great drops of blood falling down to the ground;" in large drops, probably mingled with blood. So Jesus suffered three assaults from Satan in the wilderness. Paul also prayed thrice, 2 Cor. 12 : 8. This has been erroneously called an unanswered prayer. But it was answered in the highest sense. The Father heard him always, John 11 : 42. The agony continued according to the Father's will; and the will of the Father was one with that of the Son. The angel appearing and strengthening him, (Luke 22 : 43), was also in answer to his prayer; similar to the Lord's answer to Paul's repeated petition, 2 Cor. 12 : 9. This agony also did pass away, and in composure he gave himself up to his betrayer, and went calmly to the hall of judgment. This endurance and triumph over the agony of the garden was a pledge and foretaste of full and final victory.

45. **Sleep on now.** *Sleep the remaining time, and take your rest!* The exact meaning of these words has been much discussed. Some suppose they were spoken in mournful irony; but such a view is decidedly unnatural,

46 ed into the hands of sinners. Rise, ¹ let us be going: behold, he is at hand that doth betray me.

¹ Lk. 9. 51; 12. 50.

Jesus betrayed and made prisoner.

47 AND ᵃ while he yet spake, lo, Judas, one of the twelve, came, and with him a great multitude with swords and staves, from the chief priests and elders

ᵃ Mk. 14. 43; Lk. 22. 47; John 18. 3; Ac. 1. 16.

Others suppose a question, *Do ye sleep*, etc. ? which is admissible. But it is better to take them with Aars (*Bib. World*, Oct., 1895, p. 297 f.) as an exclamation of pain or grief: *So then you are sleeping and taking rest!* a striking contrast to the conflict through which he had passed, and to his previous exhortation, "Watch and pray." This rendering avoids some objections to other translations. **The hour.** Of his sufferings by the hands of men. **Is betrayed.** So far as the act of Judas was concerned, and to the mind of Jesus, who beheld the whole as actually accomplished. **Hands of sinners.** The Jews and the Gentiles. He was betrayed by Judas, and delivered up to the Jewish rulers, and by them betrayed and delivered up to the Roman authorities, ch. 20 : 18, 19.

46. **Rise.** Awake, arise. The word in the original includes the idea of rousing from sleep. Not to escape danger, but to meet it. **Behold, he is at hand.** Look, see, he is at hand. The whole verse is a vivid picture of great earnestness and haste. "As I sat beneath the olives, and observed how very near the city was, with what perfect ease a person could survey at a glance the entire length of the eastern wall, and the slope of the hill toward the valley, I could not divest myself of the impression that this local peculiarity should be allowed to explain a passage in the account of our Savior's apprehension. Every one must have noticed something abrupt in his summons to the disciples: 'Arise, let us be going; see, he is at hand that doth betray me,' Matt. 26 : 46. It is not improbable that his watchful eye at that moment caught sight of Judas and his accomplices, as they issued from one of the eastern gates, or turned round the northern or southern corner of the walls, in order to descend into the valley. Even if the night was dark, he could have seen the torches which they carried," John 18 : 3.—DR. HACKETT, *Scripture Illustrations*, p. 266.

47-56. JESUS IS BETRAYED AND MADE PRISONER, Mark 14 : 43-52 ; Luke 22 : 47-53 ; John 18 : 2-12.

47. **While he yet spake.** While he was yet speaking. He had probably roused the three disciples from their slumbers, and rejoined the remaining eight, possibly saying similar words to them; the words in Luke 22 : 46 may have been said to all; but *immediately*, as Mark says, cometh the betrayer. **Judas, one of the twelve.** Thus styled by Mark, and Luke also, pointing him out not only as one of the apostles, but also as the apostolic criminal, whose crime and guilt were the more aggravated by the position he had held, and the knowledge and intimacy he had enjoyed with Jesus. **A great multitude.** This consisted, first, of *the band* (John 18 : 3, 12), or Roman cohort, which, consisting of 300 to 600 men, was quartered in the tower of Antonia, overlooking the temple, and ever ready to put down any tumult or arrest any disturber. Probably so much of the band as could be spared was present. Then there were *the captains of the temple* (Luke 22 : 52), with their men, who guarded the temple and kept order. Also, some of the *chief priests and elders* (Luke 22 : 52); and finally their servants, such as Malchus (John 18 : 10), and others, who had been commissioned by the Jewish authorities. **With swords and staves.** Swords and *sticks*, or *clubs*. The swords were in

ROMAN SWORDS.

the hands of the soldiers; the staves, or clubs, were probably in the hands of the guards of the temple, and of others. According to John, they also had torches

MATTHEW XXVI.   367

48 of the people. Now he that betrayed him gave them a sign, saying, Whomsoever I shall kiss, that
49 same is he: hold him fast. And forthwith he came to Jesus, and said, ˣ Hail, Master! and kissed him.
50 And Jesus said unto him, ʸ Friend, wherefore art thou come? Then came they, and laid hands on
51 Jesus, and took him. And, behold, ᶻ one of them which were with Jesus stretched out *his* hand, and drew his sword, and struck a servant of the high-

ˣ 2 Sam. 20. 9, 10; Ps. 55. 21; Pro. 27. 6.
ʸ Ps. 41. 9; 55. 13.
ᶻ John 18. 10.

and lamps, which, notwithstanding the moonlight, they might need to search the shady retreats in the garden, and the dark caverns of the valley of the Kedron. **From the chief priests and elders.** The Jewish Sanhedrim, who had obtained the soldiers, and sent them with their servants and others, under the leadership of Judas.

48. Hold him fast. Seize him, hold him fast. Judas was afraid that Jesus might escape, as he had done before, Luke 4 : 30; John 8 : 59; 10 : 39.

49. Forthwith he came. Probably a little in advance of the multitude. Jesus, a little in advance of his disciples, is met by Judas, leading his enemies; one at the head of a peaceful, the other of a warlike and inimical band. At this point comes in the account of John 18: 4-9. Jesus advances to meet them; in awe they start backward, and fall to the ground. Thus he shows that though he has power to retain his life, he willingly lays it down. At the same time he encourages the drooping hope of his disciples, and insures their safety from the public authorities.

Although Jesus discovered himself to them (John 18 : 5-8), yet Judas must give the signal agreed upon in order that the officers might take him. It was night also; and many of them were probably not acquainted with Jesus, and none so well as Judas. **Hail, Master.** *Hail, Rabbi,* as in ver. 25. *Hail* is the translation of a common term of salutation, meaning, *Joy to thee.* **Kissed him.** *Kissed him tenderly.* The verb here is a compound of the one translated kiss in the preceding verse, and denotes that he not only gave the sign, but also that the act was performed in a tender and affectionate manner, thus adding to his guilt the sin of affectation and hypocrisy. We know not which to admire or contemn the most, Judas giving or Jesus receiving the kiss. In Judas we

indeed see the depth of baseness, and in Jesus the height of endurance.

50. Friend. A term of respectful, but not always of affectionate address, meaning *comrade, companion.* See on ch. 20 : 13. **Wherefore art thou come?** The Greek pronoun is not an interrogative but a relative. Hence some verb and antecedent need be supplied, as, What is that *for which thou art come?* The Revised version renders, "Do that for which thou art come." But either rendering implies our Lord's knowledge of what Judas was doing; and we may render: "I know for what thou art come." The question by Luke naturally follows, "Betrayest thou the Son of Man with a kiss?" And Jesus had previously said (John 13 : 27), "What thou doest, do quickly." Some would insert John 18 : 4-9 here. It is admissible, but it seems more natural and more accordant with all the circumstances to place it as above. **Then came they.** When the signal was given. **Laid hands on Jesus.** Laid hold of Jesus, so as to apprehend and secure him. **And took him.** Rather, *Secured him, held him fast,* as the word is translated in ver. 48.

51. One of them. Peter, John 18 : 10. Prudence quite likely led the first three Evangelists to omit the name of Peter, in order to shield him from any odium or violence which might arise from giving his name. As Jesus healed the ear (Luke 22 : 51), Peter was not then apprehended; and although he seems to have been recognized in the palace of the high-priest by a kinsman of the servant who received the injury (John 18 : 26), yet his name may have been unknown, and he was probably lost sight of as the perpetrator. But John, who wrote after the death of Peter, supplements the other accounts by giving his name. **Sword.** Two swords were in the hands of the disciples (Luke 22 : 38),

368 MATTHEW XXVI. A.D. 30.

52 priest's, and smote off his ear. Then said Jesus unto him, ^a Put up again thy sword into thy place: ^b for all they that take the sword shall perish with
53 the sword. Thinkest thou that I can not now pray to my Father, and he shall presently give me ^c more
54 than twelve legions of angels? But how then shall the Scriptures be fulfilled, ^d that thus it must be?
55 In that same hour said Jesus to the multitudes, Are ye come out as against a thief with swords and

^a ch. 5. 39; Ro. 12. 19; 1 Thes. 5. 15; 1 Pet. 2. 21-23.
^b Ge. 9. 6; Ps. 55. 23; Eze. 35. 5, 6; Rev. 13. 10.
^c 2 Ki. 6. 17; Dan. 7. 10.
^d ver. 24; Is. 53. 7, etc.; Lk. 24. 25, 44, 46.

and more than one were proposing to resist (Luke 22 : 49); for they ask, "Lord, shall we smite with the sword?" And before the answer was given, Peter, in accordance with his impetuous nature, and doubtless emboldened by the supernatural awe which Jesus had just previously exerted on the multitude, drew his sword, and commenced the conflict, not doubting the power of Jesus to give the victory. **A servant of the high-priest.** Rather, *The servant*, who was well-known, namely, Malchus, John 18 : 10. The first three Evangelists may have omitted his name, either because he was well-known (and he may have become a disciple) or from prudential considerations. **Smote off his ear.** *Struck off, took off*, his right ear, Luke 22 : 50. The servant may have been stepping forward, as Dr. Hackett remarks, to handcuff or pinion Jesus. The blow was doubtless aimed at his head; perhaps the power of Jesus prevented a fatal stroke.

52. Jesus at once touches the ear and heals it. He now rebukes Peter, and teaches him that his submission is voluntary and in fulfillment of Scripture. **Thy sword—his place.** Into its sheath, John 18 : 11. The sword was foreign to his kingdom. In that kingdom its place is the sheath. Unsheathed, its place is in the hands of the minister of civil authority, who is an avenger for wrath to him that does evil, Rom. 13 : 4. **All they that take the sword,** etc. By taking the sword they usurp God's place, who says, "Vengeance is mine, I will repay," Rom. 12 : 19. The whole sentence expresses a general principle. They who resort to the sword must expect the sword. Christ's kingdom is not to be extended by violence or force; and they who use it for that purpose must expect the consequences, external defeat and death. This applies to the true followers of Christ, who have ever been comparatively weak, and not to worldly hierarchies, which are evidently not of that kingdom which is not of this world. Some, with much reason, regard this language as an authoritative principle or command, a repetition of Gen. 9 : 6, that the murderer shall be punished with death. Compare Rev. 13 : 10. John adds that Jesus further said, "The cup that my Father hath given me, shall I not drink it?"

53. **Thinkest thou?** Literally, *Or thinkest thou?* Or, Do you suppose that I need human aid? **Can not pray,** etc. That I have lost my power in prayer, and yield submissively because compelled to do so? **Presently give me.** *Presently,* not in the original. Literally, *will place beside me,* will send, furnish. **Twelve legions.** One to each, himself and the eleven. A legion consisted of about six thousand. Twelve legions seem to represent an indefinitely large and overwhelming number in contrast to the comparatively small number of those arresting him, and the very small and insignificant number of those disciples who would defend him. **Angels.** Not mere men, such as the Roman soldiers, or Peter and the other Apostles.

54. **But.** Not in the original. **How then,** etc., if I should now call these to my aid, acting as Judge with myriads of angels (Jude 14, 15), and not as a propitiatory and suffering Savior? **Thus it must be.** The Scriptures must be fulfilled (Ps. 22 : 1; Isa. 53 : 7-12; Dan. 9 : 26; Zech. 13 : 7), and they can not be broken, John 10 : 35. And back of them were the counsel and plan of God for the salvation of sinners, which find expression in his word, 1 Pet. 1 : 19, 20; Rev. 13 : 8.

55. **In that same hour.** Rather, *In that hour,* at that time when seized and bound. **To the multitudes.** Especially to their leaders, the chief priests,

staves for to take me? ᵉ I sat daily with you teach-
56 ing in the temple, and ye laid no hold on me. But
all this was done, that the ᶠ Scriptures of the prophets might be fulfilled. Then ᵍ all the disciples
forsook him, and fled.

* Mk. 12. 35; John 8. 2.
ᶠ ver. 54; Lam. 4. 20; Dan. 9. 26.
ᵍ ver. 31; John 16. 32; 18. 15.

Jesus before Caiaphas and the Sanhedrim.

57 ʰ AND they that had laid hold on Jesus led *him*
away to Caiaphas the high-priest, where the scribes
and the elders were assembled.

ʰ Mk. 14. 53; Lk. 22. 54; John 18. 13, 24.

---

captains of the temple and elders, Luke 22: 52. **Against a thief.** In the original *a robber*, a plunderer, one who is more than a thief. Such an array of force and weapons would be a becoming preparation against a notorious robber like Barabbas. **Staves.** See ver. 47. **I sat.** The posture of teaching, ch. 5: 1. The furthest remote from the character of a robber. **Daily.** During that week, and at other times and previous festivals. He had often been with them and among them, and that by *day*; their assault was secretly contrived and by *night*. **In the temple.** Within the courts of its sacred inclosure. **Laid no hold on me.** As they had opportunity. Your present violence is needless, and proves your malignity and moral weakness. Jesus then adds (Luke 22: 53) the reason of their present success and of his quiet submission, "This is your hour and the power of darkness."
56. **But all this was done.** This is a continuation of what Jesus says, which becomes more evident from a correct translation, *But all this has been done;* the seizing and binding him, etc., Mark 14: 49. **That the Scriptures,** etc. See on ver. 54.
Then. When they saw him arrested and bound, and learned from his words that he did not intend to deliver himself. **Forsook him and fled.** All, a little before, had declared their readiness to even die with him (ver. 35); but now all, panic-stricken, desert him. Peter and John, however, did not flee far, but follow at a safe distance, John 18: 15.
More faithful and courageous than the eleven was a young man (Mark 14: 51, 52), supposed to be Mark, who now followed Jesus, and barely escaped apprehension and violence. Nicodemus and Joseph of Arimathea a little later also took a more decided stand than they, John 19: 38, 39.

57–68. JESUS BEFORE CAIAPHAS AND THE SANHEDRIM, TRIED AND CONDEMNED, Mark 14: 53–65; Luke 22: 54, 63–65; John 18: 24. John relates that they led him first to Annas, who, after having been high-priest for several years, had been deposed, but who was still the legitimate high-priest according to the law of Moses (the office being for life, Num. 20: 28; 35: 25), and may have been so regarded by the Jews. Before him he received an informal examination (John 18: 12–14), and then, in order to have him officially tried and condemned in the eye of the Roman law, he is sent to Caiaphas. Annas appears to have possessed vast influence, and, as father-in-law to Caiaphas, doubtless exerted a very controlling influence over him. It is quite reasonable to suppose that they occupied a common official residence, and that Annas after his examination sent him across the court to the apartment occupied by Caiaphas. See also on ver. 3.
57. **Where the Scribes and the elders were assembled.** The Sanhedrim had probably assembled to receive their prisoner. The dawn of day was drawing nigh, when the second cock-crowing would remind Peter of the Savior's prediction of his three denials. Jesus now undergoes a preliminary examination, preparatory to the regular meeting in the morning (Luke 22: 66), which should condemn him and hand him over to Pilate, ch. 27: 1, 2. See on ver. 66. The usual place of holding the Sanhedrim was at the council-room in the temple; but this meeting, being extraordinary and of a secret character, was held at the residence of the high-priest.
The early hour of this meeting was very much in keeping with the habits of the people. The habit of early rising has been noticed by modern travelers in

58 But Peter followed him afar off unto the high-priest's palace, and went in, and sat with the servants, to see the end.
59 ᵢ Now the chief priests, and elders, and all the council, sought false witness against Jesus, to put
60 him to death; but found none: yea, though ᵏ many false witnesses came, *yet* found they none. At the
61 last came ˡ two false witnesses, and said, This *fellow* said, ᵐ I am able to destroy the temple of God,
62 and to build it in three days. And the high-priest arose, and said unto him, Answerest thou nothing?
63 what *is it which* these witness against thee? But

ᶦ Mk. 14. 55; Lk. 22. 63.

ᵏ Ps. 27. 12; 35. 11; Ac. 6. 11-13.

ˡ Deu. 19. 15.

ᵐ ch. 27. 40; John 2. 19-21.

Palestine. "During the greater part of the year, in Palestine," says Dr. Hackett, "the heat becomes so great a few hours after sunrise as to render any strenuous labor inconvenient. The early morning, therefore, is the proper time for work; midday is given, as far as may be possible, to rest or employments which do not require exposure to the sun. The arrangements of life adjust themselves to this character of the climate. . . . Men and women may be seen going forth to their labor in the field, or starting on journeys, at the earliest break of day. . . Being anxious to attend the services of a Jewish synagogue, I was summoned to rise for that purpose before it was light."—*Scripture Illustrations,* p. 124.

58. **Afar off.** At a distance, and scarcely near enough for a mere spectator, much less a disciple. Yet he followed him, and he seems to show more courage than any of the eleven except John; he comes to the house of the high-priest, ventures to enter into the court, and sits with the servants to see the result. **Palace.** *Court,* as in ver. 3, on which see note. Here a fire had been kindled. **Servants.** Officers and agents of the high-priest. Through the influence of John, who was acquainted with the family of the high-priest, Peter obtained access into this inner court, John 18: 16.

59. **Sought false witness against him.** They had determined on his death, but they must condemn him for some capital crime. They fail to obtain true witnesses, and they seek for false ones. **All the council.** All of those present. Nicodemus, Joseph of Arimathea, and others (John 12: 42), who did not approve of such proceedings, were doubtless absent.

60. **Found none.** They found many false witnesses, but not the evidence they desired, namely, two witnesses agreed in sustaining a definite accusation, as required by the law of Moses, Deut. 17: 6; Mark 14: 56. Hence it is immediately said, **At the last came two.**

61. **This fellow.** Rather, *This one*, or, *This man; fellow* is too disrespectful to express the true sense of the original. **I am able,** etc. He had not said this. What he had said referred to his body, and not to the temple. They misquote and misapply what he had said three years before, John 2: 19. But even now their testimony did not avail anything; for Mark tells us that they did not agree. Words against the temple were held to be of the nature of blasphemy, Acts 6: 13. Yet even this language could hardly be considered as words against the temple, since he was to build it again; and besides, there was a tradition that when the Messiah came, he was to build a much more glorious temple than the one then existing. This testimony may also have suggested the question, whether he was the Christ, the Son of God, ver. 63.

62. **The high-priest arose.** Seeing that the evidence was insufficient, the high-priest, somewhat excited, and possibly with some affected indignation, rises from his seat and questions Jesus, in the hope that he may criminate himself. **Answerest thou nothing,** etc. Dost thou not explain, or tell us whether this testimony is true or false?

63. **Held his peace.** A solemn and impressive silence, as Isaiah had foretold, Isa. 53: 7.

I adjure thee by the living God. The high-priest calls upon him to an-

A.D. 30. MATTHEW XXVI. 371

ⁿ Jesus held his peace. And the high-priest answered and said unto him, º I adjure thee by the living God, ᵖ that thou tell us whether thou be 64 ᑫ the Christ, the Son of God. Jesus saith unto him, ʳ Thou hast said: nevertheless I say unto you, ˢ Hereafter shall ye see the Son of man ᵗ sitting on the right hand of power, and coming in the clouds 65 of heaven. ᵘ Then the high-priest rent his clothes, saying, ˣ He hath spoken blasphemy; what further need have we of witnesses? Behold, now ye have

ⁿ Ps. 38. 12–14; Is. 53. 7; 1 Pet. 2. 23.
º Le. 5. 1; 1 Sam. 14. 21, 26.
ᵖ John 8. 25; 10. 24.
ᑫ ch. 16. 16.
ʳ ver. 25; ch. 27. 11.
ˢ ch. 16. 27; 24. 30; 25. 31; Dan. 7. 13, 14; Lk. 21. 27; John 1. 51;

---

swer, upon his oath by the *living* God, as distinguished from false gods. His answer, being equivalent to an oath, shows that his precept, "I swear not at all," does not forbid judicial oaths. See on ch. 5 : 34. **The Christ.** The Messiah. **The Son of God.** This appellation was given to the Messiah from Ps. 2 : 7, making the question the more definite and expressive. The Jews did not, however, understand by it the full idea which Christ in his reply and the Gospel reveals. It is also quite probable that the high-priest added this in hope that he would declare before the Sanhedrim what he had before said to the people, John 10 : 30, 33. In the final examination before the Sanhedrim (Luke 22 : 66–71), the high-priest divides the question, and uses the appellation *Son of God* in its more extended meaning. This was natural after the reply which Jesus now makes in this preparatory examination.

64. **Thou hast said.** *Thou hast* said it. Mark (14 : 62) has the direct answer, "I am." See on ver. 25. This is his first formal public declaration of his Messiahship and divinity. Alford thinks that there is a latent reference to the convictions and admissions of Caiaphas, John 11 : 49–52. **Nevertheless.** The word thus translated is emphatic, meaning, *but, besides*, something over and above what I have just confessed. If he had simply confessed himself the Messiah, the high-priest would probably have asked him other questions, and if failing to elicit further confession, would then probably have condemned him to death as a false Messiah and false prophet, the latter being included in the former, Deut. 13 : 5 ; 18 : 20. But Jesus gave special prominence to the last portion of the question, using language which would remind him of the well-known passage in Dan. 7 : 13. **Sitting on the right hand of power.** He was now *standing* as a prisoner and a criminal, but then he should sit in his glory, as Lord of lords and King of kings, at the right hand of Omnipotence, sharing and exercising sovereign supremacy. **Coming in the clouds.** As Judge. Jesus thus answers the solemn adjuration of the high-priest with a more solemn reference to his own judgment-seat, when the scene would be reversed—the prisoner the Judge, and the judge the prisoner.

65. **Rent his clothes.** His ordinary dress; his high-priestly robe was worn only in the temple. This was to be done standing, and the rent was to be from the neck straight downward, about nine inches in length. The high-priest was forbidden to rend his clothes (Lev. 21 : 10); yet it seems to have been allowable in extraordinary cases of blasphemy and public calamity, 1 Macc. 2 : 14; 11 : 71; Josephus, *Jewish War*, ii. 15. 2, 4. The practice of rending the clothes at blasphemy was based on 2 Kings 18 : 37. The unexpected answer of Jesus, declaring his divine glory and judgeship, aroused the hatred, rage, and horror of the high-priest to the utmost bounds, and he rends his garments as if too narrow to contain his exasperated emotions. This he does as if in holy indignation and horror. Terribly excited feelings and hypocrisy were doubtless mingled.

Spoken blasphemy. Impious language, which detracted from the honor of God, implying that he was the Son of God, the sharer in the power and glory of God, and the Judge of mankind. See on ch. 12 : 31. Thus Jesus confesses his true character, and for it is charged with blasphemy and condemned to death. **What further need,** etc. The lan-

66 heard his blasphemy. What think ye? They an-
67 swered and said, ʸ He is guilty of death. ᶻ Then
did they spit in his face, and buffeted him; and
ᵃ others smote *him* with the palms of their hands,
68 saying, ᵇ Prophesy unto us, thou Christ, Who is
he that smote thee?

Jesus thrice denied by Peter.

69 ᶜ NOW Peter sat without in the palace: and a
damsel came unto him, saying, Thou also wast with

Ro. 14. 10; 1
Thes. 4. 16; Rev.
1. 7.
ᵗ Ps. 110. 1; Ac.
7. 55,56; Col. 3.1.
Num. 14. 6; 2 Ki.
ᵘ 18. 37; 19. 1.
ˣ ch. 9. 3; John
10. 33, 36.
ʸ Le. 24. 16; John
19. 7.
ᶻ ch. 27. 30; Is.
52. 3.

guage of excited feelings. He takes for granted that the feelings of the Sanhedrim are the same as his own. He decides that this confession is all the evidence necessary.

66. **What think ye.** In hot haste he presses an immediate decision. **He is guilty of death.** He is deserving of death, or rather, his guilt requires death, according to the law, Lev. 24: 16; Deut. 18:20. This was an informal expression or vote. It was necessary to assemble the Sanhedrim in the morning (ch. 27 : 1 ; Luke 22 : 66-71), when it was already day, to formally try and pass sentence; for, (1) they could not, according to Jewish law, investigate any capital crime during the night; and (2), according to Roman law, a sentence pronounced before the dawn of day was invalid. Yet in this examination, given by Matthew, Jesus was really tried and condemned; the one succeeding was but a formal repetition; the main thing then was the perfection of their plans to put him to death, ch. 27 : 1. It was, however, contrary to Jewish law to pronounce the sentence of death on the same day on which the investigation took place. If they thought to elude this law by the investigation in the night, it showed hot haste. But it was no elusion, for the Jewish day commenced in the evening. The truth is, the whole trial was but a form, a judicial sham; his death had been determined upon (ver. 4; Mark 14 : 1), his conviction was a foregone conclusion.

67. **Then they spit in his face.** Expressive of the greatest contempt, Num. 12 : 14; Deut. 25 : 9. Thus a heathen would treat a slave only under the gravest provocation. Some of the Sanhedrim may have heaped upon Jesus these insults. Compare Acts 7 : 54, 57; 23 : 2. Yet "the men who held Jesus," the officers and soldiers, also did it, possi-

bly a little later, Luke 22 : 63. We may either regard this, and that described by Luke, one and the same, or this as taking place when the Sanhedrim was closing its preparatory session, and that in the interval before the final session. **Buffeted him.** Struck him with their fists. **Smote him.** *With the palms of their hands*, should be omitted. The Greek word means to strike with a stick as well as with the hand. Mark says, *the servants* or officers did this. It is probable that they smote him with their staves or rods, ver. 47. Thus insult is added upon insult. Isa. 52 : 14.

68. **Prophesy unto us, thou Christ.** Mark says (14 : 65), they covered his face to prevent his seeing. Luke speaks (22 : 64) of having blindfolded him. They thus make his Messiahship the object of insult and mockery. They treat him as a base pretender and outlaw, mingling their revilings with deeds of violence.

69-75. JESUS IS THRICE DENIED BY PETER, Mark 14 : 66-72 ; Luke 22 : 54-62 ; John 18 : 15-18, 25-27.

69. **Peter sat.** *Was sitting* while the examination was going on in the adjoining apartment. The three denials, though occurring during the different stages of the preliminary examinations, are conveniently grouped together in one narrative. **Without in the palace;** *in the court*, the interior courtyard, around which the house was built. See on ver. 3. The room where Jesus stood on trial was probably on the ground-floor, in the side or in the rear of this open court. If, as we have supposed, Annas and Caiaphas occupied a common official building, they quite likely occupied opposite side apartments. The doors being open from the court into the audience rooms, Peter could doubtless observe what was going on within.

70 Jesus of Galilee. ᵈ But he denied before *them* all,
71 saying, I know not what thou sayest. And when he was gone out into the porch, another *maid* saw him, and said unto them that were there, This *fellow*
72 was also with Jesus of Nazareth. And again he de-
73 nied with an oath, I do not know the man. And after a while came unto *him* they that stood by, and said to Peter, Surely thou also art *one* of them ;

ᵃ Is. 50. 6; Lk. 22. 63; John 19. 3.
ᵇ Mk. 14. 65; Lk. 22. 64.
ᶜ Mk. 14. 66; Lk. 22. 55; John 18. 16, 17, 25.
ᵈ vers. 33–35; ch. 10. 28; Pro. 28. 26; 29. 25.

A damsel. According to Mark, she was one of the maids or maid-servants of the high-priest. John speaks of her as the damsel who kept the door of the porch, or passage into the court. She probably observed Peter carefully when he entered with John, and afterward when he seats himself with the servants of the high-priest. Something about his appearance or manner excites her suspicion. Then she thinks she remembers seeing him with Jesus. She approaches him, looks earnestly or intently upon him (Luke 22 : 56), and says, "This man was also with him." She tells him so (Matthew and Mark), and asks him (John) if he was not one of "this man's disciples." **Jesus of Galilee.** Literally, *the Galilean.* This was a contemptuous epithet among the Jews of Judea. She may have feared being blamed for admitting him. He seems to have been in no great danger, except as he might be recognized as the one who smote Malchus. **Thou also.** Some see in the word *also* a reference to John.

70. Peter's first denial. The precise words are differently reported by the different Evangelists, but with the same meaning. This reply embraced all the forms given. The one here, **I know not what thou sayest,** I know not what thou art talking about, is a strong expression, implying a denial of the charge itself. It would seem that Peter was taken by surprise, and, in his cowardice, not only denies, but pleads ignorance. He would have her suppose that he came in as a mere observer.

71. About this time closed the informal examination before Annas, and Jesus is sent bound to the apartment of Caiaphas, John 18: 24. **Gone out into the porch.** Into the passage-way. Disturbed by the question of the woman, Peter begins to think of retreat, yet not so hasty as to excite suspicion. He goes to the porch through which he had entered into the court. At this time, according to Mark, a cock crew the first time. While standing here, with the blaze of the fire shining upon him (John 18 : 25), another maid said, **This fellow,** *this man* (see on ver. 61), **was also with Jesus of Nazareth,** *Jesus the Nazarene,* a contemptuous epithet, similar to *Galilean* in ver. 69. The maid-servant who kept the door, seeing him again, joins in the charge, saying to the bystanders, "This is one of them," Mark 14 : 69. They thereupon ask, "Art thou also one of his disciples?" John 18 : 25. These several questions, by different persons at this time, are perfectly natural, and, as recorded by the different Evangelists, show how independent were their narrations. Yet how harmonious!

72. Peter's second denial. According to the three other Evangelists, he denies that he is a disciple of Jesus. But Matthew tells us that he even denied knowing him, and that, too, with an **oath,** calling God to witness, and with the somewhat contemptuous form, **I know not the man.** As if he had come from curiosity, to learn the cause of this gathering, without any interest in it, and possibly without knowing even the name of the criminal on trial. This denial is thus a step in advance on the first. That was when he was taken by surprise, possibly somewhat confused ; this after he had had a little time to reflect, and hence more deliberate. The number now questioning him, doubtless, excited him to his rash and wicked oath. Yet even now no one appears to have intended him positive injury.

73. **After a while.** About one hour after, Luke 22 : 56. Peter was now in the court. **They that stood by.** They had, doubtless, discussed the matter among themselves, and, having observed his Galilean provincialisms, conclude that the charge of the maid-servant is true. They, therefore, say to

74 for thy ^e speech bewrayeth thee. Then ^f began he to curse and to swear, *saying*, I know not the man.
75 And immediately the cock crew. And Peter remembered the word of Jesus, which said unto him, ^g Before the cock crow, thou shalt deny me thrice. And he went out, ^h and wept bitterly.

^e Lk. 22. 59.
^f Mk. 14. 71; Jer. 17. 9.
^g ver. 34; Mk. 14. 30; Lk. 22. 61, 62; John 13. 38.
^h ch. 5. 4; Ps. 38. 18; 2 Cor. 7. 9–11.

---

him, **Surely, thou art one of them.** A strong affirmation, Thou certainly belongest to his disciples. The reason, **For thy speech bewrayeth thee,** *betrayeth thee*, shows that thou art a Galilean like him, and most of his disciples are Galileans. The pronunciation and accent of the Galileans were indistinct and less pure than those of the inhabitants of Judea. They confounded the gutturals and the two last letters of the Jewish alphabet. At the same time a relative of Malchus, whose ear Peter had cut off, asked, "Did I not see thee in the garden with him?" John 18 : 26.

74. Peter's third denial. This was an advance upon his second. He not only, with an oath, repeats what he had said in the second, that he knew not of whom they spake, but he affirms it with imprecations of divine wrath on himself if he spake not the truth. **Then began he to curse and to swear.** He began to invoke curses on himself, to take the most solemn oaths, in confirmation of the assertion, **I know not** (rather, *I do not know*, as in ver. 72) **the man.** "The mischievous interpolation, **saying,** destroys the proper connection, and gives a false sense to the preceding words."—DR. CONANT. In this lowest point of Peter's fall he gives way to profanity, an old forsaken habit, as some suppose.

But immediately **the cock crew.** The article should be indefinite, as in ver. 34; on which see. This was at the opening of the fourth watch, at three o'clock, or a little later.

75. **Remembered.** The first crowing did not seem to remind Peter of the prediction of Jesus; but this recalls it vividly to mind. Luke tells us that "the Lord turned and looked upon Peter," probably through the open door of the council-room of Caiaphas. **Went out.** Leaving the court, he passed through the porch and left the house, overwhelmed with shame at his own weakness, and especially his sins of lying, profanity, perjury, and disloyalty to Christ, and, as he thought thereon (Mark 14 : 72), he **wept bitterly.** Peter exercised true repentance, while soon after Judas kills himself in remorse, ch. 27 : 3–5. This was probably near the close of the first examination before Caiaphas.

REMARKS.

1. We may not, like Jesus, know the time of our death, yet, like him, let us be conversant with death, and in our example, teaching, and labors be prepared for it, vers. 1, 2; ch. 17 : 22, 23; John 18 : 4.

2. We should beware putting our trust in any priesthood, or ecclesiastical authority; in a Caiaphas rather than Christ, vers. 3, 4; Ps. 2 : 2; Acts 4 : 8–12; 5 : 29.

3. Formal and worldly religious officials are often worse than the people under them, ver. 5; ch. 23 : 13; Mark 11 : 18, 32.

4. Men should fear lest God should permit them to carry out their wicked designs sooner than they expect. *At the feast*, though they say, Not at the feast, ver. 5; Prov. 19 : 21.

5. Love counts nothing too precious for Jesus, ver. 7; 2 Cor. 5 : 14.

6. A covetous and selfish spirit begrudges the gifts and sacrifices of love to Christ, ver. 8; 1 Tim. 6 : 10.

7. Many hypocritically plead the wants of the poor as an excuse for withholding their offerings to Christ and his cause, ver. 9.

8. It is God's plan that the poor should always be with his people to receive their sympathy and aid, ver. 11; Deut. 15 : 11; Prov. 22 : 2; Luke 18 : 22; Rom. 15 : 26, 27.

9. Whatever honors our Savior's death is pleasing to him. For example, baptism and the Lord's Supper, ver. 12.

10. Christians share in the honors of the Gospel. Their deeds of love are held in everlasting remembrance, ver. 13; Ps. 112 : 6; Mal. 3 : 16; Acts 10 : 31.

11. Many a formal professor has turn-

ed against Jesus for the sake of worldly gain, vers. 14-16; 1 Tim. 6 : 9, 10; 2 Tim. 4 : 10; 2 Pet. 2 : 14, 15.

12. Jesus, in keeping the Passover, has taught us to attend faithfully to those ordinances which are now in force, vers. 17-19; 1 Cor. 11 : 2.

13. Jesus is the searcher of hearts, and knows all of the plans and purposes of his professed followers, vers. 20, 21; Rev. 2 : 23.

14. The sins of God's people are the more aggravated on account of their relation to him, ver. 21; Zech. 13 : 6; Heb. 6 : 6.

15. The thought of dishonoring Jesus, or sinning against him, is sad to the renewed heart, ver. 22; Mark 14 : 72; 2 Cor. 7 : 8, 9.

16. The truly humble and pious heart is ever ready to suspect itself, rather than condemn others, vers. 22; 1 Sam. 24 : 17; 2 Sam. 24 : 17; Isa. 6 : 5.

17. Christ's death was in accordance with the eternal purpose of God, ver. 24; Luke 24 : 44; Acts 2 : 23; 1 Pet. 1 : 20.

18. The wicked act freely in sinning, even though in the divine arrangement they fulfill the divine purposes, ver. 24; Acts 4 : 25-28.

19. The fear of hell may arouse the most desperate to self-examination, but it is too often only momentary, vers. 24, 25; Acts 24 : 25.

20. Self-examination is peculiarly fitting before participating in the Lord's Supper, vers. 21-26; 1 Cor. 5 : 8; 11 : 28.

21. We must feed upon Christ as the bread of life, as well as trust in his atoning blood, vers. 26-28; John 6 : 51, 54; 1 John 1 : 7.

22. The Lord's Supper is an ordinance of the new Covenant, designed to continue till Christ's second coming, vers. 28, 29; 1 Cor. 11 : 26.

23. It is our privilege at the Lord's table to look forward to the marriage supper of the Lamb, when the ordinance and the emblems will be no longer needed, since we shall be with Jesus and see him as he is, 1 John 3 : 2; Rev. 19 : 9; 21 : 3.

24. Singing is a fitting and divinely-appointed part of worship, ver. 30; Eph. 5 : 19; Col. 3 : 16; James 5 : 13.

25. Christians may greatly wander from Christ, and do great injury to themselves and his cause, vers. 31-34; Ps. 89 : 30-33; Rev. 2 : 4, 5.

26. To be forewarned of an evil is to be forearmed; but even then self-confidence is generally a precursor to a fall, vers. 31-33; Prov. 16 : 18; Rom. 12 : 3; 1 Cor. 10 : 12.

27. Learn the weakness of human resolution and the folly of trusting thereon, vers. 35, 56, 70, 72, 74; Prov. 28 : 26.

28. Christ has set us an example of prayer in enduring and overcoming suffering, vers. 36-44; Ps. 50 : 15; Isa. 26 : 16; James 5 : 13, 14.

29. They who go down into the deep valley of humiliation are generally privileged at other times to go up on the high mountain of enjoyment and blessing, ver. 37; ch. 17 : 1-5; Acts 2 : 14; 3 : 1, 4; Gal. 2 : 9; 1 Pet. 5 : 1.

30. Watchfulness and prayer are the best safeguards against temptation, vers. 38, 41; ch. 6 : 13; Eph. 6 : 18; 1 Pet. 4 : 7; Rev. 16 : 15.

31. If it was necessary for Christ to endure such agonies to save men, how hopeless the case of those who avail not themselves of his atonement, vers. 38, 39, 42; Heb. 2 : 3.

32. What self-denial and self-sacrifice should we make for him who has endured so much for us, vers. 38, 39; Rom. 12 : 1; Gal. 6 : 14; 1 Pet. 4 : 1, 2.

33. Jesus has set us an example of entire submission to the will of God, vers. 39, 42; ch. 6 : 10; Phil. 2 : 6-8; James 4 : 7.

34. Soul struggles and afflictions of various kinds are necessary, and should therefore be borne submissively, cheerfully, and with strong faith in Christ, vers. 38, 39, 41; Rom. 7 : 21-25; Gal. 5 : 17; Heb. 12 : 3-7.

35. Let us see to it that our spirits are willing, though our flesh be weak; thus shall we be objects of the divine compassion of Jesus, who will pity though he reproves, vers. 41, 43, 45; Ps. 103 : 14; Gal. 5 : 16, 18; Heb. 4 : 15; 5 : 2, 5-9.

36. Let any beware how they sleep on when Christ is betrayed among his people into the hands of sinners, ver. 45; Rev. 3 : 15, 16.

37. The time will come when all who are in a religious sleep will be compelled to awake, vers. 45, 46; Isa. 33 : 14; Prov. 1 : 24-26; 6 : 9-11; Rev. 3 : 19.

38. If one of the twelve whom Jesus chose was a traitor, how unsafe to follow those who *arrogate* to themselves an apostolic succession, ver. 47; Rev. 2 : 2.

39. Hypocritical discipleship and treacherous friendship are far more odious and injurious than open hostility. They who acknowledge Christ in word, but deny him in deed, seeking to make

Jesus finally condemned and delivered to Pilate.   Mk. 15. 1; Lk. 23. 1; John 18. 28–38; Ps. 2. 2; Ac. 4. 24–28.

XXVII. WHEN the morning was come, ¹ all the chief priests and elders of the people took counsel

gain and merchandise of Christ, are fast following in the steps of Judas, vers. 48, 49; Ps. 41 : 9; Prov. 27 : 6; Matt. 7 : 21.

40. Let each one who comes to Jesus, in any way, ask himself, Wherefore am I come? Ver. 50; Ezek. 33 : 31.

41. "It has always been the ear, the spiritual hearing and willing susceptibility, which carnal defenders of Christ's cause have taken away from their opponents, when they have had recourse to the sword of violence."—LANGE. Ver. 51.

42. Persecutors are in reality murderers, and merit death, ver. 52; Num. 35 : 17; John 8 : 40, 44; 1 John 3 : 15; Rev. 19 : 19, 21.

43. Every Christian is in the hands of his heavenly Father, who can bring the host of heaven to his aid, if necessary and best, ver. 53; 2 Kings 6 : 16, 17; Ps. 34 : 7; Heb. 1 : 14; 12 : 22.

44. The wicked can not afflict or persecute God's people except by divine permission, ver. 55; Job 1 : 5–12; 2 : 6; Ps. 31 : 15; 105 : 14, 15.

45. The persecutions of Christians have generally been characterized by secret designings, malignant cunning, and open violence, ver. 55.

46. Jesus, as a Savior, stood alone. As all human help failed him, so we must despair of all, and trust in his atonement alone, vers. 56, 57; Isa. 63 : 3–5; Acts 4 : 12.

47. It is dangerous at any time to venture into temptation, especially in our own strength and when we are following Christ afar off, ver. 58; ch. 6 : 13; Prov. 3 : 5.

48. Happy is he against whom his enemies can allege nothing, except falsely, vers. 59–61; 1 Kings 21 : 9–14; Ps. 27 : 12; 35 : 11; 64 : 5, 6; Matt. 5 : 11.

49. Evil men and false teachers commonly mingle some truth with error, ver. 63.

50. There is a time for silence and a time to speak. Jesus treated frivolous and unjust charges with silence; but declared his character and mission, vers. 61–64; Prov. 21 : 23; Isa. 53 : 7; 1 Pet. 2 : 23; Acts 4 : 20.

51. God gives the most wicked the light of his truth, so that their deeds are without excuse, ver. 64; John 15 : 22; Rom. 1 : 20.

52. He that charges others with blasphemy is sometimes himself the blasphemer, ver. 65; 1 Kings 21 : 13; Acts 6 : 13; 7 : 57.

53. They who jest at religion make light of Christians, strive to injure the cause of Christ, would have mocked him and spit upon him when upon earth, vers. 67, 68.

54. Except when duty calls, we should avoid that company and place where our reputation may be injured, vers. 69–75, and Mark 14 : 54; Ps. 1 : 1; Prov. 2 : 12; 4 : 14; 1 Cor. 15 : 33.

55. If we go not forth in God's strength, but depend on ourselves, the smallest matter may overcome us. Peter fears and falls before a maid-servant, vers. 69, 71.

56. Sin is progressive. Beware of the beginning of sin, and especially of what are called little sins, vers. 70, 72, 74.

57. Little confidence can be placed in assertions abounding with profanity, ver. 74.

58. The smallest matter in God's hands may lead to repentance, and the feeblest means result in salvation. The crowing of a cock brought Peter to himself, vers. 75, 76.

59. The fall of Peter should stand as a warning against a like sin; but his recovery should encourage those who have fallen to turn to God with humble repentance, ver. 75; Jer. 3 : 22.

60. Repentance has no merit, and can make no atonement for sin; but it should restore our confidence in those who truly exercise it, ver. 75; 2 Cor. 7 : 10.

CHAPTER XXVII.

1, 2. JESUS FINALLY CONDEMNED BY THE SANHEDRIM AND BROUGHT BEFORE PILATE, Mark 15 : 1; Luke 22 : 66–71; 23 : 1; John 18 : 28.

1. **The morning.** About five or six o'clock of Friday, the 15th of Nisan, April 7th, in the seven hundred and eighty-third year from the founding of Rome.

A.D. 30. MATTHEW XXVII. 377

2 against Jesus to put him to death: and when they had bound him, they led *him* away, and ᵏ delivered him to Pontius Pilate the governor.

ᵏ ch. 20. 19; Ac. 3. 13; 1 Tim. 6. 13.

The confession, remorse, and death of Judas.

3 ˡ THEN Judas, which had betrayed him, when he saw that he was condemned, ᵐ repented himself,

ˡ ch. 26. 14, 15; Job. 20. 5, 15-29.
ᵐ 2 Cor. 7. 10.

All the chief priests, etc. This was a meeting of the Sanhedrim in order to formally condemn him to death. See on ch. 26 : 57, 66. They also consulted as to the best means of putting him to death, and doubtless fixed upon the twofold charge of blasphemy and treason. They could condemn to death, but could not put the sentence into execution without the sanction of the Roman governor, John 18 : 31. The Jews lost the power of life and death when Archelaus was deposed, A.D. 6.

2. **Bound him.** They may have loosened or removed the bonds during trial (John 18 : 12); now they rebound him. **They led him away.** It would seem that the whole Sanhedrim present went in a body to Pilate, who was now in his official residence in Herod's palace. See on ver. 11. Their thus coming early, with a prisoner bound in fetters, was adapted to produce the impression on the governor that Jesus was a great criminal. **Delivered him.** The same word as in ch. 26 : 2, 16, etc., translated *betrayed*. As Jesus is betrayed by Judas, one of his disciples, into the hands of the Jewish authorities, so is he betrayed by the latter, his own people, into the hands of the Gentiles.

Pontius Pilate. After Archelaus was deposed, Judea and Samaria were annexed to the Roman province of Syria, and governed by procurators, the sixth of whom was Pontius Pilate. He was appointed A.D. 25, and held his office ten years during the reign of the Emperor Tiberius. He was noted for his severity and cruelty; and by several massacres, to one of which Luke refers (Luke 13 : 1), he rendered himself odious to both the Jews and Samaritans. The latter accused him of cruelty before Vitellius, the governor of Syria, by whom he was ordered to Rome to answer to the charge before the emperor. But Tiberius having died before he arrived, Pilate is said to have been banished by his successor, Caligula, to Vienna, in Gaul, and there to have committed suicide. The traveler who descends the Rhone, in the south of France, may see still standing the very tower from which, as tradition says, Pilate precipitated himself and died. The Roman historian Tacitus makes this important reference to Pilate and Christ, "The author of this name (Christian) was Christ, who was capitally punished in the reign of Tiberius by Pontius Pilate."

At the trial of Jesus, Pilate showed a lack of moral courage to do what he knew to be right. This led to his indecision, and to the various expedients to release Jesus, till at last he yields to the demands of the Jews, through fear of losing his standing as Cæsar's friend.

The governor. A term applied to pro-consuls, legates, or procurators. The first were appointed by the Roman senate a governor or president of a province for one year. The second were governors of provinces, appointed by the emperor, and had much greater power. The third, the office of procurator, pertained rather to the revenues; but sometimes it extended over every department of government in a small province, or in a portion of a large province where the pro-consul or legate could not reside. Such was the case of Pilate, Felix, Festus, and other procurators of Judea. The Roman governor's residence was at Cæsarea, but at the Passover he went to Jerusalem to preserve order.

3-10. THE CONFESSION, REMORSE, AND SUICIDE OF JUDAS. The purchase of the potter's field, in fulfillment of ancient prophecy. Found only in Matthew. Compare Acts 1 : 18, 19.

3. **Condemned.** Some suppose that Matthew here goes forward a little, and relates the remorse and suicide of Judas after the condemnation by Pilate. This is unnecessary. It is better to regard the condemnation as that of the Sanhedrim, and that he *saw* that Jesus was

and brought again the thirty pieces of silver to the
4 chief priests and elders, saying, I have sinned in
that I have betrayed ⁿ the innocent blood. And
they said, What *is that* to us? see thou *to that.*
5 And he cast down the pieces of silver in the temple,
ᵒ and departed, and went and hanged himself.

ⁿ vers. 19, 23, 24, 54; Lk. 23. 41; John 19. 4; Heb. 7. 26.
ᵒ 2 Sam. 17. 23; Ac. 1. 18.

---

condemned in the fact that he was taken and led away in a procession to Pilate. When Judas saw this, he doubtless regarded the final condemnation of Jesus by Pilate as certain. The terrible consequences of his sin burst upon him. But his case was not a singular one. The wicked never fully realize the consequences when in the act of sinning. It is not to be supposed that Matthew writes this to palliate the crime of Judas. He is everywhere spoken of as acting freely and intentionally. His great guilt was brought to view by the words of Jesus, "It had been good for that man if he had not been born," ch. 26 : 24.

Repented himself. The verb thus translated means *to change one's care, to regret,* and is not the one translated *repent* in ch. 3 : 2, the note of which please see. While Judas was bargaining with the chief priests, and seeking opportunity to betray him, his mind was taken up with the love of money and the details of the betrayal; but when he had done the deed, and received the paltry reward of his treachery, he had opportunity for reflection. The money did not afford him the anticipated pleasure, but was rather a reminder of his terrible crime. He remembered the predictions of Jesus in regard to his death, and especially in regard to himself as the traitor, and the woe he had pronounced upon him. The condemnation of Jesus by the Sanhedrim, therefore, gave Judas new proof of the sure fulfillment of these predictions. He feels that his doom is certain. He is filled with remorse and despair in view of the terrible consequences of his sin upon himself. Contrast his false repentance with the true repentance of Peter, ch. 26 : 75. **Thirty pieces,** etc. About fifteen dollars. See on ch. 26 : 15. He probably brought the money back in the morning when the priests were arranging for the festival.

4. **I have sinned.** So said Pharoah and Saul, in view of the consequences of their sins, Exod. 9 : 27; 1 Sam. 15 : 24. **Betrayed the innocent blood.** Omit the article. He acknowledges his crime : I have betrayed an innocent person to a bloody death. Such words, from one who had long been most intimately acquainted with Jesus, was a testimony to his innocence and a solemn warning to the Jewish rulers. Judas would gladly have appeased his conscience, if in any way he could have persuaded himself that Jesus was not innocent, and the chief priests and elders would have as gladly used him as a witness against Jesus, if they could. **See thou to that.** It is your business, not ours, whether you have sinned and betrayed innocent blood or not.

5. **Cast down—in** or *into* **the temple.** The original word means *temple* in the limited sense, in the *holy place* where the priests only might enter. Stung with remorse, Judas rushed into the temple, which was probably quite empty on account of the scenes connected with the crucifixion of Jesus, and, penetrating into the court of the priests, unto the entrance of the holy place, confessed his crime, and flung the money into that sacred inclosure. **Departed.** Withdrew from the temple and the chief priests into solitude, a lonely wretch. **Hanged himself.** This is entirely consistent with the statement of Peter, Acts 1 : 18. Judas may have hung himself on a tree near a precipice, over the valley of Hinnon, where, the limb or rope breaking, he would fall to the bottom, crushed, mangled, and killed. Dr. Hackett says, in regard to the heights of Hinnon (*Scripture Illustrations,* p. 275), "I measured the precipitous, almost perpendicular, walls, in different places, and found the height to be, variously, forty, thirty-six, thirty-three, thirty, and twenty-three feet. Trees still grow quite near the edge of these rocks, and no doubt in former times were still more numerous in the same place. A rocky pavement exists, also, at the bottom of the ledges; and

A.D. 30. MATTHEW XXVII. 379

6 And the chief priests took the silver pieces, ᵖ and said, It is not lawful for to put them into the trea-
7 sury, because it is the price of blood. And they took counsel, and bought with them the potter's
8 field, to bury strangers in. Wherefore that field was called, ᑫ The field of blood, ʳ unto this day.
9 Then was fulfilled that which was spoken by Jeremy the prophet, saying, ˢ ' And they took the thirty

ᵖ ch. 23. 24; Is. 61. 8.

ᑫ Ac. 1. 19.
ʳ Jos. 4. 9.

ˢ Zec. 11. 12, 13.

---

hence, on that account too, a person who should fall from above would be liable to be crushed and mangled, as well as killed. The traitor may have struck in his fall upon some pointed rock, which entered the body and caused his bowels to gush out." Matthew simply states the fact of his suicide; Peter refers to his terrible death, a fit end to his treacherous career. See on ver. 7.
6. **It is not lawful.** Regarded as unclean and abominable. It was the price of human blood, and dishonorably obtained by Judas. The principle that money basely acquired should not be used in the service of God, is involved in Deut. 23 : 18. They were conscientious in not defiling the temple treasury, but made no scruple about defiling their own hands and souls with both the blood and its price. **The price of blood;** given to secure the shedding of blood. They thus acknowledge that they paid this to secure the death of Jesus.
7. **Took counsel.** While the crucifixion was going on, or soon after. They were at a stand in regard to the use of the money of their own as well as Judas's iniquity. Their scruples are satisfied by devoting it to a benevolent object; unconsciously they fulfill prophecy. **The potter's field.** A well-known field, where clay was dug for pottery, or the manufacture of earthenware. The excavations of clay had rendered the land comparatively useless, and hence was purchased for so small a sum. Where this field was situated is uncertain. It is now pointed out on the steep southern slope of the valley of Hinnom, opposite Mount Zion, near the eastern end of the valley. Clay and ancient sepulchres are found here. It was doubtless in this locality. A pottery at Jerusalem at present obtains clay from the hill over the valley of the Hinnom. Judas may have fallen into one of these clay excavations. It is not, however, necessary to understand Peter (Acts 1 :

18) as saying that Judas fell and met his bloody end on this field; but he may mean that the field was named "field of blood" from the notorious bloody end of the traitor, wherever it occurred. Peter would also seem to intimate that Judas purchased the field himself; but the original evidently means that Judas, by his treachery, gave occasion for the purchase of the field. **To bury strangers.** Foreigners, probably Gentile proselytes, who might come up to the feasts. Others suppose foreign Jews to be meant. Compare Eph. 2 : 12, 19.
8. **Wherefore that field was called.** A two-fold reason why it was called *Aceldama, field of blood;* one given here by Matthew, because purchased with the price of blood; the other by Peter (Acts 1 : 19), from the well-known bloody death of the traitor. **Unto this day.** The time that Matthew wrote, about eight to twenty years after the crucifixion. "Skeptics have quoted this phrase in proof that Matthew was written in a later age. But it is a curious coincidence that we fell upon this phrase a few days since in a New-York newspaper, in regard to an event not more than eight years distant."—WHEDON.
9. **Jeremy.** The prophecy is found in Zech. 11 : 13. Why, then, is it referred to Jeremiah? This very difficult question may be answered variously. (1) The Syriac and Persian versions of Matthew, and several of the later Greek manuscripts, read simply "through the prophet." Some early transcriber may have inserted the name Jeremiah, supposing it to be his prophecy, from a reminiscence of Jer. 18 : 2. (2) Or some early transcriber may have mistaken the abbreviated form of Zechariah for that of Jeremiah, the only difference being in a single letter. (3) Or possibly, as the Jews (according to the Talmudic order) placed Jeremiah at the head of the prophets, his name is given as a general title

pieces of silver, the price of him that was valued,
10 whom they of the children of Israel did value; and gave them for the potter's field, as the Lord appointed me.'

Jesus is arraigned before Pilate.

11 AND Jesus stood before the governor. ᵗ And the governor asked him, saying, Art thou the King of the Jews? And Jesus said unto him, ᵘ Thou say-
12 est. And when he was accused of the chief priests
13 and elders, ˣ he answered nothing. Then said Pilate unto him, ʸ Hearest thou not how many

ᵗ Mk. 15. 2; Lk. 23. 3; John 18. 33.
ᵘ John 18. 37.
ˣ ch. 26. 63; John 19. 9.
ʸ ch. 26. 62; John 19. 10.

---

of the prophetic writings. (4) Or, with the last reason may be added, that the Evangelist had in view several prophetic passages, Jer. 7 : 32; 19 : 6; 32 : 8, 14; Zech. 11 : 12, 13. Either of these answers is a sufficient explanation. (5) Or the passage quoted may have occurred in a work of Jeremiah which has been lost. Such a work, Jerome, of the fourth century, says he saw.

And they took, etc. The *sense* of Zechariah is given rather than the *words.* **Valued—value.** Better translated, *priced—price.* The verbal correspondence between the noun *price* and the verbs *priced* and *price* is thus retained, as in the Greek. **The children of Israel did value,** or *price.* The Sanhedrim and Judas as representatives of Israel fixed the price.

10. As the Lord appointed me. Zechariah both acted and spoke, and wrote his prophecy under the command and direction of the Lord. Compare Jer. 32 : 6-9, where the prophet, by way of symbol, purchases the field at Anathoth, according to the command of the Lord. The Septuagint has the same formula, Exod. 9 : 12.

11-14. JESUS IS EXAMINED BY PILATE. THE FIRST TIME, Mark 15 : 2-5; Luke 23 : 2-5; John 18 : 28-38.

11. And Jesus stood. According to several of the oldest manuscripts, *was placed*. In the governor's palace, or prætorium (John 18 : 28), on Mount Zion, built by Herod the Great, and the official residence of the Roman governors, when at Jerusalem. Some suppose the tower of Antonia, adjoining the temple area on the north. The Sanhedrim entered not into the governor's house; for the entrance of a Jew into the house of a Gentile made him unclean till the evening, John 18 : 28. They wish Pilate to ratify and execute their sentence. This he refuses to do without knowing their accusation, and the evidence, John 18 : 29-32. They therefore appear as his accusers, bringing the charge, not of blasphemy, on account of which he had been condemned by the Sanhedrim (ch. 26 : 65, 66), but of treason against Cæsar, as king of the Jews, Luke 23 : 2. They thought that the former charge, being religious, Pilate would not entertain, but that the latter he must entertain, relating as it did both to Cæsar and himself.

At this point Matthew says, **the governor asked him,** rather, *questioned him*, the verb here expressing formal judicial questioning. **Art thou the King?** etc. It is implied that this charge had been preferred against him. Accordingly Luke (23 : 2) informs us that they charged him with seditious agitation, forbidding to pay the tribute money, and proclaiming himself Christ, a king. Before answering, Jesus brought out clearly before Pilate's mind the distinction between a civil and a spiritual kingdom, declaring that his was the latter, John 18 : 32-36. And then he answered, **Thou sayest;** *thou* hast answered it. See on ch. 26 : 25.

12. He answered nothing. He had declared his Messiahship and the spiritual nature of his kingdom to Pilate. He had nothing more to add. Their malignant charges were unworthy an answer, and his silence a reaffirmation of what he had said. Compare 1 Pet. 2 : 23.

13. How many things. Rather, *What great things*, or simply, *What things.* The reference is to the *magnitude* rather than the *number* of things. Pilate may have desired Jesus to deny

14 things they witness against thee? ᵃ And he answered him to never a word; insomuch that the governor marveled greatly.

ᵃ Is. 53. 7.

Barabbas preferred to Jesus.

15 ᵃ NOW at *that* feast the governor was wont to release unto the people a prisoner, whom they would.
16 And they had then a notable prisoner, called Barabbas.
17 Therefore when they were gathered together, Pilate said unto them, Whom will ye that I release unto you? Barabbas, or Jesus which is called Christ?
18 ᵇ For he knew that for envy they had delivered him.

ᵃ Mk. 15. 6; Lk 23. 17; John 18. 39. 40.

ᵇ Ge. 37. 11; Prov. 27. 4; 1 John 3. 12.

---

the charges, in order to help him in declaring his innocence and his acquittal. But they needed no denial; Pilate knew his innocence (ver. 18), and that the Jewish rulers would not conspire against him, because he would free them from Roman authority.

14. The governor marveled greatly. He greatly wondered that Jesus did not even make any reply, much less any explanation of the charges, *not even a word*. His silence continues till Pilate some time after referred to his power to crucify him or release him, John 19 : 10, 11.

Pilate now goes forth and declares the innocence of Jesus, Luke 23 : 4; John 18 : 28. The Jews are therefore the more violent, accusing him with stirring up the people throughout all Judea, beginning from Galilee. Learning that Jesus is a Galilean, Pilate sends him to Herod, the tetrarch of that country, who mocks him, and sends him back to Pilate, Luke 23 : 5-15. Matthew omits this reference to Herod, which is recorded only by Luke, and passes to the next expedient of Pilate to release Jesus.

15-23. BARABBAS PREFERRED TO JESUS, Mark 15 : 6-14; Luke 23 : 17-23; John 18 : 39, 40.

15. At that feast. At every Passover. **Was wont to release.** The origin of this practice is unknown; it is not mentioned in history. The custom was probably established by the Romans to conciliate the Jews, since persons would often be in prison whom the Jews would desire to liberate from Roman law. On the strength of this custom, Pilate tries to save Jesus without offending the Jews. Instead of boldly doing what he knew to be right, he weakly resorts to an expedient,

16. They. The officers and keepers of the prison, where transgressors against Roman law were confined. **Notable.** The word in Greek is used in a bad sense, and means *notorious, famous, noted.*

Barabbas. The name means *Son of his father.* Some think he was son of a rabbi. A few ancient versions and later manuscripts have *Jesus Barabbas.* Hence some regard him as a false Messiah, and see a striking providence in having a false Jesus, *Savior*, put against the true Jesus; a false son of the Father against the true and real Son of God. All this, however, is very doubtful. The contrast in verse 20 seems to be decidedly against the supposition that Barabbas was also called Jesus. We learn from the Gospels that he was a most atrocious criminal, a robber (John 18 : 40); a raiser of sedition in Jerusalem, and a murderer; and that he was bound with his companions in sedition, Mark 15 : 7; Luke 23 : 19.

17. They were gathered together. The people (ver. 15) in connection with the Jewish rulers. Pilate hoped to get a popular expression from the multitude in favor of releasing Jesus, rather than Barabbas. The reason of this hope is stated in the next verse.

18. Envy. Pilate knew that the Jewish rulers were envious against Jesus on account of his popularity with the multitude, and because they regarded him as a formidable rival. He hoped the people would demand his release. **They.** The chief priests and elders. Three times does he propose to release Jesus (Luke 23 : 22), but the people, persuaded by their rulers, to his surprise and mortification, demand Barabbas,

19 When he was set down on the judgment seat, his wife sent unto him, saying, Have thou nothing to do with ᶜ that just man: for I have suffered many things this day in a dream because of him.
20 ᵈ But the chief priests and elders persuaded the multitude that they should ask Barabbas, and destroy
21 Jesus. The governor answered and said unto them, Whether of the twain will ye that I release
22 unto you? They said, Barabbas. Pilate saith unto them, What shall I do then with Jesus which is

ᶜ ver. 4; Is. 53, 11; 1 Pet. 2. 22; 1 John 2. 1.
ᵈ Mk. 15. 11; Lk. 23. 18; John 18. 40; Ac. 3. 14, 15.

---

19. When he was set down. Rather, *And as he sat*. He was sitting upon the judgment-seat awaiting the decision of the people, and ready to pronounce the discharge of the prisoner demanded. **Judgment-seat.** John (19: 13) speaks of the official seat, upon which the magistrate sat when pronouncing judgment, as located in a place called, in Greek, the Pavement, and in Hebrew, Gabbatha, or *elevation*. This was outside of the judgment-hall, probably in front of it, on an elevated platform, paved with marble. The judgment-seat may have been portable, and placed wherever the magistrate might direct.

His wife. Her name is said to have been Claudia Procula. This incident is related only by Matthew, and it shows his accuracy; for the Roman governors had but recently been permitted by the Roman senate to take their wives along with them. **That just man.** Not only innocent, but righteous. She doubtless had some knowledge of Jesus, and was not unlikely a God-fearing heathen woman. **A dream.** An extraordinary one, from which she had *suffered much*. It was sent by God; for the time both of the dream and of sending the message to her husband, indicates an overruling Providence. Compare ch. 2: 13, 19, 22. It is remarkable that a heathen woman should plead for the Just One, when the Jewish people clamor for his death. **This day.** Probably in the morning, after Pilate had gone forth to the trial of Jesus.

20. The chief priests and elders persuaded. While Pilate receives the message from his wife, the Jewish leaders are active in counteracting the influence of Pilate's appeal in favor of Jesus. The multitude were those who had collected during the arrest and the trial; doubtless composed very largely of the street rabble, who are now as ready to condemn him as they were a few days before to praise him. The disciples and friends of Jesus, who took the lead in his triumphal entry into Jerusalem, and whom the Jewish rulers so feared that they dare not to arrest him openly, were without doubt mostly absent, through fear or ignorance. Yet persuasion was necessary to induce even the rabble to ask for the discharge of such a notorious criminal as Barabbas, and the death of such a righteous one as Jesus. The wicked and malicious conduct of the Jewish people in demanding the death of the Holy and the Just, when Pilate had decided to release him, is presented by Peter in Acts 3: 13–15.

21. *Answered.* The instigations of the priests and elders, which he overhears and observes from his judgment-seat. See on ch. 11: 25. He interposes the question: **Whether of the twain?** *Which of the two?*

22. What shall I then do? Pilate seems to have been taken with surprise that they should ask the release of Barabbas, the rebel, robber, and murderer, rather than Jesus, who had committed no crime. He is left in doubt as to what they would have him do with Jesus. Here do we behold another step of Pilate in weakly yielding himself into the power of the Jews. At first, instead of acquitting Jesus, he adopts the expedient of having the people demand his release at the feast. This fails, and expediency leads to expediency. Instead of acting as a righteous and independent judge, he now asks those who had no jurisdiction over the case, "What shall I then do with Jesus?" Though he desires to acquit him, yet the question implies and shows that his decision will be influenced by the demands of the people. He was doubtless also desirous of pleasing the people, because they might accuse him of disloyalty to Cæsar. The

called Christ ? *They* all say unto him, Let him be ᵉ Ac. 13. 28.
23 crucified. And the governor said, Why, what evil hath he done? But they cried out the more, saying, Let him be crucified.
24 When Pilate saw that he could prevail nothing, but *that* rather a tumult was made, he ᶠ took water, and washed *his* hands before the multitude, saying, I am innocent of the blood of ᵍ this just person:
25 see ye *to it*. Then answered all the people, and said,

ᶠ Deu. 21. 6, 7; Ps. 26. 6; Jer. 26 15.
ᵍ ver. 4.

complaints of the Jews received particular attention at Rome. Archelaus had been deposed partly on account of the complaints of his subjects against him. A selfish motive, therefore, operated against his moral courage, and doubtless led him to desire to conciliate the Jews, to whom he was odious, by granting their request, at least in a modified form, as by scourging and mockery. See on ver. 23.
Let him be crucified. That they all thus cried out shows how successful the rulers had been in stirring up the people. They might have asked, Let him be stoned, which was the Jewish mode of execution and their penalty for blasphemy; or they might have simply said, Let him be put to death; but they demand crucifixion, the Roman punishment for sedition. They thus also gratify their hatred against Jesus. As they demanded the release of Barabbas, who would, doubtless, have been crucified for his crimes, so they ask for Jesus the punishment which Barabbas would have received. Thus is Barabbas preferred to Jesus. Yet in this were the Scriptures and the predictions of Jesus being fulfilled, John 18 : 32. He dies an ignominious death, his body is unmutilated and not a bone broken, and he is made a curse by hanging on the tree.
23. Pilate strives to reason with them. If they insist on his death, they must show some crime meriting such a punishment. And certainly he had not done any thing demanding crucifixion. Though he finds no *evil* in him (Luke 23 : 14), yet on the principle of expediency he proposes to conciliate the Jews by the milder punishment of scourging, Luke 23 : 22. But they only answer by crying out tumultuously, **Let him be crucified.**
24, 25. PILATE DECLARES HIMSELF INNOCENT OF THE BLOOD OF JESUS, which the people imprecate upon themselves.

Found only in Matthew. As Matthew alone relates the dream and the message of Pilate's wife, so he alone relates this act, which her message, doubtless, did much in producing. The answer of the Jews also fittingly appears in a Gospel especially designed for Jews, showing the aggravated guilt of their nation.
24. **Washed his hands.** Pilate, finding that his expedients *availed* nothing, and that a popular tumult was imminent, took water and washed his hands, according to a usage of the Jews (Deut. 21 : 6-9), and of some other nations, signifying that he repudiated all responsibility for the death the people demanded. This was an impressive act, and should have caused the Jews to pause and consider. Possibly Pilate hoped that it might produce a good effect. But he had no right to pronounce what he knew to be an unrighteous condemnation; and to relieve himself of the responsibility of a judge was impossible. Washing of hands and repudiation, however solemn and public, could not relieve him or cleanse his conscience from guilt. **This just person.** *Just man*, using the same language as his wife, ver. 19. **See ye to it.** As the chief priest and the elders had said to Judas (ver. 4), so now Pilate says to the people, The responsibility and the guilt of shedding innocent blood rests on you, not on me.
25. **His blood be on us,** etc. Such was the fearful imprecation of the frantic multitude upon themselves and their children. For eighteen centuries have the Jewish people been suffering what they then madly imprecated on themselves. Forty years after, their city was taken and destroyed by the Romans, and such multitudes were crucified that room failed for the crosses, and crosses for the bodies. (Josephus, *Jewish War*, v. 11. 1.) Doubtless some of those very persons, or their children, were among those who were crucified,

26 ʰ His blood *be* on us, and on our children. Then released he Barabbas unto them: and when ⁱ he had scourged Jesus, he delivered *him* to be crucified.

ʰ Deu. 19. 10; Jos. 2. 19; 2 Sam. 1. 16; 1 Ki. 2. 32; Ac. 5. 28.
ⁱ Mk. 15. 15; John 19. 1, 16; Is. 50. 6; 53. 5; Lk. 23. 16, 24. 25.

The insults of the soldiers.

27 THEN the soldiers of the governor took Jesus into the common hall, and gathered unto him the
28 whole band *of soldiers.* And they stripped him,
29 and ˡ put on him a scarlet robe. ᵐ And when they had platted a crown of thorns, they put *it* upon his

ᵏ Mk. 15. 16; John 19. 2.
ˡ Lk. 23. 11.
ᵐ Ps. 69. 19; Is. 53. 3.

This was the decision of the multitude, and, properly speaking, of the nation, though done in partial ignorance (Acts 3 : 17); for nearly one half of the population of Judea and Galilee probably attended the Passover. Josephus estimates the number who attended at about three millions. (*Jewish War*, ii. 14. 3.) In this multitude were probably representatives of all portions of the country, and their decision against Jesus was unanimous, John 18 : 40. See on ch. 21 : 9.

26. Thereupon Pilate RELEASES BARABBAS, SCOURGES JESUS, and DELIVERS HIM TO BE CRUCIFIED, Mark 15 : 15; Luke 23 : 24, 25.

26. **And when he had scourged Jesus.** *But Jesus, having caused to be scourged.* It was a Roman custom to scourge a criminal before crucifixion. Roman scourging was more severe than Jewish. The number of lashes was not limited to forty. The whips were armed with bones or lead, to render the blow the more fearful, and to lacerate the flesh. The criminal was generally bound to a low block, in a stooping posture, and received the fearful blows upon the naked back. The scourging before crucifixion was generally exceedingly cruel, and criminals frequently died under it. Jesus was probably scourged by soldiers appointed by Pilate for the purpose. It took place outside of the governor's house, and was a fulfillment of a prediction of Jesus, ch. 20:19; and of prophecy, Isa. 50: 6; 53 : 5. Pilate seems to have been affected by the cruel scourging, and, thinking that what touched his heart might affect the hearts of others, he determines to make one more appeal to the Jewish people by showing him lacerated and bleeding, arrayed in a garb of mockery. But in vain. See John 19 : 1–16. **Delivered him to be crucified.** Matthew states the general fact, and in harmony with John's account, in that he places his delivery to crucifixion after the scourging, and the scourging before the mockery. After making this summary statement, he passes on and describes the mockery.

27–30. JESUS MOCKED BY THE SOLDIERS, Mark 15 : 16–19; John 19 : 1–16. Matthew does not describe this with reference to exact chronological order, but, in placing it in a general way just previous to his being led away to crucifixion, agrees with John, who delineates this portion of the narrative with great particularity.

27. **The common hall.** The prætorium, or governor's house; Herod's palace. See on vers. 2 and 11. Jesus is taken from near the judgment-seat, which was probably in front of the house, into the court of the house, Mark 15:16. **The whole band.** The whole Roman cohort, stationed at Jerusalem, which was a tenth part of a legion, and embraced from three to six hundred men or more. See on ch. 26 : 47. The whole company of soldiers were gathered unto Jesus to make sport with him.

28. **Stripped him,** of his outer garment, or mantle. **Scarlet robe.** Crimson military cloak of a Roman officer. Mark and John speak of it as *purple,* or purple-red, a color worn by emperors. The colors intermingled, and the names were often indefinitely applied, and, in popular language, interchanged. The cloak was put upon him in derision of his kingly dignity, and in accordance with the charge the Jews brought against him. Compare Ps. 35 : 15, 16.

29. **Had platted.** Having woven. **A crown of thorns.** The principal object was mockery; a derisive imitation of crowning kings and conquerors with wreaths of ivy, palm, or laurel. It

A.D. 30.   MATTHEW XXVII.   385

head, and a reed in his right hand: and they bow- *a* ch. 26. 67; Is. 50. 6.
ed the knee before him, and mocked him, saying, *o* Mic. 5. 1.
30 Hail, king of the Jews! And ⁿ they spit upon him, *p* Mk. 15. 20; Lk. 23. 26; John 19. 16.
and took the reed, and ᵒ smote him on the head.

Jesus led away to be crucified.   *q* ch. 21. 38, 39; Is. 53. 7.

31 ᵖ AND after that they had mocked him, they *r* Le. 4. 12, 21; Num. 15. 35, 36; 1 Ki. 21. 13; Ac. 7. 58; Heb. 13. 12.
took the robe off from him, and put his own raiment
32 on him ; ᑫ and led him away to crucify *him*. ʳ And as
they came out, ˢ they found a man of Cyrene, Si- *s* Mk. 15. 21; Lk. 23. 26.
mon by name: him they compelled to bear his

---

was, doubtless, a secondary object to make it a *painful* crown. So mean a plant as the thorn made it suitable for a mock crown, and well adapted to produce pain. It is a matter of dispute as to what species of thorn was used. Thorny plants and shrubs abound in Palestine. The *Spina Christi*, or *Christ's thorn*, is now very common near Jerusalem, and is very generally pointed out as the species of thorn used on this occasion. Another plant (a *leguminous* flexile thorn) is preferred by others. Rev. E. P. Hammond, who was in Jerusalem in December, 1866, in referring to it says, "Before leaving, Mrs. Gobat presented me with a crown of thorns, which must be similar to the one which our blessed Savior wore; for all about Jerusalem the same kind of thorn grows as in the days of our Lord. . . Each of the thorns upon the crown was, when it was given me, as sharp as a cambric needle." The latter plant is the more probable one. It is possible that this crown remained on his head during his crucifixion, since Matthew and Mark mention the removal of the purple robe, but not the crown.

A reed. A plant with a hollow-jointed stock, a common product of the wilderness of Judea and of the banks of the Jordan, and sometimes used for walking-canes. This was given him as a mock sceptre, and placed in his **right hand,** as kings generally held their sceptres in this hand. **Mocked him.** Paid him mock homage as to a king. Thus was fulfilled his prediction, ch. 20 : 19. **Hail.** *Joy to thee.* Similar to the Hebrew phrase, Let the king live forever, Neh. 2 : 3; Dan. 2 : 4.

30. Their mockery is now turned into the grossest insult and violence. To spit upon a person was expressive of the deepest contempt. Isa. 53 : 3. See on ch. 26 :

67. The pain from the stroke of the reed was heightened by the sharp, thorny crown. This mockery and violence was not required by the law. It was the lawless sport of a coarse and brutal soldiery, who knew little of Jesus except what they had heard from the Jews, and who, doubtless, regarded him as a religious fanatic. But all this Jesus bore meekly, submissively, silently, Isa. 53 : 7.

Having related the mockery of Jesus which preceded the final attempt of Pilate to release Jesus (John 19 : 1–16), Matthew proceeds to narrate the crucifixion. See on ver. 26.

31–34. JESUS IS LED FORTH TO CRUCIFIXION, Mark 15 : 20–23; Luke 23 : 26–33; John 19 : 16, 17. Luke's account is the fullest.

31. **Led him away.** Led by the centurion on horseback, who had charge of the crucifixion, ver. 54.

32. **As they came out;** the city, Heb. 13 : 12. Criminals were executed outside the city, Lev. 24 : 14; Num 15 : 35; 1 Kings 21 : 13; Acts 7 : 58. **Cyrene** was a city on the north coast of Africa. Many Jews resided there. They were accustomed to visit Jerusalem in large numbers at the great festivals, and had there a synagogue, Acts 2 : 10; 6 : 9. **Simon** was just coming in from the country when Jesus was passing out the gate, bearing his own cross (John 19 : 17), and was the father of Alexander and Rufus, probably well-known disciples among the early Christians, Mark 15 : 21; Rom. 16 : 13. He had probably recently come from Cyrene to attend the Passover. A Simeon in Acts 13 : 1, and the mother of Rufus in Rom. 16 : 13, are spoken of as disciples; but whether they are to be identified as Simon and his son is conjectural. **They compelled.** Or, rather, *impress-*

33 cross. ᶦ And when they were come unto a place called Golgotha, that is to say, a place of a skull, ᶦ Mk. 15, 22; Lk. 23. 33; John 19. 17.

ed, pressed into service, the same word being used as in ch. 5 : 41, the note on which see. Thus they did not arbitrarily assume power, but, under the direction of the centurion, who had the necessary authority under Roman law, they pressed this man into their service. The reason for selecting him was, probably, because he was a stranger and foreigner, and happened to meet them just at the time when some one was needed. It is not necessary to suppose him a disciple or a slave. **To bear his cross.** The cross was of various forms. (1) It was originally a simple stake. (2) Afterward it was made of two pieces of wood, crossed like the letter T; or (3) like the letter X; or (4) the transverse beam crossed the perpendicular one at some distance from the top, as †. The latter was, doubtless, the one used on this occasion, since the title was placed over the head. The uniform tradition is, that this was the form of the Savior's cross. The cross which Constantine commanded to be placed on his standard represented the first two letters of the Greek *Christos* (*Christ*) ☧.

Jesus bore his cross to the gate, when he was relieved or aided by Simon. Compare Isaac carrying the wood in Gen. 22 : 6. It was usual for persons condemned to crucifixion to bear their own cross. A tradition says that Jesus sunk to the ground under it. It is quite possible that, having fallen exhausted from great weariness and the loss of blood, it was put on Simon. Yet it is more in accordance with the language of Luke (23 : 26) to suppose that Simon bore only the part of the cross which was behind Jesus, and thus lightened the burden. As they pass along to the place of crucifixion, a great company of people, and of women, who also bewailed and lamented him, follow. This touching incident is related only by Luke (ch. 23 : 27-31).

33. **Golgotha.** The name in Hebrew, or, rather, Aramean, means a skull. According to Luke 23 : 33, correctly translated, it is "a place which is called *a skull*." Calvary, in the common version, is from *Calvarium*, the Latin for skull. Some suppose that it was so called from the skulls of criminals executed or buried there. But these must have been buried according to Jewish law. Why, then, should the place be named from the skull rather than from any other part of the skeleton? Why in the singular and not in the plural? Others, therefore, suppose it so called because it was a rounded and skull-like knoll. But there is no intimation in the Scriptures that it was a hill. Still, the latter explanation is the best, unless we suppose it received the name from some skull which had been found there, or lain there exposed for a time contrary to Jewish usage. From the Gospels we learn it was nigh the city (John 19 : 20), near a thoroughfare (Mark 15 : 29), by a garden, where was the sepulchre hewn in the rock, ver. 60; John 19 : 41. Tradition places it north-west of the temple, where the Church of the Sepulchre is at present situated. But this is improbable, since the site of the church must have been within the city, and Golgotha was without the gate, ch. 28 : 11; John 19 : 17. The general tendency of opinion now locates Calvary north of Jerusalem, near the Damascus gate, at the grotto of Jeremiah. This meets well all the conditions. Another site is thus described by one who knew well the modern city: "The palace of Pilate and the judgment-hall stood at the north-west angle of the Harem area, where the house of the pasha still stands. . . . It would seem that the soldiers had not far to go from the palace to Golgotha. The gate of St. Stephen's (in the eastern wall) is about two hundred yards from the palace, and leads directly into the country. Without the gate one road runs eastward across the Kidron, another northward along the narrow brow of the hill. Between these is an open space, rugged and rocky; just below it, in the shelving banks of the Kidron, are several rock tombs. This spot would seem to answer all the requirements of the narrative. The passers-by on both roads would be within a few yards of him; and his acquaintance could stand 'afar off' on the side of Olivet and see with the utmost distinctness the whole scene."—J. L. PORTER, in *Alexander's Kitto's Cyclop.*

34. **Vinegar.** Sour wine. The *wine*

34 they gave him vinegar to drink mingled with gall : and when he had tasted *thereof*, he would not drink.

The Crucifixion.

35 ˣ AND they crucified him, and parted his garments, casting lots; that it might be fulfilled which

ᶦ Mk. 15. 24; Lk. 23. 34; John 3. 14, 15; 12. 32; 19. 24.

of Mark 15 : 23. The soldiers used a cheap, sour wine, but little better than vinegar. **Mingled with gall.** The word translated *gall* denoted a very bitter substance, as wormwood, colocynth, poppy, myrrh, and the like. Mark explains the bitter ingredient to be *myrrh*. It was probably the sour wine, mingled with myrrh, wormwood, etc., which was given to criminals, according to a Jewish usage, just before crucifixion, to stupefy and deaden the pain. Compare Prov. 31 : 6, and notice the fulfillment of prophecy (Ps. 69 : 21), according to which the language of Matthew agrees. **Tasted—would not drink.** He received it, and showed that he knew what it was; but refused to drink it, since he would drink the cup of suffering to its very dregs, without any alleviation, and retain his mind with all its powers clear and unimpaired unto the end.

35-56. THE CRUCIFIXION OF JESUS, AND THE ATTENDING CIRCUMSTANCES, Mark 15 : 24-41; Luke 33 : 49; John 19 : 18-30.

ˣ 35. **Crucified him.** Crucifixion was the severest and most ignominious punishment among the ancients. It was not a Jewish, but rather a Roman mode of execution, and was inflicted on slaves and the vilest criminals. "It is an outrage," said Cicero, "to *bind* a Roman; to *scourge* him is an atrocious crime; to *put him to death* is almost parricide; but to CRUCIFY him, what shall I call it?" To a proud Roman, the cross was a symbol of infamy, and crucifixion an unspeakable disgrace.

The cross was generally first driven into the ground, and then the criminal was lifted up and fastened to it, by nails through the hands and feet, the latter being either separate or united, and about a foot or two above the ground. Sometimes the victim was first fastened to the cross, and then sunk into the earth with a sudden shock, causing the most agonizing torture. Whether a single nail was driven through the feet of Jesus, or they were nailed separately, can not be determined; but that they were *nailed* and not *tied*, as some have conjectured, is evident from Luke 24 : 39, and from the fact that nailing was usual in Roman crucifixion. Compare 22:16, and Hackett's *Smith's Dictionary of the Bible*, on CRUCIFIXION. In order that the hands might not be torn away, a large wooden pin was commonly inserted in the upright timber, passing between the legs to support the weight of the body. The unnatural position and tension of the body, the laceration of the hands and feet, which are full of nerves and tendons, and the consequent inflammation; the pressure of the blood to the head and stomach, causing severe pain and terrible anxiety, and the burning and raging thirst; all these, with no vital part wounded, made crucifixion a most excruciating and lingering death. Sometimes the wretched victim would hang three days before death came to his relief. The unusual quickness of our Savior's death arose from his previous exhausting agonies and his deep mental anguish. This terrible mode of punishment continued till it was abolished by Constantine, the first Christian emperor.

It was the third hour of the day, nine o'clock in the morning (Mark 15 : 25), when they arrived at Golgotha, and fastened Jesus to the cross. John says (ch. 19 : 14) about the sixth hour. The discrepancy can be explained by supposing that some early transcriber mistook the sign for three for that of six, the two being very nearly alike (some manuscripts of John read *third* hour); or that the time of crucifixion was somewhere between the two broad divisions, the third and sixth hours, and that Mark designates the time by the beginning, and John by the ending of the period; or that John uses the Roman mode of reckoning the day from midnight to midnight. See author's HARMONY, note on § 181. Matthew, Mark, and Luke agree in fixing the commencement of the darkness at the sixth hour, after Jesus had hung some time on the cross. While they were nailing him to the cross, he forgets, as it were, his own pains in his anxiety for their souls,

was spoken by the prophet, ʸ They parted my garments among them, and upon my vesture did they
36 cast lots. ᶻ And sitting down they watched him
37 there. And [they] ᵃ set up over his head his accusation written, THIS IS JESUS THE KING OF THE JEWS.
38 ᵇ Then were there two thieves crucified with him, one on the right hand, and another on the left.

ʸ Ps. 22. 18.
ᶻ ver. 51.
ᵃ Mk. 15. 26; Lk. 23. 38; John 19. 19.
ᵇ Is. 53. 12; Mk. 15. 27; Lk. 23. 32, 33; John 19. 18.

and prays, Father, forgive them, for they know not what they do, Luke 23 : 34. This was the first of his *seven sayings* from the cross. See on ver. 50.

Parted his garments. Persons were crucified naked. It was an ancient belief and tradition that a linen cloth was bound about his loins. From John 19 : 23, 24, it appears that the four soldiers who were engaged in the crucifixion *divided* some of the garments among themselves, but cast lots for his coat, or tunic, being an inner garment, without a seam, and woven throughout.

They thus unconsciously fulfilled prophecy, Ps. 22 : 18. **That it might,** etc. These words to the end of the verse are omitted in the oldest manuscripts, but are found in John 19 : 24. In **casting lots,** their names were probably written on slips of parchment, and cast into a vase, or a receiver of some kind, and then taken up; the one first drawn received the prize.

36. They watched him there. Four soldiers—a centurion and three others, John 19 : 23. They watched him as a guard, with little concern and with little sympathy. The wounds in crucifixion were not generally mortal, and hence the necessity of watching, lest friends should come and take him down, and preserve his life. Josephus had a friend who was taken down from the cross and lived; and many cases have occurred where they have recovered, some of them after even remaining on the cross three hours.

37. Returning a little in his narrative, Matthew refers to the superscription put on the cross, above Jesus, and states that two others were crucified with him. **And set up.** *And they set up;* that is, those who were directed by Pilate; he appears to have written the title himself, John 19 : 22. **Accusation.** The reason, or charge, for which he suffered. The crime for which a person suffered crucifixion was in some way published. Sometimes a public crier announced it; sometimes it was written on a tablet, and hung about the neck of the criminal as he was led to execution; and very commonly it was, as in this case, written on a white tablet, and put above the criminal's head on the cross. In some cases, these three may have been combined.

This is Jesus, etc. Mark has simply, "The King of the Jews;" Luke, "This is the King of the Jews;" and John, "Jesus the Nazarene, the King of the Jews." The difference in these titles may be explained: (1) That some of the Evangelists, and even all of them, may have given the sense rather than the words. (2) That the accusation was written in Hebrew, Greek, and Latin (John 19 : 20), and while the inscriptions were one in sense, they may have been very likely varied in expression, and hence the translation of them would vary. The Latin was the official language of the empire; the Greek, the language of the cultivated classes, and very common in the province; the Hebrew, or Aramean, the vernacular language of the Jews and the common people. It is quite likely that John's inscription, containing the contemptuous phrase, "the Nazarene," was the one written in Hebrew, and which would be understood by the Jews of Palestine. Pilate purposely wrote the sarcastic title, purporting that the Jews were crucifying their king, and also that he was a Nazarene. The absurdity of the charge appeared upon its very face; yet when the Jews desired it changed, Pilate would not consent. They had pressed him to crucify Jesus, working on his fears, and saying, "If thou let this man go, thou art not Cæsar's friend;" and now he has the opportunity to return the taunt, and he does it, and perseveres in it, John 19 : 12, 20–22. Pilate at the same time unconsciously proclaimed him the King of the Jews (ch. 2 : 2), the Messiah, whose claims they could not escape, and whose power they could not resist.

38. **Two thieves.** *Two robbers,* pro-

Jesus mocked on the Cross.

39 AND they that passed by reviled him, wagging
40 their heads, and saying, Thou that destroyest the temple, and buildest it in three days, save thyself. If thou be the Son of God, come down from the cross.
41 Likewise also the chief priests mocking *him*, with
42 the scribes and elders, said, He saved others; himself he can not save. If he be the King of Israel, let him now come down from the cross, and we will
43 believe him. He trusted in God; let him deliver

c Mk. 15. 29; Lk. 23. 35; Ps. 22. 6, 7; 109. 25.
d ch. 26. 61; John 2. 19.
e ch. 4. 3, 6; 26. 63, 64.
f ch. 16. 4; Lk. 16. 31.
g John 11. 47.
h ch. 2. 2; John 1. 49.
i Ps. 22. 7, 8; 71. 10, 11.

bably two associates of Barabbas, left to suffer while he was released. The Greek makes a distinction between the terms, *thief* and *robber*, John 10 : 8. **Then were—crucified.** The present tense in the original. *Then two robbers are crucified with him.* Jesus is nailed to the cross; the superscription is put above his head. Then the two malefactors who were led out with Jesus (Luke 23 : 32) are also crucified, by the same soldiers, Mark 15 : 27; Luke 23 : 33; John 19 : 18. "The crucified is decked with the title, King of the Jews; then two robbers, as the symbol of his Jewish kingdom, are crucified. This was the governor's revenge, that the Jews had overcome him and humbled him in his own estimation."—LANGE. Thus did Pilate unconsciously fulfill prophecy, "And he was numbered with the transgressors," Mark 15 : 28; Isa. 53 : 12. The time of the Passover festivities was regarded as a suitable time for the execution of criminals that an impression might be made on the multitudes assembled at Jerusalem. Compare Deut. 17 : 13. The governor, being at Jerusalem at this time, was accustomed to crucify several criminals.

39. Matthew proceeds (as far as verse 44) to relate the scoffs and insults of the passers-by, and of the chief priests, which were even taken up by the malefactors who were crucified with Jesus. These indignities are related by the first three Evangelists.
They that passed by. The people going in and out of the city on the thoroughfare near the place of crucifixion.
Wagging their heads. A contemptuous and scornful shaking of the head, fitting their words as they **reviled him**, or *blasphemed* him, for such is the word used in the original. See on ch. 12 : 31. They revile, or blaspheme his power and his divine Sonship, as is shown by the next verses. The most atrocious criminal is hardly ever mocked and derided when undergoing execution.
40. **Thou that destroyest.** See ch. 26 : 61. Jesus had spoken not of *destroying*, but of *raising up* the temple of his body, John 2 : 19. **Save thyself.** If thou possessest this power. **If thou be the Son of God.** Literally, *God's Son.* See on ch. 14 : 33. If thou be the Son of the Highest, as thou professest, ch. 26 : 63, 64. **Come down.** Shutting their eyes to all of the manifestations and evidences of his divine power and Sonship, they prescribe this last test. Ever ready to applaud success (ch. 21 : 9) and denounce failure, they conclude that Jesus is an impostor, and revile him accordingly. Some, however, did it under greater light, and with more malicious intent than others.
41. **Chief priests — scribes and elders.** The rulers, Luke 23 : 35. That the dignitaries of the Sanhedrim should thus mingle with the populace in their scoffs, shows how bitter their hatred and how terrible their malignity. **Mocking.** Held him up in derision. Their mockery was no less blasphemous than that of the people.
42. **He saved others.** They had been compelled to acknowledge his supernatural power. See, for example, Mark 3 : 22; John 12 : 10. They taunt him with having lost it now when he needs it for his own deliverance. They treat him as an impostor. **If he is the King of Israel.** If he is the Messiah. The most approved text reads, *He is the King of Israel*, which is even more ironical. They thus reproach him as a false Messiah.
43. **He trusted in God.** They spoke in derision, yet unconsciously fulfilled, Ps. 22 : 7, 8. **For he said,** etc. Re-

him now, if he will have him: for he said, ^k I am
44 the Son of God. ^l The thieves also, which were
crucified with him, cast the same in his teeth.

^k ch. 23. 63, 64.
Mk. 15. 32; Lk.
23. 39.

The supernatural darkness.

45 ^m NOW from the sixth hour there was darkness
46 over all the land unto the ninth hour. And about
the ninth hour ⁿ Jesus cried with a loud voice, say-

^m Mk. 15. 33; Lk.
23. 44; Ex. 10.
21-23; Am. 8. 9.
ⁿ Heb. 5. 7.

ferring to his answer to the high-priest, ch. 26 : 64. **The Son of God**, or, literally, *God's Son*, as in ver. 40, referring not so much to his claim to Messiahship as to divinity. Thus in these several taunts did they in their malignity speak blasphemously against the Son of Man, ch. 12 : 32.

Luke (ch. 23 : 36) states that the soldiers also mocked him.

44. **The thieves.** *The robbers.* Luke records the railings of only one. But both may at first have joined in reproaches; but one of them, being afterward convinced of the Messiahship of Jesus, repents, Luke 23 : 39-43. **Cast the same in his teeth.** *Reproached* him in like manner, or with the same thing. Thus Jesus was crucified between robbers, and reproached by them as the greatest of criminals. Thus we have recorded by the Evangelists two scoffs by the passing multitude, three by the rulers, one by the soldiers, and one by the malefactors; seven in all.

About this time probably occurred that interesting incident related in John 19 : 25-27: Jesus committing his widowed mother to the care of the beloved disciple.

45. In this and the four following verses Matthew describes the extraordinary darkness, the despouding cry of Jesus, and the remarks of some of the bystanders. Mark and Luke also record the darkness. **From the sixth—unto the ninth hour.** From twelve o'clock to three in the afternoon. Jesus had hung about three hours upon the cross. **Darkness over all the land.** Over all the land of Palestine, or over all the earth, that is, over that part of it where there was then day. The Greek word may have either the limited, or the more extended sense. The *darkness* was supernatural. It could not have been an eclipse of the sun, for that occurs only at new moon, and it was then the Passover, which was observed at full moon. Nor was it the natural precursor of the earthquake, for that was miraculous, vers. 51-53. Luke (23 : 45) adds, "The sun was darkened," after the darkening of the earth, which suggest a thickening of the atmosphere, or a dark gloom coming over the heavens, obscuring even the sun. This was evidently the first of the miraculous events attending the crucifixion. "Yea, creation itself bewailed its Lord; for the sun was darkened and the rocks were rent."—CYRIL ALEX. As the *night* of our Savior's birth was enlightened with the glory of the heavenly hosts (Luke 2 : 9), so now the *day* of his death is darkened with the gloom of a forsaken world. The darkness represented the eclipse of the Sun of Righteousness, the darkness and distress which overwhelmed his soul when the Father forsook him, and left him to meet alone the powers of death and hell.

Several heathen writers mention an extraordinary darkening of the sun about this time. Eusebius quotes the words of Phlegon, a chronicler under the reign of Hadrian : "There occurred the greatest darkening of the sun which had ever been known; it became night at midday, so that the stars shone in the heavens. Also, a great earthquake in Bithynia, which destroyed a part of Nicæa." This language may apply to a darkening of the sun, either by an eclipse or by a supernatural power, and it is said to have occurred at about the time of our Savior's death. May it not be a heathen testimony to the wonderful phenomena of that event? Tertullian, Origen, and others also boldly appealed to the Roman archives for the proof of the eclipse of the sun, as it was called, at the time of our Savior's death.

46. **About the ninth hour.** For about three hours had darkness prevailed, and Jesus continued the terrible conflict in silence. Amidst the gloom

ing, Eli! Eli! lama sabachthani? that is to say, ᵒ'My God! my God! why hast thou forsaken me?' ᵒ Ps. 22. 1.
47 Some of them that stood there, when they heard *that*, said, This *man* calleth for Elias. ᵖ ver. 34; Ps. 69. 21; Mk. 15. 36; 23. 36; John 19. 29.
48 And straightway one of them ran, and took a sponge, ᵖ and filled *it* with vinegar, and put *it* on a

---

we may suppose the mockings around the cross had ceased. Into the mysterious agonies of these hours of darkness no mind on earth is permitted to penetrate. The Evangelists let us not into its secrets, but simply record the length of the interval, and the bursting wail of agony at the close of the scene. **Eli, Eli.** Ps. 22:1. *Eli* is the Hebrew, and *Eloi* (Mark 15:34) the Aramean, the ordinary dialect of the day. The Aramean words are given to show more clearly the reference to Elijah in the next verse. **My God! my God!** The cry, not of despair, but of extreme anguish, yet of resignation and holy confidence in God as his God. **Why hast thou forsaken me?** Rather, *Why didst thou forsake me?* He was now just emerging from this terrible abandonment by the Father. We catch a glimpse of the incomprehensible height and depth of his sufferings, to which the agonies of Gethsemane were but a prelude. See on ch. 26:38. As he was made a curse for us and bore our sins, standing in the place of the sinner, the Father turned, as it were, his face from him. He who is of purer eyes than to behold evil (Habbak. 1:13) turns away from his Son when the sins of a world were laid upon him, Isa. 53:4, 5, 10; Gal. 3:13; 2 Cor. 5:21; 1 Pet. 2:24. **Why?** The interrogative form gives intensity to the expression. It is not the cry of ignorance of the cause of this abandonment, but rather the struggling of language in its weakness, to express the unfathomable woe and utter desolation of his vicarious sufferings. Yet the cry coming forth at the close of this abandonment, shows that he had endured all that was put upon him, and was coming forth victorious from the conflict. Though left to himself for a time, yet he did not forsake God. Personifying forsaken humanity under the wrath of God, he makes an atonement, cries unto God, and is heard, in that he feared (Heb. 5:7)—the presence of the Father is restored, the darkness rolls away, and light returns to the land. This language also points to the twenty-second Psalm as fulfilled in him.

46. This man calleth for Elias; for Elijah, whose coming the Jewish people were expecting. Most commentators suppose this was said in jest. If so, it betrays the most terrible depravity, an insensibility and malignant hatred almost inconceivable. It hardly seems possible that after a supernatural darkness of about three hours, these attendants would have turned into derision this deathly wail of anguish. It is more natural to suppose that amid those hours of gloom, sadness and awe pervaded their minds, and that some of them really mistook the word Eli or *Eloi* for Elias, or, in their language, *Elia*. Their superstitious fears may have been sufficiently aroused in regard to the day of judgment, which they may have supposed the coming of Elijah would usher in (Mal. 4:5), as to seize instantly upon the word Eli, as the name of that old prophet. Or some, standing by the cross, might have been foreign Jews, who did not very readily understand the language, and therefore confounded the words. Or even some of the Roman soldiers, who, amid this wonderful phenomenon, had listened attentively to the conversation of the Jews about the coming of Elijah, might have thought Jesus calling for the prophet. It seems better to adopt any of these suppositions than to suppose mockery in the midst of supernatural occurrences. And it accords better with what occurred very soon after, related in Luke 23:47, 48.

48. Immediately after this cry, John informs us that Jesus, knowing that all things were now accomplished, and that the Scripture might be fulfilled (Ps. 69:21), said, "I thirst." Moved with sympathy, one extends a sponge of vinegar to his parching lips. A feverish thirst was one of the greatest sufferings attending crucifixion. **Vinegar.** The sour wine of the soldiers. Possibly one of the guard-soldiers who crucified him did this deed of compassion. This must not be confounded with the offering of vine-

49 reed, and gave him to drink. The rest said, Let be, let us see whether Elias will come to save him.

The death of Jesus, and its attendant circumstances.

50 ¶ JESUS, when he had cried again with a loud voice, yielded up the ghost.

51 And, behold, ʳ the vail of the temple ˢ was rent in

q Mk. 15. 37; Lk. 23. 46; John 10. 11.
r Mk. 15. 38–41; Lk. 23. 45; Ex. 26. 31· 2 Chr. 3. 14.

gar in mockery by the soldiers, related in Luke 23 : 36, which took place before the season of darkness. **A reed.** A hyssop-reed, or stalk, John 19 : 29. Jesus would not receive the drugged wine which was intended to stupefy and assuage the pain, nor the wine extended to him in mockery; but this, extended to him in sympathy, he receives. The great conflict, too, was over, and now he can drink it.

49. **The rest said.** The others about the cross, in contrast to the *some* in ver. 47. It appears from John 19 : 29 that several assisted in filling the sponge with vinegar, and giving it to Jesus. May they not have been of those who had said, "This man calleth for Elias." The others, seeing what was about to be done, exclaim, **Let be,** *wait now,* let us see whether Elijah comes to his rescue. The language seems to be not in mockery, but in doubt and suspense. On the one hand was the supernatural darkness, but on the other Elijah does not immediately come. They are for waiting to see if there will be any divine interposition. According to Mark 15 : 36, the one offering him the vinegar says the same, *Wait,* etc., a response to the other party, and possibly showing a little stronger expectation that Elijah might come to deliver him.

50. In this verse Matthew relates the death of Jesus, and in the three following verses the wonderful phenomena attending it.

Cried again, etc. When Jesus had received the vinegar, he said, "It is finished," John 19 : 30. Luke (23 : 46) states that Jesus, crying again with a loud voice, said, "Father, into thy hands I commend (commit) my spirit." The latter is doubtless the one meant by Matthew.

The most probable order of the seven sayings of Jesus is as follows: 1. The prayer for his enemies, Luke 23 : 34. 2. The promise to the penitent robber, Luke 23 : 43. 3. The charge to Mary and John, John 19 : 26. 4. The cry Eli, Eli,

etc., ch. 26 : 46; Mark 15 : 34. 5. The exclamation, "I thirst," John 19 : 28. 6. The declaration, "It is finished," John 19 : 30. 7. The committing his spirit to God, Luke 23 : 46.

Yielded up the ghost. *Yielded up his spirit.* He died voluntarily, John 10: 18.

That Jesus should have died in six hours (Mark 15 : 14; John 19 : 33) instead of lingering two or three days upon the cross, was owing to the great mental agonies he endured, in comparison to which the physical pains of crucifixion were light. Intense anguish has itself been known to produce death. If the agonies of the garden caused a bloody sweat, and so affected him that an angel appeared to strengthen him, how must the greater agonies of the cross, when forsaken by the Father, have affected his already exhausted body?

Dr. Stroud, an eminent European physician, in the year 1847 advanced the theory that Jesus died of a broken or ruptured heart. It has been found that under violent and intensely excited emotions, the heart is sometimes rent or torn by the violence of its own action. The blood flows into the pericardium, the bag or sack which incloses the heart, and by its pressure gradually stops the beating. The blood then coagulates, and the watery matter is separated from the thicker substance. If the pericardium should be then pierced, there would flow out blood and water, which harmonizes with and best explains the singular phenomenon mentioned in John 19 : 34. This theory also strikingly harmonizes with the predictions in Ps. 22 : 14; 69 : 20. It also gives additional prominence to the *blood* of Christ, since then his death was literally caused by the flowing of his blood. Nor is it opposed to the Savior's declaration, "No man taketh my life from me; I lay it down of myself;" for he voluntarily took upon himself all this anguish, even unto death itself. The theory well deserves consideration.

51. **The vail of the temple.** A

twain from the top to the bottom. And the earth 52 did quake, and the rocks rent. And the graves were opened; and many bodies of the saints which 53 slept arose, and came out of the graves after his resurrection, and went into the holy city, and appeared unto many.

* Eph. 2. 13-18; Heb. 6. 19, 20; 9. 8; 10. 19-22.
t ch. 28. 2.
u Is. 26. 19.
x Dan. 12. 2; 1 Cor. 15. 51; 1 Thes. 4. 14

large, thick, inner curtain, which divided the holy place from the holy of holies, Exod. 16 : 33; Heb. 9 : 3. **Rent in twain.** Into two pieces. From Luke we learn that it was rent through the middle, Luke 23 : 45. **From the top to the bottom.** Some sixty feet. This could not have been the result of an earthquake. It was rent by the same supernatural power that produced the earthquake and raised some of the dead.

This occurred at the ninth hour, about three in the afternoon, the time of offering the evening sacrifice, when the priest would be in the holy place burning incense, and the people praying without. Into the holy of holies the high-priest entered alone once a year to make an atonement, Exod. 30 : 10 ; Lev. 16 : 15-17 ; Heb. 9 : 7. The rending of the vail symbolized the entering of Jesus, the great High-Priest of his people, into the holy of holies on high, there to present the atonement which he had made through his blood for their sins, Heb. 9 : 12-14, 25, 26. The Aaronic priesthood and atonement were no longer needed. Each worshiper became himself a priest, a new and living way of access to God was opened, the middle wall of partition between Jews and Gentiles was broken down, Heb. 10 : 12-14, 19-22; Eph 2 : 14; 1 Pet. 2 : 5. The rent of the vail, seen by the priests, would very likely be known through rumor, and substantiated by the great company of priests who afterward became obedient to the faith, Acts 6 : 7. Jesus himself may have revealed it to his disciples after his resurrection.

The rocks were rent. The quaking of the earth and rending of rocks were miraculous, possibly emblematic of the approaching destruction of the Jewish state. Large rents and fissures in the rocks have been observed by travelers near the supposed spot of crucifixion.

52, 53. **The graves were opened.** The Jewish sepulchres were natural or artificial excavations in the rocks, and their entrances were closed up with massive stones. Hence the doors or stones were removed from many of the tombs by the earthquake, showing that Jesus had entered the domain of death, and broken open its prison-house, 1 Cor. 15: 55-57; Col. 2 : 15; 2 Tim. 1 : 10. Some put a period, and others a comma, after *opened*, in order to present clearly the fact that the bodies of the saints did not rise and come into the city till "after his resurrection."

Saints. Their *bodies* were actually reanimated. Some suppose they were some of the most eminent saints of the Old Testament. Others that they were those who had recently died, such as Simeon, Anna, Zacharias, and John the Baptist. Otherwise how could it be known who they were? **Slept.** A beautiful figurative designation for the death of the righteous.

Arose, and came, etc. After his resurrection. Matthew clusters these facts together, and, in order to complete his account, mentions their resurrection, which accompanied or immediately followed that of Christ, who was the first fruits of them that slept (1 Cor. 15 : 20), and their appearance in Jerusalem. This showed that the power of death and the grave was vanquished by the death and resurrection of Christ, and is regarded by some as a literal fulfillment of his words in John 5 : 25. **Holy city.** So Jerusalem was called, as the seat of the theocracy and the place of the temple. See on ch. 4 : 5.

Appeared unto many. To such as were chosen of God (compare Acts 10 : 41), to give unmistakable evidence of their actual resurrection. What became of these risen saints is not told us. We can hardly suppose that they returned to their graves; that they were raised to die again. We rather think, with many commentators, that they rose to a glorified life, appeared to many during the forty days, and ascended with Christ, or soon after, into his glory. As Matthew wrote his Gospel for the Jews, he alone mentions this, and doubtless at the time of his writing there were those living to whom these saints appeared in Jerusalem.

54 ⁱ Now when the centurion, and they that were with him, watching Jesus, saw the earthquake, and those things that were done, feared greatly, saying, ᵃ Truly, this was the Son of God.
55 And many women were there beholding afar off, ᵇ which followed Jesus from Galilee, ministering
56 unto him: ᶜ among which was Mary Magdalene, and ᵈ Mary the mother of James and Joses, ᵉ and the mother of Zebedee's children.

ⁱ ch. 4. 5.
¹ ver 36; Mk. 15. 39; Lk. 23. 47.

ᵃ Ro. 1. 4.
ᵇ Lk. 8. 2, 3.
ᶜ Mk. 15. 40.

ᵈ John 19. 25.
ᵉ ch. 10. 2.

---

54. Matthew notices in this verse the effect of these supernatural occurrences on the **centurion** who had charge of the crucifixion, and the soldiers who were on guard with him. A centurion was a commander of a hundred men. **Feared greatly;** as they witnessed the convulsions of nature, lest terrible vengeance might be visited upon them. From Mark 15 : 39 we learn that not only the wonderful phenomena, but also the manner of Christ's death affected the mind of the centurion. He exclaims, "Certainly this was a righteous man" (Luke 23 : 47); he was not an impostor, but what he claimed to be; he was **the Son of God,** or rather, *God's Son,* as in ver. 40. The centurion does not mean *a son of a god* in a heathen sense, nor the Messiah, but that Jesus was indeed of a *divine* nature. He had doubtless heard something of what Jesus claimed to be, and the charge of the Jews against him, and the taunt, "If thou be the Son of God" (compare on ver. 40 with ch. 2 : 64), and he now expresses his convictions that he was indeed divine. There was an impress of divinity on his death as well as on his life, which has been felt and recognized by the observing of every age. Even the infidel Rousseau exclaimed, If Socrates lived and died like a sage, Jesus of Nazareth lived and died like a god.

Justin Martyr and other early writers affirm that Pilate made an official report to Tiberius of the condemnation and death of Jesus. This is very probable. He was deeply impressed not only by the dream of his wife, but also by the charge that he "made himself the Son of God," John 19 : 7, 8.

Luke also notices the effect in general. "All the people that came together to that sight, beholding the things which were done, smote their breasts and returned," Luke 23 : 48.

55. In this and the next verse Matthew refers to the women of Galilee, who witnessed his death. **Many women.** In their devotion they watched him to the last, and two of them (ver. 61) continued and saw where they buried him. They were, however, in less danger than the male followers of Jesus. Luke adds (ch. 23 : 49), "All his acquaintance." There may have been several groups. **Afar off.** Probably from the side of the Mount of Olives. See on ver. 33. **Ministering unto him.** To his wants. Benevolent women had also in Galilee supplied his wants from their own substance, Luke 8 : 3.

56. Mary Magdalene. *Mary the Magdalene,* from Magdala, now the village of Mejdel, on the west coast of the Sea of Galilee. See on ch. 15: 39. From Luke 8 : 2, and Mark 16 : 9, we learn that Jesus had wrought a signal miracle upon her in casting out seven demons. She was a woman of some property, as is evident from her ministering to the wants of Jesus, and from the position of her name (Luke 8 : 2, 3); not only in connection with, but even before that of Joanna, the wife of Chuza, Herod's steward, who, from his official position, must have acquired considerable wealth. Tradition has confounded her with the sinner in Luke 7 : 37, but without evidence or reason. Neither is she to be confounded with Mary who anointed Jesus in Bethany, John 12 : 3. She was one of the two women who saw the burial of Jesus (ver. 61), and one of those who prepared spices and ointment to embalm him. She was early at the tomb on the first day of the week, and, lingering there after the other disciples had retired, she was the first to see her Lord, Mark 16 : 1; John 20: 11–18.

Mary the mother of James and Joses. Probably the wife of Cleopas, or Alpheus, John 19 : 25. She witnessed, with Mary Magdalene, the burial of Je-

The Burial of Jesus.

57 ⸉ WHEN the even was come, there came a rich man of Arimathæa, named Joseph, who also him-
58 self was Jesus' disciple: he went to Pilate, and begged the body of Jesus. Then Pilate command-

⸉ Mk. 15. 42; Lk. 23. 50; John 19. 38.

---

sus, Mark 15 : 47. Mark (ch. 15 : 40) designates James the *less*, or the *younger*, to distinguish him from the James the son of Zebedee. See on chs. 10 : 3 and 13 : 55.
The mother of Zebedee's children. Supposed to be Salome, from comparing this passage with Mark 15 : 40 and 16 : 1. Salome is also regarded by some as "his mother's sister " of John 19 : 25. Mary the mother of Jesus is not mentioned, as she had probably gone away with John, overwhelmed with sorrow (Luke 2 : 35), soon after she was committed to his care, John 19 : 25-27.
57-61. THE BURIAL OF JESUS, Mark 15 : 42-47; Luke 23 : 50-56; John 19 : 31-42. John's account is the fullest. He relates that the Jews requested the legs to be broken and the bodies removed, so that they might not remain upon the cross on the Sabbath. The request was granted, but the legs of Jesus were not broken, because he was already dead; but one of the soldiers pierced his side, and thus two predictions of Scripture were fulfilled, John 19 : 31-37.
57. **When the even was come.** The first evening, beginning with the decline of day, about three o'clock in the afternoon. See on ch. 14 : 15. As the first evening had already come, we may suppose it to have been as late as four o'clock, or even later. The Jews were very careful to have the bodies of persons publicly executed taken down and buried before sunset, Deut. 21 : 23. "So great care did the Jews take respecting the burial of men, that even the bodies of those condemned to be crucified they took down and buried before the going down of the sun."—JOSEPHUS, *Jewish War*, iv. 5. 2.
Arimathea. Probably Ramah, called Ramathaim-Zophim, the birthplace of Samuel, 1 Sam. 1 : 19. The first book of Maccabees (11 : 34) speaks of it as transferred, together with Lydda, from Samaria to Judea, which may account for Luke's calling it "a city of the Jews," Luke 23 : 51. It has generally been located at the modern Lydda, about twenty-four miles north-west of Jerusalem. Its location, however, is uncertain. From the narrative in 1 Sam. 9 : 4-6; 10 : 2, it would seem that it lay south or south-west of Bethlehem.
A rich man. Thus was fulfilled Isa. 53 : 9, which may be translated, "And his grave was appointed with the wicked, but he was with the rich in his death." Criminals were commonly buried together, in a common sepulchre. It was expected that this would be the case with Jesus; but, by a remarkable Providence, he is buried in the new tomb of a man of wealth and rank.
Joseph. He was an honorable counselor, a member of the Sanhedrim, a good and just man, waiting for the kingdom of God, and one who had not consented to the death of Jesus, Mark 15 : 43; Luke 23 : 51. He was also himself a *disciple of Jesus;* but secretly, for fear of the Jews, John 19 : 38. While his open disciples are scattered and in dismay, two secret and timid followers are emboldened to attend to his burial.
58. **He went to Pilate.** Probably to his official residence. See on ver. 11. Mark states that he "went in boldly," *dared*, had the courage and confidence to go in to Pilate and ask the body of Jesus. Pilate had given the order to break the bones, in order to hasten death, but he is now surprised to hear that Jesus is already dead. Having learned that he had been dead for some time, Pilate grants the request. The standing of Joseph as a member of the Sanhedrim, and a man of wealth, doubtless had weight with Pilate, who, according to Mark (15 : 45), *gave the dead body* freely, as a present, without demanding money for it. We can not but admire the Providence which so ordered the circumstances of our Savior's crucifixion and burial that there could be no doubt about his death, and no deception in regard to his resurrection.
59. **A clean linen cloth.** A winding-sheet, in which the body was wrapped. The mummy cloths of the Egyptians were universally linen. John relates

59 ed the body to be delivered. And when Joseph had taken the body, he wrapped it in a clean linen
60 cloth, and ᵍ laid it in his own new tomb, which he had hewn out in the rock: and he rolled a great stone to the door of the sepulchre, and departed. ᵍ Is. 53. 9.
61 And there was Mary Magdalene, and the other Mary, sitting over against the sepulchre.

The Sepulchre sealed and guarded.

62 NOW the next day, that followed ʰ the day of   ʰ ch. 26. 17; Ps. 2. 1, 3.

(19 : 39) that Nicodemus now joined Joseph, bringing a mixture of myrrh and aloes, about a hundred pounds weight. The sheet was wrapped about in such a way as to inclose the spices next to the body. This was hurriedly done, and preparatory to the more formal embalming by the women, after the Sabbath, for which there was not now time.

60. **New tomb.** It was fitting that Jesus should be laid in a tomb where no one had before been buried. It would also prevent the assertion, after his resurrection, that some one else had been raised. Matthew alone relates that it was Joseph's. John says it was in a garden, and in the place where he was crucified. The nearness of the place and of the Sabbath may have led Joseph to bury him in his own new tomb (John 19 : 42); but once laid there, we need not suppose that Joseph would have removed it, but rather, in his devotion, would have kept it there, had Jesus not risen.

Hewn out in the rock. The tombs of the Jews were generally cut out of the solid rock; sometimes below the level of the ground, but oftener above the ground, and on the sides of hills and mountains. They were generally large and commodious, with one or more apartments with cells for depositing the dead. The tomb of Joseph was doubtless a family vault. **Rolled a great stone to the door.** This seems to imply that the tomb was excavated horizontally, or nearly so. The stone was so heavy that the women, on going to the sepulchre, were perplexed to know how to obtain its removal. Dr. Hackett saw a tomb at Nazareth, cut in the rock, and a large stone rolled against its mouth. But most of the tombs he examined near Jerusalem must have had doors, as is evident from the grooves and perforations for the hinges that still remain. "It is possible," he adds, "that the tomb used in the case of the Savior, which is said to have been new, was not entirely finished, and the placing of the stone at the entrance may have been a temporary expedient."—*Scripture Illustrations*, p. 108.

61. **The other Mary.** The mother of James and Joses, ver. 56. They were there, **sitting** over against the tomb, while the burial was going on, and after the stone had been rolled to the door, and Joseph had departed, ver. 60. They sit there as if to watch it. A very different guard was soon after stationed there through the guilty fears of the Jews.

62-66. THE SEPULCHRE SEALED AND GUARDED. Recorded only by Matthew.

62. **The day of the preparation.** Simply, *The preparation*, omitting *day*. The preparation was Friday, the day before the Jewish Sabbath, which was Saturday; the day for making ready for the Sabbath, Mark 15 : 42; Luke 23 : 54; John 19 : 31. **The next day.** *The morrow.* The Sabbath, which began Saturday eve at sunset. A Sabbath of anxiety and guilty fear to the chief priests and Pharisees, and of deep gloom and unspeakable sadness to the disciples. Some suppose that the watch was obtained in the evening, at the beginning of the Sabbath, instead of the next morning, or even later, arguing that his body was as liable to be stolen on the first as on the second night.

But it may be replied, that the chief priests and Pharisees could have had no anxiety for the first night, for it was the third day that he was to rise again; and moreover, the sanctity of the Sabbath would have been itself a guard. And as Golgotha was by a thoroughfare, and constantly exposed to observation by daytime, the eve of the first day of

the preparation, the chief priests and Pharisees came
63 together unto Pilate, saying, Sir, we remember that
ᶦthat deceiver said, while he was yet alive, ᵏ After
64 three days I will rise again. Command therefore that
the sepulchre be made sure until the third day, lest
his disciples come by night, and steal him away,
and say unto the people, He is risen from the dead:
65 so the last error shall be worse than the first. Pilate said unto them, Ye have a watch: go your way,

ᶦ John 7. 12. 47.
ᵏ ch. 16. 21; 17. 23; 20. 19; 26. 61; Mk. 8. 31; 10. 34; Lk. 9. 22; 18. 33; 24. 6, 7; John 2. 19.

the week was really the earliest time when such a guard was necessary. And this agrees better with the word translated *next day*, which more naturally refers to the next morning, or later, rather than to the preceding evening or night. Compare the use of the word in Mark 11 : 12; Acts 10 : 23; 20 : 7. It seems better, therefore, to suppose that this request was made to Pilate some time during the daytime of Saturday, and in time to have the guard stationed at the sepulchre by evening. This also explains why the women who visited the sepulchre on the morning of the resurrection were anxious about the removal of the stone, and not about the seal and the guard, because, being placed there but the evening before, they were ignorant of the fact.

Chief priests and Pharisees. Members of the Sanhedrim and leaders of the Pharisaic party. They came in a body to Pilate. That they should have done this on the Sabbath may be explained from their greatly excited and guilty fears, increased by the wonderful phenomena attending his crucifixion and death. They may have called this a religious act in behalf of their religion. They, indeed, requested the tomb to be guarded; but this they asked of Romans, who did not observe the Sabbath. Jews to this day often avail themselves of work done by Gentiles on their Sabbath. They, doubtless, came very quietly to Pilate, as they would wish to secure their object with as little notoriety as possible.

63. **That deceiver.** He had been charged with deceiving the people, and this charge they regard as confirmed by his death. **After three days,** etc. He had told this to his disciples, ch. 16 : 21; 20 : 17. He had also stated it more generally and more publicly, ch. 12 : 40; John 2 : 19; 10 : 15, 17, 18. Possibly Judas, to whom such a prediction must have been especially odious, had told it as an instance of a wild, extravagant, and absurd declaration. But how should they *remember* that which the disciples seemed to forget? Their perceptions were quickened by malice and fear. Guilt, too, aroused their imagination. They in some way knew that Jesus made such a prediction. At least, a very little at such a time as this would make them believe he did. But the disciples, who had been puzzled in regard to its meaning, were disconcerted and disheartened by their Lord's sudden and unexpected arrest and death, and altogether unprepared to exercise that spiritual perception and high faith necessary for understanding and believing such a prediction.

64. **Lest his disciples come by night.** These Jewish leaders not only style Jesus a deceiver or impostor, but they suggest that his disciples will carry out the imposition in the most shameful manner, by lying and theft. How far was this from the thoughts of those sorrowing and broken-hearted disciples! **The last error,** or deception, that he had risen, and hence was what he professed to be. **The first.** That he was the Messiah, which many had believed. They were afraid lest they should lose their power among the people and over the Jewish nation.

65. **Ye have a watch.** The watch is at your service. This guard consisted of Roman soldiers, as the word in the original and ch. 28 : 12 indicate. Hence, being in the service of the Sanhedrim, they reported to them (ch. 28 : 11), but were also accountable to Pilate, ch. 28 : 14. The guard may have been those who watched the crucifixion, or, possibly, a small guard attending upon the Sanhedrim. It was customary among the Romans, in guarding a prisoner, to employ four soldiers for each watch of three hours, making four of these sets

66 ¹ make *it* as sure as ye can. made the sepulchre sure, ᵐ sealing the stone, and setting a watch. So they went, and

¹ ch. 28. 11 15; Ps. 76. 10; Pro. 21. 30.
ᵐ Dan. 6. 17.

for a night, Acts 12 : 4. **As ye can.** *As ye know how.* The guard, and every thing necessary to securing the body and the sepulchre, were at their disposal, and they were to use their knowledge and best judgment in doing what they desired.

66. **Sealing the stone,** by means of a cord or string drawn across the stone and fastened at both ends by sealing-clay or wax, on which was stamped the seal of Pilate. Thus no one could enter the tomb without resisting public authority. Compare Dan. 6 : 17. The watch was a precaution against violence; the seal, against fraud. Thus, every means was used to prevent deception. The evidence of the resurrection of Jesus is therefore the greater. If he had not risen within three days, the Jewish rulers would doubtless have completed their triumph by throwing open the sepulchre, and pointing to his lifeless body as an evidence of his deception. But that they did not this, but resorted to a most absurd expedient (ch. 28 : 13), is an evidence of his resurrection.

REMARKS.

1. "Fanaticism is often as blind as it is malignant. The very necessity which compelled the Jewish rulers to apply for Pilate's authority for the crucifixion of Christ demonstrated his Messiahship. The sceptre had departed; it was the appointed sign that Shiloh had come."— J. P. WARREN. Ver. 2; Gen. 49 : 10.

2. Sin encourages its votaries to expect from it worldly advantages, but their possession is attended with misery. The way of the transgressor is hard, vers. 3–6; Job 20 : 12–14; Prov. 13 : 15.

3. By comparing the conduct of Judas with that of Peter, we may mark the difference between false and true repentance. In the one, remorse, turning *from* rather than *to* Christ, despair, plunging deeper into sin; in the other, sorrow, confession of sin, and turning to Christ, vers. 3–6; ch. 26 : 75; John 21 : 7, 17; Acts 1 : 25; 2 Cor. 7 : 10.

4. Suicide is a terrible crime when committed freely and in a sane mind; and in such a case may be taken as an evidence of an unrenewed state and of sins unforgiven, ver. 5; 2 Sam. 17 : 23; Acts 16 : 27.

5. From the remorse of Judas learn the misery caused by an awakened conscience, and catch a glimpse of the tortures of conscience in the world of despair, vers. 3–6; Gen. 42 : 21; Matt. 22 : 12; Mark 9 : 44.

6. No counsel, nor deeds of charity, nor memorials, can free the wicked from the penalty of their sins, vers. 6–8; Prov. 11 : 21, 31; 1 Pet. 4 : 11.

7. God foreknew the deeds of the wicked as well as those of the righteous, and will make all subserve his grand designs and purposes, vers. 9, 10; Ps. 76 : 10; Acts 2 : 23.

8. Let us seek the spirit and courage of Christ, and, like him, witness a good profession, ver. 11; 1 Tim. 6 : 13.

9. It is generally better to treat with silence than to answer the clamors and false accusations of our enemies, vers. 12–14; 1 Pet. 2 : 21–23.

10. How often is Barabbas still preferred to Jesus; self, the world, and the devil, to the Savior! vers. 15–21; Acts 3 : 14; 7 : 51, 52.

11. The best of men must at times expect to be objects of envy, ver. 18; ch. 10 : 24, 25; Gen. 4 : 4, 5; 37 : 11; Ps. 106 : 16; Acts 13 : 45.

12. God gives to every man sufficient warning to guard him against sin, and sufficient light to show him the path of duty, ver. 19; Job 33 : 14–17; Acts 14 : 17; 17 : 30, 31.

13. The ministers of a corrupt church are generally more corrupt than the people, and the leaders in their wickedness, ver. 20; Jer. 23 : 15; Mic. 3 : 5.

14. How many ask the world what they shall do with Jesus, instead of listening to God's messages, and following the dictates of their consciences! They ask, and vacillate to their own destruction, vers. 22–24.

15. How fickle are they who make the popular current instead of truth their principle of action, crying out at one time, Hosanna to the Son of David! and at another, Crucify him! vers. 22, 24; ch. 21 : 9; Acts 14 : 11, 19.

16. Pilate gave a remarkable testimony to the innocence of Jesus, a condemnation of his own act in delivering him to be crucified. Beware how you condemn yourself in not accepting Christ, while you acknowledge him a Savior, ver. 24.

17. No outward washing can cleanse from guilt, ver. 24; Rom. 3 : 20; Heb. 9 : 9–14; 10 : 4.

18. The prayers of the wicked are often answered in their own destruction, ver. 25.

19. Jesus endured cruel scourging that we might be healed, ver. 26; Ps. 129 : 3; Isa. 50 : 6; 53 : 5.

20. Jesus was mocked and treated with the greatest indignity, in order that we might be raised with him to the highest glory, vers. 27–31; Phil. 2 : 9, 10; Heb. 2 : 10; 12 : 2; Rev. 5 : 8–14.

21. We must follow Christ, bearing his cross, if we would reign with him and share his glory, ver. 32; ch. 16 : 24; Phil. 3 : 10, 11; Heb. 13 : 13, 14.

22. We should willingly and patiently endure all that our heavenly Father may put upon us, ver. 34; Acts 21 : 13; Heb. 12 : 3–5.

23. Jesus was treated as a slave, valued at the price, and suffering the death, of a slave, in order that he might give us true freedom, ver. 35; ch. 26 : 15; John 8 : 36; Gal. 5 : 1.

24. Jesus was stripped of his garments, pointing to the spiritual nakedness of the race, and the white garments he has purchased to cover us, ver. 35; Gen. 3 : 7, 10; Phil. 3 : 9; Rev. 3 : 18.

25. In Jesus on the cross, suspended between heaven and the earth, we behold a mediator between God and man, vers. 35, 36; 1 Tim. 2 : 5.

26. Jesus saved not himself so that he might save others, vers. 39–42; Rom. 5 : 6; 1 Cor. 15 : 3; 2 Cor. 5 : 15; 1 Thess. 5 : 10.

27. Adversity is not a proof of God's displeasure, nor is a want of success always an indication of final failure, vers. 40–43; Job 42 : 10; Ps. 3 : 2–4; 42 : 10, 11.

28. All classes, Jews, Gentiles, priests, rulers, people, soldiers, and servants, were turned against Jesus, in order that he might be a Savior to all, vers. 39–44; Luke 23 : 36; Gal. 3 : 28; 1 John 2 : 1, 2.

29. The darkness around the suffering and dying Jesus should remind us of the spiritual darkness of our world, and of Christ its true light, ver. 45; John 8 : 12.

30. In the darkest hour the Christian should imitate his Savior, and not lose confidence in God as his God, ver. 46, "*My God;*" Job 13 : 15; Ps. 43 : 5; Hab. 3 : 17, 18; Rom. 5 : 3–5; 2 Tim. 1 : 12.

31. If the agony of the Savior when forsaken of God for sinners was so great, what shall be the misery of those who at last shall be forsaken forever to wrath and endless despair? ver. 46.

32. As the soldiers around the cross failed to enter into the feelings and agonies of Jesus, so impenitent sinners of our day fail to be impressed with his sufferings and death, vers. 47–49; 1 Cor. 2 : 14.

33. Jesus received drink from his enemies, suggestive of a complete atonement for sinners, and of peace and goodwill to men, ver. 48; Dan. 9 : 24; Rom. 5 : 1; Eph. 2 : 14.

34. "With pleasure may we survey the awful tokens by which God owned his dying Son, and wiped away the infamy of his cross."—DODDRIDGE. Ver. 51.

35. Inasmuch as the way into the holiest of all has been opened through the rent vail of the Redeemer's flesh, let us draw near to God boldly, and in strong faith, ver. 51; Heb. 4 : 16; 9 : 12; 10 : 19–22.

36. Let the shaking of the earth, the opening of the graves, and the raising of the dead, be symbolical of the effect of Christ's death on our hearts and consciences, vers. 51–53; Acts 2 : 37; Gal. 6 : 14; Eph. 5 : 14.

37. In the death of Jesus we see evidences of his divinity. The centurion saw it. How much more should we, with our greater evidences! ver. 54; Heb. 1 : 1–4.

38. God will at all times have a people in the world, vers. 54–56; Rom. 9 : 27; 11 : 5.

39. Let us be suitably affected with the lifeless body of Jesus on the cross, and accept of the glorious fruits of his death, ver. 54; 2 Tim. 1 : 10; 1 Pet. 2 : 24.

40. God, who so wonderfully guarded the body of Jesus, will in like manner guard the dust of all them that sleep in Jesus, vers. 57–60; 1 Thess. 4 : 14.

41. In Joseph of Arimathea behold a man of wealth devoting his property to the Lord, vers. 57–60; 1 Kings 18 : 13; 1 Tim. 6 : 17–19.

The resurrection of Jesus; the visit of the women

XXVIII. IN the [a] end of the sabbath, as it began

[a] Mk. 16. 1; Lk. 24. 1; John 20. 1, 2.

42. The devotion of woman to Jesus is seen both at the cross and the sepulchre, ver. 61; 55, 56; ch. 28 : 1, etc.

43. The wicked are like the troubled sea, whose consciences give them no rest, vers. 62-64; Isa. 57 : 20; Prov. 28 : 1.

44. God permits the malice of men against him to go just so far as to subserve his purposes and the highest interest of his people, vers. 62-66; Job 5 : 12, 13; Prov. 19 : 21.

CHAPTER XXVIII.

Matthew now closes his Gospel history with a brief account of the resurrection of Jesus from the dead. The evidences which he gives are: (1) The earthquake and descent of the angel who rolled away the stone, and the effect upon the guard. (2) The testimony of the angel to the women, who had come early to view the sepulchre. (3) The appearance of Jesus to the women. (4) The report of the guard to the chief priests of all things that had occurred, and the shallow and fallacious attempt of the latter to explain away the fact of his resurrection. (5) The appearance of Jesus to his disciples in Galilee. Since Matthew wrote especially for Jewish readers, he relates (1) what the guard saw, what they reported to the chief priests, and what the chief priests attempted to do; and (2) the declaration of Jesus concerning his supreme authority, and his commission to his disciples to preach the Gospel to all nations. And, finally, as Matthew had for the most part related our Lord's ministry in Galilee, so he very appropriately gives his most signal appearance to his disciples in that region, after his resurrection, and with it closes his Gospel.

In comparing this chapter with the accounts of the resurrection as given by the other Evangelists, the fact is at once apparent that they were independent narrators. On account of the great brevity of these narratives, especially those of Matthew and Mark, great difficulty has been experienced in bringing them into complete harmony. But a careful study of these records will convince any reasonable mind that the discrepancies are only apparent. They can all be so explained us to show at once that, if we were in possession of all the details, the difficulties would not exist. But God has wisely ordered difficulties here as well as in other things, in order to give his people the more opportunity to exercise their faith in his word, and the wicked their unbelief. See author's HARMONY, Introductory note to Part VIII.

From a comparison of these four accounts, and of Paul (1 Cor. 15), we gather the following ten appearances after his resurrection: 1. To Mary Magdalene, Mark 16 : 9; John 20 : 11-18. 2. To the women, ch. 28 : 9, 10. 3. To Peter, Luke 24 : 34; 1 Cor. 15 : 5. 4. To the two disciples, Mark 16 : 12; Luke 24 : 13-31. 5. To the apostles, except Thomas, Mark 16 : 14; Luke 24 : 36-49; John 20 : 19-23. 6. To the apostles, Thomas being present, John 20 : 26-29. 7. To some of his disciples on the shore of the lake of Tiberias, John 21 : 4-22. 8. To the apostles and others, comprising above five hundred brethren, on a mountain in Galilee, ch. 28 : 16-20; Mark 16 : 15-18; 1 Cor. 15 : 6. 9. To James, 1 Cor. 15 : 7. 10. To the eleven at Jerusalem, and on the Mount of Olives, near Bethany, just before his ascension, Luke 24 : 50, 51; Acts 1 : 4-9.

Jesus doubtless appeared at other times, since he showed himself to his apostles during forty days, speaking the things concerning the kingdom of God, Acts 1 : 3; compare John 20 : 30, 31.

1-7. THE RESURRECTION OF JESUS AND ITS ACCOMPANYING INCIDENTS. The earthquake, the descent of the angel, the effect on the guard, the comforting address to the women, and the message to the disciples, Mark 16 : 1-7; Luke 24 : 1-8; John 20 : 1, 2. 1. **In the end of the Sabbath,** or more exactly, *But late on the Sabbath day*, an indefinite expression defined by the next clause, "As it began to dawn," etc. Thus Matthew seems to follow the natural division of the day from sunrise to sunrise; as perhaps had been his custom, as a publican, to reckon the civil day. The custom of reckoning from evening to evening (Lev. 23 : 32) grew out of observing feasts and

to dawn toward the first *day* of the week, came Mary Magdalene º and the other Mary to see the 2 sepulchre. And, behold, ᵖ there was a great earthquake: for ᑫ the angel of the Lord descended from heaven, and came and rolled back the stone from

º ch. 27. 56, 61.
ᵖ ch. 27. 51-53.
ᑫ Mk. 16. 5; L 24. 4; John 20. 12.

seasons, which depended on the return of the new moon. The natural day was originally regarded as closing with the morning (Gen. 1 : 5; Lev. 7 : 15). So Jonah (1 : 17) and Matthew (12 : 40) follow *day* by *night*, "three days and three nights." This view harmonizes Matthew with the other Gospels, which distinctly declare that our Lord arose in the early morning. Some, as Grimm and Godet, maintain that the expression should be translated, *After the Sabbath*. But this meaning is not clearly made out, though it may be possible.
As it began to dawn. The dawning of the day. John says, "When it was yet dark;" the light was struggling with darkness. Luke says, "Very early." Mark says, "Very early. . . At the rising of the sun." The visit of the women to the sepulchre may have occupied two or three hours from their first leaving their home until they left the sepulchre. Mary Magdalene may have gone somewhat in advance of the rest. John mentions her, and her alone, and the other Evangelists mention her first, as if peculiarly prominent in their visit to the sepulchre. As the company of women came to the sepulchre the rising sun may have shed its first beams upon them. Yet in popular usage, dawn and sunrise are often used for early morning, and Mark seems so to regard his own expression; for he says, "*Very early* in the morning," etc. There need, therefore, be no difficulty in harmonizing the Evangelists in regard to the time of the visit. There may have been different arrivals. Or, if not, one may have in mind the time of starting, another of their going, and another of their arrival or of their stay at the sepulchre. But see further on.
The first day of the week. Sunday; afterward observed by the disciples as the Lord's day, Rev. 1 : 10; Acts 20 : 7; 1 Cor. 16 : 1. Ignatius, who was educated under the Apostle John, and who was pastor of the church at Antioch for forty years, from about A. D. 70, in his letter to the Magnesians speaks of "no longer observing the Sabbath, but living in the observance of the Lord's day." The Teaching of the Twelve Apostles (ch. 14), early in th second century, says, "But every Lord's day do ye come together and break bread, and give thanks, confessing your transgressions, that your sacrifice may be pure." Justin Martyr, who wrote about A. D. 158, says (Apology I., 67), "Sunday is the day on which we hold our common assembly, because it is the first day, on which God . . . made the world and Jesus Christ our Saviour on the same day rose from the dead." Much similar testimony might be given, showing that while the Jewish Sabbath was observed more or less by early Jewish churches and Jewish converts, the Lord's day was observed by all.
Mary Magdalene and the other Mary. See on ch. 27 : 56, 61. Mark also mentions Salome, supposed to be the mother of James and John. Luke (24 : 10) speaks of Joanna and other women, the former supposed to be the one mentioned in Luke 8 : 3, the wife of Chuza, steward of Herod. **To see.** *To look at* attentively, *to view* the sepulchre, and, at the same time, to anoint and embalm his body, Mark 16 : 1; Luke 24 : 1. It is not an improbable supposition that Mary Magdalene, with the other Mary and Salome, went to view the sepulchre before the time they had agreed to meet Joanna and the other women there, who were to come about sun-rising to assist in embalming the body.
2. **Earthquake.** This probably occurred while they were on their way to the sepulchre. We learn from John (20 : 1) that when Mary Magdalene came to the sepulchre, she found the stone taken away; and from Mark, that the women, who were ignorant of the guard and the seal, were considering, while on their way, who should roll away the great stone from the door of the sepulchre; but coming, they found it rolled away, Mark 16 : 3, 4. **The angel.** This should be *An angel. The angel* misguides the reader, as if a particular an-

3 the door, and sat upon it. ʳ His countenance was   ʳ Dan. 10. 6.
4 like lightning, and his raiment white as snow: and
  for fear of him ˢ the keepers did shake, and became   ˢ ch. 27. 65, 66.
  as dead *men.*
5   ᵗ And the angel answered and said unto the   ᵗ Mk. 16. 6; Lk.
  women, Fear not ye; for I know that ye seek Jesus,   24. 5.

---

gel, the angel of the covenant, was meant. Jesus could have rolled the stone away himself, but an angel descends and does it, showing to the guard that it was done by a higher order than that of either the Sanhedrim or of Pilate—even by the mandate and a messenger of heaven. It was not necessary that the stone should be removed at all; for with his resurrection body Jesus could have come forth from the closed tomb, even as he entered and left the closed room where the disciples were assembled, John 20 : 19, 26; Luke 24 : 31. Hence, most expositors suppose Jesus rose before the rolling away the stone. It seems natural to suppose that, as an earthquake followed immediately after his death, so one preceded immediately his return to life; and hence we may suppose that he passed out of the tomb when the angel removed the stone. His resurrection may not have been seen by any human being then living; but the evidences of it were many and overwhelming, among which were the descent of the angel and the rolling away the stone. **Sat upon it.** In presence of the keepers. He removed into the sepulchre before the women arrived, Mark 16 : 5; Luke 24 : 3, 4.

3. **His countenance.** The *appearance* of his face. **Like lightning,** in its brightness. **White as snow.** The first time that heavenly messengers are said to have appeared in white; they so appeared afterward, Acts 1 : 10; compare Acts 10 : 30. The dress was in harmony with the occasion and with the tidings. Compare Mark 9 : 3; Rev. 3 : 4; 7 : 14.

4. **The keepers.** The guard of soldiers, ch. 27 : 65. **Shake.** As the earth quaked just before, so do they now *quake.* **As dead men.** The effect of the glory and splendor of heavenly visitants seem to be to overpower the senses and prostrate the strength, Dan. 8 : 27; compare Matt. 17 : 6; Rev. 1 : 17. The keepers, therefore, were not eye-witnesses of his resurrection.

5. **The angel.** He had entered the sepulchre, Mark 16 : 5. Hence, Mary Magdalene, who seems at this time not to have entered the sepulchre, saw not the angel. At seeing the stone rolled away, she, quick to draw an inference of evil, runs back to Jerusalem and tells Peter and John, "They have taken away the Lord out of the sepulchre, and we know not where they have laid him," John 20 : 2. The other women thus left by Mary Magdalene may have tarried a little, in hesitation, at the entrance of the tomb. Then they entered and searched, but found not the body of the Lord Jesus. They stand perplexed. While in this state they behold the angel. See Luke 24 : 3, 4, where it is also said, "Two men stood by them in shining garments." So, also, Mary Magdalene, on her return, saw two angels in white sitting, the one at the head and the other at the feet, where the body had lain, John 20 : 11, 12. That Matthew and Mark mention only one angel may be satisfactorily explained in various ways. They may speak only of the one who was the speaker on this occasion. Or, as the first one arose, the other may have suddenly appeared by his side to confirm his testimony. But see a similar instance in note on ch. 9 : 28. That Luke speaks of their standing, while Mark speaks of the one sitting, may also be variously explained. The former does not say that they had not been sitting, nor the latter that they did not afterward stand. The word translated *stood* in Luke 24 : 4 has reference, not so much to the *posture,* as the *suddenness* of their appearing, and may be translated, *came upon them, appeared suddenly.* Compare the use of the word in Luke 2 : 9; Acts 12 : 7. Or, combining the latter idea with a former suggestion, the one angel may have arisen, and the other appeared suddenly. Other possible explanations will occur to the thoughtful reader.

Fear not ye. *Ye* is emphatic. His foes and the guard may well be afraid; but fear not *ye,* his faithful followers, for he is risen. It is possible that they may have seen the frightened soldiers

6 which was crucified. "He is not here: for he is risen, ˣ as he said. Come, see the place where the Lord lay. And go quickly, and tell his disciples that he is risen from the dead; and, behold, ʸ he goeth before you into Galilee; there shall ye see him. Lo, I have told you.

ᵒ John 14. 19; 1 Cor. 15. 20-22.
ˣ ch. 12. 40; 16. 21; 17. 23; 20. 19.
ʸ ch. 26. 32; Mk. 16. 7.

The women return; Jesus meets them.

8   ᶻ AND they departed quickly from the sepulchre with fear and great joy; and did run to bring his disciples word.
9   And as they went to tell his disciples, behold,

ᶻ Mk. 16. 8.

fleeing from the sepulchre. The language would seem to imply that others were present, or had been present, who were also afraid.

6. **Come see the place,** etc. The language implies that the angel was in the sepulchre, in harmony with Mark and Luke. The *place* was, doubtless, a cell in the tomb, like a berth or shelf, so that the body lay parallel with the wall. John 20 : 12 seems to imply this, since Mary Magdalene saw two angels, one at the head and the other at the feet, where Jesus had lain. **Lord,** of angels as well as of men.

7. **His disciples.** To the whole company of believers then at Jerusalem. The message was also to be communicated to Peter personally, Mark 16 : 7. The importance and prominence given to this appearance in Galilee, and the fact that Jesus did appear that day, and a week later, to his apostles and others, at Jerusalem, seem to indicate that the appearance here foretold was that to believers at large, and recorded in 1 Cor. 15 : 6. Hence, the message, which would naturally be told first to the apostles, was for all. **Goeth before you into Galilee.** Jesus had foretold this, ch. 26 : 32. There should occur his great and grand manifestation to his assembled disciples. He would go, not as on former occasions, *journeying* with them, but as his resurrection body could go; he would be there on their return from the Passover, and would meet them gathered at the appointed place. He did not, however, go for more than a week, till the Paschal festival was over, and the disciples who came up to Jerusalem were ready to return, John 20 : 26. **There shall ye see him.** Some would end the message to the disciples with the preceding clause, making this an address to the women. It is better to regard it as included in the message, in harmony with that in vers. 10. From Luke (24 : 6) we learn that the angel reminded them that Jesus had foretold his crucifixion and resurrection. **Lo, I have told you.** A solemn and authoritative affirmation of the message, both to confirm their faith in it and to enable them confidently to announce it.

8–10. THE WOMEN RETURN; JESUS MEETS THEM, Mark 16 : 8.

8. **Fear—joy.** Awe at the strange and wondrous things they had seen; great joy at the glad tidings they had heard. Mark dwells upon their fear. They fled from the sepulchre; trembling and astonishment seized them. They said nothing to any one, for they were afraid. While in this state of mind Jesus appears to them. This was very fitting, both for dispelling their fear and for giving them utterance. Before his appearance *fear* preponderated; after it, *joy*. Before, they are silent; after, they hasten and tell the disciples. Matthew, in his brevity, combines the two, without going into details.

9. The first clause of this verse, *And as they went to tell his disciples,* should be omitted, according to the highest critical authorities. **Behold, Jesus met them.** This was his second appearance; for Mark (16 : 9) says expressly that Jesus "appeared first to Mary Magdalene." All attempts to explain away this evident meaning seem to me unsatisfactory. Did we know all the circumstances, difficulties would vanish. But as it is, we can conceive of more than one possible way of reconciling apparent discrepancies. Mary Magdalene, the other Mary, and Salome may have gone to view the sepulchre a little before the time they

ᵃ Jesus met them, saying, All hail! And they came and held him by the feet, and worshiped him.

10 Then said Jesus unto them, Be not afraid: go tell ᵇ my brethren that they go into Galilee; and there shall they see me.

ᵃ Mk. 16. 9; John 20. 14.

ᵇ ch. 25. 40; Ps. 22. 22; John 20. 17; Ro. 8. 29; Heb. 2. 11.

Report of the Guard.

11 NOW when they were going, behold, some of the watch came into the city, and showed unto the
12 chief priests all the things that were done. And when they were assembled with the elders, and had

had agreed to meet Joanna and the other women. See note on ver. 1, second paragraph. As they approach the sepulchre, Mary Magdalene, seeing the stone rolled away, turns back and hastens to tell Peter and John, supposing that the body of Jesus had been taken away. The two other women now hesitate, view the sepulchre, and tarry a little, till Joanna and the others arrive. Then they enter and search the tomb. They are perplexed. The good order of everything would seem to indicate that he was not stolen away. But where is he? They possibly interchange their thoughts. But behold the angels appear, telling them that Jesus is risen, and giving them a message to his disciples. They go forth quickly, rejoiced indeed at such glad tidings, yet overpowered with awe at beholding the angels. Under the influence of amazement they go not directly to the city, but take a more circuitous route. Immediately after their fleeing from the sepulchre, Peter, John, and Mary Magdalene arrive, and then occurs what is related in John 20: 3–17. Jesus having appeared to Mary Magdalene, appears immediately to the other women, who are still on their way to the disciples. **Met.** "The Evangelists never say *came*, *went*, and the like of their risen Lord."—STIER.

All hail. *Joy to thee.* The usual salutation on meeting friends, expressing joy and good wishes. **Held him by the feet.** Partly expressive of fear; for Jesus referred to their feeling of dread when he said, "Be not afraid," ver. 10; but especially of the most humble reverence as suppliants; for it is immediately said, they **worshiped him.** Suppliants often clasped the knees or the feet of those whose favor they sought. See on ch. 2: 2. "Before his passion, Jesus had been worshiped by strangers rather than by his disciples."—BENGEL. Their posture also expressed their ardent and reverential love; it gave them also evidence that it was not a phantom they saw, but the living body of Jesus.

10. **My brethren.** He still calls them brethren, though they had proved unfaithful and had deserted him; neither had his new state of existence altered his relation or feelings to them. His Father was their Father. See on ch. 25: 40. He had used the same endearing title in his address to Mary Magdalene, John 20: 17. **That they go.** *That they go away* from Jerusalem into Galilee; that they make immediate preparations to depart after the feast was over.

11–15. THE REPORT OF THE WATCH to the Jewish authorities, who bribe them to falsehood. Found only in Matthew. The whole account of the guard was especially appropriate in a Gospel written particularly for Jewish readers. It shows the honesty and faithfulness of the Evangelist.

11. **When they were going.** While the women were going, some of the watch came into the city and reported to the chief priests. While one message was being borne to the friends of Jesus, another was borne to his enemies. **The watch.** The soldiers on guard at the sepulchre at the time of the resurrection. See on ch. 27: 65. **Some** of the watch reported, but all of them were probably bribed. For they gave money to the *soldiers*, ver. 12.

12. **When they were assembled with the elders,** etc. Or, more literally, *And having assembled with the elders, and taken counsel.* The form of expression seems to suggest a secret gathering of those hostile to Jesus, rather than a

taken counsel, they gave large money unto the sol-
13 diers, saying, Say ye, His disciples came by night,
14 and stole him *away* while we slept. And if this
come to the governor's ears, we will persuade him,
15 and ᶜ secure you. So they took the money, and did
as they were taught : and this saying is commonly
reported among the Jews ᵈ until this day.

ᶜ Ac. 12. 19.
ᵈ ch. 27. 8.
ᵉ ver. 7; ch. 26. 32.
ᶠ Dan. 7. 11; Ro.

---

formal sitting of the whole council. They would hardly have undertaken such a course when Joseph of Arimathea, Nicodemus, and possibly a number of others, were present.

The report of the watch drove the Jewish authorities to desperation; in their perplexity and madness they deliberately fabricated a lie. This was the disgraceful climax of their opposition to Jesus, entirely consistent with their hypocritical character (ch. 23 : 13-33), and with the extremity into which they had voluntarily plunged themselves. **Gave large money;** *much money.* A contrast indeed to the thirty pieces of silver given to Judas. They would give but the price of a slave for Jesus, in order to put him to death; but now they are willing to give a large sum, any amount sufficient to bribe the soldiers, in order to hide his resurrection and their own shame, by perpetuating a deception. **Soldiers.** Those on guard when the angel descended.

13. **Stole him.** Most improbable on its very face. How unlikely that a few timid disciples should have made the attempt, much less carried it out, when the stone was sealed and the soldiers on guard; and, even if the soldiers had been asleep, that the disciples could have rolled away the stone and stolen the body without awaking them. **While we slept.** More improbable still, and most absurd. It was unlikely and incredible that soldiers, accustomed to military discipline, would all sleep at their post, the penalty of which was death. And it was impossible for them to know what was going on when asleep. If asleep, how did they know that the body was stolen, and the disciples did it? And had they slept, the penalty would have been inflicted upon them to the utmost, as was the case with Peter's guards afterward, Acts 12 : 19. The story has in itself the evident marks of a lie. To what straits must the Jewish rulers have been driven!

14. **To the governor's ears.** *If this shall be heard by the governor.* That they had slept, and the body had been stolen by the disciples. According to several most ancient authorities it should read, "If this shall be heard *before* the governor," that is, heard judicially and officially; if it be borne witness of before him; if a stir be made, and you are in trouble and danger. Pilate would soon return to Cæsarea. He might not hear of it, except it was brought officially before him; and if he did, he would care but little for the stories which might be circulated among the Jews at Jerusalem. **Persuade him.** They knew their influence with Pilate, and how they had carried their point in regard to the crucifixion. They understood the use of bribes, as is evident from the case of Judas and the soldiers; and they had no doubt that they would be able to *conciliate* Pilate in regard to the soldiers by their influence and money. **Secure you.** *Make you secure;* free of danger or care.

15. **This saying.** This account of the matter, concerning the disappearance of the body, that it was stolen while the soldiers slept. **Commonly reported.** Justin Martyr says, "That the Jews sent chosen men over all the world, representing the followers of Christ as an impious sect, and asserting that the body of Jesus was stolen out of the tomb by night, by his disciples, who thenceforth reported that he rose from the dead and ascended to heaven." An expansion of this lie is also found in the Talmudic tract, *Toledoth Jeschu.* The same story is still reported among the Jews. Compare Acts 28 : 22. **Until this day;** the time of Matthew's writing this Gospel. Compare ch. 27 : 8. This was probably somewhere between eight and twenty years after our Savior's ascension. The language would suggest that it was some years after the occurrences here related took place.

16-20. The APPEARANCE OF JESUS TO

The grand appearance of Jesus in Galilee; his last commission.

16 THEN the eleven disciples went away into Galilee, into a mountain ᵉ where Jesus had appointed
17 them. And when they saw him, they worshiped
18 him: but some doubted. And Jesus came and spake unto them, saying, ᶠ All power is given unto

14. 9; 1 Cor. 15. 27; Heb. 1. 2; 2. 8; 1 Pet. 3. 22; Rev. 17. 14.
ᵉ Mk. 16. 15; Ro. 10. 18; Col. 1. 23.
ᵐ Ac. 2. 38-41; 8. 12-16, 38; 16. 15, 33.

HIS DISCIPLES in Galilee, AND HIS LAST COMMISSION, Mark 16: 15-18; 1 Cor. 15: 6.

16. **Went away into Galilee.** After several appearances of Jesus, recorded by the other Evangelists. See remarks at the beginning of this chapter. After the disciples arrived in Galilee, Jesus appeared to seven of them, on the shore of the lake of Tiberias, John 21: 4—22. Matthew passes over these, and hastens to relate *the* appearance of all the appearances of Jesus to his followers: that to about five hundred brethren at once, on a mountain in Galilee.

A mountain. More exactly, *the mountain*, the one which he had probably designated, when he directed them to go into Galilee (vers. 7, 10; ch. 26: 32); and the one familiarly known to the disciples at the time of writing. Or, possibly, Jesus designated the mountain at his interview with the disciples at the lake of Tiberias. What mountain is unknown. Some suppose it to have been Tabor, about six miles south-east of Nazareth, which was a very suitable place for a general meeting; others, that it was the mount on which the Sermon had been delivered, which was even more suitable, considering its nearness to the Sea of Galilee, and to the populous plain of Gennesareth. It is worthy of note that the first and last discourses, which Matthew records, were delivered on a mountain in Galilee.

Matthew, indeed, only specifies *the eleven* as having gone to the appointed mountain; but this does not forbid the supposition, now held by the best of expositors, that the followers of Jesus were also generally there. The command to go to Galilee was given to the disciples generally (ver. 7), and hence it is natural to suppose that they would generally be there. It is also said that "some doubted," which could hardly be said of the eleven, after his appearances to them at Jerusalem. The appearance to above five hundred must be referred to Galilee, where his disciples were most numerous; for, even after his ascension, there were only a hundred and twenty at Jerusalem. The eleven are specially mentioned, as they were the apostles of Christ, and were to be the witnesses of his resurrection, Acts 1: 22. They were emphatically spoken of, being the leaders of the rest.

17. **Worshiped him.** Gave him divine homage as their Lord. See on ver. 9. **Some doubted.** The form of the expression in the original implies that the number who doubted was small. They doubted whether it was Jesus, not, as some suppose, whether to worship him. Of course they did not join the others in worship; but their doubts extended deeper, to the personal identity of Jesus, whether it was really he. These doubters could hardly have been among the apostles; for this was after his interview with Thomas, John 20: 26-29. They were doubtless some of the others present, probably of the more than five hundred who met him at once. How cautious were the early disciples in receiving the evidences of Christ's resurrection! "They doubted," as Leo has said, "that we might not doubt."

18. **And Jesus came,** etc. *And Jesus coming, spake.* He drew near to the whole company, dispelling the doubts of the few, and confirming the faith of the many.

All power is given unto me. *All authority* and consequent *power was given to me.* See on ch. 11: 27. (Ps. 2; Acts 12: 33, 34; John 5: 22; 13: 3; Matt. 25: 34). And won, and openly declared by his death and resurrection. As the Christ, the Mediator between God and men, *the God-man,* he, in his resurrection and ascension, took full possession of that glory which he had before the foundation of the world, and of that inheritance and kingdom which was the special purchase of his blood, Luke 24: 26; John 17: 5; Rom. 14: 9; Phil. 2: 9-11; Eph. 1: 20-23; 1 Pet. 3: 22; Rev. 5: 5-14. Compare Acts 12: 33, 34; Rom. 1: 4;

19 me in heaven and in earth. ᶠ Go ye therefore, and teach all nations, ᵐ baptizing them in ⁿ the name of the Father, and of the Son, and of the Holy Ghost:

ᶠ see ·Ge. 1. 26; Num. 6. 24-27; Is. 48. 16; 2 Cor. 13. 14; 1 John 5. 7.

also, Dan. 7 : 14; Rev. 17 : 14. It might also be said that the kingdom of God had come with power to these disciples. Thus began to be fulfilled the prediction of Jesus in ch. 16 : 28, on which see. Mark 16 : 15-18 fits admirably between this and the following verse.

19. Go ye, therefore. Since all power is given me in heaven and earth, therefore go. The great commission is founded upon the power and glory of Christ. His majesty, as Lord of lords and King of kings, clothes it with authority. This was spoken not to the apostles only, but to all the brethren. All were now commissioned as the propagators of the Gospel.

Teach. A too restricted translation of the original. The Greek word means *to make disciples;* hence, *disciple all nations;* convert, cause all nations to become followers of me. How they were to make disciples, may be seen by his previous charge (Mark 16 : 15), "Go ye into all the world and preach the Gospel to every creature; he that believeth and is baptized shall be saved, and he that believeth not shall be damned."

All nations. *All the nations.* Not only the Jews, but also the Gentiles; "every creature." The restriction in ch. 10 : 5 was now removed. Beginning at Jerusalem, they were to preach the Gospel in Judea, in Samaria, and unto the uttermost parts of the earth, Luke 24 : 47; Acts 3 : 6. How, then, did the apostles have any doubt in regard to going to the Gentiles with the Gospel, and receiving them into the church? Acts 10 : 28. Their doubt was probably not in regard to the *fact*, but the *way* in which it should be accomplished. They were doubtless in much darkness about it, awaiting further developments and the guidance of the Spirit. They most probably expected the Gospel would be preached to the Gentiles as they became proselytes to Israel, and were circumcised, Acts 2 : 10; 11 : 3. Hence they began to preach the Gospel to the Jews among all nations, Acts 11 : 19. The spiritual nature of Christ's kingdom is here seen, that Christ commands, to *make disciples of*, not *subdue* all nations.

Baptizing. On the meaning of the word, see ch. 3 : 6. The use of the present participle points to baptism as following the *teaching* or *discipling*. They were to baptize **them**, referring not to nations, but to the antecedent *disciples*, implied in the preceding verse. A previous instruction and conversion are thus implied. The idea is not, Make disciples by baptizing and instructing them to observe my precepts and ordinances; but make disciples by your preaching and their believing, convert them to my doctrines and principles, John 4 : 1; Matt. 27 : 58. Yet it should be noted that the *baptizing* and *teaching to observe* are included in complete *discipling*, and in full *discipleship*, Acts 14 : 21. How they were to begin to disciple is shown by the command, *Preach the Gospel to every creature; he that believeth* (Mark 16 : 15, 16); and by the uniform example of the early disciples in preaching the Gospel and baptizing those that believed. Such passages as Acts 2 : 37-41; 8 : 12, 34-39; 17 : 30-33, are the best comments on the apostolic mode of discipling. No instance can be found in the New Testament of baptizing before professed faith. Neither is there any instance, expressed or implied, of an infant baptized upon the faith of its parent. The first thing, then, in *discipling*, is to preach Christ, and lead men to believe on him, Acts 9 : 20-22; then they are to profess their discipleship, or "put on Christ," by baptism; then observe Christ's ordinances and precepts, Acts 2 : 42; 1 Cor. 11 : 2. The discipling of the heart begins in faith and continues in the service of faith in every duty; that of the life, or rather outward manifestation of discipleship, commences in confessing the faith, professing it in baptism, and observing the ordinances and precepts of the Gospel. Baptism is thus the *initiatory* rite into the church.

In the name. Literally, *Into the name*. *In the name*, meaning *in reference to the name*, may be grammatically defended, as is done by Dr. Conant, by ch. 10 : 41, *in the name of a prophet*, and ch. 18 : 20, *gathered together in my name*. He also says, "*Into the name* is not an English phrase, and, though a literal form of the Greek, does not give the sense." By being baptized, in reference to the name of the Trinity, **a** person solemnly and

20 °teaching them to observe all things whatsoever I have commanded you. And, lo, ᵖI am with you alway, *even* unto the end of the world. Amen.

°Ac. 2. 42.
ᵖch. 18. 20; Is. 41. 10; John 14. 18–23; Ac. 18. 9, 10.

publicly recognizes the relations of the act to the Triune God, and the relation into which it brings him, thus signifying his allegiance and subjection to God. Yet in Rom. 6 : 3, 4, are found the phrases, "baptized *into* Jesus Christ," "baptism *into* death," and in Gal. 3 : 27, "baptized *into* Christ." It may, therefore, be asked, Why not with equal propriety say, *baptize into the name of the Trinity?* meaning into a profession of belief in him, of fellowship with him, and of subjection to him. It is certainly an objection to the phrase, *in the name,* that it naturally suggests the idea, *by the authority,* which idea is not the one here intended. The authority is found in the command and in the power and majesty of Christ, ver. 18. Whichever view, therefore, we take, we are not to regard the expression as meaning, by the authority of the Father, the Son, and the Holy Spirit; but rather involving a professed allegiance and subjection to, and fellowship with the three Persons of the one God.

The name. The Being which his name represents, as revealed in his word; all the manifestations of the triune God, attributes, relations, as revealed in the Gospel. All that the name imports, and of which it is an index. See on ch. 6 : 9; see also Luke 1 : 49; Heb. 2 : 12. The singular is used: *name,* not *names,* pointing to the unity in trinity, and to the equality of the Father, Son, and Holy Spirit. There is thus a reference to the different parts which the Father, the Son, and the Holy Spirit take in the work of salvation, and to the unity of the Godhead, the fountain of all blessing. The plural would have implied three distinct beings. The singular implies that the three, though in a sense distinct, are yet one. The fact of the trinity is revealed, but the precise mode of its existence is one of the secret and mysterious things of God. Compare 2 Cor. 13 : 14. The singular also points clearly to only *one* immersion. If a *three-fold* immersion had been intended, the form would have been either *in the names of,* or *in the name of the Father, and in the name of the Son,* etc. The old custom of immersing at the utterance of each name, still practiced by the Greek Church, is first mentioned by Tertullian, and appears to have arisen from the superstitions and corruptions which gave birth to infant baptism.

The language of this last commission implies that this was not the institution of the ordinance. It was the *extending* to all nations, the preaching of the Gospel, baptism, and the observances of Christ's commands. As well might it be said that here began Gospel preaching, as that Gospel baptism here had its origin or beginning. Baptism, as a Gospel ordinance, was instituted by John at the dawn of the new dispensation, ch. 11 : 12, 13; Mark 1 : 1–5. Jesus submitted to it as a Gospel ordinance, and as an example, ch. 3 : 15; the three persons of the Godhead were present to sanction it; pointing also to the fact that, after Christ had arisen and ascended, and the Holy Spirit had come, believers should be baptized, in reference to the name of the triune God, into an open allegiance and subjection to him. After the baptism of Jesus, his disciples baptized under his direction, John 4 : 1, 2. And now as he is about to leave the world and to send the Holy Spirit, which would complete a full manifestation of the Trinity, he enjoins upon his disciples the complete formula which would correspond to the completeness of revealed truth and to the full organization of his churches. Baptism, administered by John, in view of the coming Messiah, or by the disciples of Jesus in his name as the Messiah, was valid, as it corresponded to the revelations of truth and to the development of Christ's kingdom. But after the full manifestation of the Son, and of the Holy Spirit, baptism, to be valid, must be administered in the name of the Father and of the Son and of the Holy Spirit. See on ch. 3 : 1, 15, 17; 11 : 12, 13.

20. **Teaching them.** Converts are to be taught as well as baptized. Thus will they be able to act out their discipleship, fulfilling its terms and complying with all its requirements. **All things whatsoever I have commanded you.** In his previous instructions, both before and after his cruci-

fixion. They were to *carry out*, not *originate*. The doctrines, precepts, and ordinances of Christ, and not the traditions of men, constitute Christian faith and practice. The Lord's Supper was one of the things which he had commanded them to observe. We here get a view of the divine order—Faith, Baptism, the Lord's Supper. Notice here the ones thus commanded, "Teaching *them*," those baptized, "to observe," etc. The practice of the early churches illustrates this, Acts 2 : 41–47; 14 : 22; 16 : 40; 1 Cor. 11 : 20–34. See also on ch. 26 : 30.

Lo. *Behold.* Calling attention to a great and glorious promise. **I am with you.** By a living union, John 14 : 20; 15 : 5; by the Holy Spirit, John 14 : 16. Jesus is Immanuel, *God with us*, ch. 1 : 23. Matthew, at the beginning of his Gospel, thus presents him in his incarnation, as foretold by the prophet; and now, at the end of his Gospel, in his promised continued presence with his followers. The promise is in harmony with his name and character, Gal. 2 : 20; Rev. 21 : 3. The words *with you* are not to be confined to the apostles, but referred to the whole multitude of disciples then gathered together. As Alford, a dignitary of the Episcopal Church, has justly said, "Descending into literal exactness, we may see that 'teaching them to observe all things whatsoever I commanded you,' makes *them* into *you* as soon as they are discipled. The command is to the universal church, to be performed, in the nature of things, by *ministers* and *teachers*, the manner of appointing which is not here prescribed, but to be learnt in the unfoldings of Providence in the Acts of the Apostles, who, by his special ordinance, were the founders and first builders of that church, *but whose office, on that very account, precluded the idea of succession or renewal*." Compare our Savior's prayer for all believers, John 17 : 20, 21. **Always.** Literally, *All the days*. Never absent a single day, not even the darkest.

Even. Should be omitted, as there is nothing answering to it in the original. **Unto the end of the world.** Until the consummation of the present dispensation or world, before the second coming of Christ. With that advent will commence "the world to come." "The word *unto* does not set a term to Christ's presence, but to his *invisible* and *temporal* presence, which will be exchanged for his *visible* and *eternal* presence at his last coming. Now Christ is *with us;* then, when he shall appear in glory, we shall be *with him* where he is (John 17 : 24), and shall see him as he is, 1 John 3 : 2."—DR. SCHAFF, in *Lange*.

Matthew closes his Gospel with the last commission, including this grand promise to his followers in all ages of the Gospel dispensation. He omits the record of the *ascension*. The *fact*, however, is implied in the promise of his constant presence with his disciples, and in ch. 24 : 30; 25 : 14, 31; 26 : 64. **Amen.** So let it be, and so it shall be. The word, however, should be omitted, according to the highest critical authorities. It was added by copyists to the later manuscripts.

REMARKS.

1. As woman was first to sin, so woman has ever been first to seek and find a risen Savior, ver. 1; Gen. 3 : 6; 1 Tim. 2 : 14.

2. The same power which was exercised in the resurrection of Christ will be exercised in the resurrection unto life of all his followers, ver. 2; John 5 : 29; 1 Cor. 15 : 20–23; 1 Thess. 4 : 16.

3. How will the wicked tremble when Christ comes to raise the dead and judge the world! vers. 3 : 4; Rev. 1 : 7; 6 : 15–17.

4. No power of man can prevent the resurrection and judgment, or thwart the purposes of God, vers. 2–4; Acts 2 : 24; Matt. 13 : 41–43; Job 9 : 12; 11 : 10, 12.

5. Angels are ministering spirits to the righteous. The power and glory which shall cause the wicked to tremble at the resurrection and the judgment, will cause the righteous to rejoice, ver. 5; Luke 21 : 28; 1 Cor. 15 : 51, 52; 1 Thess. 2 : 19; 4 : 17, 18.

6. The empty grave of Jesus teaches his Messiahship, his death and resurrection, his humiliation and exaltation, the atonement fully made, and the salvation of believers sure. The believer should not, therefore, fear the grave, ver. 6; 1 Cor. 15 : 55–57.

7. How appropriately is the first day of the week named the Lord's Day, and how fitting to observe it as the day of Christian rest! If the day when God rested from the work of creation was

hallowed and observed, how much more the one when Christ rested from the greater work of redemption. Some have argued that the Lord's Day is but the restoration of the original Sabbath of creation, a change having been made at the reënactment of the Sabbath among the Jews (Deut. 5 : 15). This is a curious and interesting question. Certain it is that, as the original Sabbath was the first day of completed creation, so the Lord's Day was the first day of completed redemption. But, aside from conjectures, there was, in the nature of things, a reason for a change in the day. It was fitting that that day of unparalleled darkness, when Jesus lay in the grave, should be the last of Jewish Sabbaths, and that the birthday of immortality and of Christ's finished work should ever after be the day of the Christian's rest. How could those early disciples recall the former but with sorrow, and how could they remember the latter but with joy? It is enough to know that they ever after observed the first day of the week, and that it comes down to us with the sanction of apostolic authority and example, vers. 1–6; John 20 : 19, 26; Acts 20 : 7; 1 Cor. 16 : 2; Rev. 1 : 10.

8. We are not to seek the living among the dead. We are to exercise faith in a *living* Savior, ver. 7; John 14 : 19; Rev. 1 : 17, 18.

9. How compassionate is Jesus toward his fallen yet penitent disciples! He sends a special message to Peter, who had denied him, and afterward wept bitterly, ver. 7; Heb. 5 : 2.

10. As all the previous appearances to the disciples were preparatory to the grand appearance to the collective body of disciples in Galilee, so are all of the manifestations of grace preparatory to the great gathering of all believers at last in glory, ver. 7.

11. We should run in the way of God's commandments, ver. 8; Ps. 119 : 32; Isa. 40 : 31; Hab. 2 : 2; Heb. 12 : 1.

12. Jesus will meet those that seek him, vers. 6, 9; John 20 : 14–17, 27; James 4 : 8.

13. Jesus is an object of divine worship. He is divine, vers. 9, 17; Acts 7 : 59; 9 : 14; Col. 3 : 24; Heb. 1 : 6. Compare Acts 10 : 25; 14 : 14, 15; Rev. 19 : 10; 22 : 9.

14. The guilt of the wicked is sometimes more keen-sighted than the faith of God's people, vers. 11, 12; ch. 27 : 63, 64; Luke 24 : 11.

15. False teachers are afraid of facts, and of the dissemination of knowledge, vers. 12, 13; Luke 11 : 52.

16. Sin leads to sin, and crime to crime, vers. 12–14; Isa. 30 : 1; 2 Tim. 3 : 13; James 1 : 15.

17. Money is a power in the world. There is no crime but may be traced to a love of it, ver. 15; Acts 8 : 18, 19; 1 Tim. 6 : 10; 2 Pet. 2 : 13–15.

18. They who would fully enjoy a risen Savior must go where he appoints, ver. 16; Ps. 87 : 2; Luke 24 : 49.

19. How unbelieving the human heart, and how kind the treatment of Jesus toward his doubting disciples! ver. 17; ch. 12 : 20; 14 : 31; John 20 : 27.

20. Christ, whose authority and dominion are supreme, is the ground of our confidence, the source of our blessings, and our present and eternal safety, ver. 18; John 3 : 35; Col. 1 : 12–20; Rev. 11 : 15.

21. The grand mission of Christ's disciples is to convert the world. Each should in some way labor for this end. Every one should strive to make disciples, ver. 19; ch. 5 : 16; Acts 1 : 8; 8 : 4.

22. As Christ, our supreme Lawgiver and Head, has fixed a regular order for his churches to follow in discipling the nations, no one has a right to change that order, as they do who put baptism before faith, or the Lord's Supper before baptism, vers. 19 : 20; Lev. 10 : 1, 2; Isa. 1 : 12; Rev. 22 : 18, 19.

23. Each of the persons of the Trinity are interested, not only in baptism, but also in the whole scheme of salvation, and in every disciple, ver. 19; Eph. 2 : 18, 20, 22; Tit. 3 : 4–6.

24. We are not only to observe and do, but also teach the commands of Christ, who is the Lawgiver of his church, ver. 20; John 15 : 14; 1 Cor. 11 : 1.

25. The promised presence of Jesus with his disciples unto the end is an encouragement to observe and teach all that he has commanded, ver. 20; Acts 18 : 9, 10; 23 : 11; Phil. 4 : 13; 2 Tim. 4 : 17, 18; Rev. 2 : 12; 3 : 10.

INDEX.

	PAGE
Abandonment on the cross	391
Abomination of desolation	329, 330
Accuracy of Matthew	243
Accusation on the cross	388
Aceldama	379
Adultery, law of	76
Agony in Gethsemane	363–366
Alabaster	352
Alms, 86; how to give	87
Angel at the sepulchre	402
Angels, 23, 248; ministering to Jesus, 56; their relation to Christians	248
Anise	319
Annas	351, 369
Annihilation	349
Anointing the head	92
Anointing at Bethany	352
Anxiety for food and raiment	95
Apostles, 135; selection, 134; catalogue of, 135; mission of	134, 135
Appearances of Jesus after the resurrection, 400; to Mary Magdalene, 404; to the other women, 404; to the five hundred in Galilee	406, 408
Aramathea, 395; Joseph of	395
Archelaus	36
Ass, and colt of, 282; Jesus riding on, 282, 283; foal of	283
Authority of Christ questioned	291, 292
Babes	159, 288
Band, Roman	366
Baptism, 42, 43, 44, 46, 49, 408; of suffering, 275; proselyte baptism, 39, 40; in the Holy Ghost and fire, 46, 47; of Christ, 48, 49, 50; infant baptism, 262, 407; relation to Lord's Supper	361, 407, 409
Baptismal formula	407–409
Bar	228
Barabbas, 381; preferred to Jesus	383
Bartholomew	137
Baskets	208, 222, 226
Beam	99
Beelzebub, 168; the charge of Pharisees against Jesus	168, 169
Bethany, 281, 282, 288; supper and anointing at	352

	PAGE
Bethlehem	27, 31
Bethphage	281, 282
Bethsaida Julias	206, 207
Betrayed	351
Binding and loosing on earth	232, 233
Blasphemy, 122; different kinds, 171; against the Holy Spirit, 170–172; against the Son	171, 172
Blessed, happy	66
Blindness, wilful and judicial	184
Blood of new covenant	360
Books, ancient form of	17
Borders of garments	314
Bottles, old	127
Brass in New Testament	139
Bread, daily	90
Bread at the Lord's Supper, 358; not the real body of Christ	358, 359
Brothers of Jesus	177, 199, 200
Buffet	372
Burial of Jesus	395
Cæsar	305
Cæsarea Philippi	227
Caiaphas, 351; Jesus before	369, 372
Calvary	386
Camel, 319; and needle's eye	265
Camel's hair	42
Canaanitish woman	218–220
Capernaum	57
Carpenter	199
Celibacy	260
Censorious spirit, warned against	98, 99
Centurion	110
Children, little, 260; Christ blessing, 261; their connection with the kingdom of heaven	261, 262
CHRIST, meaning of, 18; its use, 18; king of Jews and of Israel, 28, 50; his office and work, 24, 26, 51; divinity, 41, 133, 228; the Judge, 146, 147; false Christs	327
Christ in Egypt, 33, 34; a Nazarene, 37, 38; temptation of, 52–56; early ministry in Judea, 56, 57; later ministry in Judea, 257; last journey to Jerusalem	257
Christ forgiving sins	123, 133
Christ and Jonah in the storm	117

INDEX

Christ's sufferings with sickness, 114; Christ's sonship............ 371
Christians, why hated of all, 143, 3.8; God's care for them, 249, 330, 331; representatives of Christ............................. 348
Church, meaning of, 231; in classic Greek, 231; in the Septuagint, 231; in the New Testament....231, 232
Cleansing the temple............285, 286
Closet..................................... 83
Coasts..................................... 227
Cock, the................................ 362
Cock-crowing........................... 362
Conversion and regeneration...... 245
Commandments, 309; great and small, 72, 309; on keeping them, 263; great and first, 309; the second................................... 310
Conscious existence after death.... 312
Council..............................74, 141
Court, of a house...................... 351
Courts, 141; Christians before..... 142
Covenant, new.......................... 360
Crown of thorns........................ 385
Crucifixion.............................. 387
Christ's first prediction of, 274; time of................................. 387
Crosses, 386; Jesus and Simon bearing..................................... 386
Cubit...................................... 95
Cummin.................................. 319
Cup.. 359
Custom or revenues................... 134
Cutting asunder........................ 338
Cyrene.................................... 385

Damnation............................... 321
Darkness over the land............... 390
Darnel, 189; American................ 190
Daughter................................. 129
Day, heat of, etc....................... 271
Death, a sleep....................129, 130
Death of Jesus, how................... 392
Debts...................................... 90
Defilement............................... 218
Decapolis, 63; inhabited by whom. 220
Demoniacs, two healed, 117; dumb healed, 131; blind and dumb..... 168
Denarius............................270, 353
Destruction.............................. 102
Devil....................................... 52
Devils, 62; in dry places, 176; possession of, 62, 63; Pharisees and exorcists casting out................ 169
Dinner..................................... 300
Dipping in the dish.................... 357
Disciple, meaning of, etc............ 66
Discipling................................ 407
Discipleship, requirements of..... 115, 116, 147, 264

Discipline, church........249, 250, 256
Ditch...................................... 217
Divine sovereignty.................... 158
Divorce, law of, 77, 78; only cause for............................78, 257-259
Divorces................................. 23
Doctor of divinity, title of....315, 316
Doctrine................................. 226
Dogs, 100; little dogs................ 219
Doves, harmless as.................... 141
Drowning, execution by............. 247
Dust, shaking from the feet....... 140

Early rising in the east.............. 370
Egypt...................................... 33
Elders..................................... 30
Eli.. 391
Elias, 237, 238, 391; John the Baptist................................239, 240
Enemy, Jewish idea of................ 82
Ephratah.................................. 31
Ethnarch.................................. 36
Eunuchs.................................. 260
Evening, two.......................207, 224
Evil............................418, 80, 91
Eye, the single, 93; the evil........ 94
Eye of the needle..................... 265
Exclusion from church............... 250
Exchangers............................. 345

Faith...................................... 319
Faith, power of........................ 241
Faith by proxy......................... 112
Falling from grace.................... 255
False Christs......................327, 332
Famines before the destruction of Jerusalem............................. 327
Fan or winnowing shovel........... 48
Farthing.............................76, 146
Fasting, 92; Jewish fasts, 126; Christ's disciples fasting....126, 127
Father, not to be called........315, 316
Fatling................................... 300
Feast of unleavened bread......... 355
Feeding the five thousand....207, 208
Feeding the four thousand, 221, 222; the two feedings compared...... 221
Fertility of the east.................. 182
Fevers at Capernaum................ 113
First day of the week................ 401
First last, and last first.............. 268
Fig-tree, 289, 335; its leaves, etc., 289; the curse of.............289, 290
Flax, smoking.......................... 167
Flesh and blood....................... 228
Floods in Palestine, 105; in Bengal. 106
Following Christ...................... 148
Forgiveness, spirit of, 91; how often exercised, 252; on not exercising it..................................253, 254
Foul....................................... 234

INDEX.

	PAGE
Fowls in Palestine	362
Frankincense	32
Friend	367
Fruit of the vine	360
Fruits	103, 104
Future life	308
Gadara	118
Galilee	37, 58, 60, 61
Galilean, 373; speech	374
Gall	387
Gate, strait, 102; of cities	103
Gehenna	75
Genealogies, 18; of Christ reconciled, 19, 20; why Gentiles in it, 20; other difficulties explained, 21, 22; reflections on	26
Generation	335
Genesaret, land of, 211; its fine temperature	211
Gentiles	58, 97, 274
Gerasa	118
Gergesenes	117, 118
Gersa	118
Gethsemane, 363, 366; Christ in	363–366
Gift	318
Giving	81
Goats	347
"God forbid"	295
Gnat, straining at	319
Golden rule, 101; compared with the maxims of others	102
Goodman	337
Golgotha	386
Gomorrah	141
Gospel, meaning of	17, 62
Gospel, the, producing divisions, 147; preached to the whole world	329
Gospel of Matthew, 17; in what language first written, ix. x.; when written, x.; design and arrangement	x–xii. 18
Gospels, the age when written, v.; received as authoritative inspired writings by the early churches, v. vi.; the unity of the four Gospels. vii.	
Governments ordained of God	80
Governor	377
Governors of Judea, during Christ's life	36
Grapes	103
Greeks desiring to see Jesus	285
Hades, 157; gates of	232
"Heart of the earth"	175
Heaven	157
Heavy laden	150
Heavy burdens	314
Hell, 75, 157; gates of	232
Hem of garment	211

	PAGE
Herod the Great, 27, 28; cruelties, 34, 35; death, 33, 35, 36; family	36
Herod Antipas, 203; his opinion of Jesus, 203; his relation to John, 204; his oath	205
Herodias	203
Herodians, 304; reply of Jesus to	304, 306
High-priest	351
Holy	100
Homage, paying	30
Hosanna	284
Hour	220, 270
Householder	198, 269
Housetop	330
Humility and obedience	51
Hymn at Lord's Supper	361
Hypocrites	86
Idle words	173
Image, superscription	305
Impressment, Roman	81, 385, 386
Infant baptism	215, 222, 262, 407
Infant salvation	262
Israel, 111; house of	138
Israel, land of	35
Jairus' daughter	128
James and John, 60, 136, 137; their several calls	60
Jeremiah	227
Jericho, 277, 278; two blind men healed at, 278, 279; apparent discrepancies explained	278, 279
Jerusalem, 28; going up to, 273; its destruction foretold and the fulfillment	330, 331, 333
Jesus, meaning of, 18, 24; birth of, 22; time of birth, 27; forsaken on the cross, 391; seven sayings on the cross	392
Jews, last state worse than the first, 176, 177; their imprecations	383, 384
John's Gospel, credibility of	159
John the Baptist, 39, 153; Elias, 155; relation to Christ, 40, 41, 51, 59, 126, 154, 155; cast into prison, 56; disciples of, 126; message of, 150–153; his death	205
Jordan	44
Joseph	22, 26
Joseph of Arimathea	369
Jot	72
Judas, 137; Iscariot, 137, 139, 378; engages to betray Jesus, 354; what led to the act, 354; pointed out as traitor, 356, 357; betrays with a kiss, 367; confession, remorse, and death, 378; place of his death	378
Judea, wilderness of	40, 48

INDEX

	PAGE
Judged according to words	173
Judgment	74, 166, 319
Judgment, the final	346, 349
Keys, 232; of the kingdom, etc.	232
Kingdom of heaven, 40, 41; degrees in the, 73; the greatest in	245, 246
Labor	159
Laborers in the vineyard, 269; meaning of parable	272
Last first, and first last	273
Law, made of none effect, 215; among Christians	215
Law and prophets, 71; how fulfilled, 72; Christ came not to destroy, 72; law and Gospel, 73, 85; law spiritually expounded	73–83, 85
Lawyer	309
Leaven, 192, 225; parable of 192; meaning doctrine, teaching	226
Lebbeus	137
Legions	368
Leper	108
Leprosy, 108; an emblem of sin	109
Life, 103, 148; eternal	349
Light of the world, Christ and Christians	71
Lilies	95
Little ones	247
Locust	42
Lord	110
Lord's Day	401, 410
Lord's prayer, a model, 89; its doxology	91
Lord's Supper, 358–360; its proper name, 359; significance of the bread, 358, 359; of the cup	359, 360
Lots, casting	388
Love to our neighbor, law of	82
Lowering	224
Lunatic	63, 240
Magdala	222
Malchus	368
Mammon	94
Mark	369
Markets, 155; children in the	155
Marriage of the King's son	299–302
Marriage relation	268, 339, 340
Marriage among the Jews, 22, 339; the ancient law of, 258; lawful exceptions from, 260; among the Hindoos	341
Mary, mother of James the Less	395
Matthew, viii.; the language in which he wrote, ix. x.; when he wrote, x.; design of his Gospel, x. xi.; arrangement, xi. xii.; beginning and close	409
Matthew	137

	PAGE
Matthew, call of, etc., 124; relating things by twos	130
Mary Magdalene, 394; Jesus appearing first to	404
Mary, mother of Jesus, 22, 26, 32; had other children, 26; not an object of worship	38
Mary, sister of Martha	352
Measure of meal	192
Meek, the	67
Memorial of Mary	354
Merciful, the	68
Mercy	319
Mercy desired, not sacrifice	163
Mill	336
Minister	277
Ministers called of God	64, 149
Minstrels	129
Mint	319
Miracles, 107; words used to designate, 107; of Christ, 107, 108, 169; of God's messengers, 108; their connection with spiritual healing.	122
Money-changers	286, 287
Morning	224
Moses	237
Moses' seat	313
Mote	99
Moth	93
Mount of Beatitudes	66
Mountain, used figuratively	241
Mourning, true	67
Mourning for the dead	129
Murder, law of	74
Mustard, parable of, 190, 191; Dr. Hackett on, 191; the plant or the tree	191
Myrrh	32
Mysteries	183
Name, that is, of God, 90, 408; in the name of	408
Names, significant among the Jews.	25
Naphtali	57, 58
Nazareth, 37; Christ's second rejection at	199
Nazarene	37
Needle's eye	265
Neighbor, 82; Jewish idea of	82
Net, 59, 196; parable of fishing, 196, 197; contrasted with parable of the tares	197
New cloth	127
Nicodemus	369, 396
Nineveh	175
Nob	162
Numbers, their symbolical use in Scripture	134, 135
Oaths, law of, 78, 79, 318, 319; profane oaths common among the	

INDEX.

	PAGE
Jews, 79; judicial oaths, 79; one administered to Jesus........370,	371
Offenses, duty in respect to, 75, 76, 249, 250; causes of...........77,	247
Offerings and gifts before the altar.	75
Ointment	353
Olives, Mount of................	281
One greater than the temple.......	163
Omniscience of Jesus..........122,	123
Outer darkness....................	112
Oven...........................	96
Palace...........................	372
Palsy, 63, 110; healing of at Capernaum......................121,	122
Parables of Christ, 181, 182; teaching by, 181; why Christ spoke in, 183, 184; exposition of, 188; the seven in ch. xiii................	198
Parentage of Christ..........310,	311
Passover, 350, 356; number of lambs killed at, 284; as kept by later Jews...................... 355,	356
Peacemakers......................	69
Pence...........................	253
Penny............	270
Pearls, 100, 196; parable of goodly.	196
Perfect, what to be.........83, 84,	264
Peter, 136; his rank among the apostles, 136, 230; meaning of, 229; styled Satan, 234; denials foretold, 361, 363; his denials, 373,	374
Peter's confession, 229; repentance, 374; Peter's wife's mother......	113
Persecution, 187; to be expected, 144, 145; not to be feared......	145
Pharisees, 45, 313; first organized opposition to Jesus, 165, 166, 258; their requirements..........313,	314
Philip	137
Phylacteries	314
Pieces of silver....................	355
Pinnacle of the temple.	54
Pontius Pilate, 377; Jesus before, 380; his wife, 382; her dream and message, 383; his expediency, 382, 383; washing his hands	383
Porch	373
Potter's Field....	379
Prayer, 87, 98; times of, 88; place of, 88; Lord's prayer, 89; encouragements to..............100,	251
Preaching tours throughout Galilee; the first, 60, 61; the third.......	132
Priests, chief.....................	30
Prophecy, typical...............24,	25
Prophet, 103, 148; false, 103, 104; without honor in his own country, 200; false.................	328
Proselytes. 317,	318
Publicans, 85; and sinners.....124,	125

	PAGE
Punishment, future, 74, 75, 145, 146, 349; degrees of................	75
Purses...........................	139
Rabbi, Rabboni...................	315
Raca..........................	74
Rachel bewailing her children......	35
Rama............................	35
Ransom, Christ giving himself a...	277
Reed............................	385
Reeds, 153; bruised...............	167
Regeneration, the.............. ...	266
Region and shadow of death.......	58
Remission of sins.................	360
Render, 305; what to Cæsar and what to God................305,	306
Rending the clothes, 371; the high-priest...........................	371
Repentance...... ....40, 50,	51
Resurrection, 306, 307; proof of a.	308
Resurrection of saints.............	393
Resurrection of Jesus, 400-402; Matthew's account, 400; accompanying circumstances.......401,	402
Retaliation, law of, 79-81; in regard to personal violence, 80; legal suits, 80; public authority.......	81
Retirement of Jesus fulfilling prophecy......................166,	167
Revelation, different modes of.....	23
Rich man entering the kingdom...	265
Righteousness, 68, 86; Christian and Pharisaical........................	73
Right hand.......................	311
Roads in the east	182
Robbers.........................	287
Rock, 229; in respect to Peter, 229, 230; Christ the rock, 230, 231; Lightfoot on the, 230; in the Peshito version.....................	230
Rust	93
Sabbath, 162, 178; what lawful on the, 162, 165; Christ the lord of, 164; Christian................	401
Sackcloth........................	157
Sadducees, 45, 308; reply of Jesus to.........................306-308	
Salt, 70; losing its savor...........	70
Saints, who and how applied......	17
Salutation 83,	140
Samaritans.......................	138
Sandals..........................	46
Sanhedrim, 30; place of meeting, and early meeting, 369, 370; condemning Jesus..................	377
Sawn asunder....................	338
Scarlet robe.....................	384
Scourging, Roman...............	384
Scribe, one instructed............	198
Scribes....................80, 105,	313

INDEX.

	PAGE
Scrip	139
Scriptures, 297; must be fulfilled	368
Sea of Galilee	59
Sealing the stone	398
Second coming of Christ, 326, 333; time of	336
Selfishness and self-love	310
Sentence of death, when pronounced	372
Sermon on the Mount and Sermon in the Plain	65
Sepulchre, 320; whited, 320; Christ's	396
Servant	110, 111, 277
Serpents, wise as	141
Seven sayings of Jesus on the cross	392
Sheba	175
Sheep, lost, 138; among wolves	141
Showbread	163
Sidon	157
Silence enjoined by Jesus, why.110,	131
Sign from heaven	174, 224
Sign of Jonah	174
Signs of the times	224
Sin, a debt, 90; a lapse or fall	92
Simon Barjona	228
Simon the leper	352
Simon of Cerene	385
"Six days before the Passover"	281
Sodom	141, 158
Son, how used	18
Son of David	130
Son of God, 53, 371; of the living God	228
Sons of God	69
Sonship of Christ	243
Son of Man, 115; coming in his kingdom	235
"Son of Man be come"	143, 144
Soul	234
Sovereignty of God	272
Sower, parable of, 182, 186; Drs. Hackett and Thomson on	182, 183
Sparrows	149
Spikenard	353
Spirit, a	210
Spirit-flesh	365
Spitting in the face	372
Star in the east, 29, 31; where seen, 29,	32
Staves	139, 366
Stony places	182
Stone of the corner, 297; Christ as a stone	298
Strewed	344
Sucklings	288
Sun darkened, etc.	334
Superscription	305
Swearing by the temple	318
Swine, 100, 119; demons sent into, 119; destruction of	119
Swords, Roman	366

	PAGE
Synagogues	61
Synopsis of chapters xxiv. xxv.324,	325
Synopsis of the Four Gospels	xiii.
Syria	62
Syro-Phœnicia	218
Tabernacles	238
Table, sitting at, 124; spiritual meaning of	111, 112
Talent, of silver, of gold	252
Talents, parable of	342–346
Talmuds of Jerusalem and Babylon.	214
Tares, 189; parable of, 189, 193, 194; Catholics and Donatists on	194
Tempest stilled, 114–116; on the Sea of Galilee	116
Temple, 286, 325; cleansed....285,	286
Temptation	90
Temptation of Christ; place, etc., 52–56, 63,	64
Tempting	224
Ten virgins, parable of	339–342
Tetrarch	36
Thaddeus	137
Thief—*robber*	369
Thieves	287
Thieves, or robbers, crucified with Jesus	389, 390
Thieves breaking through	93
Thomas	137
Thorns and thistles	103, 182
Thrashing-floor	48
"Three days and three nights"	175
Throne of glory, 267; disciples on twelve thrones	267
Thorns, crown of	385
Tithe	319
Tittle	72
Tomb, new	396
Tombs	118, 320, 396
Tormentors	254
Tower	294
Tradition of elders	213, 214
Transfiguration, the, 237; where	237
Treasures	93
Treasures, hidden; parable of, 195; explanations of, 196; Dr. Thomson on	195
Trespasses	92
Tribulation	187
Tribute-money	305
Tribute, sacred	242
Trial of Jesus	372
Triumphal entry into Jerusalem.281,	284
Trumpet, sound of a	334
Two sons, parable of	292
Tyre	157
Unclean, what is really	216, 217
Unmerciful servant, 252–255; meaning of the parable of	254, 255

	PAGE		PAGE
Upbraid	156	Wicked husbandmen, parable of, 293–296; meaning of	296, 297
Usury	345	Widows' houses	317
Vail of temple rent, etc.	393	Wild honey	42
Vain repetitions	88	Wine; at the Passover, 356, 359; at the Lord's Supper	359, 360
Verses first introduced into the English Bible	iv	Wine-press	244
Vinegar	387	Wisdom of God	321
Vipers, generation of	173	Wise men, Magians	28
Vineyard	294	Withered hand	164
Vision	139	Woe	317
Vision of angels at the sepulchre	402	Woes against the Pharisees	317
		Wolves in sheep's clothing	103
Walking on the water, Jesus and Peter	209	Worship, meaning of word	30, 219
Wars before the destruction of Jerusalem	327	Yoke, 160; Christ's	160
Washing the hands, 214; Talmud on.	214	Young man whom Jesus loved	263, 264
Watch at the sepulchre, 397, 398; their incredible story	405	Zachariah, the son of Barachias	321, 322
Watches of the night	209	Zebedee's wife and children, 274; ambitious request of	274, 275
Wedding-garment	301	Zebulon	57, 58
Whitened sepulchres	320	Zion	283

APPENDIX.

EVIL, OR THE EVIL ONE, WHICH?

For over fifteen centuries the question has been discussed whether *poneron* in the Lord's Prayer (Matt. 6 : 13) should be rendered "evil" or "the evil one"; in other words, whether the word is neuter or masculine, whether it is used as an abstract or a concrete term. The Greek Fathers generally took the latter view; Augustine and the Latins after him took the former view. Among moderns, Erasmus, Beza, Bengel, Olshausen, Meyer, Grimm, Plumptre and others regard the word as masculine, a designation of Satan; Luther, Melancthon, Tholuck, Ewald, Bleek, Stier, Lange, Alford, Conant, Cramer, and others take the word in the neuter, as an abstract noun, meaning moral evil generally. With such an array on either side, it appears at once that the question is not to be decided by learned names. It is rather one in which the decision must be reached by historical and exegetical reasoning.

There are seven undoubted examples in the New Testament where this word designates Satan: Matt. 13 : 19; Eph. 6 : 16; 1 John 2 : 13, 14; 3 : 12; 5 : 18, 19. Some would claim the expression in Matt. 13 : 38 as clearly meaning "the children of the evil one"; but this is at least doubtful; for, as Cramer remarks, the parallel phrase, "sons of the kingdom," naturally requires the rendering "sons of evil." And this too would be a Hebraism as natural as "a child of hell" in Matt. 23 : 15, or "the sons of disobedience" in Eph. 5 : 6. The Revised version and the Improved version have marked the word as at least doubtful in four instances, by rendering it "the evil one" in the text, and putting the alternate rendering "evil" in the margin: Matt. 5 : 37; 6 : 13; John 17 : 15, and 2 Thess. 3 : 3. But the Bible Union version regards them as undoubted examples of the abstract noun "evil." It is, however, acknowledged by all that the word is in the neuter gender, meaning evil in the abstract, in Luke 6 : 45; Acts 28 : 21; Rom. 12 : 9; 1 Thess. 5 : 22, and in several instances where the plural is used, as in Luke 3 : 19. The word occurs over seventy times in the New Testament. It thus appears that there is but one undoubted example in the Gospels, and only one in the Epistles of Paul, where the word should be rendered "evil one," as applied to Satan; while the five other examples are found in the First Epistle of John, written at the close of the apostolic age, when, perhaps, Satan and evil spirits were gaining greater prominence in Christian thought and doctrine. But all this is not decisive, since in the doubtful passages the word may be translated either way, and in either case it makes good English, as it is good Greek. It is necessary, therefore, to look further.

In favor of the rendering "evil," it may be said that "the evil one" is not the usual designation of Satan in the New Testament. About seventy times he is styled Satan or devil—thirty of these in the Gospels, and ten of them in Matthew. These against only two undoubted examples outside of John's First Epistle certainly create a presumption for the rendering "evil" in this passage.

This presumption is strengthened by turning to the Old Testament. Satan is never called the evil one, either in the Hebrew or in the Septuagint. Satan is, indeed, seldom mentioned in the Old Testament; but the idea of evil is general and prominent. The Hebrew word for evil, when used substantively, almost always has the article, but meaning "that which is evil." And this affords a presumption that the Aramaic original of the Lord's Prayer was the same. It may also be added that, in the prayer book of the orthodox Jews, the ancient prayers representing devotions far back near apostolic times nowhere designate Satan as the evil one, but petition "deliverance from all evil." This throws light on Jewish habits of thought and upon the meaning of the word to the ancient Jew, which might seem doubtful to many in our day. "No one," says an eminent scholar, "so far as I know, has ever alleged an instance in which the Hebrew or Aramaic words for evil mean Satan. The Peshito version of the New Testament, however, seems to favor 'evil one,' since it is in the masculine in the Lord's Prayer. But the Syriac has no neuter gender. Dr. Isaac H. Hall, a recognized authority in Syriac scholarship, says of this version: 'I think, however, it favors the rendering "evil." The masculine is common enough for abstracts of all sorts. So far as I have read Syriac, the writers generally look upon the phrase as "evil," not "the evil one."'" Such considerations strengthen the probability that Jesus intended to teach us to say, "Deliver us from evil."

But, on the other hand, the Greek Fathers preferred "the evil one." Indeed, it seemed to have been a favorite designation of Satan with them. They even substituted "evil one" for Satan in quoting Scripture. Their frequent use of this term is in striking contrast to its rare use in the New Testament. But in this we may discover a growing tendency to give undue prominence to evil spirits. Some of them made the sufferings and death of Christ a ransom paid to Satan for our release. Great importance was attached to exorcism, to casting out evil spirits by rites and ceremonies. With such doctrinal views and tendencies, it would not be strange if they did magnify the agency of Satan in doubtful passages of the New Testament. Their acumen and scholarship certainly were not superior to many of the present day, and their exegesis was strikingly inferior. There was certainly nothing in their historical and exegetical training to fit them to decide a question like this. Indeed, their exaggerated and perverted views concerning Satan and evil spirits disqualified them in a measure as impartial judges.

But what light does the petition itself throw on this point? Turning to the Lord's Prayer, we discover at once that the clause, "Deliver us from evil," or "the evil one," is not a separate petition. It is antithetical to the preceding clause, "Bring us not into temptation," and unfolds it. Temptation may suggest the tempter, but it also suggests all solicitations and exposures to sin, and the next clause naturally a correspondingly comprehensive deliverance. It seems too narrow to limit it to Satan and to the mention of his name. I do not think our Lord's hearers would have so limited the phrase. It would not accord with their mode of thought. Like the other petitions which precede it, it seems broad and deep, embodying the shrinking of the Christian soul from all trying exposures to evil, and its longing for deliverance from all the power and forms of sins. With this view, it fittingly stands as the last and closing petition of the Lord's Prayer, sweeping the whole horizon of moral evil.

In view of all this, it seems to me that a decided preference should be given to the rendering "evil." But, in view of the many eminent scholars who favor the other side of the question, I would place "the evil one" in the margin, but retain "evil" in the text.

See an able discussion in *Bibliotheca Sacra*, 1891, pp. 332 f. and 686 f.

www.ingramcontent.com/pod-product-compliance
Lightning Source LLC
Chambersburg PA
CBHW020100020526
44112CB00032B/594